Communications
in Computer and Information Science 848

Commenced Publication in 2007
Founding and Former Series Editors:
Alfredo Cuzzocrea, Xiaoyong Du, Orhun Kara, Ting Liu, Dominik Ślęzak,
and Xiaokang Yang

More information about this series at http://www.springer.com/series/7899

Hanning Yuan · Jing Geng
Chuanlu Liu · Fuling Bian
Tisinee Surapunt (Eds.)

Geo-Spatial Knowledge and Intelligence

5th International Conference, GSKI 2017
Chiang Mai, Thailand, December 8–10, 2017
Revised Selected Papers, Part I

 Springer

Editors
Hanning Yuan
Beijing Institute of Technology
Beijing
China

Jing Geng
Beijing Institute of Technology
Beijing
China

Chuanlu Liu
Beijing Institute of Technology
Beijing
China

Fuling Bian
Wuhan University
Wuhan
China

Tisinee Surapunt
Beijing Institute of Technology
Beijing
China

ISSN 1865-0929   ISSN 1865-0937 (electronic)
Communications in Computer and Information Science
ISBN 978-981-13-0892-5   ISBN 978-981-13-0893-2 (eBook)
https://doi.org/10.1007/978-981-13-0893-2

Library of Congress Control Number: 2018944420

Printed on acid-free paper

This Springer imprint is published by the registered company Springer Nature Singapore Pte Ltd.
part of Springer Nature
The registered company address is: 152 Beach Road, #21-01/04 Gateway East, Singapore 189721, Singapore

Preface of GSKI 2017

The 5th 2017 International Conference on Geo-Spatial Knowledge and Intelligence (GSKI 2017) was held in Chiang Mai, Thailand, during December 8–10, 2017. The conference aims to bring together researchers, engineers, and students working in the areas of geo-spatial knowledge and intelligence. GSKI 2017 featured a unique mix of topics including smart city, spatial data acquisition, processing and management, modeling and analysis, and recent applications in the context of building a healthier ecology and resource management. The conference provided a forum for sharing experiences and original research contributions on these topics. Researchers and practitioners alike were invited to submit their contributions to GSKI 2017.

We received 579 submissions from various parts of the world. The International Program Committee worked very hard to have all papers peer-peer reviewed before the review deadline. The final program consisted of 142 papers. There were five keynote speeches. All the keynote speakers are internationally recognized leading experts in their research fields, who have demonstrated outstanding proficiency and have achieved distinction in their profession. The proceedings were published as two volumes in Springer's *Communications in Computer and Information Science* (CCIS) series. Some excellent papers were selected and recommended to the special issue of *Journal of Environmental Science and Pollution*, a Science Citation Index Expanded journal. We would like to mention that, owing to the limitation of the conference venue capacity, we were not able to include many fine papers in the program. Our apology goes to these authors.

We would like to express our sincere gratitude to all the members of international Program Committee and organizers for their enthusiasm, time, and expertise. Our thanks also go to many volunteers and staff for the long hours and hard work they generously contributed to GSKI 2017. We are very grateful to Professor Thomas Blaschke and Professor Shihong Du for their support in making GSKI 2017 possible. The generous support from Beijing Institute of Technology is greatly appreciated. Finally, we would like to thank all the authors, speakers, and participants of this conference for their contributions to GSKI 2017.

May 2018

Hanning Yuan
Jing Geng
Chuanlu Liu
Fuling Bian
Tisinee Surapunt

5th Annual 2017 International Conference on Geo-Spatial Knowledge and Intelligence [GSKI 2017]

http://www.GSKI2017.org/
December 8–10, 2017, Chiang Mai, Thailand

Publisher

 Springer

Organization

Keynote Speakers

Thomas Blaschke	University of Salzburg, Austria
Nopasit Chakpitak	Chiang Mai University, Thailand
Shihong Du	Peking University, China
Wang Shuliang	Beijing Institute of Technology, China
F. Benjamin Zhan	Texas State University, USA

Honorary Chairs

Zeeshan Ahmad	Nanjing University of Science and Technology, China
Fuling Bian	Wuhan University, Wuhan, China
Erin M. Hodgess	University of Houston, USA
Phongsak Phakamach	North Eastern University, Thailand

General Chair

Wang Shuliang	Beijing Institute of Technology, Beijing, China

Co-chairs

İsmail Rakıp Karaş	Karabuk University, Turkey
Zongyao Sha	Wuhan University, Wuhan, China

International Program Committee

Arun Agarwal	Siksha 'O' Anusandhan University, India
Ramesh K. Agarwal	Washington University, USA
Naveed Ahmed	Yonsei University, South Korea
Zeeshan Ahmad	Nanjing University of Science and Technology, China
Ulas Akkucuk	Bogazici University, Turkey
Mohammed A. Akour	Yarmouk University, Jordan
Iyad Al Khatib	Politecnico di Milano, Italy
Mohamad Al Ladan	Haigazian University, Lebanon
Shadi G. Alawneh	Oakland University, USA
Alberta Albertella	Technische Universität München, Germany
Mehdi Ammi	University of Paris-Sud, France
Jose Anand	KCG College of Technology, India
Tomasz Andrysiak	UTP University of Science and Technology, Poland
Ho Pham Huy Anh	Ho Chi Minh City University of Technology (HUT), Vietnam

Rkia Aouinatou — LRIT Laboratory, Rabat, Morocco
Kamran Arshad — Ajman University of Science and Technology, UAE
M. Arunachalam — K.L.N College of Information Technology, India
Bahareh Asadi — Islamic Azad University of Tabriz, Iran
Anjali Awasthi — Concordia University, Canada
Tchangani Ayeley — University Toulouse III, France
Nur Sukinah Aziz — TATI University College, Malaysia
Megat Farez Azril — Universiti Kuala Lumpur, Malaysia
Jianjun Bai — Shaanxi Normal University, China
Sen Bai — Chongqing Communication Institute, China
Yuqi Bai — Tsinghua University, China
K. Balakrishnan — Karpaga Vinayaga College of Engineering and Technology, India
Mirko Barbuto — Roma Tre University, Italy
Abul Bashar — Prince Mohammad Bin Fahd University, Saudi Arabia
Sabine Baumann — Technische Universität München, Germany
Muhammed Enes Bayrakdar — Duzce University, Turkey
Emna Ben Slimane — National Engineering School of Tunis, Tunisia
Marija Boban — University of Split, Croatia
Leszek Borzemski — Wroclaw University of Technology, Poland
Alexandra Bousia — University of Thessaly, Greece
Peter Brída — University of Zilina, Slovakia
Nor Amani Filzah Bt. Mohd Kamil — University Tun Husseion Onn Malaysia, Malaysia
Manfred F. Buchroithner — Technische Universität Dresden, Germany
Changsheng Cai — Central South University, China
Alberto Cano — Virginia Commonwealth University, USA
Fali Cao — Xi'an Jiaotong University, China
Hongjun Cao — Ocean University of China, China
Yanan Cao — Institute of Information Engineering, China
Yuan-Long Cao — Jiangxi Normal University, China
Yue Cao — University of Surrey, UK
Gina Cavan — Manchester Metropolitan University, UK
Saman Shojae Chaeikar — K. N. Toosi University of Technology, Iran
Chee-Ming Chan — Universiti Tun Hussein Onn Malaysia, Malaysia
Meng-Chou Chang — National Changhua University of Education, Taiwan, China
Ray-I Chang — National Taiwan University, China
Wong Man Sing Charles — The Hong Kong Polytechnic University, SAR China
Chin-Ling Chen — Chaoyang University of Technology, Taiwan, China
Deng Chen — Wuhan Institute of Technology, China
Duanduan Chen — Beijing Institute of Technology, China
Hongli Chen — ZheJiang Sci-Tech University, China
Hsing-Chung Chen — Asia University, Taiwan, China
Jianjiao Chen — Georgia Institute of Technology, USA
Jianping Chen — China University of Geosciences, China

Jyh-Cheng Chen	National Yang-Ming University, Taiwan, China
Ken Chen	Chengdu University of Technology, China
Siwei Chen	National University of Defense Technology, China
Tao Chen	Tsinghua University, Beijing, China
Wei Chen	China University of Mining and Technology, China
Yanying Chen	Meteorological Science Institute of Chongqing, China
Bo Cheng	Beijing University of Posts and Telecommunications, China
Bo Cheng	Earth Observation and Digital Earth Chinese Academy of Sciences, China
James Cheng	Manchester Metropolitan University, UK
Qiang (Shawn) Cheng	University of Kentucky, USA
Cheng-Yuan	Huafan University, Taiwan, China
Yee-Jin Cheon	University of Science and Technology, South Korea
Simon K. S. Cheung	The Open University of Hong Kong, SAR China
Hung-Chun Chien	Jinwen University of Science and Technology, Taiwan, China
Gihwan Cho	Chonbuk National University, South Korea
Chi-Wai Chow	National Chiao Tung University, Taiwan, China
Edwin Chow	Texas State University, USA
Rajdeep Chowdhury	JIS College of Engineering, India
George Christakos	San Diego State University, USA
Basile Christaras	Aristotle University of Thessaloniki, Greece
Ying-Chun Chuang	Kun Shan University, Taiwan, China
Arie Croitoru	George Mason University, USA
Shengcheng Cui	Chinese Academy of Sciences, China
Yaodong Cui	Guangxi University, China
Agnieszka Cydzik-Kwiatkowska	University of Warmia and Mazury in Olsztyn, Poland
D. M. D'Addona	University of Naples Federico II, Italy
Arianna D'Ulizia	University of Rome La Sapienza, Italy
Rocío Pérez de Prado	University of Jaén, Spain
Jan Dempewolf	University of Maryland, USA
Weihua Dong	Beijing Normal University, China
Zhenjiang Dong	Nanjing University of Science and Technology, China
Chunjiang Duanmu	Zhejiang Normal University, China
Rahul Dutta	Oracle India Pvt. Ltd., India
Ahmed Moustafa Elmahalawy	Menoufia University, Egypt
Ahmet H. Ertas	Karabuk University, Turkey
Ismail Erturk	Kocaeli University, Turkey
Oscar Esparza	Universitat Politècnica de Catalunya, Spain
Kong Fah	University of Greenwich, UK
Ahmad Fakharian	Islamic Azad University, Iran
Hong Fan	Institute of Remote Sensing and Digital Earth Chinese Academy of Sciences, China

Ping Fang   Tongji University, China
Kuishuang Feng   University of Maryland, USA
David Forrest   University of Glasgow, UK
Ximing Fu   Tsinghua University, China
Gurjot Singh Gaba   Lovely Professional University, Jalandhar, India
Chenfei Gao   AT&T Labs, USA
Jinzhu Gao   University of the Pacific, USA
Lianru Gao   Chinese Academy of Sciences, China
Qiang Gao   Beihang University, Beijing, China
Zhenguo Gao   Harbin Engineering University, China
Krzysztof Gdawiec   University of Silesia, Poland
Jing Geng   Beijing Institute of Technology, China
Rozaida Ghazali   Universiti Tun Husssein Onn Malaysia, Malaysia
Grigoras Gheorghe   Gheorghe Asachi Technical University of Iasi,
                              Romania
Apostolos Gkamas   University Ecclesiastical Academy of Vella, Greece
Andrzej Glowacz   AGH University of Science and Technology, Poland
Adam Glowacz   AGH University of Science and Technology, Poland
Luis Gomez Deniz   University of Las Palmas de Gran Canaria, Spain
Prosanta Gope   Singapore University of Technology and Design,
                              Singapore
Aldy Gunawan   Singapore Management University, Singapore
Jeonghwan Gwak   Gwangju Institute of Science and Technology,
                              South Korea
Malka N. Halgamuge   The University of Melbourne, Australia
Maria Hallo   Notre Dame University of Belgium, Belgium
Saouli Hamza   University Khider Mohamed, Biskra, Algeria
Shuqing Hao   China University of Mining and Technology, China
Maguid H. M. Hassan   The British University in Egypt, Egypt
Anhua He   China Earthquake Administration, China
Anqi He   Queen Mary University of London, UK
Qian He   Guilin University of Electronic Technology, China
Trong-Minh Hoang   Posts and Telecommunication Institute of Technology,
                              Vietnam
Gassan Hodaifa Meri   Pablo de Olavide University, Spain
Erin M. Hodgess   University of Houston, USA
Soon Hyung Hong   Korea Advanced Institute of Science and Technology,
                              South Korea
Fangyong Hou   National University of Defense Technology, China
Yi-You Hou   Southern Taiwan University of Science and
                              Technology, Taiwan, China
Hui-Mi Hsu   National Ilan University, Taiwan, China
Wenchen Hu   University of North Dakota, USA
Yu-Chen Hu   Providence University, Taiwan, China
Yupeng Hu   Hunan University, China
Fangjun Huang   Sun Yat-sen University, China

Fei Huang	Ocean University of China, China
Gordon Huang	University of Regina, Canada
Jen-Fa Huang	National Cheng Kung University, Taiwan, China
Qinghui Huang	Tongji University, China
Shian-Chang Huang	National Changhua University of Education, Taiwan, China
Shuqiang Huang	Jinan University, China
Wanchen Huang	Wu Feng University, Taiwan, China
I-Shyan Hwang	Yuan Ze University, Taiwan, China
Lain-Chyr Hwang	I-Shou University, Taiwan, China
Min-Shiang Hwang	Asia University, Taiwan, China
Mahmood K. Ibrahem Al Ubaidy	Al-Nahrain University, Iraq
Hamidah Ibrahim	Universiti Putra Malaysia, Kuala Lumpur, Malaysia
Mohd Haziman Wan Ibriahim	Universiti Tun Hussein Onn Malaysia, Malaysia
Choi Jaeho	Chonbuk National University, South Korea
Yogendra Kumar Jain	Samrat Ashok Technological Institute, India
Sadaqat Jan	University of Engineering and Technology, Pakistan
Jin Su Jeong	Technical University of Madrid, Spain
Fuucheng Jiang	Tunghai University, Taiwan, China
Liangxiao Jiang	China University of Geosciences, China
Zhiyu Jiang	University of Chinese Academy of Sciences, China
Fusheng Jin	Beijing Institute of Technology, China
Behshad Jodeiri Shokri	Hamedan University of Technology, Iran
Hanmin Jung	Korea Institute of Science and Technology Information, South Korea
Yasin Kabalci	Nigde University, Turkey
Amjad Kallel	Ecole Nationale d'Ingénieurs de Sfax, Tunisia
Massila Kamalrudin	Universiti Teknikal Malaysia Melaka, Malaysia
Chi-Wai Kan	Hong Kong Polytechnic University, SAR China
Dimitris Kanellopoulos	University of Patras, Greece
Ismail Rakip Karas	Karabuk University, Turkey
Ali Karrech	University of Western Australia, Australia
Sedat Keleş	Çankırı Karatekin University, Turkey
Elsayed Esam M. Khaled	Assiut University, Egypt
Syed Abdul Rehman Khan	Iqra University and Brasi School of Supply Chain Management, Pakistan
Najeeb Ullah Khan	CECOS University, Pakistan
Manoj Khandelwal	Federation University, Australia
Ittipong Khemapech	University of the Thai Chamber of Commerce, Thailand
Hyunsung Kim	Kyungil University, South Korea
Chan King-ming	Hong Kong, SAR China
Janusz Klink	Wroclaw University of Technology, Poland
Marcin Kowalczyk	Warsaw University of Technology, Poland

Artur Krawczyk	AGH University of Science and Technology, Poland
Piotr Kulczycki	Polish Academy of Sciences, Poland
Ashok Kumar Kulkarni	Malla Reddy Institute of Medical Sciences, Thailand
Andrew Kusiak	The University of Iowa, USA
Guoming Lai	Guangdong Polytechnic of Science and Technology, China
Wen Cheng Lai	National Taiwan University of Science and Technology, Taiwan, China
Alain Lambert	University of Paris-Sud, France
Huey-Ming Lee	Chinese Culture University, Taiwan, China
Jiann-Shu Lee	National University of Tainan, China
Tzong-Yi Lee	Yuan Ze University, Taiwan, China
Bai Li	Zhejiang University, China
Chaokui Li	Hunan University of Science and Technology, China
Guoqing Li	Institute of Soil and Water Conservation, CAS & MWR, China
Hongjun Li	Beijing Forestry University, China
Hongyi Li	Jiangxi University of Finance and Economics, China
Mengxue Li	University of Maryland, USA
Ming-Jian Li	University of Wisconsin Madison, USA
Tianhong Li	Peking University, China
Wenwen Li	Arizona State University, USA
Xiaolei Li	Wuhan University, China
Ying Li	Dalian Maritime University, China
Zengxiang Li	Institute of High Performance Computing, Singapore
Zhaoyang Li	Jilin University, China
Zhenhong Li	University of Glasgow, UK
Chiangchi Liao	National Kaohsiung First University of Science and Technology, Taiwan, China
Guo-Shiang Lin	Da-Yeh University, Taiwan, China
Lily Lin	China University of Technology, Taiwan, China
Yi-Kuei Lin	National Taiwan University of Science and Technology, Taiwan, China
Yo-Sheng Lin	National Chi Nan University, Nantou, Taiwan, China
Yun Lin	Harbin Engineering University, China
Zhiting Lin	Anhui University, China
Bin Liu	Dalian University of Technology, China
Binyi Liu	Tongji University, China
Chang-Yu Liu	South China Agricultural University, China
Chengyu Liu	Shandong University, China
Jiangwei Liu	National Institute for Materials Science, Japan
Lei Liu	Beijing University of Technology, China
Lin Liu	University of Cincinnati, USA
Quanyi Liu	Tsinghua University, China
Shuai Liu	Inner Mongolia University, China

Shuo Liu	Institute of Remote Sensing and Digital Earth Chinese Academy of Sciences, China
Weimo Liu	George Washington University, Washington, USA
Yan Liu	The University of Queensland, Australia
Yu Liu	Peking University, China
Roberto Llorente	Universitat Politècnica de València, Spain
Elena Simona Lohan	Tampere University of Technology, Finland
Yongmei Lu	Texas State University, USA
Arnulfo Luévanos Rojas	Autonomous University of Coahuila, México
Edwin Lughofer	Johannes Kepler University Linz, Austria
Dandan Ma	University of Chinese Academy of Sciences, China
Qianli Ma	University of California, USA
Xiuyan Ma	Dalian University of Technology, China
José Manuel Machado	University of Minho, Portugal
Dionisio Machado Leite	Federal University of Mato Grosso do Sul, Brazil
Elżbieta Macioszek	Silesian University of Technology, Poland
Mojtaba Maghrebi	University of New South Wales, Australia
Basel Ali Mahafzah	The University of Jordan, Jordan
Abdallah Makhoul	University of Bourgogne Franche-Comté, France
Bappaditya Mandal	Institute for Infocomm Research, Singapore
Parvaneh Mansouri	Azad University, Iran
Guojun Mao	Central University of Finance and Economics, China
Amin Riad Maouche	M'Hamed Bougara Univerity of Boumerdes, Algeria
Stephan Mäs	Technische Universität Dresden, Germany
Samaneh Mashhadi	Iran University of Science and Technology, Iran
Imran Memon	Zhejiang University, China
Lei Meng	Nanyang Technological University, Singapore
Aleksandra Mileva	Goce Delchev University, Macedonia
Jolanta Mizera-Pietraszko	Institute of Mathematics and Computer Science, Opole University, Poland
Helmi Zulhaidi Mohd Shafri	Universiti Putra Malaysia, Malaysia
Nursabillilah Binti Mohd Ali	Universiti Teknikal Malaysia Melaka, Malaysia
Sheikh Ahmad Izaddin Sheikh Mohd Ghazali	Applied Sciences, Malaysia
Rosmayati Binti Mohemad	Universiti Malaysia Terengganu, Malaysia
Sathaporn Monprapussorn	Srinakharinwirot University, Thailand
Abderrahmen Mtibaa	Texas A&M University, Qatar
Alan Murray	Arizona State University, USA
Faizal Mustapha	Universiti Putra Malaysia, Malaysia
Houda Mzoughi	National Engineering School of Sfax, Tunisia
Barbara Namyslowska-Wilczynska	Wroclaw University of Science and Technology, Poland
Andrea Nanetti	Nanyang Technological University, Singapore
Roberto Nardone	University of Naples Federico II, Italy

Panayotis Nastou	University of the Aegean, Greece
Anand Nayyar	KCL Institute of Management and Technology, India
Alexey Nekrasov	Southern Federal University, Russia
Loc Nguyen	International Engineering and Technology Institute, Vietnam
Thang Trung Nguyen	Ton Duc Thang University, Vietnam
Bongani Ngwenya	Solusi University, Zimbabwe
Fan Ning	Beijing University of Posts and Telecommunications, China
Ruipeng Ning	East China Normal University, China
Alfrendo Satyanaga Nio	Nanyang Technological University, Singapore
Klimis Ntalianis	Athens University of Applied Sciences, Greece
Michael S. Okundamiya	Ambrose Alli University, Nigeria
Togay Ozbakkaloglu	The University of Adelaide, Australia
Sanjeevikumar Padmanaban	University of Johannesburg, South Africa
Jinghu Pan	Northwest Normal University, China
Weichun Pan	Zhejiang Gongshang University, China
Ti Peng	Southwest Jiaotong University, China
Phongsak Phakamach	Royal Thai Army, Thailand
Phongsak Phakamach	North Eastern University, Thailand
Bartłomiej Płaczek	University of Silesia, Poland
Ioan Lucian Popa	University of Alba Iulia, Romania
Dmitry Popov	Moscow State University of Printing Arts, Russia
Ashok Prajapati	IEEE Computer Society South-East Michigan, USA
B. Priya	Rajalakshmi Engineering College, India
Fengxiang Qiao	Texas Southern University, USA
Jiahu Qin	University of Science and Technology of China, China
Chen Qiu	Michigan State University, USA
Qiang Qu	Innopolis University, Russia
Tran Cao Quyen	University of Engineering and Technology, Pakistan
Rana Rahim-Amoud	The Lebanese University, Tripoli, Lebanon
Md Arafatur Rahman	University of Naples Federico II, Italy
Muhammad Tauhidur Rahman	King Fahd University of Petroleum and Minerals, Saudi Arabia
Hari Mohan Rai	Krishna College of Engineering, Ghaziabad, India
R. Raja	Alagappa University, India
Seethalakshmi Rajashankar	SASTRA University, India
Partha Pratim Ray	Sikkim University, India
Mohd Adib Bin Mohammad Razi	Universiti Tun Hussein Onn Malaysia, Malaysia
Fares Redouane	University of Science and Technology, Algeria
Luca Reggiani	Politecnico di Milano, Italy
Erfeng Ren	Qinghai University, China
Natalia Revollo Sarmiento	University of Buenos Aires, Argentina
Matt Rice	George Mason University, USA
Petri Rönnholm	Aalto University, Finland

Zulkifli Mohd Rosli	Universiti Teknikal Malaysia Melaka, Malaysia
Huada Daniel Ruan	Beijing Normal University, Hong Kong Baptist University United International College (UIC), China
Xiukai Ruan	Wenzhou University, China
Rukhsana Ruby	Shenzhen University, China
Paul Loh Ruen Chze	Nanyang Polytechnic, Singapore
Zuraidi Saad	Universiti of Teknologi MARA, Malaysia
Maytham Safar	Kuwait University, Kuwait
Youssef Said	National Engineering School of Tunis, Tunisia
Amirhossein Sajadi	Case Western Reserve University, USA
Furkan Hassan Saleh Rabee	University of Kufa, Iraq
Carlos Humberto Salgado	Universidad Nacional de San Luis, Argentina
Jaime Santos Reyes	Systems Engineering Department, Mexico
Arun K. Saraf	India
Biju T. Sayed Mohammed	Dhofar University, Oman
Hassene Seddik	ENSIT Tunisia, Tunisia
Indranil SenGupta	North Dakota State University, USA
Delia B. Senor	Mapua Institute of Technology Manila, Philippines
Zongyao Sha	Wuhan University, China
Imran Shafique Ansari	Texas A&M University at Qatar, Qatar
B. Shanmugapriya	Sri Ramakrishna College of Arts and Science for Women, India
Chun Shi	Hainan Normal University, China
Khor Shing Fhan	Universiti Malaysia Perlis, Malaysia
Muh-Tian Shiue	National Central University, China
Andy Shui-Yu Lai	Technological and Higher Education Institute of Hong Kong, SAR China
André Skupin	San Diego State University, USA
Sarmad Sohaib	University of Engineering and Technology, Pakistan
Ivo Stachiv	National Taiwan University, China
Anthony Stefanidis	George Mason University, USA
Ching-Liang Su	Da Yeh University, Taiwan, China
K. M. Suceendran	Tata Consultancy Services, India
Jianguo Sun	Harbin Engineering University, China
Le Sun	Victoria University, Australia
Rui Sun	Beijing Normal University, China
Wen-Tsai Sung	National Chin-Yi University of Technology, Taiwan, China
Fengqi Tan	University of Chinese Academy of Sciences, China
Xicheng Tan	Wuhan University, China
Cheng-Yuan Tang	Huafan University, New Taipei, Taiwan, China
Qian Tang	Xidian University, China
Zhu Tang	National University of Defense Technology, China
Kai Tao	Nanyang Technological University, Singapore
Daniel Thalmann	Nanyang Technological University, Singapore

Paul Torrens	University of Maryland, USA
Ljiljana Trajkovic	Simon Fraser University, Canada
Bor-Wen Tsai	National Taiwan University, China
Juin-Ling Tseng	Minghsin University of Science and Technology, Taiwan, China
Kurban Ubul	Xinjiang University, China
Kuniaki Uehara	Kobe University, Japan
Wilfried Uhring	University of Strasbourg, France
Najam ul Hasan	Dhofar University, Oman
Raul S. Ulloa Herrera	Instituto Nacional de Pesca de Mexico, Mexico
Sina Vafi	Charles Darwin University, Australia
J. L. van Genderen	University Twente, The Netherlands
Laura Mónica Vargas	National University of Córdoba, Argentina
Pariwate Varnakovida	Prince of Songkla University, Thailand
Alexandru Vulpe	University Politehnica of Bucharest, Romania
Rong-Jong Wai	National Taiwan University of Science and Technology, Taiwan, China
Farn Wang	National Taiwan University, Taiwan, China
Guodong Wang	South Dakota School of Mines and Technology, China
Guodong Wang	University of Chinese Academy of Sciences, China
Hongzhi Wang	Harbin Institute of Technology, China
Huamin Wang	Wuhan University, China
Jian Wang	Wuhan National Laboratory for Optoelectronics, Huazhong University of Science and Technology, China
Jinling Wang	University of New South Wales, Australia
Lixin Wang	Paine College, USA
Lulu Wang	Hefei University of Technology, China
Tao-Ming Wang	Tunghai University, Taiwan, China
Xiaofeng Wang	Chang'an University, China
Yongzhi Wang	Jilin University, China
Yuhua Wang	Wuhan University of Science and Technology, China
Zhendong Wang	Jiangxi University of Science and Technology, Jiangxi, China
Lifeng Wei	Beijing University of Civil Engineering and Architecture, China
Peng-Sheng Wei	National Sun Yat-Sen University, Taiwan, China
Yi-Fei Wei	Beijing University of Posts and Telecommunications, China
Bing Wen	Xinjiang Institute of Ecology and Chinese Academy of Science, China
Qingke Wen	Institute of Remote Sensing and Digital Earth Chinese Academy of Sciences, China
Janusz Wielki	University of Warsaw, Poland
Yair Wiseman	Bar-Ilan University, Israel
Yair Wiseman	Holon Institute of Technology, Israel

Ming Ming Wong	Sarawak Campus, Malaysia
Mike Worboys	The University of Maine, USA
Ben Wu	Princeton University, USA
Qunyong Wu	Fuzhou University, China
Wei-Chiang Wu	Da-Yeh University, Taiwan, China
Yong Xia	Northwestern Polytechnical University, Xian, China
Meng Xianyong	Zhuhai College of Jilin University, China
Wanan Xiong	University of Electronic Science and Technology of China, China
Chuanfei Xu	Concordia University, Canada
Qing-zheng Xu	Xi'an Communications Institute, China
Tianhua Xu	University College London, UK
Xin Yan	Wuhan University of Technology, China
Chaowei Yang	George Mason University, USA
Hui Yang	Beijing University of Posts and Telecommunications, Beijing, China
Huijun Yang	Northwest A&F University, China
Jingyu Yang	Shenyang Aerospace University, Shenyang, China
Liang Yang	Guangdong University of Technology, China
Liping Yang	Huazhong Agricultural University, China
Ting Yang	Tianjin University, China
Nicole Yang Lai Fong	Taylor's University Malaysia, Malaysia
Xiaojun Yang	Florida State University, USA
Jun Ye	Sichuan University of Science and Engineering, China
Qiang Ye	Nanjing Institute of Physical Education and Sports, China
Chien-Hung Yeh	Feng Chia University, Taiwan, China
Shih-Chuan Yeh	De Lin Institute of Technology, Taiwan, China
Ben-Shun Yi	Wuhan University, Wuhan, China
Peng-Yeng Yin	National Chi Nan University, Taiwan, China
Lee Beng Yong	Universiti Teknologi MARA Sarawak, Malaysia
Huan Yu	Chengdu University of Technology, Chengdu, China
Weiyu Yu	South China University of Technology, China
Xianchuan Yu	Beijing Normal University, China
Cheng Yuan	Huafan University, Taiwan, China
Hanning Yuan	Beijing Institute of Technology, China
Yang Yue	Juniper Networks, USA
Chau Yuen	Singapore University of Technology and Design (SUTD), Singapore
Noor Zaman	King Faisal University, Saudi Arabia
Muhammad Zeeshan	National University of Sciences and Technology, Pakistan
F. Benjamin Zhan	Texas State University, USA
Xianglin Zhan	Civil Aviation University of China, China
Di Zhang	Waseda University, Japan
Jianxun Zhang	Chongqing University of Technology, China

Keynote Speakers of GSKI 2017

Geospatial Data Science and Knowledge Discovery in Environmental Health Research

F. Benjamin Zhan

Texas State University, USA

Prof. F. Benjamin Zhan is Professor of Geographic Information Science in the Department of Geography at Texas State University. He was the founding director of the Texas Center for Geographic Information Science, and served as director of the center from 2003 to 2015. Among other honors, Professor Zhan was recipient of the Presidential Award for Excellence in Scholarly/Creative Activities at Texas State University, and held a Chang Jiang Scholar Guest Chair Professorship at Wuhan University in China from 2008 to 2011.

Abstract. There are over 80, 000 chemicals lurking in the environment and in everyday items. How some of these chemicals affect human health, particularly human reproductive health, remains unknown. The availability of geographically referenced environmental monitoring data and health outcome data makes it possible to examine the associations between maternal exposure to some of these chemicals and health issues in offspring. This presentation reports a data-driven approach for investigating these associations. The presentation first outlines the components of geospatial data science to support environmental health research. It then reports the datasets, analysis procedures, and results of two case studies based on large geographically referenced datasets. The first case study examines the association of maternal residential proximity to industrial facilities with toxic air emissions and birth defects in offspring. The second case study investigates the association of maternal residential exposure to some chemicals in the environment and low birth weights in offspring. Results from the two case studies demonstrate the power and potential of using geospatial data science to support environmental health research.

Spatial Data Mining: Theory and Application

Shuliang Wang

Beijing Institute of Technology, China

Shuliang Wang, PhD, a scientist in data science and software engineering, is a professor at the Beijing Institute of Technology in China. His research interests include spatial data mining and software engineering. For his innovatory study of spatial data mining, he was awarded the Fifth Annual InfoSci-Journals Excellence in Research Awards of IGI Global, IEEE Outstanding Contribution Award for Granular Computing, and one of China's National Excellent Doctoral Thesis Prizes.

URL: http://www.springer.com/gp/book/9783662485361#aboutAuthors

He is Guest Editor of:

(1) *International Journal of Systems Science*
(2) *International Journal of Data Warehousing and Mining*
(3) *Lecture Notes in Artificial Intelligence*

Abstract. The talk offers a systematic and practical overview of spatial data mining, which combines computer science and geo-spatial information science, allowing each field to profit from the knowledge and techniques of the other. To address the spatiotemporal specialties of spatial data, the authors introduce the key concepts and algorithms of the data field, cloud model, mining view, and Deren Li methods. The data field method captures the interactions between spatial objects by diffusing the data contribution from a universe of samples to a universe of population, thereby bridging the gap between the data model and the recognition model. The cloud model is a qualitative method that utilizes quantitative numerical characters to bridge the gap between pure data and linguistic concepts. The mining view method discriminates between the different requirements by using scale, hierarchy, and granularity in order to uncover the anisotropy of spatial data mining. The Deren Li method performs data preprocessing to prepare it for further knowledge discovery by selecting a weight for iteration in order to clean the observed spatial data as much as possible. In addition to the essential algorithms and techniques, the contribution provides application examples of spatial data mining in geographic information science and remote sensing. The practical projects include spatiotemporal video data mining for protecting public security, serial image mining on nighttime lights for assessing the severity of the Syrian crisis, and the applications in the government project "The Belt and Road Initiatives."

The Development of Geomatics Systems Based on Government Policy for Driving Thailand 4.0

Nopasit Chakpitak
Chiang Mai University, Thailand

Chakpitak Nopasit is Dean of the International College Chiang Mai University, Thailand. He was Dean of the College of Arts, Media and Technology, Chiang Mai University between 2004 and 2011. He was then promoted to be an assistant to the president, academic and international affairs, Chiang Mai University during 2011–2014. Before working at Chiang Mai University, he was responsible for many projects related to electronic engineering. His research interests lie in knowledge engineering and AI application in the power industry. Moreover, he collaborates and organizes conferences that linked to European and Asian countries.

Abstract. Thailand is an agricultural country which provides a huge amount of cultivation information. However, there is no system to properly organize and analyze this information. With the rapid growth of technology, geomatics systems are playing an important role in helping the Ministry of Agriculture and Cooperatives with decision-making. The Thai government's policy is to improve the economy, termed "Thailand 4.0." Tourism part is the most important factor to drive the Thai economy. The government has launched the 12th National Development Plan for the period 2017–2021, which involves the wealth of the nation and focuses on agriculture, light industry, heavy industry, and industry for the future. In the past, Thailand has had a middle-income trap, an inequality trap, and an imbalance trap. Thus, the government's policy encompasses the best practices that can be improved by three engines: the productive growth engine, the inclusive growth engine, and the green growth engine. Therefore, the national development plan can help Thailand to accomplish the goal of prosperity, security, and sustainability.

Smart Knowledge-Based Remote Sensing Analysis

Thomas Blaschke

University of Salzburg, Austria

Professor Blaschke's research interests include methodological issues of the integration of GIS, remote sensing, and image processing including aspects of participation and human–environment interaction. He has held several lecturer, senior lecturer, and professor positions in Germany, Austria, and the UK as well as temporary affiliations as guest professor and visiting scientist in Germany and the USA, including about 115 journal publications. He is author, co-author, or editor of 17 books, has received several academic prizes and awards including the Christian Doppler Prize in 1995 and was elected as a corresponding member of the Austrian Academy of Sciences in 2015. He has been project leader in various international and national research projects and serves on various editing boards of international journals, conference committees, and a dozen national research councils.

Publications: https://scholar.google.at/citations?user=kMroJzUAAAAJ&hl=de

Abstract. In response to the ever-increasing amount of spaceborne imaging sensors, a research group at the University of Salzburg developed a methodology for "smart" (knowledgeable), effective, and efficient Earth observation (EO) image-content extraction. It utilizes content-based image retrieval systems. The methodology is based on a priori 4D spatiotemporal scene domain knowledge to be mapped onto the image domain in terms of 2D image features and spatial constraints. This 4D to 2D mapping capability holds the solution to the vision problems, where the semantic gap from sensory data to high-level information products must be filled in. Another pivotal component is the concept of (geographic) object-based image analysis – GEOBIA or OBIA in short. OBIA aims for the generation of geographic information (in GIS-ready format) from which new spatial knowledge can be obtained. I will outline how OBIA methods and methodologies can structure the complexity of our environment and, likewise, the complexity of measurements into scaled representations for further analysis and monitoring tasks.

Segmentation Scale Selection in Geographic Object-Based Image Analysis (GEOBIA)

Shihong Du
Peking University, China

Shihong Du is currently Associate Professor of GIScience in the School of Earth and Space Sciences at Peking University and the vice director of the Institute of Remote Sensing and GIS. His research interests include spatial knowledge representation and reasoning, as well as intelligent mining and understanding of geospatial data including GIS and remote sensing data. He authored/co-authored over 80 journal articles and two books, and was awarded the New Century Excellent Talents in University and Second Place Award of National Science and Technology Progress in Surveying and Mapping.

Abstract. Geographic object-based image analysis (GEOBIA) with very-high-resolution (VHR) images plays an important role in geographical investigations, but its uncertainty in segmentation scale significantly affects the accuracy and reliability of GEOBIA results, e.g., object segmentations and classifications. Therefore, a scale-selection method is needed to determine the optimal scale for GEOBIA, which, however, can be influenced by three factors, i.e., categories, surrounding contrasts, and internal heterogeneities of objects. Thus, if we want to select the optimal scale, the three factors should be totally considered. The existing scale selections including supervised and unsupervised methods partly considered these three factors, but could not resolve all of them, thus, this issue is still open and needs further study. This report reviews five kinds of scale-selection methods, compares their advantages and disadvantages, and discusses the future direction of scale selections.

Contents – Part I

Smart City in Resource Management and Sustainable Ecosystem

The Research on 3D Modelling and Visualization of the Quaternary
in Tongzhou Area, Beijing.................................... 3
    Mingchao Zhang, Wei Li, Qiong Yan, Mingyi Zhang,
    and Wanjuan Liang

The Snow Disaster Risk Assessment of Township Population-Livestock
in Guoluo State of Qinghai Province............................ 13
    Changjun Xu, Tianyun Xue, and Yan Zhu

Spatial Autocorrelation of Urban Economic Growth in Shandong Province,
China by Using Time-Series Data of Per Capita GDP 23
    Jun Zhao, Yue Wang, and Xin Wang

Using Local Moran's I Statistics to Estimate Spatial Autocorrelation
of Urban Economic Growth in Shandong Province, China 32
    Jun Zhao, Yue Wang, and Wenxiu Shi

MIC for Analyzing Attributes Associated with Thai Agricultural Products ... 40
    Tisinee Surapunt, Chuanlu Liu, and Shuliang Wang

Historical Development of Corporate Social Responsibility Concept
in Kazakhstan... 48
    Ulsara Zhantore Nematullakyzy and XiaoHu Zhou

Information Security in the Smart Grid: Survey and Challenges 55
    Fei Wang, Zhenjiang Lei, Xiaohua Yin, Zhao Li, Zhi Cao,
    and Yale Wang

A Power Grid GIS Cloud Framework Based on Docker and OpenStack..... 67
    Xin Ji, Bojia Li, Junwei Yang, and Qiangxin Hu

A Factor Analysis-Based Detection Approach to Network Traffic
Anomalies for Power Telecommunication Access Networks............. 75
    Peng Ji, Hongyu Zhang, Wen Xu, Xianjing Liu, Qinghai Ou,
    Wenjing Li, and Le Qiu

Semi-formal Verification with Supporting Tool by Automatic Application
of Hoare Logic... 83
    Shingo Fukuoka, Yixiang Chen, and Shaoying Liu

A Fault Detection Device for Wind Power Generator Based
on Wireless Transmission.   96
    Guanqi Zhang, Xinyan Zhang, Lulu Yang, and Jialiang Luo

Multi-users Cooperation in Spectrum Sensing Based on HMM Model
for Cognitive Radios.   106
    Wenwei Yang, Weiyun Chen, Messaykabew Mekonen, and Tuanfa Qin

A VoLTE Encryption Experiment for Android Smartphones.   115
    Shaoru Liu, Yao Wang, Quanxin Zhang, and Yuanzhang Li

A Novel Differential Dipoles Frequency Reconfigurable Antenna   126
    Guiping Jin, Chuhong Deng, and Guangde Zeng

Classification of Network Game Traffic Using Machine Learning   134
    Yuning Dong, Mi Zhang, and Rui Zhou

How to Insure Reliability and Delay in Multi-controller Deployment.   146
    Hongyan Cui, Tao Yu, Lili Zheng, Tao Wang, Guoping Zhang,
    and Zongguo Xia

Interference-Avoid-Concept Based Indoor VLC Network
Throughput Optimization   158
    Yan Chen and Hongyu Yang

A Comparative Acoustic Analysis of Mongolian Long Tunes
of Pastoral and Hymn   168
    Guangming, Yuhua Qi, and Guoqiang Chen

RSSI Based Localization with Mobile Anchor for Wireless
Sensor Networks.   176
    Yakun Zhao, Juan Xu, and Jiaolong Jiang

Mobile Device Selection Based on Doppler Shift with High Resolution   188
    Lingfei Yu and Xixi Chang

The Double-Coverage Algorithm for Mobile Node Deployment
in Underwater Sensor Network   198
    Xue Wang, Nana Li, Fang Liu, and Yuanming Ding

Goodwill Asset, Ultimate Ownership, Management Power
and Cost of Equity Capital: A Theoretical Review   212
    Haoqian Shi

Total-Neighbor-Distinguishing Coloring by Sums of the Three Types
of Product Graphs.   221
    Xiahong Cai, Shuangliang Tian, and Huan Yang

Research on the Fruit and Vegetable Cold Chain Preservative System
Based on Compressive Sensing................................. 229
   Ying Zhang, Ruqi Cheng, Yangyang Li, and Shaohui Chen

A Heterogeneous Architecture Based Power Control for Cooperative Safety
Systems.. 238
   Pulong Xie, Fuqiang Liu, Nguyen Ngoc Van, and Lijun Zu

Monitoring of the Ground Subsidence in Macao Using the PSI Technique... 250
   Shaojing Jiang, Fenghua Shi, Bo Hu, Weibo Wang, and Qianguo Lin

An Application of a Location Algorithm Integrating Beidou and WSN in
Agricultural IOT.. 262
   Tao Chi, Lei Wang, and Ming Chen

Spatial Data Acquisition Through RS and GIS in Resource Management and Sustainable Ecosystem

A Distinct Approach for Discovering the Relationship of Disasters
Using Big Scholar Datasets 271
   Liang Zheng, Fei Wang, Xiaocui Zheng, and Binbin Liu

Design of Sensor System for Air Pollution Monitoring 280
   *Hua Fan, Junru Li, Yulin Qin, Quanyuan Feng, Dagang Li,
   Daqian Hu, Yuanjun Cen, and Hadi Heidari*

China Crude Oil Purchase Decision Under Considering Disruption Risk 289
   Wei Pan and Cheng Hu

Variation of NDVI in Wetland of Nansihu Lake Based
on Landsat Images 297
   Fang Dong and Xiaoying Chi

Mapping Heavy Metals in Cultivated Soils Based on Land Use Types
and Cokriging.. 305
   *Jinling Zhao, Chuang Liu, Qixiang Song, Yan Jiang, Qi Hong,
   and Linsheng Huang*

Detection of Redundant Condition Expression for Large Scale
Source Code.. 312
   Dandan Gong, Wensheng Xu, Chunfang Qiu, and Libei Zhou

Airplane Fine-Grained Classification in Remote Sensing Images
via Transferred CNN-Based Models 318
   Li Yan, Shouhong Wan, Peiquan Jin, and Chang Zou

Object Detection Based on Deep Feature for Optical Remote
Sensing Images.   327
   Xujiang Zhao, Shouhong Wan, Chang Zou, Xingyue Li,
   and Li Yan

Ship Detection from Remote Sensing Images Based on Deep Learning   336
   Ziqiang Yuan, Jing Geng, and Tianru Dai

Congestion Analysis Based on Remote Sensing Images.   345
   Hanning Yuan, Jiakai Yang, Xiaolei Li, and Shengyu Ma

Detection of Oil Spill Through Fully Convolutional Network.   353
   Yan Li, Xiaofei Yang, Yunming Ye, Lunan Cui, Binfeng Jia,
   Zhongming Jiang, and Shaokai Wang

A Secure and Energy-Efficient Data Aggregation Protocol
Based on Wavelet.   363
   Jiana Bi and Qiangkui Leng

Efficient Processing of the SkyEXP Query Over Big Data   372
   Zhenhua Huang, Chang Yu, Yong Tang, Yunwen Chen, Shuhua Zhang,
   and Zhonghua Zheng

Research on Comprehensive Benefits of Urban Rail Transit System
Based on the Joint Evaluation Methods   384
   Hongjiao Xue, Ping Yang, and Hong Zhang

Experimental Analysis of Space Acoustic Field Positioning Characteristics
of Plecotus Auritus Pinna Model.   397
   Sen Zhang, Xin Ma, Yufeng Pan, and Hongwang Lu

Spectrum Zoom Processing for Low-Altitude and Slow-Speed
Small Target Detection   405
   Xuwang Zhang, Jinping Sun, and Songtao Lu

Knowledge-Aided Wald Detector for Range-Extended Target
in Nonhomogeneous Environments   414
   Nan Wang, Jinping Sun, and Wenguang Wang

Data Deterministic Deletion Scheme Based on DHT Network
and Fragmentation Deletion   426
   Yongsheng Zhang, Nengneng Li, Ranran Cui, and Yueqin Fan

Wavelet Entropy Analysis for Detecting Lying Using Event-Related
Potentials.   437
   Yijun Xiong, Junfeng Gao, and Ran Chen

Improved CRC for Single Training Sample on Face Recognition   445
  Wei Huang and Liming Miao

Combating Malicious Eavesdropper in Wireless Full-Duplex Relay
Networks: Cooperative Jamming and Power Allocation   452
  Ronghua Luo, Jun Lei, and Guobing Hu

Short-Term Subway Passenger Flow Prediction Based on ARIMA   464
  Danfeng Yan, Junwen Zhou, Yao Zhao, and Bin Wu

Bounded Correctness Checking for Knowledge with eCTLK   480
  Fei Pu

Ecological and Environmental Data Processing and Management

AHP-Based Susceptibility Assessment on Debris Flows in Semiarid
Mountainous Region: A Case of Benzilan-Changbo Segment in the
Upper Jinsha River, China.   495
  Jian Chen, Yan Li, Wendy Zhou, Chong Xu, Saier Wu,
  and Wen Yue

Influence of Index Weights on Land Ecological Security Evaluation:
The Case Study of Chengdu Plain Economic Zone, China   510
  Ruoheng Tian, Chengyi Huang, Liangji Deng, Conggang Fang,
  Weizhong Zeng, Yongjiang Lei, Lianxin Yang, and Chao Xue

An Empirical Study on the Effect of Eco Agriculture Policy
in Erhai River Basin   520
  Xiaoyan Yan and Youde Wu

Study on the Evolution of Industrial Division of Labor and Structure
in Central Yunnan Urban Agglomeration   527
  Yan Li and Xiaoyan Yan

The Transition Probabilities from Captive Animal's Behavior
by Non-invasive Sensing Method Using Stochastic
Multilevel State Model   534
  Phudinan Singkahmfu, Pruet Boonma, Wijak Srisujjalertwaja,
  Anurak Panyanuwat, and Natapot Warrit

The Temporal Precipitation in the Rainy Season of Koxkar Glacier
Based on Observation Over Tianshan Mountain in Northwest of China   543
  Chuancheng Zhao, Shuxia Yao, Jian Wang, and Haidong Han

Graph-Based Tracklet Stitching with Feature Information for Ground
Target Tracking   550
  Jinbin Fu, Jinping Sun, and Peng Lei

Study In-band & Out-of-band in Monopole Antennas
and the Effect of Curved Ground Surface........................... 558
  Mabrook Masoud A, Donglin Su, and Junjun Wang

Multi-scale Feature Based Automatic Screen Character Integrity Detection... 569
  Chenhong Sui, Nan Zhu, and Xu Qiao

An Algorithm Towards Energy-Efficient Scheduling for Real-Time Tasks
Under Cloud Computing Environment............................ 578
  Tongtong Sun, Ye Tao, and Ruichun Tang

Execution Time Forecasting of Automatic Test Case Generation
Based on Genetic Algorithm and BP Neural Network 592
  Ershun Luo, Dahai Jin, Bo Zhang, and Mingnan Zhou

An Improved Interconnection Network for Data Center Based
on BCube Structure... 601
  Jianfei Zhang, Weiwu Ren, and Guannan Qu

Message Passing Algorithm Based on Cut-Node Tree 608
  Huanming Zhang

Energy Efficiency Optimization in SFR-Based Power
Telecommunication Networks................................. 615
  *Honghao Zhao, Siwen Zhao, Rimin Jiang, Haiyang Huang,
  Xiangdong Jiang, and Ling Wang*

Constructing Algorithm of MLMS Data Center Network 629
  Jianfei Zhang, Weiwu Ren, and Guannan Qu

Research on Election of Distributed Wireless Multi-hop
Self-organized Network 637
  Xiaodong Shang, Xu Li, and Xin Tong

Application of CO_2 Gas Monitoring System in the CO_2 Geological
Storage Project 652
  Shaojing Jiang, Xufeng Li, Weibo Wang, Lisha Hu, and Qianguo Lin

Key Technologies of Comprehensive Monitoring of Safety Production
in Networked Coal Mine 660
  *Jie Tian, Hongyao Wang, Louyue Zhang, Pufan Zhu, Yaosong Hu,
  and Shan Song*

Author Index 671

Contents – Part II

Advanced Geospatial Model and Analysis for Understanding Ecological and Environmental Process

Feature Point Detection and Target Tracking Based on SIFT and KLT 3
Huajing Zheng and Changchang Chen

Research on the Handwriting Character Recognition Technology Based on the Image Statistical Characteristics 13
Yongfeng Sun, Zhonghua Guo, and Weijiang Qiu

A Listwise Approach for Learning to Rank Based on Query Normalization Network 21
Chongchong Zhu, Fusheng Jin, Yan Li, and Tu Peng

Soft Frequency Reuse Scheme with Maximum Energy Efficiency in Power Telecommunication Networks 31
Lina Cao, Daosheng Li, Fei Xia, Xiaobo Huang, Siwen Zhao, and Shuang Liu

Mining High Utility Co-location Patterns Based on Importance of Spatial Region 43
Jiasong Zhao, Lizhen Wang, Peizhong Yang, and Hongmei Chen

Analyzing Community Structure Based on Topology Potential over Complex Network System 56
Kanokwan Malang, Shuliang Wang, and Tianru Dai

Static Detection Method for C/C++ Memory Defects Based on Triad Memory Model 69
Yuxia Wang, Fusheng Jin, Xiangyu Han, and Runan Wang

An Immune Neural Network Model for Aeroengine Performance Monitoring. 79
Wei Wang, Shengli Hou, and Jing Guo

Based on AHP and Minimum Spanning Tree of Fuzzy Clustering Analysis of Spatial Sequence Arrangement of Old Dismantling Area 88
Juanmin Cui, Wenguang Ji, and Yang Jae Lee

An Improved Method on the Wave Height of Ocean Surface Based on X-Band Radars. 98
Yi Wang, Mingyuan He, Haiyang Zhang, and Jingjing Ge

Short-Term Operation Optimization of Cascade Hydropower Reservoirs
with Linear Functional Analysis   107
    Yanke Zhang, Jinjun You, Changming Ji, and Jiajie Wu

Digging More in Neural World: An Efficient Approach for Hyperspectral
Image Classification Using Convolutional Neural Network   117
    Adnan Iltaf, Matee Ullah, Junling Shen, Zebin Wu, Chuancai Liu,
    and Zeeshan Ahmad

An Intelligent Cartographic Generalization Algorithm Selecting Mode
Used in Multi-scale Spatial Data Updating Process   127
    Junkui Xu, Dong Li, Longfei Cui, and Xing Zhang

A Cross-National Analysis of the Correlated Network Structure
of Marine Transportation in the Indian Ocean Rim Association   135
    Shuguang Liu, Xiaoxin Yang, and Han Zhang

A Software Reliability Combination Model Based on Genetic
Optimization BP Neural Network   143
    Runan Wang, Fusheng Jin, Li Yang, and Xiangyu Han

Practical Experience of the Use of RGB Camera Images in UAV
for the Generation of 3D Images in the Accurate Detection Distance
of Vegetation Risk in Right-of-Way Transmission Line   152
    Mauricio G. M. Jardini, Augustinho José Menin Simões,
    José Antonio Jardini, Jose Mauricio Scovino de Souza,
    and Ferdinando Crispino

An Exploratory Study and Application of Data Mining: Railway
Alarm Data   161
    Yichuan Yang, Hanning Yuan, Dapeng Li, Tianyun Shi, and Wen Cheng

Research on Smooth Switching Technology of UAV Complex Flight
Control Laws   170
    Xianwei Hao, Aiqun Xiao, Duo Li, and Ying Wang

Study on the Spatial and Temporal Pattern of Qinghai Lake Area
in the Past 50 Years   178
    Baokang Liu, Yu'e Du, Weiguo He, Shuiqiang Duan,
    and Tiangang Liang

An Algebraic Multigrid Preconditioner Based on Aggregation
from Top to Bottom   192
    Jianping Wu, Fukang Yin, Jun Peng, and Jinhui Yang

COKES: Continuous Top-k Keyword Search in Relational Databases   205
    Yanwei Xu and Yicheng Yang

Core Competencies Keywords Discovering Algorithm
for Employment Advertisements   218
   Xiaoping Du, Lelai Deng, Xingzhi Zhang, and Qinghong Yang

A Clothing Image Retrieval System Based on Improved Itti Model   232
   Yuping Hu, Chunmei Wang, Hang Xiao, and Sen Zhang

Study on a Kind of War Zone Equipment Material's Urgency
Transportation Problem for Multi-requirement Points   243
   Peng Dong, Peng Yu, Kewen Wang, and Gongda Yan

A New Algorithm for Classification Based on Multi-classifiers Learning   254
   Yifeng Zheng, Guohe Li, and Wenjie Zhang

An Information Distance Metric Preserving Projection Algorithm   263
   Xiaoming Bai and Chengzhang Wang

Bug Patterns Detection from Android Apps   273
   Waheed Yousuf Ramay, Arslan Akbar, and Muhammad Sajjad

An Improved PHD Filter Based on Dynamic Programming   284
   Meng Fang, Wenguang Wang, Dong Cao, and Yan Zuo

Type Analysis and Automatic Static Detection of Infeasible Paths   294
   Fuping Zeng, Wenjing Liu, and Xiaodong Gou

A New Perspective on Evaluation Software of Contribution Rate
for Weapon Equipment System   305
   Huadong Yang, Fang Liu, and Yongdun Yan

Research on Sentiment Analysis of Online Public Opinion Based
on Semantic   313
   Zhengtao Jiang and Lu Liu

A New Method of Dish Innovation Based on User Preference
Multi-objective Optimization Genetic Algorithm   322
   Zijie Mei and Yinghua Zhou

Algorithm for Calculating the Fractal Dimension of Internet
AS-Level Topology   334
   Jun Zhang, Hai Zhao, and Wenbo Qi

An Improved GPSR Routing Algorithm Based on Vehicle
Trajectory Mining   343
   Peng Zhou, Xiaoqiang Xiao, Wanbin Zhang, and Weixun Ning

Design and Implementation of a Self-powered Sensor Network Node   350
   Jun Jiao, Moshi Wang, and Lichuan Gu

Mining Association Rules from Multidimensional Transformer
Defect Records.   364
  Yi Yang, Yujie Geng, Yi Ju, Xuan Zhao, and Danfeng Yan

A Modeling Algorithm to Network Flows in OTN Based on E1 Business . . .   375
  Fei Xia, Fanbo Meng, Zongze Xia, Xiaobo Huang, and Li Song

Computing Offloading to Save Energy Under Time Constraint Among
Mobile Devices.   383
  Xiaomin Zhou, Yong Zhang, and Tengteng Ma

A New Weighted Connection-Least Load Balancing Algorithm Based
on Delay Optimization Strategy   392
  Guangshun Li, Heng Ding, Junhua Wu, and Shuzhen Xu

An Extensible PNT Simulation Verification Platform Based on Deep
Learning Algorithm.   404
  Shuangna Zhang, Li Tian, and Fuzhan Yue

A Binary Translation Backend Registers Allocation Algorithm Based
on Priority   414
  Jun Wang, Jianmin Pang, Liguo Fu, Zheng Shan, Feng Yue,
  and Jiahao Zhang

Applications of Geo-Informatics in Resource Management and Sustainable Ecosystem

A New Information Publishing System for Mobile Terminal
by Location-Based Services Based on IoT   429
  Li Zhu and Guoguang Ma

An Improved Spatial-Temporal Interpolation and Its Application
in the Oceanic Observations.   437
  Huizan Wang, Ren Zhang, Hengqian Yan, Shuliang Wang,
  and Lei Liu

The Spatial-Temporal Simulation of Mankind's Expansion
on the Tibetan Plateau During Last Deglaciation-Middle Holocene   447
  Tianyun Xue, Changjun Xu, and Sunmei Jin

Remote Environmental Information Real-Time Monitoring and Processing
System of Cow Barn.   457
  Faquan Yang, Chunsheng Zhang, and Ling Yang

The Application of Big Data Technology in Competitive Sports Research . . .   466
  Xiaobing Du

UMine: Study on Prevalent Co-locations Mining from Uncertain Data Sets . . .   472
  Pingping Wu, Lizhen Wang, Wenjing Yang, and Zhulin Su

Research for Distributed and Multitasking Collaborative
Three-Dimensional Virtual Scene Simulation 482
    Jing Zhou

Comparisons of Features for Chinese Word Segmentation 492
    Xiaofeng Liu

Forecasting of Roof Temperature in a Grey Prediction Model
with Optimal Fractional Order Accumulating Operator................. 500
    Yuan Zhang, Xiaoyong Peng, and Wei Hu

Wa Language Syllable Classification Using Support Multi-kernel Vector
Machine Optimized by Immune Genetic Algorithm.................... 513
    Meijun Fu, Wenlin Pan, Hua Yang, and Huazhen Dong

A Novel Method for Detecting the Degree of Fatigue
Using Mobile Camera 524
    Qing Yu, Ludi Wang, Ying Xing, Xiaoguang Zhou, and Wei Zhou

WPNet: Wallpaper Recommendation with Deep Convolutional
Neural Networks... 531
    *Hang Yu, Quan Cheng, Jiejing Shao, Boyang Yu, Guangli Li,
and Shuai Lü*

Equipment Maintenance Support Decision Method Research Based
on Big Data... 544
    Ziqiang Wang and Yuanzhou Li

Research on a New Density Clustering Algorithm Based on MapReduce.... 552
    Yun Wu and Zhixiong Zhang

Bounded Correctness Checking for Extended CTL Properties
with Past Operators.. 563
    Fei Pu

A Cloud Based Three Layer Key Management Scheme for VANET 574
    Wanan Xiong and Bin Tang

An Evaluation Method Based on Co-word Clustering Analysis – Case
Study of Internet + Innovation and Entrepreneurship Economy........... 588
    Yunjie Ji, Yao Jiang, and Ling He

An Empirical Case of Applying MFA on Company Level 596
    Lina Wang and Koen Milis

PAPR Reduction Using Interleavers with Downward Compatibility
in OFDM Systems 611
    Y. Aimer, B. S. Bouazza, S. Bachir, C. Duvanaud, K. Nouri, and C. Perrine

Design and Implementation of Wireless Invoice Intelligent Terminal Based
on ARM 622
   Yuexia Zhang, Shuang Chen, and Yijun Jia

The Design and Implementation of Swarm-Robot Communication
Analysis Tool... 631
   Yanqi Zhang, Bo Zhang, and Xiaodong Yi

The Research and Implementation of the Fine-Grained Implicit
Authentication Framework for Android 641
   Hongbo Zhou and Yahui Yang

Fair Electronic Voting via Bitcoin Deposits 650
   Xijuan Wu, Baodian Wei, Haibo Tian, Yusong Du, and Xiao Ma

Research and Development of Door Handle Test Equipment Electrical
System Based on Automatic Control Technology 662
   *Kang Gao, Hangjian Guan, Chengyang Wei, Zhuang Ouyang,
Zhijie Wang, and Xiaoping Huang*

Analysis and Solution of University Examination Arrangement Problems.... 670
   Dengyuhui Li, Yiran Su, Huizhu Dong, Zhigang Zhang, and Jiaji Shen

Analyzing the Information Behavior Under the Complexity Science
Management Theory 684
   Rongying Zhao, Mingkun Wei, and Danyang Li

Risk Explicit Interval Linear Programming Model for CCHP System
Optimization Under Uncertainties 695
   Ling Ji, Lucheng Huang, and Xiaomin Xu

Wireless Sensor Network Localization Approach Based on Bayesian MDS.... 709
   Zhongmin Pei

Empirical Study on Social Media Information Influencing
Traveling Intention 717
   Chunhui Huang

Evolution of Online Community Opinion Based on Opinion Dynamics 725
   Liang Yu, Donglin Chen, and Bin Hu

Research on the Growth of Engineering Science and Technology Talents
from the Perspective of Complex Science. 736
   Haifeng Zhao and Weijia Jiang

Research on the Relationship Between Entrepreneurship Learning
and Entrepreneurship Ability Based on Social Network 746
   Gang Hao, Qing Sun, and Yingying Ding

Using C Programming in Analytic Hierarchy Process and Its Application
in Decision-Making.   760
    Gebin Zhang and Jianmin Zhang

Author Index   769

Smart City in Resource Management and Sustainable Ecosystem

The Research on 3D Modelling and Visualization of the Quaternary in Tongzhou Area, Beijing

Mingchao Zhang[1,2(✉)], Wei Li[3], Qiong Yan[2], Mingyi Zhang[4],
and Wanjuan Liang[1]

[1] Development Research Center of China Geological Survey,
45 Fuwai Street, Xicheng District, Beijing 100037, China
cgszhangmc@163.com
[2] China University of Geosciences, Beijing 100083, China
[3] The 7th Gold Detachment of Chinese Armed Police Force,
Yantai 264000, China
[4] Wuhan Geotechnical Engineering and Surveying Co. Ltd.,
Wuhan 430022, China

Abstract. Urban 3D geological modeling is a typical application of 3D information technology in urban geological area, which significantly promotes expression of result of urban geological investigation, upgrades capability of evaluating and predicting urban geological resources and environment, and has important supporting function to urbanization construction in China. By establishing model of 3D geological body of quaternary formation in Tongzhou area, the geological information was transformed into visual 3D geological body and been visually display, which simplifies management of underground space in city, and the visualization system were completed to realize various function, which has both theoretical and practical importance to evaluation of underground resource, protection of supergenetic ecological environment, and rational development of underground resource, and provides scientific basis for decision-making in engineering construction planning and development, management and development of groundwater resources, pollution monitoring, and ground subsidence.

Keywords: 3D modelling · Visualization · The quaternary
Tongzhou area · Urban geology

1 Introduction

With progress of modeling technique, evaluation of urban engineering geological environment with 3D model of geological body is conducted gradually. Combination of urban geological work and urban planning, establishment of 3D urban geological model, and comprehensive evaluation of urban engineering geological environment under the condition of 3D visualization is one of hotspots in the geological study recently [1–4]. Moreover, through combining 3D GIS (Geographic Information System) and 3D visualization with several methods about description, analysis and evaluation of urban

© Springer Nature Singapore Pte Ltd. 2018
H. Yuan et al. (Eds.): GSKI 2017, CCIS 848, pp. 3–12, 2018.
https://doi.org/10.1007/978-981-13-0893-2_1

geological characteristics and models, 3D urban geological information system has been constructed in the foreign countries with advanced GIS, urban remote sensing, database, 3D visualization, and computer network technologies, which enhances research on the urban geological work [5–9]. Based on achievements from previous geological survey and regional geological investigation, e.g. data of Quaternary section and drilling holes, the paper focuses on establishing 3D model of Quaternary geological body, establishing visual display of 3D model, converting the geological information into visual 3D geologic images, which provides scientific basis for decision-making in development and management of urban underground space, engineering construction planning and development, management and development of groundwater resources, pollution monitoring, and research on ground subsidence.

2 Status of 3D Modeling

In the 3D modeling and visualization of geological body, the research on information processing, data organization, spatial modeling and digital expression in formation and its surroundings is conducted with modern spatial information theory, realizing true 3D display and visualization interaction. The technology is capable of recovering the structure, morphological characteristics, and spatial distribution of geological bodies under the surface, and rotation, virtual wandering, slice analysis, and virtual drilling in the targeted objects are manipulated randomly, which facilitates dynamic observation of internal details, and acquaintance with relationship between the objects and surrounding geological environment, and provides support for quantitative analysis, exploration, and utilization of geological information. The concept of 3D modeling and visualization of geological body was firstly presented by SW Houlding (1993) in Canada, and it has been developed rapidly with computer and geospatial information technologies, and become hotspot in several fields, e.g. petroleum exploration, mathematical geology, geotechnical engineering, hydropower investigation, and visualization in scientific computing. The 3D modeling methods presented by scholars worldwide are divided into two types. The first is "entity modeling", which is realized through mathematical algorithms, e.g. determination of boundaries of geological body with sections, and the 3D visualization is realized with multi-2D sections. The second is visual computation which is constructed with geological statistical modeling, and the sampling data is converted into volumetric data with 3D interpolation.

In the meanwhile, there emerged a series of professional software with function of 3D geological modeling, e.g. Surpac from SSI in Australia, MicroMine from Micro-Mine, GOCAD from Université Henri Poincaré-Nancy, which are widely applied in petroleum, and engineering, mining, and geological industries. Several scholars and research institutes in China are dedicated to development of 3D geological modeling software, e.g. Ttina3DM (3D geological modeling software), GeoView (3D geoscience visualization information system), and research on 3D visualization system for geological survey, and they have made impressive achievements in 3D spatial data models, analogic tri-prism and quasi tri-prism volume (QTPV). This paper focuses on 3D visualization modeling with Surpac.

With the mature 3D visualization modeling technology and 3D GIS software, the metallogenic prediction based on 3D GIS has become the hotspot [10–12]. In last decade, with rapidly developing computer 3D technology, an increasing number of scholars initiate research on blind deposit with large scale in 3D view, and they have made great progress. Simulation and inversion of geological process, and 3D quantitative prediction and visual expression of blind deposit are realized through integration of true 3D platform of geological simulation and model for statistical prediction of mineral resources.

3 Overview of Geology

Tongzhou is located in the southeast of Beijing, and north end of The Beijing-Hangzhou Grand Canal (Fig. 1). The plain area of Beijing is located in the northwest margin of North China Plain, surrounded by mountains in its western, northern, and northeast sides, and adjacent to Jun Du Shan and Yanshan Mountain in north, and Western Hill and Tai-hang Mountains in west. The plain is resulted from alluviation by Yongding River, Chaobai River, Wenyu River, Juma River and Jucuo River, with elevation between 20 m and 60 m, southeast trend, and slope from 1% to 3%.

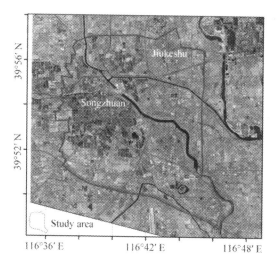

Fig. 1. Geographical location of the study area.

The landform in Tongzhou is divided into alluvial plain, fluvial terrace, riverbed and flood plain, sandy flood fan and sand dune, depression, mining earth and sandpit, etc. Tongzhou is covered with many surface river systems, including the North Grand Cannel, Wenyu River, Liangshui River, Tonghui Cannel, Xiaozhong River, Yunchaojian River and Yudai River, etc., which are dominated by Chaobai River and the North Grand Cannel.

The exposure formation in Tongzhou is Quaternary (Q) diluvial-alluvial loose sediment, below which is underlying subterrane dominated by Ji Xian System (Jx), Qingbaikou System (Qn), and Cambrian System (∈). The study area is located in the alluvial-proluvial plain of Yongding River, Chaobai River, and Wenyu River, with typical multilayer rock-soil structure. Within 30 m below surface, there exist two layers of relatively thick sandy soil, which is intercalated with clayey soil layer. From west to east, the sandy soil increases and thickens, and the burial becomes shallow, with minimum thickness of only 1 m and maximum thickness of 18.5 m. The burial depth is more than 15 m near western Guo Jia Chang, and less than 5 m in eastern Xiao Dou Ge Zhuang.

Located in the northeast part of Daxing Uplift, the study area is dominated by Nanyuan-Tongxian Fault, which is distributed in NE direction with strike between 35°–50°, length around 110 km long, fault plane trend of NW, and dip between 50°–75°. Tongzhou covers middle and north sections of Nanyuan-Tongxian Fault. The middle section lies between Fengtai overlapping sag and Daxing overlapping uplift, by which Tertiary sedimentation is controlled. The fault activity was strong during Tertiary, and weakened since Quaternary. The north section showed signs of activity in Early and Middle Pleistocene.

The active fault is dominated by Nanyuan-Tongxian Fault, which is main controlling fault in southern plain area of Beijing, and it separates Beijing overlapping sag and Daxing overlapping uplift. The fault is distributed in NE direction, origins from Tashang in Zhuoxian, Hebei in south, extends along Yandiaowo, Matou, Liangjianfang, and Hulufa in Fangshan area, through Yongding River to the northeast, and spreads among Nanyuan Town, Dahongmen, Gaobeidian, Dingfuzhuang, Shuangbutou, Pingjiatong, and Beiwu, Shunyi, with total length of about 110 km. The fault shows "S" shape in the plane, with general strike of NE 35°–50°, which changes sharply in Nanyuan Town, and stabilizes at 45° averagely to the south of Nanyuan Town, shows NNE 20°–30° from Nanyuan Town to Dahongmen, and changes to 50° to the north of Dahongmen. The fault plane has dip of NW 50°–75°.

The burial depth of ground water is below 6 m along Heizhuanghu - Liyuan - Songzhuang, gradually decreases in both sides, and keeps above 3 m around Louzizhuang and Cangtou. The ground water is divided into phreatic water and confined water within 30 m below surface, where regionally exists the upper stagnant water.

Generally, the burial depth of phreatic water in Quaternary pore is between 0.7 m–9 m, with water level elevation between 12 m–24 m. The lithology of aquifer is dominated by silty-fine sand and silt layer. The burial depth of confined water head is generally between 14 m–20 m, with water level elevation between 0 m–8 m. The lithology of aquifer is dominated by Quaternary silty-fine sand, medium-coarse sand, rounded pebble and silt layer. Two and more layers of confined groundwater occurred regionally.

4   3D Modeling

The research on 3D modeling covers data collection, organization, and pre-treatment, and the data include 219 copies of exploration drilling hole data, 4 copies of section data, 59 copies of vectorization drilling holes data, 47 copies of deep drilling holes data, high-resolution remote sensing image of 157.85 km^2, and 1:1000 ground elevation data (resolution is 30 m).

4.1   Processing of Basic Data

a. Exploration line section

The map of exploration line section, a basic map reflecting geologic engineering results, is finished by comprehensively collecting engineering data in exploration lines and achievements of geologic research on surface, and reflects the formation, and permeability. It is a cross-section diagram integrating the information of geological body drawn by geological engineering professionals with the drilling hole information based on geological requirements. The section reflects the real geological conditions. The collected map of exploration line sections are presented in picture formats (Fig. 2A). However, in practical works, the map of AutoCAD version is applied. Thus, the map of picture format is converted to the file compatible with AutoCAD through vectorization in MAPGIS and similar software.

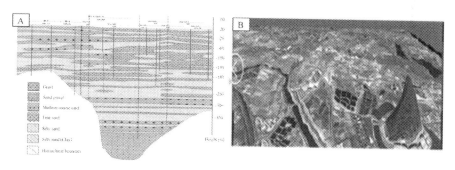

Fig. 2. A- Prospecting line profile map, B- Model of elevation terrain.

b. Model of elevation terrain

The study applied DEM data with resolution of 30 m from Aster satellite, generated the contour lines with 30 m interval after processing data based on practical precision, imported the data into MapGIS software to eliminate the excess lines impacting establishment of surface model for examination and check, converted the correct line file into.dxf file in CAD, imported.dxf file into Surpac (3D modeling software), and generated DTM model of surface terrain in Tongzhou (Fig. 2B).

c. Processing of drilling hole data

The study collected 219 copies of basic drilling hole data, 190 of which were applied. The borehole data, the first-hand information logged by geological

personnel in the drilling site, play a very important role in establishing the geological section and acquiring the geological information in deep formation. The
collected drilling hole data are present in Excel and Access file, and include
coordinate of drilling hole head, inclinometer data, and lithology analysis table,
which are converted into file of Excel format, and saved as text file (.csv) after
format modification, and imported into Surpac to establish drilling hole database
and 3D drilling hole model (Fig. 3A).

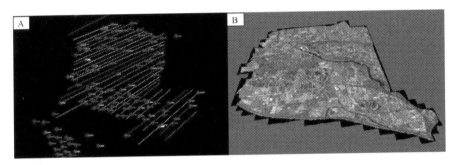

Fig. 3. A- 3D drilling hole model, B- 3D terrain model.

4.2   3D Modeling of Quaternary Formation

In 3D geological modeling, the surface model is generated based on digital terrain
model (DTM), and the construction of underground model is resulted from generation
of 3D wire frame of geological bodies, and Boolean calculation between geological
bodies. The modeling of 3D geological structure aims at transforming spatially uneven
and disperse geological information into visual, continuous, and vivid 3D image of
geological body through fitting with mathematical surfaces and modern computer
graphics, dealing with association relationship between rock interface and structural
surface, striving for reflecting overall perspective of geological structure, and dis-
playing the geological bodies and their structures in the visual way, which strengthens
intuition and accuracy of geological analysis as far as possible.

a. 3D terrain model
   The terrain in 3D scene is defined in continuous function of altitude f: R2- >R3 in
   2D plane, and the terrain surface is expressed with altitude field evenly sampled in
   the digital elevation data (Fig. 3B). The altitude field is expressed with regular grid
   in the standard file, and the terrain is always expressed and drawn with triangular
   net in graphics. If the terrain is expressed with regular net, the finest sampled
   rectangular region is separated in diagonal with finest triangular net, forming two
   triangles. Thus, the triangles in the terrain is quadrupled with the size of terrain.

b. 3D engineering model
   According to the design and arrangement in drilling hole engineering, the data were
   further organized and screened, and the 3D engineering model was build (Fig. 4A).

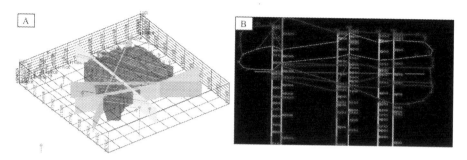

Fig. 4. A- 3D engineering model, B- Overlay map of exploration lines profile and drilling holes.

d. 3D model of geological body

The two-dimension section data in different azimuths were imported into 3D modeling software to check whether the geological bodies in each section are compatible with the geological rule and logical laws. Then, the geological bodies of lithology is defined in each section (Fig. 4B). After overall screening the data and information in exploration line section, the geological body is divided into sand layer and soil layer. The sand layer covers medium sand, fine sand, and silty sand, and the soil layer covers silt, silty clay, clay, and clayey silt.

According to drilling hole data and formation distribution, the connection and wedge out of geological body were adjusted until they are compatible with the geological rule, generating 3D model of single geological body (Fig. 5A).

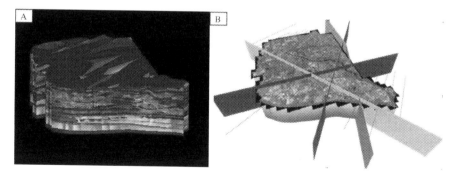

Fig. 5. A- 3D model of geological body, B- 3D model of geological structure.

Finally, different 3D models of single geological body were combined to form the 3D model of geological structure. The model is dominated by fine sand and silty clay, which are intercalated with each other. The sand is near the surface, and the soil is in the majority in the deep formation. The sand layer is dominated by fine sand, followed successively by medium sand and silty sand. The soil layer is dominated by silty clay, which is followed successively by clay (higher content in deep formation), clay silt (mostly occurs in the northwest part of model), and silt (Fig. 5B).

5 3D Visual Display

The construction of 3D scene is to integrate the data of different sources in the real world with optimized algorithm, and establish the uniform spatial platform.

5.1 Construction of 3D Scene

a. Scene database
   The scene database controls all body data and relation data in 3D scene. The system covers a number of model data, thus the scene database is in charge of simplification and compression of data and structural storage, data query and extraction, and information recovery.
b. Object-oriented modeling
   Since the entities and relationship in the system are complicated, the object-oriented modeling effectively simplifies the design of system.
c. Scene engine
   The scene engine is in charge of drawing 3D visualization system and realizing accidents and information system. The research on scene engine focuses on resolving the complexity of scene and contradiction between computer image and calculation performance.
d. Interaction model
   The interaction model is the interface between 3D visual system and clients, and it is in charge of receiving and understanding the interaction orders from clients and converting the orders into internal behavior of system.

5.2 3D Visualization

In order to realize visual and vivid expression of 3D visualized circumstance, various instrument models are expressed with 3D fine models. In general, the 3D modeling is conducted 3D modeling software, e.g. 3DMax and Creator, and the models are imported into 3D scene based on the space coordinates. Due to huge workload in treating the model, the final files resulted from common modeling methods would create huge data volume, thus causing great difficulty in operation of system. Therefore, the procedure of 3D modeling should not only ensure that the 3D model are compatible with real conditions, but also requires simplification, which is designed in terms of modeling methods and chartlet application.

For parts of regular buildings with relatively simple shapes, e.g. pier, pillar, and platform, the modeling is completed with basic geometries. The basic geometries cover sphere, cylinder, box, and their variation shapes, which are parameterized, and they are established and adjusted easily. For relatively complicated buildings, they are split and refined, and then fitted together with modeling basic geometries in space coordinates or relative coordinates with positioning methods. For convenience of further operation of model and pasting material in the surface of model, the models are merged. For complicated and irregular buildings, e.g. landmark building, special model, and door, the models are split and divided, and established with 2D figures and 3D models, with which the spline curves of typical section of buildings is produced, and the 3D models are generated through Extrude, Lathe, and Loft.

Generally, the landmark builds have special shape, which could not be made with above methods, and they could be edited and manipulated in dots, lines, surfaces, and bodies of sub-level objects in 3D models to ensure that the 3D models are compatible with real shapes of buildings.

The material guarantees real visualization effect of 3D models of landmark builds, and the visual effects cover color, texture, reflection, refraction, and roughness and texture of surface, which are simulated in material design and show visual characteristics of some materials.

In simulation system, the purposes of applying material in 3D model cover real expression of texture of building and replacement of detail modeling in the building through chartlet, which realizes reducing data volume of model file.

The chartlet is obtained through processing a variety of graphic information. The pixel of chartlet should be kept as low as possible, and the title should be applied possibly in laying stone, pavement, and vegetation. Some details, e.g. doors, windows, step, cannelure, are expressed by chartlet, which rapidly reduces data volume of model and meets the requirements on appearance of buildings. For expression of fence, the replacement modeling is achieved through texture and transparent disposal.

After treatment and research, the 3D model of geological body in Quaternary formation in Tongzhou area is visually display. The 3D visualized system was customized to realize 3D inquiry, 3D sectioning, and 3D interaction positioning and property inquiry, calculation of volume and area, and analysis of spatial distribution of soil layers.

6 Conclusions

With collected geological data, and based on complex structural development and lithology, various geomorphic units, and uneven distribution of drilling hole data, the spatial distribution and structure of Quaternary formation in Tongzhou area was investigated. The model of Quaternary formation in Tongzhou area was established in 3D modeling software, in which 3D visualization system was developed based on the requirements, realizing 3D inquiry, 3D sectioning, 3D interaction positioning and property inquiry, calculation of volume and area, and analysis of spatial distribution of soil layers. The model basically reflects the geological conditions of Quaternary formation in study area, realizing visualization of geological structure, and providing basis for establishing geological conceptual models.

Urban 3D geological modeling is a typical application of 3D information technology in urban geological area, which significantly promotes expression of result of urban geological investigation, upgrades capability of evaluating and predicting urban geological resources and environment, and has important supporting function to urbanization construction in China.

By establishing model of 3D geological body of Quaternary formation in Tongzhou area, the geological information was transformed into visual 3D geological body, which simplifies management of underground space in city, and the visualization system were completed to realize various function, which has both theoretical and practical importance to evaluation of underground resource, protection of supergenetic ecological environment, and rational development of underground resource, and provides scientific basis for decision - making in engineering construction planning and development, management and development of groundwater resources, pollution monitoring, and ground subsidence.

Acknowledgments. This work was supported by the Geological Survey Project "Research and development of geological information product system and social service" (DD20160353) of China Geological Survey.

References

1. Wu, C.L., Niu, R.Q., Liu, G., Kong, C.F., Lei, S.T., Liu, P.D.: Construction aim and solution of the urban geological information system. J. Geol. Sci. Technol. Inf. **22**(3), 67–72 (2003)
2. Zhu, L.F., Wu, X.C., Yin, K.L., Liu, X.G.: Study of management and service system of urban 3D geological data supported by 3D GIS. J. Huazhong Univ. Sci. Technol. (Urban Sci. Ed.) **20**(4), 40–46 (2005)
3. Mark, J.: Three-dimensional geological modelling of potential-field data. J. Comput. Geosci. **27**(4), 455–465 (1994)
4. Liu, Y.: Geomatics and earth observation science (EOS) for disaster management: an overview. J. Geomech. **14**(3), 212–220 (2008)
5. Ehlen, J., Harmon, R.: GeoComp 99: GeoComputation and the geosciences. J. Comput. Geosci. **27**(27), 899–900 (2001)
6. Christian, J.: 3D geoscience modeling: computer techniques for geological characterization. J. Earth-Sci. Rev. **40**(3–4), 299–301 (1994)
7. Wang, M., Bai, Y.: The status quo and development tendency of 3D geosciences modeling. J. Soil Eng. Found. **20**(4), 27–29 (2006)
8. Wang, R., Li, Y., Liu, Y., Xiang, Z.: Import and determination methods for virtual borehole in Geo -3D modeling. J. Geol. Prospect. **43**(3), 102–107 (2007)
9. Hou, E., Wu, L.: Present state and developing trend in the research on main issues of - 3D geoscience modeling. J. Coal Geol. Explor. **28**(6), 5–8 (2000)
10. Qu, H.G., Pao, M., Liu, X.Q., Yu, C.L.: Urban 3-D geological modeling and its application to urbanization. J. Geol. Bull. China **34**(7), 1350–1358 (2015)
11. Zeng, Q., He, X.: Mathematical model and display method of three dimensional geological modeling. J. Eng. Geol. Comput. Appl. **3**, 1–8 (2006)
12. Li, Y., Guosheng, Q., Chen, J.: Realization of 3D subsurface geological modeling software in urban areas based on borehole data. J. Geol. Bull. China **24**(5), 470–475 (2005)

The Snow Disaster Risk Assessment of Township Population-Livestock in Guoluo State of Qinghai Province

Changjun Xu[1,2,5P(✉)], Tianyun Xue[3], and Yan Zhu[4]

[1] Geomatics Technology and Application Key Laboratory of Qinghai Province,
Xining 810001, China
39950625@qq.com
[2] Provincial Geomatics Center of Qinghai, Xining 81001, Qinghai, China
[3] Institute of Surveying and Mapping Qinghai Province,
Xining 810000, Qinghai, China
[4] School of Geographic Science, Qinghai Normal University,
Xining 810000, China
[5] No. 13, Yellow River Road, Chengxi District, Xining, Qinghai, China

Abstract. Applying the natural disaster risk theory and selecting 3 Meteorological index and 12 social economic statistics index, quantitative analysis is carried out on risk of township snow hazard, population-livestock risk vulnerability (exposure sensitivity and adaptability) and snow disaster risk respectively with 40 townships in 5 counties in Guoluo state of Qinghai province as an evaluation unit, by using the AHP analytic method and the clustering analysis method, combining the GIS and RS tools. The results show that: Snow disaster risk of towns in Guoluo is totally higher. Among them, there are 3 towns in Jiuzhi County with comprehensive higher snow disaster risk of livestock-population such as Zhiqingsongduo town. There are 21 towns in Gande county with higher snow disaster risk such as Qingzhen town. There are 8 towns in Banma county with medium snow disaster risk such as Jika town. There are 8 towns in Maqin county with low snow disaster risk such as Xiadawu town. On the basis of those results, this article discusses the preventive measures such as: construction of regional snow disaster risk management model and establishment of the snow disaster response system.

Keywords: Township · Snow disaster · Risk assessment · GIS

1 Introduction

The IPCC Fourth Assessment Report [1] concluded that the cold activity in the northern hemisphere was significantly increased during the second half of the twentieth century. With the global warming, the probability of extreme weather events increased significantly [2] the extreme heavy rainfall events in the northern hemisphere increased by an average of 2%–4% [3]. In the past few decades, the trend of precipitation growth is obvious [4] in west part of China, the largest snow depth in the country has increased significantly. The frequency and intensity of extreme weather events may increase.

© Springer Nature Singapore Pte Ltd. 2018
H. Yuan et al. (Eds.): GSKI 2017, CCIS 848, pp. 13–22, 2018.
https://doi.org/10.1007/978-981-13-0893-2_2

Guoluo area located in southern Qinghai Plateau is one of the main pastoral areas in Qinghai Province. It is also a high incidence of snow disaster area. It's always said that 'three years a small disaster, five years of two disasters, a decade of a big disaster' [5], and this area's snow disaster is serious. In the past, the research on the snowstorm in Guoluo area is mainly aimed at the cause, mechanism, temporal and spatial distribution characteristics of the meteorological significance of the study [6–9]. The actual loss caused by the snowstorm is not only determined by the intensity of the meteorological factors, but also by the population, the industrial form, the economic development, the transportation and other infrastructure construction, the disaster prevention and disaster prevention ability and the disaster prevention consciousness of the masses and so on. This paper intends to carry out the snowstorm risk assessment of the township unit in Guoluo area, which has certain theoretical significance and great practical value. It is the basis for regional disaster prevention, disaster relief, disaster reduction, land planning and socio-economic development plans, and ultimately achieves regional sustainable development.

1.1 Overview of the Study Area

Guoluo is located in the southeastern part of Qinghai Province, and located in the hinterland of the Qinghai-Tibet Plateau. The area of Guoluo is about 76,000 km^2 and its average elevation is more than 4200 m. Guoluo's climate is cold and hypoxia, and its average annual precipitation is 400–700 mm. The average annual temperature is -4°C, and there is no absolute frost-free period throughout the year. Its terrain is that the northwest part is high, southeast part is low. Its northwest is a gentle plateau; alpine and gully are mainly gathered in its southeast. The existing available grassland is about 58467 km^2, and the grassland is dominated by alpine meadow vegetation, accounting for 76.48% of the total land area. There are a small amount of natural forest land and cultivated land. The regional economy is based on animal husbandry which is made up of the yak and sheep, and now the existing livestock are 462 thousand.

Nowadays, Guoluo is composed of six counties, namely Maqin, Maduo, Gande, Dari, Bama, Jiuzhi. According to the statistics in 2012, there are 44 townships and 28466 households (including 27115 shepherd households), with a total population of 185,600 (including 140,200 agriculture and animal husbandry population people). Tibetan population of 91.86%, and total output value of agriculture and animal husbandry is 619 million yuan.

2 Materials and Methods

2.1 Data

The annual snow depth and snow duration of this paper are from 58 meteorological stations in Qinghai and Sichuan from 1960 to 2012, which 39 meteorological stations in Qinghai Province and 19 meteorological stations in Sichuan Province (Fig. 1). The TM remote sensing images of the Guoluo area were downloaded from the Landsat-7 satellite, an international scientific data service platform. The time period is the 2000 year which is the typical year from October to May. And the snow area of Guoluo area is extracted. The data of the national economic and social development of the township administrative units such as the population, the number of livestock, the livestock commodity rate, the per capita village income, the highway mileage and so on are from Compilation of Statistical Data on National Economic and Social Development in 2012 of the county bureau of statistics. The information is mainly collected form the other five counties of the Guoluo area in addition to Maduo County (4 townships). It is covered the national economic and social development data of the 40 townships, including Maqin County (8 townships), Dari County (10 Townships), Gande County (7 townships), Bama County (9 townships), Jiuzhi County (6 townships).

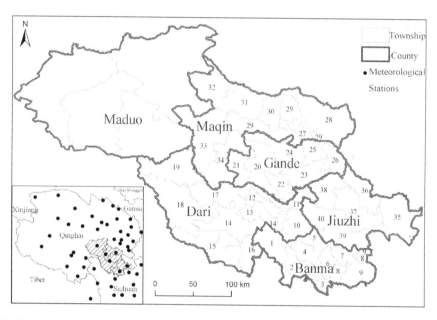

Fig. 1. Guoluo county-level administrative division and the use of meteorological site map (Figure for the township number, consistent with Table 3)

2.2   Methods

The risk of snowstorm is the result of the combination of the disaster factors and the inherent vulnerability of the insurance body. The hazard of snow disaster is the frequency and intensity of snow activity in Guoluo area. The vulnerability of snowstorms refers that the effects of natural, social, economic and environmental factors, in the face of potential hazards, the exposed body of the disaster and the inherent sensitivity of the risk-taker in response to external strikes [10], as well as the ability of its associated human anti-risk. Exposure is that the number or the value of the risk-taker are exposed to the impact of the risk factor, which is a necessary condition for the existence of natural and natural disaster risks. Sensitivity refers to the ability of the risk-taker to respond to the snowstorm and its strength. Disaster capacity is the ability, the measures and means to cope with snowstorms in the region. The vulnerability of snowstorms is related to the extent of exposure and the sensitivity of the risk-taker and the ability to respond to disaster events related to socio-economic [11] and cultural backgrounds. According to the above evaluation module, this paper selects the corresponding evaluation index.

Snow disaster hazard assessment method is more mature. The method uses snow depth, snow duration and snow area ratio as the evaluation index. Due to the limitation of the vulnerability assessment statistic, this paper only assesses the snowstorm hazard of the township population and livestock separately. Population exposure is the number of selected population, the number of township households. Livestock exposure is selected the cattle, horses, sheep population at the end of a year. Population sensitivity is based on the number of low-income poor people. Livestock sensitivity is the proportion of livestock in total livestock, livestock mortality, and livestock survival rate indicators. Ability to cope with disaster of the township is based on the highway mileage, per capita income and livestock commodity rate of the county level and above (Table 1).

Table 1. The hierarchy system of the snowstorm risk assessment index in Guoluo

Target layer	Criteria layer		Index layer
The natural physical properties of snowstorms	Risk of disaster		Snow depth, snow duration, ratio of snow area
Snowstorm vulnerability	Exposure	population	Population, number of households
		livestock	At the end of the year the number of cattle stocks, the number of hurdles stocks, the number of sheep stocks
	Sensitivity	population	The number of low - income poverty
		livestock	Large livestock accounted for the proportion of total livestock, animal mortality, survival rate of newborn animal
	Ability to cope with disaster		County level and above highway mileage, per capita income, livestock commodity rate

Specific assessment methods are as follows:

Standardization of indicators: In order to eliminate the magnitude difference of the indicators, this paper first standardized the 15 evaluation indexes of 40 townships, the formula is:

$$X_I = (X_i - X_{min})/(X_{max} - X_{min}) \tag{1}$$

X_I is the normalized index value, X_{max}, X_{min} are the maximum and minimum values of a certain index.

Determination of indicator weight: First, we use the analytic hierarchy process to determine the weight value of the index [12], and then judge the importance of the above 15 indicators according to the experts in the snow disaster study, establish the judgment matrix, and finally calculate the eigenvectors of the judgment matrix to obtain the weight vector. And calculate the random consistency ratio CR to test, when CR < 0.10, the results are satisfactory consistency. By calculating CR < 0.10, all of the judgment matrix pass the consistency test. Finally, we get the weight of 15 index data (Table 2).

Calculation of snowstorm risk assessment: The hazard risk formula is:

$$H = \sum_{i=0}^{i} q_i \times I_i \tag{2}$$

In the formula, H is the hazard index of snow disaster. L is the number of hazard risk indicators, and qi is the weight of hazard risk index of the i-th.

Population and livestock vulnerability is calculated as follows:

$$V = \frac{\left(\sum_{i=0}^{m} q_{ei} \times E_i \right) \times \left(\sum_{i=0s}^{n} q_{si} \times S_i \right)}{\sum_{i=0}^{k} q_{di} \times D_i} \tag{3}$$

V is the vulnerability index. qei, qsi and qdi are the weights of the exposure, sensitivity, and coping abilities of the i-th. Ei refers to the exposure index of the i-th. Si refers to the sensitivity index of the i-th. Di refers to the adaptive index of the i-th.

Eventually get the snowstorm risk index R:

$$R = \sqrt{H \times V} \tag{4}$$

This paper calculates the risk of population and livestock snowstorm respectively. And then seek the square root of the two, you can get risk index of snowstorm comprehensive, which is based on population - livestock.

This paper completes the calculation of hazard risk, vulnerability and snowstorm risk index according to the above process. Using the size of each index, combined with the township of the evaluation index of the cluster analysis results, this paper began grading.

In addition, in the evaluation of livestock exposure, the horse and cattle were converted into sheep units. The proportion of various types of livestock and sheep in Qinghai Province is: 1 head yak = 4 sheep; 1 horse = 6 sheep.

Table 2. The weight of the snowstorm risk assessment index in Guoluo

	Risk of disaster	Vulnerability					Level weight
		Exposure		Sensitivity		Ability to cope with disaster	
		Population exposure	Livestock exposure	Population sensitivity	Livestock Sensitivity		
Snow depth	0.38						
Snow days	0.37						
Ratio of snow area	0.25						
Population		0.75					0.2475
Number of households		0.25					0.0825
The number of cattle at the end of the year			0.317				0.1046
The number of horses at the end of the year			0.437				0.1442
The number of sheep at the end of the year			0.246				0.0812
The number of low - income poverty				1			0.33
Large livestock accounted for the proportion of total livestock					0.458		0.1511
Animal mortality					0.289		0.0954
Survival rate of newborn animal					0.253		0.0835
Per capita income						0.433	0.1429
Livestock commodity rate						0.31	0.1023
County level and above highway mileage						0.257	0.0848

Note: The weight of the hazard risk and vulnerability is 1, and the weight value of exposure, sensitivity and adaptability in vulnerability is 0.33.

Table 3. The snow disaster risk, vulnerability and risk assessment in Guoluo

County	Number	Township	Hazard risk				Population Vulnerability and Risks				Livestock Vulnerability and Risks		
			Snow depth	Snow days	Ratio of snow area	Risk index	Ability	Exposure	Sensitivity	Risk index	Exposure	Sensitivity	Risk index
Banma	1	Daka	0.744	0.411	0.007	0.436	0.077	0.020	0.099	2.449	0.012	0.172	3.464
	2	Jika	0.756	0.293	0.006	0.397	0.087	0.006	0.123	1.414	0.006	0.086	2.000
	3	Zhiqin	0.733	0.191	0.002	0.350	0.107	0.011	0.217	2.000	0.012	0.116	2.449
	4	Makeke	0.787	0.235	0.008	0.388	0.083	0.002	0.001	1.414	0.009	0.141	2.449
	5	Duogongma	0.790	0.236	0.003	0.388	0.098	0.009	0.092	1.414	0.011	0.154	2.828
	6	Slaitang	0.763	0.118	0.002	0.334	0.096	0.008	0.108	1.414	0.008	0.152	2.449
	7	Jianritang	0.843	0.082	0.003	0.351	0.077	0.019	0.154	2.449	0.007	0.150	2.449
	8	Yaerrang	0.811	0.067	0.009	0.335	0.074	0.013	0.108	2.000	0.004	0.141	2.449
	9	Dengta	0.831	0.044	0.007	0.334	0.091	0.028	0.074	2.000	0.009	0.153	2.828
Dari	10	Manzhang	0.780	0.338	0.000	0.421	0.092	0.019	0.082	2.449	0.007	0.153	3.000
	11	Deang	0.790	0.351	0.000	0.430	0.081	0.011	0.069	1.732	0.008	0.127	3.000
	12	Wosia	0.724	0.523	0.002	0.469	0.077	0.008	0.074	2.000	0.003	0.152	2.828
	13	Jimazhen	0.703	0.570	0.006	0.480	0.078	0.019	0.071	2.828	0.005	0.078	2.828
	14	Saba	0.680	0.617	0.003	0.487	0.108	0.006	0.076	2.000	0.001	0.060	2.000
	15	Shanhongke	0.522	0.588	0.004	0.417	0.081	0.022	0.077	2.449	0.004	0.153	2.449
	16	Xiakongke	0.610	0.500	0.007	0.419	0.083	0.016	0.074	2.449	0.009	0.084	3.000
	17	Jianshe	0.610	0.802	0.000	0.529	0.140	0.026	0.085	2.828	0.008	0.049	2.828
	18	Sangrima	0.474	0.878	0.007	0.507	0.070	0.015	0.071	2.828	0.001	0.155	2.828
	19	Fuhetu	0.393	1.000	0.011	0.522	0.086	0.006	0.070	2.000	0.001	0.156	2.000
Gande	20	Kequ	0.635	0.480	0.005	0.420	0.148	0.088	0.195	3.464	0.330	0.016	3.464
	21	Shangongma	0.607	0.689	0.005	0.487	0.097	0.031	0.093	3.464	0.000	0.039	2.000
	22	Xiagongma	0.728	0.390	0.004	0.422	0.073	0.041	0.094	3.000	0.005	0.132	3.000
	23	Ganglong	0.737	0.262	0.005	0.378	0.082	0.045	0.103	2.449	0.002	0.105	1.414
	24	Qingzhen	0.546	0.303	0.010	0.322	0.125	0.079	0.111	2.449	0.009	0.131	2.449
	25	Jiangqian	0.579	0.160	0.003	0.280	0.125	0.034	0.085	1.414	0.000	0.103	1.000
	26	Xiazangke	0.754	0.178	0.001	0.353	0.099	0.062	0.109	2.449	0.007	0.074	2.000
Maqin	27	Dawuzhen	0.381	0.163	1.000	0.455	0.059	0.266	0.171	3.464	0.002	0.080	2.449
	28	Lajia	0.375	0.000	0.001	0.143	0.221	0.195	0.196	2.000	0.046	0.080	2.000
	29	Dawu	0.387	0.190	0.011	0.220	0.248	0.062	0.011	1.000	0.015	0.083	1.414
	30	Dongqing	0.304	0.123	0.002	0.162	0.246	0.007	0.002	1.000	0.003	0.128	1.000
	31	Huishan	0.167	0.284	0.006	0.170	0.206	0.006	0.001	1.000	0.011	0.126	1.414
	32	Xiadawu	0.000	0.382	0.009	0.144	0.143	0.002	0.072	1.000	0.004	0.089	1.000
	33	Youyun	0.413	0.922	0.003	0.499	0.106	0.029	0.099	2.828	0.002	0.029	2.000
	34	Dangluo	0.548	0.790	0.008	0.503	0.152	0.045	0.130	3.464	0.008	0.004	2.000
Jiuzhi	35	Zhiqinguos	1.000	0.332	0.002	0.503	0.190	0.163	0.262	4.000	0.024	0.038	2.828
	36	Menrang	0.969	0.252	0.000	0.462	0.173	0.012	0.177	2.828	0.012	0.034	2.000
	37	Suohurima	0.987	0.247	0.003	0.467	0.222	0.047	0.259	3.464	0.017	0.037	2.828
	38	Wasai	0.875	0.252	0.001	0.426	0.143	0.032	0.211	3.000	0.013	0.134	3.000
	39	Baiyu	0.900	0.168	0.005	0.406	0.108	0.062	0.330	2.828	0.013	0.159	2.828
	40	Waeryi	0.852	0.266	0.001	0.423	0.137	0.031	0.232	3.000	0.007	0.126	2.449

3 Result

The risk of the population of the snowstorm in the central area of Guoluo is relatively high (Fig. 2), including Jiuzhi, Gande, Dari township and in the southern part of Maqin county. These counties suffer from high risk of snowstorms, such as the Zhiqing-songduo town, Suohurima town in the Jiuzhi county, Kequ town, Shanggongma town, Xiagongma town in Gande county, Dawu town, Youyun town, Dangluo town in Maqin county, Sangrima town in Dari county.

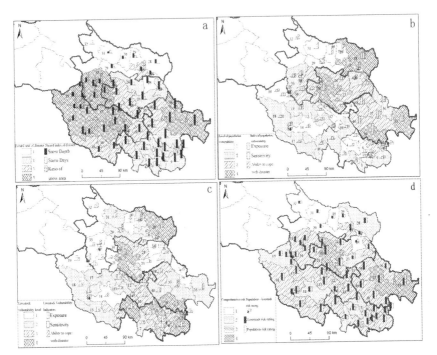

Fig. 2. Assessment results of the snow disaster risk in Guoluo Township. (a) risk of disaster, (b) population vulnerability, (c) livestock vulnerability, (d) snowstorm risk and comprehensive risk of population, livestock

The higher risk areas of snow livestock disaster are Kequ town and Xiagongma town in Gande county, Manzhang town, Deang town and Xiahongke town in Dari county, and Wasai town in Jiuzhi county. But the towns in Maqin county have lower risk of livestock disaster.

Population and livestock comprehensive snowstorm risk of these areas reach the level four, including Zhiqingduosong town and Suohurima town in Jiuzhi, Kequ town in Gande county and so on. The most of the other towns in Jiuzhi, Gande, Dar and part of township in Banma belongs to the level three. Snow disaster comprehensive risk is low in the Xiadawu, Xueshan, Dongqingou, Dawu, Cangmahe in the northwest part of Maqin County, and in the Jiangqian township in Gan county. The risk of other towns is level two.

4 Application of Snow Disaster Risk Assessment

Based on the risk assessment of township-level unit snow disaster in Guoluo, the following measures are put forward:

We should build a regional snowstorm risk management model and a snowstorm response system: Snow risk management is a system based on strengthening scientific research work on snowstorms and improving regional socio-economic development.

The scientific research of snow disaster is the pioneer of regional snow disaster prevention and control, and the level of social and economic development is the key to the prevention and control of snowstorm. The measure is to establish a complete snowstorm monitoring and forecasting information system.

According to the risk assessment results, we have developed a program so that the township can cope with different levels of snowstorm: The government should actively construct and plan life and production and other relief supplies to ensure that food and materials to maintain the basic needs of people's lives and production during the snowstorm, and build township-level relief supplies reserve center. When snowstorms occur, relief supplies can be quickly distributed and reach the affected villages and towns. We ensure the necessary disaster relief and disaster relief capability. We do our best to defense disasters and reduce snow losses.

The relevant laws and regulations are perfect, and the public awareness of disaster prevention is improved: Snowstorms are related to all aspects of the area, and in particular to the livelihoods of farmers and herdsmen. Therefore, the implementation and improvement of some relevant laws and regulations will play a role in disaster prevention and mitigation at the system and legal level.

5 Summary

In this paper, the basic theory of natural disaster risk assessment is used to quantitatively analyze the risk of snow disaster, the vulnerability, exposure, sensitivity and ability to cope with disaster of demographic and livestock in Guoluo area. This paper calculates the risk of population and livestock snowstorm and its comprehensive risk based on both. Township is the basic administrative unit and important participants, performers for disaster prevention, disaster prevention and disaster relief. Therefore, it is necessary to carry out the risk assessment of the snowstorm at the township level, but there are also unsound problems in the socio-economic development of the township. Therefore, it is possible to increase the collection and construction of social and economic development data in the township scale of the study area in the future, which will make the result more accurate and guide the disaster prevention and preparedness work effectively for all levels of government, so as to reduce the snow disaster and improve the scientific basis. And all levels of government snow disaster emergency plan has been improved, making the snow disaster emergency management capabilities have been enhanced, the natural disaster emergency management of the scientific management has improved.

Acknowledgments. This paper was funded by the Geomatics Technology and application key laboratory of Qinghai province, Grant NO.2017-z~914. Also thanks for supporting my colleagues, and thanks for the reviewers.

References

1. Solomon, S.D., Qin, M., Manning, Z.: The physical science basis contribution of working group 1 to the fourth assessment report of the IPCC. J. Comput. Geom. **18**(2), 95 (2007). Climate Change 2007
2. David, R.E., Gerald, A.M.: Climate extreme: observations modeling and impacts. J. Sci. **5487**(289), 2068–2074 (2000)
3. Easterling, M.: Observed variability and trends in extreme climate events. J Bull. Am. Meteorol. Soc. **81**(3), 417–425 (2000)
4. The Editorial Committee: National Assessment Report on Climate Change. Science Press, Beijing (2007)
5. Wang, S.: China Meteorological Disaster Ceremony, Qinghai Volume. Meteorological Press, Qinghai (2007)
6. Jin, L.Y., Wu, Y.S., Qin, N.S.: Temporal and spatial distribution of temperature and precipitation anomalies in the southern part of Qinghai Plateau and its relationship with snowstorm. J. Plateau Meteorol. **15**(4), 405–412 (1996)
7. Lee, P.J.: Analysis on the Spatial and Temporal Distribution of Snowstorm and the Snowstorm in Pastoral Area in the Qinghai - Tibet Plateau, p. 15. Meteorological Press, Beijing (1998)
8. Zhou, L.S., Wang, Q.C., Li, H.H.: Study on real - time pre - assessment method of snowstorm disaster in blizzard in eastern pastoral area of Qinghai - Tibet Plateau. J. Nat. Disasters **10**(2), 58–65 (2001)
9. Dong, W.J., Wei, Z.G., Fan, L.J.: Climatic characteristics of snowstorm in eastern pastoral area of Qinghai - Tibet Plateau. Plateau Meteorol. J. Plateau Meteorol. **20**(4), 402–406 (2001)
10. Ge, Q.S.: A Preliminary Study on Comprehensive Assessment of Natural Disaster Risk in China. Science Press, Beijing (2008)
11. Birkmann, J.: Measuring Vulnerability to Hazards of National Origin. UNU Press, Tokyo (2006)
12. Xu, J.H.: Mathematical methods in contemporary geography. Higher Education Press, Beijing (2002)

Spatial Autocorrelation of Urban Economic Growth in Shandong Province, China by Using Time-Series Data of Per Capita GDP

Jun Zhao[1(✉)], Yue Wang[2], and Xin Wang[2]

[1] School of Civil Engineering and Architecture, University of Jinan,
Jinan 250022, Shandong, China
{Jun.Zhao,cea_zhaoj}@ujn.edu.cn
[2] Business School, University of Jinan, Jinan 250002, Shandong, China
{Yue.Wang,Xin.Wang}@ujn.edu.cn

Abstract. Urban spatial distribution will impact the development of economic in the specific geographic areas. To find out the relationship and influence of spatial autocorrelation to urban economic growth, we use global Moran's I method to measure spatial autocorrelation of economic growth for the 17 cities in Shandong province, China. Through calculating the Moran's Index, Z score and P value by using Per Capita GDP in the period from 2000 to 2015, the results reflect that spatial clustering pattern of each city is gradually enhanced in the past 16 years. That is, with the gradual increase of GDP per capita in Shandong, the spatial autocorrelation of each city is gradually increased. There is a positive correlation between spatial distribution and urban economic growth in the cities.

Keywords: Urban economic · Spatial autocorrelation · Global Moran's I
Spatial clustering

1 Introduction

On the background of global economic integration, people live in an internet made society and information society. There is closely relationship between the urban development and social economic. Especially in recent years, huge changes happened in urban and urban groups. Growth of urban present more and more agglomeration effect. Shandong, one of the developed provinces, is located between the capital economic circle and the Yangtze River economic belt in the east of China. The geographical position is superior, and the regional economic development is steady growth and basically balance. It archives GDP (Gross Domestic Product) of 6.7 trillion yuan in 2016 [1]. There are two sub-provincial cities (Jinan, Qingdao) and 15 prefecture-level cities. And it has advantage of geography, resource and labor force. As of historic, policy, natural factors, there are big differences of economic among the local cities in Shandong. The developed level is shown reduce tendency from east to west, and from north to south. For example, Linyi city, the biggest prefecture-level city for the population and area in Shandong, is located on the southwest of the province. Its GDP is no

© Springer Nature Singapore Pte Ltd. 2018
H. Yuan et al. (Eds.): GSKI 2017, CCIS 848, pp. 23–31, 2018.
https://doi.org/10.1007/978-981-13-0893-2_3

more than a half for Qingdao, the Eastern coastal city. So, the issues about relationship and difference of urban economic growth among the 17 prefecture-level cities in Shandong should be conducted.

Recently, there are lots of research on the urban economic development, but most of methods are mainly traditional econometric model, and the spatial factors are not considered. Moreover, the relevant theories and practices of urban economy show that there is diffusion or aggregation effect between cities, and the development of urban economy itself is affected by spatial factors. As traditional methods do not consider spatial aspects, it is difficult to truly reflect the impact of geographical position. Therefore, this paper uses spatial autocorrelation to analyze the pattern of urban economic development in Shandong, which is followed by the Moran's I index to reflect the relationship of urban economic growth in 17 cities of Shandong province.

Spatial statistical analysis is the extension of the traditional statistical analysis method. Spatial regression, spatial autocorrelation, geography weighted regression and other methods provide an accurate understanding of spatial location and spatial interaction [2]. Some authors explored the feature of regional linkage and the spatial correlation among China's regional Per Capita GDP from 1998 to 2009. They find that there exists global spatial autocorrelation all over the country, and this kind of autocorrelation has been increasing since 1998 [3]. Some investigation has been conducted for the finite-sample properties of Moran's I test statistic for spatial autocorrelation in tobit models suggested by Kelejian and Prucha [4]. A method is proposed to test the correlation of two random fields when they are both spatially autocorrelated. It recovers the null distribution considering the autocorrelation. With simulation model, any test based on the independence of two (or more) random fields is constructed [5]. Geo-referenced user-generated datasets like those extracted from Twitter are increasingly gaining the interest of spatial analysts. Such datasets oftentimes reflect a wide array of real-world phenomena. However, each of these phenomena takes place at a certain spatial scale. Therefore, user-generated datasets are of multiscale nature. It focuses on the popular local G statistics. The method has been compared with the original one on a real-world Twitter dataset. Experiments show that the approach can be able to better detect spatial autocorrelation at specific scales, as opposed to the original method [6]. When analyzing data is collected with a geographical dimension, it is important to be able to test for spatial autocorrelation. The presence of spatial autocorrelation might unveil ignored explanatory variables or just be a factor necessary to consider when further analyzing the data [7]. Spatial autocorrelation statistics detect the presence of interdependence between the values of data at neighboring locations. spatial analysis identify the problem-ridden and developed territories within the EU based on the characteristics of those which describe driving forces of competitiveness, also in terms of long-term potentiality, and those which are direct or indirect outcomes of a competitive society and economy [8]. Based on the fifth and sixth census data in China, studying on the spatial autocorrelation of the population in Shandong province has been focused. The global Moran I statistic is used to quantify the spatial clustering of the population in the whole province both in 2000 and 2010 years, respectively [9]. Another research is to identify the homogeneity of GDP and Per Capita GDP (GPI per capita) in the European Union as a whole and at the level of change caused by the accession of new countries in years 1973, 1981, 1986, 1995, 2004 and 2007. To identify the presence of spatial structure Moran index is used too [10].

2   Methodology

Spatial statistical analysis refers to a method of statistical analysis based on the theory of regional variables with spatial distribution characteristics. Research objects focus commonly on the spatial interactions and their transformation laws about the things or phenomena with geospatial information characteristics. We know that mapping and visualization can be used to analyze regional geospatial phenomena. In the study of the urban economic growth, it is difficult to simply figure out the rules that are hidden behind the numbers, and the lengthy figures make it difficult to grasp the key, especially the comparison between economic and social phenomena. With the help of spatial analysis tools such as ArcGIS, spatial location data can be matched with spatial attribute data to realize visual representation of spatial attribute data, which can help to carry on spatial analysis of attribute data. The complicated attribute data, especially social and economic data, is easily used to compare differences between cities, and show the performance of urban economic characteristics.

Spatial statistical analysis first assumes that all variables in the study areas are independent and have spatial autocorrelation with each other. Then in spatial or temporal context, this correlation is defined as autocorrelation. That is, spatial autocorrelation is one of the most important characteristics of spatial data. It refers to the potential interdependence between some variables in observational data within the same distribution area. Spatial autocorrelation is a fundamental property used to measure geographic data. That is, the degree of interdependence between data at a location and other locations. This dependency is often called spatial dependence. Geographic data may not be independent of each other, but are relevant because of spatial interaction and spatial diffusion. One of the examples of relations is called spatial autocorrelation phenomena. Spatial autocorrelation implies that values of objects located in a close vicinity are more similar one to another contrary to distant objects values. This phenomenon favors forming of spatial clusters characterized by similar values. Various measures are used to check if selected objects are characterized by similar values of a variable. The most frequently used statistics for spatial autocorrelation examination are Moran's I Statistics [11].

Moran's I statistics of can be expressed as:

$$I = \frac{n}{S_0} \frac{\sum\limits_{i=1}^{n} \sum\limits_{j=1}^{n} w_{i,j} z_i z_j}{\sum\limits_{i=1}^{n} z_i^2} \tag{1}$$

Where,

i and j are spatial features
n is the total number of spatial features

$w_{i,j}$ is the spatial weight of between feature i and j

z_i is the differences between attribute value and average of attribute value

$$Z_i = (x_i - \bar{X}) \tag{2}$$

x_i is the attribute value

$\bar{X}$ is the average of attribute value

S_0 is the aggregation of spatial weight

$$S_0 = \sum_{i=1}^{n} \sum_{j=1}^{n} w_{i,j} \tag{3}$$

3   Data Analysis

Based on the statistical analysis of the imbalance of urban economic development in Shandong, the Per Capita GDP of 17 cities above the prefecture level in Shandong from 2000 to 2015 is selected, and the urban economic development of Shandong is based on the datasets.

3.1   Overview of Urban Economics in Shandong

There is a good geographical location in Shandong since the reforming and opening in recent years. The economic layout of Shandong passes the Bohai Sea Economic Circle and Shandong Peninsula Blue Economic Zone. Economy has made great development in the past years. The level of economic development in Shandong from 2000 to 2015 is shown in Figs. 1 and 2 by using Per Capita GDP as an indicator.

From above two figures, we can see that the level of Per Capita GDP in Shandong is higher than in domestic. Shandong is one of the developed provinces in China. Secondly, The Per Capita GDP of 2015 is 6.88 times that of 2000 in Shandong. It shows the speed of economic is going up in the past 16 years. But we should know that there is tendency of going down in the growth rate of Per Capita GDP not only in Shandong but also domestic in recent years (2012–2015).

3.2   Global Moran's I

Global Moran's I, the spatial analysis tool in ArcGIS can measures spatial autocorrelation based on position and feature values. In the case of a given set of features and related attributes, the patterns used to evaluate analysis results are clustering, scattered, and random. The significance of the index was assessed by calculating the global Moran's index, Z score, and P value.

We have established the spatial geographical database of 17 cities in Shandong, China, which is built on the Xi'an coordinate system of 1980. Through the spatial transformation tool, *Feature to Point* in ArcMap, the area-features of the 17 prefecture-level municipal administrative regions are taken into 17 point-features

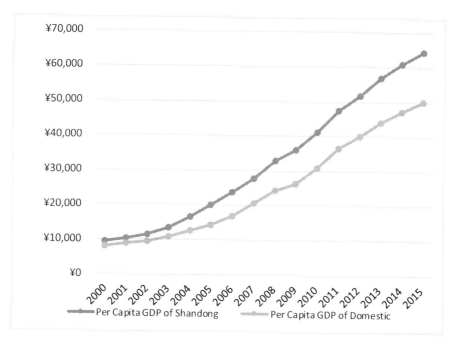

Fig. 1. Comparison of Per Capita GDP between Shandong and Domestic from 2000 to 2015 (Color figure online)

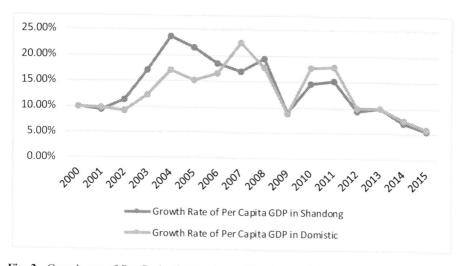

Fig. 2. Growth rate of Per Capita GDP between Shandong and Domestic from 2000 to 2015 (Color figure online)

Fig. 3. Distribution of 17 prefecture-level municipal administrative regions in Shandong province

(centroids), which are the spatial variables of spatial autocorrelation analysis, as shown in Fig. 3.

Then the datasets Per Capita GDP of 17 cities in Shandong from 2000 to 2015 are input into the ArcGIS spatial database, and global Moran's I statistics in the ArcMap is carried out. The results are shown in Table 1.

Table 1. Global Moran's I index of Per Capita GDP of 17 cities in Shandong province from 2000 to 2015

Year	Moran's I index	Z score	P value
2000	0.018023	1.940061	0.052372
2001	0.023081	2.051976	0.040172
2002	0.026519	2.123004	0.033754
2003	0.022019	2.032532	0.0421
2004	0.023122	2.070495	0.038406
2005	0.021715	2.09061	0.036563
2006	0.02755	2.228412	0.025853
2007	0.031182	2.322415	0.020211
2008	0.022411	2.164743	0.030407
2009	0.029636	2.300385	0.021426
2010	0.023633	2.166614	0.030264
2011	0.024798	2.203418	0.027565
2012	0.023911	2.199135	0.027868
2013	0.023278	2.186349	0.02879
2014	0.02326	2.165997	0.030311
2015	0.031907	2.343366	0.019111

In Table 1, all the 16 Moran's I indexes are more than zero. They show positive correlation with spatial distribution among the 17 cities. Value is larger, more significant with cluster pattern. The P value and the Z score are used to interpret the significant degree of spatial cluster pattern in Fig. 4.

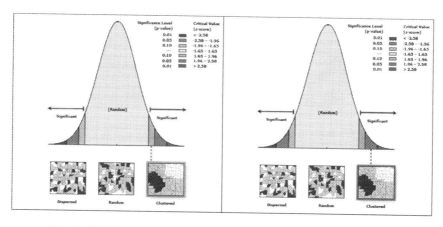

Fig. 4. Significant degree of spatial clustering pattern in 2000 and 2015

The left picture of Fig. 4 shows the significant degree in 2000, and the right one shows the significant degree in 2015. The global Moran's I index for Per Capita GDP in 2000 indicates a significant level of spatial clustering of "clustering" under significance of 10%, which is on the right side of the distribution curve with a score of 1.940061 in the interval of [1.65, 1.96]. The global Moran's I index for Per Capita GDP

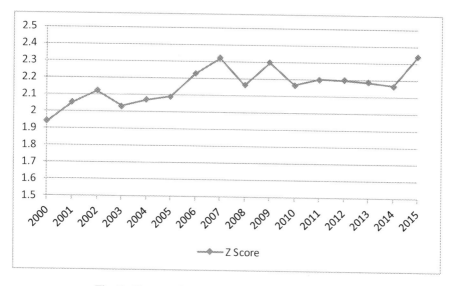

Fig. 5. Z score of global Moran's I from 2000 to 2015

in 2015 indicates that the spatial distribution pattern is "clustering" under the significance of 5%, which is located on the right side of the distribution curve with the Z score of 2.343366 in the interval of [1.96, 2.58]. Spatial autocorrelation of the Per Capita GDP in 2015 is more significant than that in 2000.

Further analysis is the different values of Z score in the period from 2000 to 2015, as shown in Fig. 5. The Z scores including the three years of 2003, 2008 and 2010 are decreased, which are compared with the previous year. They indicate that the degree of spatial clustering pattern has weakened in significance. In the past 16 years, the data of Per Capita GDP reflected the spatial clustering pattern of each city is gradually enhanced. That is, with the gradual increase of GDP per capita in Shandong, the spatial autocorrelation of each city is gradually increased.

4 Conclusion

Global Moran's I statistics by using time-series data of Per Capita GDP gives a full range of positive correlation between economic growth and spatial distribution in specify geographic area. And this correlation is going up with time to go. In the past 16 years the urban economics are shown in a steady growth trend in Shandong province. In addition, spatial clustering pattern is presentation of spatial autocorrelation. The more obvious for spatial clustering, the faster for urban economic growth. But issues about the economic development of each city is different clearly due to the difference of geographical position. To illustrate, we should carry on the research for the differences of spatial clustering pattern between the 17 cities with local Moran's I analysis.

Acknowledgements. This work was supported by the National Social Science Fund Project, China (grant number 17BJL055), the Humanities and Social Science Research Project, Ministry of Education, China (grant number 13YJA790038) and 2016 sponsorship of teacher visiting abroad in University of Jinan.

References

1. Shandong Provincial Bureau of Statistics, China. http://www.stats-sd.gov.cn/
2. Qiao, J., Li, X.: Spatial structure of city-and-town concentrated area in Henan Province. Geogr. Res. **25**, 213–222 (2006). (in Chinese)
3. Pan, W.: Regional linkage and the spatial spillover effects on regional economic growth in China. Soc. Sci. China **3**, 125–139 (2013). (in Chinese)
4. Amaral, P.V., Anselin, L.: Finite sample properties of Moran's I test for spatial autocorrelation in tobit models. Pap. Reg. Sci. **93**, 773–781 (2014)
5. Viladomat, J., Mazumder, R., McInturff, A., McCauley, D.J., Hastie, T.: Assessing the significance of global and local correlations under spatial autocorrelation: a nonparametric approach. Biometrics **70**, 409–418 (2014)
6. Westerholt, R., Resch, B., Zipf, A.: A local scale-sensitive indicator of spatial autocorrelation for assessing high- and low-value clusters in multiscale datasets. Int. J. Geogr. Inf. Sci. **29**, 868–887 (2015)

7. Holmberg, H., Lundevaller, E.H.: A test for robust detection of residual spatial autocorrelation with application to mortality rates in Sweden. Spat. Stat. **14**, 365–381 (2015)
8. Melecky, L.: Spatial autocorrelation method for local analysis of the EU. Procedia Econ. Finan. **23**, 1102–1109 (2015)
9. Shen, S.L., Wu, X.Q., Wang, C.W.: Research on spatial autocorrelation of the population in Shandong Province. In: Zeng, Z., Bai, X. (eds.) Proceedings of the 2016 2nd Workshop on Advanced Research and Technology in Industry Applications, vol. 81, pp. 1284–1287 (2016)
10. Vavrek, R., Ardielli, E., Gonos, J.: Members of the European union as a single economic unit and its spatial autocorrelation. In: Proceedings of the 3rd International Conference on European Integration 2016 (ICEI 2016), pp. 1060–1067 (2016)
11. Maleta, M., Calka, B.: SGEM: examining spatial autocorrelation of real estate features using Moran statistics. Inf. Geoinf. Remote Sens. **2**, 841–847 (2015)

Using Local Moran's I Statistics to Estimate Spatial Autocorrelation of Urban Economic Growth in Shandong Province, China

Jun Zhao[1], Yue Wang[2(✉)], and Wenxiu Shi[2]

[1] School of Civil Engineering and Architecture, University of Jinan,
Jinan 250022, Shandong, China
Jun.Zhao@ujn.edu.cn
[2] Business School, University of Jinan, Jinan 250002, Shandong, China
{Yue.Wang, se_wangy, Wenxiu.Shi}@ujn.edu.cn

Abstract. Urban economic development in the past years has been in steady growth trend in Shandong, China. But between cities show differences each other. To find out the influence of spatial autocorrelation to urban economic growth, local Moran's I statistics are applied with Capita GDP datasets of 17 cities from 2000 to 2015. Four kinds of visual presentation for the spatial clustering show spatial autocorrelation of urban economic growth with the time of going. Cities in east coastal region present H-H clustering. Cities in central west region show L-L clustering. There are unbalanced for urban economic growth in Shandong province due to geographical distribution.

Keywords: Urban economic · Spatial autocorrelation
Spatial clustering · Local Moran's I

1 Introduction

There is closely relationship between the urban development and social economic. Especially in recent years, huge changes happened in urban and urban groups. Growth of urban present more and more agglomeration effect. Shandong, one of the developed provinces, is located between the capital economic circle and the Yangtze River economic belt in the east of China. The geographical position is superior, and the regional economic development is steady growth and basically balance. There are two sub-provincial cities (Jinan, Qingdao) and 15 prefecture-level cities. And it has advantage of geography, resource and labor force. As of historic, policy, natural factors, there are big differences of economic among the local cities in Shandong. The developed level is shown reduce tendency from east to west, and from north to south. For example, Linyi city, the biggest prefecture-level city for the population and area in Shandong, is located on the southwest of the province. Its GDP is no more than a half for Qingdao, the western coastal city. So, the issues about relationship and difference of urban economic growth among the 17 prefecture-level cities in Shandong should be conducted.

As traditional statistics do not consider spatial aspects, it is difficult to truly present the impact of geographical position. This paper uses Geographic Information System

© Springer Nature Singapore Pte Ltd. 2018
H. Yuan et al. (Eds.): GSKI 2017, CCIS 848, pp. 32–39, 2018.
https://doi.org/10.1007/978-981-13-0893-2_4

(GIS) and spatial statistics to analyze the pattern of urban economic development in Shandong province. It is followed by local Moran's I statistics to reflect the difference of urban economic growth of the cities in Shandong province.

Spatial autocorrelation, one of methods for Spatial statistical analysis, provide an accurate understanding of spatial location and spatial interaction. Spatial autocorrelation statistics detect the presence of interdependence between the values of data at neighboring locations. Spatial analysis identify the problem-ridden and developed territories within the EU based on the characteristics of those which describe driving forces of competitiveness, also in terms of long-term potentiality, and those which are direct or indirect outcomes of a competitive society and economy [1]. Simultaneously, technical support for the quantitative study of urban economic are provided. Issues was separately discussed through centralized degree of city-and-town from the following three angles such as the growth of node, and the linkage of traffic network, traffic flows, volume of telecommunications and the level of regional development [2]. Some authors explored the feature of regional linkage and the spatial correlation among China's regional per capita GDP from 1998 to 2009. They find that there exists global spatial autocorrelation all over the country, and this kind of autocorrelation has been increasing since 1998. Meanwhile, the local spatial correlation is gradually being shown [3]. Some investigation has been conducted for the finite-sample properties of Moran's I test statistic for spatial autocorrelation in tobit models suggested by Kelejian and Prucha [4]. A method is proposed to test the correlation of two random fields when they are both spatially autocorrelated. In this scenario, the assumption of independence for the pair of observations in the standard test does not hold. The method recovers the null distribution considering the autocorrelation [5]. When analyzing data is collected with a geographical dimension, it is important to be able to test for spatial autocorrelation. The presence of spatial autocorrelation might unveil ignored explanatory variables or just be a factor necessary to consider when further analyzing the data [6]. Georeferenced user-generated datasets like those extracted from Twitter are increasingly gaining the interest of spatial analysts. Such datasets oftentimes reflect a wide array of real-world phenomena. However, each of these phenomena takes place at a certain spatial scale. Therefore, user-generated datasets are of multiscale nature. Such datasets cannot be properly dealt with using the most common analysis methods, because these are typically designed for single-scale datasets where all observations are expected to reflect one single phenomenon. Experiments show that the approach can be able to better detect spatial autocorrelation at specific scales [7]. Based on the fifth and sixth census data in China, studying on the spatial autocorrelation of the population in Shandong province has been focused. The global Moran I statistic is used to quantify the spatial clustering of the population in the whole province both in 2000 and 2010 years, respectively. And the local Moran I statistic is employed to assess the spatial autocorrelation degree between one city and others [8]. Based on the given data of as content in the soil, Anselin elocal spatial autocorrelation model is used to carry on local spatial clustering. It can cluster the similar attribute values to a class [9]. Another research is to identify the homogeneity of GDP and Per capita GDP (GPI per capita) in the European Union as a whole and at the level of change caused by the accession of new countries in years 1973, 1981, 1986, 1995, 2004 and 2007. To identify the presence of spatial structure Moran index is used too [10].

2 Methodology

2.1 Datasets

Local Moran's I statistics mainly focus on inside relations between the 17 cities. Based on the statistical data of the urban economic development in Shandong, the Per capita GDP of 17 cities on the prefecture level in Shandong from 2000 to 2015 is selected, which can illustrate the urban economic development in the past 16 years [11]. We have established the spatial geographical database of 17 cities in Shandong, China. And input the datasets as attribute data into database. So, the 17 groups of time-series sample are used to carry on the local Moran's I statistics.

2.2 Moran's I

Spatial statistical analysis first assumes that all variables in the study areas are independent and have spatial autocorrelation with each other. Then in spatial or temporal context, this correlation is defined as autocorrelation. Spatial autocorrelation is one of the most important characteristics of spatial data. It refers to the potential interdependence between some variables in observational data within the same distribution area. Spatial autocorrelation statistics are a fundamental property used to measure geographic data. That is, the degree of interdependence between data at a location and other locations. This dependency is often called spatial dependence. Geographic data may not be independent of each other, but are relevant because of spatial interaction and spatial diffusion. One of the examples of relations is called spatial autocorrelation phenomena. Spatial autocorrelation implies that values of objects located in a close vicinity are more similar one to another contrary to distant objects values. This phenomenon favors forming of spatial clusters characterized by similar values. Various measures are used to check if selected objects are characterized by similar values of a variable. The most frequently used statistics for spatial autocorrelation examination are Moran's I Statistics [12].

Moran's I statistics of can be expressed as:

$$I = \frac{n}{\sum_{i=1}^{n}\sum_{j=1}^{n} w_{i,j}} \frac{\sum_{i=1}^{n}\sum_{j=1}^{n} w_{i,j} z_i z_j}{\sum_{i=1}^{n} z_i^2} \tag{1}$$

Where, n is the total number of spatial features, i and j are spatial features, $w_{i,j}$ is the spatial weight of between feature i and j, z_i is the difference between attribute value and average of attribute values $Z_i = (x_i - \bar{X})$, x_i is attribute value, $\bar{X}$ is average of attribute value.

3   Local Moran's I Statistics

To interpret the spatial differences among the 17 cities in Shandong, GeoDA software are run on. Functions of scatter plot, cluster map and significance map present the results. Note that distance threshold has a great influence on the spatial autocorrelation between regions, and the spatial weight matrix will change due to the distance threshold. Through calculating and judgement, the Euclidean distance between the centroids of 17 cities and the centroid of Shandong is in the range of [110881 m, 606594 m]. To illustrate the influence of the distance threshold on results of local Moran's I, and consider the actual effect of the geographical distribution of the cities around Shandong, three results of local Moran's I are given for the three-distance thresholds of 110881 m (110 km), 250000 m (250 km) and 500000 m (500 km), as shown in Table 1.

Table 1. Local Moran's I index

Year	110 km	250 km	500 km
2000	0.129337	0.15154	−0.0942085
2001	0.145856	0.16577	−0.0952701
2002	0.162753	0.182148	−0.0954742
2003	0.137103	0.164752	−0.0962237
2004	0.138794	0.169974	−0.100683
2005	0.150235	0.149664	−0.102875
2006	0.181589	0.161412	−0.105141
2007	0.183606	0.163114	−0.10618
2008	0.170501	0.141805	−0.112468
2009	0.204066	0.16535	−0.113604
2010	0.200898	0.160888	−0.119334
2011	0.200943	0.162394	−0.124673
2012	0.186292	0.161027	−0.125493
2013	0.177368	0.162636	−0.126174
2014	0.176198	0.169154	−0.124991
2015	0.203326	0.194488	−0.129976

When the distance thresholds are 110 km and 250 km, local Moran's I indexes are more than zero, indicating that there is positive correlation between the cities in the spatial distribution. When the distance threshold is 500 km, indexes are negative, and the spatial distribution is negative correlation. In other words, no spatial correlation. However, under the 110 km distance threshold condition, spatial clustering is not significant. The 250 km distance threshold setting is effective for the spatial clustering.

The 250 km distance threshold is used to generate spatial weight matrix for local Moran's I cluster map of 2000–2015. Spatial autocorrelation between cities show different clustering patterns with the change of Per capita GDP. Here are the results of 2000–2015, as shown in Fig. 1.

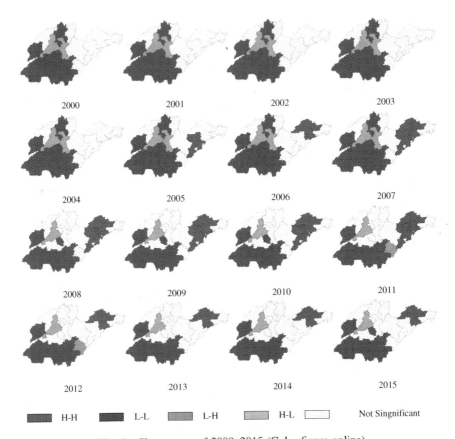

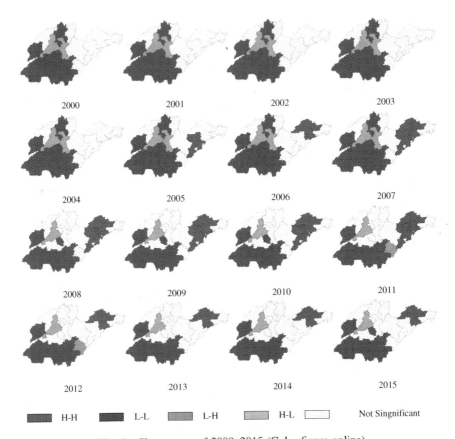

Fig. 1. Cluster map of 2000–2015 (Color figure online)

Noted that H-H is high clustering region surrounded by low clustering region, L-L is low clustering region surrounded by low clustering region. Both show positive correlation. H-L is high clustering region surrounded by low clustering region, L-H is low clustering region surrounded by high clustering region. Both show negative correlation.

During 2000–2004, Jinan city and Zibo city (pink region), two central western regions of Shandong, are clustered by H-L clustering. Surrounding cities (blue region) are L-L clustering. No H-H clustering is shown among the other cities. Then from the beginning of 2005, Qingdao city and Yantai city (red region), the eastern developed area are H-H clustering. Only Jinan City (pink region) is clustered by H-L clustering. Surrounding cities (blue region) are L-L clustering.

In addition, we took the classification statistics for clustering shown in Table 2, which are according to the classification of cluster pattern in Fig. 1.

Table 2. Classification statistics for clustering

Year	H-H	L-L	L-H	H-L	Not significant
2000	0	8	0	2	7
2001	0	8	0	2	7
2002	0	8	0	2	7
2003	0	8	0	2	7
2004	0	8	0	2	7
2005	1	8	0	2	6
2006	0	8	0	2	7
2007	1	8	0	2	6
2008	2	6	0	1	8
2009	2	6	0	1	8
2010	2	6	0	1	8
2011	2	5	1	1	8
2012	2	5	1	1	8
2013	1	5	0	1	10
2014	1	5	0	1	10
2015	1	6	0	1	9

However, in the past 16 years, L-L clustering present a downtrend. At the same time, the number of *Not Significant* present uptrend. It means that Spatial autocorrelation between cities will be more unclear, and spatial differences between cities became gradually clear. It can also be seen in Fig. 2.

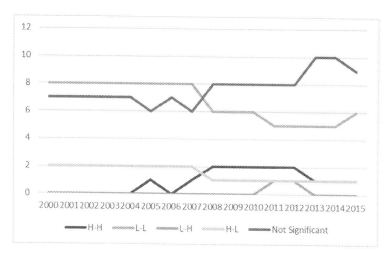

Fig. 2. Cluster pattern change trend from 2000 to 2015 (Color figure online)

4   Conclusion

Before the local Moran's I analysis, we took the global Moran's I statistics by using a total of 16 years of Per capita GDP data with the 17 cities of Shandong from 2000–2015. The results gave a full range of positive spatial autocorrelation between economic growth and spatial distribution of geographical area. And this correlation is going up with time to go. Due to the differences of geographical distribution, the urban economic growth of Shandong in recent years is dumbbell-shaped pattern. The eastern coastal areas are rich in marine resources, frequent economic activities, and spatial clustering pattern was highly clustered. However, the economic development in central western regions are relatively slow. With time of going, the clustering pattern of the surrounding areas is also changing constantly. Qingdao city and Yantai city located in east coastal region are H-H clustering, their economic present strengthen increase. Cities in central west region show L-L clustering. Their economic present low growth. This tendency shows that the urban economic growth in different regions is different due to spatial cluster pattern. That is, there is unbalanced in economics growth in the cities.

Acknowledgements. This work was supported by the National Social Science Fund Project, China (grant number 17BJL055), the Humanities and Social Science Research Project, Ministry of Education, China (grant number 13YJA790038) and 2016 sponsorship of teacher visiting abroad in University of Jinan.

References

1. Melecky, L.: Spatial autocorrelation method for local analysis of the EU. Procedia Econ. Finan. **23**, 1102–1109 (2015)
2. Qiao, J., Li, X.: Spatial structure of city-and-town concentrated area in Henan province. Geogr. Res. **25**, 213–222 (2006). (in Chinese)
3. Pan, W.: Regional linkage and the spatial spillover effects on regional economic growth in China. Soc. Sci. China **3**, 125–139 (2013). (in Chinese)
4. Amaral, P.V., Anselin, L.: Finite sample properties of Moran's I test for spatial autocorrelation in tobit models. Pap. Reg. Sci. **93**, 773–781 (2014)
5. Viladomat, J., Mazumder, R., McInturff, A., McCauley, D.J., Hastie, T.: Assessing the significance of global and local correlations under spatial autocorrelation: a nonparametric approach. Biometrics **70**, 409–418 (2014)
6. Holmberg, H., Lundevaller, E.H.: A test for robust detection of residual spatial autocorrelation with application to mortality rates in Sweden. Spat. Stat. **14**, 365–381 (2015)
7. Westerholt, R., Resch, B., Zipf, A.: A local scale-sensitive indicator of spatial autocorrelation for assessing high- and low-value clusters in multiscale datasets. Int. J. Geogr. Inf. Sci. **29**, 868–887 (2015)
8. Shen, S.L., Wu, X.Q., Wang, C.W.: Research on spatial autocorrelation of the population in Shandong province. In: Zeng, Z., Bai, X. (eds.) Proceedings of the 2016 2nd Workshop on Advanced Research and Technology in Industry Applications, vol. 81, pp. 1284–1287 (2016)

9. Fu, J.M., Li, Y.F.: A locating method based on the Anselin elocal spatial autocorrelation model which researches in the heavy metal pollution source. In: Ma, B., Zhou, D. (eds.) Proceedings of the 2016 3rd International Conference on Materials Engineering, Manufacturing Technology and Control, vol. 67, pp. 1694–1698 (2016)
10. Vavrek, R., Ardielli, E., Gonos, J.: Members of the European union as a single economic unit and its spatial autocorrelation. In: Proceedings of the 3rd International Conference on European Integration 2016 (ICEI 2016), pp. 1060–1067 (2016)
11. Shandong Provincial Bureau of Statistics, China. http://www.stats-sd.gov.cn/
12. Maleta, M., Calka, B.: SGEM: examining spatial autocorrelation of real estate features using moran statistics. Inf. Geoinf. Remote Sens. 2, 841–847 (2015)

MIC for Analyzing Attributes Associated with Thai Agricultural Products

Tisinee Surapunt[(✉)], Chuanlu Liu, and Shuliang Wang

School of Software, Beijing Institute of Technology, No. 5, 100081 Haidian, Beijing, China
kitty_nat_t@hotmail.com

Abstract. A prediction system of Thai agricultural products will purpose as our future work. The large amount of data is necessary and precise to predict the trend. Due to the high-efficiency prediction, only the associated attributes are preferred and well prepared in the next process. MIC is one statistical method to measure a correlation coefficient of pairwise variables on an immense dataset. After that their correlation coefficient shows the ranking of variables relationship. Thus, the pre-processing of data is done before executing. In this paper will present the theoretical of MIC and related works. The general concepts of MIC and the special ideas will be described.

Keywords: MIC · Agricultural production · Prediction production

1 Introduction

To determine the dependency among the variables, a correlation coefficient is required as a quantitative measurement. Base on the statistical theory, there are various methods to present the correlation coefficient such as the distance correlation, the Spearman's rank correlation coefficient, the Pearson correlation coefficient. The distance correlation is a Euclidean distance-based measure which illustrates the relationship between two random variables or two vectors of arbitrary. The notion is known as the Brownian distance covariance [1, 2]. The Spearman's rank correlation coefficient and the Pearson correlation coefficient present on the similar dependency values but focus on the different variable types. The Spearman method works with the monotonic relationship while the Pearson works with linear relationship [3, 4]. The zero value of correlation coefficient indicates an independent relationship between 2 variables. In addition, an interval scale between −1 and 1 implies the dependent relationship between 2 variables. A positive defines the direct relationship but a negative reveals the inverse relationship [5, 6].

In the era of big data, the data keeps on growing. The computation process has to deal with the abundant of variables [7, 8]. Thus, the related variables will be chosen for optimizing the run-time. The MIC is one statistical method which is discovered by Reshef et al. [9]. It stands for Maximum Information Coefficient. The kind of linear and non-linear relationship variables are manipulated by MIC. The score can capture roughly by R^2 when the data relationship is linear regression function. Thus, the result will be the interval integer between 0 and 1. When result is 0, the same meaning with

© Springer Nature Singapore Pte Ltd. 2018
H. Yuan et al. (Eds.): GSKI 2017, CCIS 848, pp. 40–47, 2018.
https://doi.org/10.1007/978-981-13-0893-2_5

other methods is interpreted. Meanwhile, the result indicates closely to 1, the pairwise variable is a direct relationship [4, 10].

The associated attributes extraction of Thai agricultural products is a data mining process which is done by meshing the decision rules. We anticipate that the MIC method is possible to perform simply with Thai agricultural products attributes. The MIC will be accountable for the data analysis on an immense dataset. The result of interval integer will present the mutual information of pairwise variables. The considered top-scoring will show how strong of the relationship between each pairwise variables are. Then, the associated pairwise attributes of Thai agricultural products will be selected to process in the further steps. Our case study will apply MIC method on Thai agricultural products dataset. After that, a prediction system will be developed to forecast the Thai agricultural products trend in each seasoning as a final result in the future work.

Hence, in this paper will illustrate an overview of MIC methodology and other related fields is described. The second section is related work which illustrates how MIC applies in various fields. In addition, many researchers worked on the performance and accuracy of MIC. Then, the third section is the MIC methodology. The MIC theory and the acquired mutual values processes will be described. At last section is conclusion and future work.

2   Related Work

Due to the enormous variables in various fields, researchers applied MIC to solve their issues. It demonstrates that MIC is a popular method to measure the correlation coefficient. Then, the associated variables will be selected. Thus, MIC play an important role in the pre-processing of data.

The agricultural statistical data mining [8] was described the methods to simplify associated attributes. They handled the agricultural data from the statistic yearbook of China from 1982 to 1990. The output was accurate and big variance when statistical methods have more relevant rules. Therefore, the attributes were generalized by implying the classification rules. Then, the redundant attributes were discovered and removed. The simplified attributes cannot change and effect to the result. Wei et al. [11] presented a Bayesian network structure learning algorithm which based on MIC. An initial undirected graph was generated in his algorithm. The idea described the degree of dependency between two nodes X_i and X_j which can be determined by the MIC. The MIC result described the dependencies between two nodes following the ranking rule. Hence, the network node connectivity was determined and the network structure was build. Moreover, Zhang et al. [12] obtained an undirected graph by measuring the degree of two random variables dependency in order to build the Bayesian network structure. Then, Zeng et al. [13] also made use of MIC to construct an initial Bayesian network with the greedy algorithm. The result was to modify locally the initial network, the screening and the correlation factor. Since the MIC is robust to outliers, it can be used as a criterion for evaluating a network. To construct models which well fits the data and reduce classification error, Zeng and Zheng [14] proposed a deep belief networks based on MIC principle. When the MIC was used in dimensionality reduction, the unreliability of the reconstruction error was also improved. The comparative of traditional methods showed the deep belief networks in the experiment. The recognition effectively rate can be better.

Other related works in language recognition, medical and searching based which can be enhanced their accuracy and performance by applying MIC concept [15–17]. The closed relationship variables in the power system static voltage stability margin was explored by MIC in order to select the optimal input variables [18]. A case of Xiangxi River was predicted the monthly streamflow [19]. The streamflow was measured and characterized the nonlinearity between the hydro-meteorological variables by MIC. In addition, the continuous optimization problems were purposed to quantify the level of variable interactions. The MIC measures the novel exploratory landscape analysis [20]. Since MIC has been detected linear and nonlinear correlation between pairwise variables but the triplet did not apply directly. Among three variables can be examined by MIC. The concept of total correlation is to measure only one-dimensional manifold dependency [21].

3   MIC Methodology

The purpose of MIC is to evaluate the dependency of pairwise variables following two heuristic properties. The generality and equitability properties are discovered to show classes of relationships. Because of an adequate dataset, the generality property illustrates the wide range of associated values. There is no limit for MIC to presents various form of function such as linear function, exponential function, or periodic function [9]. The equitable measure of dependency will be examined the similar scores whether there are matters with the relationships or not. The noise level is difficult to append in several functional relationships however the noisy relationship exists. MIC can also depict the perfect score seems as noiseless [22, 23]. Thus, the equitability is imperative when non-related variables have to be equal to added-noisy relationship [24]. Not only the variables relationships are realized, the data exploration should also emphasize. The dimensionality of datasets can be an effective capability to prioritize the significant relationships [25–28].

The equitability property is formalized to evaluate the quantity value of an association between 2 variables without bias. The fundamental information theory is accepted when the MIC detects nonlinear correlations in the equitability dataset. The mutual information is called as a quantitative measure between 2 associated variables and presented a mathematical proof [11, 29, 30]. The pre-processing of data is the MIC means to apply the mutual information on the continuous random variables. In this research selects some of the important aspects which are illustrated by Reshef et al. [24].

3.1   The MIC Characteristic

Most of the associated variables are computed their association with the quantitative score by MIC. The MIC categorizes their association by the score between 0 and 1 which is examined by the following proof. Among different functions are performed by MIC, the different MIC scores present as shown in Fig. 1. The 2 random variables

X and Y are focused. Y is a function of X which is not constant. Then the data of function (X, Y) will obtain the MIC score which tends to 1. When the function (X, Y) is a finite union of differentiable curves with the form c(t) = [x(t), y(t)] while t is an interval integer between 0 and 1, the data of function (X, Y) will also acquire the MIC score which also tends to 1. If X and Y are statistically independent, the zero values of dx/dt and dy/dt should be prepared on finitely many points. The data of function (X, Y) meets zero value although a sample size grows. In addition, the proof of Reshef et.al. [9] presented the equitable property on the noisy function which was bounded below a function of R^2. The simulation experiment confirmed that the MIC's equitability is the noiseless function because the MIC score tends to 1.0 ($R^2 = 1.0$) with different statistic methods [31–34].

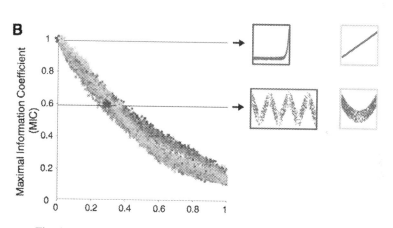

Fig. 1. The scatterplot of MIC scores among different function [9]

3.2 The Utility of Maximization and Normalization Based on the Definition of MIC

The maximization and normalization are MIC specific features [24]. They were explored before their properties. To make use of those features, the researchers omitted specific features from the MIC behavior. Then, the statistical result will be noticed. Thus, the 3 considerations can exclude maximization or normalization and both respectively. Firstly, the maximization is omitted a variation on MIC. The mutual information can simply equipartition of each grid instead of all grids. The maximal possible mutual information is calculated afterwards. The MIC can determine as

$$\text{MIC}_{\text{without maximize}}(D) = \frac{max}{xy < B(|D|)} \frac{I^E(D, x, y)}{log_2 min\{x, y\}} \tag{1}$$

Secondly, when the normalization is omitted, the $log_2 min\{x, y\}$ can consider the variant of MIC. In fact, the $log_2 min\{x, y\}$ is the upper bound on the maximum mutual information for all grids. Thus, the normalization provides the possible value between 0 and 1, and the different resolution among grids are compared.

$$\text{MIC}_{\text{without normalize}}(D) = \genfrac{}{}{0pt}{}{max}{xy < B(|D|)} I^*(D, x, y) \qquad (2)$$

Thirdly, both maximization and normalization are omitted.

$$\text{MIC}_{\text{without maximize and normalize}}(D) = \genfrac{}{}{0pt}{}{max}{xy < B(|D|)} I^E(D, x, y) \qquad (3)$$

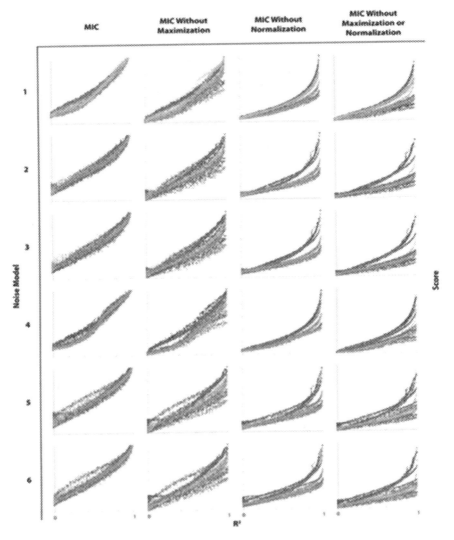

Fig. 2. The characteristics of MIC with 3 different variant features on noise model [24]

Finally, the scatter plots of Fig. 2. present the distinguish between the variant of MIC against noise model. The most independent scatter plot is MIC with maximization. The measure mutual information with equal partition of each grid effects to MIC score. The MIC with 2 features presented the strongly associated relationship. The scatter plot of each noise model examines the similar score.

4   Conclusion and Future Work

The association between variables is defined by the MIC correlation coefficient The MIC score is the quantitative interval scale between 0 and 1. MIC score which is close to 1 indicates the dependent pairwise, while MIC score which is close to 0 indicates the independent pairwise. So, only the associated variables are preferred in the following processes. Not only the time is saved, but the system will also execute more accurate because of the reduction of variables and classification errors. Moreover, the redundant features are also removed. It implies that the MIC can manipulate and examine the relationship between variables as the pre-processing of data. In the future, our research will focus on the prediction system of Thai agricultural products trend. Due to the growing dataset of Thai agricultural products, MIC is efficient to discover the associated attributes.

Acknowledgments.   This work was supported by National Key Research and Development Plan of China (2016YFB0502604, 2016YFC0803000), National Natural Science Fund of China (61472039), and Frontier and Interdisciplinary Innovation Program of Beijing Institute of Technology (2016CX11006), International Scientific and Technological Cooperation and Academic Exchange Program of Beijing Institute of Technology (GZ2016085103).

References

1. Székely, G.J., Rizzo, M.L.: Brownian distance covariance. Annal. Appl. Stat. **3**(4), 1236–1265 (2009)
2. Székely, G.J., Rizzo, M.L., Bakirov, N.K.: Measuring and testing dependence by correlation of distances. Annal. Stat. **35**(6), 2769–2794 (2007)
3. A comparison of the pearson and spearman correlation methods (2016). http://support. minitab.com/en-us/minitab-express/1/help-and-how-to/modeling-statistics/regression/ supporting-topics/basics/a-comparison-of-the-pearson-and-spearman-correlation-methods/
4. Huang, Y., Luo, T., Wang, X., Hui, K., Wang, Wen-Jie, He, Ben: On evaluating query performance predictors. In: Zu, Q., Vargas-Vera, M. (eds.) ICPCA/SWS 2013. LNCS, vol. 8351, pp. 184–194. Springer, Cham (2014). https://doi.org/10.1007/978-3-319-09265-2_20
5. Mukaka, M.M.: A guide to appropriate use of correlation coefficient in medical research. Malawi Med. J. **24**(3), 69–71 (2012)
6. Benesty, J., Huan, Y., Chen, J.: Pearson correlation coefficient. In: Benesty, J., Huan, Y. (eds.) Noise Reduction in Speech Processing. Springer Topics in Signal Processing, pp. 1–4. Springer, Heidelberg (2009)
7. Wang, S., Yuan, H.: Spatial data mining: a perspective of big data. Int. J. Data Warehous. Min. **10**(4), 50–70 (2014)

8. Li, D., Wang, S., Li, D.: Spatial Data Mining: Theory and Application. Springer, Heidelberg (2016). https://doi.org/10.1007/978-3-662-48538-5

9. Reshef, D.N., et al.: Detecting novel associations in large data sets. Science **334**(6062), 1518–1524 (2011)

10. Wang, S., et al.: Fast search local extremum for maximal information coefficient (MIC). J. Comput. Appl. Math. **327**, 372–387 (2018)

11. Wei, Z.Q., Hong-Zhe, X.U., Wen, L.I., et al.: Bayesian network structure learning algorithm based on maximal information coefficient. Appl. Res. Comput. (2014)

12. Zhang, Y., Zhang, W., Xie, Y.: Improved heuristic equivalent search algorithm based on maximal information coefficient for bayesian network structure learning. Neurocomput. J. **117**(14), 186–195 (2013)

13. Zeng, Q.Q., Zeng, A., Pan, D., et al.: Bayesian network structure learning algorithm based on maximal information coefficient. Comput. Eng. J. **43**(8), 225–230 (2017)

14. Zeng, A., Zheng, Q.M.: Deep belief networks research based on maximum information coefficient. Comput. Sci. J. (2016)

15. Lei, L.I., Liu, J., Zhang, H.K.: Topics identification and evolution trend of network public opinion based on co-occurrence analysis. Inf. Sci. J. (2016)

16. Wang, P., Zhang, S.C.: Method for the correlation analysis of data with time delay based on maximal information coefficient. Lectron. Measur. Technol. **9**, 112–115 (2015)

17. Liu, H., Rao, N., Yi, L., et al.: Maximal information coefficient on identifying differentially expressed genes of permanent atrial fibrillation. Chin. J. Biomed. Eng. **34**, 8–16 (2015)

18. Zhou, S.P., Chen, J., Liu, C., et al.: Assessment method of power system static voltage stability margin. Electron. Des. Eng. **6**, 066 (2014)

19. Fan, Y.R., Huang, G.H., Li, Y.P., et al.: Development of PCA-based cluster quantile regression (PCA-CQR) framework for streamflow prediction. J. Appl. Xiangxi River Watershed, Appl. Soft Comput. **51**, 280–293 (2017)

20. Sun, Y., Kirley, M., Halgamuge, S.: Quantifying variable interactions in continuous optimization problems. IEEE Trans. Evol. Comput. **1–1**, 99 (2016)

21. Li, Y.J., Zhang, Y.H.: Detecting measure for trivariate one-dimensional manifold dependences. Acta Electronica Sinica **44**, 639–645 (2016)

22. Reshef, Y.A., et al.: Theoretical foundations of equitability and the maximal information coefficient. arXiv preprint arXiv:1408.4908 (2014)

23. Kinney, J.B., Atwal, G.S.: Equitability, mutual information, and the maximal information coefficient. Proc. Nat. Acad. Sci. **111**(9), 3354–3359 (2014)

24. Reshef, D., et al.: Equitability analysis of the maximal information coefficient, with comparisons. arXiv preprint arXiv:1301.6314 (2013)

25. Tenenbaum, J.B., De Silva, V., Langford, J.C.: A global geometric framework for nonlinear dimensionality reduction. Science **290**(5500), 2319–2323 (2000)

26. Roweis, S.T., Saul, L.K.: Nonlinear dimensionality reduction by locally linear embedding. Sci. **290**(5500), 2323–2326 (2000)

27. Guyon, I., Elisseeff, A.: An introduction to variable and feature selection. J. Mach. Learn. Res. **3**(Mar), 1157–1182 (2003)

28. Hastie, T., Tibshirani, R., Friedman, J.: The Elements of Statistical Learning. In: Data Mining, Inference, and Prediction, Guide to Biometrics. Springer, Heidelberg (2002)

29. Speed, T.: Mathematics, a correlation for the 21st century. Sci. J. **334**(6062), 1502–1503 (2011)

30. Kinney, J.B., Atwal, G.S.: Equitability, mutual information, and the maximal information coefficient. Proc. Nat. Acad. Sci. U.S.A **111**(9), 3354 (2014)

31. Delicado, P., Smrekar, M.: Measuring non-linear dependence for two random variables distributed along a curve. Stat. Comput. **19**(3), 255 (2009)

32. Kraskov, A., Stögbauer, H., Grassberger, P.: Estimating mutual information. Phys. Rev. E **69**(6), 066138 (2004)
33. Moon, Y.-I., Rajagopalan, B., Lall, U.: Estimation of mutual information using kernel density estimators. Phys. Rev. E **52**(3), 2318 (1995)
34. Rényi, A.: On measures of dependence. Acta mathematica hungarica **10**(3–4), 441–451 (1959)

Historical Development of Corporate Social Responsibility Concept in Kazakhstan

Ulsara Zhantore Nematullakyzy[✉] and XiaoHu Zhou

The School of Economics and Management, Nanjing University of Science and Technology, XiaoLingWei. 200, 210094 Nanjing, China
13921445141@163.com, njustzhx@njust.edu.cn

Abstract. In recent times, there has gained an increasing interest in corporate social responsibility concept initiatives have emerged in developing countries, in particular Kazakhstan. However, many of these studies investigate in the Western and Chinese context of CSR, preferring to rely on theories and hypotheses from studies undertaken developed countries. The Kazakhstani CSR initiatives include laws, and regulations, governmental instructions, non-governmental organizations standard guidance. We develop a historical CSR concept with chronological evaluation. Based on the social, economic, political-environments, with completely different legal systems and cultural influences. This paper contributes to extend mainly considering specific context, and stages of evaluation CSR.

Keywords: Corporate social responsibility · Historical development
Kazakhstan

1 Introduction

With the constantly increase in all over world's corporations are involved in corporate social responsibility activities. The most of research papers are written in Western and Chinese context, not raised the question about developing countries CSR concept such as Kazakhstan. CSR content in Chinese academic literature and texts are developed as follows: CSR's content is richer and includes charitable donation, fund raising, environment protection, and etc. (Xiao and Xu 2011). Responsibility of China (Huang and Zhao 2016) issued by the Chinese Academy of Social Sciences, the CAGR of Chinese CSR development index reached 16.80% since 2009. In this research that considers about CSR concept and historically development make focus on traditional, cultural, legitimacy differentiations. In China, the authoritative and widely used database is given by Rankings CSR Ratings (RKS). In different circumstance is the concept of CSR has a relatively long history in Western countries (Carroll 1999; Whetten 2002). The KLD index given by American KLD company is the most accepted and widely used. However, recently has been more and more corporations are joining to disclosure CSR information to public. The majority of the world's population lives in developing countries and each country experiences its own unique social, political and environmental issues (United Nations 2013). These countries are in the process of industrialization and are often characterized by unstable governments, higher levels of unemployment, limited technological capacity, unequal distribution of income,

H. Yuan et al. (Eds.): GSKI 2017, CCIS 848, pp. 48–54, 2018.
https://doi.org/10.1007/978-981-13-0893-2_6

unreliable water supplies and underutilized factors of production. A few papers have specifically reviewed studies on developing countries. For example, (Belal and Momin 2009) categories the work on developing countries into three groups: studies of the volume or extend of reporting; studies of the perceptions of CSR by managers; and studies of the perception of CSR by stakeholders; In all the studies reviewed there is little discussion of the context, other than a description of the country, and no real thought about the theoretical assumptions being made.

This paper presents discussions emphasized on contextual issues or various factors that evidences or potential to influence CSR in developing countries. It focusses on improved consideration in CSR historically research, with particular emphasis one regional such as Kazakhstan have similarities to the emerging market countries, but economy is set against a background the Post-Soviet Union, and has important influence in social, environmental and policy areas. The paper is structured as follows: The next section introduces some broad contextual factors that warrant consideration in the literature on CSR. Next, specific contextual issues are examined: the role of historically development of CSR, differentia's on political ideology; the influence of cultural understandings; and the impact of historical economic context. Finally, conclusion and recommendations for future research works are suggested.

2 Contextual Considerations

The researcher, who first proposed the concept of CSR, is Oliver Sheldon. He defined CSR as a businessman who satisfies the internal and external requirements. Before the 1960's, scholars used social responsibility of businessman as the CSR undertake. Bowen, who is the father of Corporate social responsibility and who is the first systematically defined CSR, also pointed out that the businessman has the responsibility to develop policies in accordance with established social goals and values, and a businessman's voluntary performance of social responsibility is the effective method to improve the economy and achieve economic goals. Adams (2004) talks about the social, political, cultural and economic context, so some consideration of what this might mean is needed as each of these concepts themselves cover a variety of aspects, and indeed overlap. While papers are talk about the "social context" in which the companies being examined operate, this is not well defined and the little consideration is given to what means. This paper chooses to highlight to only one regional, and this is discussed briefly below in broad terms, framework of CSR historical development and followed by a discussion of some specific aspects of identified as providing fertile grounds for future research.

2.1 Political System

Many organizations, associations with the support of government constantly are conducting a lot of activity to enhance the awareness about CSR in the country by arranging seminars, workshops. One case for is in this process, in the month of September 2015, the American chamber of commerce, with support from Eurasia Foundation of Central Asia (EFCA), the ministry of industry and trade of Kazakhstan and the Kazakhstan press club, held training on "CSR in Kazakhstan – The Role of

Government and Media" for journalists of regional mass media and representatives of key ministries. The goal of the training was to improve the quality of CSR coverage in the media and to strengthen the role of CSR in Kazakhstan. Many domestic companies till now have not found out for themselves, to create a place for the concept of "the corporate and social responsibility of business". Consonant to the program of the National Democratic Party "Nur Otan" the holding will attempt to maximally address the social programs and assure they will correspond to the essential needs of the society. The reasons for slow development of the social responsibility of business in Kazakhstan – high political interference and the imperfect legislation, lack of knowledge and complexity of the CSR concept.

2.2 Social-Cultural Environment

In a recent theoretical paper, Matten and Moon (2008) used a historically developed institutional perspective to delineate how and why differences exist in CSR across countries. They proposed that different social norms and cultural values contribute to variation in assumptions regarding different stakeholder interests. Kazakhstan is a multi national country for about have 135 nationalities. The majority is Islamic nation with a strong Central Asian heritage. In so being, the values, beliefs, norms and interpretation of meaning of events, of Kazakhstan will be distinct. What may be desirable or appropriate in Kazakhstan. Yet, for some time now there have been concerted efforts by developed Western nations, to impose their social values and beliefs unto developing nations such as Kazakhstan. Attempts by developing nations in insisting on their differences are usually brushed-off as being regressive or rooted in religious fundamentalism (Donnely 1999). Gupta et al. (2002) provide a brief overview of various research in over fifty years – all by Western scholars to boot – that invariably point to social differences amongst people from different parts of the world. Therefore, in adopting a basis for their CSR, Kazakhstan enterprises need to be cognizant of two factors in view of Kazakhstan's social landscape. The first is that all of the CSR theories that have been proposed over the years emanate from the West. In so being, they may not be congruent to the Kazakh's social milieu. And secondly – which is closely connected to the first the fundamentals of normative CSR theories, based on social values, beliefs and morality, may impinge on the sensitivities of the Kazakh's multi-racial society.

2.3 Economical and Strategy System

As well as government control, culture and political factors, the stage of economic development a country is in is also an important contextual factor that may impact CSR. Kazakhstan is a developing nation aspiring to join the ranks of developed nations of the world by the year 2030. This corresponds with the principles of the "Strategy 2030" plan launched which has since served as the nation's blueprint for development. Kazakhstan's stable and steadily growing economy – on a pace to become one of the three fastest-growing economies in the world in 2015 – is the main draw for foreign investors. Kazakhstan's gross domestic product (GDP) has grown at nearly double the rate of the rest of the world from 2011 onward and is predicted to continue that rate to

2014. Kazakhstan 2050 strategy the G-Global forum, all of which aim to increase competitiveness, create new markets and promote better policies for growth. Investors also appreciate the country's telecommunications infrastructure, the establishment of which is a priority for the government. 2012 saw a 30% growth in broadband connections and Kazakh telecom hopes to provide Internet and telecommunication services to all rural settlements by next year. The system of corporate taxation was another attractive feature, as was the government's promotion of sustainable development. Kazakhstan achieved its goal of entering the top 50 most competitive countries in 2013, and has maintained its position in the 2014–2015 World Economic Forum Global Competitiveness Report that was published at the beginning of September 2014.

The majority of work that considers sociocultural, political and economical factors have impacts on maintain aspects of CSR, such as national identity, values, social organization and language, could be incorporated. The teachings of many religions focus on social responsibility, the relationship with the natural environment, treatment of others, fairness, justice, etc., so there is a natural expectation that religion-based organizations may be more likely to engage in CSR. A more nuanced consideration of how this manifest itself in different societies would improve understanding of the drivers and motivations of these activities CSR context.

3 Historical Development of CSR

The most of literature on CSR classifies countries only into developed or developing. The Western world examines countries that are "developing" (Belal and Momin 2009; Momin and Parker 2013), but little depth is included about where they are in their development journey and how the potential conflict between economic and social goals impacts CSR. The issue of CSR in Kazakhstan was first raised by Nursultan Nazarbayev at the II Congress of Entrepreneurs in Astana (Nazarbayev 2005). The President of RK argued that Kazakhstan needed its own model of corporate social responsibility which would be based on best world practices taking into account the peculiarities of economics, social relationships, multinational culture and traditions of the country. The model should include the resolution of ecological problems, social and regional issues, and activities directed towards economic prosperity and welfare of citizens of Kazakhstan (Nazarbayev 2005). In his speech President strived to inspire local and international companies to engage in social activities. Gaukhar Kopbasarova, the Director of the center for Corporate Governance and Business Ethics in Kazakhstan, states that "companies and corporations that have international investors are more effective in this regard. At their level, CSR is a must" (Kopbasarova 2010) But there is evidence that small and medium enterprises are also trying to be socially responsible. In 2015 more than 300 small, medium, and large companies took part in the contest on corporate social responsibility named "Paryz" which was established by the President of RK (Fabrika Novostei 2015).

In the initial period of evaluation that Kazakhstani enterprises were not interested in the activities in the field of CSR. Therefore, this stage is defined as "the stage of silence". In the second stage is in 1990–2000, social responsibility brought about aversion, and sometimes even objection and aggression of the majority of the business leaders or economic publicists, convinced of the fact that free market is a cure for all problems. It was from this period at there appeared the development of specific, though partial projects, including the selected, significant areas of the functioning of companies in the field of CSR 200-2010. The last stage of the development of social responsibility, 2010 is the stage initially chaotic, since there was an attempt to link CSR to other strategies (Table 1). In other developing countries the importance of local economic, cultural, and religious factors that shape the business environment, and understandings of charity and philanthropy, need to be taken into account. Empirical work in this area is lacking (Lund-Thomsen 2016). For example, an improved brand image, increased market or customer share, employee retention, mitigated regulatory risks, and reduced tax burden, are considered mostly irrelevant" (Global Insights 2013). Business leaders engage in CSR for a range of business, humanitarian, social, religious, and political

Table 1. Historically development CSR in Kazakhstan, the author's own research

Stage 1	
Elements of the framework	1990–2000
Legislation	Newly set up, unclear responsibilities of boards, dispersed ownership structure, creation of closed privatization
Business culture	A lot of discretion, learning by doing, misusing opportunities, management dominated boards, lack of the CSR interest
Business sector	Newly created Stock Exchange, almost no regulation, all joint-stock companies allowed to be publicly trade
Stage 2	
Elements of the framework	2000–2010
Legislation	Securities Commission created, some protection of small shareholders introduced, responsibilities of boards partially clarified, amendments to bankruptcy low reducing the scope for owners to strip funds from a failing company before bankruptcy proceedings can be completed and giving more scope for voluntary settlement with creditors
Business culture	Concentration of ownership, more active Supervisory Boards representing mainly owners, development of the specific CSR projects
Business sector	Massive outlisting of companies
Stage 3	
Elements of the framework	2010-nadal
Legislation	Opening of closed funds, amendments to the Commercial Code (plus second - round implications for other legislation particularly that relating to the securities markets), improvements in related areas but no progress in law enforcement
Business culture	Increased adoption of ethical codes by companies and associations, linking CSR to the other strategies
Business sector	Privatization of major banks, adoption of a code by Principles of Corporate Governance

reasons. Key amongst them is a belief that "giving back" to society discharges religious obligations to the poor, and an awareness that being seen to contribute to national development goals is important (Global Insights 2013). Hence, the conception of CSR in this region is culturally determined, but also shaped by the economic environment.

4   Conclusion and Recommendation

CSR has been a hot topic in the past and present. CSR research in Kazakhstan, in parallel has risen the business sector, government sector and academia. The historical development stages developed according to after taken the independence of Kazakhstan country. In the beginning of 1990s business ethics were gaining first initial stages and until now in the process of developing corporate's social responsibility.

Today, research in the CSR in Kazakhstan is mainly linked to what specific aspects the various research institutions are already addressing. Similarly, the universities of Kazakhstan, with long in developing country studies, has focus on social development issues in its CSR focus.

With the growing also of Kazakhstani business, we may see more CSR engagement be corporation in the future. The challenge for Kazakhstani companies in this context will be follow up increased on CSR with actual and measurable performance in this area, which goes marketing and profiling. A more modern form of CSR, where mastering the social issues are being seen as an integrated competitive advantage.

The reconsidering of CSR with contextual understanding on evidence, like as different political social, cultural, economical and strategic environments impact on evaluation and consequently influence the value of viewing activities to benefit society and natural environment.

The contribution of this paper is contextual CSR research. This study is a cross-cultural research that we focused on specially one region, and national status idea of Kazakhstani companies. Developed the historically evaluation of CSR stages.

References

Adams, C., Zutshi, A.: Corporate social responsibility: why business should act responsibly and be accountable. Aust. Account. Rev. **14**(34), 31–39 (2004)

Gupta, V., Hanges, P.J., Dorfman, P.: Cultural clusters: methodology and findings. J. World Bus. **37**(1), 11–15 (2002)

Huang, H., Zhao, Z.: The influence of political connection on corporate social responsibility—evidence from Listed private companies in China. Int. J. Corp. Soc. Responsib. **1**(1) (2016)

Lund-Thomsen, P., Lindgreen, A., Vanhamme, J.: Industrial clusters and corporate social responsibility in developing countries: what we know, what we do not know, and what we need to know. J. Bus. Ethics, **133**(1), 9–24 (2016)

Maignan, I., Ferrell, O.C., Ferrell, L.: A stakeholder model for implementing social responsibility in marketing. Eur. J. Market. **39**(9/10), 956–977 (2005)

Malik, M.: Value-enhancing capabilities of CSR: a brief review of contemporary literature. J. Bus. Ethics **127**(2), 419–438 (2015)

Marquis, C., Qian, C.: Corporate social responsibility reporting in China: symbol or substance? Organ. Sci. **25**(1), 127–148 (2013)

Matten, D., Moon, J.: Implicit and explicit CSR: a conceptual framework for a comparative understanding of corporate social responsibility. Acad. Manag. Rev. **33**(2), 404–424 (2008)

Wang, H., Tong, L., Takeuchi, R.: Corporate social responsibility: an overview and new research directions thematic issue on corporate social responsibility. Acad. Manag. J. **59**(2), 534–544 (2016)

Zhu, Q., Zhang, Q.: Evaluating practices and drivers of corporate social responsibility: the Chinese context. J. Clean. Prod. **100**, 315–324 (2015)

Zhu, Q., Liu, J., Lai, K.: Corporate social responsibility practices and performance improvement among Chinese national state-owned enterprises. Int. J. Prod. Econ. **171**, 417–426 (2016)

Schlegelmilch, B.B.: Global marketing ethics and CSR. Global Marketing Strategy. MP, pp. 195–220. Springer, Cham (2016). https://doi.org/10.1007/978-3-319-26279-6_10

Rahman Belal, A., Momin, M.: Corporate social reporting (CSR) in emerging economies: a review and future direction. In: Accounting in Emerging Economies, pp. 119–143. Emerald Group Publishing Limited (2009)

Rao, K., Tilt, C.: Board composition and corporate social responsibility: the role of diversity, gender, strategy and decision making. J. Bus. Ethics, 1–21 (2015)

Greenwood, R., Meyer, R.E.: Influencing ideas a celebration of DiMaggio and Powell (1983). J. Manag. Inq. **17**(4), 258–264 (2008)

Pope, S.: The tiny trumpet: the surprisingly weak relationship from advertising to corporate social responsibility—a systematic literature review and a panel study of the world's largest and most international companies. In: Elgar, E., Boubaker, S., Cummings, D., Nguyen, D. (eds.) Forthcoming in the "Handbook of Finance and Sustainability" (2016)

Whetten, D.A., Rands, G., Godfrey, P.: What are the responsibilities of business to society. In: Handbook of strategy and management, pp. 373–408 (2002)

Information Security in the Smart Grid: Survey and Challenges

Fei Wang[1], Zhenjiang Lei[2], Xiaohua Yin[1], Zhao Li[2], Zhi Cao[1], and Yale Wang[3(✉)]

[1] Information and Telecommunication Branch, State Grid Liaoning Electric Power Co., Ltd., Shenyang, China
{wf,leizj,caoz}@ln.sgcc.com.cn
[2] ICT Department, State Grid Liaoning Electric Power Co., Ltd., Shenyang, China
{leizj,lz}@ln.sgcc.com.cn
[3] College of Electronic and Information, Nanjing University of Aeronautics and Astronautics, Nanjing, China
yalewang@nuaa.edu.cn

Abstract. The Smart Grid is a revolutionary regime of existing power grids, which is more efficient, reliable, clean and intelligent. However, Smart Grid is facing serious cyber security issues, as millions of intelligent electronic devices are inter-connected by communication networks, which has significant impact on the reliability and usability of the Smart Grid. In this paper, the security threats from both software and hardware levels are reviewed. According to the specific features of Smart Grid, various countermeasures are discussed, which can be the solution for the cyber security issues of Smart Grid. This paper emphasizes the threats and countermeasures from hardware level. Future works based on the discussion is also provided.

Keywords: Smart grid · Cyber security · Attacks and countermeasures
Hardware security

1 Introduction

Previous studies have shown that the energy conversion efficiency of traditional power grids is only 1/3, and 8% of the electrical energy is lost during transmission. 20% of the capacity of the power generation equipment is only used to meet the peak demand of 5% [1]. These facts show that the whole grid has a very low level of intelligence and efficiency. Due to the enormous pressure of current global resources and the needs of better environmental, the demand for energy-saving emission reduction and sustainable development is increasing. At the same time, the power market services is constantly improving, in which the reliability and quality requirements are also rising. This requires the future power grid must be able to provide a more secure, reliable, clean, cheap power supply. In order to meet the needs of users' variety of independent power selection, and provide more quality services, many countries have proposed to build the next generation of intelligent, efficient and safe grid, *i.e.,* Smart Grid [2].

© Springer Nature Singapore Pte Ltd. 2018
H. Yuan et al. (Eds.): GSKI 2017, CCIS 848, pp. 55–66, 2018.
https://doi.org/10.1007/978-981-13-0893-2_7

Smart Grid need to be distributed over a highly distributed and hierarchical network consisting of seven domains (as shown in Fig. 1): Bulk generation, Transmission, Distribution, Customer, Markets, Service provider, and Operations. The information network of the Smart Grid includes backbone and local area network (LAN). Backbone networks connect different components, which are connected by wired communications such as optical fiber communications. Monitoring, Operation, Transmission and Distribution can be monitored through Supervisory Control and Data Acquisition (SCADA). Local area networks are used for communication in various parts, usually including a series of self-organizing terminals, such as electricity meters, sensors, data collectors, and other terminal intelligent electronic devices installed on the power infrastructure. These terminal devices usually use wireless technologies such as WiFi and ZigBee to be connected.

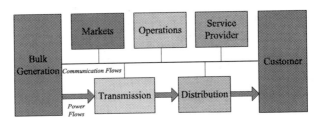

Fig. 1. The conceptual model for Smart Grid.

Compared with conventional power grid, the Smart Grid is expected to fully integrate real time two-way communication into millions of power devices. However, being highly dependent on the information network makes the Smart Grid facing the same information security issues as in the Internet and the Internet of things (IoT), which seriously threatens the security and reliability of the Smart Grid. Existing Smart Grid issues have shown that intrusion attacks can cause serious consequences [3], such as large-scale power outages [4], infrastructure damage [5], disclosure of user information [6], etc. Therefore, according to the structure of smart grid and features of terminal devices, a comprehensive analysis of the information security threats is needed. Research on Smart Grid information security defense technology has become one of the highest priorities in designing Smart Grid [7].

In this paper, we review the emerging information security threats and the security countermeasures that can be applied in Smart Grid. The remainder of this paper is organized as follows. Section 2 provides the difference between the Smart Grid and the conventional Internet. In Sect. 3, the classification of information security objectives in the Smart Grid is given. Attacks targeting availability, integrity and confidentiality at software and hardware levels are investigated in Sect. 4 and Sect. 5 respectively. Finally, the summary and future work is given in Sect. 6.

2   Differences Between Smart Grid and Internet

Compared with the conventional Internet, the Smart Grid has its special requirements in performance, time requirements and communication model, which brings new challenges to the security and defense technology of Smart Grid [8]:

- Performance Metric: Internet takes data throughput as the most important measurement metric, while the power communication network needs to ensure real-time messaging and non real-time monitoring and management. Therefore, in Smart Grid power systems, delay is more important than throughput.
- Time Requirements: IP traffic in the Internet usually requires latency of 100–150 ms, while in the Smart Grid, traffic flow delays are from milliseconds to minutes. Therefore, the communications in Smart Grids have more stringent time requirements.
- Communication Model: The Internet supports any point-to-point communication. In conventional power communication systems, there is usually one-way communication, such as electronic devices sending their data to the control center. While in the Smart Grid, it needs to control two-way communication between the central and terminal devices.

Due to the above mentioned differences between Internet and the Smart Grid, the information security objectives of Smart Grid are different, which are further discussed in the following section.

3   Security Objectives and Attack Classification of Smart Grid

3.1   Security Objectives of Smart Grid

The information security objectives can be summarized as follows [8]:

- Availability: Timely and steady access to information is necessary, and it concerns the smooth delivery of power. To ensure real-time and low latency requirements, dedicated encryption chips are needed to achieve acceleration.
- Integrity: The permissions to modify the information need to be strictly controlled, and the integrity of the information needs to be verified. Loss of integrity will result in unauthorized modifications or damage, which further results in erroneous decisions on power grid management.
- Confidentiality. Data encryption is essential for all network communications to protect personal privacy and proprietary information.

3.2 Classification of Smart Grid Security Issues

According to the security objectives of Smart Grid, attacks can be classified as follows [8]:

- Attacks targeting availability: the common attacks are called denial-of-service (DoS) attacks, which attempt to delay, block or corrupt the communication in the Smart Grid.
- Attacks targeting integrity: they aim at deliberately and illegally modifying or disrupting data exchange in the Smart Grid.
- Attacks targeting confidentiality: they intend to acquire unauthorized information from network resources in the Smart Grid.

This classification takes into account the means of attacks. However, the defense

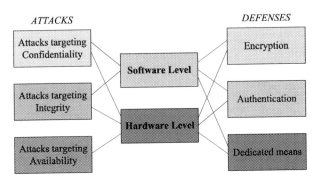

Fig. 2. Classification of information security issues in Smart Grid.

techniques can be implemented at both software level and the hardware level. Moreover, by applying hardware security techniques for terminal authentication and data encryption, the security of the system can be enhanced significantly. In the following sections, we will review the information security threats and defense techniques of Smart Grid in both software level and hardware level, as shown in Fig. 2.

4 Security at Software Level

The terminal devices in Smart Grid need to communicate with their users continuously. Therefore, as a large-scale communication network, it faced with similar threats to the Internet and IoT at network layer, protocol layer, and application layer.

4.1 Attacks at Software Level

If adversaries want to get the encrypted information in the communication, they need to find ways to get the secret key first. In a Man-in-the-Middle (MITM) attack [9], the attacker connects itself to the communication devices and then receives the network messages between them. Sophisticated MITM attack can decrypt data by passing a fake encryption key [10]. This illegal way of getting plain text needs to break the encryption system. In a replay attack, an attacker intercepts a packet received by a target host and steals its authentication credentials, and then resends it to the authentication server to obtain illegal authentication [11].

False data injection (FDI) attack is one of the important threats to the Smart Grid currently. It is directed to a network that has a large number of metering devices, and by injecting false data into the measurements of metering devices distributed in the grid, makes the state estimation result offset from the non-attack state. It can escape the bad data detection mechanism, and affect the operation control of power system [12]. Compared with traditional physical attacks, FDI attack can be transmitted many times without being detected. Line interrupts caused by physical attacks may be masked if FDI was coordinated with physical attacks [13]. Common software based attacks also include impersonation attacks, denial attacks, and so on [14]. These attacks are based on the assumption that the adversaries can obtain secret keys and break through the authentication system in different ways, and then modify the data in the network to achieve the goal of destroying or gaining personal benefits.

4.2 Defenses at Software Level

According to the characteristics of the attacks mentioned above, identity authentication and data encryption are the key technologies and basis for defending against cyber attacks. Therefore, the software level defense techniques include encryption and authentication algorithms and protocols, and some dedicated defenses in addition:

- Encryption: the application of cryptography is a direct way to prevent the enemy from getting information, and it can prevent data from being tampered with to a certain extent [15, 16]. This encryption method can withstand eavesdropping attacks, and protect user privacy. The security of cryptography is based on the fact that breaking the encrypted data at a high cost. However, the use of cryptography need to store and exchange secret keys. Storage of keys at software level requires the use of non-volatile memory (NVM), where the data can be obtained by physical attacks.

- Authentication: the application of digital signature can make the two sides of information exchange realize identity authentication, and prevent the information from being maliciously destroyed and tampered [17, 18]. The principle of digital signature is that the sender sends a message and a summary encrypted with his/her private key. The recipient can verify the integrity and the origin of the information according to the received data. This method can resist replay attack, deny attack and impersonation attack.

- Dedicated defenses, for specific attacks, dedicated defense methods can be use by studying their data characteristics, such as data detection methods for FDI attacks [19]. For MITM attacks, the defender can use the dynamic encryption method to increase the frequency of key replacement, make the attacker getting an outdated secret key [20, 21].

The advantage of the software level defense techniques is that it does not need additional hardware cost or modification. The disadvantage is obvious as it adds the computational burden to the terminal devices, and the storage of secret keys in non-volatile memories has a high risk. It cannot provide a strong authentication, and software authentication methods can also be broken down by some sophisticated software methods, such as replay attacks [11].

4.3 Threats from Quantum Computer

It is worth mentioning that quantum computer technology continues to make break-throughs. In 1994, Shor's algorithm [22] is proposed as a typical representative of quantum algorithms. Many previously reliable cryptographic algorithms have been shown to be able to be cracked by quantum computers in a short time. Most of today's cryptographic systems do not take into account the threats of quantum computer attacks during the development process [23].

At software level, quantum computer attacks can only be resisted by applying post quantum encryption algorithms, such as lattice-based cryptography [24], code-based cryptography [25], hash-based Signature [26] and multivariate Cryptography [27]. Post-quantum cryptography is a cryptosystem that is believed to be able to withstand attacks by quantum computers. Such encryption techniques are based on difficult problems in specific mathematical domains, and do not rely on any quantum theory phenomenon, but their computational security can withstand any known form of quantum computation attacks. More importantly, they have high compatibility with current network systems. In post-quantum cryptography, lattice-based cryptography has significant advantages in both efficiency and security, and it is likely to be adopted by the NIST standard of cryptography in US.

However, the computation overhead and storage requirements of the post-quantum encryption algorithm are very large, which is more detrimental to the computing power and the smart meter with limited hardware resources.

5 Security at Hardware Level

The advanced metering system (AMI) is an important component of the Smart Grid infrastructure, and AMI is made up of more than millions of smart meters. Unlike other networks, these terminals (smart meters) in the Smart Grid are basically working in unattended environments, which puts them at greater risk of direct attacks (physical attacks). At the same time, with the development of more and more sophisticated software based information security technologies in other networks, the proportion of Smart Grid attacks against hardware gradually increase.

At hardware level, the adversary uses physical attacks to destroy the information exchange or get secret key. Similarly, the defense methods at this level refer to the method by hardware implementation and countermeasures.

5.1   Attacks at Hardware Level

Attacks at hardware level refer to physical attacks, and the denial of service (DoS) attacks against availability in the previous classification methods fall into this category, such attacks do not require breaking through authentication and encryption system, which affect normal device operations by depleting the computing resources of the grid and blocking normal communications [28]. For this storage form in the random access memory by the continuous power supply of the battery or non-volatile memory, the key can be obtained by means of invasive attack or semi-invasive attack [29]. In addition, the number and variety of physical attacks against Smart Grid authenticated encryption chips are increasing, with the most serious threat being Side Channel Attacks (SCAs) [30]. The security of modern cryptography system is based on the security of the cryptographic key.

SCA technique utilizes the physical information that is leaked by chips and hardware circuits running the encryption algorithm, and uses this physical information to recover the key quickly. This physical information includes power consumption [30], electro-magnetic signal [31], time consumption [32], fault output [33], etc. This leads to the mathematically secure cryptography no longer secure. SCA technology can greatly reduce the key space by monitoring the physical information of the hardware circuit, and then restore the key in a limited time in a limited time. SCAs can be simply divided into passive and active attacks. Passive attacks only observe the behavior of the chip processing data and collect the available side channel information without interfering with the chip operation, just as mentioned above [30–32]. Active attack means that the attacker tampered with the normal operation of the chip, such as introducing errors into the chip computing process and initiating a fault attack. In 1997, Biham and Shamir first proposed differential fault attacks, and analyzed the DES [33]. After that, the researchers used this method to improve the analysis of DES, and extended to 3DES, AES, SM4 and other block ciphers. In recent years, researchers use new physical leaks, combined with fault attacks, and proposed the idea of combined bypass leak fault analysis.

In addition, there are attacks against Physical Unclonable Function (PUF) [37], such as cloning attacks [34] modeling attacks [35] and machine learning attacks [36]. A cloning attack is a physical means to copy the response of the target hardware and is used to copy authentication responses. In [34], the adversary reprograms the tendency of a cell using focused ion beam circuit edit, thus effectively cloning the challenge-response pairs behavior of the SRAM PUF. In modeling attacks, they assume that an adversary has collected a large number of all possible CRPs of a given Strong PUF (usually between several hundred to a few million CRPs, depending on the exact Strong PUF design). By using numeric methods and an internal, parametric model of the PUF, the adversary then tries to extrapolate the behavior of the PUF on the other, yet unknown CRPs. And machine learning algorithms are a natural and very powerful tool in deriving unknown CRPs.

5.2   Defenses at Hardware Level

Before introducing the security and defense measures of the hardware level, we first introduce a hardware technique called Physical Unclonable Function (PUF). PUF is an emerging hardware security authentication technology, with the advantages of unclonable, real-time generation of keys, high security and so on [37]. PUF can extract the random disorders introduced between the internal integrated circuit or disorders from connection lines due to the inconsistency of the manufacturing process and use these random disorders to generate an encrypted signal (response) with certain rules. Intuitively, PUF is the 'fingerprint' of the hardware, which is unique to the physical object. The main task of PUF is to extract and characterize these 'fingerprints' effectively. PUF can generate different but specific responses according to different challenges, and a corresponding challenge and its response is called challenge-response pair (CRP). According to the number of CRPs, PUFs can be divided into strong PUFs and weak PUFs [38]. Strong PUFs derive a more complex challenge-response behavior from the physical disorders. Typically, many physical components are involved in the generation of a response, and there are a very large number of possible challenges that can be applied to the Strong PUFs. The prime application of Strong PUF is challenge-response based identification and system authentication. In contrast, a Weak PUF has got very few, fixed challenges, commonly only one challenge per PUF instance. Weak PUF essentially is a new form of storing secret keys in vulnerable hardware, offering an alternative to ROM, Flash or other non-volatile memories.

Hardware level defense methods can also be divided into three kinds: encryption, authentication and dedicated defense:

- Encryption: using weak PUF to generate the secure key. It can be used to generate and store keys, which can replace non-volatile memory [38]. When the device is powered on, the response signal (secrete key) of the PUF can be automatically generated, and when it's powered down, the response signal is automatically annihilated [39]. This way is more secure than using non-volatile memory to store keys.
- Authentication: implement by hardware of strong PUF [40]. A strong PUF has many CRPs, and each CRP can be used only once and needs to be erased from the list subsequently. The advantages of this approach are high security, low cost, and lightweight [41, 42].
- Dedicated defense: point at one specific physical attack. Such as data detection for DoS attack [43], data detection for side channel attack [44], shielding method for intrusion attack [45] and so on. In the defense of the side channel attacks, there are traditional ways of wave dynamic differential logic combined with differential routing [46], and masking techniques [47]. In addition, the industry is more inclined to use random delay means [48] and white-box cryptography [49] to achieve low-cost protection.

The greatest advantage of hardware level defense method is that it can isolate the risk of leaking the key at software level. These hardware based methods can realize the high security of authentication and lightweight of computation, and improves the ability of the equipment to resist the DoS attack. Its only disadvantage is the need to add special hardware to the device.

5.3   Hardware Implementation of Post-quantum Cryptography

At software level, the application of post quantum cryptography against quantum computer attacks has the disadvantages of high computational complexity and high storage space requirements. At hardware level, the computation speed can be improved on the basis of quantum cryptography after hardware implementation. In the implementation of embedded microprocessors based on lattice-based cryptography, in 2014, Boorghany et al. [50] proposed the first implementation of lattice-based cryptographic system. They evaluated the implementation of four kinds of lattice-based authentication protocols on 8 bit AVR and 32 bit ARM processors. Oder et al. [51] introduced the efficient implementation of the Bimodal Lattice Signature Schemes (BLISS) on 32 bit ARM Cortex-M4F processors. In 2015, Clercq et al. [52] implemented a Ring-LWE encryption scheme on the same ARM platform. Pöppelmann et al. [53] compared the Ring-LWE encryption and BLISS implementation on the ATxmega128 processor. In the aspect of reconfigurable hardware implementation, BLISS signature scheme has developed into a potential alternative to RSA or ECC. Güneysu et al. [54] implemented a variant of Ring-LWE based lattice signature algorithm on hardware. This work takes advantage of recent advances in lattice-based cryptography and optimizes the implementation of embedded systems. Its implementation in Xilinx Spartan/Virtex-6 shows that the proposed scheme is scalable, and has a low area consumption, and its performance even exceeds the classical algorithms such as RSA. Howe et al. [55] proposed a hardware architecture for optimizing circuit area by using Lattice-based encryption over standard lattices and implemented on Xilinx Spartan-6 FPGA.

6   Summary and Future Work

This review paper provides a review of information security issues in Smart Grids, at both software level and hardware level. Software level defense methods are simple for implementation and do not need to increase the cost, but need to sacrifice the computational processing ability of the terminal devices. Strong authentication cannot be obtained at software level, the key storage method is not safe enough. Risk always exists at software level. The defense measures at hardware level have higher security in providing authentication and key storage, and the ability to resist DoS attacks has also improved. But it needs to increase hardware costs and will also encounter new attacks at this level. Threats from the most advanced technology of quantum computer and corresponding defensive measures have also been mentioned.

Some of the information security threats mentioned in this paper are not widely encountered by Smart Grid at present, such as cloning attacks and side channel attacks on hardware, and attacks from quantum computers. However, according to the attacks on Internet and IoT, these threats are inevitable with the development of the Smart Grid. The Smart Grid needs to be developed and perfected by taking account into these cyber security threats.

Future works should look are hardware solution closely to provide high level security countermeasures. It is suggested that PUF based authentication, SCA resistant encryption chip and post-quantum cryptography chip are highly demanding in future Smart Grid.

References

1. Fang, X., Misra, S., Xue, G., et al.: Smart Grid: the new and improved power grid: a survey. IEEE Commun. Surv. Tutor. **14**(4), 944–980 (2012)
2. National Institute of Standards and Technology: NIST framework and roadmap for Smart Grid interoperability standards, release1.0, January 2010. http://www.nist.gov/publicaffairs/releases/upload/smartgridinteroperabilityfinal.pdf
3. Metke, A., Ekl, R.: Smart Grid security technology. In: IEEE Conference on Innovative Smart Grid Technologies (ISGT), pp. 1–7 (2010)
4. Guo, Q., Xin, S., Wang, J., et al.: Comprehensive security assessment for a cyber physical energy system: a lesson from Ukraine's blackout. Autom. Electr. Power Syst. (5), 145-147 (2016)
5. Li, Z., Tong, W., Jin, X.: Construction of cyber security defense hierarchy and cyber security testing system of Smart Grid: thinking and enlightenment for network attack events to national power grid of Ukraine and Israel. Autom. Electr. Power Syst. **40**(8), 147–151 (2016)
6. Tian, X., Li, L, Sun C, et al. Review on privacy protection approaches in smart meter. J. East China Norm. Univ. (Nat. Sci.) (5), 46–60 (2015)
7. Ericsson, G.: Cyber security and power system communication-essential parts of a Smart Grid infrastructure. IEEE Trans. Power Deliv. **25**(3), 1501–1507 (2010)
8. Wang, W., Lu, Z.: Cyber security in the Smart Grid: survey and challenges. Comput. Netw. **57**(5), 1344–1371 (2013)
9. Conti, M., Dragoni, N., Lesyk, V.: A survey of man in the middle attacks. IEEE Commun. Surv. Tutor. **18**(3), 2027–2051 (2016)
10. Yang, Y., Mclaughlin, K., Littler, T., et al.: Man-in-the-middle attack test-bed investigating cyber-security vulnerabilities in Smart Grid SCADA systems. In: IET International Conference on Sustainable Power Generation and Supply, pp. 1–8 (2013)
11. Tran, T., Shin, O., Lee, J.: Detection of replay attacks in Smart Grid systems. In: IEEE International Conference on Computing, Management and Telecommunications, pp. 298–302 (2013)
12. Liu, Y., Ning, P., Reiter, M.K.: False data injection attacks against state estimation in electric power grids. In: ACM Conference on Computer & Communications Security, pp. 21–32 (2009)
13. Deng, R., Xiao, G., Lu, R., et al.: False data injection on state estimation in power systems-attacks, impacts, and defence: a survey. IEEE Trans. Ind. Inform. **13**(2), 411–423 (2017)
14. Liu, G., Zhang, S.: Analysis of smart grid information security threats and countermeasures. Microcomput. Appl. (5), 8–10 (2017)
15. Li, F., Luo, B., Liu, P.: Secure information aggregation for Smart Grids using homomorphic encryption. In: IEEE International Conference on Smart Grid Communications, pp. 327–332. IEEE (2010)
16. Seferian, V., Kanj, R., Chehab, A., et al.: Identity based key distribution framework for link layer security of AMI networks. IEEE Trans. Smart Grid 1–16 (2016)
17. Saxena, N., Grijalva, S.: Efficient Signature scheme for delivering authentic control commands in the Smart Grid. IEEE Trans. Smart Grid 1–13 (2017)
18. Li, Q., Cao, G.: Multicast authentication in the Smart Grid with one-time signature. IEEE Trans. Smart Grid **2**(4), 686–696 (2011)
19. Zhao, J., Zhang, G., Scala, M.L., et al.: Short-term state forecasting-aided method for detection of Smart Grid general false data injection attacks. IEEE Trans. Smart Grid **8**(4), 1580–1590 (2017)

20. Saxena, N., Grijalva, S.: Dynamic secrets and secret keys based scheme for securing last mile Smart Grid wireless communication. IEEE Trans. Ind. Inform. **13**(3), 1482–1491 (2016)
21. Liu, T., Liu, Y., Mao, Y., et al.: A dynamic secret-based encryption scheme for Smart Grid wireless communication. IEEE Trans. Smart Grid **5**(3), 1175–1182 (2014)
22. Shor, P.W.: Polynomial time algorithms for discrete logarithms and factoring on a quantum computer. In: Adleman, L.M., Huang, M.-D. (eds.) ANTS 1994. LNCS, vol. 877, p. 289. Springer, Heidelberg (1994). https://doi.org/10.1007/3-540-58691-1_68
23. Chen, L., Jordan, S., Liu, Y., et al.: Report on Post-Quantum Cryptography. NIST (2016). https://doi.org/10.6028/NIST.IR.8105
24. Abdallah, R., Shen, S.: A lightweight lattice-based security and privacy-preserving scheme for Smart Grid. In: Global Communications Conference, pp. 668–674. IEEE (2014)
25. Sendrier, N.: Code-Based Cryptography: State of the Art and Perspectives, pp. 44–50 (2017)
26. Mozaffari-Kermani, M., Azarderakhsh, R.: Reliable hash trees for post-quantum stateless cryptographic hash-based signatures. In: IEEE International Symposium on Defect and Fault Tolerance in VLSI and Nanotechnology Systems, pp. 103–108. IEEE (2015)
27. Wang, J., Cheng, L., Su, T.: Multivariate cryptography based on clipped Hopfield neural network. IEEE Trans. Neural Netw. Learn. Syst. 1–11 (2016)
28. Jin, D., Nicol, D.M., Yan, G.: An event buffer flooding attack in DNP3 controlled SCADA systems. In: Simulation Conference, pp. 2619–2631. IEEE (2012)
29. Mohamed, E., Bulygin, S., Zohner, M., et al.: Improved algebraic side-channel attack on AES. In: Proceedings of IEEE International Symposium on Hardware-Oriented Security and Trust (HOST), pp. 146–151 (2012)
30. Kocher, P., Jaffe, J., Jun, B.: Differential power analysis. In: Wiener, M. (ed.) CRYPTO 1999. LNCS, vol. 1666, pp. 388–397. Springer, Heidelberg (1999). https://doi.org/10.1007/3-540-48405-1_25
31. Yoshikawa, M., Nozaki, Y.: Electromagnetic analysis attack for a lightweight cipher PRINCE. In: IEEE International Conference on Cybercrime and Computer Forensic, pp. 1–6. IEEE (2016)
32. Couvreur, A., Marquez-Corbella, I., Pellikaan, R.: A polynomial time attack against algebraic geometry code based public key cryptosystems. In: IEEE International Symposium on Information Theory, pp. 1446–1450. IEEE (2014)
33. Biham, E., Shamir, A.: Differential fault analysis of secret key cryptosystems. In: Kaliski, B. S. (ed.) CRYPTO 1997. LNCS, vol. 1294, pp. 513–525. Springer, Heidelberg (1997). https://doi.org/10.1007/BFb0052259
34. Helfmeier, C., Boit, C.: Cloning physically unclonable functions. In: IEEE International Symposium on Hardware-Oriented Security and Trust, pp. 1–6. IEEE (2013)
35. Rührmair, U., Sölter, J., Sehnke, F., et al.: PUF modeling attacks on simulated and silicon data. IEEE Trans. Inf. Forensics Secur. **8**(11), 1876–1891 (2013)
36. Vijayakumar, A., Patil, V., Prado C., et al.: Machine learning resistant strong PUF: possible or a pipe dream? In: IEEE International Symposium on Hardware Oriented Security and Trust, pp. 19–24. IEEE (2016)
37. Suh, G., Devadas, S.: Physical unclonable functions for device authentication and secret key generation. In: Design Automation Conference, DAC 2007, pp. 9–14. ACM/IEEE (2007)
38. Rührmair, U., Holcomb, D.: PUFs at a glance. In: Design, Automation & Test in Europe Conference & Exhibition, pp. 1–6. IEEE (2014)
39. Lim, D., Lee, J., Gassend, B., et al.: Extracting secret keys from integrated circuits. IEEE Trans. VLSI Syst. **13**(10), 1200–1205 (2004)
40. Chang, C., Zheng, Y., Zhang, L.: A retrospective and a look forward: fifteen years of physical unclonable function advancement. IEEE Circuits Syst. Mag. **17**(3), 32–62 (2017)

41. Suh, E., Devadas, S.: Physical unclonable functions for device authentication and secret key generation. In: Proceedings of the 44th Annual Design Automation Conference (DAC), pp. 9–14 (2007)

42. Anderson, H.: A PUF design for secure FPGA-based embedded systems. In: Proceedings of the 15th Asia and South Pacific Design Automation Conference (ASP-DAC), pp. 1–6 (2010)

43. Yang, J., Chen, Y., Trappe, W.: Detecting spoofing attacks in mobile wireless environments. In: IEEE Communications Society Conference on Sensor, Mesh and Ad Hoc Communications and Networks, SECON 2009, pp. 1–9. IEEE (2009)

44. Yu, S., Gui, X., Lin, J.: An approach with two-stage mode to detect cache-based side channel attacks. pp. 186–191 (2013)

45. Ling, M., Wu, L., Li, X., et al.: Design of monitor and protect circuits against FIB attack on chip security. In: Eighth International Conference on Computational Intelligence and Security, pp. 530–533. IEEE Computer Society (2012)

46. Tiri, K., Hwang, D., Hodjat, A., Lai, B.-C., Yang, S., Schaumont, P., Verbauwhede, I.: Prototype IC with WDDL and differential routing – DPA resistance assessment. In: Rao, J. R., Sunar, B. (eds.) CHES 2005. LNCS, vol. 3659, pp. 354–365. Springer, Heidelberg (2005). https://doi.org/10.1007/11545262_26

47. Nikova, S., Rechberger, C., Rijmen, V.: Threshold implementations against side-channel attacks and glitches. In: Ning, P., Qing, S., Li, N. (eds.) ICICS 2006. LNCS, vol. 4307, pp. 529–545. Springer, Heidelberg (2006). https://doi.org/10.1007/11935308_38

48. Martin, R., Demme, J., Sethumadhavan, S.: Timewarp: rethinking timekeeping and performance monitoring mechanisms to mitigate side-channel attacks. ACM SIGARCH Comput. Archit. News **40**(3), 118–129 (2012)

49. Wyseur, B.: White-Box Cryptography. Encyclopedia of Cryptography and Security, pp. 1386–1387. Springer, Boston (2011). https://doi.org/10.1007/978-1-4419-5906-5

50. Boorghany, A., Sarmadi, S.B., Jalili, R.: On constrained implementation of lattice-based cryptographic primitives and schemes on smart cards. ACM Trans. Embed. Comput. Syst. **14**(3), 42 (2014)

51. Oder, T., Poppelmann, T., Güneysu, T.: Beyond ECDSA and RSA: lattice-based digital signatures on constrained devices. In: IEEE Conference on 51st Annual Design Automation Conference (DAC), no. 2, pp. 638–643 (2014)

52. Clercq, R., Roy, S., Vercauteren, F., et al.: Efficient software implementation of ring-LWE encryption. In: Design, Automation & Test in Europe Conference & Exhibition (DATE), pp. 339–344 (2015)

53. Pöoppelmann, T., Oder, T., Güneysu, T.: Speed records for ideal lattice-based cryptography on AVR. Cryptology ePrint Archive, p. 382 (2015)

54. Güneysu, T., Lyubashevsky, V., Pöppelmann, T.: Lattice-based signatures: optimization and implementation on reconfigurable hardware. IEEE Trans. Comput. **64**(7), 1954–1967 (2015)

55. Howe, J., Moore, C., O'Neill, M., et al.: Lattice-based encryption over standard lattices in hardware. In: 53rd Annual Design Automation Conference (DAC), p. 162 (2016)

A Power Grid GIS Cloud Framework Based on Docker and OpenStack

Xin Ji[1(✉)], Bojia Li[2], Junwei Yang[1], and Qiangxin Hu[3]

[1] China Electric Power Research Institute, Haidian District,
Beijing 100192, China
{jixin,yangjunwei}@epri.sgcc.com.cn
[2] University of La Verne, 950 3rd Street, La Verne, CA 91750, USA
bojia.li@laverne.edu
[3] School of Computer Science and Technology,
North China Electric Power University, Beijing 071003, China
hhhqiangxin@qq.com

Abstract. The fast development of intelligence power grid has posed increasingly great demand over power grid GIS. To establish a cloud based power grid platform is of great importance to information sharing, information exchange and GIS based application. In this paper, we combine Docker and OpenStack to build a containerized based cloud power grid GIS platform management framework. To take advantage of Docker container's characteristics such as lightweight, low system overhead, high system resource utilization, easy deployment with multiple running instances and great extensibility, we combine OpenStack to manage the resource in a uniform supervisor which simplify development, testing and maintenance and enhance the system efficiency. Compared with classic cloud based deployment method in a simulated system, our framework can reduce GIS based application deploy time greatly and poses better extensibility as cloud node numbers increase.

Keywords: Cloud computing · OpenStack · Docker · Container
Virtualization

1 Introduction

GIS has been widely applied in power systems since the last century in the form of applications such as intelligent power grid analysis, remote sensing based electricity transmission line selection system, and real time electricity line monitoring system etc. [1, 2]. All these application systems have specific functions while they are not easy to scale, of huge system complex, of high demand to system hardware [3]. Generally, these systems have the following disadvantages when applied to power grid informatization:

(1) These systems would lead to great waste of resources. Currently, many power grid companies in China have established their own GIS based systems. These GIS systems have different technology framework and functions, utilize different developing program languages, operating systems, database systems and

© Springer Nature Singapore Pte Ltd. 2018
H. Yuan et al. (Eds.): GSKI 2017, CCIS 848, pp. 67–74, 2018.
https://doi.org/10.1007/978-981-13-0893-2_8

middlewares, which make it great waste of resource due to system business-business data interface difference and repeated system implementation.

(2) Information interchange and share are inefficient. Due to GIS applications differences of various power incorporations, data interchange between central company and sub-branch companies is not efficient which obstacles the data sharing in companies management system.

(3) System has long development circle. Existing GIS systems are loosely managed during the development process; they have complex development environment settings. Services of development, testing and maintaining are kept by software programmers independently where they deploy software settings, middleware and dependencies on their own leading to high error rate and low resource reuse.

The emergency of cloud computing and Docker based container technology has provide new solution to classic GIS based power grid software applications. With the combination of Docker container technology and OpenStack, an open source cloud technology, power grid GIS applications are easily implemented to fulfill requirements such as fast scalability to large number of nodes, smooth information interchange, and efficient resource reuse, etc. In this paper, we aim to integrate cloud computing into our GIS based platform to efficiently make use of data and system resources, reduce development cost, and improve information exchange between different sections. On the other hand we expect the combination of cloud based technology into our GIS systems to provide highly concurrent request and real time advanced monitoring and analysis abilities [4].

This paper is organized as follows. We would briefly introduce basics of GIS power grid systems in Sect. 2. In Sect. 3, we introduce state-of-art container technology, Docker. High level of integration of OpenStack and Docker is described in Sect. 4. In Sect. 5, we present technical structure of Docker container management in power grid GIS platform and experimental study results compared with traditional methods. Conclusion is given in Sect. 6.

2 GIS Based Grid Power Platform

Power grid GIS system is a management system which abstracts and manages objects in a power grid such as power facilities, substation, transmission-distribution network and power load, forming a product management system [5]. Through power grid GIS platform, we can query power facilities state information and other GIS information. Basic GIS information in power grid GIS based systems is composed of image map data and vector map data which are stored in sliced manner to enhance map loading velocity and fulfill efficient query and browsing requirements of users. So to establish a digital power grid GIS system to manage and display resources in a power grid would make great contribution, from data management point of view, to product and sales.

Power grid GIS system has the following characteristics which make it necessary to use more scalable and efficient framework to deploy applications and manage systems.

(1) High real time response. Power grid need to react in real time highly to information and data in the system. Data in the system needs to be collected and stored for real time computing and analysis.

(2) High reliability and accuracy. Power grid GIS systems should be able to store data once and output data more times and keep the data consistency. To fulfill related standards of information system in power industry, power grid GIS systems should be highly reliable and accurate.

(3) Supporting topology and transformation. In a power system, real time system is of high volume, interfaces are complicated, users are enormous and power facilities are always dispersed and versatile which means the power grid GIS system needs topology and transformation ability to react to emergent situations.

(4) Shared resources. Currently, high level of central power grid companies own their GIS systems which are running in a intra- network and are not shared with other power grid companies. So in a new framework, the GIS system of a power grid company should share resources with other companies.

(5) High degree of safety. From a national security point of view, power grid data are one of the most important data sources of a country. Location information of power facilities are fundamental infrastructure data of a country so a GIS based power grid system should be highly safe.

3   Docker Container

Docker is an open source project based on Linux containers which is written in go and developed by Dotcloud (A PaaS Company) [6]. Docker is a container engine which takes advantage of the Linux Kernel features such as namespaces and control groups to create containers on top of an operating system and automates application deployment on the container. Docker provides lightweight environment to run users' application system and is efficient to provide workflow for moving users application from developers laptop, test environment to production. Architecture of Docker is illustrated in Fig. 1 [7].

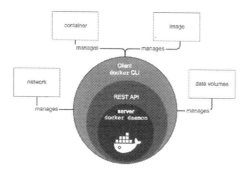

Fig. 1. Architecture of Docker.

Docker can help users construct and deploy containers, users only need to package the related application programs into the container in which more than one thread can be running. Generally, image is considered as the construction phase of Docker's life circle, while container is the initiation and execution phase. Docker does not consider the content of the container when it is running operations such as initiating, starting, restarting, closing and deleting image. All contents of the container, which could be database, web server and application software servers, are loaded in the same way.

4   Integration of Docker and OpenStack

OpenStack, as an open source cloud management software, can be used to monitor many kinds of clouds such as private cloud, public cloud and other clouds. Docker and OpenStack can complement each other greatly. Compared with virtual machine, Docker is considered as lightweight which would make full use of the IaaS resources. Docker centers on application in PaaS of the cloud framework while OpenStack works mainly for IaaS of the cloud which could provide network, computing and storage services. Components structure of OpenStack is shown in Fig. 2 [8].

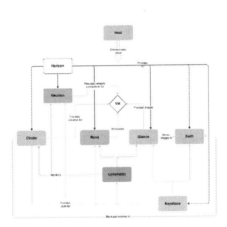

Fig. 2. OpenStack component architecture [8].

Glance is an image service project which provides a service where users can upload and discover data assets that are meant to be used with other services. Glance image services include discovering, registering, and retrieving virtual machine (VM) images. Glance has a RESTful API that allows querying of VM image metadata as well as retrieval of the actual image [9].

One of the commonly used method of integration Docker with OpenStack is to use the Nova project. Docker is a common way to manage LXC containers on a single machine. However, when Docker is used behind Nova, it would be much more powerful since it's possible to manage several hosts which will then manage hundreds of containers.

Containers don't aim to be a replacement for VMs, they are just complementary for specific use cases. Nova support for VMs is currently advanced due to the variety of hypervisors running VMs [10]. Docker aims to go the second level of integration. Integration structure of Docker and OpenStack is shown in Fig. 3 [11].

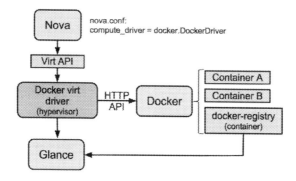

Fig. 3. Docker container and OpenStack integration.

5 Power Grid GIS Containerization Management Framework

As Docker is based on LXC (Linux Container), the compatibility to Linux operating system of Docker is great. In this paper, we propose to setup Docker engine on the Linux based server of power grid GIS platform, and release and deploy applications of power grid GIS system in the form of Docker based image. As Docker can fulfill the parameters setting during release and deployment, system efficiency has been greatly improved. During the runtime, the platform would initiate Docker instances in second according to real time system load status [12–14]. As in the bottom level of Docker has utilized cgroups and namespaces mechanisms, Docker instances of PaaS could run in their own spaces and safety and isolation of Docker instance thread have been guaranteed. The proposed power grid GIS containerization management framework is shown in Fig. 4.

As we can see from Fig. 4, in the top level, there are commonly used applications of the power grid GIS system. The application level is connected with the Docker client server. There is a daemon thread, Docker Daemon, running in the backend of Docker framework which consists of Docker server, Docker engine and Job. Docker Daemon responses requests from Docker client through Docker Server module, and these requests are processed in the Docker Engine. The Docker Daemon would initiate and run specific Job, apply image from Docker Registry, pull image with graph driver and run some local operations, set network parameters with network driver, and execute internal operations of containers with exec driver, etc. The lib Container level includes network connection, application protection, namespaces, and cgroup etc. The bottom level is the base service and infrastructure. Base services include elastic computing

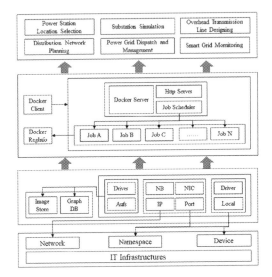

Fig. 4. Power grid GIS containerization management framework.

resources, database resources, distributed file system and job scheduling. The infrastructure includes hosts (physical machine), network, storage and other hardware.

6 Simulated Analysis and Application

In this section, we present simulate study of the proposed framework. Due to hardware limitations, we analyze performances over a simulated platform. The application used in our simulation study is one of our GIS applications—galloping warning. We used some virtual machines to simulate the cloud. The hardware used in this paper is with Intel Core i7-6700HQ processor, 8 GB DDR4 memory. Softwares used in this paper include win7, boot2docker, Ubuntu14.02.

To reduce experiment randomness, we set the cloud node numbers as 2, 10, 50, 100 and 300. Benchmark of the simulation is application deploy time over different number of nodes. The experiments have been run for 5 times, then we take the averaged deploy time. The result is shown in Fig. 5.

As we could see from Fig. 5, when the deploy nodes number is relatively small, both Docker based and the traditional method consume similar deploy time. However, as the nodes number increases over 100, Docker based deploy method consumes half time compared with the traditional one. When node numbers reaches 300, Docker based method outperforms the traditional one with nearly 3 times less of deploy time. As we could expect, Docker based method can be well extended to large scale number of nodes in a cloud.

To verify the container application efficiency, we deployed and tested Docker over our GIS based platform. As Docker container is lightweight, it would make the system low load and make full use of the system resources. Compared with deploy method,

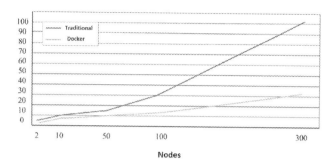

Fig. 5. Experimental results.

when deploy GIS applications, Docker based deploy method could run more instances, especially when the nodes number in the cloud is large. On the other hand, as Docker provides the container with a standardized deploy method, single GIS based application and its environment could be packed into image and run across multiple platforms. Programmers of development, test and maintaining could encapsulate GIS based application and its settings in the form of image to eliminate online and offline inconsistency which would greatly simplify the whole life circle of the application and enhance efficiency.

7 Summary

In this paper, we propose to utilize LXC engine based Docker container technique as power grid GIS platform's PaaS. With the Docker container integrated into the platform management system, application deployment and maintain has been greatly simplified, system safety is also guaranteed. We verify the effectiveness of the framework in a simulated GIS based system, the result show that our framework outperforms traditional deploy methods greatly as cloud nodes number increases.

Acknowledgement. This work is supported by science and technology project of China State Grid Corporation-Research and Application of Grid GIS Platform Based on Cloud Computing (Grant No. SGTYHT/15-JS-191).

References

1. Markovic, D.S., Zivkovic, D., Branovic, I., Popovic, R., Cvetkovic, D.: Smart power grid and cloud computing. Renew. Sustain. Energy Rev. **24**(Suppl. C), 566–577 (2013). https://doi.org/10.1016/j.rser.2013.03.068
2. Zhou, Y., Xu, T., Fu, L.: Electric power GIS system architecture based on CIM and SOA. Power Syst. Technol. **38**(4), 1115–1121 (2014)
3. Panteli, M., Kirschen, D.S.: Situation awareness in power systems: theory, challenges and applications. Electr. Power Syst. Res. **122**, 140–151 (2015)

4. Lian, H., Di, X., Shen, Z., Feng, M.: Detailed power distribution network planning based on the description of load characteristics. Paper presented at the China international conference on electricity distribution (CICED) (2014)

5. Cuffe, P., Keane, A.: Visualizing the electrical structure of power systems. IEEE Syst. J. **11**(3), 1810–1821 (2017)

6. Turnbull, J.: The Docker Book: Containerization is the New Virtualization. James Turnbull (2014)

7. Docker: Docker Engine (2017). https://docs.docker.com/engine/docker-overview/#docker-engine

8. OpenStack (2017). https://rmohan.com/?p=3606

9. OpenStack Glance (2017). https://docs.openstack.org/glance/latest/

10. Tihfon, G.M., Park, S., Kim, J., Kim, Y.-M.: An efficient multi-task PaaS cloud infrastructure based on Docker and AWS ECS for application deployment. Clust. Comput. **19**(3), 1585–1597 (2016)

11. OpenStack and Docker Integration (2017). https://wiki.openstack.org/wiki/Docker

12. Green, R.C., Wang, L., Alam, M.: Applications and trends of high performance computing for electric power systems: focusing on smart grid. IEEE Trans. Smart Grid **4**(2), 922–931 (2013)

13. Lin, Y., Yongning, Z.: A review on wind power prediction based on spatial correlation approach. Autom. Electr. Power Syst. **38**(14), 126–135 (2014)

14. Spector, A.Z.: Achieving application requirements. In: Mullender, S. (ed.) Distributed Systems. ACM Press Frontier Series, pp. 19–33. ACM, New York (1989). http://doi.acm.org/10.1145/90417.90738

A Factor Analysis-Based Detection Approach to Network Traffic Anomalies for Power Telecommunication Access Networks

Peng Ji[1]([⊠]), Hongyu Zhang[1], Wen Xu[2], Xianjing Liu[2], Qinghai Ou[3], Wenjing Li[3], and Le Qiu[4]

[1] State Grid Liaoning Electric Power Company Limited,
Shenyang 110006, China
merry_99@sina.com
[2] State Grid Dalian Electric Power Supply Company, Dalian 116011, China
[3] State Grid Information and Telecommunication Group Co., LTD,
Beijing 102211, China
[4] State Grid Info-Telecom Great Power Science and Technology Co., Ltd,
Fuzhou 311003, China

Abstract. With new network applications quickly appearing in power telecommunication access networks, Network traffic exhibits new abnormal behaviors. How to find out the abnormal traffic parts is very difficult. This paper bring forth a new anomaly detection approach to network traffic. Firstly, we take network traffic in power telecommunication access networks as a time series. Secondly, the factor analysis method is used to describe them. According to the factor decomposed theory, network traffic is divided into different factor components. Thirdly, the empirical mode decomposition is carried out for these two components. In this case, a quick anomaly detection algorithm is presented. Simulation results show that our approach is feasible and promising.

Keywords: End-to-end network traffic · Anomaly detection
Factor analysis · Empirical mode decomposition

1 Introduction

With the rapid development of network technologies, network applications in power telecommunication access networks exhibit new traffic types and this results in network traffic quickly rising. Then new network traffic anomalies quickly appears in power telecommunication access networks. Network traffic anomalies have impact on network performance and users' experience quality [1, 2]. How to effectively detect and find out abnormal and anomalous components in network traffic has become a larger challenge [3, 4]. More importantly, anomalous network traffic implies users' and network devices' abnormal behaviors. Through detecting the anomalous network traffic, operators can effectively perform active defense for their networks. Therefore, network traffic anomaly detections are very significant in current network operations, which has become a very import research topic at present. This has received very extensive attentions from academic and industrial communities [5–8].

© Springer Nature Singapore Pte Ltd. 2018
H. Yuan et al. (Eds.): GSKI 2017, CCIS 848, pp. 75–82, 2018.
https://doi.org/10.1007/978-981-13-0893-2_9

Anomaly detections about network traffic are studied extensively. The time-frequency domain method was proposed to find anomalous components in network traffic [1, 5, 9]. They attained the fairly accurate detection results for abnormal network traffic. The Pattern-of-life [2] and empirical mode decompositions [3] were used to perform the correct detections of network traffic. In this way, network traffic features were extracted via different metrics or mode functions. The parameter-based detection method was proposed to find the abnormal part of aggregate network traffic [10]. Wang et al. used robust regression to extract traffic anomalies [6]. In such a case, network traffic was described as a period signals to model network traffic due to self-similar nature. Additionally, a new detection method was presented to find the abnormal part of network traffic for multimedia applications [7]. Their method could effectively find out and recognize anomalous network traffic. Through modeling network events, a model-based detection approach was proposed to find out abnormal situations in networks [11]. To more effectively and accurately detect anomalous network traffic, the spectral kurtosis analysis was proposed to recognize and diagnose abnormal parts in network traffic [12]. Dynamic anomaly detection approaches were proposed to identify abnormal parts of dynamic environments [4]. The compressive sensing theory could used to characterize network traffic [13]. This motivates us to use the signal processing technologies to detect network traffic anomalies.

Different from these methods, this paper proposes a new quick detection approach to capture the traffic anomaly components in power telecommunication access networks, which combines the factor analysis with the empirical mode decomposition method. Firstly, we take network traffic as a time series, which is used to construct a random traffic matrix. Secondly, the factor decomposition is performed for the random traffic matrix. In this way, network traffic is divided into common and specific components, in which common components denotes the common features in network traffic while specific components describe the specific features in network traffic. Thirdly, we exploit the empirical mode decomposition to decompose these two components. We build the different empirical mode functions to characterize them, respectively. In this case, we can effectively describe the features of network traffic. Then we present a quick anomaly detection algorithm to perform the accurate recognition of anomalous network traffic. Simulation results show that our approach is feasible and promising

The rest of this paper is organized as follows. Our method is derived in Sect. 2. Section 3 presents the simulation results and analysis. We then conclude our work in Sect. 4.

2 Problem Statement

Generally, network traffic in power telecommunication access networks changes with time. Accordingly, we can take them as a time series. Assume that $y(t)$ stands for network traffic at time t. Then time series $y = \{y(t)|t = 1, 2, \ldots\}$ denotes network traffic over time. Without loss of generality, assume network traffic $\tilde{y} = \{y(t)|t = 1, 2, \ldots, n\}$ with length n where n is an integer. According to network traffic $\tilde{y}$, we can attain the following random matrix:

$$Y = \{y_i\}_{n \times 1} = \{y(1), y(2), \ldots, y(n)\} \tag{1}$$

Where $y_i(i = 1, 2, \ldots, n)$ are the observed random vector, its mean vector is $E(Y) = 0$, and its covariance matrix is $Cov(Y) = R$. Next, we perform the factor decomposition for network traffic Y in Eq. (1). By the factor analysis theory, Y can be decomposed as the following equation:

$$\begin{cases} y(1) = a_{11} Y_{c1} + a_{12} Y_{c2} + \ldots + a_{1p} Y_{cp} + Y_{s1} \\ y(2) = a_{21} Y_{c1} + a_{22} Y_{c2} + \ldots + a_{2p} Y_{cp} + Y_{s2} \\ \ldots \\ y(n) = a_{n1} Y_{c1} + a_{n2} Y_{c2} + \ldots + a_{np} Y_{cp} + Y_{sn} \end{cases} \tag{2}$$

Where Y_{ci} (where $i = 1, 2, \ldots, p$ and $p \leq n$) are not observed random vector, its mean vector is $E(Y_c) = 0$ (where $Y_c = \{Y_{c1}, Y_{c2}, \ldots, Y_{cp}\}$), and its covariance matrix is $Cov(Y_c) = 1$. This means that each component in Y_{ci} is independent of each other. $Y_{sj}(j = 1, 2, \ldots, n)$ and $Y_{ci}(i = 1, 2, \ldots, p)(p \leq n)$ are independent of each other, equation $E(Y_s) = 0$ holds (where $Y_s = \{Y_{s1}, Y_{s2}, \ldots, Y_{sn}\}$), and all components in Y_s are independent of each other.

We select the k top common factors in network traffic. Then the below equation can be attained:

$$Y = \{y_i\}_{n \times 1} = AY_c + Y_s \tag{3}$$

Where Y_c denotes the common factors and Y_s describes the specific factors in network traffic, and A is known as the factor loading matrix. The model in Eq. (3) can be used to characterize the features of network traffic.

Accordingly, according to Eqs. (2)–(3), a new time series can be obtained as follows:

$$\begin{aligned} \tilde{y}_c &= \{\tilde{y}_c(t) | t = 1, 2, \ldots, p\} \\ &= \{y_{1,c}, y_{2,c}, \ldots, y_{p,c}\} \end{aligned} \tag{4}$$

Where $\tilde{y}_c$ characterizes the common factors features in network traffic $\tilde{y}$.

Then another time series $\tilde{y}_s$, which describes the specific factors features in network traffic $\tilde{y}$, can be denoted as:

$$\begin{aligned} \tilde{y}_s &= \{\tilde{y}_s(t) | t = 1, 2, \ldots, n\} \\ &= \{y_{1,s}, y_{2,s}, \ldots, y_{n,s}\} \end{aligned} \tag{5}$$

In this case, network traffic is divided into two parts $\tilde{y}_c$ and $\tilde{y}_s$. Now we use the empirical mode decomposition method to extract the features in $\tilde{y}_c$ and $\tilde{y}_s$, respectively. As mentioned in [3], we exploit empirical mode decompositions to split network traffic into different intrinsic mode function components. Each intrinsic mode function component reflects the true hidden information in network traffic; each intrinsic mode function component is mutually orthogonal. Accordingly, we use the empirical mode decomposition to convert network traffic into the orthogonal intrinsic mode function components.

Therefore, for $\tilde{y}_c = \{\tilde{y}_c(t)|t = 1, 2, \ldots, p\}$ denoting the common features of network traffic, according to the empirical mode decomposition method, we attain:

$$\tilde{y}_c(t) = \sum_{i=1}^{m} g_{i,c}(t) + r_{m,c}(t) \tag{6}$$

Where $r_{m,c}$ is the residue component which represents the average trend of $\tilde{y}_c(t)$.

Similarly, for $\tilde{y}_s = \{\tilde{y}_s(t)|t = 1, 2, \ldots, n\}$ denoting the specific feature of network traffic, we obtain:

$$\tilde{y}_s(t) = \sum_{i=1}^{m} h_{i,s}(t) + s_{m,s}(t) \tag{7}$$

Where $s_{m,s}$ is the residue component which represents the average trend of $\tilde{y}_s$.

Now, we propose our detection algorithm. As mentioned in [x], the steps of our algorithm is as follows:

Step 1: Give network traffic $\tilde{y} = \{y(t)| t = 1, 2, \ldots, n\}$, the number k of common factors in network traffic.

Step 2: According to Eq. (1), attain random matrix Y.

Step 3: Standardize the raw data to eliminate the difference between the variables in the order of magnitude and dimension. Obtain correlation matrix R $(R = Cov(Y))$ of standardized data, eigenvalues and eigenvectors of correlation matrix R. And calculate variance's contribution rate and cumulative variance's contribution rate, and determine factors Y_c and Y_s.

Step 4: If the common factor solution is obtained, the typical representative variables of each common factor are not very prominent. Then the factor rotation is needed, and the main factor satisfying the appropriate rotation is obtained.

Step 5: Once the factor analysis model is established, there is also an important role to apply factor analysis models to evaluate the status of each sample throughout the model. Let the linear combination of the common factor Y_c represented by the variable y be the factor score function, from which the common factor score for each sample is calculated. The number p of equations in the factor scoring function is less than the number n of the variables, so the factor score cannot be calculated accurately and the factor score can only be estimated. Estimated factor scores are more common. And use regression estimation method, Bartlett estimation method, and Thomson estimation method to attain them.

Step 6: $\tilde{y}_s$ is obtained via the factor analysis method. Set $r_0(t) = \tilde{y}_c(t)$ and $c = 1$.

Step 7: Set $i = 1$. Then initialize the threshold a and the maximum iterative step S.

Step 8: Initialize $k = 0$ and $e_{i+1,k}(t) = r_i(t)$. Set the spline function $s(t)$ be a cubic spline, $s = 3$, $v = P$ and $P > 0$.

Step 9: Find out local maxima and minima of $e_{i+1,k}(t)$, use a $s(t)$-based spline interpolation method to create two spline curves $s_u(t)$ and $s_l(t)$, get $m_{i+1,k} = (s_u(t) + s_l(t))/2$, and set $e_{i+1,k+1}(t) = e_{i+1,k}(t) - m_{i+1,k}$.

Step 10: If $e_{i+1,k+1}(t)$ satisfies the conditions of an intrinsic mode function component, go to Step 14.

Step 11: If $v > m_{i+1,k}$, set $v = m_{i+1,k}$ and $e(t) = e_{i+1,k+1}(t)$.

Step 12: If $s = 3$, then set the spline function $s(t)$ be a B-spline, $s = b$ and go back to Step 9.

Step 13: If $k \leq S$ and the following equation holds $\sum_{t=1}^{N} \frac{[e_{k-1}(t) - e_k(t)]}{e_k^2(t)} > a$, then set $k = k+1$, $s = 3$, and go back to Step 9. or set $e_{i+1,k+1}(t) = e(t)$ otherwise.

Step 14: Get the *ith* intrinsic mode function component $f_{i+1}(t) = e_{i+1,k+1}(t)$, and set $r_{i+1}(t) = r_i(t) - f_{i+1}(t)$.

Step 15: If the residue $r_{i+1}(t)$ is not a monotonic function, then set $i = i+1$, and go back to Step 8.

Step 16: If $c = 1$, let $g_{i,c}(t) = f_i(t)$ and $r_{m,c}(t) = r_{i+1}(t)$, attain the feature function set $g_c(t) = \{g_{1,c}(t), g_{2,c}(t), \ldots\}$, let $r_0(t) = \tilde{y}_s(t)$, $c = 2$, and go back to Step 4.

Step 17: Let $h_{i,s}(t) = f_i(t)$ and $s_{m,s}(t) = r_{i+1}(t)$, attain the feature function set $h_s(t) = \{h_{1,s}(t), h_{2,s}(t), \ldots\}$.

Step 18: Perform the feature extraction for $\tilde{y}_c$ and $\tilde{y}_s$ according to $g_c(t)$ and $h_s(t)$.

Step 19: Filter the features attained via $g_c(t)$ and $h_s(t)$, find out anomalous traffic components, and save resulting detection results into the file.

3   Simulation Result and Analysis

Now we carry some tests to validate our approach for network traffic in power telecommunication access networks. In our simulations, anomalous network traffic is injected into normal background network traffic at four different time slots of 300, 700, 1100, and 1500 with the duration of 80, respectively. To avoid the random errors, we run 50 times simulation to attain the average detection results. The detection threshold is decided automatically according to our detection algorithm. We evaluate the feature extraction ability based on the factor decomposition, the feature extraction ability based on the empirical mode decomposition, and anomaly detection ability. We use the real data from the Abilene backbone network to perform the simulation process.

Figure 1 shows network traffic and factor decomposition results, in which Fig. 1(a) and (b) denote the normal and abnormal network traffic, respectively, while Fig. 1(c) and (d) describe the common and specific components extracted from abnormal network traffic in Fig. 1(b). From Fig. 1(a) and (b), we can see that normal and abnormal traffic have no distinct difference, which leads to the larger challenge for anomaly detection ability of algorithms. Figure 1(c) and (d) state that the common features and specific features of abnormal network traffic can be correctly extracted via our algorithm. We can find that the common component traffic reflects the common characteristics of network traffic. This indicates that our algorithm is effective.

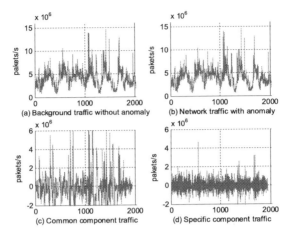

Fig. 1. Network traffic and factor decompositions.

Figure 2 plots the empirical mode decompositions for common component traffic. From Fig. 2, we can clearly see that the common component traffic can be characterized by 10 empirical mode functions accurately. It is very clear that the different empirical mode functions can capture the different features of the common component traffic. Likewise, Fig. 3, plots the empirical mode decompositions for specific component traffic. From Fig. 3, we can see that the specific component traffic can be described by 10 empirical mode functions accurately. Figure 3 shows that different empirical mode functions can capture different features of specific component traffic. This states that our algorithm is promising.

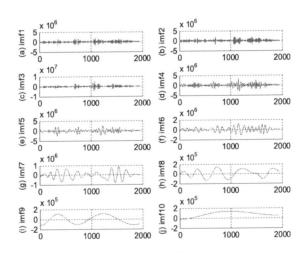

Fig. 2. Empirical mode decompositions for common component traffic.

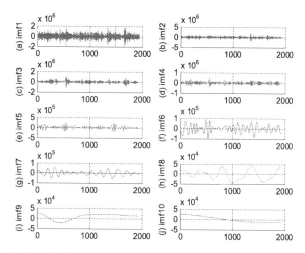

Fig. 3. Empirical mode decompositions for specific component traffic.

Figure 4 shows traffic anomaly detection results via our algorithm, where the decided detection threshold is 0.6 and the dot-ling pulse curve denotes time slots at which the anomalous traffic is injected. It is very interesting that the detection curve can accurately highlights time slots at which anomalous network traffic happens. We use the detection threshold to be able to correctly find out the abnormal and anomalous network traffic. Consequently, we can perform the accurate anomaly detection for network traffic. This further demonstrates that our algorithm can effectively find out the anomalous traffic.

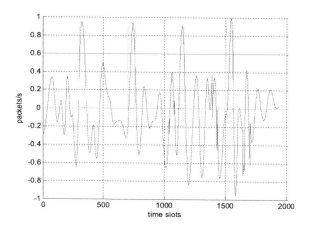

Fig. 4. Traffic anomaly detection results

4   Conclusions

This paper proposes a new quick detection approach to detect the anomaly components in network traffic, which combines the principal component analysis with the empirical mode decomposition method. Through converting network traffic series into a traffic matrix, the principal component decomposition is performed for the matrix. Accordingly, the principal and non-principal components of network traffic are attained. We use principal components to denote the principal features in network traffic while non-principal components to describe the secondary features in network traffic. The empirical mode decomposition issued to decompose these two components. Then the different empirical mode functions are constructed to capture and characterize them, respectively. Finally, a quick anomaly detection algorithm is presented to perform the accurate recognition of anomalous network traffic. Simulation results show that our approach is promising

References

1. Jiang, D., Xu, Z., Zhang, P., et al.: A transform domain-based anomaly detection approach to network-wide traffic. J. Netw. Comput. Appl. **40**(2), 292–306 (2014)
2. Aparicio-Navarro, F.J., Chambers, J.A., Kyriakopoulos, K., et al.: Using the pattern-of-life in networks to improve the effectiveness of intrusion detection systems. In: Proceedings of the ICC 2017, pp. 1–7 (2017)
3. Yuan, Z., Jiang, D., Tang, Q., et al.: A time-frequency analysis-based detection algorithm for network traffic anomaly. In: Proceedings of the COIN 2013, pp. 1–4 (2013)
4. Xiong, W., Hu, H., Xiong, N., et al.: Anomaly secure detection methods by analyzing dynamic characteristics of the network traffic in cloud communications. Inf. Sci. **2014**(258), 403–415 (2014)
5. Jiang, D., Yao, C., Xu, Z., et al.: Multi-scale anomaly detection for high-speed network traffic. Trans. Emerg. Telecommun. Technol. **26**(3), 308–317 (2015)
6. Wang, Z., Yang, J., Zhang, S. et al.: Robust regression for anomaly detection. In: Proceedings of the ICC 2017, pp. 1–6 (2017)
7. Jiang, D., Yuan, Z., Zhang, P., et al.: A traffic anomaly detection approach in communication networks for applications of multimedia medical devices. Multimed. Tools Appl. **75**(22), 1–25 (2016)
8. Thatte, G., Mitra, U., Heidemann, J.: Parametric methods for anomaly detection in aggregate traffic. IEEE Trans. Netw. **19**(2), 512–525 (2011)
9. Jiang, D., Qin, W., Nie, L., et al.: Time-frequency detection algorithm of network traffic anomalies. In: Proceedings of the ICIIM 2012, pp. 1–4 (2012)
10. Thatte, G., Mitra, U., Heidemann, J.: Parametric methods for anomaly detection in aggregate traffic. IEEE/ACM Trans. Netw. **19**(2), 512–525 (2011)
11. Eriksson, B., Barford, P., Bowden, R., et al.: Basisdetect: a model-based network event detection framework. In: Proceedings of the IMC, pp. 451–464 (2010)
12. Jiang, D., Yao, C., Zhang, W., et al.: A detection algorithm to anomaly network traffic based on spectral kurtosis analysis. In: Proceedings of the ITSim 2013, pp. 980–983 (2013)
13. Jiang, D., Nie, L., Lv, Z., et al.: Spatio-temporal Kronecker compressive sensing for traffic matrix recovery. IEEE Access **4**, 3046–3053 (2016)

Semi-formal Verification with Supporting Tool by Automatic Application of Hoare Logic

Shingo Fukuoka[1,3](✉), Yixiang Chen[2], and Shaoying Liu[3]

[1] East China Normal University, Shanghai Shi, China
13120605586@stu.hosei.ac.jp
[2] School of Computer Science and Software Engineering,
East China Normal University, 3663 Zhongshan N Rd, HuaShiDa,
Putuo Qu, Shanghai Shi, China
yxchen@sei.ecnu.edu.cn
[3] Hosei University, 3-7-2, Kajino Cho, Koganei Shi, Tokyo 184-0002, Japan
sliu@hosei.ac.jp

Abstract. Software development is costly endeavors. In general, the cost can be reduced by checking whether the program meets the specification. Usually, software is composed of several modules so that by checking the correctness of each module, developers can find the causes of errors efficiently. Formal verification and specification-based testing are effective techniques to verify programs. Formal verification based on Hoare logic can establish the correctness of programs from the theoretical point of view. However, it is regarded as an impractical technique for realistic programs, due to some challenges, On the other hand, specification-based testing is able to detect errors, and it is easy to perform. Therefore, it is frequently used for realistic developments. However, in most cases, the testing cannot guarantee the correctness of programs. As we described above, both of these techniques cannot do satisfactory job alone. To solve this problem, a novel verification approach was suggested, which is called testing-based formal verification (TBFV). In this paper, we aim to automate application of Hoare logic to Java programs based on the previously proposed TBFV. At the same time, we try to reveal the feasibility of TBFV through developing a supporting tool for Java programs and conducting a case study. At the same time, to achieve an effective automatic verification, we add the function of automatic boundary testing in the result evaluation step in the supporting tool. As a result, our supporting tool has achieved a semi-formal automation of Hoare logic application, which can help reduce the cost of verification process.

Keywords: Specification-based testing · Hoare logic · Program correctness
Formal specification · Testing-based formal verification

1 Introduction

Given a formal specification and an implementation, how to verify whether the implementation conforms to the specification is an important issue in the aspect of software reliability.

Also at practical level, importance of testing is increasingly noticed and regarded as one of significant processes. Recently, most companies conduct testing to ensure their

H. Yuan et al. (Eds.): GSKI 2017, CCIS 848, pp. 83–95, 2018.
https://doi.org/10.1007/978-981-13-0893-2_10

products. However, owing to the character of testing, some challenges still remains to ensure the system is correct at practical level.

Formal verification based on Hoare logic [1] can establish the correctness for programs by applying the axioms for each statement. But due to the difficulty in deriving appropriate loop invariant and managing side effect, complex data structures, and method invocations, despite of its high potential, formal verification based on Hoare logic is considered to be impractical for realistic programs.

On the other hand, specification-based testing (SBT) is widely spread out as a practical technique. SBT is much easier to perform than other verification techniques, even automation with formal specification is possible for various systems [2, 3]. Because of this characteristic, SBT has been adopted in many realistic developments. However, it is difficult for SBT to cover all the domains of inputs in each process. Therefore, SBT cannot prove the correctness in the program in most cases. In other words, SBT can detect errors but it cannot obtain program correctness. In the case of detecting errors, even if all the paths are traversed by using test cases, SBT may still not find some errors remaining on the traversed paths.

The underlying idea of this paper is known as Testing-Based Formal Verification (TBFV) proposed by Liu [4], which focuses on the superior points of combining both formal verification and specification-based testing. This paper aims to show how effective TBFV is through the development of a supporting tool for TBFV. The source language that we consider is Java. Java is one of the most successful and frequently-used languages for various systems. In these years, Java is increasingly adopted by embedded systems, such as smartphones and industrial robots. Therefore, we consider the supporting tool for Java code would become practical and beneficial. At the same time, in our research by executing boundary testing for derived assertion on the same step, we try to achieve more automation and more efficiency than original TBFV. The rest of the paper is organized as follows. Section 2 gives a brief intro-duction to Hoare Logic and the concept of TBFV. In Sect. 3, we explain and the structure of our supporting tool. Section 4 describes the result of demonstration with case study. In Sect. 5, we conclude the result of this research. Finally, in Sect. 6, we point out the present challenges which and the future research direction.

2   Preliminaries

2.1   Hoare Logic

Hoare logic is established based on predicate logic and provides a set of axioms to define the semantics of programming languages.

For each program construct, such as sequence, selection, or iteration, an axiom for defining its semantics is defined. These axioms can be used to reason about the cor-rectness of programs written in a programming language. For the relevance of the axioms to this paper, we introduce the axiom for assignment and for non-changing statement in this section.

2.1.1   The Axiom for Assignment

Let $x := E$ be an assignment: assigning the result of evaluating expression E to variable x.

The axiom for assignment is

$$\overline{\{Q[E/x]\}x := E\{Q\}}$$

It states that the assignment $x := E$ is correct with respect to the given post-assertion Q and the derived pre-assertion $Q[E/x]$. The pre-assertion is a predicate which is derived from substituting E for all occurrences of x in Q. The post-assertion Q must be satisfied by x after the execution of the assignment. To make sure that post-assertion Q would be true, expression E must satisfy the post condition, because x would be changed E after the execution of assignment. Therefore, after the execution, it is guaranteed for post-assertion to be satisfied.

2.1.2   The Axiom for Non-change Statement

Let S be one of the three kinds of program segments: decision, "return" statement, and print out statement. TBFV set the original axiom for this statement, and it is called the axiom for non-change statement.

The axiom for non-change statement is

$$\overline{\{Q\}S\{Q\}}$$

The axiom states that the pre-condition and post-condition for these three kinds of program segments are the same because all of them doesn't change states.

2.2   Testing-Based Formal Verification

This section briefly introduces the relevant parts of TBFV. TBFV and our supporting tool have almost same structure. And it is composed of the following three parts.

2.2.1   Derivation of Traversed Paths

Test cases which are generated by formal specification-based testing (FSBT) to discover all the paths in the program. FSBT is a specific specification-based testing approach that takes pre- and post-condition into account in test case generation [5]. This approach treats a specification as a disjunction of functional scenarios. The concept of functional scenario is defined as follows:

Definition. Let $S_{post} \equiv (C_1 \wedge D_1) \vee (C_2 \wedge D_2) \vee \ldots \vee (C_n \wedge D_n)$, where each $C_i(i \in \{1, \ldots, n\})$ is a predicate called "guard condition" that contains no output variable in S_{ov}; D_i is a predicate called "defining condition" that contains at least one output variable in S_{ov} but no guard condition. Then, a functional scenario f_s of S is a conjunction $\sim S_{pre} \wedge C_i \wedge D_i$, and the expression $(\sim S_{pre} \wedge C_1 \wedge D_1) \vee (\sim S_{pre} \wedge C_2 \wedge D_2) \vee \ldots \vee (\sim S_{pre} \wedge C_n \wedge D_n)$ is a called a functional scenario form (FSF).

Our research uses FSBT to derive the paths. FSBT generate test cases where input variables satisfy a functional scenario. If each functional scenario defines an independent function and the guard conditions completely cover the restricted domains, it means that generated test cases respectively undertake each function of the process. Therefore, by using test cases that are generated by FSBT, it is ensured that each path would be traversed at least once and certainly obtains all the paths in the program.

A test case is a set of input variables, which has nothing to do with output variables. Hence, on test cases generation, we don't need to consider without input variables. FSBT generates test cases for each disjunction and based on only condition about input variables in functional scenario. The condition is called test condition.

Test conditions can be denoted:

$$\left(\sim S_{pre} \wedge C_1 \right) \vee \left(\sim S_{pre} \wedge C_2 \right) \vee \ldots \vee \left(\sim S_{pre} \wedge C_n \right),$$

Each conjunction states test condition and FSBT generates at least one test case for each conjunction.

2.2.2   Application of Hoare Logic

Assume p is a traversed path by using a test case. To verify the correctness of p with respect to the functional scenario, TBFV form a path triple

$$\left\{ \sim S_{pre} \right\} p \left\{ C_i \wedge D_i \right\}$$

The path triple has same structure with Hoare triple, but is specialized to a single path rather than the whole program. It means that if the pre-condition is true before path p is executed, the post-condition $C_i \wedge D_i$ will be true. Repeatedly applying the axiom for assignment or non-change statement, we can derive a pre-assertion, denoted by p_{pre}, to form the following expression:

$$\left\{ \sim S_{pre}(\sim x/x) \right\} \left\{ p_{pre}(\sim x/x) \right\} p \left\{ C_i \wedge D_i(\sim x/x) \right\}$$

where $\sim S_{pre}(\sim x/x), p_{pre}(\sim x/x) \, and \, C_i \wedge D_i(\sim x/x)$ are a predicate logic as a result of substitution every decorated input variable $\sim x$ for the corresponding input variable x respectively, based on Hoare logic. We distinguish x and $\sim x$ to avoid confusion between the input variables and the updated variables. However, to simplify the notation, in this paper, we denote $\sim S_{pre}, p_{pre} \, and \, C_i \wedge D_i$ instead of $\sim S_{pre}(\sim x/x)$, $p_{pre}(\sim x/x) \, and \, C_i \wedge D_i(\sim x/x)$

2.2.3   Evaluation Result

In the test result evaluation step, we need to derive p_{pre}

$$\sim S_{pre} \Rightarrow p_{pre}$$

If the implication is correct, this path is correct with respect to the path triple. We consider that automatic proof of the implication may be impossible. Automatic verification tool has been developed in these years such as ATP. However, even if we use ATP to prove the implication. It depends on complexity of the implication. If the implication is so complicated that ATP cannot prove the implication.

3   The Supporting Tool

The structure of our supporting tool is showed in the picture below (Fig. 1).

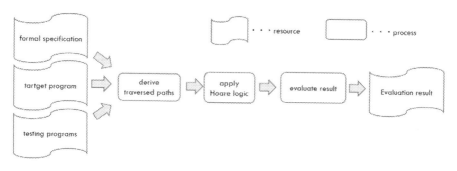

Fig. 1. The whole picture of the supporting tool

As you can see from the figure above, the inputs of our supporting tool are a formal specification, a target program which implements a formal specification and testing programs. Its structure resembles original TBFV. The different point is the result evaluation step. In the result evaluation step, our supporting tool conducts boundary testing automatically. Based on the result of boundary testing, the supporting tool judges the correctness of the path. If all the testing result is true, the tool judge the path correct in aspect of testing. On the contrary, if the result contains one more false, it means that the path contains errors. This function can help the developers to find existing errors. We have also developed a comprehensible GUI for the tool to facilitate the user in using the tool. Moreover, because of GUI, the developers can conduct TBFV step by step and know intermediate results (Fig. 2).

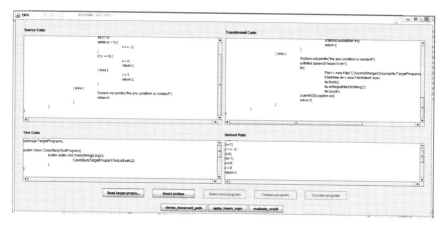

Fig. 2. GUI image for our supporting tool

4 Case Study

We have conducted a case study to show the feasibility and effectiveness of the supporting tool. We also expect it to be able to help the reader understand the structure of our tool. At the same time, we have found some points to be improved on development and they are addressed in Sect. 6.

The formal specification is written in SOFL specification language [6] below, which has similar structure with operation definition in VDM-SL. Thus, for people who have experienced using VDM-SL or other specification languages, SOFL specifications should be comprehensible.

Here is the formal specification of case study.

```
process isEven(x : int) z : nat0
pre x >= 0
post x % 2 = 0 and z = 0 or x % 2 ! = 0 and z = 1
end process
```

The specification states that the process *isEven* requires one input variable x and one output variable z. x can take the value in the range of integer and z can take the value in the range of integer which is greater than or equal to 0. x must be greater than or equal to 0 before execution, which is restricted by pre-condition. Otherwise, the pre-condition is violated and anything can be happened after execution. If x satisfies pre-condition, this process judges whether x is even or odd, and output z as a result.

The Java program below is implementation of case study.

```java
int isEven(int x) {
    if (x >= 0) {
        int z = 0;
        while (x > 1) {
            x = x - 2;
        }
        if (x == 0) {
            z = 0;
            return z;
        } else {
            z = 1;
            return z;
        }
    } else {
        //"the pre condition is violated!");
        return 0;
    }
}
```

The program should contain three paths, one is the case where x satisfies the pre-condition and is even number, another is the case where x satisfies the pre-condition as well and is odd number, and the other is the case where x doesn't satisfy the pre-condition. As I mentioned above, in test case generation based on TBFV, the derivation of functional scenarios from formal specification is essential. In this example, three functional scenarios can be derived:

(1) $x >= 0$ and $x \% 2 = 0$ and $z = 0$
(2) $x >= 0$ and $x \% 2 = 1$ and $z = 1$
(3) $x < 0$ and anything

By using FSBT, automatic generation of testing program is possible. As of now, our supporting tool does not support automatic testing program generation. Therefore, the developers need to generate test cases and testing programs by themselves. To obtain the correctness of whole program, verification for each path is required. However, in this paper, since the verification process is same for other paths, we only verify the first path with the test case $\{(x, 8)\}$.

Here is testing program for case study.

```
package TargetPrograms;

public class CaseStudyTestProgram{
        public static void main(String[] args){
                CaseStudyTargetProgramTest.isEven(8);
        }
}
```

Not to override the original program, our tool creates the copy of the original program. And the copy program is inserted print out statements between statements appropriately. Hence, the testing program is required to call the copy program like case study (Figs. 3 and 4).

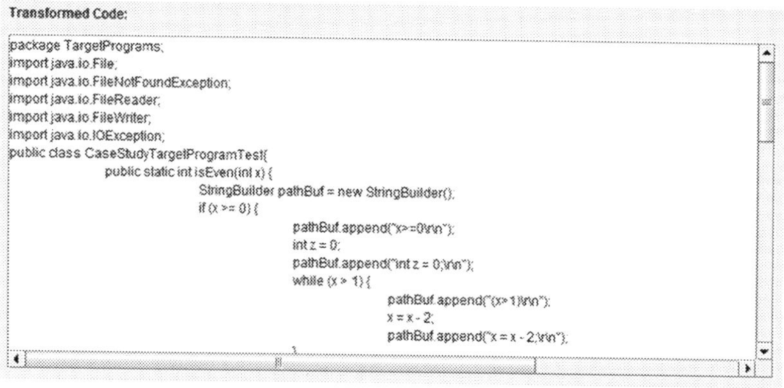

Fig. 3. Automatically probed program by the support tool

Fig. 4. Derived path by the execution of testing program

We think it is inconvenient to show the entire derived path and explain its works in pictures, it may be confusing. So we copied them in text below.

$$
\begin{aligned}
&x>=0 \\
&\text{int } z = 0; \\
&(x>1) \\
&x = x - 2; \\
&(x>1) \\
&x = x - 2; \\
&(x>1) \\
&x = x - 2; \\
&(x>1) \\
&x = x - 2; \\
&(x,0) \\
&!(x>1) \\
&x==0 \\
&z = 0; \\
&\text{return } z;
\end{aligned}
$$

As you can see, by using TBFV, all the iterations are decomposed into sequences after execution. Therefore, the developer does not need to take loop invariants into account. We think this point is the most valuable advantage of TBFV.

Here is the result of the application of Hoare logic.

$\{((((\,x-2\,)-2\,)-2\,)-2\,)\,\%\,2=0$ and $0=0\}$
x>=0
$\{((((\,x-2\,)-2\,)-2\,)-2\,)\,\%\,2=0$ and $0=0\}$
int z = 0;
$\{((((\,x-2\,)-2\,)-2\,)-2\,)\,\%\,2=0$ and $0=0\}$
(x>1)
$\{((((\,x-2\,)-2\,)-2\,)-2\,)\,\%\,2=0$ and $0=0\}$
x = x - 2;
$\{(((\,x-2\,)-2\,)-2\,)\,\%\,2=0$ and $0=0\}$
(x>1)
$\{(((\,x-2\,)-2\,)-2\,)\,\%\,2=0$ and $0=0\}$
x = x - 2;
$\{((\,x-2\,)-2\,)\,\%\,2=0$ and $0=0\}$
(x>1)
$\{((\,x-2\,)-2\,)\,\%\,2=0$ and $0=0\}$
x = x - 2;
$\{(\,x-2\,)\,\%\,2=0$ and $0=0\}$
(x>1)
$\{(\,x-2\,)\,\%\,2=0$ and $0=0\}$
x = x - 2;
$\{x\,\%\,2=0$ and $0=0\}$
(x,0)
$\{x\,\%\,2=0$ and $0=0\}$
!(x>1)
$\{x\,\%\,2=0$ and $0=0\}$
x==0
$\{x\,\%\,2=0$ and $0=0\}$
z = 0;
$\{x\,\%\,2=0$ and $z=0\}$
return z;
$\{x\,\%\,2=0$ and $z=0\}$

Now, we can obtain the path triple with the derived assertion for this path.

$\{x>=0\}$
$\{((((x-2)-2)-2)-2)\%2=0$ and $0=0\}$
x>=0
int z = 0;
(x>1)
x = x - 2;
(x>1)
x = x - 2;
(x>1)
x = x - 2;
(x>1)
x = x - 2;
(x,0)
!(x>1)
x==0
z = 0;
return z;
$\{x \% 2 = 0$ and $z = 0\}$

Now if we succeed to prove $\sim S_{pre} \Rightarrow p_{pre}$, then it means there is no error on this path.

Specifically, if we can prove the implication

$$\{x \geq 0\} \Rightarrow \{(x - 8) \% 2 = 0 \, and \, 0 = 0\},$$

we can conclude that there are no errors on this path.

We denote $(x - 8)$ instead of $((((x - 2) - 2) - 2) - 2)$ to help the readers understand the explanation.

In result evaluation step, which the domains of input variables are limited in the range of the value which satisfies the test condition that is used in test case generation. Otherwise, x would be out of the domain for undertaken functional scenario. The supporting tool requires formal specification is well-formed. In other words, if input variables satisfy one functional scenario, the same values must not satisfy other functional scenarios. In any values of input variables, they satisfy only one test condition (Fig. 5).

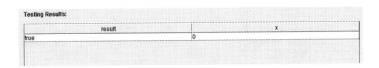

Fig. 5. Automatic boundary testing results for the path

In our tool, our aim is to check whether the implication would be true for restricted domains of inputs variables. Hence, the supporting tool checks only the boundary values which satisfy functional scenario. For case study, x must satisfy $\{x \geq 0 \, and \, x \% 2 = 0\}$. Now, it is obvious that 0 can only be used as boundary value (Fig. 6).

Fig. 6. Error detection based on boundary testing

The result of testing here is too weak to obtain the correctness for this path. However, if the result is false, then we can find out the program contains at least an error on the path. Therefore, we consider that the automatic boundary testing result is still helpful.

Then, how can we obtain the correctness for this path. As we mentioned in Sect. 4, to obtain the correctness, mathematical proof is essential. The tool requires users to prove the implication to obtain the correctness for this path. In case study, the propositional logic formula below should be derived:

$$\forall_{x < N \cup \{0\}}, x \geq 0 \, and \, x \% 2 = 0, (x - 8) \% 2 = 0 \, and \, 0 = 0$$

Here is mathematical proof for case study:

Let m be a natural number, then any even number can be denoted 2 m. Then $2m - 8$ is equal to $2(m - 4)$, which is divisible by 2. Hence, if x is integer which is greater than or equal to 0 and divisible by 2, $(x - 8) \% 2 = 0$, would be true (1).

$0 = 0$ is always true, despite of the variables' values (2).

Now, by (1) and (2), we can conclude

$$\forall_{x < N \cup \{0\}}, x \geq 0 \, and \, x \% 2 = 0, (x - 8) \% 2 = 0 \, and \, 0 = 0$$

As a result, we can conclude that there are no errors on this path. The developer has to prove the implication by hands in this step.

5 Conclusion

On evaluation result step, we adopt boundary testing for full automation of Hoare logic. However, it is not strong enough to obtain the correctness. Therefore, we plan to change boundary testing to SMT solver, and then we can check whether the implication is correct in the range of the domains that is allowed in program language. To achieve the adoption of SMT solver, our first job is to transform the implication written in first order logic to follow the specific notation rule of the SMT solver.

Although we believe that the tool still has problems and functions needing to be improved, it can help the developer efficiently carry out the proof of the implication for individual traversed paths than the whole program due to the fact that the whole program is decomposed into individual paths. Therefore, our present tool can help reduce the developer's efforts and the development cost to some degree.

6   Future Work

For method invocation, some challenges still remain. Our tool can manage internal method invocation, such as subroutine calls. However, the situation which the tool can deal with is limited. Because the supporting tool cannot process the return value of subroutine call, our tool cannot deal with subroutines with the void type for the returned value. The void type is the type for the result of a function that returns normally, but does not provide a result value to its caller. Subroutine call also results in a path sequential as the result of executing its body. Therefore, our tool can manage subroutine calls without special treatment. If we improve the supporting tool to be able to deal with the return value of method invocation, we can expand the range of programs to which our tool can be applied. Another weakness of the tool is that it is not capable of automatically generating test programs based on FSBT. Therefore, developers have to generate test cases and write testing programs by hand. To generate a test case by using FSBT, we have to transform the post-condition in formal specification into disjunctive normal form. However, the automatic transformation method from post-condition into disjunctive normal form is already established [7]. In addition, Takumi Amitani, who is the master student at Hosei University, has been working on this part simultaneously. Thus, we plan to combine our tool with test case generation module after the work has been finished. After that, our tool can achieve fully automatic application of Hoare logic and we believe that our supporting tool can show high potential then.

Acknowledgments. I'm grateful to Kangli He for helping me edit this paper. And I thank East China Normal University for financial support to attend the conference. This work was supported by JSPS KEKENHI Grant Number 26240008 and Defense Industrial Technology Development Program JCKY 2016212B004-2.

References

Hoare, C.A.R.: An axiomatic basis for computer programming. Commun. ACM **12**(10), 576–580 (1969)

Liu, D., Liu, Y., Zhang, X., Zhu, H., Bayley, I.: Automated testing of web services based on algebraic specifications. In: 2015 IEEE Symposium on Service-Oriented System Engineering (SOSE), San Francisco Bay, US, 30 March 30–3 April 2015 (2015)

Chupilko, M., Kamkin, A., Kotsynyak, A., Protsenko, A., Smolov, S., Tatarnikov, A.: Specification-based test program generation for arm vmsav8-64 memory management units. In: 2015 16th International on Workshop Microprocessor and SOC Test and Verification (MTV), Austin, US, 3–4 December (2015)

Liu, S.: Utilizing hoare logic to strengthen testing for error detection in programs. In: Proceedings of the Turing Centenary Conference, Manchester, UK, pp. 229–238 (2010)

Liu, S.: A decompositional approach to automatic test case generation base on formal specification. In: 4th IRRR International Conference on Secure Software Integration and Reliability Improvement (SSIRI 2010), 9–11 June 2010, pp. 147–155. IEEE CS Press, Singapore (2010)

Liu, S.: Formal Engineering for Industrial Software Development Using the SOFL Method. Springer, Heidelberg (2004). https://doi.org/10.1007/978-3-662-07287-5

Liu, S., Hayashi, T., Takahashi, K., Kimura, K., Nakayama, T., Nakajima, S.: Automatic transformation from formal specifications to functional scenario forms for automatic test case generation. In: 9th International Conference on Software Methodologies. Tools and Techniques (SoMet2010), Yokohama, Japan, 29 September–1 October 2010. IOS International Publisher (2010) (Page to appear)

A Fault Detection Device for Wind Power Generator Based on Wireless Transmission

Guanqi Zhang$^{(\boxtimes)}$, Xinyan Zhang, Lulu Yang, and Jialiang Luo

School of Electrical Engineering, Xinjiang University, No. 1230, Yanan Road,
Tianshan District, Urumqi 830049, Xinjiang, China
19296980@qq.com, 272639840@qq.com, 134466134@qq.com,
xjcxzxy@126.com

Abstract. In the light of the fact that the detection data is small, the fault diagnosis of the wind turbine often occurs. A multi-channel data acquisition based on wireless transmission wind turbine fault monitoring device is presented in this paper. The system used sensors to collect fan status data, and processes the signals by 32 bit digital signal processor DSP (TMS320F28335). The LabVIEW software system and the MCGS (Monitor and Control Generated System) configuration software display synchronously. The simulation experiments show that compared with the traditional wind generator online detection device, it can collect more data under various operating conditions, and provide a reliable basis for fault diagnosis.

Keywords: Multi-channel · Wireless transmission
Wind power generator · Data detection

1 Introduction

With the rapid development of wind power, the maintenance of fan failures is also a difficult problem. The wind farm is generally located in a remote and hostile environment, and the engine room is at the height of 50–80 m, which causes great difficulties for fault detection and maintenance [1]. The wind turbine monitoring system needs remote real-time monitoring of the fan, the cable transmission mode will be limited by the terrain, and the response time is long. Therefore, this device adds wireless transmission mode, so that the condition monitoring system is not limited by geographical conditions, so it is convenient to build [2].

The traditional wind generator fault monitoring device can only detect a characteristic quantity, which cannot fully reflect the fault characteristics and evolution process of the system, and cannot transmit data remotely. So, it is important for wind turbine fault diagnosis to design an on-line detecting device of wind generator which can detect many signals simultaneously. To solve this problem, experts have done some research. In the document [3, 4], the vibration signals of the key parts of wind turbines are collected, stored and displayed in order to provide reference for the fault diagnosis of wind turbines. The [5] design of a remote fault diagnosis system function analysis of multi-channel F2812 based data system, data acquisition, feature extraction, fault diagnosis together to embed DSP, achieve good real-time fault diagnosis.

© Springer Nature Singapore Pte Ltd. 2018
H. Yuan et al. (Eds.): GSKI 2017, CCIS 848, pp. 96–105, 2018.
https://doi.org/10.1007/978-981-13-0893-2_11

According to the fault characteristics of wind turbine under various operating conditions show, this paper designs a detection device for wireless transmission signal generator based online fault detection scheme, using LabVIEW software, MCGS software and DSP combination. With rich peripherals and powerful data processing function lower machine DSP main control chip, PC to realize data acquisition and display by MCGS software and LabVIEW software system, and the practicability of the device is verified by experiment.

2 Overall Design of the Detection Device

The detection device consists of two parts: upper computer and lower computer (Fig. 1). The host computer is responsible for interacting with users, data analysis, data organization and so on. The lower machine is an executive unit that receives the master device command [6]. In this article, the host computer is the software system written by LabVIEW and the MCGS on-line monitoring configuration software, and the lower computer is the DSP system designed with DSP chip. The system is a pretreatment device are connected to the conditioning circuit of DSP28335 main control board on the signal through the voltage sensor, current sensor, vibration sensor, magnetic sensor, temperature sensor, sensor noise based on the data sent to the host computer through the serial communication.

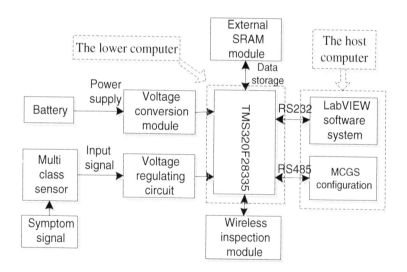

Fig. 1. Block diagram of overall structure

The lower computer adopts TMS320F28335 chip as the core processor, and designs the DSP system and its peripheral circuit. The main function of the DSP system is to carry out a variety of signal acquisition to the wind generator at the scene, and to upload the collected data to the host computer in real time, and to provide raw data for fault analysis and fault diagnosis.

The host computer uses two interface modes to display. LabVIEW system has the characteristics of easy to write and visual interface. It is used to display the collected data and the waveform after Fourier transformation. MCGS configuration software has the characteristics of friendly interaction, which is used to display the collected data, real-time data curve and historical data curve.

The communication between the host computer and the DSP system adopts RS232 and RS485 serial communication respectively.

3   Lower Computer Design

The detection device uses 32 bit floating point DSP processor TMS320F28335 as the master chip. The use of its rich peripheral module receives the signal processing, communication processing circuit to build hardware platform, it mainly includes the analog acquisition module, enhanced quadrature decoder pulse module, serial communication module and wireless detection module.

3.1   Analog Acquisition Module

The ADC conversion module of the device hardware platform using F28335 in data acquisition, analog digital conversion module is provided by the internal module of a 12 bit precision conversion, there are 2 independent sampling holder (S/H) can work in a state of simultaneous or sequential sampling. The signal voltage regulation circuit is shown in Fig. 2.

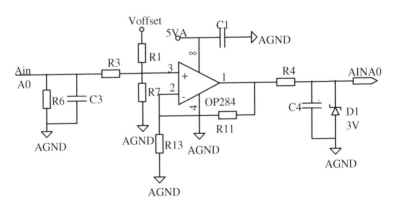

Fig. 2. Signal voltage regulation circuit

3.2   Enhanced Quadrature Decoder Pulse Module

EQEP F28335 module for enhanced orthogonal decoding module type, mainly used in the motion control system, which provides a direct interface encoder, the eQEP module can get the position, direction and speed information of the wind turbine, so the use of eQEP module to detect the rotational speed signal of fan.

3.3 Serial Communication Interface Module

There are 3 serial communication interfaces on the F28335. Since SCIA has been shared with other pins, SCIB and SCIC can only be selected. The two serial ports use two different protocols RS232 and RS485 respectively, transceiver driver and external interface, providing RS232 and RS485 communication. Device selection and host computer, PC select RS232 communication mode, and MCGS select RS485 communication mode.

3.4 Wireless Detection Module

The device adopts a wireless transmission module, and enlarges the practical application range of the device. Using ARM (STM32F103BRT6) NRF24L01 as wireless detection module to transmit real-time data from the vibration and noise signal, using lithium battery as its energy source, which has the advantages of small volume and convenient use.

4 Host Computer Design

4.1 Test System Control Flow Design

Because of the unique advantages of DSP in collecting signal processing, the bottom sensor collects data from multi-channel signals through DSP chip for data filtering and FFT processing to the host computer, and the control flow chart of the detection system is shown in Fig. 3.

4.2 Lab VIEW Software System

The system uses graphical programming language LabVIEW to prepare virtual instruments to display the vibration, voltage, current, noise, temperature, speed and other information of the wind power generator. LabVIEW has two basic windows, the front panel and the program block diagram. The front panel is used to set up the settings window for collecting, storing and processing FFT, and the program block diagram is used to write and display the graphical source code of program [7]. The front panel as shown in Fig. 4.

LabVIEW system uses VISA serial port [8] to realize real time communication. The serial data received by passive receiving, serial communication procedures used in the communication system in order to ensure the correctness of data received by the data frame of the baud rate is 9600 bits, 8 bits, 1 stop bit. LabVIEW serial port to receive data flow chart, as shown in Fig. 5.

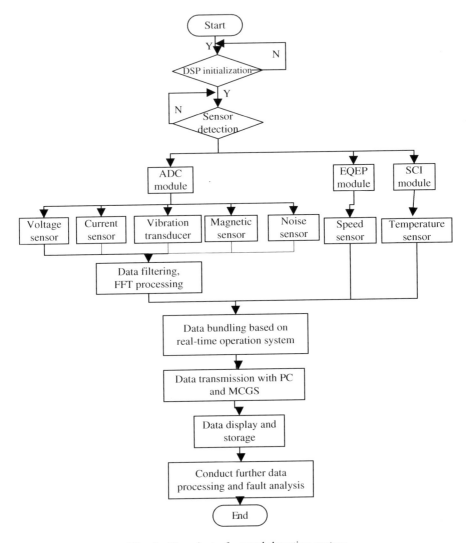

Fig. 3. Flowchart of control detection system

4.3 MCGS Software System

MCGS real-time monitoring system is mainly composed of monitoring and operation control of two parts [9–13].

Monitoring includes multi-channel sensors, the collected signals are displayed in real-time at the human-computer interaction interface, and the operation control includes monitoring personnel to modify the display parameters at the human-computer interaction interface. In the process of configuration detection system, control system of the first configuration are analyzed, through the analysis of the software design, set up ten users: window cover, main interface, real-time data display, data acquisition,

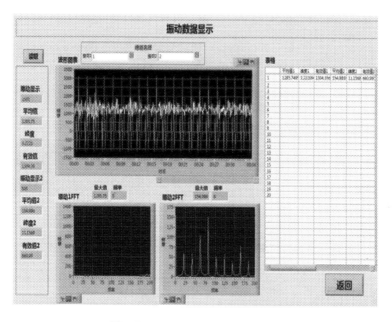

Fig. 4. Front panel design diagram

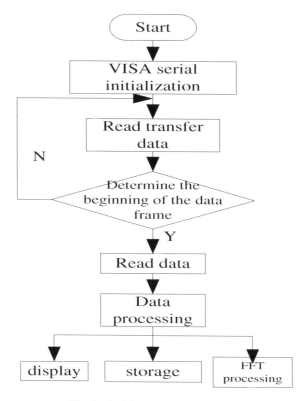

Fig. 5. Serial receive data flowchart

vibration table voltage signal acquisition data, current signal acquisition, data collection of temperature signal and noise signal, the data acquisition data electromagnetic speed data collection, data collection. It shows real-time data, real-time data curve and historical data curve change.

5   System Debugging Operation and Data Analysis

In order to verify whether the wind turbine fault diagnosis system designed according to the above content is effective, the field test is carried out in this paper. The simulation experiment of this device is to collect data of many kinds of signals in the case of simulating the direct drive wind turbine. The field data acquisition diagram is shown in Fig. 6.

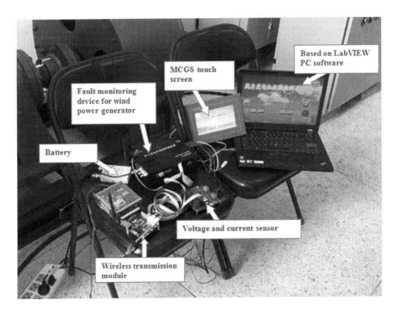

Fig. 6. Physical figure of the field testing device

The sampling frequency is 10000 Hz, the sampling time is 2 s, the detection device of multi-channel signal acquisition to data storage in the set in the excel table in simple, this paper analyzes the vibration signal of the acquisition, the denoised vibration signal and spectral diagram as shown in Fig. 7. We also analyze the current signals of the fan under the fault of bearing and the eccentricity of the spindle under normal and abrupt wind speed conditions, such as Figs. 8 and 9.

As can be seen from Fig. 7, a noticeable mutation can be seen in the time domain vibration signal after Fourier transformation. There is a slight fluctuation near the 15 Hz, and there is a big fluctuation near the 95 Hz, so the fan can be found to be out of order. Figure 8 shows a set of current spectrum diagrams under the different faults of

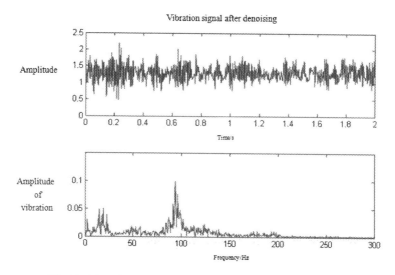

Fig. 7. Time domain and frequency domain of vibration signal

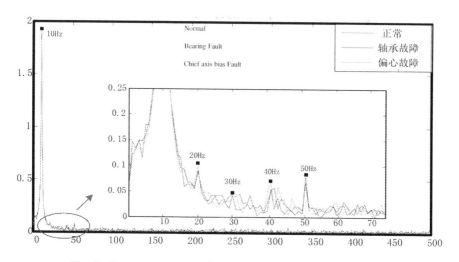

Fig. 8. Frequency analysis of stator current under normal condition

the unit under normal operating conditions. Under normal operating conditions, the amplitude of fundamental wave is more obvious than the harmonic amplitude, and the 2 and 5 harmonic changes are the weakest. The amplitude of the fundamental wave current is about 1.9 A. The current harmonic components are abundant and are distributed in the 0–500 Hz band. The overall harmonic level is low and the power quality

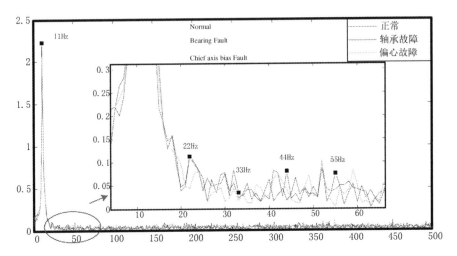

Fig. 9. Frequency analysis of current under different fault of the unit under wind speed abrupt condition

is good. When the simulated wind speed is abrupt, the generator rotor accelerates slowly in the sampling period, and the basic frequency of the current is no longer 10 Hz. The frequency spectrum of the generator outlet current collected under the working condition is analyzed, as shown in Fig. 9. As you can see from the diagram, the basic frequency of the current is 11 Hz, which proves the slow acceleration of the rotor. Compared with normal operating conditions, the basic frequency component increases from less than 2 A to close to 2.2 A, and the 4 and 5 harmonic changes are relatively obvious. The experiment shows that the fault detection device can collect the symptom information better, and it is helpful to the subsequent fault diagnosis.

6   Conclusion

Based on the traditional fault detection device of wind power generator technology analysis, design a fault detecting device of wind-driven generator based on multiple signal, at the same time as the data to the host computer display using LabVIEW software and MCGS software. The device solves the problem that the fault symptom information is single, and breaks through the limitation of the detection environment, so as to give full play to the advantages of wireless detection. The device can meet the requirements of users and realize the real-time performance of data transmission, providing the basis for subsequent fault diagnosis.

Acknowledgment. This research was financially supported by the National Natural Science Foundation of China (Grant No. 51367015 & No. 51667018).

References

1. Xuefeng, C., Jimeng, L., Hang, C., et al.: Research and application of condition monitoring and fault diagnosis technology in wind turbines. J. Mech. Eng. **9**, 45–52 (2011)
2. Yasen, I., Wang, Y.: Condition monitoring system of wind turbine blade based on wireless transmission. Mech. Eng. **7**, 103–104 (2017)
3. Wang, H.: Large Wind Turbine Vibration Monitoring System Design and Implementation. Shenyang University of Technology, Shenyang (2014)
4. Wenwen, D.: Vibration Status Monitoring and Fault Diagnosis of Wind Turbine. East China University of Science and Technology, Shanghai (2014)
5. Gao, Y., Pan, H., Wu, S.: System for wind turbine gearbox remote fault diagnosis based on DSP and neural network. Instrum. Tech. Sens. **1**, 67–70 (2011)
6. Du, S.: The transmission between the host computer and the lower computer. Comput. CD Softw. Appl. **15**, 45–47 (2012)
7. Bingcai, Z., Lin, L., Guangfeng, G.: Data acquisition and signal analysis based on LabVIEW. Instrum. Tech. Sens. **12**, 74–75 (2007)
8. Xianjun, W.: Serial port sampling data processing using LabVIEW. Electron. Meas. Technol. **37**(3), 107–111 (2014)
9. Yang Y, Zhang D.: High-voltage motor test system based on PLC and MCGS configuration software. Electr. Power Autom. Equip. (2008)
10. Zhang, Y., Tang, D.S.: Application of MCGS configuration software in sodium reduction process during tantalum smelting. Rare Metals Cem. Carbides **58**(14), 8171 (2010)
11. Wang, K.M., Li, X.-Z.: Applied study of monitoring and control system in coal mine based on MCGS configuration software. J. Taiyuan Univ. Technol. (2008)
12. Zhao, L.B.: Flotation medicine control system based on MCGS configuration software. Hydrometall. China (2006)
13. Wang, L.: Research on traffic control system based on MCGS configuration software. Foreign Electron. Meas. Technol. **3**, 17 (2009)

Multi-users Cooperation in Spectrum Sensing Based on HMM Model for Cognitive Radios

Wenwei Yang[1], Weiyun Chen[1], Messaykabew Mekonen[2], and Tuanfa Qin[3(✉)]

[1] School of Computer and Electronic Information, Guangxi University, Nanning, China
545336325@qq.com, 1229170755@qq.com
[2] School of Electrical Engineering, Guangxi University, Nanning, China
mesay.kabew@hotmail.com
[3] Guangxi Key Laboratory of Multimedia Communications and Network Technology, Guangxi University, Nanning, China
tfqin@gxu.edu.cn

Abstract. In order to solve the problem of frequent spectral state transition in the traditional cognitive radio network, the existing spectrum sensing is less reliable and the "hidden terminal" is added to reduce the interference to the main user. In this article raised introducing multiple secondary users to cognitive radio network and carrying out Hidden Markova Model (HMM) to main user's spectrum. Recursion calculating forecast probability of user's next time slot spectrum status is "busy" or "leisure." All counting of the secondary users "busy" and "leisure" frequency. If the percentage is "busy" exceeds a certain value, so could judge following time slot spectrum status is "busy," otherwise it is "leisure." The simulation results show that the algorithm is 10%–20% higher than the average energy sensing algorithm, and it is more obvious at low level. This paper improves the perceived reliability while rapidly detecting the spectrum, and greatly reduces the interference to the primary user.

Keywords: Cognitive radio · Spectrum sensing · Hidden Markova Model
Collaborative sensing · Hidden terminal

1 Introduction

In this information age and rapid development of the mobile intelligent terminal, wireless spectrum resources have become one of the most valuable resources in modern society [1]. Due to the unreasonable application, it caused lower utilization ratio of spectrum resources, some happen congestion, and some are idle. Acquired from American federal Communication Committee, the average spectrum utilization rate is only 15%–85% [1], and formed a high waste of spectrum resources. Based on above background, Mitoladia et al. [2]. Raised cognitive radio technique concept, and its springing up and development provides a new path to solve spectrum resources. Through allowing unauthorized secondary user adaptively perceives, learns spectrum space of the authorized frequency range and making use of spectrum space to carry out signal transmission to improve the utilization rate of the spectrum. The prerequisite to

H. Yuan et al. (Eds.): GSKI 2017, CCIS 848, pp. 106–114, 2018.
https://doi.org/10.1007/978-981-13-0893-2_12

cognitive radio is spectrum sensing technique, attract many scholars and researchers to working on it [3]. Signal checking to the main user transmitter and receiver is the main two testing ways in spectrum sensing technique, cyclostationary characteristic value checks [4], energy check [5], and matching filter check [6]. These types of primary checking methods, from the perspective of the secondary user number, so spectrum sensing was divided into single user sensing [7] and multi-users sensing [8]. These methods separately have own advantages and disadvantages, among which unique user energy checking could carry out fast checking speed, and don't need to know more prior conditions, that could achieve quickly but it is easily affected by fading channel at the same time. According to energy check algorithm is easily affected by fading channel, Digham et al. [9] raised capability check algorithm under the multipath fading channel; Sun et al. [10] built spectrum sensing algorithm under dynamic time-varying fading channel. Although many scholars acquired many excellent results in a spectrum check algorithm, due to certain shadow effect, fading and hidden terminal, etc. Environment factors caused spectrum status frequently converted, with bad checking effect [11].

Aimed at above problems there is scholar raised spectrum collaborative sensing [12, 13], multi-users collaborative sensing refers to carry out fusion processing to multi unauthorized cognitive users' sensing data at different geographical positions. Finally, the center node should confirm the main user whether using frequency range should be checked. But it doesn't consider secondary users' sensing blindness and brought check delay due to blindly check and check energy consumption reduced spectrum sensing performance.

This paper starts from problems of many spectrum statuses convert in traditional cognitive radio, the empty spectrum not easily to sensing and current lower current spectrum sensing reliability and "hidden terminal" plus reducing interference to the primary user, etc. raised one type of multi-users' collaborative spectrum sensing based on HMM model. Through HMM prediction and combining last time slot spectra observed value better-judged spectrum status of following time slot, then combining multi-users' sensing, increasing the reliability of spectrum sensing.

2 Multi Users Collaborative Spectrum Sensing Algorithm Based on HMM Model

2.1 HMM Model

To use the principle of HMM chain modeling to its main user in communication channel cognitive radio system, and making of spectrum check capability to perceive user is important. Based on its sensing result and predicted spectrum status, by last time slot in communication channel information reducing secondary user common sensing purposeless, and reducing caused check delay and check energy consumption. A general random process which can't intuitive observed random transfer sequence and described the relationship between this status and directly observed sequence formed two random processes of HMM model. Put HMM model into cognitive radio system, because the secondary user can't directly observe convert status between actual spectrum status and leisure and busy, so it could take convert status as the hidden process of HMM, as shown in Fig. 1 [14]. A random process which could Intuitively observe relationships between sequences is a visual observation sequence related to actual status sequence acquired through secondary user carries out sensing to main communication channel status. Hence, we can carry out modeling to secondary user's spectrum sensing process through HMM model and reach predicted spectrum status. Among which, an unknown quantity of state $L = 2$, expressed as $K = \{0, 1\}$, 0 is unoccupied spectrum, 1 expressed occupied, so hidden status sequence of communication channel at T time slot is $Q = \{q_1 \cdots q_t \cdots q_T\}$, q_t is spectrum status within t moment. Intuitively observed quantity of spectrum status is $N = 2$, expressed as $H = \{0, 1\}$, 0 expressed as this communication channel is unoccupied and 1 is occupied, then observation sequence could express as $O = \{o_1 \cdots o_t \cdots o_T\}$, o_t is the checking result of secondary user within t moment. Initial probability distribution of spectrum status could express as $\prod = \{\pi_0, \pi_1\}$, Initial probability when main communication channel is leisure and busy separately expressed as π_0, π_1. The probability matrix which seen transferred status expressed with $A = \{a_{ij}\}_{2\times2}$, among which $b = p\left\{q_{t+1} = \frac{Z_j}{q_t} = Z_i\right\}$ is probability when Z_i moment transferred to Z_j at following time status under this moment t. Emission matrix namely refers to intuitively observed probability matrix is $B = \{b\}_{2\times2}$, expressed probability when secondary user observed is H_K when status is H_K moment.

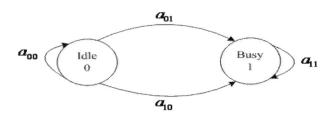

Fig. 1. Hidden state transition probability model

2.2 Multi-users Collaborative Sensing Technology

2.2.1 Centralized Collaborative Sensing

Centralized collaborative sensing as shown in Fig. 2, including multiple secondary users and one fusion center and the secondary users, send checked spectrum status result to fusion center through controlling communication channel. The center, through carrying on analysis of multiple secondary user results, then making the corresponded judgment about the main user's spectrum status, then sending the primary user's status result in every secondary user.

2.2.2 "K Order" Judgement

When above K Cognitive users checked main user signal among N sensing users, fusion center will judge main user is existed. Otherwise it will be judged as non-existent in essence, "K order" is general form of "and", "or" rule, when $K = 1$, it will become "or" criteria; when $K = N$, become "and" rule.

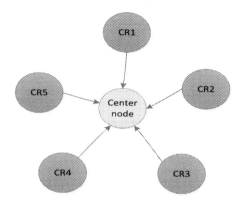

Fig. 2. Centralized collaboration awareness model

Its checking model as shown in formula (1);

$$\begin{cases} H_1 : \sum_{i=1}^{N} D_i \geq K \\ H_0 : \sum_{i=1}^{N} D_i < K \end{cases} \tag{1}$$

Among which D_i is expressed spectrum sensing result of the i sensing user.

2.3 Multi-users Collaborative Spectrum Sensing Algorithm Based on HMM Predicted Model

In short, the basic process of the algorithm is; According to the observation sequence $O = \{o_1 \cdots o_t \cdots o_T\}$ of SU as training sequence to estimate HMM parameter, then making use of estimated HMM parameter and sensing sequence $O = \{o_1 \cdots o_t \cdots o_T\}$ to predict probably status of communication status in the following moment. Then, according to spectrum status in the following time slot predicted by every secondary user, through reasonable judgment, finally acquired spectrum, which is the most approach to the real situation, hence carrying out reasonable and fast occupation.

Detail algorithm process as shown Fig. 3;

Initializing HMM parameter model $\lambda = \{\Pi, A, B\}$: Through carrying out HMM modeling at main user communication channel in spectrum status of cognitive radio could acquire HMM parameter model $\lambda = \{\Pi, A, B\}$; $A = \{a_{ij}\}_{2 \times 2}$; $B = \{b\}_{2 \times 2}$.

Running accumulation and energy, the check algorithm to carry out spectrum sensing, then acquiring an observation value sequence $O_i = \{o_{it} \in K | t = 1, 2, \cdots T\}$ of every sensing node at T time slot. Status space of observation value sequence $K = \{0, 1\}$, 0 expressed the secondary user judged this time slot is leisure, 1 expressed judgment is busy; and taking stated observation value sequence $O_i = \{o_{it} \in K | t = 1, 2, \cdots T\}$ as training sequence;

Running Baum-Welch algorithm to carry out training of HMM parameter Π and A and B, and acquiring estimated HMM parameter $\hat{\lambda}_i = \{\hat{\pi}_i, \hat{A}_i, \hat{B}_i\}$;

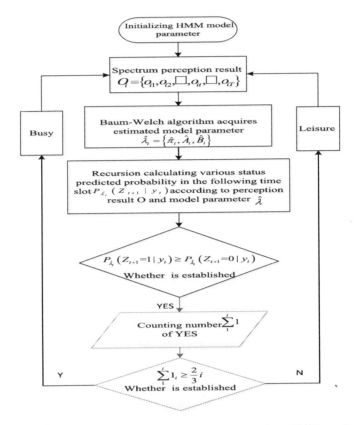

Fig. 3. Flow diagram of the spectrum sensing algorithm based on HMM predictive model multiuser collaboration

According to the sensing result of last status $Q_i = \{q_{i1}, q_{i2}, \cdots, q_{it}, \cdots, q_{iT}\}$ and HMM parameter $\hat{\lambda}_i$ to recursion calculating predicted probability $P_{\hat{\lambda}_i}(Z_{t+1} = 1|y_t)$ of various spectrum status in the following time slot, to compare multiple nodes predicted probability at this spectrum;

Comparing spectrum status predicted probability of various nodes in the time slot, if $P_{\hat{\lambda}_i}(Z_{t+1} = 1|y_t) \geq P_{\hat{\lambda}_i}(Z_{t+1} = 0|y_t)$ is established, hen judging this time slot spectrum sensing is busy for this node, otherwise it is leisure;

Collecting spectrum sensing frequency of "busy" and "leisure" at various nodes, if frequency of "busy" exceeds 2/3 of nodes frequency, then judging spectrum status in this time slot is "busy," otherwise it is "leisure," and return results to sensing result sequence;

Counting all the frequency of secondary user's sensing Counting all, the frequency of the secondary user's sensing spectrum status is "busy" or "leisure" in the following time slot. If "busy" percentage exceeds the preset threshold, then judging spectrum status is "busy" in the following time slot. Otherwise, it is "leisure," output spectrum status result, and return the result to spectrum sensing for the data fusion center.

3   Experimental Results Analysis

We use MATLAB software to build the experimental platform to carry out simulation analysis to checking the performance of multi-users collaborative algorithm based on HMM model. Comparing its checking probability, false alarm probability at single user HMM sensing, multi-users HMM and common energy sensing which not adopts HMM model, and discussing the performance of the algorithm.

The initial observed value of the HMM model parameter of main user communication channel applies HMM modeling should set up random sequence, and it should, use a value above 0 and less than 1 for emission probability matrix A. Reached speed of the data packet is 0.5 p\s, and leisure and busy length are both 1 and experiment carries out checking to 40-time slots, and each time slot collects 20 samples, for contrasting checking capability of multi nodes collaborative sensing algorithm based on the HMM model in a low level environment. Then, designed and introduced −5 dB and −10 dB carries out a comparison to algorithm and other type algorithm, for the purpose to improve simulation frequency, setting up simulation frequency is 5000 times, carrying out fitting to all acquired various second arousers checking probability.

Figures 4 and 5 show the fitting curves of single-user and triple-user and five user probing probability of normal energy sensing and HMM models under different signal-to-noise ratios, respectively. Compared with their detection probabilities, the detection probability of HMM model is about 20% higher than that of ordinary energy alarm, and the detection probability of multi-point cooperative spectrum sensing algorithm based on HMM model is higher than that of ordinary energy sensing and the simulation results show that the algorithm improves the detection probability of the spectrum and reduces the detection delay of the system, and improves the throughput of the system accordingly.

Figure 6 shows the comparison of the perceptual algorithms under different SNR values. In contrast to Fig. 6, the probability of detection of common energy sensing is

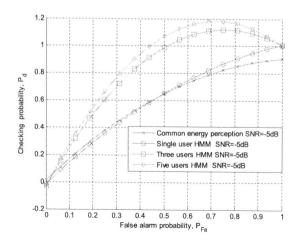

Fig. 4. SNR = −5 dB under the algorithm SU sensing ability comparison

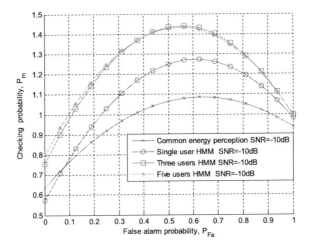

Fig. 5. SNR = −10 dB under the algorithm SU sensing ability comparison

reduced by about 20% when the SNR is reduced by −5 dB, using HMM single node perceived detection probability Down about 5%, the decline in the amount of ordinary energy sensing compared to a lot of small, for the use of more aware nodes, but the detection probability of a little increase, about 5% increase. The simulation results show that the multi node cooperative spectrum sensing based on HMM model is helpful to improve the system's successful detection probability in the complex wireless environment where the main user's signal strength is low and hidden terminal, so as to improve the system performance.

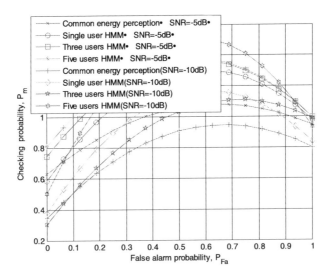

Fig. 6. Comparison of anti-jamming capabilities of the algorithm

4 Conclusions

Form the MATLAB simulation, contrasting checking success probability of sensing algorithm and common energy sensing algorithm based on HMM model, contrasting checking success probability and false alarm probability based on HMM single user sensing and multi-users sensing. The simulation result is shown, this article raised algorithm with high checking success rate, and lower false alarm probability and with more excellent error code performance. Conquering problems of frequent convert of spectrum status in traditional cognition radio network, lower reliability for current spectrum status and "hidden terminal" plus reducing interference to main user etc. It improves reliability of perception while quickly checked spectrum, and greatly reduced interference to main user. Because this article to perceive spectrum with a way of energy accumulation, thus some wireless transmission method similar to black broadcast, etc. high energy with profoundly impact to the algorithm, next step should research and consider access in safety aspect, further improving practicability and accuracy of the algorithm.

Acknowledgments. This research was supported in part by the National Natural Science Foundation of China (No. 61761007); in part by Guangxi Natural Science Foundation (No. 2016GXNSFAA380222)

References

1. Federal Communication Commission: Spectrum Policy Task Force Report. ET Docket no. 02-155.FCC (2002)
2. Mitola, J., Maguire, G.Q.: Cognitive radio: making software radios more personal. IEEE Pers. Commun. **6**(4), 13–18 (1999)
3. Khan, F., Nakagawa, K.: Comparative study of spectrum sensing techniques in cognitive radio networks. In: 2013 World Congress on Computer and Information Technology (WCCIT), pp. 1–8 (2013)
4. Wang, X., Wang, F., et al.: Spatial Sensing of PCA and RVM for stationary stability. Telecommun. Technol. **54**(7), 893–898 (2014)
5. Liu, C.: A connected-components-based multi-scale wavelet approach for wideband spectrum sensing. In: International Informatization and Engineering Associations, Atlantis Press, Proceedings of 2015 3rd International Conference on Machinery, Materials and Information Technology Applications International Informatization and Engineering Associations, Atlantis Press, p. 6 (2015)
6. Yan, H.: Study on Spectrum Sensing Problem in Cognitive Radio System. Journal of Jilin University (2013)
7. Zhao, X.: A multi-threshold spectrum sensing algorithm based on the phototropism theory for cognitive radio. In: Proceedings of 2014 4th IEEE International Conference on Information Science and Technology. IEEE Beijing Section, p. 4 (2014)
8. Shu, D.M.: A cooperative spectrum sensing based on the decision fusion for cognitive radio networks. In: Proceedings of 2014 International Conference on Communication Technology and Application (CTA2014), p. 9. Advanced Science and Industry Research Center (2014)
9. Digham, F.F., Alouini, M.S., Simon, M.K.: On the energy detection of unknown signals over fading channels. IEEE Trans. Commun. **5**(1), 21–24 (2007)

10. Sun, M.-W., Zhao, L., Xu, Q.-C.: Spatial sensing algorithm under dynamic time-varying fading channel. J. Commun. **35**(7), 63–69 (2014)
11. Fanous, A., Sagduyu, Y.E., Ephremides, A.: Reliable spectrum sensing and opportunistic access in network-coded communications. IEEE J. Sel. Areas Commun. **32**(3), 400–410 (2014)
12. Chaudhary, A., Dongre, M., Patil, H.: Energy-decisive and upgrade cooperative spectrum sensing in cognitive radio networks. Procedia Comput. Sci. **79**, 683–691 (2016)
13. Dong, S., Zhang, J.: Based on energy efficiency collaborative spectrum sensing time optimization. Comput. Technol. Dev. **27**(3), 176–180 (2017)
14. Choo, K.H., Tong, J.C.: Recent applications of Hidden Markov Models in computational biology. Genomics Proteomics Bioinform. **2**(2), 84–96 (2004)

A VoLTE Encryption Experiment for Android Smartphones

Shaoru Liu[1], Yao Wang[1], Quanxin Zhang[2], and Yuanzhang Li[2(✉)]

[1] School of Computer Science and Technology,
Beijing Institute of Technology, Beijing 100081, China
[2] Research Center of Massive Language Information Processing
and Cloud Computing Application, Beijing 100081, China
541272783@qq.com, popular@bit.edu.cn

Abstract. With the increasing popularity of 4G networks, communication technology based on VoLTE protocol has gradually become more and more mature. However, the public pay more attention to data security in the communication. We modify the baseband protocol of mobile phone with C language and assembly language in Android system and the encryption scheme for VoLTE protocol adds the key agreement and the improved RC4 encryption algorithm by capturing and analyzing the RTP packets in the communication. Finally, end-to-end VoLTE encrypted communication is implemented to protect user communication security and avoid the third party stealing data.

Keywords: VoLTE · Baseband · Android

1 Introduction

VoLTE protocol is based on IMS (IP Multimedia Subsystem) IP data transmission technology and the 4G network voice services business which can be in the same network at the same time to achieve data and voice services. VoLTE technology has the advantage of shorter turn-on time, higher quality audio and video calls and a drop rate equal to zero [1].

As the IP phone needs to communicate with the traditional telecommunications network, in the physical, user information and the corresponding support system share the same IP network [2]. The IP telephony implementation is based on the TCP/IP protocol, so the common attack technology for IP can also be used to attack VoLTE traffic. However, the systematic research on the security of VoLTE communication is lagging behind the rapid development of business [3]. In the face of the increasing number of communications leaked insecurity, public concern about the security needs of mobile networks, the need to speed up the VoLTE protocol for voice calls security research.

The main work of this paper includes the following aspects.

Update the code of platform baseband. Analyze the baseband code in the experimental platform and modify the hardware baseband program that handles the VoTLE call. So that the handling of VoLTE calls does not affect other functions in the baseband. At the same time, we design a program to send and receive DTMF signal packets This is to achieve the key negotiation.

© Springer Nature Singapore Pte Ltd. 2018
H. Yuan et al. (Eds.): GSKI 2017, CCIS 848, pp. 115–125, 2018.
https://doi.org/10.1007/978-981-13-0893-2_13

Voice data encryption scheme. After the "#" entered by the user, the key negotiation processing section is started. The encryption and decryption key is generated by key negotiation according to the keys from both sides of the call. After the user enters "*", the encrypted call ends and the normal communication state is restored. Improved RC4 algorithm to make it more suitable for voice encryption.

Test on the real machine. Through the capture and analysis of the voice packets in the communication process, we compared the contents of the same voice packet before and after decryption and decryption. They are the same. This proves that this scheme can complete the encryption and decryption based on VoLTE protocol.

The structure of the paper is organized as follows: Sect. 2 mainly presents the study background and related work. In Sect. 3, we discuss the modification of the baseband program on the experimental platform, and realize the processing of the VoLTE call without affecting the other functions in the baseband. In Sect. 4, we analyze the scheme of VoLTE call encryption, including the method of key negotiation and the improvement of RC4 algorithm. In Sect. 5, we discuss experimental results and verify that VoLTE call encryption is achievable. In Sect. 6, we point out the shortcomings and the next direction of this scheme.

2   Study Background and Related Work

2.1   VoLTE Protocol Communication Process

IMS (IP Multimedia Subsystem) is considered to be the next generation of network architecture to achieve a large convergence of communication network, to satisfy the terminal customers a variety of new business needs [4] LTE network voice services solutions - VoLTE, it is based on the IMS system. The VoLTE communication process is the same as the business process of voice communication in two core networks [5].

VoLTE communication process mainly includes three stages: turn on the terminal, call establishment, call release. Firstly, the UE initiates a call, establishes a wireless connection with eNodeB, completes EPS registration, data initialization, and IMS registration, user authentication and so on. Secondly, the VoLTE call is established, the IMS VoIP session and the EPS bearer are established, and then the normal voice conversation can be performed. Finally, the IMS VoIP session and the dedicated bearer will be released and the VoLTE call ends after the call is completed [6].

2.2   IMS Framework in the Android System

To achieve VoLTE communication, Android as the main mobile terminal system need to have high-definition voice, high-definition video communication capabilities, and support LTE and IMS networks [7].

As the Fig. 1 shows, Ims Phone Call Tracker is the class that monitors the IMS phone, the Phone or Ims Phone Call Tracker can directly create and call the Ims Manager class. Ims Manager is the IMS core management module, the starting point for all IMS activities. Ims Manager can call Ims Config, Ims Call and Ims Ut according to the specific request to reach the Vender RIL and its communication. Ims Config provides an interface for dynamic control of IMS capabilities and parameters. Ims Call is used to handle transactions related to IMS Call. And matters related to IMS supplementary services are handled by Ims Ut. In order to standardize the chip manufacturers, Android defines Iims Service, Iims Config, Iims Call Session and IImsUt and other interfaces. These interfaces are implemented by the chip manufacturer, and the upper interface does not need to be changed [8].

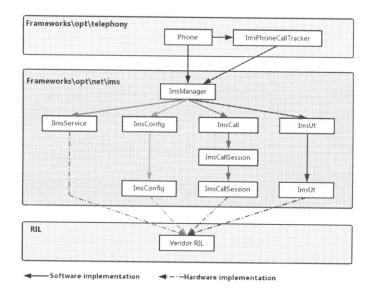

Fig. 1. IMS framework in the android system

3 Platform Baseband Code Update

3.1 Environment Building and Initialization

This paper the Coolpad mobile phone as the experimental platform, the basic parameters are: Android version 5.1, kernel version 3.10.65, baseband version MOLY.LR9. W144.MD. LWTG.CMCC.MP.V42.P23, processor MT6735 1.0 GHz.

Select CMCC as the communication service provider in this experiment. Compared to China Unicom and China Telecom two companies, CMCC support for VoLTE agreement is more stable and mature [9].

In the experiment, the experimental platform Coolpad mobile phone obtain super administrator privileges through the ROOT operation, and then capture and deal with RTP data packets.

3.2 Baseband Code Modification Scheme

The execution process of the program which modify the experimental platform baseband code shown in Fig. 2.

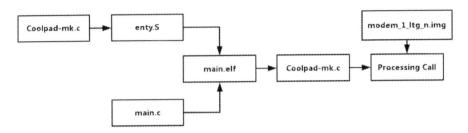

Fig. 2. The execution process of the program

modem_1_ltg_n.img is a hardware baseband program for handling VoTLE calls, which contains the associated functions and their addresses in ROM, respectively: call initialization ROM: 0065479C, send voice data ROM: 00655338, receive voice data ROM: 006557C2, send key data ROM: 0065680A and receive button data ROM: 006558BC.

Coolpad-mk.c is the interface of modem_1_ltg_n.img baseband and modifier. In a free space, specify all code start fields CODE_AREA_BEGIN and end fields CODE_AREA_END.

Entry. S is a fictional function that implements the call initiation, send/receive voice data, send/receive key function processing in the baseband, and implements the interface function for connecting the Coolpad-mk.c and main.c programs.

The function in main.c implements the fictitious function in entry.S. The processing of the RTP packet before and after reception is implemented in the ex_rtp_send and ex_rtp_receive functions, respectively. The ex_send_dtmf and ex_play_dtmf functions are used to capture and process activities that send keystrokes and receive keystrokes during a call. main.c function logic structure shown in Fig. 3.

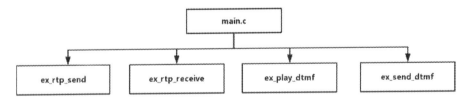

Fig. 3. Main.c function logic structure

Main.elf Compile with the function to modify the send/receive voice and keystroke packets main.c program and interface entry.S, and again through the Coolpad-mk.c function ROM address, return to the original baseband in the corresponding address. So that the management for the VoLTE call has no effect on other functions in the baseband.

3.3   Capture and Analysis RTP Packet

RTP (Real-time Transport Protocol) is a network transmission protocol to support real-time data transmission in the network. RTCP (Real-time Transport Control Protocol) is mainly used for transmission control information, real-time monitoring of data packets and network changes in order to respond in a timely manner. VoLTE communication technology use RTP/RTCP protocol for real-time transmission of voice, video and other data [10].

RTP packets not only carry the voice information, but also the two sides of the phone key information. DTTF (Dual Tone Multi Frequency) can reliably distinguish between key signal and voice information [11]. DTMF contains high frequency group and low frequency group, and each group has four kinds of frequencies, each transmission key number is composed of a high frequency signal and a low frequency signal, a total of 16 combinations, namely *, #, 0–9, A–D, as listed in Table 1.

Table 1. DTMF frequency combination table

	1209 Hz	1336 Hz	1477 Hz	1633 Hz
697 Hz	1	2	3	A
770 Hz	4	5	6	B
852 Hz	7	8	9	C
941 Hz	*	0	#	D

In this experiment, the RFC 2833 method is used to detect the DTMF transmission signal. The same DTMF key information will have multiple RTP packet transmissions, with the same timestamp to identify the same key, and the end of the last packet will be set 1 to indicate that the key packet is over.

During the sending process, the *ex_send_dtmf* function of the *main.c* program gets the DTMF information.

Through the IDA analysis modem_1_ltg_n.img baseband, the original program to send DTMF signal function address 0065680A in the ROM, the specific code to achieve the process shown below.

```
ROM:00656802        MOVW R0, #0x341
ROM:00656806        STRB.W      R1, [R2,#0x292]
ROM:0065280A        LDRSB.W     R2, [R2,#0x293]
ROM:0065280E        LDR    R1,  =aSDtmfQ_idxDCod   ;   "%s:   DTMF
q_idx=%d, codec=%d"
ROM:00652810        STR    R2, [SP,#0x20+var_20]
ROM:00652812        LDR    R2, =aLtecsr_madia_3 ; "ltecr_media_dtmf_req"
ROM:00652814        BL.W   x_log_sub_274FC
```

entry.S will save the address and jump to the ex_send_dtmf function to execute. The ex_send_dtmf function is used to identify the keys that are sent. "*" And "#" special symbols in the RTP packet, respectively, 10 and 11 transmission. While the other transfer numbers are themselves.

The principle of receiving DTMF signal packets is the same as sending. The difference is that for the same button will receive a large number of packets, and we need to locate the flag packet to end the button. The receive processing DTMF signal packet function is implemented in ex_play_dtmf. The address of the DTMF signal is received and processed as 006558BC in ROM, and its execution code is shown below.

```
ROM:006558BC    LDRB   R5, [R4,#0xD]
ROM:006558BE    AND.W  R5, R5, #0x80
ROM:006558C2    LDR    R2, =0xF2011B61
ROM:006558C4    UXTB   R5, R5
ROM:006558C6    CBZ    R5, loc_6558E2
ROM:006558C8    MOVS   R4, #0
ROM:006558CA    MOVW   R0, #0x341
ROM:006558CE    STRB   R4, [R2]
ROM:006558D0    LDR    R1,  =aSStopPlayingDt ; " %s: Stop Playing
DTMF %x!!"
ROM:006558D2    LDR    R2, =aLtecsr_voice_2 ; " ltecsr_voice_rtp_dl_cb"
ROM:006558D4    BL.W   x_log_sub_274FC
```

The ex_play_dtmf function extracts the key signals in the received DTMF packet. According to the special field changes, the function determines the start and end of the same key packet.

4   Voice Data Encryption Scheme

4.1   Encryption and Decryption Process

End-to-end VoLTE communication encryption is mainly achieved in the main.c program. Before transmitting the data packet, the sender encrypts the RTP packet which carries the voice information with the negotiation key. After receiving the encrypted data packet, the receiver decrypts the voice data with the same decryption key as the encryption key, and completes the normal call process. "#" indicates that the encryption process is officially started and "*" indicates the end of the encryption process.

Enter "#" starts the part of key agreement. Before the key agreement succeeds (key_length is less than 8), the RTP packet data is set to all zero and no effective data is transmitted. After the key agreement succeeds (key_length is 8), both the sender and the receiver will invoke rc4Init to initialize the key so that both sides can hold the same key to encrypt or decrypt the data. When the sender sends a packet, the ex_rtp_send function calls the rc4Cipher function to encrypt, and the receiver receives the encrypted voice packet then the ex_rtp_receive function calls the same rc4Cipher function to decrypt the data. The encryption processing structure is shown in Fig. 4.

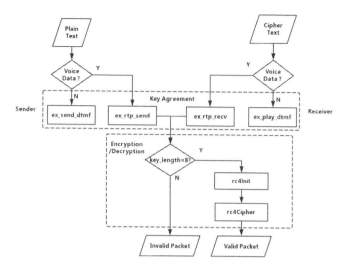

Fig. 4. The encryption processing structure

4.2 Key Structure

The encryption and decryption keys of the encryption are determined by sender and receiver. The key is an 8-byte array of characters whose first four bytes are from the number entered by the sender and the last four from the receiver. Any sides press "#" to enter the encrypted process, if one or both sides of the communication type less than four keys then the total length of the key is not 8, RTP packet is set to 0, no valid data will be transmitted.

The ex_send_dtmf function handles the key from sender, as shown below.
If (key $\neq$ 10) AND (key $\neq$ 11) Then
If key = 0 Then
key = key + 12
key_send [send_num%4] $\leftarrow$ key
send_num++
If send_num $\geq$ 4 Then
send_string_cmp = 1

The global variable key_send is a 4-byte char array, which stores the keys from the sender. The send_num is an integer global variable with an initial value of 0 and it records the number of the key from the sender. Since "0" is a special character, the idle value 12 is assigned to the key when the "0" is sent. After judging that the send button is neither 10 (*) nor 11 (#), it is stored in the key_send array in turn. If the length of send keys is longer than 4, these keys will be rewritten from key_send [0] and the original data will be covered. Meanwhile the variable send_string_cmp that identifies whether the key_send array is changed will be set to 1.

The principle of handling the key of the receiver is the same as that of the sender to ensure that both keys are the same. The ex_play_dtmf function handles the key from the receiver. And the key_recv array stores the key from the sender. The variable recv_string_cmp identifies the change of key_recv.

The send key and the receive key merge process are implemented in the ex_rtp_send and ex_rtp_receive functions. When the length of keys from both sides is 4 and the total key length is 8, the key will be combined. The sender and the receiver can be distinguished according to calling_flag and called_flag. The key agreement process is shown in Fig. 5.

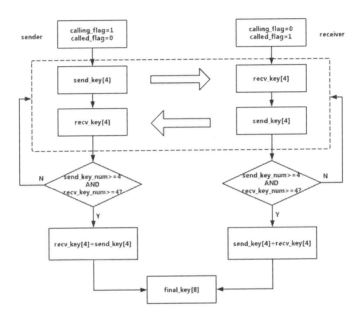

Fig. 5. The key agreement process

4.3   RC4 Encryption Algorithm Improvement

The RC4 encryption algorithm was designed by Ronald Rivest, one of the inventors of RSA, and was published in 1994. RC4 algorithm is a symmetric stream encryption algorithm cluster, and its key length is variable, mainly by the initialization algorithm and pseudo-random sub-key generation algorithm composed [12]. Because RC4 is symmetric encryption, it is required that both algorithms which produce the pseudo-random subkey are synchronized, and the encrypted and decrypted subkeys are always consistent. In view of the actual call, the case of packet loss occurs, it is difficult for the two sides to achieve self-synchronization. Therefore, the RC4 encryption algorithm needs to be further improved to meet the practical application environment.

The RC4 encryption algorithm is improved for the random subkey generation part. RC4 initialization operation and the original RC4 is the same way, when send_string_cmp or recv_string_cmp variable recognition key state is 1, call RC4 initialization function, when the variable is 0, the key does not need to perform initialization.

The improvement of the RC4 encryption algorithm is for the random subkey generation part. During the call, the serial number of each RTP packet is unique and stable. Regardless of packet loss or not, the serial number of the packet obtained by the sender and receiver is the same for the same packet. The sender and the receiver perform the same operation on the packet serial number, and assign the parameters to i and j so that both the encryption and decryption keys are always the same, thus ensuring the normal encrypted call. The specific improvement is as follows: set the variables ii and jj are the result of the serial number except 256 and mod 256, and pass the parameters to the rc4 Cipher function, assign the variables i and j to participate in the subkey generation process.

5 Discussion

5.1 Key Negotiation Process

The two sides of the communication are verified by the experimental data. During the call, the sender presses the "#" key to start the encryption call processing, and then press 1, 2, 3, 4, 8, 9, 1 as the sender's key, the receiver press 5, 6, 7, 8, 0 as the receiver's key. In the process of key negotiation, the receiver sends the key for the first four bytes, and the sender is the last four, and the two sides of the negotiation key in real time with any one of the changes in the transmission key changes, so that the communication Both keys are always consistent, as listed in Table 2.

Table 2. Key negotiation process

Sender	Key_send	Receiver	Key_recv	Key
1	01 00 00 00	5	05 00 00 00	– – – – – – – –
2	01 02 00 00	6	05 06 00 00	– – – – – – – –
3	01 02 03 00	7	05 06 07 00	– – – – – – – –
4	01 02 03 04	8	05 06 07 08	– – – – – – – –
8	08 02 03 04	–	05 06 07 08	05 06 07 08 08 02 03 04
9	08 09 03 04	–	05 06 07 08	05 06 07 08 08 09 03 04
1	08 09 01 04	–	05 06 07 08	05 06 07 08 08 09 01 04
–	08 09 01 04	0	0c 06 07 08	0c 06 07 08 08 09 01 04

5.2 Voice Packet Encryption and Decryption

Data packets before and after decryption as shown in Fig. 6, rtp_send_buffer_201.BIN is the unencrypted data from the sender. And rtp_send_encrypt_buff_202.BIN is encrypted by the RC4 algorithm.

In the experiment, the receiver receives the two packets: rtp_recv_encrypt_275. BIN, rtp_recv_decrypt_buff_276.BIN. According to the serial number information in the first four bytes of the packet, rtp_recv_encrypt_275.BIN is carrying the same voice data as rtp_send_encrypt_buff_202.BIN. rtp_recv_decrypt_buff_276.BIN is the

```
root@CP8722:/data/nvram/md/NVRAM # hexdump -C rtp_send_buffer_201.BIN
hexdump -C rtp_send_buffer_201.BIN
00000000  80 62 01 f5 00 06 d4 c0  35 d9 1b 6c f0 e7 d8 22  |.b......5..l..."|
00000010  c4 08 67 7b 89 aa f7 07  32 af 72 7b 05 a3 38 7e  |..g{....2.r{.8~|
00000020  e3 46 b4 40                                       |.F.@|
00000024
root@CP8722:/data/nvram/md/NVRAM # hexdump -C rtp_send_encrypt_buff_202.BIN
hexdump -C rtp_send_encrypt_buff_202.BIN
00000000  80 62 01 f5 c1 37 f7 6d  0f d0 f2 57 fe b1 f7 e5  |.b...7.m...W....|
00000010  da 99 0f 20 63 19 ba 2d  68 21 da 3b 65 78 1d 7f  |... c..-h!.;ex..|
00000020  dd bd 35 7f                                       |..5.|
00000024
```

Fig. 6. Data packet before and after encryption

```
root@CP8722:/data/nvram/md/NVRAM # hexdump -C rtp_recv_encrypt_275.BIN
hexdump -C rtp_recv_encrypt_275.BIN
00000000  80 62 01 f5 c1 37 f7 6d  0f d0 f2 57 fe b1 f7 e5  |.b...7.m...W....|
00000010  da 99 0f 20 63 19 ba 2d  68 21 da 3b 65 78 1d 7f  |... c..-h!.;ex..|
00000020  dd bd 35 7f                                       |..5.|
00000024
root@CP8722:/data/nvram/md/NVRAM # hexdump -C rtp_recv_decrypt_buff_276.BIN
hexdump -C rtp_recv_decrypt_buff_276.BIN
00000000  80 62 01 f5 00 06 d4 c0  35 d9 1b 6c f0 e7 d8 22  |.b......5..l..."|
00000010  c4 08 67 7b 89 aa f7 07  32 af 72 7b 05 a3 38 7e  |..g{....2.r{.8~|
00000020  e3 46 b4 40                                       |.F.@|
00000024
```

Fig. 7. Data packet before and after decryption

plaintext data package decrypted by RC4 algorithm from rtp_recv_encrypt_275.BIN, as shown in Fig. 7.

Each byte of the rtp_send_buffer_201.BIN before the sender encrypted and the rtp_recv_decrypt_buff_276.BIN decrypted by the receiver is the same. This fully proves that VoLTE end-to-end encryption calls can be achieved.

6   Conclusion

This paper realizes End-to-end encryption and decryption calls based on VoLTE protocol. There are still some shortcomings of this scheme, mainly including the following two aspects:

The key in the encryption and decryption scheme is relatively simple. At present we can't provide a higher intensity of the key negotiation method, the user's communication security still has some risk. If we can provide a more complex key, we can further protect the user's privacy from destruction and theft.

Can't handle the communication between human and machine encryption. At present we can only encrypt the communication between people, such as 10086 and other intelligent voice services can't be protected. If we can distinguish between different call objects, targeted design for different encryption schemes, we will make the whole design more complete and more available.

In the future work, we will further study and improve the shortcomings in this scheme, and we hope that the design of VoLTE call encryption for Android smartphones can contribute a little strength for the field of data protection.

References

1. Wen, K., Miao, Y.: QoS guaranteed cross-layer scheduling algorithm in LTE downlink multiple traffic system. Appl. Res. Comput. **08**, 2488–2491 (2013)
2. Sun, P.: Performance analysis and optimization of VoLTE. Beijing University of Posts and Telecommunications (2015)
3. Wang, J.: Study on security of VoLTE system and resolution strategy. Inf. Secur. Technol. (12), 55–56+61 (2014)
4. Anonymous: ZTE demonstrates first VoLTE call. M2 Presswire (2010)
5. Khalid, W.: IMS performance enhancement using hybrid techniques. Hunan University (2013)
6. Xiao, Z.Y.: User plane for VOLTE. Appl. Mech. Mater. **2865**(462), 198–202 (2014)
7. Zhang, C., Cheng, W., Hei, X.: Measurement study of 3G mobile networks using android platform. Comput. Sci. **02**, 24–28 (2015)
8. Huang, Y., Chen, M.: Architecture characteristics and analysis of mobile device applications. Chin. J. Comput. **02**, 386–396 (2015)
9. Song, J.: Research on development strategy of SIM card of China mobile group. Beijing University of Posts and Telecommunications (2008)
10. Liao, X., Miao, J., Zhu, Z., Zhang, Y., Lin, X.: Applicationg on call signal system and call control of HMP. J. Comput. Appl. **07**, 1847–1849 (2008)
11. Dai, H.: Research on the generation and decoding algorithms of DTMF signal. Inf. Technol. **11**, 88–91 (2008)
12. Hou, Z., Meng, M., Zhu, X., Liu, D.: Analysis and improvement of RC4 stream cipher algorithm. Comput. Eng. Appl. (24), 97–101+108 (2015)

A Novel Differential Dipoles Frequency Reconfigurable Antenna

Guiping Jin, Chuhong Deng[(⊠)], and Guangde Zeng

School of Electronic Information Engineering,
South China University of Technology, Guangzhou 510641, China
gpjin@scut.edu.cn, 136121248@qq.com, 529428668@qq.com

Abstract. A Novel Differential Dipoles Frequency Reconfigurable Antenna is proposed in this letter. The antenna consists of a pair of half-wave dipoles which are connected in parallel through a coplanar stripline, and a rectangular ground with a "H" shape slot on the center and four small rectangular cuts on four angles. In order to achieve the frequency reconfigurable characteristic, four PIN diodes are placed on the four ends of the dipoles, the current path can be controlled by the On or Off state of these PIN diodes. The effect of switch configuration either at On or Off state were studied. Simulation and measurement results show that the proposed antenna can operate at 2.60 GHz and 3.50 GHz bands. Good agreement between simulation and measurement results is achieved. The proposed antenna has compact size and can be fabricated easily and very suitable to be integrated with RF front-end circuits.

Keywords: Antenna · Differential · Frequency reconfigurable
PIN diodes · Dipoles

1 Introduction

With the development of wireless communications, frequency reconfigurable antennas for mobile terminals are demanded. To meet these requirements, many antennas with frequency reconfigurable characteristics have been successfully designed for wireless applications [1–3].

As the increasing demand in the wireless communication market has led to the need for compact and fully integrated radio frequency (RF) front-end products, for which differential signals are preferable. Usually, in order to connect a single port antenna with differential integrated circuits, a balun is needed. However, the use of a balun causes extra loss and lower efficiency. When the antenna is excited with a differential signal, the balun is no longer necessary. Thus, differential antennas are more suitable for differential signal operation due to the direct integration with differential circuits. Recently, several kinds of differential antennas operating at a single frequency or dual-frequency have been reported [4–8].

© Springer Nature Singapore Pte Ltd. 2018
H. Yuan et al. (Eds.): GSKI 2017, CCIS 848, pp. 126–133, 2018.
https://doi.org/10.1007/978-981-13-0893-2_14

1.1 Input Impedance of Differential Antenna

The differential antenna can be treated as a two-port network. Based on the Z parameters of the two ports, the differential voltage is:

$$V_d = V_1 - V_2 = (Z_{11} - Z_{21})I_1 - (Z_{22} - Z_{12})I_2. \tag{1}$$

where V_d is the differential voltage, V_1 and V_2 are the driving voltages of the two ports, and I_1 and I_2 are the driving currents of the two ports. For the differential antenna, the driving currents of the two ports satisfy:

$$I_1 = -I_2 = I. \tag{2}$$

Hence, the input impedance of the differential antenna can be described as:

$$Z_d = \frac{V_d}{I} = 2(Z_{11} - Z_{21}) = 2(Z_{22} - Z_{12}) \tag{3}$$

where Z_{11} is the self impedance of port 1 and Z_{21} is the mutual impedance between the two ports.

1.2 Odd and Even Mode Excitation of Two Port Networks

The key parameter at the interface between the feed circuit and the differential antenna is the odd mode reflection coefficient. Actually, an even mode excitation of the two ports will not excite a radiating mode in differential antenna, so the majority of even mode power would be reflected back to the source. When the two ports of balanced antenna are excited with an odd mode signal, the excitation at port 2 is constrained to be equal in amplitude but perfectly out of phase with that at port 1. Using the normalized incident and reflected waves at two ports, the reflection coefficient at port 1 can be expressed as

$$\Gamma_{odd} = \frac{b_1}{a_1}\bigg|_{a_2=-a_1}. \tag{4}$$

where, Γ_{odd} is the odd mode reflection coefficient, a_1 and a_2 are the normalized incident waves at two ports, and b_1 is the normalized reflected wave at port 1. Based on the definition of S parameters of two ports networks, the odd mode reflection coefficient can be described as:

$$\Gamma_{odd} = \frac{b_1}{a_1}\bigg|_{a_2=-a_1} = \frac{S_{11}a_1 + S_{12}a_2}{a_1}\bigg|_{a_2=-a_1} = S_{11} - S_{12}. \tag{5}$$

In the same way, when the two ports are excited with an even mode signal, the excitation at port 2 is equal in amplitude and phase with that at port 1. The even mode reflection coefficient Γ_{even} at port 1 would be:

$$\Gamma_{even} = \frac{b_1}{a_1}\bigg|_{a_2=a_1} = S_{11} + S_{12}. \tag{6}$$

Therefore, the S parameters of two-port networks can be used to calculate the reflection coefficients.

In conclusion, it is very creative and necessary to design a frequency reconfigurable antenna which can also connect with differential circuit. In this communication, a novel differential dipoles frequency reconfigurable antenna is presented. The objective of this paper is to design and analyze the differential dipoles frequency reconfigurable antenna where the RF switches (PIN diodes) are employed at the slots to achieve the frequency reconfigurable. By controlling the length and current distribution from the RF switch, the antenna can operate in dual frequency either at 2.60 GHz or 3.50 GHz. The configuration of the RF switch either to On or Off state will influence the odd mode impedance of the antenna we proposed. In this design, an ideal switch (copper strip line) is used based on the basic concept of the RF switch configuration. In Sects. 2 and 3, antenna design and frequency reconfiguration are explained, and the antenna performances in term of the frequency, odd mode reflection coefficient and the characteristic of the radiation pattern and radiation efficiency of simulations results are displayed. Section 4 is the study of the frequency reconfigurable characteristic. Finally, the conclusions are presented in Sect. 5.

2 Antenna Design

The configuration of the proposed antenna is shown in Fig. 1. The antenna consists of a pair of half-wave dipoles, which are connected in parallel through a coplanar stripline, what's more, two short striplines are added on the center of each coplanar stripline, they are placed on the up side of the substrate, a rectangular ground with a "H" shape slot on the center and four small cuts on the four angles which is placed on the down side of the substrate, the whole antenna is fed by differential signals through two coaxial cables, the two circular holes are driving points. As Fig. 1(a), it is the configuration of the whole antenna structure, four PIN diodes are places on the four slots of the two half-wave dipoles' ends on the up side of the antenna to achieve the frequency of reconfigurable characteristic, the resonance impedance of the proposed antenna can be controlled by the On or Off state of the four PIN diodes, the configuration of the up side and down side are shown in Fig. 1(b) and (c), respectively, the basic dimensions of the antenna is shown in Table 1.

The proposed antenna can change the frequency by changing the states of the PIN diodes loaded on the slots of the two half-wave dipoles' ends on the up side of the antenna. In simulation, we use four copper strip lines to replace the four diodes, when simulate the On state, the four copper strip linescan connect the four ends and the two half-wave dipoles, when simulate the Off state, the four copper strip lines are set as are deleted which means the four ends and the two half-wave dipoles are disconnected. While in the real prototype of the whole antenna, four identical DC bias circuits are applied to control the four PIN diodes. Figure 2 gives one DC bias circuit (the DC bias circuit of other diodes are the same as it), the bias circuit is implemented to control the state of the diode, the model of the diode is BAR64-02 V, the model of the inductances is LQG15HH220NJ02, and the reason of using these two inductances is to prevent the AC on the antenna and avoid influencing the radiation of the antenna. The proposed antenna can well realize the characteristic of frequency reconfiguration when the On/Off state of all diodesare properly controlled by the DC voltage.

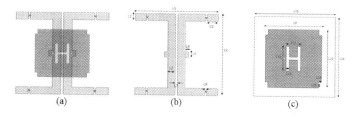

Fig. 1. Configuration of the antenna. (a) Configuration of the whole antenna structure. (b) Configuration of the up side. (c) Configuration of the down side.

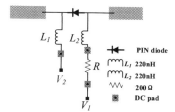

Fig. 2. DC bias circuit

Table 1. Basic dimensions of the antenna.

Name	Length(mm)	Name	Length(mm)
L1	55	L9	32.5
L2	5	L0	30.5
L3	6.5	L11	8.4
L4	3	L12	14
L5	4	L13	1.7
L6	55	L14	1.5
L7	2.1	L15	1.75
L8	1	L16	66

3 Simulation and Measured Results

The Novel Differential Dipoles Frequency Reconfigurable Antenna is simulated with the commercial software Ansoft Designer (HFSS) and fabricated on a FR4 substrate having a dielectric constant of 4.4, the loss tangent of 0.02, and the thickness of 1.6 mm. Figure 3 shows the prototype of the whole antenna, Figs. 4(a) and (b) show the simulated and measured odd mode reflection coefficient of the proposed antenna on two states, respectively. When all switches are Off, the measured frequency is 2.60 GHz, when all switches are On, the measured frequency is 3.50 GHz.

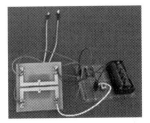

Fig. 3. Prototype of the whole antenna

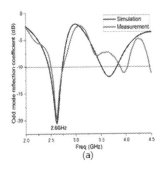 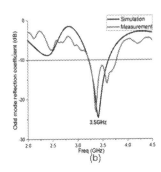

Fig. 4. Odd mode reflection coefficient of the antenna. (a) Off State at 2.60 GHz. (b) On state at 3.50 GHz.

Good agreement between the simulated and measured results is obtained except the influence caused by the material and fabrication tolerances.

Figures 5(a) and (b) show the simulated radiation patterns, it can be seen that good radiations in E-planes and H-planes are obtained. Also, the simulated results during On and Off states are shown in Table 2, the peak gain in 2.60 GHz band is 5.12 dBi, and that in 3.50 GHz band is 5.61 dBi, respectively, it can be observed that the antenna's radiation patterns and gains on two states are similar, and the antenna has an impedance bandwidth of 10.38% covering 2.44–2.71 GHz and an impedance bandwidth of 11.43% covering 3.31–3.71 GHz.

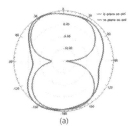 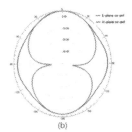

Fig. 5. Simulated radiation pattern of the antenna. (a) Off State at 2.60 GHz. (b) On state at 3.50 GHz.

Table 2. Simulated results during On and Off states.

Switches state	Off	On
Resonant frequency(GHz)	2.61	3.50
Odd mode reflection coefficient(dB)	−21.43	−24.52
Bandwidth(MHz)	270	400
Impedance bandwidth	10.38%	11.43%
Gain(dBi)	5.12	5.61

Figures 6(a) and (b) show the simulated radiation efficiency on two states, it can be seen that the radiation efficiency covering 2.4 GHz–2.8 GHz and 3.3 GHz–3.7 GHz are between 80%–90%.

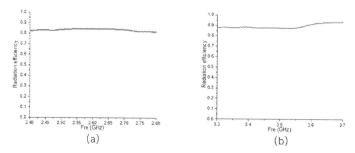

Fig. 6. Simulated radiation efficiency of the antenna. (a) Off State. (b) On state.

4   Study of the Frequency Reconfigurable Characteristic

Figure 7 shows the simulated results of surface current of the antenna.

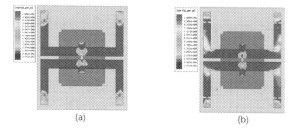

Fig. 7. Simulated results of surface current of the antenna. (a) Off state at 2.60 GHz. (b) On state at 3.50 GHz.

Figure 7(a) shows the electric current distribution of the proposed antenna in mode 1, all switches are off, the antenna operates at 2.60 GHz, it can be observed that the current distributes mostly on the arms of the dipoles, and the current can't flow through the PIN diodes. Figure 7(b) shows the electric current distribution of the proposed antenna in mode 2, all switches are on, the antenna operates at 3.50 GHz, the current mainly gathers nearby the ends of the dipoles, and the current can flow through the PIN diodes.

The state of the four PIN diodes have an influence on the impedance of the dipoles through changing its construction, as we know, if the construction changes, the impedance of it also changes correspondingly, so it is necessary to design a feeding network which can solve the impedance dismatching problem caused by the change of the radiation construction. The "H" shape slot on the center of the rectangular ground is to lengthen the electric current path and separate the differential signals, in addition, the four small rectangular cuts on four angles of the rectangular ground on the down side and the two short striplines added on the center of each coplanar stripline on the up side are to adjust the impedance matching of the antenna. In conclusion, these designations enable the antenna to operate well at two states with just one feeding network, and achieve the frequency reconfigurable characteristic.

5 Conclusion

In this letter, a Novel Differential Dipoles Frequency Reconfigurable Antenna is designed and simulated. By controlling four PIN diodes' On and Off state on the four slots on the end of the dipoles, frequency reconfigurable characteristic is achieved. The proposed antenna can work either at 2.60 GHz or 3.50 GHz and have similar radiation patterns and gains at two states, and good agreement between simulation and measurement results of odd mode reflection coefficient is achieved. Since all of the structures are printed on the one substrate, it is of low cost and compact size and can be fabricated easily and very suitable to be integrated with RF front-end circuits. The proposed antenna is suitable for wireless communication applications, and the operating band can be controlled easily to meet different requirements of practical applications, like satellite broadcast, LTE and Wimax.

Acknowledgments. Our thanks to ACM SIGCHI for allowing us to modify templates they had developed.

References

1. Ramli, N., Ali, M.T., Yusof, A.L., Ya'acob, N.: Frequency reconfigurable stacked patch microstrip antenna (FRSPMA) for LTE and WiMAX applications. In: 2013 International Conference on Computing, Management and Telecommunications (ComManTel), pp. 55–59, 21 March 2013
2. Nasrabadi, E., Rezaei, P., Saghayi, S.: Design of compact frequency reconfigurable antenna with defected ground structure for UWB applications. In: Antennas and Propagation Society International Symposium (APSURSI), pp. 1258–1259. IEEE, July 2014
3. Varsha, J., Sumi, M.: A novel pattern and frequency reconfigurable antenna. In: Inventive Computation Technologies (ICICT), vol. 3, pp. 1–5, 26 January 2017
4. Han, L., Zhang, W., Chen, X., Han, G., Ma, R.: Design of compact differential dual-frequency antenna with stacked patches. IEEE Trans. Antennas Propag. **58**(4), 1387–1392 (2010)

5. Xiao-kuan, Z., Chao, Z., Long, Z., Chen-xin, Z.: Design of a compact differential dual-frequency antenna. In: IEEE Conference Publications, pp. 207–210, 07 November 2013
6. Li, W.-A., Tu, Z.-H., Chu, Q.-X., Wu, X.-H.: Differential stepped-slot UWB antenna with common-mode suppression and dual sharp-selectivity notched bands. IEEE Antennas Wirel. Propag. Lett. **15**, 1120–1123 (2015)
7. Liu, N.-W., Zhu, L., Choi, W.-W., Zhang, J.-D.: A novel differential-fed patch antenna on stepped-impedance resonator with enhanced bandwidth under dual-resonance. IEEE Antennas Propag. Soc. **64**, 4618–4625 (2016)
8. Tu, Z.-H., Li, W.-A., Chu, Q.-X.: Single-layer differential CPW-fed notch-band tapered-slot UWB antenna. IEEE Antennas Wirel. Propag. Lett. **13**, 1296–1299 (2014)

Classification of Network Game Traffic Using Machine Learning

Yuning Dong[(✉)], Mi Zhang, and Rui Zhou

College of Telecommunications and Information Engineering,
Nanjing University of Posts and Telecommunications, Nanjing, China
{dongyn,1015010409}@njupt.edu.cn, zhourui7891@163.com

Abstract. With the rapid development of the Internet, different kinds of network games are emerging. The classification of network game flow is important to improve the quality of service. In this paper, we propose an approach to identify network game traffic. It firstly filters the game traffic data based on protocol filtering and IP filtering to reduce background noise as much as possible. Then, to remove irrelevant and redundant features, Pearson correlation coefficient and information gain ratio are used as the criteria to choose features. By analyzing various statistical features of game traffic, it is found that employing the three features, ratio of inbound to outbound data packets, downlink packet size information entropy and downlink Packets per second, is able to yield better classification performance. The experimental results show that the proposed method is feasible and can achieve higher accuracy than an existing method.

Keywords: Classification of network game traffic · Statistical features
IP filtering · SVM

1 Introduction

Accurate identification and classification of network application traffics is very important for network resource management and QoS (quality of service) support. Nowadays, mainstream online games include MMORPG (Massively Multi-Player Online Role Playing Game), FPS (First-Personal Shooting Game) and RTS (Real-time Strategy Game). The variety of game types and server structures make it a huge challenge to identify game traffics. Typical classification approaches [1] of multimedia traffic include port-based, DPI (Deep Packet Inspection)-based and flow statistical feature-based methods.

With the development of machine learning algorithms, classification algorithms [2] such as decision trees [3], Bayesian classification, neural networks, K-Means, C5.0 are widely used in the field of network traffic identification. Meanwhile, researchers constantly look for new features to effectively and accurately identify new applications including online games.

In this paper, we propose a new framework of network game traffic classification, which uses protocol filtering and IP filtering to preprocess raw data and explores new

© Springer Nature Singapore Pte Ltd. 2018
H. Yuan et al. (Eds.): GSKI 2017, CCIS 848, pp. 134–145, 2018.
https://doi.org/10.1007/978-981-13-0893-2_15

features for effective recognition of game flows. An SVM [4] (Support Vector Machine) algorithm is adopted to carry out classification experiments.

The main contributions of this paper are three folds: we propose to filter game flow data based on IP subnet for the first time, which can effectively remove background noise. In addition, Pearson correlation coefficient and information gain ratio are used as the criteria to choose features. Thirdly, our analysis shows that the ratio of inbound to outbound data packets, downlink packet size information entropy, and downlink PPS (Packets per second) are suitable for the recognition of game traffics, and can achieve better performance than existing methods.

2   Related Work

The recognition of game flow in transport layer was introduced in [5, 6]. They divided network games into the TCP-based applications and UDP-based applications based on different transport protocol. Various statistical features including PPS, bps, the average packet size, the maximum/minimum packet size and MODE, are used to analyze the P2P and the C/S model features. HMM (Hidden Markov Model) [7, 8] was used to identify HTTP traffic, QQ (an instant message application), and other video and audio streams, using two statistical features IPT and package size. "Thin client" game was studied in [9], where end users simply upload instructions, and all operations are executed on the server. The packet size, IPT and bit rate were employed for data statistics on the downlink and uplink respectively. The authors found that there are great differences in the three types of characteristics of thin client games compared with live, traditional games, video and other applications.

Online games classification at the packet level was studied in [10], i.e., inter-arrival time and packet size. Based on the supervised machine learning, the classification of team member roles in the multiplayer game Dota2 was introduced in [11]. The authors used feature selection and analyzed the classification effect of different supervised learning algorithms. The difference [12] between the game applications (Minecraft and Quake 3 Urban Terror) and audio, video streaming was studied in different scenarios. The authors employed five different supervised learning classifiers to classify these four applications. Experimental results show that latency and packet loss are of significance for game applications.

3   Data Acquiring and Filtering of Game Flow

WireShark (http://wiki.wireshark.org/) is used to grab the game flow data in a campus network and for each game application we capture 60 data flows while each flow lasts 30 min. Before obtaining data, we close all other applications to reduce interference. Selected games are Fantasy Westward Journey, against the war, furnace stone legend, LOL, DOTA2 (http://xyq.163.com/; http://nz.qq.com/; http://www.hearthstone.com.cn/home/; http://lol.qq.com/; http://www.DOTA2.com.cn/) and DOTA, as listed in Table 1.

Table 1. Game description

Game name	Issue time	Game category	Transport protocol
Furnace stone legend	2014	CARDS	TCP
Fantasy Westward Journey	2003	MMORG	TCP
Against the war	2011	FPS	UDP
DOTA (11 against Platform)	2011	RTS	TCP
LOL	2011	RTS	UDP
DOTA2	2014	RTS	UDP

In order to acquire the real data for experiment, we pre-processed the raw data with following steps: (1) removal of data without interaction with the host IP; (2) Protocol filtering. According to [5], transport layer protocol is used to filter the game traffic; (3) IP filtering. Using these methods to preprocess the raw data, it is found that there still exist a small number of background packets. In order to remove these packets, we propose a new filtering method based on IP subnet.

The Pareto principle is widely used in social science and enterprise management science. It is also known as the twenty-eighty law, such as the 20% people occupy 80% wealth of society in social science, in psychology 20% people possess 80% of human knowledge. According to this theory, when only the game application is running, a small number of IP sub networks should contain the majority of data packets. From the statistics of the IP addresses in the six types of games interacting with the host IP, it is found that the IP addresses of each network game are mainly distributed in the same subnet. By descending order on the basis of the number of packets contained in each IP subnet, the results are shown in Fig. 1. As shown in Fig. 1, let the horizontal coordinate be X and the longitudinal coordinate be Y; it manifests that, for the IP subnets arranged as above, the percentage of subset in X contains the number of packets in the data stream with a percentage of Y.

We can see that the curves rise rapidly when the percentage of packets is less than 90%, which means thatthe main IP subnets contain majority of game traffic data. In this case, the percentage of subnets is less than 12%, which means that a small number of IP subnets appear at a higher frequency. The data appeared in the less seen IP sub networks can be seen as noise data and will be removed. Therefore, 90% and 12% are chosen as thresholds for percentage of total packets and proportion of IP subsets respectively.

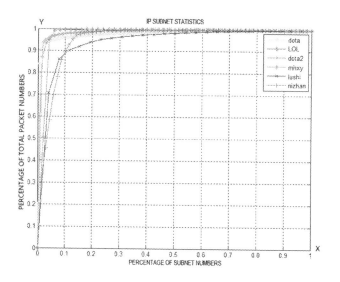

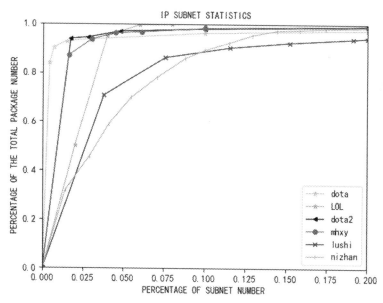

Fig. 1. The main IP subnet statistics

4 Flow Feature Selection

In this paper, we adopt the method of feature selection based on correlation, and use multiple correlation indexes to judge synthetically. The combination of the Pearson correlation coefficient [13] and the information gain ratio [14] are used to as the criteria to evaluate the correlation among the variables in feature selection, as detailed below.

4.1   Pearson Correlation Coefficient (PCC)

The Pearson correlation coefficient [13] is a simple way to reflect the relationship between features and class variables. The PCC is used to reflect the linear correlation between the two variables of the statistic. For two variables X and Y, the PCC is calculated as follows:

$$p_{x,y} = \frac{cov(X,Y)}{s_X s_Y} = \frac{\sum_{i=1}^{n}(x_i - \bar{x})(y_i - \bar{y})}{\sqrt{\sum_{i=1}^{n}(x_i - \bar{x}) * \sum_{i=1}^{n}(y_i - \bar{y})}} \tag{1}$$

The PCC is in the range of -1 to 1. When the value is 1, that two variables have complete positive correlation; for the value of -1, two variables have complete negative correlation; for value of 0, two variables are irrelevant. In addition, the PCC has certain application condition: the two independent variables generally obey normal or nearly normal distribution. According to [12], the skewness coefficient (SC) and kurtosis coefficients (KC) are usually used as the indices to judge whether the variable is in accordance with the normal distribution. Generally the absolute value of the skewness coefficient (SC) less than 1 can be considered close to the normal distribution. For a variable X, the SC is the third-order normalization moment of the variable X.

4.2   Information Gain Ratio (IGR)

The statistical features of game flow and corresponding class labels are integrated to form an $M * N$ dimensional matrix S. In the matrix S, the first $N-1$ columns represent $N-1$ different flow features $(A_1, A_2,.., A_{N-1})$and the Nth column is the class C. According to [14], IGR of any feature A_q and C can be calculated by Eq. (2):

$$G(C \mid A_q) = \frac{H(C) + H(A_q) - H(C,A_q)}{H(C)} \tag{2}$$

where, $H(C)$ is the information entropy of class C, $H(C, A_q)$ is the mutual information entropy of feature A_q and C, they can be calculated by the following formula.

$$H(C) = -\sum_{i=1}^{M} p(c_i)log_2 p(c_i) \tag{3}$$

$$H(C,A_q) = -\sum_{i=1}^{M}\sum_{j=1}^{N} p(c_i a_j)log_2 p(c_i a_j) \tag{4}$$

The $G(C|A_q)$ is in the range of 0 to 1. When the value is 0, the feature A_q and class C is irrelevant, and when the value is 1, the feature A_q is closely related to class C. In the real circumstances, we usually need to discretize continuous features using the results of [15].

4.3   Correlation Coefficients

In the real circumstances, we usually need to discretize continuous features using the results of [15]. In general, the degree of correlation can be divided into three levels: 0 to 0.4 for weak correlation, 0.4 to 0.7 for moderate correlation, 0.7 to 1 for significant correlation. In this paper, the thresholds are set to be 0.4 and 0.7 for irrelevant features and redundant features respectively. PCC and IGR are used to as correlation coefficients. However, it is found that the PCC is not consistent with the correlation index of IGR in some cases. In this work, a lot of experiments show that only when two variables meet the applicable condition of PCC, using the PCC as an indicator can improve recognition performance. When the two variables do not meet the applicable conditions of PCC, using IGR as an indicator can improve the classification accuracy.

By analysing various statistical features based on the above methods, we find that the use of three features, ratio of inbound to outbound data packets, downlink packet size information entropy and downlink PPS, can achieve higher accuracy. These features are defined as follows:

(1) *Ratio of inbound to outbound data packets (RIOP)*. The ratio of the total number of downlink data packets after filtering to the total number of uplink data packets;
(2) *Entropy of packet size downlink (EPSD)*. The information entropy of the downlink packet size.;
(3) *Downlink PPS (DPPS)*. The average number of downlink packets transmitted in data stream per second.

The corresponding feature maps are shown in Fig. 2 and 3, where mhxy is Fantasy Westward Journey, nizhan represents Against the war and lushi is on behalf of Hearthstone legend. Using the combination of DPPS and EPSD, it is shown that the four games Fantasy Westward Journey, furnace stone legend, LOL and DOTA2 have relatively concentrated distribution with less overlap. DOTA and Against the war need to use the combination of RIOP and DPPS to identify as shown in Fig. 3.

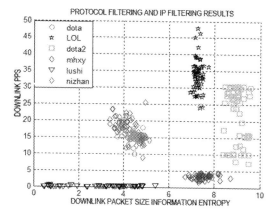

Fig. 2. Distribution maps EPSD – DPPS after protocol filtering and IP filtering

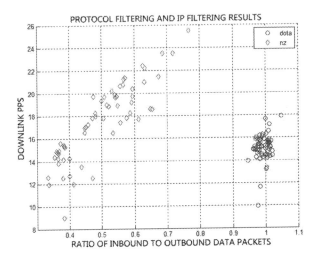

Fig. 3. Distribution maps RIOP – DPPS after protocol filtering and IP filtering

5   Experimental Results

This paper proposes a new framework, including four main steps: acquiring data, filtering data using protocol filtering and IP filtering, feature selection and classification result. The performances are compared with the method of [5].

5.1   Support Vector Machine

SVM [4] is a binary classification algorithm, which divide the feature space into two categories based on machine learning method. In SVM, the input data is (x_i, y_i) where x_i represents eigenvalue and y_i indicates the genus (-1 or 1). According to the distribution of feature points, SVM algorithm is divided into linearly separable and inseparable cases.

(1) *Linear Separable*

The formula of the hyper plane is defined as,

$$w \cdot x + b = 0 \tag{5}$$

The formula of classifier is defined as,

$$w \cdot x + b \geq 1$$
$$w \cdot x + b \leq -1 \tag{6}$$

where w is the weight vector and b a fixed value.

(2) *Linear Inseparable*

Because of the existence of noise, the feature space cannot be classified by a linear function. So the relaxation variable $\xi_i \geq 0$ is introduced, and the formula of classifier is defined as,

$$y_i(w \cdot x_i + b) - 1 + \xi_i \geq 0 \, i = 1, 2, 3 \ldots \tag{7}$$

For the above two cases, SVM aims to increase the distance between the two categories and reduce the classification error as much as possible. So it can be deduced that (w, ξ_i) should meet the following constraints:

$$\min(\frac{1}{2} \parallel w \parallel^2 + C \sum_{j=1}^{M} \xi_i) \tag{8}$$

where C is the penalty factor, $C \geq 0$, in the case of linearly separable, $C = 0$.

LIBSVM is used to implement SVM, which can achieve better performance for multi-class recognition.

5.2 Experimental Results

In the experiment, we select 30 data flow samples out of 60 randomly as a training set and the remaining 30 data flow samples as a test set. Each feature combination is tested for 30 times, and the final results are the average of 30 runs. Recall and precision are commonly used to reflect the completeness and accuracy of the classification, which can be calculated by:

$$Precision = \frac{TP}{TP + FP} \tag{9}$$

$$Recall = \frac{TP}{TP + FN} \tag{10}$$

where, TP is the True Positive; FP the False Positive; FN the False Negative.

F-measure is used to weigh and average recall and precision as follows:

$$F - measure = \frac{2 * precission * recall}{precission + recall} \tag{11}$$

Experiments with different feature combinations and methods are performed, and the following results are obtained:

(1) Using the IP filtering and selecting EPSD, DPPS and RIOP as features combination, we find that better recognition performance can be achieved by adding IP filtering. Meanwhile, the three features can accurately identify the game flow and the three performance metrics of recall, precision and F-measure can all reach to 99% or more.

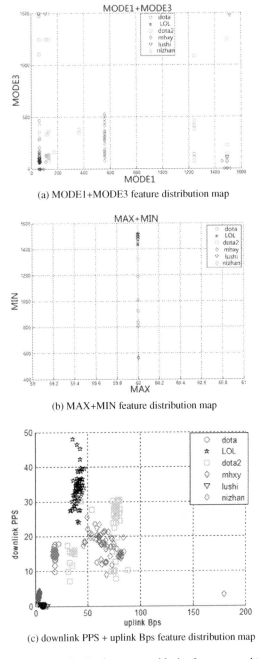

(a) MODE1+MODE3 feature distribution map

(b) MAX+MIN feature distribution map

(c) downlink PPS + uplink Bps feature distribution map

Fig. 4. Features distribution maps with the features used in [5]

(2) Extract the features used in [5], including MIN (minimum packet size), MAX (maximum packet size), downlink PPS, Bps (uplink bps) and MODE, MODE = {MODE1, MODE2, MODE3}. Where the MODE1 is the most frequent packet size value while MODE2 is the second highest one and MODE3 is the third highest one. The features of PPS and Bps are respectively selected from the downlink PPS and uplink bps. The corresponding feature distribution map as shown in Fig. 4. From (a) and (b), it can be seen that the distribution of the same game application is not concentrated, and the feature distribution of different games overlap a lot. Figure 4(c) shows that downlink PPS and uplink bps of different games distribute relatively separate while the distribution of the same game is relatively concentrated. However, we can clearly find the distribution of DOTA2 has a large span and more overlap with other games.

Using LIBSVM, experimental results are obtained as shown in Fig. 5, where left column and right column respectively correspond to experimental results from [5] and

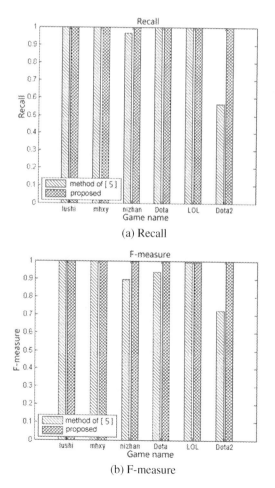

(a) Recall

(b) F-measure

Fig. 5. Performance comparisons between the method of [5]

the proposed method. It is seen that the performance is poorer when the seven features applied in [5] are used to identify game flow.

In summary, experimental results show that: (1) by adding the IP filtering, the recognition performance is improved. Using the proposed three features for game flow recognition, recall, precision and F-measure are close to 100%, some of the games can reach 100%; (2) Compared with the seven features applied in [5], the accuracy is higher by use of RIOP, EPSD and DPPS these three features.

6   Conclusion

This paper presents a new approach to classification of network game traffic, which uses protocol filtering and IP filtering for raw data pre-processing to reduce the interference. The experimental results show that this method is feasible and effective. In addition, feature selection is employed to remove irrelevant and redundant features in the classification process. This paper uses the PCC and the IGR as the criteria to choose features. It is found that the three features, EPSD, RIOP and DPPS, are suitable for the game traffic recognition and can achieve higher precision, recall and F-measure values than an existing method. For the future work, we will study online recognition of game traffic and test the feasibility of this method for online recognition. In addition, it is necessary to capture more data from different games, so that we can apply this approach to classify other types of game applications.

Acknowledgments. The authors would like to thank National Natural Science Foundation of China (No. 61271233) and the HIRP program of Huawei Technology Co. Ltd to sponsor this work in part.

References

1. Dainotti, A., Pescape, A., Claffy, K.: Issues and future directions in traffic classification. IEEE Netw. **26**, 35–40 (2012)
2. Deebalakshmi, R., Jyothi, V.L.: A survey of classification algorithms for network traffic. In: Second International Conference on Science Technology Engineering and Management (ICONSTEM) IEEE, pp. 151–156 (2016)
3. Nair, L.M., Sajeev, G.P.: Internet traffic classification by aggregating correlated decision tree classifier. In: 7th International Conference on Computational Intelligence, Modelling and Simulation (CIMSim 2015), pp. 135–140 (2015)
4. Jiang, D., Long, L.: P2P traffic identification research based on the SVM. In: Wireless and Optical Communication Conference (WOCC), IEEE, pp. 683–686 (2013)
5. Han, Y.T., Park, H.S.: Game traffic classification using statistical characteristics at the transport layer. ETRI J. **32**, 22–32 (2010)
6. Han, Y.T., Park, H.S.:UDP based P2P Game Traffic Classification with Transport Layer Behaviors. In: 14th Asia-Pacific Conference on Communications, pp. 1–5 (2008)
7. Mu, X., Wu, W.: A parallelized network traffic classification based on hidden markov model. In: International Conference on Cyber-Enabled Distributed Computing and Knowledge Discovery IEEE Computer Society, pp. 107–112 (2011)

8. Maia, J.E.B., Filho, R.H.: Internet traffic classification using a hidden markov model. In: 10th International Conference on Hybrid Intelligent Systems, pp. 37–42 (2010)
9. Claypool, M., Finkel, D., Grant, A., Solano, M.: Thin to win? network performance analysis of the OnLive thin client game system. In: 11th Annual Workshop on Network and Systems Support for Games, pp. 1–6 (2012)
10. Cheand, X., Ip, B.: Packet-level traffic analysis of online games from the genre characteristics perspective. J. Netw. Comput. Appl. **35**, 240–252 (2012)
11. Eggert, C., Herrlich, M., Smeddinck, J., Malaka, R.: Classification of player roles in the team-based multi-player game Dota 2. In: Chorianopoulos, K., Divitini, M., Hauge, J.B., Jaccheri, L., Malaka, R. (eds.) ICEC 2015. LNCS, vol. 9353, pp. 112–125. Springer, Cham (2015). https://doi.org/10.1007/978-3-319-24589-8_9
12. Middleton, S.E., Modafferi, S.: Scalable classification of QoS for real-time interactive applications from IP traffic measurements. Comput. Netw. **107**, 121–132 (2016)
13. Neto, A.M., et al.: Pearson's correlation coefficient for discarding redundant information in real time autonomous navigation system. In: IEEE International Conference on Control Applications IEEE, pp. 426–431 (2007)
14. Chen, Z., Peng, L., Zhao, S., Zhang, L., Jing, S.: Feature selection toward optimizing internet traffic behavior identification. In: Sun, X.-h., Qu, W., Stojmenovic, I., Zhou, W., Li, Z., Guo, H., Min, G., Yang, T., Wu, Y., Liu, L. (eds.) ICA3PP 2014. LNCS, vol. 8631, pp. 631–644. Springer, Cham (2014). https://doi.org/10.1007/978-3-319-11194-0_56
15. Yuan, J., et al.: T-drive: driving directions based on taxi trajectories. In: Proceedings of the 18th SIGSPATIAL International Conference on Advances in Geographic Information Systems, pp. 99–108 (2010)

How to Insure Reliability and Delay in Multi-controller Deployment

Hongyan Cui[1]([✉]), Tao Yu[2], Lili Zheng[1], Tao Wang[1],
Guoping Zhang[3], and Zongguo Xia[4]

[1] Key Laboratory of Network System Architecture and Convergence,
Beijing University of Posts and Telecommunications, Beijing 100876, China
cuihy@bupt.edu.cn, 811539149@qq.com
[2] Institute of Network Science and Cyberspace,
Tsinghua University, Beijing 100084, China
[3] The China Academy of Corporate Governance and Business School,
Nankai University, Tianjin 300071, China
[4] University of Massachusetts, Beijing University of Posts
and Telecommunications, Boston, USA

Abstract. In this paper, we researched the multi-controller deployment problem. Because the switch is completely dependent on the controller, if a forwarding plane failure happens, it may lead to communication interruption between the switch and its controller, the switch will become a "headless fly", so ensuring the reliability of the communication between the switch and its controller is necessary. Because the controller and its management within the domain of the exchange of communications will be very frequent, we want to ensure reliability while making the delay between the controller and the switch become short. Therefore, our algorithm mainly considerate the following two aspects: (1) Increase the communication reliability between the switch node and the controller node. (2) Minimize the delay between the controller and the switch, that is, minimize the average delay between the controller and the switches which under its management. The concrete implementation is divided into the following steps: First, model the network, consider the stability of the forwarding plane and the delay between the switch and the controller to establish the optimization target. And then propose a two-stage algorithm. Finally, perform the simulation on the real network topology. The results of the test show that the solution is working and functional.

Keywords: SDN · Multi-controller · Reliability · Delay

1 Introduction

In a large-scale network, one logically centralized controller cannot handle the whole network traffic and it will become network bottleneck. Therefore, multiple distributed controllers should be allocated in different regions of the network.

© Springer Nature Singapore Pte Ltd. 2018
H. Yuan et al. (Eds.): GSKI 2017, CCIS 848, pp. 146–157, 2018.
https://doi.org/10.1007/978-981-13-0893-2_16

In the SDN distributed architecture, the controller needs to complete two parts of the function:

(1) Between the controller and the switch, the controller needs to manage all the switches within the domain and maintain the local network topology state;
(2) Between the controllers, the controller needs to interact with other controllers to achieve the entire network's connection.

Therefore, multi-controller architecture is mainly concerned with two aspects: the extra delay between the controllers and the rapid growth of information sharing between controllers. The extra controller latency is primarily the communication overhead between controllers to establish flow tables or make other controller decisions. In order to reduce the delay between the controllers, all controllers can share the arrival event information through a distributed storage system. However, this will result in a sharp increase in shared information, for the shared information includes not only the topology information, but also the arrival of the flow, link failure and the entire network traffic congestion information of the entire network. To reduce the load of shared information, Koponen T, etc. proposes a concept of a controller and its switches within the management domain as a virtual node [1]. This method can effectively hide the underlying topology information.

More specifically, a physical network is partitioned into multiple logical networks, each of which is managed by a controller that knows exactly all of the underlying topology information within its managed logical area, when communicating with other controllers, the controller doesn't need to know the concrete network managed by other controllers, but to treat other controller-managed network abstraction as a logical node. Each controller and its managed network is a logical node, we use the logical nodes to achieve the communication between different partitions, such as routing and so on, as shown in Fig. 1.

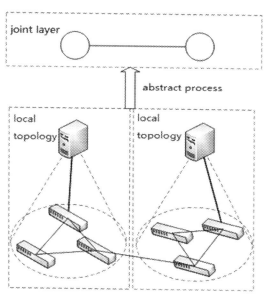

Fig. 1. The local topology is abstracted as a virtual node.

2 Related Work

Reference [2] indicated that one logically centralized controller cannot handle the whole network traffic and it will become network bottleneck. Therefore, multiple distributed controllers should be allocated in different regions of the network.

Reference [3] investigated multi-controller placement problem for software-defined network aiming at minimum the propagation latency between switches and associated controllers. Distinct from the standard clustering-based partition approaches, a modified exemplar-based clustering method based on affinity propagation is presented to address the problem.

Reference [4] proposed a dynamic and self-learning schedule method (DSL), for the reliability of controllers in a software defined network (SDN). This method is original and easy to deploy, and optimizes the combination of multiple controllers.

Reference [5] focused on two specific questions: given a topology, how many controllers are needed, and where should they go? The paper examined fundamental limits to control plane propagation latency on an upcoming Internet2 production deployment, then expand our scope to over 100 publicly available WAN topologies. It verified that the answers depend on the topology.

Reference [6] proposed POCO, a framework for Pareto-based Optimal COntroller placement that provides operators with Pareto optimal placements with respect to different performance metrics.

Reference [7] defined a capacitated controller placement problem (CCPP), taking into consideration the load of controllers, and introduce an efficient algorithm to solve the problem.

Reference [8] presented a metric to characterize the reliability of SDN control networks, and several placement algorithms are developed. Their approaches can significantly improve the reliability of SDN control networks without introducing unacceptable latencies.

Reference [9] proposed a mathematical model for the controller placement problem in SDN. More precisely, given a set of switches that must be managed by the controller (s), the model simultaneously determines the optimal number, location, and type of controller(s) as well as the interconnections between all the network elements.

Reference [10] proposed a solution that considers at the same time three critical objectives for the optimal placement of controllers: (i) the latency and communication overhead between switches and controllers; (ii) the latency and communication overhead between controllers; (iii) the guarantee of load balancing between controllers.

Reference [11] proposed construction method of more dependable virtual switches focusing on bi-connectivity and reduction of shared information using the virtual switches.

Reference [12] proposed a framework for deploying multiple controllers within a WAN. The framework dynamically adjusts the number of active controllers and delegates each controller with a subset of Openflow switches according to network dynamics while ensuring minimal flow setup time and communication overhead.

3   Formulation

An undirected graph $G = (V, E)$ represents a physical network, which V represents a set of switches, E representing a set of links between switches in the network. The distance $d(u, v)$ between the switch u and the switch v is the shortest path between the switch u and the switch v $(u, v \in V)$.

Controller set $C = \{c_1, c_2, \ldots, c_k\}$ divided the network into k sub-maps, each sub-map corresponds to a controller. The switch collection is $\lambda = \{G_1, G_2, \ldots, G_k\}$, $G_i = (V_i, E_i)$ represents the local network topology that controlled by the controller c_i. We use the in-band control, that is, each controller only connections to one switch in physical. So the controller c_i is deployed at the location of its directly connected switch. For ease of description, we consider the controller and its directly attached switches as a unit. $G^c = (V^c, E^c)$ represents that each controller and its local network topology is abstracted as a control node, V^c corresponds to a set of control nodes, E^c represents the link set of each control domain. $I(v_i, c_i)(v_i \in V_i)$ indicates whether the node v_i can reach the controller c_i through the local network topology. If the node $v \in V_i$ can't reach the controller node c_i through E_i, $I(v, c_i) = 0$. Conversely, if the node can reach the controller node c_i through E_i, $I(v, c_i) = 1$. If link e fails, the number of nodes that are unreachable is $I(e)$. When link e fails, the number of affected links between the virtual node and another virtual node is $AP(e)$.

Object to:

$$\min \left(\frac{\sum\limits_{e \in E} I(e)}{\sum\limits_{v \in V} \min\limits_{c \in C} d(v, c)} \right) \tag{1}$$

Subject to:

$$\cup_{i=1}^{k} V_i = V; \tag{2}$$

$$\cup_{i=1}^{k} E_i + E^c = E \tag{3}$$

$$G_i \cap G_j = \Phi, \forall i \neq j, i, j \in k \tag{4}$$

$$I(e) = \sum\limits_{V_i \in V} \sum\limits_{v \in V_i} I(v, c_i) \tag{5}$$

$$totalAP = \sum\limits_{e \in E} AP(e) \tag{6}$$

Equation (2) and (3) indicate that the subdivided sub-network must cover the entire network; Eq. (4) represents that one node and link can only allocate one subnet; The formula (5) is the number of switches which disconnected to the controller when a single link failure occurs. Equation (6) represents the affected links between controllers when a single link failure occurs.

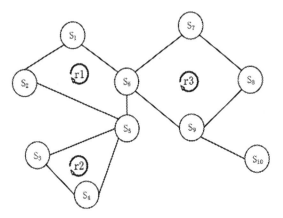

Fig. 2. A sample of decompose algorithm

4   Algorithm

In order to meet the requirements of reliability and average delay at the same time, we propose the ring based k-medoids algorithm.

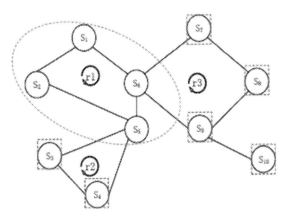

Fig. 3. Ring decomposition (1)

The ring based k-medoids algorithm is divided into two stages. In the first stage, we met the requirement of reliability, divided the network into a number small clusters and isolated points. In the second stage, we improved the k-medoids initial point selection scheme, using the ring based k-medoids algorithm to cluster the small clusters of the first stage to ensure the average delay.

In the first stage, we divided the switches into a number of small clusters according to the physical topology. As shown in Fig. 2, each node represents a switch, the lines represent the physical links between switches.

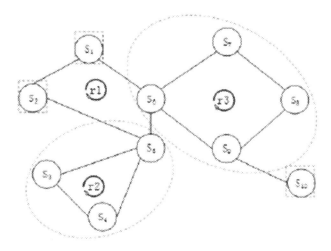

Fig. 4. Ring decomposition (2)

There are three basic rings in the network: r_1, r_2, r_3. In the multi-controllers deployment scene, each switch only be managed by one controller. So when we divide them, each node can only belongs to one domain. But the three basic rings in the figure have a common vertex, so part of them need to be split. There are two forms to split as follows.

The network has many rings, and rings may have common vertexes, once choose a ring, the others then will be split. As shown in Fig. 4, if we choose r_3, then we need to split r_1. Nodes left in r_1 are 1, 2, 5. Node 5 can be contained in r_2, while node 1 and node 2 cannot belong to any other rings, so we called node 1 and node 2 as unreliable nodes UR(r_3). To achieve the reliability of the network as much as possible, we need to select the solution with least unreliable nodes. As shown in Fig. 3, r_1 is retained, r_2, r_3 are being split, and the figure is divided into 7 parts, with 6 unreliable nodes. While in Fig. 4, we can keep r_2, r_3 at the meantime, only to split r_1, and the figure is divided into 5 parts, with 3 unreliable nodes. The solution with less unreliable nodes has a better reliability, so choose the solution in Fig. 4 can ensure a better fault tolerance.

If we choose to retain r_1, only the nodes on the adjacent ring will be affected. So we only need to compare the number of unreliable nodes caused by retaining r_1, we defined it as IncreUR(r_i). Pseudo code description of the algorithm above shown in Table 1:

After the decomposition process, we get a set of rings λ and a collection of isolated points I. Given the K value, we will use the distance dimension to aggregate these clusters.

In order to illustrate our algorithm better, we first introduce the standard k-medoids algorithm. The standard k-medoids algorithm use Euclidean distance, but in the actual network, the two nodes may not directly connected, so we use the shortest path to represent the distance between the nodes (Tables 2 and 3).

Table 1. Cluster algorithm based on ring

Input:$G = (V, E)$ V is the node in the network, E is the link between nodes
N_r is the collection that composed by ring r and its adjacent rings
Set after decomposition $\lambda \leftarrow \Phi$
Initialization: Using the depth-first algorithm to find all the sets of rings C, and all nodes that do not belong to any of the set I
While $C \neq \emptyset$ do
Select the ring r_i that with the minimum IncreUR(r_i)
$\lambda \leftarrow r$
Delete the rings containing node r_i in C
Add the IncreUR(r_i) to I
End while
Return $\lambda \& I$

Table 2. The standard k-medoids algorithm

Input: $G = (N, E)$ k
Step 1: Initialize the k classes and randomly select k nodes as the center of k classes
$C = \cup(c_1, c_2, ..., c_k)$
Step 2: The nodes $v \in V$ are assigned to one of the classes according to the shortest path
If
$$d(v, c_i) < d(v, c_j) \forall j \in \{1, 2, ..., k\}, i \neq j \ v \in R_i$$
Step 3: Update the center of each class $C' = \cup (c'_1, c'_2, ..., c'_k)$, so that the sum of the shortest path of the points in each class to its center is minimum.
Step 4: Repeat steps 2 and 4 until the center point of each class no longer changes

K-medoids is sensitive to the selection of the initial point, which may lead to a local optimal solution. The general use of k-medoids will run several times to find one of the best solution.

We use another new initialization scheme, we first randomly selected a point as the first clustering center. For each element in the set to be clustered (possibly a ring, or a node), calculate the distance between the element and the center of the selected cluster, assign the element to the nearest cluster center. And then recalculate the center point of each divided subclass, select the farthest element from the center of the subclass as the next cluster center, repeat the above steps until k cluster centers are selected.

Table 3. The polymerization process based on k-medoids

Input: $G = (N, E)$ring sets λ and I, k, ρ

$\ell = \{r_1, r_2 ..., r_n\}$ $I = \{n_1, n_2, ..., n_m\}$

Step 1: Initialize collections that require clustering, $Y \leftarrow \{\lambda, I\}, C \leftarrow \emptyset$

Step 2: A node is randomly selected from Y as the first center

Step 3: Perform the k-medoids algorithm described above and find the actual center point of the entire networkc_1', finding the furthest node c_2' from c_1' as the second center point. $C = \{c_1', c_2'\}$

Step 4: Perform the k-medoids algorithm described above and find the actual center point of the sub-networkc_1', c_2', selecting the node that is farthest from the actual center point in the sub-network as the next node.

Step 5: Perform the step 4, until the network is divided into k sub-networks.

---

5   Evaluation

We choose the real network topology Internet2 OS3E to evaluate our ring-based k-medoids algorithm. In the experiment, we used the inband deployment and assume that all switches physically connected to the controller. Finally, we validate the reliability and the average delay performance of our algorithm in the event of a single link breakdown.

The topology diagram of OS3E is shown in Fig. 5, it is composed of 37 city nodes, we got the city's latitude and longitude information, tag the city's node information and the connection state by using GML (Geography Markup Language). By analyzing the simulation results, we expect to answer the two problems as follows: given a network topology, the impact of the controllers' number on the performance of our optimized target; and our algorithm's performance on reliability and delay. In this section, we will compare our algorithm to the standard k-medoids algorithm in reference. The standard k-medoids select the initial points randomly, while random initial points may cause only partial optimization. So we run the standard k-medoids algorithm 100 times, and take the average.

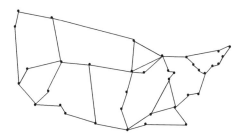

Fig. 5. OS3E topology

We selected the network topology information based on the GML mark, it only provides the nodes' latitude and longitude and the connection state between nodes. The distance between nodes is calculated by the latitude and longitude. We use the way provided by Google Maps to calculate:

The distance between Node $(Lat_1, Lung_1)$ and Node $(Lat_2, Lung_2)$ is:

$$S = 2\arcsin\sqrt{\sin^2\frac{a}{2} + \cos(Lat_1) * \cos(Lat_2) * \sin^2\frac{b}{2}} * 6378.137 \qquad (7)$$

In the formula above, a $= Lat_1 - Lat_2$ indicates the distance between two latitudes. b $= Lung_1 - Lung_2$ indicates the distance between two longitudes. 6378.137 is the radius of the earth, in kilometers. The distance calculated by the formula has almost accuracy with Google Maps, the difference is in the range of 0.2 m. OS3E belongs to a wide area network in the United States, when calculating the delay, the main delay is the propagation delay, so the delay in the following simulation is the propagation delay, which calculated by the following formula:

$$t_{ij} = d_{ij}/(2 * 10^8) \qquad (8)$$

We first simulate our algorithm, because the algorithm requires a certain number of controllers k, so we first study the effect of k to the delay.

The effect of k on the delay of the controller and the switch:

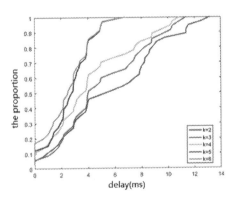

Fig. 6. Cumulative Distribution Function of delay in different number of controllers

Figure 6 shows the Cumulative distribution function of the delay of the algorithm under different number of controllers. As we can see in Fig. 6, when k becomes larger, it can effectively reduce the delay between switches and controllers. But when k increases to 6, it has no obvious reduce compared to when k is 5. So we can see that the more controllers deployed in the network the better performance it will have, but when the number reaches a certain number, increasing the number of controllers can only bring a relatively small income of reducing delay.

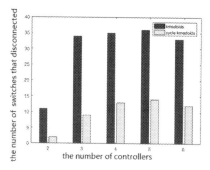

Fig. 7. The switches that disconnected to controller when a single link failure occurs

Figure 7 shows the number of nodes that are disconnected from the controller when a single link failure occurs in the network, it is the value calculated in Eq. 5. From the figure we can clearly see that our algorithm can effectively reduce the number of the isolated points compared to the standard k-medoids algorithm. In the event of a single link failure, our algorithm can make the communication between the switch and the controller more reliable, reduce the number of switches that disconnected to the controller, so that the network has better reliability.

As we can see in Fig. 8, our algorithm can effectively reduce the number of links between controllers which are affected by a single link failure, it is the value calculated by the formula 6. It can be seen, that our algorithm can ensure a better reliability when a single link failure occurs.

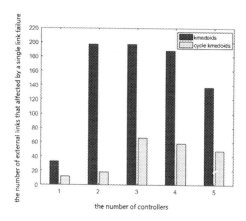

Fig. 8. The affected links between controllers when a single link failure occurs

In Fig. 9, we see that our algorithm cause a little more latency compared to the standard k-medoids algorithm, but we can keep the virtual nodes a better reliability by sacrificing a little delay performance, so to ensure a better network performance when a single link failure occurs.

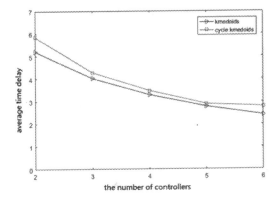

Fig. 9. Average time delay under different number of controllers

6   Conclusion

In this paper, we first introduces the scene of the algorithm, in order to ensure the reliability of the virtual nodes as much as possible, use the concept that treat the controller and its sub-network as a virtual node in distributed architecture. At the meantime, the communication between the controller and the switches that under its management is frequent, and the delay between the controller and switch is also a very important consideration. We consider the impact of reliability and latency on the network, proposed a two-stage algorithm. In the first stage, with the assumption that there is only a single link failure, we proposed an idea that providing backup paths by using ring network, divided the network into some ring networks and isolated points. In the second stage, we proposed a k-medoids solution with improved initial points selection method, which can cluster the clusters and isolated points according to time delay. Then we implemented our algorithm in actual network topology Internet OS3E, and compared it with the standard k-medoids algorithm. We used Python for simulation, the simulation result shows that our algorithm cause a little more time delay compared to the standard k-medoids algorithm, but it effectively reduces the number of disconnected switches when a single point failure occurs.

Acknowledgments. This work was supported by the project supported by the Research Project of CCF-QimingxingchenHongyan (CCF-VenustechRP2016004), National Natural Science Foundation of China: Grant No. 2015BAK16B04, Basic Research Fund of China Academy of safety and Technology:Grant No. 2016JBKY03.

References

1. Koponen, T., Casado, M., Gude, N., et al.: Onix: a distributed control platform for large-scale production networks. In: OSDI, vol. 10, pp. 1–6 (2010)
2. Heller, B., Sherwood, R., McKeown, N.: The controller placement problem. In: Proceedings of the First Workshop on Hot Topics in Software Defined Networks, pp. 7–12. ACM (2012)

3. Zhao, J., Qu, H., Zhao, J., et al.: Towards controller placement problem for software-defined network using affinity propagation. Electron. Lett. **53**(14), 928–929 (2017)
4. Li, J., Wu, J., Hu, Y., et al.: DSL: dynamic and self-learning schedule method of multiple controllers in SDN. ETRI J. **39**(3), 364–372 (2017)
5. Farshin, A., Sharifian, S.: MAP-SDN: a metaheuristic assignment and provisioning SDN framework for cloud datacenters. J. Supercomput. **73**, 4112–4136 (2017)
6. Lange, S., Gebert, S., Zinner, T., et al.: Heuristic approaches to the controller placement problem in large scale SDN networks. IEEE Trans. Netw. Serv. Manag. **12**(1), 4–17 (2015)
7. Yao, G., Bi, J., Li, Y., et al.: On the capacitated controller placement problem in software defined networks. IEEE Commun. Lett. **18**(8), 1339–1342 (2014)
8. Hu, Y., Wendong, W., Gong, X., et al.: Reliability-aware controller placement for software-defined networks. In: 2013 IFIP/IEEE International Symposium on Integrated Network Management (IM 2013), pp. 672–675. IEEE (2013)
9. Sallahi, A., St-Hilaire, M.: Optimal model for the controller placement problem in software defined networks. IEEE Commun. Lett. **19**(1), 30–33 (2015)
10. Ksentini, A., Bagaa, M., Taleb, T., et al.: On using bargaining game for optimal placement of SDN controllers. In: 2016 IEEE International Conference on Communications (ICC), pp. 1–6. IEEE (2016)
11. Nagano, J., Shinomiya, N.: Efficient switch clustering for distributed controllers of OpenFlow network with bi-connectivity. Comput. Netw. **96**, 48–57 (2016)
12. Bari, M.F., Roy, A.R., Chowdhury, S.R., et al.: Dynamic controller provisioning in software defined networks. In: Proceedings of the 9th International Conference on Network and Service Management (CNSM 2013), pp. 18–25. IEEE (2013)

Interference-Avoid-Concept Based Indoor VLC Network Throughput Optimization

Yan Chen[✉] and Hongyu Yang

School of Aeronautics and Astronautics,
University of Electronic Science and Technology of China,
2006 Xiyuan Ave, West High-Tech Zone, Chengdu 611731, China
{blastchen,yanghy}@uestc.edu.cn

Abstract. In this paper, based on the analysis of indoor VLC optical link characteristics and the aid of graph theory the idea of interference-avoid is introduced to remove the signal interference from adjacent optical access points and thus the network throughput is optimized. The interference-avoidance is achieved on the network management layer by a central resource schedule scheme following our adjusted proportional fairness schedule (PFS) rule. In this schedule rule a new priority model is proposed to take into account the delay and fairness while optimizing the throughput. Simulations proved the proposed scheduling scheme can improve the throughput for small-to-moderate scale networks compared to the present work without compromise the fairness and latency performances.

Keywords: Visible light communications · Resource scheduling
Priority fairness · Interference graph

1 Introduction

Ever since Nakagawa and his group proposed to combine the illumination and communication functions together based on fast modulated LEDs [1], visible light communications (VLC) have become more and more attractive to the next generation wide band wireless communication networks. The wavelength range of visible light is 400–700 nm, the spectrum width is more than 3×10^6 GHz, which is 10^4 times of that of the existing communication spectrum. VLC technology uses the intensity modulation to modulate the signal on the white LED carrier and the link transmission rate can be up to more than 1 Gbps. It will greatly reduce the time spending on high-definition movie downloading and other broadband data applications. VLC technology has been widely seen as an important way to mitigate the RF spectrum crisis.

Over the past decade, researches in VLC field have focused on the development of modulation bandwidth of LEDs, modulation and coding technology and light receiving methods of visible light devices. Technology on physic layers and link layershas made great progress. System coverage, data transmission rate and transmission distance have been greatly improved [2–4]. Point-to-point VLC technology has reaches its mature stage.

© Springer Nature Singapore Pte Ltd. 2018
H. Yuan et al. (Eds.): GSKI 2017, CCIS 848, pp. 158–167, 2018.
https://doi.org/10.1007/978-981-13-0893-2_17

Since Harald Haas coined the term of Li-Fi VLC is not merely a point-to-point communication technology but a solution to broadband wireless network access [5]. The research focus has changed from point-to-point physical link to network application of VLC technology [6]. The natural characteristic of VLC has brought to indoor VLC network challenges of coverage, multiple access and high signal interferences. The communication areas are confined by the illuminating area of LEDs, so we need more optical access points (APs) to achieve perfect signal coverage. Since illumination is a wide-easily-acquirable resource so the coverage issue is easy to deal with. When multiple user terminals enter the same coverage of an optical AP, the potential links between the same AP and the different user terminals cause conflictions among users. Due to the high transmitting power of LEDs, the inter-channel-interferences (ICI) become a main noise in the in-door VLC systems and it undermines the network throughput. OFDMA, OCDMA, TDMA have been applied to solve this multi-access issue [7–10].

In this paper the idea of interference-avoidance is introduced to remove the ICIs of indoor VLC networks and therefore the throughput optimization is achieved. Based on this idea a network resource scheduling scheme is proposed to resolve the problem of multiple access and ICI cancellation. What's more, through a newly proposed priority model for the scheduling scheme, the fairness and delay performances are balanced while optimizing the throughput.

2 Link Character and Problem Formulation

Figure 1 shows a typical layout of a user centric (UC) indoor VLC networks [11]. The dotted line denotes a LOS (line-of-sight) link between a user, such as a smart phone, a personal computer, and a LED served as the access point (AP).

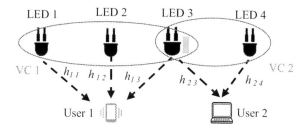

Fig. 1. An UC indoor VLC networks.

In an indoor VLC network there are multiple optical APs, the LEDs, and multiple users. Naturally if signal of any AP enters the FOV of a user's terminal there would be a potential line-of-sight (LOS) link between them. The optical channel gain for LOS link from AP j to user i is denoted as h_{ij} [12].

$$h_{ij} = \begin{cases} \frac{A_i(k+1)m}{2\pi d_{ij}^2} \cos^k(\phi_{ij}) \cos(\psi_{ij}) T_i g_i & (\phi_{ij} \leq FOV_i) \\ 0 & (\phi_{ij} > FOV_i) \end{cases} \tag{1}$$

where A_i is the physical area of the detector for user i, ϕ_{ij} is the angle of irradiance, Ψ_{ij} is the angle of incidence, d_{ij} is the distance between LED j and a detector's surface of user i. T_i and g_i are the filter transmittance and focus gain of user I respectively. m is the order of Lambertian emission and it is given by the semi-angle at half illuminance of an LED $\Phi_{1/2}$.

In a user centric (UC) VLC networks downlink all the APs within a user's FOV form a cell and they transmit the same signal to a user. The transmitting cell formation for user i is elastic and changes with the user's location. So the shape and number of APs in the transmitting cell are not fixed therefore the author of [13] calls it virtual cell (VC), as VC 1 and VC 2 in Fig. 1.

According to Shannon's Theorems, the normalized data rate of downlinks to user i in an UC-VLC downlink networks based on virtual cells is

$$\rho_i = \log_2\left[1 + \left(\sum\nolimits_{j \in VC} h_{ij}P_{ot}R\right)^2 / (\sigma_s^2 + \sigma_t^2 + I_i)\right] \tag{2}$$

where the σ_s^2 and σ_t^2 denote the shooting noise and thermal noises respectively. And $I_i = \left(\sum\nolimits_{j \notin VC} h_{ij}P_{ot}R\right)^2$ is the ICI imposed by neighbor VCs for other users. Such as signal transmitted from LED3 in Fig. 1 is an ICI for both user1 and user2.

The thermal and shooting noises are relatively fixed and mostly decided by the environment and hardware characteristics. Due to the high emitting power level required by illumination the ICI overwhelms the noises and it varies intensely with the VCs layouts and user locations.

For the entire VLC downlinks the sum date rate of all users, from 1 to K, in a timeslot is the throughput Υ we study in this paper.

$$\Upsilon = \sum\nolimits_{i=1}^{K} \log_2\left[1 + \left(\sum\nolimits_{j \in VC} h_{ij}P_{ot}R\right)^2 / (\sigma_s^2 + \sigma_t^2 + I_i)\right] \tag{3}$$

The throughput represents the data transmitting ability of a VLC networks and it's the most important performance matters to both the users' experience and the network management. A high QoS scheduling scheme aims to achieve throughput as high as possible. Equation (3) indicates that we could accomplish this by either raising the transmitting optical power or mitigating the noises. The former way will raise both the signal and noise power and decrease the SNR instead. Thermal σ_s^2 and shooting σ_t^2 noises are unavoidable, nevertheless ICI are quite dependent on the locations and cell forming of VLC networks.

For the high transmitting power character of the indoor VLC system the ICIs overwhelms shooting and thermal noises, therefore by removing ICIs the network throughput is optimized as in Eq. (4).

$$\Upsilon_{\max} = \lim_{I_i \to 0}\left\{\sum\nolimits_{i=1}^{K} \log_2\left[1 + \left(\sum\nolimits_{j \in VC} h_{ij}P_{ot}R\right)^2 / (\sigma_s^2 + \sigma_t^2 + I_i)\right]\right\} \tag{4}$$

Theoretically the resource scheduling program can identify the conflictions between users with links to the same AP, which causing ICIs, and by allocating Aps to users without conflictions at the same timeslot the ICI noise are avoided. In brief, by interference-avoiding concept the main noise, ICIs, in VLC networks are mitigated and hence the network throughput is optimized.

3 Resource Scheduling Based on Interference-Avoiding Concept

3.1 Interferences Description in Graph Theory

Figure 2 is an interference graph of an indoor VLC networks. The blue solid lines represent the interference caused by the adjacent users. And a dotted line denotes a LOS link between a user and a Ap.

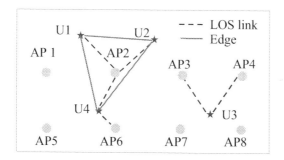

Fig. 2. Interference graph of indoor VLC networks. (Color figure online)

In graph theory interferences are typically described by interference graphs [14] where interferences and users are represented by edges and vertices respectively. User set without ICIs is in fact the Independent Set (IS) of the interference graph. All the users without ICIs can be represented by the Maximum Independent Set (MaxIS) of the interference graph. A MaxIS of an interference graph is the independent set with the most vertices. For Fig. 2 the MaxIS could be {1, 3}, {2, 3} or {4, 3}. Now the scheduling problem has been transformed into MaxIS searching problem in graph theories. Due to its NP-complete character the heuristic algorithm is needed to solve it with an acceptable time [15].

3.2 Interference-Avoiding Scheduling Under PFS Principle

Proportional Fairness Scheduling (PFS) is a widely used principle in wireless network resource management for its good balancing between throughput and fairness. In this paper it's adopted and we try to adjust it to meet the requirement of optimizing the throughput of VLC access networks downlinks. In a PFS process the central control needs to calculate the priority factor $p_{i,k}$ for every user at the beginning of each times lot by $p_{i,k} = f(r_{i,k}) = r_{i,k}/\langle r_{i,k} \rangle$. By taking fairness into consideration the PFS calculates the priority factor for user i in slot k by its data rate requirements for present slot $r_{i,k}$ against its average data rate $\langle r_{i,k} \rangle$.

In order to take latency into consideration, the exponential rule developed by Shakkottai and Stolyar is adopted [16].

$$p_{i,k} = f(r_{i,k}) \cdot q(D_{i,k})$$
$$= \frac{r_{i,k}}{\langle r_{i,k} \rangle} \cdot \exp\left[\left(D_{i,k} - \langle D'_{i,k} \rangle\right) / \left(1 + \sqrt{\langle D'_{i,k} \rangle}\right)\right] \tag{5}$$

where $\langle D'_{i,k} \rangle = \left(\sum_{j=1, j \neq i}^{K} D_{i,k}\right)$ is the average delay of all the users other than user i. The exponential form of $p_{i,k}$ makes it sensitive to a large latency variation and leads a fact that user whose latency divide far away from the average results in a higher priority factor. Otherwise for a small latency difference the exponential term $q(D_{i,k})$ is close to 1 and the policy becomes virtually the original PFS rule.

Combining the principle of PFS and interference graph theory, every vertex, i.e. every user, has a priority at each timeslot therefor the interference graph changes to the Weighted Interference Graph (WIG). In a WIG the weight for a user is the priority factor calculated by scheduling program at the present timeslot. Under the PFS principle, the scheduling scheme needs to find the users with the highest sum of priority first. And at the same time in order to optimize the throughput the scheduling scheme needs to find the users with the lowest ICIs. In a WIG the user set with the highest sum of priority and lowest ICIs is in fact the Maximum Weighted Independent Set (MWIS) of the graph. Now the resource scheduling problem actually becomes a MWIS find problem. The Greedy algorithm is one of the simple and efficient heuristic algorithms for searching MWIS and here we adopt the MIN-Greedy algorithm [15] in the simulations of our scheduling scheme.

The interference-avoiding schedule algorithm is listed below.

Scheduling algorithm
1   Input initial system parameter matrix (as in Tab. 1)
2   **for** each simulation cycle **do**
3   Randomly generate users' geometry locations
4   **for** each time slot k **do**
5   update $h_{i,k}$, $p_{i,k}$;
6   build the weighted interference graph (WIG);
7   MIN-Greedy algorithm for WMIS searching;
8   **end for**
9   Allocate the APs to users in MWIS;
10   Allocate the idle APs;
11   Calculate capacity and delayed timeslots for every user;
12 **End for**
13 Calculate throughput, SFI and average latency

3.3 Proposed Three-Term Priority Model

In order to enlarge the throughput, we insert a function $G_{i,k}(\cdot)$ in the priority model $p_{i,k}$ in Eq. (5). Throughput is directly related to SNR and in an indoor wireless communication environment SNR is mainly decided by channel conditions. By giving higher priority to user with better channel condition the scheduling is capable of achieving a higher throughput. It is well known the Carrier-to-noise ratio (CNR) is a typical parameter to reflect the channel condition so we choose CNR to reform priority models. As we've discussed before in the indoor VLC systems ICI overwhelms the system noise so at the end we use Carrier-to-Interference ratio (CIR) to replace CNR. The proposed priority model has a three-term form denoted as

$$p_{i,k} = f\left(r_{i,k}\right) \cdot G\left(CIR_{i,k}\right) \cdot q\left(D_{i,k}\right) \tag{6}$$

Since the channel conditions are time-varying so function $G_{i,k}(\cdot)$ is formed as channel condition of both the past and the present as

$$G\left(CIR_{i,k}\right) = 1/T_C \cdot CIR_{i,k-1} + \left(1 + 1/T_C\right) \cdot CIR_{i,k} \tag{7}$$

where T_C determines the weighting given to historical values.

Based on Eq. (7) we increase the nonlinearity order of the latency difference term $q(D_{i,k})$ and the fairness term $f(r_{i,k})$ in order to balance the fairness and latency performance while increasing the throughput. We did thousands of simulations before the proposed three-term priority model reaches its final form as

$$p_{i,k} = F\left(r_{i,k}\right) \cdot G\left(CIR_{i,k}\right) \cdot Q\left(D_{i,k}\right)$$

$$= \exp\left(\frac{r_{i,k}}{\langle r_{i,k} \rangle}\right) \cdot G\left(CIR_{i,k}\right) \cdot 8^{1 + \sqrt{\frac{D_{i,k} \langle D'_{i,k} \rangle}{\langle D'_{i,k} \rangle}}} \tag{8}$$

4 Simulations and Analysis

To make a fair comparison between our proposed priority model, as in Eq. (8), and the two-term priority model used in the present work [14], we adopted the same simulation parameters. In simulations the 8*8 LEDs are equally separated by distance of 2 m. For number of users from K = 1 to 16, we did the scheduling simulations. For each simulation we did 5000 cycles and for each cycle the scheduling is performed for 50 timeslots. Table 1 shows the key parameters used in the simulations.

Table 1. Simulation parameters

Parameter	Value	Parameter	Value
L*W*H (m)	3*3*3	FOV (°)	50
h (m)	0.8	A (mm^2)	0.785
N	64	$\Phi_{1/2}$ (°)	70

System performance indicators of throughput, as in Eq. (4), fairness and latency are calculated to evaluating our scheduling and new priority model, as in Eq. (9).

$$SFI = \frac{\underset{ij}{Max}|\langle\rho_i\rangle - \langle\rho_j\rangle|}{1/k\sum_{i=1}^{K}\langle\rho_i\rangle} \quad (i,j = 1,\ldots K)$$

$$Ave\_Latency = (1/SIMU) \cdot \sum_{i=1}^{SIMU}\left[\sum_{i=1}^{K} delay(u_i)/K\right] \tag{9}$$

where $\langle\rho_i\rangle$ is the average data rate of user i. SFI is the Schedule Fairness Index (SFI) and smaller SFI value means better fairness among users. If SFI = 0, the absolute fairness is achieved.

Figure 3 is the throughput comparison between scheduling applying our proposed three-term priority model and the 2-term model used in [14].

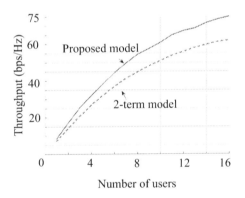

Fig. 3. Throughput comparison

From Fig. 3 we can see that scheduling with our proposed priority model achieves a better throughput with all different number of users. The average throughput increment is about 20%. This is due to the consideration of user's channel condition in the priority model which leading scheduling scheme able to flexibly assign APs to the users with higher CIR. As number of users grows the improvement is even bigger which means our proposed priority model works better on scenario with large user scales.

Figure 4 is the fairness performance comparison between scheduling applying our proposed three-term priority model and the 2-term model used in [14].

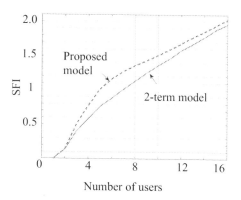

Fig. 4. Fairness performance comparison

Figure 4 shows that our scheduling scheme achieve a fairness performance close to that of Ref. [14] 's with a small degradation on a small number of users around $K = 6$. This degradation may due to the inserting of CIR which makes scheduling work on the favor of users with better channels and improves the throughput, however it potentially breaks a little bit of the balance between throughput and fairness. Note that when number of users grows larger our proposed scheduling scheme tend to achieve as better. This may arise from the fact that when number of users grows the networks become more crowded and users tend to have similar channel conditions and the undermine effect of CIR on SFI reduces gradually.

Figure 5 is the latency performance comparison between scheduling applying our proposed three-term priority model and the 2-term model used in [14].

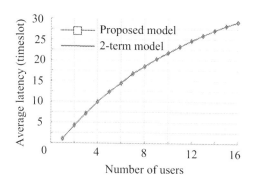

Fig. 5. Latency performance comparison

From Fig. 5 we can see the two scheme achieves almost the same time latency performance against all different number of users. As we have seen previously that the

CIR term in the proposed model has some extent of undermining effect on the performance of fairness, nevertheless it doesn't happen on the latency performance.

Generally, we can say that the proposed priority model improved the indoor VLC networks scheduling performance and achieved a balance among all the system indicators.

5 Conclusions

We studied the multi-user scheduling and resource allocations in UC-VLC networks downlink. By application interference graph the ICI-avoiding scheduling and allocation problem is transformed into MWIS searching problem. A new priority factor model is established to fully cover the three main objectives of a high QoS networks scheduling and allocation. Compared to the 2-term model applied in [14], scheduling schemes applying our proposed priority model achieves better throughput and similar latency performance on any occasions although exhibiting a small degradation on fairness on small user scale occasions. Our works is on the simulation level and further researches should be taken in order to take the improvement into practice applications, including the real-time estimating of channel gain matrix and the CIR information of all users.

Acknowledgments. This work is supported by the Chinese Fundamental Research Funds for the Central Universities (No. A03017023701231).

References

1. Tanaka, Y., Haruyama, S., Nakagawa, M.: Wireless optical transmissions with white colored LED for wireless home links. In: Proceedings of the Personal Indoor and Mobile Radio Communications, PIMRC 2000, London, UK, 18–21 September 2000, pp. 1325–1329. IEEE, New York (2000). http://doi.IEEE.org/10.1109/PIMRC.2000.881634
2. Rajbhandari, S., McKendry, J.J.D., Herrnsdorf, J., Chun, H., Faulkner, G., Haas, H., Watson, I.M., O'Brien, D., Dawson, M.D.: A review of gallium nitride LEDs for multi-gigabit-per-second visible light data communications. Semicond. Sci. Technol. **32**(2), 1–49 (2017). http://doi.iop.org/10.1088/1361-6641/32/2/023001
3. Tsonev, D., Chun, H., Rajbhandari, S.: A 3-Gb/s single-LED OFDM-based wireless VLC link using a gallium nitride μLED. IEEE Photonics Technol. Lett. **26**(7), 637–640 (2014). http://doi.IEEE.org/10.1109/LPT.2013.2297621
4. Jalajakumari, A.V.N., Xie, E., McKendry, J., Gu, E., Dawson, M.D., Hass, H., Henderson, R.K.: High-speed integrated digital to light converter for short range visible light communication. IEEE Photonics Technol. Lett. **29**(1), 118–121 (2017). http://doi.IEEE.org/10.1109/LPT.2016.2624281
5. Haas, H.: Wireless data from every light bulb. TEDGlobal, July 2011. http://www.ted.com/talks/harald_haas_wireless_data_from_every_light_bulb?language=en
6. Burchardt, H., Serafimovski, N., Tsonev, D., Videv, S.: VLC: beyond point-to-point communication. IEEE Commun. Mag. **52**(7), 98–105 (2014). http://doi.IEEE.org/10.1109/MCOM.2014.6852089

7. Khalid, A.M., Ciaramella, E., Cossu, G., Corsini, R.: Bi-directional 400 Mbit/s LED-based optical wireless communications for nondirected line of sight transmission. In: Proceedings of the Optical fiber communication conference, OFC 2014, California, USA, 9–13 March 2014, OSA, San Francisco, United States, Th1F.2. (2014). https://doi.org/10.1364/OFC.2014.Th1F.2

8. Minh, H., O'Brien, D., Faulkner, G., Bouchet, O., Wolf, M., Grobe, L., Li, J.: A 1.25-Gb/s indoor cellular optical wireless communications demonstrator. IEEE Photon. Technol. Lett. 22(21), 1598–1600 (2010). https://doi.org/10.1109/lpt.2010.2073696

9. Yang, S.H., Kim, H.S., Son, Y.H., Han, S.K.: Reduction of optical interference by wavelength filtering in RGB-LED based indoor VLC system. In: Proceedings of the Opto-Electronics and Communications Conference, OECC 2011, Kaohsiung, Taiwan, 4–8 July 2011, pp. 551–552. IEEE, New York (2011)

10. Chen, C., Serafimovski, N., Haas, H.: Fractional frequency reuse in optical wireless cellular networks. In: Proceedings of the International Symposium on Personal Indoor and Mobile Radio Communications, London, UK, 8–11 September 2013, pp. 3594–3598. IEEE, New York (2013). http://doi.IEEE.org/10.1109/PIMRC.2013.6666773

11. Li, X., Zhang, R., Wang, J., Hanzo, L.: Cell-centric and user-centric multi-user scheduling in visible light communication aided networks. In: Proceedings of the International Conference on Communications, ICC 2015, IEEE Press, London, UK, 8–12 June 2015, pp. 5120–5125. IEEE, New York (2015). https://doi.org/10.1109/icc.2015.7249136

12. Barry, J.R.: Wireless Infrared Communications. Kluwer Academic Press, Boston (1994)

13. Dai, L., Zhou, S., Yao, Y.: Capacity analysis in CDMA distributed antenna systems. IEEE Trans. Wirel. Commun. 4(6), 2613–2620 (2005). http://doi.IEEE.org/10.1109/TWC.2005.858011

14. Tao, Y., Liang, X., Wang, J., Zhao, C.: Scheduling for indoor visible light communication based on graph theory. Opt. Express 23(3), 2737–2752 (2015). https://doi.org/10.1364/OE.23.002737

15. Sakai, S., Togasaki, M., Yamazaki, K.: A note on greedy algorithms for the maximum weighted independent set problem. Discret. Appl. Math. 126(2), 313–322 (2003). http://doi.acm.org/10.1016/S0166-218X(02)00205-6

16. Shakkottai, S., Stolyar, A.: Scheduling algorithms for a mixture of real-time and non-real-time data in HDR. Teletraffic Sci. Eng. 4, 793–804 (2003). https://doi.org/10.1016/S1388-3437(01)80170-0

A Comparative Acoustic Analysis of Mongolian Long Tunes of Pastoral and Hymn

Guangming$^{(\boxtimes)}$, Yuhua Qi, and Guoqiang Chen

Northwest University for Nationalities, Lanzhou, Gansu, China
997988293@qq.com, 1306615517@qq.com, 877867573@qq.com

Abstract. In this paper, two Mongolian long-tune folk songs with different subjects are taken as experimental objects, and research them in the experimental phonetics method. The fundamental parameters such as fundamental frequency (F0), energy, formant and duration were extracted from the vocal signals; the acoustic parameters were compared and analyzed. The results show that there are many differences in the acoustic parameters when singing, Fist: the energy and the F0 of Mongolian Pastoral Songs are higher than the hymn, which shows the acoustic characteristics of the melodious loud and clear and the Formant parameter reflects the singer's singing level, and their different the me concentrate on differences of the energy and F0.

Keyword: Mongolian long - tuned energy F0 acoustic analysis

1 Introduction

The Mongolians are those people who are good at singing and dancing. Nomadism is their primary life style. They gather in the north of our country. By their diligence, wisdom and courage, they constantly create their own history and culture, especially in folk song, they have made great achievements. Of course, folk songs occupy a very important position in the Mongolian people's lives, called "the art flowers of the grassland" Mongolian folk songs mainly include short tone and long tone, in which the long tone's characteristics are particularly prominent, beautiful melody, lyric soothing rhythm with a wide grassland atmosphere. Mongolian long tunes can be divided into the following types from the theme: hunting songs, pastoral, hymn, banquet songs and so on.

Hymn, it called "Magtagalunduu", in Mongolian. From the contents, Hymn can be divided into two categories; one is singing the historical figure, and another is to praises for mountains, lakes and hometown. In the mode, Hymn usually uses a large number of levy-style and palace style, which reflects the Mongolian long tone even Mongolian's magnificent temperament. Pastoral, it called "Mara Qin Malcinuduu", in Mongolian it reveal the lifeway of the Mongolian, and is a folk song style of impromptu sing when herdsmen are grazing. Most of the pastoral contents are about the grassland, the Mongolian praised by the grassland and the horses to express their satisfaction of a good life and their vision to the future, their joy are concentrated in pastoral songs.

© Springer Nature Singapore Pte Ltd. 2018
H. Yuan et al. (Eds.): GSKI 2017, CCIS 848, pp. 168–175, 2018.
https://doi.org/10.1007/978-981-13-0893-2_18

Since the founding of new China, Inner Mongolia government from government and relevant departments they have done a lot of works to protect the Mongolian folk art, but with the change of people's life style and the impact of foreign cultures, Mongolian long tone's future situation is worrying, showing a decline trend. It is the older famous singing artists have passed away, a large number of excellent unique singing way in long tunes are facing lost, the so-called "people dead and arts die away". Rescue and protection of Mongolian folic song has become an urgent matter, and systematic, science, comprehensive research will play a role in promoting long-tunes protection. In the protection of Mongolian long-tune, we should ensure that the originality of songs, then take voice, video signals of the heritage people's long-tune. Otherwise, because of the intangible cultural heritage has a strong plasticity and variability, it is easy to take shape and change in its preservation and transmission process, contrary to intention of protecting the culture and promoting the original. In other words, to deal with the traditional and modern, protection and inheritance, inheritance and development and other relations, which is an issue that we are faced with [1].

In the international, with the development of signal processing technology and computer science, the speech vocalization study has made unprecedented development. In China, the study of the phonation types of various national languages began in the 1990s (BaoHuaiqiao et al. 1992; Kong Jiangping 2001). Recently, linguists had also conducted multimodal research on Mongolian folk songs, such as HU A-xu and Gegentana from the Northwest University for Nationalities. They have studied the acoustic features of Mongolian folk songs, aiming to explore the physiological features of Mongolian folk songs, summarize the voice characteristics in different way of singing and the relationship between the parameters [2]. Another one is GAO Shan, who studied Mongolian short and long tunes from the physiology and acoustics, gathered multidimensional signals and analysed Mongolian folk songs from singing voices and breathing features. However, the article mainly studies the Mongolian folk songs breathing parameters to presents their breathing characteristics [3]. In this article, we choose two different themes of long tune: hymn and pastoral. "The tall Alashan" is the Hymn, The BlackHorse" is the pastoral song, from the energy, fundamental frequency (F0) and other acoustic parameters to present their acoustic characteristics.

2 Experimental Method

2.1 Introduce Singers and Audio Materials

The singer who has a fine long-tuned singing skills, and has own understanding deeply about Mongolian folk songs. About recording materials, we selected the representative song of Mongolian long tunes (see from Table 1).

2.2 Recording Equipment

The recording software glottal is Adobe Audition 1.5, the hardware equipment mainly includes glottis instrument (EGG), external sound card, lavalier microphone, computer,

Table 1. Singers and songs information

Singer	Gender	Song name	Theme
Erden Saran	Female	Tall Alashan	Hymn
Erdeng Saren	Female	Black horse	Pastoral

mixer and so on. Recording dual-channel signals simultaneously. Sampling frequency is 22 kHz, resolution is 16-bit.

Using praat to extract the basic frequency value and energy value of two songs, the data were analyzed features by Excel presented comparatively the acoustic characteristics of different themes in two songs.

3 Acoustic Analyses

From the two spectrograms, we can see that the energy distribution is more uniform, and there is no obvious differences between these songs, the energy is mainly concentrated in 0–2000 Hz, high-energy resonance peak close to the national singing and BelCanto's, which is mainly due to the fake sound, airflow resistance is relatively weak, so overtone is relatively small and weak. Due to throat laryngeal go up and down enlarge the pharynx and elongated the voice channel, that certainly strengthen the produce of low-frequency resonance. Full bass is a basic condition to get gorgeous rich high-frequency harmonic overtone, that is why long-tone is not only rich in high-frequency, but also low frequency is very fully, also is the reason that songs with the penetration [4].

Spectrogram
See Figs. 1 and 2.

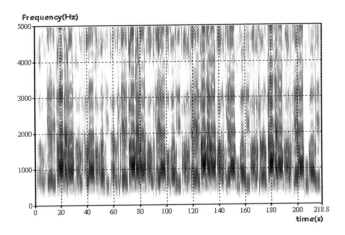

Fig. 1. Tall Alashan's spectrogram

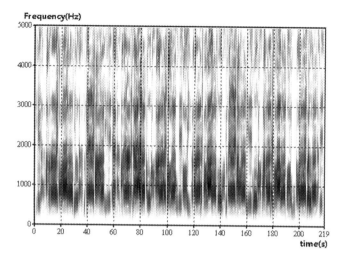

Fig. 2. Black horse's spectrogram

3.1 Energy Analysis

Energy represents the level of the volume, display the level of air flow and tone vibration's amplitude when the singer is singing. The singer expresses his own emotion from the two long-tunes through changing the energy. Energy distributions as shown in Figs. 3 and 4, there are the energy distributions of two long-tunes (Table 2).

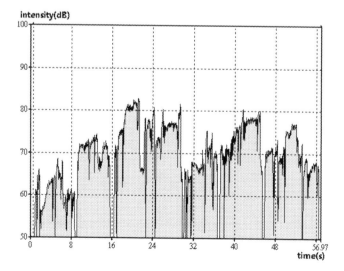

Fig. 3. High-Alashan (hymn) energy distribution map

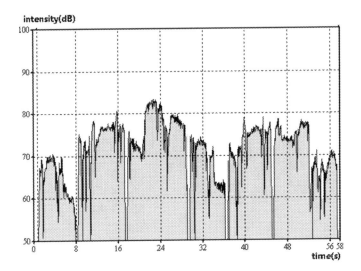

Fig. 4. Black horse (pastoral) energy distribution map

Table 2. Energy comparison parameter table

Parameter song	Highest energy (dB)	Minimum energy (dB)	Energy average (dB)	Duration (s)
Tall Alashan	82.79	12.92	67.14	56.97
Black horse	83.43	15.55	69.32	56.58

As can be seen from the figure, the pastoral's energy values generally higher than the hymn's. The average energy difference between pastoral songs and praise songs is 2.18 dB. Compared with the common singing method, the energy of long tune is not high but very concentrated, and the undulating is not obvious. Indicating that the singing long-time need to pay attention to guide singers' own breath to form a strong support point in order to evenly control the breathing, and control freely the intensity changing. At the same time, in the jumping process of different rhythm, the energy uniformity, stability and continuity of voice physiological mechanisms need better and strong singing skills [5]. The contrast analysis of two different songs showing that hymn tone is simple and powerful, with a little decorative sound, its energy is undulating. Pastoral has wide voice range and high-capacity, the momentum is quite broad, with a bright colours and the inherent lyricism.

3.2 Pitch Analysis

The fundamental frequency is the lowest natural frequency of the periodic vibration of the vocal cords, and its performance in the voice is pitch, in the physiological it is the speed of vocal cord vibration. As shown in Figs. 5 and 6, there is the pitch distribution of two long-tunes.

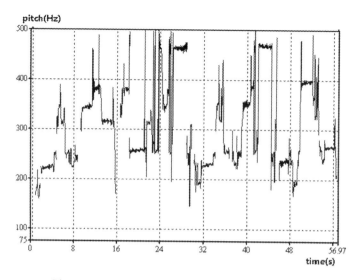

Fig. 5. High-Alashan (hymn) time-frequency diagram

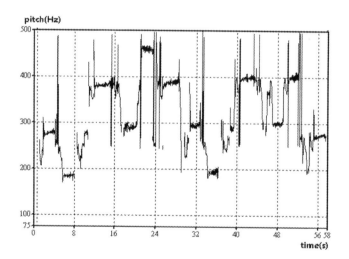

Fig. 6. Black horse (pastoral) time-frequency diagram

As can be seen from the Table 3, In Hymns, its Lowest pitch value is 145.99 Hz in the 26 s, and in the 26 s–40 s, appears valley pitch zone, hymn in 24 s appeared the maximum fundamental frequency of 499.76 Hz, and in 18 s–24 s the peak frequency of the fundamental frequency continues to appear. About the pastoral, the lowest basic frequency of 169.34 Hz appeared in 6 s, and during 6 s–8 s there is a fundamental frequency trough, and the peak of fundamental frequency appeared in 24 s, and the peak in 21 s–26 s continued to occur. The average fundamental frequency of pastoral songs and hymns differ by 9.11 Hz, the difference between the minimum fundamental frequency and the maximum fundamental frequency is 23.35 Hz and 0.16 Hz, respectively. The fundamental frequency of pastoral is higher than hymn. From above comparative analysis that Mongolian long-tune attache's great importance to breathing training, it plays a very important role to singers and singing technology. Two long-tunes maintain a balance and stability in certain pitch range, and form a number of voice ranges, in the course of emotional changes, its melody will suddenly increase or decrease. So it sounds rhythm freely, high-pitched, melodies. Hymn tone high-pitched,

Table 3. Comparison table of fundamental frequency

Parameter song	Basic frequency min(Hz)	Basic frequency max(Hz)	Basic frequency mean(Hz)	Duration (s)
Tall Alashan	145.99	499.76	310.76	56.97
Black horse	169.34	499.92	319.87	56.58

rhythmic neat and clear, the melody is also undulating, and reflects the Mongolian magnificent temperament. Pastoral, shows beautiful tune, its melody ups and downs sharply, rhythm stretch, has a wide grassland atmosphere.

4   Conclusions

In this article, we comparatively analyses the energy and pitch of two long-tunes. It is concluded that the average energy value of hymn is 67.14 dB and the average pitch is 310.76 Hz. The average energy value of the pastoral song is 69.32 dB, the average pitch value is 319.87 Hz. The energy and fundamental frequency values of pastoral songs are higher than hymn's. And also reflects the characteristics of different themes long tune, hymn's features is that the tone is simple and powerful, neat rhythm, with little decorative sounds, the melody is also undulating. Pastoral features, in the tunes, the general high-tolerance, rhythm is free, momentum is quite wide, melodic ups and downs sharply, with a bright colour and the inherent lyricism. The tone of two long-tunes are more stable high-pitched, fully express the emotions and vast distant feelings. In this article, by contrast and analyse the acoustic features of the Mongolian long tones in different themes, provide theoretical and data basis for studying sing skill of Mongolian long tones, fundamental frequency and energy as important acoustic parameters, singing style and performance form have close relationship. Only can we fully understand this relationship, it's not so long for researching the national oral culture in-depth and promoting the inheritance and protection of it. In this article, there are maybe some shortcomings in research method. In content, only select one song in different themes to analyse the acoustic characteristics, so maybe there are some individual differences in the results. I hoped that more scientific and more comprehensive research methods will be gradually explored in the future research, which will expand rescarch content and make the results more universal.

Acknowledgments. A Comparative Study of Mongolian Heroic Epic Jiang Geer and Tibetan Heroic Epic Gesar, National Natural Science Foundation of China (12XMZ061).

References

1. Gao, S.: Numerical Research on Mongolian Short and Long Tone Based on Physiology and Acoustics. Northwest University for Nationalities (2012)
2. Hu, A., Gegentana: Mongolian long tone of voice characteristics of acoustic analysis. Technology information (2013)
3. Fang, H., Li, Y.: Mongolian long tune folk song "two horses of the Lord" acoustic analysis. Northwest University for Nationalities (2012)
4. Yu, S.: Study on the Resonance Characteristics and the Formation Mechanism of Singers in Different Singing Styles. Music Research (2010)
5. Wu, Z.: Experimental Phonetics Summary. Higher Education Press, Beijing (1989)

RSSI Based Localization with Mobile Anchor for Wireless Sensor Networks

Yakun Zhao[✉], Juan Xu, and Jiaolong Jiang

College of Electronics and Information Engineering,
Tongji University, Shanghai 201804, China
{1631516, jxujuan, 1631515}@tongji.edu.cn

Abstract. Localization is one of the key issues of wireless sensor networks. Because of the energy and hardware constraints of sensor nodes, we usually use RSSI (Received Signal Strength Indicator) as a ranging method. In this paper, we proposed an RSSI-based localization algorithm, which takes use of the RSSI values received by sensor node from mobile anchor node to estimate the position of sensor node. We used mobile anchor moving along specific trajectory to locate the unknown nodes, study four different trajectories and analyze the simulation result. Our research indicates that reducing the time interval of transmitting beacons can improve the positional accuracy when using as few anchor nodes as possible. The relative position of anchor's trajectory and the unknown node has an influence on the location result, and an appropriate trajectory can optimize the localization accuracy.

Keywords: Localization · RSSI · Mobile anchor · Wireless sensor networks

1 Introduction

A Wireless Sensor Network (WSN) [1] is a distributed sensor network consisting of many inexpensive micro sensor nodes deployed in the monitoring area, a multi-hop self-organizing network connected through wireless communication system. The purpose of WSN is to perceive, collect and process information of the target in the monitoring area, and send it to the observer.

One of the most basic functions of a sensor network is to determine the location where an event happens or at where a node gets the message. However, the randomly distributed sensor nodes cannot know their position in advance, so they must be located in real time. While the battery energy of sensor nodes is limited, considering the constraints of energy consumption and hardware, RSSI based ranging method is economical.

In this paper, we proposed an RSSI-based localization algorithm: use few anchor nodes to locate all the unknown nodes in the monitoring area, the anchor node moves along a specified straight line uniformly. Specifically, the sensor node receives beacons broadcast by the mobile anchor and establishes a corresponding sequence according to the RSSI value, then uses the least squares method to fit the sequence. Through calculation, we can find the projection of the sensor node on the trajectory, thus obtain the perpendicular line of this trajectory. The intersection of such two lines is the position of the sensor node.

© Springer Nature Singapore Pte Ltd. 2018
H. Yuan et al. (Eds.): GSKI 2017, CCIS 848, pp. 176–187, 2018.
https://doi.org/10.1007/978-981-13-0893-2_19

The rest of the paper is organized as follows: In Sect. 2, we present an overview of related works. The system model is given in Sect. 3. Section 4 describes the algorithm. In Sect. 5, we simulate the location algorithm and analyze the simulation result. Conclusions and prospects are outlined in Sect. 6.

2 Related Works

The localization approaches can be broadly divided into two categories: range-based and range-free. Range-based schemes estimates the distance between sensor node and anchor node through radio signal, and calculates the position of sensor through proper method. The basic ranging methods are Time of Arrival (TOA) [2], Time Difference of Arrival (TDOA) [3], Angle of Arrival (AOA) [4], and Received Signal Strength Indicator (RSSI). While TOA/TDOA/AOA methods are expensive and difficult to realize, for the energy consumption is high and additional hardware is needed, which makes them unsuitable for wireless sensor networks. RSSI-based localization needs no extra hardware and the energy consumption is lower, which is economical and convenient for wireless sensor networks. After acquiring the distance between nodes or the direction of propagation, methods like Trilateration, Triangle Measuring and Maximum Likelihood are generally used to calculate sensor's coordinate.

The concept of mobile anchor is first proposed in [5]: one sensor node receives beacon from multiple anchor positions, using any ranging method, such as Trilateration, node position is determined as the weighted average of position estimates.

Yao and Jiang proposed a distributed refinement algorithm based on the error analyzing of range-based WSN localization [6]. In each iteration, the refinement position of node is obtained through geometric method.

Chen [7] proposed a movement path planning algorithm of auxiliary locating beacon node in wireless sensor networks (MPPA). MPPA uses mobile sinks to locate nodes in the monitoring area and obtains the beacon's trajectory which can cover the entire area through the ant colony optimization.

Shao [8] minimized the energy consumption considering estimation errors through optimal power allocation for the anchor nodes. In this paper, average energy of the received beacon is used to estimate the relative distance between anchor and unknown nodes.

In [9], RSSI trend based localization is introduced; the position of sensor nodes can be estimated through two RSSI trends from the anchor. It is quite novel and considers error reduction mechanism, but there are still some problems: use multiple anchor nodes, and the trajectories of anchor nodes are quite random. The randomness of trajectory means each time when trajectory changes its expression should be recalculated, this calculation is additional and eliminable for the sensor node. In our paper, the trajectory of mobile anchor is specified, we can know its expression in advance, and thus there is no need to calculate it repeatedly.

3 System Model

3.1 Assumption

The network we consider has sensor nodes that are not aware of their positions and anchor nodes aware of their geographic positions. Suppose that anchor nodes can move in the monitoring field in a straight line with a uniform speed, and broadcast their position information through beacons periodically. The RSSI value increases as the anchor node comes close to the sensor node and decrease when anchor node moves away. Assuming that the channel is lognormal shadowing, the RSSI value at a distance d from the transmitter is given by (1) and (2) [10]:

$$RSSI(d) = P_t - P_L(d) \tag{1}$$

$$P_L(d) = P_L(d_0) + 10\eta \log_{10}\left(\frac{d}{d_0}\right) + X_\sigma \tag{2}$$

where P_t is the transmission power, $P_L(d_0)$ is the path loss at the distance d, d_0 is the reference distance which is usually 1 m. η is the path loss exponent, ranges from 2 to 5. X_σ is a Gaussian random variable, which mean is 0.

3.2 Polynomial Model of RSSI Values

We appoint a group of beacon points along an anchor's trajectory; the first point is called reference point or initial point. Since anchor moves with uniform speed along the trajectory and broadcasts beacon periodically, distance between every two beacon points remains the same. We call the distance between a beacon point and the reference point relative distance. As shown in Fig. 1, the RSSI value changes with relative distance, when the RSSI received by unknown node gets larger, the distance between beacon point and unknown node gets shorter. The closest point to the unknown node corresponds to the max RSSI values. Use polynomial least square curve fitting method [11] to obtain a polynomial for the RSSI sequence. Let P(x) denotes a *j-th* order polynomial defined as follows:

$$P(x) = a_0 + a_1x + a_2x^2 + \cdots + a_jx^j \tag{3}$$

In this paper, j = 2, which means we have a quadratic polynomial R(d) of the relative distance d:

$$R(d) = a_0 + a_1d + a_2d^2 \tag{4}$$

As shown in Fig. 2, those circles represent beacon points, (x_s, y_s) is the coordinate of anchor's initial position and (x_d, y_d) is the coordinate of a beacon. The angle between anchor's trajectory and the horizontal line is θ, which can be calculated by (5).

$$\theta = \arctan\left(\frac{y_d - y_s}{x_d - x_s}\right) \tag{5}$$

3.3 Filtering of RSSI Values

Through some nodes are within the communication range of anchor node, as shown in Fig. 2, beacon sent at the point (x_d, y_d) can be received by the unknown node, but compared with the RSSI values at those points in the middle of the trajectory, it is too low. Moreover, due to the Gaussian characteristic of the channel interference, point with quite low RSSI value will have a negative effect on the polynomial modeling of this RSSI sequence. Thus, there is a need for a threshold th, all values less than th should be taken out of the calculation.

Theoretically, the RSSI value increases as the anchor node comes close to the sensor node and decrease when anchor node moves away. While some nodes have just a single RSSI tendency, under this circumstance, sensor node's projection on the trajectory cannot be calculated. We use more anchor nodes moving along different trajectories to solve this problem. Some nodes are quite near to the trajectory, resulting in the RSSI value at this point is much larger than those at other points. Under this circumstance, we consider this point as the max RSSI point.

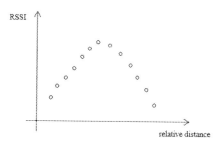

Fig. 1. Relationship of RSSI and relative distance

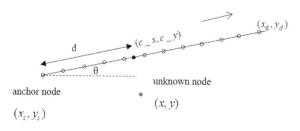

Fig. 2. The unknown node and the trajectory

3.4 Maximum RSSI Based Localization

It is known that the shortest distance between sensor node and the anchor node trajectory is the line connecting sensor node and its projection (i.e. the maximum RSSI point or the closest point) on the trajectory. To locate the sensor node, we need projections on two different anchor trajectories. With the projections, we can obtain the perpendicular lines, and the intersection of such two lines is the position of the sensor. In Fig. 3, there are two trajectories, i.e. Line 1 and 2. Let (x, y) denotes the coordinate of sensor node, (c_x_1, c_y_1) and (c_x_2, c_y_2) denote the coordinate of the closest points to the sensor node on Line 1 and 2. Let Line 3 and 4 be the perpendicular line of Line 1 and 2 separately.

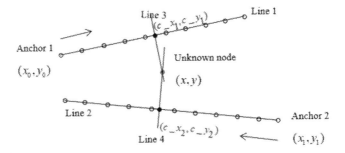

Fig. 3. Calculation of the coordinate of the unknown node

Suppose the slope of Line 1 is k_1, the slope of Line 2 is k_2. Thus, the slope of Line 3 is $-1/k_1$, and Line 4 is $-1/k_2$.

So the expression of Line 3 is:

$$y = -\frac{1}{k_1}(x - c\_x_1) + c\_y_1 \tag{6}$$

Line 4 is given by (7):

$$y = -\frac{1}{k_2}(x - c\_x_2) + c\_y_2 \tag{7}$$

With (6) and (7), the coordinate of unknown nodes can be obtained as follows:

$$\begin{cases} x = \dfrac{k_1 c\_x_2 - k_2 c\_x_1 + k_1 c\_y_2 - k_2 c\_y_1}{k_1 - k_2} \\ y = \dfrac{c\_x_1 - c\_x_2 + c\_y_1 - c\_y_2}{k_1 - k_2} \end{cases} \tag{8}$$

4 Description of Algorithm

The basic idea of the algorithm is to calculate the nearest point on anchor's trajectory to the unknown node through a set of RSSI values, and this point is sensor node's projection on the trajectory, which has the max RSSI value. With such point and given slope of a trajectory we can obtain the perpendicular line of the trajectory, the intersection of two such perpendiculars is the coordinate of the unknown node.

The detail of the proposed algorithm is as follows.

(1) Initialization

Initialize the trajectory of the anchor node. Anchor node moves from the point (x_0, y_0) and moves along a line having the slope $k = tan\ \theta$.

(2) Anchor advertises itself to the unknown nodes

For each trajectory, every unknown node receives an RSSI sequence.

(3) Process the data

(a) After filtering, a set of RSSI values is presented.

(b) Applying polynomial least square curve fitting method to a set of RSSI values, we have Eq. (4).

(c) Choose the maximum one from the values, and suppose it is the *m-th* point.

(d)
$$y_{max} = RSSI(m) + p \tag{9}$$

$$y_{max} = RSSI(m - s) \text{ or } y_{max} = RSSI(m + s) \qquad \cdot \tag{10}$$

p is adjustable to the actual situation ensuring the line $y = y_{max}$ does not intersect with $R(d)$.

s ensures that $y = y_{min}$ has two intersections with $R(d)$.

(e)
$$y_{mid} = (y_{min} + y_{max})/2 \tag{11}$$

(f) Solve the equation $R(d) = y_{mid}$.

- If the solution is two virtual roots, let $y_{max} = y_{mid}$ and then go back to (e).
- If the solution is two real roots x_1 and x_2, and $|x_1 - x_2| \geq abs$. Then let $y_{min} = y_{mid}$ and go back to step (e), else continue with step (g).

(g) Let $d\_m = (x_1 + x_2)/2$, d_m is the relative distance of unknown node's projection on this trajectory.

(h) Calculate the coordinate of the projection, i.e. (c_x, c_y).

$$c\_x = x_0 + d\_m \cdot \cos\theta \tag{12}$$

$$c\_y = y_0 + d\_m \cdot \sin\theta \tag{13}$$

θ can be calculated according to Eq. (5).

(i) With point (c_x, c_y) and slope k we can obtain the perpendicular line of the trajectory, there we have two perpendicular lines represented by (6) and (7) separately, the coordinate of the unknown node is given by Eq. (8).

5 Simulation and Analysis

5.1 Simulation Parameters

Not all the coordinates of unknown nodes can be obtained in the monitoring field. There are two main reasons, firstly, along the entire anchor node trajectory, some unknown nodes receive a single RSSI value tendency, increasing or decreasing; secondly, although some unknown nodes have two tendencies of RSSI values, the number of beacon points of one tendency is too small resulting in a bad curve fitting. For the first case, we consider use different trajectories of anchor nodes, the number of anchor nodes corresponding to different trajectories are not necessarily the same, such as W-type trajectory need only an anchor node, while X-type trajectory requires two nodes, and X-Square-type needs three. For the second case, we reduce the time interval of every two beacons, that is, reduce the positional interval h of every two beacon points.

In Table 1, there are the parameters we choose to be applied in our simulation.

Table 1. Simulation parameters

Parameter	Value
Simulation field(m × m)	100 × 100
Number of unknown nodes	20
Number of anchor nodes	1, 2, 3
Distance between beacons h (m)	3, 5
Channel Model	Lognormal Shadowing
Path loss exponent η	2
Standard deviation of X_σ	4
Transimission Power P_t(W)	1
Threshold th(W)	3×10^{-7}

5.2 Simulation Results and Analysis

In this paper, assuming sensor nodes are uniformly distributed. We study the localization of unknown nodes randomly distributed in five cases and four anchor nodes' trajectories, and analyze the location of unknown nodes in the case of shortening the time interval of every two beacons. Moreover, we compare our algorithm with the traditional Trilateration [12], to reduce the error we use 50 anchor nodes.

As shown in Fig. 4, it is the distribution of unknown nodes in the target area, five different symbols represent five different cases. Take one of the cases as an example, Figs. 6, 7, 8 and 9 shows different trajectories of the anchor nodes separately.

The segments represent the trajectories of the anchor nodes, the empty circles represent the beacon nodes, and the triangles represents the unknown sensor nodes.

Let M be the number of located unknown nodes, d be the distance between the calculated coordinate and the actual position, and M_2 the number of nodes whose d is no more than 2 m. Figure 5 shows the difference of M_2 of different trajectories and the traditional Trilateration. Obviously, the location result of Trilateration is the worst, and the number of anchor nodes used in Trilateration is far more than that in the algorithm we propose. Traditional Trilateration directly adopts the distance given by RSSI values and the lognormal shadowing model, due to the existence of path loss, the calculated position of unknown node is not as accurate as we expect. Thus, Traditional needs more anchor nodes to avoid accumulated error. Error of the algorithm we propose mainly results from path loss too, but it is acceptable. What's more, fewer anchor nodes are used in our algorithm.

In our simulation, we use five different distributions, for every one there are some digital features as shown in Tables 2 and 3. N is the number of anchor nodes; h is the distance between every two beacons; $\bar{d}$ is the mean of d; $\sigma(d)$ is the standard deviation of d; $E(\bar{d})$ is the mean of $\bar{d}$; $E[\sigma(d)]$ is the mean of $\sigma(d)$; E(M) is the mean of M; E(M_2) is the mean of M_2. We can draw a conclusion from Tables 2 and 3:

- The mean and standard deviation of d decreases as h decreases, while M and M_2 increases as h decreases.
- There are four kinds of trajectories, among them V-type is the simplest, and the digital features are the worst. As the trajectory of anchor becomes complex, digital features become better.
- None of the former three kinds of trajectories can locate all the sensor nodes in the monitoring field.
- Inspired by the X-type trajectory, we consider the X-Square-type trajectory. As shown in Table 2, coordinates of all unknown nodes can by calculated and other features are superior to the other three trajectories.

Our algorithm is effective; moreover, the relative position of unknown nodes and anchor's trajectory has an impact on the accuracy of localization.

Table 2. Digital features of localization

Features	Type of trajectory			
	V	X	W	X&S
N	1	2	2	3
h(m)	5	5	5	5
$E(\bar{d})$	2.2984	0.8377	2.1679	1.0145
$E[\sigma(d)]$	1.1856	0.6818	1.4532	0.7999
E(M)	7.8	10.2	13.4	20
E(M_2)	3.4	9.4	6.8	17.2

Table 3. Digital features of localization

Features	Type of trajectory		
	V	X	W
N	1	2	2
h(m)	3	3	3
E($\bar{d}$)	1.7449	0.5902	1.7885
E[σ(d)]	1.1086	0.4907	1.0859
E(M)	8.2	10.4	15
E(M_2)	5.2	10	9

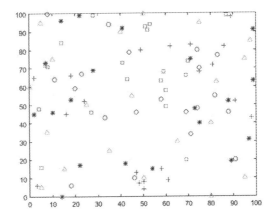

Fig. 4. Distribution of sensor nodes in the monitoring field

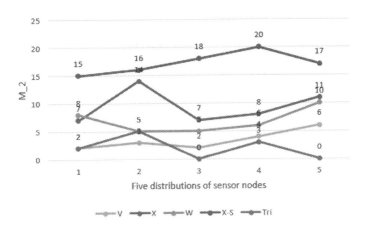

Fig. 5. Comparison of M_2 with traditional Trilateration

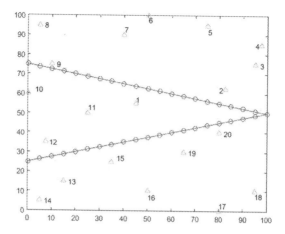

Fig. 6. V-type trajectory with single anchor node

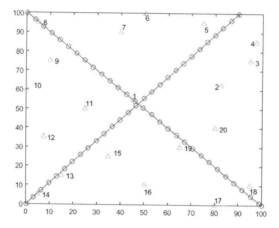

Fig. 7. X-type trajectory with double anchor nodes

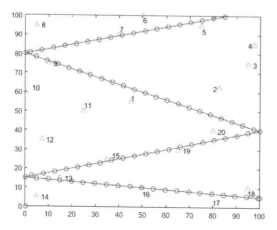

Fig. 8. W-type trajectory with single anchor node

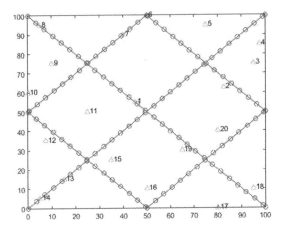

Fig. 9. X-Square-type trajectory with three anchor nodes

6 Conclusion and Prospects

In this paper, we studied an RSSI based localization technique for wireless sensor networks with few anchor nodes. Anchor nodes uniformly move along specific trajectory, making sure the communication range covers all the sensor nodes. We specified four different trajectories, and analyzed the simulation data. This RSSI based wireless sensor network localization with mobile anchor can be used in many open areas, such as pasture, farmland, theater and so on.

We draw a conclusion that the algorithm we proposed did works. Moreover, reducing the time interval of transmitting beacons can improve the accuracy of localization. The relative position of anchor's trajectory and the unknown node has an influence on the location result, and an appropriate trajectory can optimize the result.

The number of anchor nodes used in our simulation is quite few, and sensor nodes need no extra hardware, which makes the algorithm effective and economical for wireless sensor networks. However, there is a problem that once new sensor nodes are added into the monitoring field, the anchor nodes need to move again to locate the newly added nodes.

Furthermore, all of our assumptions are in a two-dimensional space, while, actually the three-dimensional space is more practical and fits more kinds of monitoring fields. Therefore, the study of multidimensional localization is the focus in our future research.

Acknowledgments. This study is supported in part by the National Natural Science Foundation of China under Grant No. 61202384, the Ministry of Science and Technology under the National Science and Technology Support Program project under Grant No. 2015BAG19B02 and the Fundamental Research Funds for the Central Universities under Grant No. 22120170186.

References

1. Akyildiz, I.F., Su, W., Sankarasubramaniam, Y., Cayirci, E.: A survey on sensor networks. IEEE Commun. Mag. **40**(8), 102–114 (2002). http://ieeexplore.ieee.org/document/1024422/
2. Sichitiu, M., Ramadurai, V.: Localization of wireless sensor networks with a mobile beacon. In: IEEE International Conference on Mobile Ad-Hoc and Sensor System (Fort Lauderdale, USA, 25–27 October 2004), pp. 174–183 (2004). http://ieeexplore.ieee.org/document/1392104/
3. Pradhan, S., Shin, S., Kwon, G.-R., Pyun, J.Y., Hwang, S.-S.: The advanced TOA trilateration algorithms with performance analysis. In: 50th Asilomar Conference on Signals, Systems and Computers (Pacific Grove, CA, USA, 06–09 November 2016), pp. 923–928 (2016). http://ieeexplore.ieee.org/document/7869184/
4. Cao, H., Chan, Y.T., So, H.C.: Maximum likelihood TDOA estimation from compressed sensing samples without reconstruction. IEEE Sig. Process. Lett. **24**(5), 564–568 (2017). http://ieeexplore.ieee.org/document/7880621/
5. Kong, F., Wang, J., Zheng, N.: A robust weighted intersection algorithm for target localization using AOA measurements. In: Advanced Information Management, Communicates, Electronic and Automation Control Conference (Xi'an, China, 03–05 October 2016), pp. 23–28 (2016). http://ieeexplore.ieee.org/document/7867106/
6. Yao, Y.-B., Jiang, N.-L.: Distributed refinement algorithm for WSN localization. J. Commun. **36**(1), 1–10 (2015)
7. Chen, Y., Wan, J., Su, Z., Zhang, R.: Study on Movement Path Planning Algorithm of Auxiliary Locating Beacon Node. J. Sichuan Univ. (Eng. Sci. Edn.) **49**(2), 160–168 (2017)
8. Shao, J.F., Tian, W.Z.: Energy-efficient RSSI-based localization for wireless sensor networks. Inf. Technol. **18**(6), 973–976 (2016)
9. Sahu, P.K., Wu, E.H.-K., Sahoo, J.: DuRT: dual RSSI trend based localization for wireless sensor networks. IEEE Sens. J. **13**(8), 3115–3123 (2013). http://ieeexplore.ieee.org/document/6502185/
10. Rappaport, T.S.: Wireless Communications: Principles and Practice
11. Björck, Å.: Numerical Methods for Least Squares Problems
12. Rusli, M.E., Ali, M., Jamil, N., Din, M.M.: An improved indoor positioning algorithm based on RSSI-trilateration technique for Internet of Things (IOT). In: On International Conference on Computer and Communication Engineering (Kuala Lumpur, Malaysia, 26–27 July 2016), pp. 72–76 (2016). http://ieeexplore.ieee.org/document/7808286/

Mobile Device Selection Based on Doppler Shift with High Resolution

Lingfei Yu[1(✉)] and Xixi Chang[2]

[1] Department of Computer Science and Technology, Zhejiang Gongshang University Hangzhou College of Commerce, Hangzhou 310018, Zhejiang, People's Republic of China
linphie@163.com
[2] School of Computer Science and Engineering, University of Electronic Science and Technology of China, Chengdu 611731, Sichuan, People's Republic of China

Abstract. For traditional mobile device selection, the source device needs to know the device ID of the target device in advance for interaction, which is not friendly for users. In this paper, a device selection scheme based on Doppler shift with high resolution is proposed. User who holds the source device makes a pointing action towards the target device, while the source device emits ultrasonic wave. According to Doppler Effect, the neighboring devices of the source device will return the device ID and Doppler frequency shifts, and the source device selects the device with the maximum frequency shift as the target device. When there are 2 or more devices with the same frequency shift, more accurate frequency differences between these devices are calculated by cross ambiguity function, in order to decide the target device with unique maximum Doppler frequency shift. Simulation results show that CAF-DS achieves higher device selection accuracy than Spartacus.

Keywords: Device selection · Doppler effect · Cross ambiguity function
Frequency shift

1 Introduction

With the development of mobile Internet and widespread popularity of smartphones, more and more applications require mobile devices interact with each other to exchange information. For example, Bluetooth earphone matches the specified audio device and receives audio data. People exchange their electronic name card with the interaction between their smartphones.

Device interaction consists of three phases: Device Scanning, Selection of Target Device and Device Matching. Different from Internet, device scanning in mobile Internet is to find devices in the vicinity of users, rather than devices in the same network, which makes the selection of the target device a bottleneck of mobile device interaction. Target device is usually selected from the device list created by device scanning and interacts with the source device after device matching. Users must get the *ID* of the target devices before device interaction. For example, when people exchange their electronic name card, they need to know the *ID* of smart phone of the other.

H. Yuan et al. (Eds.): GSKI 2017, CCIS 848, pp. 188–197, 2018.
https://doi.org/10.1007/978-981-13-0893-2_20

Similarly, a smart phone matches the right Bluetooth ear phone with the known *ID* of the ear phone from scanned device list.

Obviously, the challenge of device interaction for mobile Internet is to find and select the target device first in the physical world, and then to connect the target device for interaction. There have been some studies on the selection and interaction of mobile devices recently. NFC [1] can be used for device selection, but with the limitation of 4 cm between the source device and the target device. Point&Connect [2] and Spartacus [3] can choose the target devices up to 5 m, using acoustic sensing techniques or Doppler effect. However, Spartacus requires that the angle between the source device and two other devices should be larger than 20°. It means the distance between the two other devices would be larger than 1.8 m when they are 5 m away from the source device, which cannot be satisfied in real world for the crowed smartphones.

In this paper, a cross ambiguity function based mobile device selection method (CAF-DS) is presented. CAF-DS requires user to initiate an interaction with the target device by pointing his phone towards target phone. Based on Doppler effect, there may be a phone with the maximum Doppler frequency shifts, which is the target device. If there are several phones with the same Doppler frequency shifts when the phones come too close, then cross ambiguity function is used to calculate the higher resolution Doppler frequency shifts to determine the target phone with the maximum Doppler frequency shifts.

The remainder of this paper is organized as follows. Section 2 discusses the related works. Doppler effect and CAF is described in Sect. 3. In Sect. 4, the proposed scheme is presented in detail. Section 5 introduces simulations and discusses the results. The last section concludes the paper.

2 Related Works

There have been some works to study mobile device selection and interaction. QR code is a popular technique for device interaction [4, 5], but it cannot interact with the target device if the target device has no display function.

GPS can also be used to identify and select the target device. Drawil et al. [6] proposed a GPS based localization algorithm, which has lower location accuracy and cannot localize indoor. WIFI based localization [7] resolves indoor location, depending on the collection of WIFI fingerprint, which also achieves lower accuracy.

NFC [8] requires that mobile devices should be less than 4 cm apart in order to ensure the communication among devices. However, the distance of 4 cm restricts the applications of NFC in real world. Simon et al. [9] exploit infrared spectroscopy to choose the target device, which can select the target device with high accuracy. Unfortunately, infrared transmitter is not equipped on most of mobile devices, especially smartphones. MOO [10] developed a RFID business card for e-Card exchanging. Like NFC, the RFID based method also requires the target device is close to the source device.

[11] enables a user to send information from the user's PDA to other mobile devices with a "toss" or "swing" action. If users swing their devices at the same time, their devices can be matched. It is not easy to identify and synchronize the "swing" action of devices. SyncTap [12] is a simple method that users of the source device and

the target device press and release a button simultaneously. However, synchronous operation of users is difficult.

Point&Connect [2] proposed a novel device selection scheme, which uses a pointing gesture to initiate interactions between a mobile device and its target. However, the system requires an initial channel of communication. Similarly, Spartacus [3] explores Doppler effect, and selects the target device with the peak Doppler frequency shifts. However, if other devices are less than 1.8 m from the target device when the source device is 5 m away the target device, it will achieve poor accuracy.

3   Doppler Effect and Cross Ambiguity Function

3.1   Doppler Effect

The Doppler effect is the change in frequency of a wave for an observer moving relative to its source. When the source of the waves is moving towards the observer, each successive wave crest is emitted from a position closer to the observer than the previous wave. Therefore, each wave takes slightly less time to reach the observer than the previous wave. Hence, the time between the arrivals of successive wave crests at the observer is reduced, causing an increase in the frequency [13]. The relationship between observed frequency f and emitted frequency f_0 is given by:

$$f = \frac{c + v_R}{c - v_S} f_0 \tag{1}$$

where c is the velocity of waves in the medium, v_R is the velocity of the receiver relative to the medium, and v_S is the velocity of the source relative to the medium.

Doppler shift is the difference between f and f_0, which could be used to choose the target device. As in Fig. 1, A is the source device, C is the target device, and W is the angle between line AC and line AB. Assume that A moves towards C with the velocity v_S along the line AC. The velocity observed by B is $v_S cos W$. According to Eq. (1), the observed frequency of device B, f_B is lower than that of device C, f_C, which means device C observes the maximum frequency shift. That is, the device with the maximum Doppler frequency shift is the target device if the source device moves towards its neighboring devices. Of cause, W poses significant influence on the accuracy of Doppler frequency shift. When W is too small, other device (device B) is very close to device C, the Doppler frequency shifts of them may be no different due to low resolution Doppler shift based on Eq. (1). In this case, a high resolution Doppler shift calculation should be introduced.

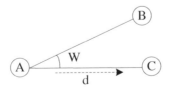

Fig. 1. Selecting the target device based on Doppler shift

3.2   Cross Ambiguity Function

Cross Ambiguity Function [14] is a method to compute the cross correlation between two signals, which not only gets the frequency shift between them, but also gets the time delay between them. In the area of radar, CAF can be used to calculate the high accuracy of Doppler shift with 0.1 Hz resolution so that it can select the target device with the maximum frequency shift accurately.

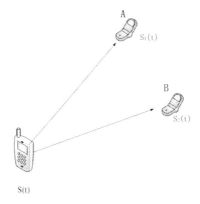

Fig. 2. Two device receiving signals from the source device

As shown in Fig. 2, the source device emits signal $S(t)$, and $S_1(t)$ and $S_2(t)$ are the signals received by the receiver device A and B. The distance between the device A and the source device is different from the distance between the device B and the source device, leading to different time delay and frequency shift. The signals received by the receiver device A and B can be expressed by:

$$S_1(t) = S(t) + n_A(t) \tag{2}$$

$$S_2(t) = S(t) + n_b(t) \tag{3}$$

where t_d and f_d are the time delay and frequency shift of the receiver device B relative to the receiver device A. $n_A(t)$ and $n_B(t)$ are independent white Gauss noise.

The cross ambiguity function is given by:

$$A(\tau, f) = \int_0^T S_1(t)S_2^*(t+\tau)e^{-j2\pi f_t}dt \tag{4}$$

where T is the integration time; while τ and f are, respectively, the time delay and frequency shift parameters to be searched simultaneously for the values that cause $A(\tau, f)$ to the peak. The outputs of CAF calculation include the expected signal and noise. To distinguish the peak frequency shit, the *SNR* of output signal should be larger than 20 dB.

4   Implementation of CAF-DS

As in Fig. 3, the source device A wants to interact with the device C. For traditional mobile device interaction scheme, the source device A scans the neighboring devices and constructs a device list containing the device B, C and D. Then the source device A chooses the device C whose *ID* is known by A in advance to establish a connection, which degrades the interaction efficiency and is not friendly for users.

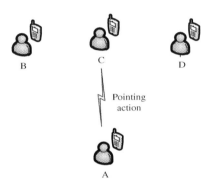

B   C   D

Pointing
action

A

Fig. 3. Source A wants to interact with target device C

To improve user experiences, CAF-DS does not need to know any information about the target device such as the device *ID* in advance. User just holds his smartphone, making a pointing action towards the target device. Because of relative motion between the source device and the target device, each neighboring receiver device observes a different frequency from that of original signal, leading to different Doppler frequency shifts for each receiver device based on Eq. (1). The receiver device with the maximum Doppler frequency shift is the target device. In Fig. 3, the source device A moves towards the device C, and the device C will observe the maximum frequency shift. Then the source device A initiates a connection with the target device C according to the device *ID* sent by the device C.

However, if the receiver devices B, C and D are very close for each other, the Doppler shifts of the three receiver devices calculated by the Eq. (1) may be the same for lacking of enough resolution. At this time, the source device A gives a cross ambiguity function instruction to notify all receiver devices with the same frequency shifts to perform CAF computing. With the calculation of CAF, which providing high resolution accuracy, the target device with the maximum Doppler frequency shift with high resolution will be selected from the receiver devices.

4.1   Design of Source Device

Figure 4 shows the procedure of the source device. The source device generates ultrasonic at 20 kHz frequency, which is emitted by the speaker of the smartphone after it is transformed from digital signal to analog signal by DAC. The microphones of the neighboring receiver devices will receive the original signal. Now user holding the source device makes a pointing action towards the device he wants to interact. All the receiver will observe a frequency shift due to Doppler effect and they send the Doppler frequency shifts computed by Eq. (1) and the device *ID* of them back to the source device.

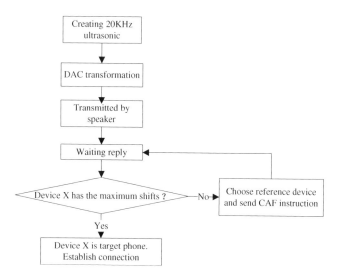

Fig. 4. Procedure of the source device

If the receiver device X has the maximal Doppler frequency shift, meaning it is the target device, the source device will interact with it. However, if there are several receiver devices with the same frequency shift, meaning the W is too small and those receiver devices are too close, the source device will choose a reference device among them and transmit a CAF instruction to it. The CAF calculation will be performed by the reference device between it and any other receiver devices with the same frequency shift. The high resolution relative frequency shifts between the reference device and any other receiver devices will be computed, which can be used to determine the target device with a unique maximum Doppler frequency shift with high resolution accuracy.

4.2 Receiver Device

The procedure of the receiver device is shown in Fig. 5. Received ultrasonic sent from the source device, Butterworth bandpass filter is used to filter signals lower than 19 kHz or greater than 21 kHz. The signals between 19 kHz and 21 kHz are under-sampled to decrease the sample rate and calculation. The undersampled signals are transformed from time domain to frequency domain by *FFT* and the frequency shifts can be extracted in each frame. The peak frequency is the Doppler frequency shift of the receiver device. Then the receiver device will send its Doppler frequency shift and *ID* back to the source device by audio encoding.

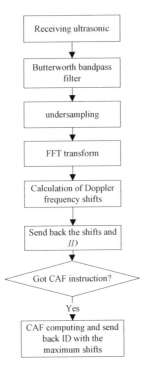

Fig. 5. Procedure of the receiver device

If the receiver device receives the CAF instruction from the source device, it means the receiver device is the reference device, denoting that there are other receiver devices having the same Doppler frequency with it, and it will perform CAF calculation between it and any other receiver devices based on (4). With the relative frequency shifts calculated by CAF, it can determine a unique target device with the maximum Doppler frequency shift, whose *ID* will be returned to the source device for the following interaction.

4.3   Cross Ambiguity Function Computation

When the reference device receives the CAF instruction, it calculates the relative frequency shift with each of the receiver devices which have the same Doppler frequency shift computed by Eq. (1). Then it will get the maximum frequency shift based on the relative frequency shift and decides which receiver device is the target device.

As in Fig. 6, three receiver devices have the same Doppler frequency shift calculated by Eq. (1). Assume that the source device selects the device 1 as the reference device and sends it the CAF instruction and information about the device 2 and the device 3. The device 1 performs CAF calculation based on Eq. (4) with the device 2 and the device 3, respectively. By CAF calculation, it can get the relative frequency shift f_1 between the device 1 and the device 2 and the relative frequency shift f_2 between the device 1 and the device 3. Compared f_1 with f_2, it can determine which the

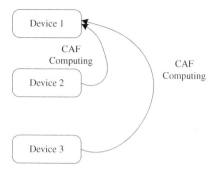

Fig. 6. CAF computing

receiver device has the maximal value of Doppler frequency shift with high resolution accuracy, whose device *ID* will be sent to the source device for the following interaction.

5 Performance Evaluation

5.1 Simulation Setup

The network topology is as in Fig. 1. There are three students and each of them holds a smartphone. The smartphone held by student *A* is the source device and the smartphone held by student *C* is the target device, which is *d* meters away from the source device. Another smart phone held by the student *B* is also *d* meters away from the source device with a directional angle *W*. For each experiment, the student *A* holding the smartphone makes a pointing action towards the target device 50 times and the peak velocity is about 3 m/s.

5.2 Simulation Results

At first, we compare CAF-DS with Spartacus [3] in terms of target device selection accuracy under different distance to the source device and different angle *W*, and the results are shown in Figs. 7 and 8, respectively.

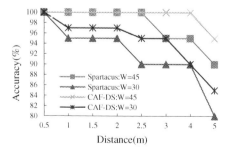

Fig. 7. The impacts of d on accuracy

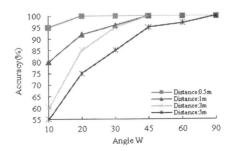

Fig. 8. The impacts of W on accuracy under different distances

Figure 7 plots the target device selection accuracy with the increasing distance d, which the angle W is set to 30° and 45°. The larger the distance d is, the more the acoustic attenuates, leading to lower accuracy. Keeping the distance d stable, the target device selection accuracy increases with the enlargement of the angle W. The reason is that the larger the angle W, the more different of Doppler frequency shift of the target device from other receiver devices. Compared with Spartacus, CAF-DS achieves higher accuracy. As in Fig. 7, the accuracy of CAF-DS reaches 100% when W is 45° and the distance d is less than 4 m, compared with 95% accuracy of Spartacus. When the distance d is 5 m, CAF-DS and Spartacus achieve 95% and 90% accuracy. But when the angle W is 30°, the accuracies of CAF-DS are 95% and 85% with the distance d is 3 m and 5 m, which have 5% more than that of Spartacus.

Figure 8 describes how the angle W influences the target device selection accuracy under different distance d. The accuracy increases with the increasement of the angle W. Within 3 m, CAF-DS achieves 95% accuracy when the angle W is 30° and 100% accuracy when the angle W is 45°. Within 5 m, CAF-DS achieves 85% accuracy when the angle W is 30° and 95% accuracy when the angle W is 45°. Noticeably, the accuracy of CAF-DS still has about 90% accuracy when the angle W is less than 20 within 2 m.

The target device selection accuracy under different noisy conditions is shown in Fig. 9. The performance of CAF-DS in environment noise has higher accuracy than in music and speak conditions, while the accuracy in speak condition has poorest performance. However, CAF-DS reaches about 87% accuracy in noisy conditions, which has little influence on the performance of CAF-DS.

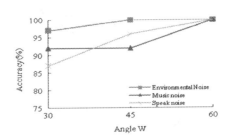

Fig. 9. The impacts of different noisy conditions

6   Conclusions

In this paper, a high accuracy mobile device selection scheme based on cross ambiguity function is presented. User holding the source device makes a pointing action towards the target device, while the source device emits a 20 kHz ultrasonic signal. According to Doppler effect, the target device will observe the maximum Doppler frequency shift. If there are several devices having identical frequency shifts, the CAF calculation is employed to compute Doppler frequency shift with high resolution accuracy, so that a unique target device with maximal frequency shift can be determined. Simulation results show that CAF-DS achieves higher accuracy than Spartacus, especially when the angle W is small.

Acknowledgments. This work is supported in part by National Science Foundation of China under Grants numbers, 61370204 and Zhejiang Provincial Natural Science Foundation under Grant number LQ16F02001.

References

1. 18 Creative & Useful Ways to Use NFC Tags with Your Smartphone (2014). http://trendblog.net/creative-and-useful-ways-to-use-nfc-tags-with-your-smartphone
2. Peng, C., Shen, G., Zhang, Y., Lu, S.: Point&connect: intention based device pairing for mobile phone users. In: Proceedings of the 7th International Conference on Mobile Systems, Applications, and Services, MobiSys 2009, pp. 137–150 (2009)
3. Sun, Z., Purohit, A., Bose, R., Zhang, P.: Spartacus: spatially-aware interaction for mobile devices through energy-efficient audio sensing. In: Proceeding of the 11th Annual International Conference on Mobile Systems, Applications, and Services, MobiSys 2013, pp. 263–276 (2013)
4. QR Code. http://www.nttdocomo.co.jp/english/service/imode/make/content/barcode/tool/
5. Semacode. http://semacode.com/
6. Drawil, N.M., Amar, H.M., Basir, O.A.: GPS localization accuracy classification: a context-based approach. IEEE Trans. Intell. Transp. Syst. **14**, 262–273 (2013)
7. Liu, H., et al.: Accurate WiFi based localization for smartphones using peer assistance. IEEE Trans. Mob. Comput. **13**, 2199–2214 (2014)
8. NFC versus Bluetooth. http://www.nearfieldcommunicationnfc.net/nfc-vs-bluetooth.html
9. Simon, J., Vojko, F., Matjaz, D.: Towards a low-cost mobile subcutaneous vein detection solution using near infrared spectroscopy. Sci. World J. **2014**, 1–15 (2014)
10. MOO Gives Out RFID Business Cards. http://www.rfidjournalcom/articles/view?10056, 2013
11. Mayrhofer, R., Gellersen, H.: Shake well before use: authentication based on accelerometer data. In: LaMarca, A., Langheinrich, M., Truong, K.N. (eds.) Pervasive 2007. LNCS, vol. 4480, pp. 144–161. Springer, Heidelberg (2007). https://doi.org/10.1007/978-3-540-72037-9_9
12. Rekimoto, J., Ayatsuka, Y., Kohno, M.: SyncTap: an interaction technique for mobile networking. In: Chittaro, L. (ed.) Mobile HCI 2003. LNCS, vol. 2795, pp. 104–115. Springer, Heidelberg (2003). https://doi.org/10.1007/978-3-540-45233-1_9
13. https://en.wikipedia.org/wiki/Doppler_effect
14. Seymour, S.: Algorithms for ambiguity function processing. IEEE Trans. Acoust. Speech Signal **3**, 588–599 (1981)

The Double-Coverage Algorithm
for Mobile Node Deployment
in Underwater Sensor Network

Xue Wang[1], Nana Li[2], Fang Liu[2], and Yuanming Ding[3(✉)]

[1] College of Information Engineering,
Dalian University, Dalian 116622, Liaoning, China
wangxue@dlu.edu.cn
[2] Communication and Network Laboratory, Dalian University,
Dalian 116622, Liaoning, China
lnn311@163.com, 352142607@qq.com
[3] Network and Information Center, Dalian University,
Dalian 116622, Liaoning, China
dingyuanming@dlu.edu.cn

Abstract. The deployment of sensors is of importance in underwater wireless sensor networks (UWSNs) in the area of underwater short distance communication. Aiming at the problem of blind coverage and excessive energy consumption in the deployment of sensors in UWSNs, from the perspective of no vulnerability coverage monitoring area and on the basis of current coverage control method, mobile sensor nodes are introduced to double cover the target area around the UWSNs' coverage control, and the double-coverage algorithm based on the deployment of mobile sensors is proposed. Firstly, the sensor node sensing model is established and the target area is divided into grid. Further, the deployment of mobile nodes is modeled and analyzed on the basis of the divided grid. Then the sensor node mobility model is designed and the double-coverage algorithm based on sensor node deployment is proposed. Finally, the rationality and effectiveness of the proposed algorithm is verified by simulation experiments. The simulation results show that the proposed algorithm can reduce the number of mobile nodes, which save the cost. At the same time, the energy consumption of sensor nodes is reduced as well under the same conditions and to a certain extent, the average energy consumption of mobile nodes in the network is evenly distributed. The algorithm effectively improves the coverage quality of UWSNs and greatly prolong the network lifetime.

Keywords: Sensor · Nodes deployment · Mobile nodes model
Coverage control · Underwater wireless sensor networks (UWSNs)

1 Introduction

Underwater wireless sensor networks (UWSNs) node deployment is a basic problem in underwater wireless short range communication. These are many problems in the deployment of sensor nodes in UWSNs, such as coverage blind area and excessive

© Springer Nature Singapore Pte Ltd. 2018
H. Yuan et al. (Eds.): GSKI 2017, CCIS 848, pp. 198–211, 2018.
https://doi.org/10.1007/978-981-13-0893-2_21

energy consumption, which affect the overall performance of the network [1]. Reasonable and efficient deployment sensor nodes coverage algorithm can effectively improve the quality of coverage of UWSNs, contribute to faster and more efficient to complete the coverage task, balance the whole network energy consumption, reduce the cost of hardware, prolong the network life cycle, so as to improve the monitoring capacity of the system [2, 3]. Therefore, it is of great practical significance to study the coverage algorithm of sensor nodes deployment in underwater wireless sensor networks.

At present, there are some achievements in the research of node deployment algorithm for underwater wireless sensor networks. Reference [4] proposes a distributed density control algorithm based on environmental monitoring and adaptive dormancy. The algorithm extends the service life of the system by leaving only part of sensor nodes working, other nodes enter a dormant state. It is simple and easy to realize the aim, but cannot guarantee complete coverage of the monitoring area. The literature [5] presents an algorithm based on K coverage algorithm. The algorithm takes advantages of the relationship between coverage and connectivity in wireless sensor networks, improving the network performance. However, the network nodes need to be precise positioning, and the energy consumption of the sensor nodes is very large. Reference [6] puts forward the double-coverage algorithm for monitoring area. The algorithm achieves without vulnerability coverage, but cannot uniform deployment of the total distance of mobile nodes, which leads to the sensor nodes premature failure because of uneven energy consumption and the more mobile sensor nodes number.

In view of the above analysis, we propose a 2-coverage algorithm based on mobile sensor nodes deployment. The algorithm is the angle from the waters covered monitoring of vulnerabilities, the deployment of mobile nodes through the design of target area mesh, which reduce the moving distance of the sensor nodes, and the resolution of each node due to the node moving distance uneven and may cause the problem of premature failure [7]. The simulation results show that the proposed algorithm can distribute the energy consumption as evenly as possible in the same conditions compared with other algorithms.

2 Network Architecture and Model Building

2.1 Network Architecture

At present, the architecture of underwater wireless sensor network is mainly divided into three categories [8, 9]: 2D static sensor networks, 3D static sensor networks, and 3D sensor networks with Autonomous Underwater Vehicle (AUV). The discussion in this paper is based on the 3D sensor network with AUV. As is shown in the Fig. 1.

The underwater sensor network with AUV consists mainly of some mobile nodes in static underwater sensor networks. The mobile node is provided with a plurality of acoustic/optical transceiver [10, 11], realizing horizontal and vertical data transceiver. The existence of the mobile node can cover the blind area of the fixed node failure so as to improve the network coverage quality.

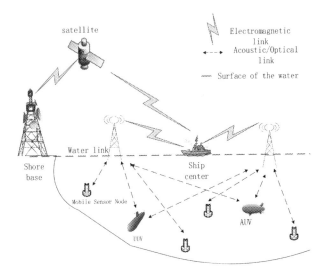

Fig. 1. Architecture of UWSNs with AUV.

2.2 Modeling and Analysis of Node Deployment

2.2.1 Node Sensing Model

In order to solve the problem of node deployment and sensor network coverage, must establish the node sensing model [12, 13]. The node's sensing model describes the radius of the nodes and the detection capability, which is determined by the physical properties of the sensor.

As is shown in the Fig. 2. The sensor nodes usually use 0–1 sensing model to describe the sensing ability and the radius of the underwater sensor nodes in UWSNs. And R_s is adjustable. If the coordinates of the node A is (x_a, y_a), the probability that the node C (x_c, y_c) is detected by the sensor node A is:

$$P_s(A, C) = \begin{cases} 1, d(A, C) \le R_s \\ 0, d(A, C) > R_s \end{cases} \tag{1}$$

The distance between C and A is $d(A, C) = \sqrt{(x_a - x_c)^2 + (y_a - y_c)^2}$. When the target is detected within the sensing range, the probability if detection is 1; otherwise the probability of detection is 0 when the detected target is located outside the sensing range of the node.

2.2.2 Nodes Mesh Model

The sensing radius of the sensor node is limited, but we need to complete monitoring water to maximize the coverage requirements with sensor nodes as few as possible. It requires the coverage area of each node is maximized. So we should reduce the

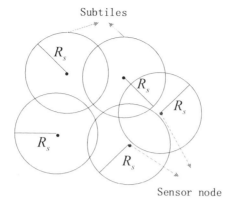

Subtiles

Sensor node

Fig. 2. Schematic diagram of 0–1 sensing model.

coverage overlap in waters and make full use of the sensing range of each sensor node. In generally, the covering model is usually a regular triangle or quadrilateral [14].

First of all, it is necessary to divide the underwater wireless sensor network with Voronoi in order to compare these models [15, 16]. It is assumed that the regular polygon is used to cover 100% of the water area without any holes. At the same time, the angle of the regular polygon is considered to be implemented on the same point. A inner angle of a n edge shape is $(n - 2) \times 180°/n$. Then the equation satisfies:

$$x \times \frac{(n - 2) \times 180°}{n} = 360° \tag{2}$$

The above formula can be converted to: $x = 2 + 4/n - 2$. Both x and n are integers, and $3 \leq x \leq 6$, so the value is $n = 3, x = 6$; $n = 4, x = 4$; $n = 6, x = 3$. It is Equilateral triangle, quadrangle and hexagon. If the radius of the node is R_s, according to Voronoi partition, the node is placed at the center of a regular polygon, then the coverage of the nodes of the equilateral triangle, quadrilateral, hexagon, as is shown in Fig. 3(a), (b) and (c).

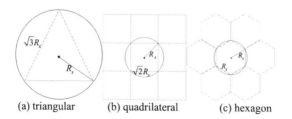

(a) triangular   (b) quadrilateral   (c) hexagon

Fig. 3. Schematic diagram of Voronoi partition.

If all the nodes are placed at the center of the triangle, each node is the same as the case, and the coverage area of the node is the difference between the coverage area of the node and the area of the inscribed triangle:

$$S_{3-cover} = \pi R_s^2 - \frac{3\sqrt{3}R_s^2}{4} \tag{3}$$

The coverage rate is: $S_{triangular}/S_{circle} \approx 41.37\%$. And the overlap area of the node is the difference between the coverage area of the node and the area of the square:

$$S_{4-cover} = \pi R_s^2 - 2R_s^2 \tag{4}$$

The coverage rate is: $S_{quadrilateral}/S_{circle} \approx 63.66\%$. And the overlap area of the node is the difference between the coverage area of the node and the area of the inscribed hexagon:

$$S_{6-cover} = \pi R_s^2 - \frac{3\sqrt{3}}{2}R_s^2 \tag{5}$$

The coverage rate is: $S_{hexagon}/S_{circle} \approx 82.74\%$. From the above analysis, it is found that the coverage rate of the hexagonal repeat coverage area is the smallest and it has the highest coverage. So the grid model of nodes in UWSNs is hexagon.

2.2.3   Mobile Node Deployment Model

According to the Reference [6], it divides the covering water into a regular hexagonal grid, and then divides each hexagonal mesh into two triangles and a rectangle. In order to 2-cover the rectangular area, the four mobile sensor nodes are placed on the four vertices of the rectangle. Although there is a double coverage by the method is used to monitor the waters, there is a certain coverage vulnerability. It is find that only 28% of the sensing waters covered rectangular sensing waters after calculation as is shown in the Fig. 4.

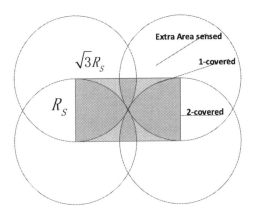

Fig. 4. Schematic diagram of mobile node at the vertex.

While the 3/4 mobile sensor nodes are placed on the three vertices of an isosceles triangle. After calculation, only 39% of the perceived water is inside the isosceles triangle as is shown in the Fig. 5.

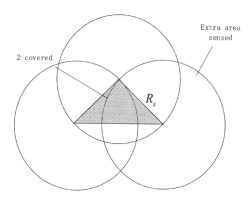

Fig. 5. Schematic diagram of mobile node in triangle vertex.

The algorithm in Reference [6] can not make the energy consumption of the mobile nodes evenly. It may cause the energy depletion of earlier sensor node of long distance, and it used to many mobile sensors so as to cost a lot. On the basis of the above model, this paper proposed a new deployment model of Four-Sensor-Triangle (FST). As is shown in Fig. 6, it used two kinds of sensors with different sensing ranges. A kind of sensor named A, it's radius of sensing is R_s, another kind of sensor named B, which radius is $2R_s$. After calculation, the model covers 58% of the sensing area.

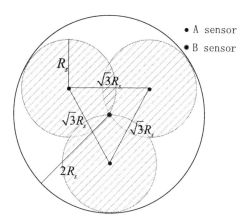

Fig. 6. FST deployment model.

2.2.4   Mobility Model

As is shown in Fig. 7, it divided the monitoring waters into a rectangular, which length is l, and the width is w. The rectangular area is divided into regular hexagonal grids. A type of sensor is placed at the apex of a regular triangle while B type sensor placed in the center of the triangle.

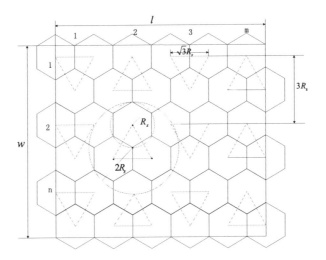

Fig. 7. Schematic diagram of mobile node deployment.

It is supposed that there are m number FSTs arranged along length l and n number of FSTs along width w. The following mathematical relations can be established to find out the values of m and n.

$$l = \frac{\sqrt{3}}{2}(3m - 1)R_s \tag{6}$$

$$w = \left[3(n - 1) + \frac{5}{2}\right]R_s \tag{7}$$

3   The 2-Coverage Algorithm Based on Mobile Node Deployment

3.1   Basic Assumptions

A sensor node in a network is meant for collecting and to transmit the data to the base station through available paths. Sensor nodes are equipped with limited power source. In many cases it is not possible to replenish the power source. Hence there is a need to save the energy of the sensor nodes.

The following assumptions are made:

(1) All sensor nodes are deployed in 2D, and all sensor nodes are aware of their location after initial deployment.
(2) Sensing are of a sensor is a circular area of its sensing range.
(3) Without considering any obstacles, the sensors are randomly distributed in the monitoring area, ignoring the regional boundary effect.
(4) Without considering the localization problem, it is assumed that the mobile node carries GPS, which is able to get the coordinates of itself in real time.

3.2   Algorithm Description

The placement and movement of mobile sensor nodes are shown in Fig. 8. In the Fig. 8, the three are located in the triangle of a kind of sensor with the number A1, A2, A3, another FST center in the B sensor with the number B.

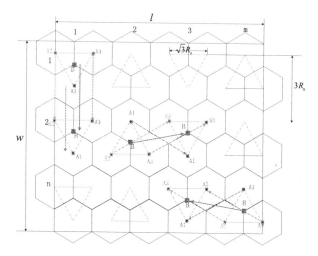

Fig. 8. Schematic diagram of node movement.

The algorithm steps are summarized as follows:

Step 1: Initially three small sensor nodes with the number A1, A2, A3 are placed at the vertices and large sensor node at the center of the equilateral triangle. This 2-covers the area under the sensing range of three small sensor nodes.

Step 2: In order to cover the next FST, all mobile sensor nodes are moved vertically downward. This movement may be upward or downward depending on the current column in which sensor are.

Step 3: Step 2 is repeated, until entire column is traversed. Now the sensors reach the bottom or top of a column and need to be shifted horizontally to the adjacent column.

Step 4: As is indicated in the Fig. 8.

- The top or the bottom sensor node with the number A1 of the FST model moves to the bottom or top position of its adjacent next FST.
- The lower left or upper left sensor node with the number A2 of the FST model moves to the upper left or lower left of the next FST.
- The sensor node with the number A3 in the lower right or upper right of the FST model moves to the upper right or lower right of the Next FST.
- The large sensor node with the number B in the FST model moves to the center of the next model.

Step 5: Step 3 and Step 4 are repeated, until the rectangular monitoring area is completely 2-coverd.

3.3   Performance Evaluation

3.3.1   Total Distance Traveled

Distance between the vertices of two vertically adjacent FST is $3R_s$. FST is divided into number of n rows. So, to traverse one column, three A and a B mobile nodes travel of $4 \times (n-1) \times 3R_s$. On reaching the vertical end, to move to the next column, three A sensor nodes traveled a distance of $3R_s$. The B sensor nodes traveled a distance of $\sqrt{7}R_s$. FST consists of m number of columns and m number of rows.

So, the total distance L traverled by all deployed mobile sensor nodes is given by.

$$L = \left[4 \times (n-1) \times 3R_s \times m + 3 \times (3R_s + \sqrt{7}R_s) \right]/2 \tag{8}$$

3.3.2   Numbers of Mobile Sensor Nodes

According to the algorithm proposed, there are $(m \times n)$ FSTs in a rectangular, which length is l, and the width is w. Each FST makes up by three A nodes and a B node. So the number of nodes is $(m \times n \times 4)$.

3.3.3   Extra Area Sensed

To 2-cover the entire FST, $m \times n \times 3\pi R_s^2$ and $m \times n \times \pi(2R_s)^2$ is sensed.

So, the extra area sensed (EAS) together by A and B sensor nodes is:

$$EAS = \pi mn[(2R_s)^2 + 3R_s^2] - 2lw \tag{9}$$

4   Results and Analysis

The simulation is carried out using MATLAB R2014a to verify the validity and practicability of the algorithm. The distribution areas of underwater sensor nodes choose a rectangle area of 4500*2000 units. And sensing range of small node number of A1, A2, A3 is varied from 45 to 65, at an increment of 5 units. The simulation parameters are shown in Table 1.

Table 1. Total number of sensing nodes

Rectangle area	Sensing range	Number of node	Experiment times	A type of node	B type of node
4500*2000	45–65	20000	30	A1, A2 and A3	B

The simulation results of the relationship between the total moving distance of sensor nodes and sensor sensing radius are shown in Fig. 9. The horizontal ordinate is the sensing range of small nodes and the ordinate is the total distance of the sensor nodes in the Fig. 9. The simulation results are compared with the algorithm proposed in the Reference [6].

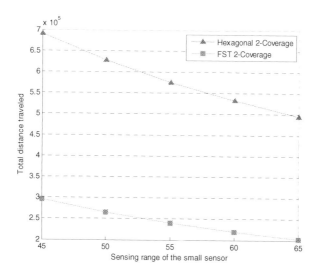

Fig. 9. Comparison of total distance traveled by mobile sensor nodes.

As can see in the Fig. 9, the total distance traveled of the two algorithms decreases with the increase of sensor range in case of mobile sensor nodes with different sensing range. The total distance traveled proposed in this paper is less than that in [6] when achieve no vulnerability coverage.

The simulation results of the relationship between the moving distance of each node in the unit FST and the sensor radius are shown in Fig. 10. The abscissa is the number of sensor nodes, which are represented by different colors. Sensor nodes with the same color as the same number. The ordinate indicates the distance traveled of each sensor node in the unit FST.

As is shown in Fig. 10, the distance traveled of each node in the unit FST of the Reference [6] is uneven while that in the algorithm proposed is well-distributed. The algorithm can make the energy consumption of each nodes more uniform so as to avoid the failure of individual nodes due to excessive energy consumption.

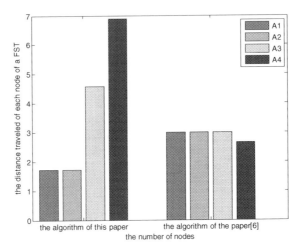

Fig. 10. Comparison of the distance traveled of each node in the same range. (Color figure online)

The simulation results of the relationship between the quantity of mobile sensor nodes and sensor sensing radius are shown in Fig. 11. The horizontal ordinate is the sensing range of small nodes and the ordinate is the quantity of mobile sensor nodes.

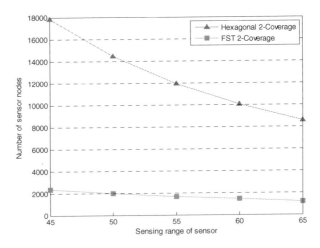

Fig. 11. Comparison of the total number of mobile nodes.

As is indicated in Fig. 11, the total number of mobile nodes used in the algorithm proposed is less than that in the algorithm of the Reference [6] when achieve no vulnerability coverage.

Table 2. Total number of sensing nodes

Sensing range (Rs)	Hexagonal coverage (Number of nodes)	FST algorithm (Number of node)	% of reduction in total sensing nodes
45	95594963.81	7901249.99	91.73%
50	95474326.65	7958006.42	91.66%
55	95103455.01	8014823.92	91.57%
60	95323530.30	8071702.51	91.53%
65	97636370.71	8128642.19	91.67%

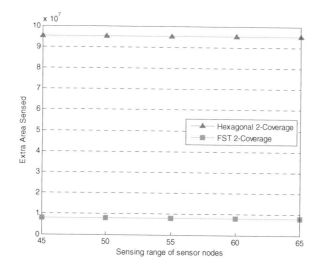

Fig. 12. Comparison of the extra sending area of mobile nodes.

The simulation results of the sensing area of mobile sensor nodes are shown in Table 2 and Fig. 12.

Table 2 gives the extra sensing area and percentage reduction of the two algorithms and is graphically shown in Fig. 12.

As is show in Fig. 12, the extra area sensed of mobile sensor node with the algorithm proposed is less than that in Reference [6] when the mobile sensor is under different circumstance.

5 Conclusion

Aiming at the problem of blind coverage and uneven energy consumption in the deployment of UWSNs, this paper proposed a 2-covered algorithm of the mobile sensor nodes. The difference between the proposed algorithm and the existing algorithm is that the mobile energy consumption of the mobile node is averaged by a new mobile model, so as to avoid the premature failure of the sensor nodes due to the uneven energy consumption.

The simulation results show that the algorithm proposed is better complete the no vulnerability coverage of nodes, reducing the extra area sensed, improving the quality of coverage and maximizing the homogenization of the energy consumption under certain conditions. In addition, the number of mobile nodes is reduced and the hardware cost is saved to a certain extent.

The paper mainly introduces the algorithm for covering the target area. The proposed algorithm can 2-covered the target area. And it has achieved the expected basic effect. But there are some problems and shortcomings in the algorithm. In the future work, will study the following two aspects:

(1) In the actual environment, the water environment will have an impact on the communication range of the nodes. In the future, the focus of consideration is to consider the double coverage of the communication range.
(2) The water environment will affect the path of nodes and the communication energy consumption of nodes in the communication process. Next, we will focus on the mobile sensor coverage algorithm in consider of the communication energy consumption.

Acknowledgments. This work was supported by the National Natural Science Foundation of China (61540024).

References

1. Wang, H., Liu, M., Zhang. S.: An efficient depth-adjustment deployment scheme for underwater wireless sensor networks. In: Proceedings of the 34th Chinese Control Conference, Hangzhou, China, pp. 7771–7776 (2015)
2. Zhang, Y., Li, X., Fang, S.: A research on the deployment of sensors in underwater acoustic wireless sensor networks. In: Proceedings of the 2nd International Conference on Information Science and Engineering, Hangzhou, China, pp. 4312–4315 (2010)
3. Chen, X., Bi, H., Liu, Y.: Energy map-based the healing protocol of coverage holes in wireless sensor networks. AISS: Adv. Inf. Sci. Serv. Sci. **3**(5), 570–579 (2013)
4. Wang, X., Xing, G., Zhang, Y., Lu, C., Pless, R., Gill, C.: Integrated coverage and connectivity configuration in wireless sensor networks. In: Proceedings of International Conference on Embedded Networked Sensor Systems, New York, pp. 28–39 (2003)
5. Xing, G., Wang, X., Zhang, Y.: Integrated coverage and connectivity configuration for energy conservation in sensor networks. ACM Trans. Sens. Netw. **1**(1), 36–72 (2005)
6. Purohit, G.N., Verma, S., Sharma, M.: Hexagonal coverage by mobile sensor nodes. Int. J. Comput. Netw. Secur. **2**(4), 41–44 (2010)
7. Khan, J.U., Cho. H.S.: A data gathering protocol using AUV in underwater sensor networks. Oceans, Taipei, pp. 1–6 (2014)
8. Bhambri, H., Swaroop, A.: Underwater sensor network: architectures, challenges and applications. In: Proceedings of the 2014 International Conference on Computing for Sustainable Global Development, New Delhi, pp. 915–920 (2014)
9. Iyer, S., Rao, D.V.: Genetic algorithm based optimization technique for underwater sensor network positioning and deployment. In: Proceedings of the 2015 IEEE Underwater Technology (UT), Chennai, pp. 1–6 (2015)

10. Johnson, L.J., Green, R.J., Leeson, M.S.: Hybrid underwater optical/acoustic link design. In: Proceedings of the 2014 16th International Conference on Transparent Optical Networks, Graz, pp. 1–4 (2014)
11. Singh, M., Singh, T.: Prevailing is sues and research confront in underwater acoustic sensor networks. Int. J. Comput. Sci. Inf. Technol. Secur. 3(4), 86–90 (2014)
12. Zhang, C., Bai, X., Teng, J.: Constructing low-connectivity and full-coverage three dimensional sensor networks. IEEE J. Sel. Areas Commun. 7(28), 984–993 (2010)
13. Liu, B., Towsley, D.: A study of the coverage of large-scale sensor networks. In: IEEE International Conference on Mobile Ad-hoc and Sensor Systems, Fort Lauderdale, FL, pp. 475–483 (2004)
14. Zhang, H., Hou, J.: Maintaining sensing coverage and connectivity in large sensor networks. Ad Hoc Sens. Wirel. Netw. 2(1), 89–124 (2004)
15. Mirzargar, M., Entezari, A.: Voronoi splines. IEEE Trans. Sig. Process. 58(9), 4572–4582 (2010)
16. Wang, Z., Wang, B., Xiong, Z.: A novel coverage algorithm based on 3D-Voronoi cell for underwater wireless sensor networks. In: Proceedings of the 2015 International Conference on Wireless Communications & Signal Processing, Nanjing, China, pp. 1–5 (2015)

Goodwill Asset, Ultimate Ownership, Management Power and Cost of Equity Capital: A Theoretical Review

Haoqian Shi[✉]

School of Accounting, Hangzhou Dianzi University, No. 1158, No. 2 Street,
Xiasha Higher Education Zone, Hangzhou, Zhejiang, China
shihaoqian@hotmail.com

Abstract. This study provides a theoretical review on the possible correlation between goodwill asset and cost of equity capital. Up to now previous literatures document mixed economic consequences of goodwill asset, and the correlation cannot be determined with ease. Both positive correlation and negative correlation might be observed. Further, such a relationship is expected to be moderated by ultimate ownership and management power, with a more significant correlation when the sample is a state owned enterprise or when management power is strong. However, these hypotheses above need to be tested and supported empirically by future study.

Keywords: Goodwill asset · Management power · Ultimate ownership · Cost of equity capital

1 Introduction

Business combination (also known as merge and acquisition) is regarded as one of the method of growth in the business life cycle, which is known and commonly used for its advantages (for example, less time is taken, acquirer can enter into a market with a rapid speed, and management control is not diluted, etc.), in contrast with internal growth and strategic alliance. Goodwill is the economic consequence of business combination, and should be recognized in the consolidated financial statement. As per CAS (2006) (Its official name is Accounting Standards for Business Enterprises (ASBE), issued by Ministry of Finance (MoF) in 2006. But Chinese Accounting Standards (CAS) is used more widely in previous literatures.), goodwill is defined as "the difference between the consideration paid by acquirer and the fair value of identifiable net asset of acquiree at the date of acquisition". Therefore, goodwill is directly caused by business combination, and a company with a positive goodwill at year end is expected to have had business combination activity. These two concepts are closely correlated, and it is expected to foresee that goodwill asset might be related to the economic consequence of business combination, or even itself.

Up to now, most previous literatures concentrate on the economic consequence caused by subsequent measurement of goodwill (i.e. impairment), and their results are similar, without much disagreement. Goodwill impairment is related to the downward

© Springer Nature Singapore Pte Ltd. 2018
H. Yuan et al. (Eds.): GSKI 2017, CCIS 848, pp. 212–220, 2018.
https://doi.org/10.1007/978-981-13-0893-2_22

expectation of investors and analysts, indicating a decline of future profitability (Li et al. 2011), and the accuracy of earning expectation made by analysts is reduced (Qu et al. 2016), in together with a decline in share price and equity market return (Qu et al. 2017). This negative influence is exacerbated by the estimation of recoverable amount in the determination of goodwill impairment. As the estimation of recoverable amount is highly subjective, earning management, such as profit smoothing and big-bath taking, might arise, thus reducing the quality of financial reporting (Ramanna and Watts 2012; Lu and Qu 2016). However, few studies focus on the initial measurement (i.e. whether the company has goodwill at year end or not) of goodwill asset. As stated above, goodwill is directly caused by business combination and is related to the economic consequence of business combination. Creditors and investors are two major kinds of stakeholders, and they can respond to business combination activity by adjusting cost of debt and cost of equity. Xu et al (2017) has documented a positive relationship between goodwill increase and cost of debt, indicating creditors are in favor of business combination, but the correlation between goodwill asset and cost of equity remains unexplored. In addition, companies listed in A-share market prefer equity financing than debt financing (Huang and Zhang 2001; Yan et al. 2001), which is different from those overseas public companies, and not in line with the traditional pecking order theory proposed by Myers (1984) and Myers and Majluf (1984). As a consequence, probing into the correlation between goodwill asset and cost of equity capital can be worthwhile and meaningful, both theoretically and practically.

This study provides a theoretical review on the possible correlation between goodwill asset and cost of equity capital. Up to now previous literatures document mixed economic consequences of goodwill asset, and their correlation cannot be determined with ease. Both positive correlation and negative correlation might be observed. Further, such a relationship is expected to be moderated by ultimate ownership and management power, with a significant correlation when the sample is a state owned enterprise or when management power is strong.

The contributions of this study are twofold: First, it enriches the literatures on the economic consequence of goodwill asset by studying its relationship with cost of equity capital, which has been seldom concentrated on before. Second, it incorporates ultimate ownership and management power into business combination and discusses their moderating effect in detail. The correlation might be more significant correlation when the sample is a state owned enterprise or when management power is strong. This necessitates the reform and marketization of state owned enterprise as well as the importance of restricting management power from abusing, especially in state owned enterprise.

The reminder of this study is organized as follows. Section 2 discusses the possible correlation on goodwill asset and cost of equity capital. Section 3 specifies the possible correlation on goodwill asset, ultimate ownership and cost of equity capital. Section 4 presents the possible correlation on goodwill asset, management power and cost of equity capital. Section 5 concludes the discussion above.

2 Goodwill Asset and Cost of Equity Capital

2.1 Negative Economic Consequences Documented

As per CAS (2006), goodwill is "the difference between the consideration paid by acquirer and the fair value of identifiable net asset of acquiree at the date of acquisition". This definition is regarded to be flawed as it focuses on the measurement on goodwill only, but the nature and connotation of goodwill are not covered. Therefore, the hierarchy of conceptual framework is not satisfied(The hierarchy of conceptual framework requires that an item or a transaction should be properly classified as an accounting element first before it can be recognized and measured. With regard to goodwill, the definition above only reveal "how to value goodwill" rather than "what is goodwill". However, this situation is not rare since the classification of some elements is still in ambiguity, such as other comprehensive income. It is notable that overriding the hierarchy of conceptual framework can avoid these disagreements, giving application guides to practitioners, making accounting practice more convenient, but still it is an expedient to do so.). Because of the imperfect definition, the goodwill recognized in consolidated financial statement would not be in consistent with what it should be, i.e. some of the recognized goodwill does not meet the definition of asset. Since its key definition is "difference between consideration and fair value of net asset", both of consideration and fair value of net asset can be manipulated, leading to the inaccuracy valuation problem. Johnson and Petrone (1998) divide the recognized goodwill into six subsections, including (1) the excess fair value of recognized assets over reacquisition target book values, (2) the fair value of previously unrecognized assets, (3) the ability of the enterprise to earn, on a going-concern or stand-alone basis, a higher return on a collection of net assets than would be expected if those net assets were not acquired separately, (4) the fair value of synergies from combining the acquirer's and target's businesses and net assets, (5) payment resulting from over- (under-) valuation of the consideration used, and (6) over- (under-) payment by the acquirer in the course of bidding. Further they document that goodwill that should be recognized in consolidated financial statement (also known as core goodwill) only consists of (3) and (4) above. Their work is followed by Henning et al. (2000) who define RESID (abbreviated for residual goodwill) as the sum of (5) and (6), also they use firm-year observations from 1990 to 1994 based on US capital market and indicates that RESID accounts for about 30% of total goodwill recognized. Moreover, RESID has a significantly negative correlation with share price and shareholder's return. However, it is notable that up to now a detailed customer due diligence (CDD) is usually expected to be taken before acquisition, with one of its task being to determine the valuation of the acquiree, so most of valuation mistakes can be diminished, or eliminated. As a consequence, many literatures attribute the causation of excessive goodwill to over-payment by the acquirer, and further excessive payment can be explained by management hubris and management overconfidence (Malmendier and Tate 2008; Ferris et al. 2013; Huang et al. 2015). Excessive goodwill caused by over-payment, if divided as per Johnson and Petrone (1998), contains only a small fraction of core goodwill, and most of the remaining part is RESID, related to hubris and overconfidence. It can be reasonably expected that these RESID could not generate excessive return, but do damage to the financial interests of investors.

A lot of literatures have documented the economic consequence of goodwill assets. Zheng et al. (2014) find evidences that purchased goodwill can enhance return on asset (ROA) at the year of acquisition, but future ROA will decline. Wang et al. (2017) indicates that companies with a positive goodwill asset have a relatively high future share price crash risk. If these negative economic consequences are perceived by investors, they are confronted with a higher risk exposure. As a defective behavior, they are inclined to request for a higher rate of return for higher risk, leading to the rise of cost of equity capital. Based on the theory and analysis above, hypothesis H1a is as follows.

H1a: *Ceteris paribus*, companies with positive goodwill assets have a higher cost of equity capital than those do not have.

2.2 Positive Economic Consequences Documented

However, some literatures document another different conclusion from above. As is discussed, the definition of goodwill has its interior drawbacks but could serve as an expedient so that accounting practice can be treated with more ease. But another concept of goodwill called "excessive earning concept" could reveal its connotation and nature. This kind of concept holds that goodwill is the value of gaining excessive earning owned by a company. Because a company opens for business for a longer time, and it can make more profit than its competitors, goodwill is then owned by this company. Given the definition above, excellent staff employed by company, good reputation created by company and high efficient management style used by company can all be treated as goodwill, but these internal goodwill cannot be measured with reliability, so they cannot be recognized as an asset in the financial statement. Business combination can make them explicit by firm valuation used in customer due diligence and bargaining between acquirer and acquiree, and goodwill should be recognized in the consolidated financial statement, since valuation report and bargain process provide reliable measurement conditions. However, synergy effect is the precondition for obtaining excessive earnings (Lin 2005; Du et al. 2011), and one of the driving factors for business combination is for synergy effect (Ye and Li 2008). Putting all things together, business combination is partly aimed for the excessive earnings created by synergy effect. Goodwill, as economic consequence of business combination, is expected to be associated with positive economic consequence. This theory is support by previous literatures. Purchased goodwill is supposed to enhance the financial performance at the year of acquisition (Lv and Fan 2016), lead to positive excessive earnings (Fu et al. 2016) and cumulative abnormal return (Guo and Yu 2016). Also, it is related to a significant increase in share price (Hu et al. 2012) and higher equity value (Du 2010). All discussed above indicates that goodwill asset could serve as a signal that a company is capable to obtain excessive earning in the future. Once the signal is perceived by investors, they tend to be more optimistic about the operation and business of the company. With lower uncertainty and risk exposure, they might ask for a lower cost of equity. Based on the theory and analysis above, hypothesis H1b is as follows.

H1b: *Ceteris paribus*, companies with positive goodwill assets have a lower cost of equity capital than those do not have.

3 Goodwill Asset, Ultimate Ownership and Cost of Equity Capital

There are two types of ultimate shareholders for companies listed in China: state owned and non-state owned. Many aspect of them are different such as ownership structure, business objective and governance mechanism, so it is necessary to treat them separately in this study. For state owned enterprise, it is owned by "all citizens", but "all citizens" is a kind of collective concept. In fact, the concept is more notional than realistic because every citizen is a kind of individual concept, and they cannot gather together to be involved in the operation of business in a state owned enterprises. This issue is called "ownership absence", making senior management in state owned enterprise be subject to less restriction and supervision. Thus state owned enterprise has a more serious agency problem (Lu and Qu 2016). Moreover, compensation contract for senior management in state owned enterprise tends to have more restrictions and prohibitions, so that they are not able to gain much personal financial interests from their normal reward. To satisfy their need, they turn to abuse their unrestricted and unsupervised management power to intervene the operation of business, making an empire building for themselves, but the interest of minority shareholders has been compromised (Li and Dong 2015). In addition, the objective of state owned enterprise is not purely for profit maximization, but they are also responsible for taking up political tasks such as maintaining social stability, reducing unemployment rate and serving as a benchmark on providing good staff benefit (Chen et al. 2011; Xiao 2016). Consequently, its corporate governance efficiency would be reduced unavoidably. As for non-state owned enterprise, these pitfalls above can be mitigated to a large extent. The owner and manager of non-state owned enterprise are both individuals, rather than a collective concept such as all citizens, so the issue of ownership absence does no longer exist. Also the supervision on management is proved to be more efficient in non-state owned enterprise than state owned enterprise, evidenced by higher information disclosure quality and less financial performance variability (Quan and Wu 2010). In terms of management compensation, most non-state owned enterprise hire professional managers, and some are family business so they appoint a family member to act as a senior manager. For professional managers, agency problem still exists, but they have a clear career path on condition that they use their talent and ability to run the company well. Once the corporate performance has been improved, they can naturally have more salary and get promoted quickly, without the need to damage the interest of minority shareholders, on condition that the labor market for professional managers is highly efficient and well organized. To sum up, state owned enterprise has a more serious agency problem and lower corporate governance efficiency, with its senior managers are more inclined to obtain personal benefit. These drawbacks above could lead to information asymmetry, causing a higher cost of equity.

Based on the theory above, synergy effect is not the only target that can explain business combination by state-owned enterprise. Other possible reasons include political purpose (such as to combine another state owned enterprise which is nearly in bankruptcy, to protect state-owned property), management's will for higher salary and position, or even the outcome of male hormone(This indicates some non-efficiency investments are made when senior managers are lacking in supervision and restriction. In fact, these investments are not worthwhile at all.), made by senior management. But business combination by non-state owned enterprise tends to be less aggressive and more rational. It can be reasonably expected that investors should have a positive attitude toward rational investment, but negative attitude toward irrational investment. Consequently, hypothesis H2 is as follows.

H2: *Ceteris paribus*, goodwill assets have a more significant effect on cost of equity capital in state owned enterprise than that in non-state owned enterprise.

4 Goodwill Asset, Management Power and Cost of Equity Capital

As stated above, excessive consideration payment can be explained by management overconfidence and hubris, but one question remains unsolved. Overconfidence and hubris are both regarded as an implicit state of mind while overpayment is a kind of explicit behavior. Up to now no consensus has been reached on what makes an implicit state of mind externalized, but dominating theory attributes it to management power. Management power is defined by Finkelstein (1992) as the ability for managers to execute their own wills, and could be the profound influence owned and exerted by managers, usually beyond their specified control rights, when the internal governance is weak and external institutional factor is not in place (Quan et al. 2010). Managers with a higher power could control the decision right of a company with ease, with a negative economic consequence such as more variations in share price fluctuations (Adams et al. 2005), less cash dividend paid, and more non-efficiency investments made (Wang et al. 2014). In addition, Chen et al. (2017a, b, c) prove chief executive officer (CEO) with strong power is more inclined to financial statement fraud, and this correlation is reinforced by management overconfidence. Ham et al. (2017) also document chief financial officer (CFO)'s narcissism (Narcissism consists of overconfidence and hubris. These two concepts can almost be used interchangeably in respect of psychology but one distinction should be clarified. Overconfidence only refers to the cognitive perception of reality while hubris includes not only cognition but also behavior. This study does make no distinction between them and regards them as one concept.) is positive related to earning management, less timely recognition of loss, weaker internal control and higher probability of financial restatement. Therefore, management power can partly explain the externalization of management overconfidence and hubris, and further they lead to a series of negative economic consequences. In respect of business combination, if managers of the acquirer have higher power, they are more likely to initiate the process quickly, to reduce negotiating time and less likely to deal with the completion (Aktas et al. 2016). All these irrational behaviors make future profitability and going concern assumption more risky and unpredictable. Being exposed to more risks, investors are sure to require a higher rate of return, and cost of equity capital will rise naturally. Based on the theory and analysis above, hypothesis H3 is as follows.

H3: *Ceteris paribus*, goodwill assets have a more significant effect on cost of equity capital in companies with a high management power than those with a low management power.

5   Concluding Remark

This study provides a theoretical framework on the possible correlation between goodwill asset and cost of equity capital. Up to now previous literatures document mixed economic consequences of goodwill asset, and the correlation cannot be determined with ease. Both positive correlation and negative correlation might be observed. Further, such a relationship is expected to be moderated by ultimate ownership and management power, with a more significant correlation when the sample is a state owned enterprise or when management power is strong.

However, this study is subject to some limitations. As for the limited time and effort, only "goodwill asset at year", rather than "increase in goodwill" and "decrease in goodwill" (as used by Wang et al. 2017) is used. Moreover, this study only presents a theoretical review, with no further work being carried out. All the hypotheses are left unsupported and unproved by empirical evidence. These pitfalls could suggest some possible areas for future study.

References

Adams, R., Almeida, H., Ferreira, D.: Powerful CEOs and their impact on corporate performance. Rev. Financ. Stud. **18**(4), 1403–1432 (2005). https://doi.org/10.1093/rfs/hhi030

Aktas, N., Bodt, E., Bollaert, H., Roll, R.: CEO narcissism and the takeover process: from private initiation to deal completion. J. Financ. Quant. Anal. **51**(1), 113–137 (2016). https://doi.org/10.1017/s0022109016000065

Chen, G.H., Sun, L.R., Sun, J.: Environmental uncertainty, senior management power and cost of equity capital. Res. Financ. Econ. Issues **6**(2017), 79–85 (2017a). (In Chinese)

Chen, H.W., Chen, Z.Y., Lobo, G., Wang, Y.Y.: Effects of audit quality on earnings management and cost of equity capital: evidence from China. Contemp. Acc. Res. **28**(3), 892–925 (2011). https://doi.org/10.1111/j.1911-3846.2011.01088.x

Chen, M., Qu, X.H., Sun, X.J.: Whose cost of equity capital reduces after IFRS convergence and why? Heterogeneity evidence from Chinese stock market. Chin. J. Acc. Stud. **5**(1), 1–27 (2017b). https://doi.org/10.1080/21697213.2017.1304539

Chen, Y., Fan, X., Cheng, Y.: CEO power, overconfidence and financial reporting fraud. Mod. Financ. Econ. J. Tianjin Univ. Financ. Econ. **10**(2017), 78–89 (2017c). https://doi.org/10.19559/j.cnki.12-1387.2017.10.007. (In Chinese)

Du, X.Q.: Nature of goodwill and its impact on equity valuation: theory and evidence based on CAS (2006). In: Conference Proceedings of Goodwill Accounting Seminar, (Beijing, China, 26 June 2010), pp. 8–28 (2010). (in Chinese)

Du, X.Q., Du, Y.J., Zhou, Z.J.: Study on the connotation and recognition of goodwill. Acc. Res. **1**(2011), 11–16 (2011). (In Chinese)

Ferris, S., Jayaraman, N., Sabherwal, S.: CEO overconfidence and international merger and acquisition activity. J. Financ. Quant. Anal. **48**(1), 137–164 (2013). https://doi.org/10.1017/s0022109013000069

Finkelstein, S.: Power in top management teams dimensions, measurement and validation. Acad. Manage. J. **35**(3), 505–538 (1992). https://doi.org/10.2307/256485

Fu, C., Wang, J.Y., Fu, D.G.: Has goodwill been overstated with its merging? Empirical evidence from A-share market listed companies in China. Chin. Econ. Stud. **6**(2016), 109–123 (2016). https://doi.org/10.19365/j.issn1000-4181.2016.01.009. (In Chinese)

Guo, X.M., Yu, R.J.: Does goodwill indicate corporate ability of excess earning? J. Beijing Jiaotong Univ. (Soc. Sci. Edn.) **1**, 87–97 (2016). https://doi.org/10.16797/j.cnki.11-5224/c.20160122.011. (In Chinese)

Ham, C., Lang, M., Seybert, N., Wang, S.: CFO narcissism and financial reporting quality. J. Acc. Res. **55**(5), 1089–1135 (2017). https://doi.org/10.1111/1475-679X.12176

Henning, S., Lewis, B., Shaw, W.: Valuation of the components of purchased goodwill. J. Acc. Res. **38**(2), 375–386 (2000). https://doi.org/10.2307/2672938

Hu, Y., Zhang, X.Y., Ji, R.L.: A study on value-relevance of consolidated goodwill based on the data of A-share listed companies from 2007 to 2009. J. Beijing Technol. Bus. Univ. (Soc. Sci.) **5**, 72–78 (2012). https://doi.org/10.16299/j.1009-6116.2012.05.013. (In Chinese)

Huang, Q.H., Sun, L., Zhang, J.: Quantitative analysis of hubris effect of state-owned enterprise's merger and acquisition. Res. Econ. Manage. **6**, 104–111 (2015). https://doi.org/10.13502/j.cnki.issn1000-7636.2015.06.014. (In Chinese)

Huang, S.A., Zhang, G.: An analysis on the stock financing preference of Chinese listed companies. Econ. Res. J. **11**(2001), 11–20 (2001). (in Chinese)

Johnson, T., Petrone, K.: Commentary: is goodwill an asset? Acc. Horiz. **12**(3), 293–303 (1998). https://doi.org/10.2139/ssrn.143839

Li, X.R., Dong, H.Y.: Senior management power, frim ownership and cost of equity. Econ. Sci. **4**(2015), 67–80 (2015). https://doi.org/10.19523/j.jjkx.2015.04.007. (In Chinese)

Li, Z.N., Shroff, P., Venkataraman, R., Zhang, X.Y.: Causes and consequences of goodwill impairment losses. Rev. Acc. Stud. **16**(2011), 745–778 (2011). https://doi.org/10.1007/s11142-011-9167-2

Lin, J.X.: Discrimination of internally generated goodwill, externally purchased goodwill and negative goodwill. J. Xiamen Univ. (Arts Soc. Sci.) **5**, 109–114 (2005). (In Chinese)

Lu, Y., Qu, X.H.: Goodwill impairment and management compensation: empirical evidence from Chinese A-share market. Contemp. Acc. Rev. **9**(1), 70–88 (2016). (In Chinese)

Lu, Y., Qu, X.H.: Earnings management motivations of goodwill impairment - the empirical evidence from Chinese A-share market. J. Shanxi Univ. Financ. Econ. **7**, 87–99 (2016). https://doi.org/10.13781/j.cnki.1007-9556.2016.07.008. (In Chinese)

Lv, Z.H., Fan, S.M.: The influence of purchased goodwill on firm's financial performance. J. Southeast Univ. (Philos. Soc. Sci.) **S2**, 17–20 (2016). https://doi.org/10.13916/j.cnki.issn1671-511x.2016.s2.006. (in Chinese)

Malmendier, U., Tate, G.: Who makes acquisitions? CEO overconfidence and the market's reaction. J. Financ. Econ. **89**(1), 20–43 (2008). https://doi.org/10.1016/j.jfineco.2007.07.002

Myers, S.: The capital structure puzzle. J. Financ. **39**(3), 574–592 (1984). https://doi.org/10.1111/j.1540-6261.1984.tb03646.x

Myers, S., Majluf, N.: Corporate financing and investment decisions when firms have information those investors do not have. J. Financ. Econ. **13**(2), 187–221 (1984). https://doi.org/10.1016/0304-405X(84)90023-0

Qu, X.H., Lu, Y., Wang, J.: Goodwill impairments and analysts' earnings forecasts - from the perspective of earnings management. J. Shanxi Univ. Financ. Econ. **4**, 101–113 (2016). https://doi.org/10.13781/j.cnki.1007-9556.2016.04.009. (In Chinese)

Qu, X.H., Lu, Y., Zhang, R.L.: Value relevance of goodwill impairments: empirical evidence from Chinese A-share market. Res. Econ. Manage. **3**, 122–132 (2017). https://doi.org/10.13502/j.cnki.issn1000-7636.2017.03.013. (In Chinese)

Quan, X.F., Wu, S.N.: CEO power, information disclosure quality and corporate performance variability: empirical evidence from the listed companies in SZSE. Nankai Bus. Rev. **4**, 142–153 (2010). (in Chinese)

Quan, X.F., Wu, S.N., Wen, F.: Managerial power, private income and compensation rigging. Econ. Res. J. **11**(2010), 73–87 (2010). (in Chinese)

Ramanna, K., Watts, R.: Evidence on the use of unverifiable estimates in required goodwill impairment. Rev. Acc. Stud. **17**(2012), 749–780 (2012). https://doi.org/10.1007/s11142-012-9188-5

Wang, M.L., He, Y.R., Lin, H.T.: Managerial power, cash dividends and enterprises' investment efficiency. Nankai Bus. Rev. **2**(2014), 13–22 (2014). (in Chinese)

Wang, W.J., Fu, C., Fu, D.G.: Is M&A goodwill the prior signal of stock price crash risk? From the perspectives of accounting function and financial security. J. Financ. Econ. **9**(2017), 76–87 (2017). https://doi.org/10.16538/j.cnki.jfe.2017.09.006. (In Chinese)

Xiao, Z.P.: The effect of ultimate ownership structure on cost of equity capital: empirical evidence from Chinese listed companies. J. Manage. Sci. Chin. **19**(1), 72–86 (2016). (In Chinese)

Xu, J.C., Zhang, D.X., Liu, H.H.: Does purchased goodwill information affect the cost of debt. J. Cent. Univ. Financ. Econ. **3**(2017), 109–118 (2017). (In Chinese)

Yan, D.W., Geng, J.X., Liu, W.P.: An empirical research on the right issue financing behavior of Chinese listed companies. Acc. Res. **9**(2001), 21–27 (2001). (In Chinese)

Ye, H., Li, S.M.: The theory review of merge and acquisition. J. Guangdong Univ. Financ. **1**(2008), 115–128 (2008). (In Chinese)

Zheng, H.Y., Liu, Z.Y., Feng, W.D.: Can merger and acquisition goodwill promote company performance? - Empirical evidence from Chinese A-shares listed companies. Acc. Res. **3**(2014), 11–17 (2014). (In Chinese)

Total-Neighbor-Distinguishing Coloring by Sums of the Three Types of Product Graphs

Xiahong Cai[(✉)], Shuangliang Tian, and Huan Yang

Mathematics and Computer Institute, Northwest Minzu Universty,
Xibei Xincun No. 1, Chengguan District, Lanzhou, Gansu, China
1850697869@qq.com

Abstract. We consider a proper total coloring σ of edges and vertices in a simple graph G and the sum $f(v)$ of colors of all the edges incident to v and the color of a vertex v. We say that a coloring σ is distinguished adjacent vertices by sums, if every two adjacent vertices have different values of f, the σ is called total neighbor distinguishing coloring by sums. In this paper, we determine exact value of these parameters for the Cartesian product, direct product and semi strong product of infinite paths, and finite graph of the semi strong product.

Keywords: Infinite path · Finite graph · Product graph
Neighbor sum distinguishing total coloring
Neighbor sum distinguishing total chromatic number

1 Introduction

In 2004, Zhang et al. [1] for the first time gave the adjacent vertex distinguishing total coloring of the concept, The adjacent vertex distinguishing total coloring of the graph G is the normal total coloring of G that satisfies any two adjacent vertex color sets are different. Zhang et al. [1] studied the adjacent vertex distinguishing total chromatic number of some graphs such as cycle, complete graph, complete bipartite graph, fan, wheel and tree. And on this basis put forward the following conjecture: For connected simple graph G with order at least 2, we have $\chi_a''(G) \leq \Delta(G) + 3$. Wang [2] proved that the maximum degree of a graph G is 3, there is $\chi_a''(G) \leq 6$.

In 2011, Monika and Mariusz [3] gave the total neighbor distinguishing coloring by sums of graph: Suppose that $\sigma : V \cup E \rightarrow \{1, 2, \cdots, k\}$ is a proper total coloring of G, For a vertex v, let $f(v)$ denote the total sum of colors of the edges incident to v and the color of v. We try to answer the question, how large k have to be to guarantee that there is a proper coloring of vertices and edges with k colors, so that the function f distinguishes adjacent vertices of G. The smallest such k the smallest such k is called the total neighbor distinguishing coloring by sums, and denoted by $\chi_\Sigma''(G)$.

By the concept of total neighbor distinguishing coloring by sums. It is clear that there are the following the lemmas:

Lemma 1.1. [3]. For connected simple graph G with order at least 2, we have $\Delta(G) + 1 \leq \chi''(G) \leq \chi_a''(G) \leq \chi_\Sigma''(G)$.

H. Yuan et al. (Eds.): GSKI 2017, CCIS 848, pp. 221–228, 2018.
https://doi.org/10.1007/978-981-13-0893-2_23

Where $\Delta(G)$ is the maximum degree of graph G, $\chi_a''(G)$ is adjacent vertex distinguishing total coloring of the graph G.

Lemma 1.2. [3]. If there a adjacent maximum degree vertex in the connected simple graph G with order at least 2, we have $\chi_a''(G) \geq \Delta(G) + 2$.

Lemma 1.3. [3]. Let G is connected branches be $G_1, G_2, \cdots G_w$, where every graph G_i with order at least 2, we have $\chi_\Sigma''(G) = \max\{\chi_\Sigma''(G_i)|i = 1, 2, \cdots, w\}$.

Monika et al. gave a conjecture about total neighbor distinguishing coloring by sums of graph G: For every graph $G = (V, E)$, the total neighbor distinguishing coloring by sums $\chi_\Sigma''(G)$ satisfies the inequality $\chi_\Sigma''(G) \leq \Delta + 3$, and proved this conjecture about complete graphs, cycles, bipartite graphs is established. Dong and Wang [4] proved the following two conclusions (1) G is a graph with at least two vertices, if mad $\Delta(G) < 3$ then $\chi_\Sigma''(G) \leq k + 2$, where $k = \max\{\Delta, 5\}$. (2) Let G is a planar graph with at least two vertices. If $g(G) \geq 6$ and $\Delta(G) \geq 5$, the $\chi_\Sigma''(G) \leq \Delta(G) + 2$. Li and Liu et al. [5] research the neighbor sum distinguishing total colorings of $K4$-minor free graphs and got the following result: $\chi_\Sigma''(G) \leq \Delta + 3$, if $\Delta(G) \geq 4$, then $\chi_\Sigma''(G) \leq \Delta + 2$. About the planar graph, Li and Cheng et al. [6, 7] researched neighbor sum distinguishing total colorings of planar graphs with maximum degree are 13 and 14, verification the conjecture that neighbor sum distinguishing total colorings is true, The specific result are: (1) If G is a planar with a maximum degree of at least 13, we have $\chi_\Sigma''(G) \leq \Delta + 3$; (2) If G is a planar with a maximum degree of at least 13, we have $\chi_\Sigma''(G) \leq \Delta + 2$.

As one of the most important tools in the research of graph's topology, graph structure computation provides an effective method for studying graph coloring. It is helpful to study the chromatic number with more complicated structure by studying various kinds of coloring chromatic number of simple graph and different structure calculation of the graph. The structure of graph operations include: Cartesian product, direct product, strong product and semi strong product, the specific concept is as follows [8].

Let $G = (V(G), E(G))$ and $H = (V(H), E(H))$ be two graphs.

(1) The Cartesian product $G \square H$ has vertex set $V(G \square H) = V(G) \times V(H)$ and edge set

$$E(G \square H) = \{(u_1, v_1)(u_2, v_2)|u_1u_2 \in E(G) \text{ and } v_1 = v_2, \text{ or } u_1 = u_2 \text{ and } v_1v_2 \in E(H)$$

(2) The direct product $G \wedge H$ has vertex set $V(G \wedge H) = V(G) \times V(H)$ and edge set

$$E(G \wedge H) = \{(u_1, v_1)(u_2, v_2)|u_1u_2 \in E(G) \text{ and } v_1v_2 \in E(H)\}$$

(3) The semi strong product $G \bullet H$ has vertex set $V(G \bullet H) = V(G) \times V(H)$ and edge set

$$E(G \bullet H) = \{(u_1, v_1)(u_2, v_2)|u_1u_2 \in E(G) \text{ and } v_1v_2 \in E(H), \text{ or } u_1 = u_2 \text{ and } v_1v_2 \in E(H)\}$$

(4) The strong product $G \boxtimes H$ has vertex set $V(G \boxtimes H) = V(G) \times V(H)$ and edge set

$$E(G) \boxtimes H) = \{(u_1, v_1)(u_2, v_2) | u_1 u_2 \in E(G) \text{ and } v_1 v_2 \in E(H) \text{ or } u_1 u_2 \in E(G) \text{ and }$$
$$v_1 = v_2 \text{ or } u_1 = u_2 \text{ and } v_1 v_2 \in E(H)\}$$

In this paper, we also need to use the following lemma:

Lemma 1.4. For any integer $n \geq 3$, $K_{n,n}$ is a n-regular complete bipartite graph, it has a proper edge coloring, it makes a perfect match in $K_{n,n}$, different edge has different colors.

Lemma 1.5. Let K_n be a complete graph of order $n \geq 1$, then

$$\chi_\Sigma''(K_n) = \begin{cases} n+1; & \text{if } n \text{ is even,} \\ n+1; & \text{if } n \text{ is odd.} \end{cases}$$

Let P_∞ is a infinite path, the vertex set $V(P_\infty)$ is an integer set and when the two adjacent vertices x and y in the vertex set $V(P_\infty)$ If and only if $|x - y| = 1$.

Let P_m, P_n be a finite path, and $V(P_m) = \{0, 1, \cdots, m-1\}, V(P_n) = \{0, 1, \cdots, n-1\}$ are the vertex set of a finite path P_m, P_n severally, where two vertices x and y are adjacent for every $x \in \{0, 1, \cdots, n-1\}$ $y \in \{0, 1, \cdots, m-1\}$ if and only if. If and only if $|x - y| = 1$.

In this paper, we study the total neighbor distinguishing coloring by sums of the Cartesian product, direct product and semi strong product of infinite paths, and finite graph of the semi strong product. We refer to the books [9, 10] for graph theory terminology and notation not defined in this paper.

The coloring problem in graph theory is mainly used in optimization, Specifically see reference [11–15].

2 Main Result

Theorem 2.1. $\chi_\Sigma''(P_\infty \square P_\infty') = 6$

Proof. Since $P_\infty \square P_\infty'$ is a 4-regular infinite graph, we have $\chi_\Sigma''(P_\infty \square P_\infty' \geq 6$. we only need to construct a Total-neighbor-distinguishing coloring by sums of $P_\infty \square P_\infty'$. Assumed that the color set is $\{1, 2, 3, 4, 5, 6\}$, for any integer x, y, let

$$\sigma'((x,y)(x+1,y)) = (x+y)_6 + 1,$$
$$\sigma'((x,y)(x,y+1)) = (x+y+2)_6 + 1,$$
$$\sigma(x,y) = (x+y+3)_6 + 1.$$

It can be easily seen that the total chromatic number of $P_\infty \square P_\infty'$ is equal to 6.

(1) We proved that σ' is the proper edge coloring of $P_\infty \square P_\infty'$ Let $u = (x, y)$ is any vertex in $P_\infty \square P_\infty'$, by the definition of the coloring σ', we have

$$\sigma'((x,y)(x,y+1)) = (x+y+2)_6 + 1$$
$$\sigma'((x,y)(x+1,y)) = (x+y)_6 + 1$$
$$\sigma'((x,y-1)(x,y)) = (x+y+5)_6 + 1$$
$$\sigma'((x-1,y)(x,y)) = (x+y+1)_6 + 1$$

Obviously σ' is the proper edge coloring of $P_\infty \square P'_\infty$.

(2) We proved that σ is the proper vertex coloring of $P_\infty \square P'_\infty$

Let $u = (x,y)$ is any vertex in $P_\infty \square P'_\infty$, by the definition of the coloring σ, we have $\sigma(u) = (x+y+3)_6 + 1$.

Let $u = (x,y)$ and $v = (x',y')$ are any adjacent vertices in $P_\infty \square P'_\infty$, let $\sigma(u) = \sigma(v)$, there are $(x',y') = (x,y\pm 1)$, or $(x',y') = (x\pm 1,y)$, Whether $(x',y') = (x,y\pm 1)$, or $(x',y') = (x\pm 1,y)$ we have $\sigma(v) = (x+y+3\pm 1)_6 + 1$. On account of $\sigma(u) = \sigma(v)$, there are contradictions $(0)_6 = (\pm 1)_6$, so $\sigma(u) \neq \sigma(v)$. Obviously σ is the proper vertex coloring of $P_\infty \square P'_\infty$.

(3) We proved that the color of any vertex is different from the color it is associated with $P_\infty \square P'_\infty$.

By the definition of the coloring σ and σ', obviously that the color of any vertex is different from the color it is associated with $P_\infty \square P'_\infty$.

(4) We proved that every two adjacent vertices have different values of f.

Let $u = (x,y)$ is any vertex in $P_\infty \square P'_\infty$, by the definition of the coloring $f(u)$, we have

$$f(u) = (x+y)_6 + (x+y+1)_6 + (x+y+2)_6 + (x+y+3)_6 + (x+y+5)_6 + 5$$

Let $u = (x,y)$ and $v = (x',y')$ are any adjacent vertices in $P_\infty \square P'_\infty$, let $\sigma(u) = \sigma(v)$, there are $(x',y') = (x,y\pm 1)$ or, $(x',y') = (x\pm 1,y)$, Whether $(x',y') = (x,y\pm 1)$, or $(x',y') = (x\pm 1,y)$ we have

$$f(v) = (x+y\pm 1)_6 + (x+y+1\pm 1)_6 + (x+y+2\pm 1)_6 + (x+y+3\pm 1)_6 + (x+y+5\pm 1)_6 + 5$$

On account of $f(u) = f(v)$, there are contradictions $(4)_6 = (5)_6$, so $f(u) \neq f(v)$. Obviously every two adjacent vertices have different values of f.

We can see from the above analysis, we have $\chi''_\Sigma(P_\infty \square P'_\infty) = 6$.

Theorem 2.2. $\chi''_\Sigma(P_\infty \wedge P'_\infty) = 6$

Proof. Since $P_\infty \wedge P'_\infty$ can be decomposed into two disjoint infinite paths Cartesian product sub graph, we have $\chi''_\Sigma(P_\infty \wedge P'_\infty) = 6$.

Theorem 2.3. $\chi''_\Sigma(P_\infty \bullet P'_\infty) = 8$

Proof. Since there a adjacent maximum degree vertices in the $P_\infty \bullet P'_\infty$, we have $\chi''_\Sigma(P_\infty \bullet P'_\infty) \geq 8$, we only need to construct a total neighbor distinguishing coloring by sums of $P_\infty \bullet P'_\infty$. Since $P_\infty \bullet P'_\infty$ can be decomposed into $(P_\infty \wedge P'_\infty)$ and $\bigcup_{i \in Z} H_i, Z$ is a integer set. H_i is induced subgraph with $\{v_{ij}|j \in Z\}$ in $P_\infty \bullet P'_\infty$. Clearly, if $i \neq j$, H_i and H_j are disjoint path. We can distinguish two steps to construct the total neighbor distinguishing coloring by sums of $P_\infty \bullet P'_\infty$. For any integer x, y, Assumed that the color set is $\{1,2,3,4,5,6,7,8\}$. The first, the color set $\{1,2,3,4,5,6\}$ is used to color the edge of the $(P_\infty \wedge P'_\infty)$, recorded as σ'_1. The second, the color set $\{7,8\}$ is used to color the edge of the P_∞, recorded as σ'_2. σ'_1 and σ'_2 will be combined as σ'. The third, the color set $\{1,2,3,4,5,6\}$ is used to color the vertexes of the $P_\infty \bullet P'_\infty$, recorded as σ. Let

$$\sigma'_1((x,y)(x+1,y+1)) = (x+2y)_6 + 1$$
$$\sigma'_2((x,y)(x+1,y)) = (x+y)_2 + 7$$
$$\sigma(x,y) = (x+2y+1)_6 + 1$$

It can be easily seen that the total chromatic number of $P_\infty \bullet P'_\infty$ is equal to 8.

(1) We proved that σ' is the proper edge coloring of $P_\infty \bullet P'_\infty$

Let $u = (x,y)$ is any vertex in $P_\infty \bullet P'_\infty$, by the definition of the coloring σ', we have

$$\sigma'((x,y)(x+1,y)) = (x+y)_2 + 7$$
$$\sigma'((x,y)(x-1,y)) = (x+y+1)_2 + 7$$
$$\sigma'((x,y)(x+1,y+1)) = (x+2y)_6 + 1$$
$$\sigma'((x,y)(x-1,y+1)) = (x+2y+5)_6 + 1$$
$$\sigma'((x,y)(x-1,y-1)) = (x+2y+3)_6 + 1$$
$$\sigma'((x,y)(x+1,y-1)) = (x+2y+4)_6 + 1$$

Obviously σ' is the proper edge coloring of $P_\infty \bullet P'_\infty$.

(2) We proved that σ is the proper vertex coloring of $P_\infty \bullet P'_\infty$

Let $u = (x,y)$ is any vertex in $P_\infty \bullet P'_\infty$ by the definition of the coloring σ, we have

$$\sigma(u) = (x+2y+1)_6 + 1$$

Let $u = (x,y)$ and $v = (x',y')$ are any adjacent vertices in $P_\infty \bullet P'_\infty$, let $\sigma(u) = \sigma(v)$, consider the following three cases.

Case1. If $(x',y') = (x \pm 1, y)$

$$\sigma(v) = (x+2y+1 \pm 1)_6 + 1$$

on account of $\sigma(u) = \sigma(v)$, there is contradiction $(\pm 1)_6 = (0)_6$, so $\sigma(u) \neq \sigma(v)$.

Case2 If $(x',y') = (x \pm 1, y \pm 1)$

$$\sigma(v) = (x \pm 1 + 2y \pm 2 + 1)_6 + 1$$

on account of $\sigma(u) = \sigma(v)$, there are contradictions $(1 \pm 2)_6 = (0)_6, (-1 \pm 2)_6 = (0)_6$ so $\sigma(u) \neq \sigma(v)$.

(3) We proved that the color of any vertex is different from the Color it is associated wit $P_\infty \bullet P'_\infty$.

By the definition of the coloring σ and σ', obviously that the color of any vertex is different from the color it is associated with $P_\infty \bullet P'_\infty$.

(4) We proved that every two adjacent vertices have different values of f Let $u = (x, y)$ is any vertex in $P_\infty \bullet P'_\infty$, by the definition of the coloring $f(u)$, we have

$$f(u) = (x+2y)_6 + (x+2y+1)_6 + (x+2y+3)_6 + (x+2y+4)_6 + (x+2y+5)_6 + 19$$

Let $u = (x, y)$ and $v = (x', y')$ are any adjacent vertices in $P_\infty \bullet P'_\infty$, let $f(u) = f(v)$, there are $(x', y') = (x \pm 1, y)$ or $(x', y') = (x \pm 1, y \pm 1)$.

Case1. If $(x', y') = (x \pm 1, y)$
on account of $f(u) = f(v)$, there are contradiction $(3)_6 = (2)_6$, $(1)_6 = (2)_6$, so $f(u) \neq f(v)$.

Case2. If $(x', y') = (x \pm 1, y \pm 1)$

$$f(v) = (x \pm 1 + 2(y \pm 1))_6 + (x \pm 1 + 2(y \pm 1) + 1)_6 + (x \pm 1 + 2(y \pm 1) + 5)_6 + (x \pm 1 + 2(y \pm 1) + 3)_6 + (x \pm 1 + 2(y \pm 1) + 4)_6 + 2$$

on account of $f(u) = f(v)$, there are contradiction $(5)_6 = (2)_6, (1)_6 = (2)_6$, $(1)_6 = (4)_6$, so $f(u) \neq f(v)$.
Obviously every two adjacent vertices have different values of f.
We can see from the above analysis, we have $\chi''_\Sigma(P_\infty \bullet P'_\infty) = 8$.

Theorem 2.4. For any integer $n \geq 3$, we have $\chi''_\Sigma(P_2 \bullet K_n) = 2n$.

Proof. Since $P_2 \bullet K_n$ has adjacent maximum vertices, we have $\chi''_\Sigma(P_2 \bullet K_n) \geq 2n$. We only need to construct a total neighbor distinguishing coloring by sums of $P_2 \bullet K_n$. Because $P_2 \bullet K_n$ can be decomposed into two K_n and a $(n-1)$-regular bipartite, Let the vertex set is $\{X_1, X_2\}. X_1 = \{v_{11}, v_{12}, \cdots, v_{1n}\}$, $X_2 = \{v_{21}, v_{22}, \cdots, v_{2n}\}$, there are vertices v_{1i} and v_{2i} are not adjacent.

Case1. If n is even, we have $\chi''_\Sigma(K_n) = n+1$. Assumed that the color set is $\{1, 2, \cdots, 2n\}$. The first, the color set $\{1, 2, \cdots, n+1\}$ is used to color the two K_n, each vertex is missing a different color. The second, the color set $\{n+2, \cdots, 2n\}$ is used to color the $(n-1)$-regular bipartite. Obviously there is $\chi''_\Sigma(P_2 \bullet K_n) = 2n$.

Case2. If n is odd, Assumed that the color set is $\{1, 2, \cdots, 2n\}$. The first, the color set $\{1, 2, \cdots, n\}$ is used to color the K_n. The second, the color set $\{n+1, \cdots, 2n\}$ is used to color the $(n-1)$-regular bipartite. Because $K_{n-1,n-1} + M$ isomorphic to $K_{n,n}$, there is

$M = \{v_{1i}v_{2i}|i = 1, 2, \cdots n\}$, by Lemma 1.4 we use the color set k_2 to color the $K_{n,n}$, making each edge of M stained with different colors, Finally delete the edge in M, we can be with the total neighbor distinguishing coloring of $P_2 \bullet K_n$.

We can see from the above analysis, we have $\chi''_\Sigma(P_2 \bullet K_n) = 2n$.

Theorem 2.5. For any integer $m \geq 3$, $n \geq 3$, we have $\chi''_\Sigma(P_m \bullet K_n) = 3n - 1$.

Proof. Since $P_m \bullet K_n$ has adjacent maximum vertex, we have $\chi''_\Sigma(P_m \bullet K_n) \geq 3n - 1$. we only need to construct a total neighbor distinguishing coloring by sums of $P_m \bullet K_n$.

Let $G = P_m \bullet K_n$, G' represents all the copies of G in K_n delete the resulting graph, Assumed that the vertex set is $\{X_0, \cdots, X_{n-1}\}$, there is $X_i = \{v_{i1}, v_{i2}, \cdots, v_{im}\}$. Let $G_{i,i+1}$ represents all the edges between X_i and X_{i+1} form a set of derived subgraphs, obviously $G_{i,i+1}$ is a $(n-1)$-regular bipartite, there are vertices v_{1i} and v_{2i} are not adjacent.

Case1. If n is even, we have $\chi''_\Sigma(K_n) = n + 1$. We can distinguish three steps to construct the Total neighbor distinguishing coloring by sums of $P_m \bullet K_n$. Assumed that the color set is $\{1, 2, \cdots, 3n - 1\}$. The first, the color set $\{1, 2, \cdots, n + 1\}$ is used to color the edge of all the K_n, each vertex is missing a different color $\{j\}$ in X_i. The second, the color set $\{n + 2, \cdots, 2n + 1\}$ and $\{2n + 2, \cdots, 3n - 1\}$ is used to color the G'. If $(i)_2 = 0$, we used the color set $\{n + 2, \cdots, 2n + 1\}$ to color the $G_{i,i+1}$; If $(i)_2 = 1$, we used the color set $\{2n + 2, \cdots, 3n - 1\}$ to color the $G_{i,i+1}$. we have $\chi''_\Sigma(P_m \bullet K_n) = 3n - 1$.

Case2. If n is odd, equivalent, We can distinguish three steps to construct the Total-neighbor-distinguishing coloring by sums of $P_m \bullet K_n$.

Assumed that the color set is $\{1, 2, \cdots, 3n - 1\}$. The first, the color set $\{1, 2, \cdots, n\}$ is used to color the edge of all the K_n, the color set is the same for each vertex. The second, the color set $\{n + 1, \cdots, 2n + 1\}$ and $\{2n + 2, \cdots, 3n - 1\}$ is used to color the G'. If $(i)_2 = 0$, we used the color set $\{n + 1, \cdots, 2n + 1\}$ to color the $G_{i,i+1}$; If $(i)_2 = 1$, we used the color set $\{2n + 2, \cdots, 3n - 1\}$ to color the $G_{i,i+1}$, we have $\chi''_\Sigma(P_m \bullet K_n) = 3n - 1$.

We can see from the above analysis, we have $\chi''_\Sigma(P_2 \bullet K_n) = 2n$.

3 Conclusion

In this paper, we studied that the Cartesian product, direct product and semi strong product of infinite paths, and finite graph of the semi strong product. we determine exact value of these product graphs. We can obtain the following result about this paper studies the product graph $\chi''_\Sigma(G) = \Delta(G) + 1$.

Acknowledgments. This research was financially supported by Key Laboratory of Streaming Data Computing Technologies and Applications, State Ethnic Affairs Commission of China (No.14XBZ018) and Innovative Team Subsidize of Northwest Minzu University and Central University for Northwest Minzu University of the basic scientific research business expenses of the special funds to support graduate projects (Yxm2017103, Yxm2017105).

References

1. Zhang, Z., Chen, X.E., Li, J., et al.: On adjacent-vertex-distinguishing total coloring of graphs. Sci. China Ser. A Math. **48**(3), 289–299 (2005)
2. Wang, H.: On the adjacent vertex-distinguishing total chromatic numbers of the graphs with Δ (G) = 3. J. Comb. Optim. **14**(1), 87–109 (2007)
3. Monika, P., Mariusz, W.: On the total-neighbor-distinguishing index by sums. Graphs Comb. **31**(3), 771–782 (2015)
4. Dong, A.J., Wang, G.H.: Neighbor sum distinguishing total colorings of graphs with bounded maximum average degree. Acta Math. Sin. Engl. Ser. **30**(4), 703–709 (2014)
5. Li, H.L., Liu, B.Q., Wang, G.H.: Neighbor sum distinguishing total colorings of K4-minor free graphs. Front. Math. China **30**(6), 1351–1366 (2013)
6. Li, H.L., Ding, L.H., Liu, B.Q.: Neighbor sum distinguishing total colorings of planar graphs. J. Comb. Optim. **32**(3), 906–916 (2016)
7. Cheng, X.H., Huang, D.J., Wang, G.H., et al.: Neighbor sum distinguishing total colorings of planar graphs with maximum degree Δ. Discret. Appl. Math. **190**(C), 34–41 (2015)
8. Jaradat, M.M.M.: On the edge coloring of graph products. Int. Math. Math. Sci. **2005**(16), 296–301 (2005)
9. Bondy, J.A.: Graph Theory with Applications. American Elsevier, New York (1976)
10. Diestel, R.: Graph Theory. Springer, Heidelberg (2005)
11. Su, Z., Wang, T., Hamdi, M.: JOTA: Joint optimization for the task assignment of sketch-based measurement. J. Comput. Commun. **102**, 17–27 (2017)
12. Wang, T., Hamdi, M.: Presto:towards efficient online virtual network embedding in virtualized cloud data centers. J. Comput. Netw. **106**, 196–208 (2016)
13. Wang, T., Su, Z., Xia, Y., Qin, B., Hamdi, M.: Towards cost-effective and low latency data center network architecture. J. Comput. Commun. **82**, 1–12 (2016)
14. Wang, T., Su, Z., Xia, Y., Hamdi, M.: Rethinking data center networking: architecture, network protocols, and resource sharing. J. IEEE Access **2**, 1481–1496 (2014)
15. Su, Z., Wang, T., Hamdi, M.: COSTA: cross-layer optimization for sketch-based software defined measurement task assignment. In: IEEE/ACM International Symposium on Quality and Service (IWQoS 2015) (2015)

Research on the Fruit and Vegetable Cold Chain Preservative System Based on Compressive Sensing

Ying Zhang[1(✉)], Ruqi Cheng[1], Yangyang Li[1], and Shaohui Chen[2]

[1] College of Electronic Information and Optical Engineering,
Tianjin 300071, China
caroline_zy@nankai.edu.cn
[2] National Engineering and Technology Research Center for Preservation
of Agriculture Products, Tianjin 300384, China

Abstract. According to the present stage low-level information of China's cold chain preservation, a kind of fruit and vegetable cold chain preservation perception system is designed. Based on compressed sensing theory of non-related measurement data using the sparsity of the signal, remove the data redundancy. Introducing BATIMP algorithm which has good performance in data reconstruction to explore the Cold Chain networking data transmission strategy and the degree of accuracy, establish the efficient information sharing mechanism, realizing the vegetables, fruits and other agricultural products remote intelligent monitoring from the storage, transportation and sales etc. Solve the problem of redundancy of mass data for Chinese traditional sensing mechanism, and provides great convenience for monitoring environmental parameters of agricultural products.

Keywords: Cold chain logistics · Temperature and humidity
Compressive sensing · Sensory perceptual system

1 Introduction

In China, the development of cold chain [1] logistics of agricultural products is still in the starting stage [2], and the cold chain logistics system of intelligent large-scale and systematic development is not maturity [3]. Compared with the developed countries, the corrosion rate of fruit and vegetables in China is about 15% higher than that of the developed countries. The cold chain products of fruit and vegetable produce up to 100-billion-yuan loss per year [4]. To establish a perfect cold chain technology system and a perfect technology system for cold chain information management, maximize the quality and safety of products, and reduce the consumption of special supply chain system, which is an important stage [5] of the development of China's cold chain logistics.

The emergence of Internet of things technology has effectively improved the technological level and information level of supply chain, and has great theoretical and practical significance for reducing the decay rate of fresh agricultural products. However, large-scale cold chain monitoring network node deployment will increase data

© Springer Nature Singapore Pte Ltd. 2018
H. Yuan et al. (Eds.): GSKI 2017, CCIS 848, pp. 229–237, 2018.
https://doi.org/10.1007/978-981-13-0893-2_24

redundancy [6]. Therefore, using the reasonable data distribution mechanism [7] for acquisition, transmission [8] and processing of cold chain data networking, solve the major contradiction between the limited resources of the large-scale networking solutions [9] and the processing of massive data [10]. Based on compressed sensing theory of non-related measurement data using the sparsity of the signal, remove the data redundancy and establish the fresh fruit and vegetable cold chain preservation system, constructing the Cold Chain Logistics Monitoring Perception Transmission Model, and introducing Sensing and Reconstruction Mechanism of Cold Chain Data to explore the networking data transmission strategy and the degree of accuracy, and establish the efficient information sharing platform, involving BATIMP algorithm into the traditional Cold Chain System to improve the performance in data transmission and data recovery and finally realize the vegetables, fruits and other agricultural products remote intelligent monitoring from the storage, transportation and sales etc.

2 Structure of Cold Chain Fresh Preservative Perception System

Fruit and vegetable cold chain preservation perception system, as shown in Fig. 1, mainly includes cold chain information sensing terminal, embedded data aggregation system, information sharing data management center. The micro environment of fruit and vegetable products in warehousing, logistics and other links determines the fresh-keeping period of agricultural products. The key parameters are temperature, humidity, concentration of oxygen and carbon dioxide gas.

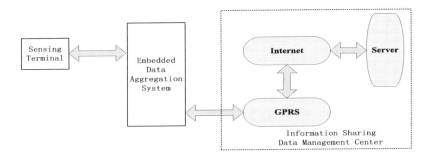

Fig. 1. Block diagram of cold chain preservation perception system

Therefore, based on the ARM processing chip, control sensors to collect environmental data as temperature and humidity, the concentration of oxygen and carbon dioxide gas. Transmit to the remote server through Si4463 module in wireless mode and information sharing management center provides data processing, early warning of environmental parameters, shelf life prediction, and consumer traceability query processing. To realize the whole process, seamless monitoring and early warning of the supply chain link of fruit and vegetable agricultural products, and provide reliable information guarantee for the storage, transportation and transaction of agricultural products. This paper mainly studies the environmental parameters acquisition model and transmission reconstruction method of cold chain of fruits and vegetables based on compressed sensing technology. Taking the perception and reconstruction of temperature data as an example, this paper discusses the intelligent optimization of environmental information perception of fruits and vegetables and other agricultural products cold chain logistics links.

3   Transmission Model of Cold Chain Logistics Monitoring Perception

A set of $\Lambda_N := \{1, 2, \ldots N\}$ as N acquisition node sequences of cold chain monitoring system, the original data collected by each node is d_i, d is the readings in each round of N nodes acquisition, namely $d = \{d_i\}, i \in \Lambda_N, d_i \in R_N$. Define Ψ as the sparse matrix, the vector x can get its sparse expression via sparse base $\{\psi_{ij}\}$ using K nonzero vector $\theta \in \Sigma_K \left(\text{or } \|\theta\|_2 = K\right)$:

$$\mathbf{d} = \vec{\Psi} \cdot \vec{\theta} \tag{1}$$

Mean

$$\begin{bmatrix} y_1 \\ y_2 \\ \vdots \\ y_M \end{bmatrix} = \begin{bmatrix} \varphi_{11} & \varphi_{12} & \cdots & \varphi_{1N} \\ \varphi_{21} & \varphi_{22} & \cdots & \varphi_{2N} \\ \vdots & \vdots & \ddots & \vdots \\ \varphi_{M1} & \varphi_{M2} & \cdots & \varphi_{MN} \end{bmatrix} \cdot \begin{bmatrix} d_1 \\ d_2 \\ \vdots \\ d_N \end{bmatrix} + \begin{bmatrix} z_1 \\ z_2 \\ \vdots \\ z_M \end{bmatrix} \tag{2}$$

Figure 2 depicts the cold chain preservation system compressive sensing structure. The N dimensional original sensing signal, after M step of measurement, obtains the M measurement value and add to other corresponding values according to the network topology. From the whole network, amount to the original vector multiplying with network measurement matrix N, get an M dimensional measurement vector y, while $z = \{z_i\}, i \in [1, 2, \ldots, M]$ is the channel transmission noise, and each measurement process is:

$$y_m = \sum_{n=1}^{N} \varphi_{mn} d_n + z_m \tag{3}$$

In the process of reconstruction, the receiver according to the obtained measurement vector y, approximate the sparse representation $\widehat{\theta}$ of the original signal via reconstruction matrix $\Phi\Psi$. Reconstruct the$N$ node original signal through sparse inverse reconstruction $\widehat{\mathbf{d}}$, while w is sparse transform noise, assuming to follow WGN $w \sim N(0, \sigma^2 I)$. Therefore, each sensor node reconfiguration value is:

$$\widehat{d}_n = \sum_{k=1}^{K} \psi_{nk} \widehat{\theta}_k + w_n \tag{4}$$

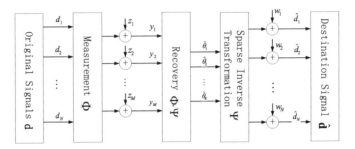

Fig. 2. Compression sensing process of space sparse signal model

4 Sensing and Reconstruction Mechanism of Cold Chain Data

Analyze the sparsity of the fruit and vegetable cold chain data using the Chirplet Dictionary Two-step Optimization Algorithm, and determine the sparse domain. Figure 3 describes the detailed flow of the two-step optimization matching tracking algorithm in the Chirplet dictionary.

The length of the original signal d of the environment parameter is N, and the analytical $d(n)$ is analyzed, to obtain the complex analytic signal $f(n)$. If the signal itself is complex, then $f(n) = d(n)$. $D = \{c_r\}_{r \in \Gamma}$ is over complete-dictionary, $D \in H$, Γ is the

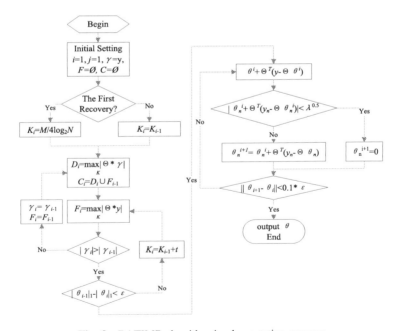

Fig. 3. BATIMP algorithm implementation process

index set of D, c_r is Chirplet atom determined by the parameter r. Initialize the residual $res\_d_0 = f(n)$, and pick Q atoms out of the time-frequency distribution during each iteration, ordering $m = 0$, and approximation error is ε.

Calculate the time-frequency distribution of residual res_d_m, and Q time-frequency atoms are matched from it.

Step 1: $\theta_0(n, m) = \theta(n, m)$, $q = 1$, search for the time-frequency center (p, k) of matched atom, confirming the discrete parameter group:

$$(p_q, k_q) = \arg\max_{(n,m)} \theta_q(n, m) \tag{5}$$

Step 2: search (j, l, i) as the dimension, frequency modulation and phase parameters of time-frequency atoms in Chirplet time-frequency dictionary.

$$(j_q, l_q, i_q) = \arg\max_{(j,l,i)}\left\{\sum_m res\_d_m(n)c^*_{(j,p,k,l,i)}(n)\right\} \tag{6}$$

If $q = Q$, stop iterating, or else step into step 3, and correct the time-frequency distribution.

Step 3: Time-frequency correction:

$$\theta_{q+1}(n, m) = \theta_q(n, m) - \theta_{p_q, k_q, j_q, l_q}(n, m) \tag{7}$$

$q = q + 1$, return to step 1 for the next atom matching.

At the end of the iteration, we get Q matching atoms:

$$\left\{c_{r_q(m)}(n), r_q^{(m)} = \{p_q, k_q, j_q, l_q\}, q = 1, 2, \ldots, Q\right\} \tag{8}$$

Making Q matched atoms as a subspace V_m, calculate the orthogonal projection of the residual signal res_d_m in the subspace.

$$P_{V_m} = \left(s_1^{(m)}, s_2^{(m)}, \ldots, s_Q^{(m)}\right) = \arg\min_{c_q}\left\{\left\|res\_d_m - \sum_{q=1}^{Q} s_q c_{r_q^{(m)}}(n)\right\|_2^2\right\} \tag{9}$$

When the approximation of the residuals is satisfied to:

$$res\_d_{m+1} = res\_d_m - P_{V_m} = res\_d_m - \sum_{q=1}^{Q} s_q^m c_{r_q^{(m)}}(n) \leq \varepsilon\|d(n)\|_2^2 \tag{10}$$

Over the iteration, otherwise repeat it. Finally get the approximated signal:

$$d = res\_d_{m+1} + \sum_{r=0}^{m} P_{V_r} = res\_d_{m+1} + \sum_{r=0}^{m}\sum_{q=1}^{Q} s_q^{(r)} c_{r_q^{(r)}}(n) \tag{11}$$

Thus, the sparse matrix $\Psi = [c_{r_1}, c_{r_2}, \ldots c_{r_m}]$ is obtained.

Reconstruct the compressed cold chain preservation data by using the Group Atoms Matching Pursuit algorithm (GAMP). Select candidate multiple optimal atomic composition from over-complete atomic dictionary per round, and choose the appropriate atom from the candidate set. When the residual reaches a certain threshold, it shows that the sparse decomposition reaches enough precision, and the iteration can be stopped.

Initialization: Assumed that N is the length of signal d to be decomposed, and $\{a_k\}$ is the atom of over-complete atomic library, $k \in D$, the initial value for the residual signal r_0 is d, iter = 0 iteration, and residual threshold ε, supported set $\Omega = \varnothing$.

Step 1: calculate the inner product between the residual r_{i-1} and $\{a_k\}$ to choose q largest inner product atoms, forming the candidate set T.

$$T = \{a_{k_i}\}_q = \{\max_{k \in \mathbf{D}} \langle r_{i-1}, a_k \rangle\}_q \tag{12}$$

Step 2: select the most relevant atoms from T, and save to the support set Ω

$$\Omega = \Omega \cup \max \langle T, d \rangle \tag{13}$$

Step 3: update the residual r_i

$$r_i = d - \left\langle \{a_k\}_{Omega}, d \right\rangle \{a_k\}_\Omega \tag{14}$$

Step 4: Simplify over-complete atomic library, and remove the selected optimal atoms from it.

$$\{a_k\}_i = \{a_k\}_{\overline{\Omega}} \tag{15}$$

Step 5: Loop step 1 to step 4, till the iteration termination condition is satisfied as:

$$r_i < \varepsilon \tag{16}$$

Step 6: Get the sparse base Ψ of signal d

$$\Psi = \{a_k\}_\Omega \tag{17}$$

The Backtracking Adaptive Threshold Iterative Matching Pursuit (BATIMP) algorithm is used to reconstruct the cold chain preservative signals, further improve the precision of reconstruction.

The basic idea of BATIMP algorithm is to realize the adaptive of sparse degree by adjusting the step length of candidate set. Adopting stage reconstruction process. The estimation of the sparse coefficient is carried out based on the threshold iteration during each stage, and complete the reconstruction of target signal using sparse representation inverse process.

As shown in Fig. 3, the implementation of the specific algorithm is as follows:

Step 1: Initialization: iteration number $i = 1$, stage number $j = 1$, the residual $r = y$, estimate the sparsity of the signal, as the initial step length t, the initial size of the candidate set $L = t$.

Step 2: Sparse value pre-estimation: Θ is recovery matrix, at the jth stage, select support set by stage wise matching tracing method, and calculate the inner product $|\Theta T * r|$, looking for L biggest column vector atoms most relevant with residual in the reconstruction matrix, in the set S_j, to obtain the candidate set $C_j = F_{j-1} \cup S_j$.

Step 3: Calculate the inner product $\left| Theta_{C_j}^{T} * y \right|$, looking for L atoms most relevant with measurement vector y, in support set F, estimated value θ of sparse signal is obtained by the least square operation.

Step 4: The threshold iterative backtracking optimization of support set: new estimates value obtained in step 3 will be compared with the one get in previous stage. Terminate the current stage if $\left\| \theta_{i-1} - \theta_i \right\|_2 < \varepsilon$, update residuals and support sets. Return to step 3 to estimate sparse using current L and candidate set. Otherwise, increase the candidate set step length L by t size, and back to step 2, to the next stage.

5 Results and Analysis

The cold chain preservation system collect data such as temperature and humidity. Deploy 80 nodes to control the different cold chain transport warehouse, to real-time collect and record the change of temperature and humidity. It poll once each 5 min to collect data to the information center for high-precision reconstruction following the cold chain logistics monitoring system perception transmission model. Figure 4 shows that a contrast diagram of the original temperature and the reconstructed data collected by one node according to the time slot. The certain node has constant temperature at 2 °C.

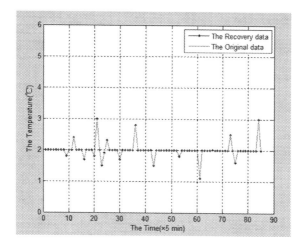

Fig. 4. Contrast diagram of the original temperature and the reconstructed data

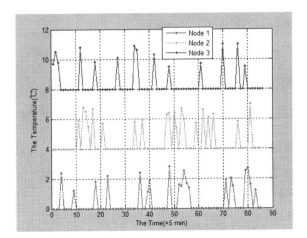

Fig. 5. The monitoring result of multi nodes

When the temperature change is more than 1 degrees, the control center sends the control instruction to keep the cold chain store constant temperature. Figure 5 is the monitoring result of multi nodes. Three temperature sensors are selected, which are kept at 8 °C, 4 ° C, 0 °C respectively.

Figure 6 shows the different sparsity of the signal through the measurement matrix in different dimensions and the BATIMP to get the accuracy of reconstruction, which is the average of 1000 times operation. K here is the sparsity degree of data. It can be seen that the signal with lower sparsity is able to reconstruct the original data accurately through a lower measurement dimension. That is to say, the stronger sparsity or compression is, the less measurement consumption is required to get the accurate reconstruction.

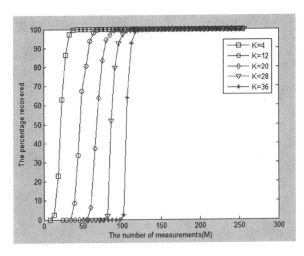

Fig. 6. Different sparsity of the signal through the measurement matrix in different dimensions

6 Conclusion

For the problem of China's agricultural products warehousing and logistics at the present stage, according to the modern agricultural products cold chain logistics construction, introduced the theory of compressed sensing to study the large-scale network deployment. The sensing transmission model of cold chain logistics monitoring network is established, and the sensing and reconstruction of fresh and cold storage data of fruits and vegetables is studied. Taking the temperature data as an example, studied the reconstruction effect of the cold chain storage environment data through the BATIMP algorithm. Based on compressed sensing, fruit and vegetable cold chain fresh-keeping system solves the problem of redundancy of mass data for traditional sensors, and runs stably, which provides great convenience for monitoring environmental parameters of agricultural products such as warehousing and logistics.

Acknowledgments. Supported by Key Projects of Tianjin Science and Technology Support Plan: Research and development of fruit and vegetable cold chain circulation support technology of Internet of things (No. 15ZCZDNC00240).

References

1. Chen, N.: The current situation and the countermeasures of China's cold chain logistics development. Logistics Eng. Manag. **39**(01), 14–15 (2017)
2. Lin, H.D., Gao, G.J.: Transportation safety countermeasure analysis on cold-chain logistics of fresh agricultural products. Adv. Mater. Res. **860–863**, 3123–3127 (2014). Energy Development
3. Guo, H.-X., Shao, M.: Process reengineering of cold chain logistics of agricultural products based on low-carbon economy. Asian Agric. Res. **4**(2), 59–62 (2012)
4. Ren, W.-z, Wang, L.-L.: The analysis of typical mode of domestic and foreign food cold-chain logistics. Guangdong Agric. Sci. **2**, 212–214 (2013)
5. Jie, L.: Issues of food-related cold-chain logistics management in China. In: International Conference on Logistics Systems and Intelligent Management, ICLSIM 2010, vol. 3, pp. 1319–1322 (2010)
6. Jun, X., Zhongwei, W.: The construction of symbiotic synergistic mode of forest fruit industry and cold chain logistics in China. In: Logistics for Sustained Economic Development - Infrastructure, Information, Integration - Proceedings of the 2010 International Conference of Logistics Engineering and Management, ICLEM 2010, vol. 387, pp. 487–494 (2010)
7. Zhang, Y., Sun, G., Li, Z.: Balanced energy consumption adaptive sensing algorithm for multi-layer wireless sensor network. J. Comput. Inf. Syst. **10**(10), 4451–4458 (2014)
8. He, J., Sun, G., Zhang, Y., et al.: Data recovery in heterogeneous wireless sensor networks based on low-rank tensors. In: 21st IEEE Symposium on Computers and Communication, ISCC, Messina, Italy (2016)
9. He, J., Sun, G., Zhang, Y., et al.: Data recovery in wireless sensor networks with joint matrix completion and sparsity constraints. IEEE Commun. Lett. **19**(12), 2230–2233 (2015)
10. Xu, Y., Sun, G., Zhang, Y., et al.: Sparsity adaptive look ahead matching pursuit algorithm for compressed sensing. J. Comput. Inf. Syst. **1**(18), 6829–6836 (2015)

A Heterogeneous Architecture Based Power Control for Cooperative Safety Systems

Pulong Xie[1(✉)], Fuqiang Liu[1], Nguyen Ngoc Van[2], and Lijun Zu[3]

[1] School of Electronic and Information Engineering,
Tongji University, Shanghai, China
puloxie@126.com, dragonking18@163.com
[2] School of Electronics and Telecommunications,
Hanoi University of Science and Technology, Hanoi, Vietnam
ng_ng_van@yahoo.com
[3] China UnionPay, Shanghai, China
zulijun@unionpay.com

Abstract. While using the cooperative vehicle safety systems based on Vehicle Ad-hoc Network more frequently, the performance of the Vehicle Ad-hoc Network in high vehicle density could not meet the requirements of the increasing road safety due to the channel congestion condition. Though there is a lot of research about the congestion control in Vehicle Ad-hoc Network, the feedbacks of the Vehicle Ad-hoc Network limit the Quality of Service in vehicle connectivity. In this paper, we proposed a heterogeneous architecture to achieve superior performance in congestion condition, interworking the Vehicle Ad-hoc Network with the cellular network 3GPP LTE. The congestion state was determined in LTE cellular network and the control algorithm of adjusting the transmitting power was implemented in Vehicle Ad-hoc Network. Furthermore, if the network congestion reached a critical value, partial data would be transmitted through LTE cellular network. Finally, we proved that the network performance in terms of packet reception probability and channel busy ratio was optimized as illustrated by our simulation results.

Keywords: Heterogeneous architecture · Channel Busy Ratio
Power adjustment · Congestion control

1 Introduction

With the deep-going research in Vehicle to Everything (V2X) communication in recent years, Vehicle Ad-hoc Network (VANET) has been a focus of attention. VANET is a kind of special mobile self-organizing network used in vehicle wireless communication, with the characteristics of high mobility, rapid change of network topology and predictable node direction. The dedicated short-range communication (DSRC), based on IEEE 802.11p [1], is the centerpiece of VANET, and authorized to work on the 5.9 GHz band, whose radio is based on matured Orthogonal Frequency-Division Multiplexing (OFDM) technology, consisting of seven channels with channel bandwidth 10 MHz. However, considering the large number of road and vehicle communication modules and cost, the DSRC technology coming into actual application also

© Springer Nature Singapore Pte Ltd. 2018
H. Yuan et al. (Eds.): GSKI 2017, CCIS 848, pp. 238–249, 2018.
https://doi.org/10.1007/978-981-13-0893-2_25

need a lot of work. Meanwhile, because LTE possess a sound foundation and wide communication range, as well as high transmission speed, large capacity and stability characteristics, therefore, more and more researchers consider realizing the V2X communication by utilizing the LTE network.

In Cooperative Vehicle Safety (CVS) systems, the vehicles need to broadcast their safety information such as velocity, position and steering wheel angle etc. to the surrounding vehicles, providing support to Advanced Driver Assistance System (ADAS) application, for example, vehicle collision warning and overtaking warning, so the network performance should be high reliable and low latency. However, in high vehicle density condition, vehicle in VANET will constantly transmit safety information to the surrounding vehicles with a certain period of time, causing network congestion and resulting in low packet reception probability; but if all vehicles send beacons to each other via LTE, the network delay will be too high to meet the requirements.

To address the problem of network congestion, the scholars proposed many approaches, mainly divided into three types: first method is to adjust the beacon packet size, the smaller the packet is, the shorter the transmission time will be, thus the Channel Busy Ratio (CBR) [2] will be lower; second factor is beacon frequency, the higher the frequency is, the more beacons will exist in the network, and the worse the network performance will be, but high frequency could ensure the freshness of the vehicle data, so it cannot be too small, this value is always set to 10 Hz; the last one is transmission power, which can directly affect the communication range of the vehicles. In this paper, our congestion control method focus on the transmission power in heterogeneous network.

However, the VANET has its own limitations because of its distributed network structure. There is no central control point and each node communications with each other in equivalent position, flooding data in the network, thus producing a large number of redundant data packets, and leading to serious network congestion, that is to say, broadcast storm [3]. But the LTE cellular network could perform centralized network control and its flat structure supports low-latency transmission, hence the LTE could assist to solve the network congestion problem in VANET.

In this paper, we propose a heterogeneous architecture to acquire a better performance in vehicle density. We optimize the detection of the congestion state via LTE base station to obtain the current congestion state in a global perspective. Then utilize a Linear Memoryless Range Control algorithm (LMRC) [4] and an improved algorithm Stateful Utilization- based Power Adaptation (SUPRA) [5] to achieve power control in VANET MAC layer. Therefore, we can effectively prevent the vehicle node from misjudging the current congestion state in VANET by itself, and enhance the success rate of beacon received.

The reminder of the paper is organized as follows. Section 2 will present the discussion of related work of congestion control based on the power adjustment. In Sect. 3, we will introduce the theory of the LMRC and the improved control algorithm SUPRA, then propose the heterogeneous architecture and present how it works to enhance the network performance. Section 4 evaluates the proposed scheme via simulation and Sect. 5 concludes this paper.

2   Related Previous Work

Network congestion often occurs when the information transmitting in the network exceeds the network capacity for relatively long periods of time. The main goal of congestion control is to ensure the timely transmission of vehicle safety information and receiving information with high probability. This safety information, or called beacons in VANET, including position, velocity, direction and other messages related to a moving vehicle. The main problem in controlling congestion with beacons is how to attain the optimized frequency or appropriate transmission power to broadcast beacons to meet the requirements of the CVS application.

In this paper, we mainly discuss the power control in which many scholars has done a lot of research. As proposed in [6], a fairness–based power control algorithm named FPAV via solving a max-min optimized problem to find the optimum transmission range of every node and it ensures the bandwidth allocated fairly under the premise the congestion. At the meanwhile, a fully distributed strategy named D-FPAV based on FPAV is proposed in [7]. Contrary to the FPAV, this strategy is motivated by the safety requirements of safety applications and achieves more fairness, but it needs more time to calculate the optimized power. In ref. [8], a low-overhead transmission power control scheme has been proposed, time channels could be occupied by several vehicles, as a result, fostering a fair channel reservation scheme.

Also, there are other methods to adjust the transmission power, for example, a scheme proposed in [2], through adaptively changing the power based on limited feedback of CBR from the network, the value of CBR could remain the optimal value. In [9], each node broadcasts its latest power and overload (the number of received packets), then the node could dynamically adjust its own power based on strict criterion to control the load of periodic beacons on the channel. Paper [4] proposes an approach of changing the communication range linearly according to the average channel occupancy rate (also named CBR), this parameter could be obtained by observing the Clear Channel Assessment (CCA) from PHY to MAC layer in IEEE 802.11p.

However, as mentioned above, if only using VANET in CVS application, though adopting the congestion control method, the network performance cannot well satisfy the demand of applications. As performance evaluated in [10] between IEEE 802.11p standard and LTE technology for vehicular networks in terms of delay, reliability, and scalability, LTE could offer superior network capacity and end-to-end delay, but the delay will increase as the network load increases. As for IEEE 802.11p, though it can offer acceptable performance for sparse network topologies and typical transmission frequency, its performance decreases extremely serious for lacking coordinated channel access, utilizing distributed congestion control algorithms and joint power/rate adaptation mechanisms. Nevertheless, LTE can guarantee to gain network performance to a certain extent by assisting scheduling and access control through base station.

Then some researchers begin to study how to utilize LTE network in vehicular environments. In [11], the author analyzes the performance of UMTS cellular network in real vehicular environment, and describes a centralized real-time driver assistance system. Whereas, only the response delay of centralized server is analyzed, ignoring the performance of communication between vehicles. Paper [12] proposes a centralized location service architecture based on the heterogeneous network, inter-vehicle communication is done over 802.11p network while unicast location updates and queries are routed through cellular network such as LTE, so the performance could be better in high vehicle density network, but congestion control scheme has not been mentioned in this paper.

Base on the above congestion control mechanism in VANET and the application of LTE cellular network in vehicular environment, we propose a heterogeneous framework that is mainly based on the VANET network and supplemented by LTE cellular network to attain superior performance in congestion state by adjusting the transmission power and offload partial data. Not like in VANET, the detection of congestion state no longer relies on the judgment of each vehicle. Instead, the state will be determined by LTE base station from a global perspective. Then the LMRC and improved algorithm SUPRA will be adopted to calculate the optimized transmission power, if the congestion reaches a threshold value, partial messages will be transmitted through LTE cellular network, therefore we could enhance the performance of the network.

3 Proposed Scheme

In congestion control, firstly we need to detect the current state of network and determine whether the network is congested. Hence we propose a semi-distributed and semi-centralized congestion detection mechanism based on CBR and describe the congestion state by state machine, then change the transmitting power by LMRC or SUPRA algorithm and transmit partial messages through LTE if the congestion state reaches a threshold value. Here we will introduce some knowledge used in our architecture as follows.

3.1 Channel Busy Ratio as Feedback Measure

The use of CBR as a feedback measure is motivated by the unique relationship of the broadcast throughput of a VANET, the broadcast throughput is defined as the number of copies of a packet delivered per unit time from a vehicle to its neighbors up to its communication range. CBR could be measured by calculating the ratio of time that the channel has been sensed busy in a given time window T (in the order of milliseconds to seconds) at the MAC level, that is to say, CBR is the ratio of mini time slots T_{slot} duration that is busy in time window T, the T_{slot} could only be idle or busy in time window T. Therefore, the CBR can be calculated as follows [2]:

$$\text{CBR} = \frac{\sum_{i=1}^{[T/T_{slot}]} \Lambda_i}{[T/T_{slot}]} \tag{1}$$

Where Λ_i is 1 representing busy slots and 0 for idle slots, and $[T/T_{slot}]$ is the number of min slots in the measured window; for ease of presentation, T is the given time window, T_{slot} is the min slot time, $[T/T_{slot}]$ means the number of T_{slot} in time T. Actually, CBR could be considered as a local feedback available for each node in the

network and CBR can be used as an indicator of the system performance. It is calculated in the MAC layer by using CCA from the PHY layer of 802.11p. The state
machine and two existing power control methods all use CBR and are summarized in
the following sections.

3.2   State Machine (SM) Description

As Fig. 1 depicts, the state machine consists of three kinds of states and two time
periods. The three states are as follows: *Relaxed, Normal* and *Restrictive*, respectively
standing for the channel is idle, normal and congestion. Two time periods include
NDL_time Up indicating the increasing of CBR value, and *NDL_time Down* standing
for the decreasing of CBR value.

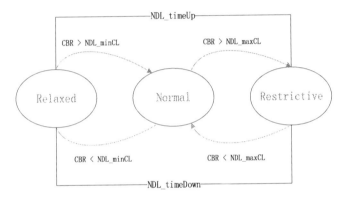

Fig. 1. State machine to describe the congestion state

At the same time, *NDL_minCL* indicates how fast the SM could react to the
increasing of CBR, and *NDL_maxCL* stands for how quickly the SM could react to the
decreasing of CBR. The beginning state of SM remains *Relaxed*. During the *NDL_
timeUp* period, if current CBR is greater than *NDL_minCL*, the SM will switch from
Relaxed to *Normal*; if the CBR is also larger than *NDL_maxCL*, then the SM will shift
to *Restrictive*. In *NDL_ timeDown* period, when the current CBR is less than *NDL_
maxCL*, the SM will toggle back to *Normal* from *Restrictive*; and when the CBR is still
smaller than *NDL_minCL*, the SM will switch back to *Relaxed*.

3.3   Congestion Control Algorithm Based Power Adjustment

3.3.1   Linear Memoryless Range Control Algorithm (LMRC)

The power control introduced in paper [2], which is based on limited feedback from the
network and called linear memoryless range control, robustly maintains the system
performance near optimal operation points. The idea is to provide a robust scheme of
power adjustment that does not need know the optimal operation point. The approach
can be described using the following equation to update the power (or transmission
range) as a function U_k.

$$P_{k+1} = f(U_k) = \begin{cases} P_{\max} & U_k < U_{\min} \\ P_{\min} + \frac{U_{\max}-U_k}{U_{\max}-U_{\min}}(P_{\max} - P_{\min}) & U_{\min} \leq U_k < U_{\max} \\ P_{\min} & U_k > U_{\max} \end{cases} \quad (2)$$

Where U_k is the last measured CBR (at the time k), U_{min} is the minimum desired CBR value, in this paper, it equals to the *NDL_minCL*. U_{max} is the maximum desired CBR, also, in this paper, it equals to the *NDL_maxCL*. The values for (U_{min}, U_{max}) are chosen based safety requirements. When the network is congested, the LMRC can keep the CBR within a certain range by updating the equation so as to ensure the reception probability. However, LMRC algorithm may converge very slowly or even diverge.

3.3.2 Stateful Utilization-Based Power Adaptation (SUPRA)

The SUPRA is an improved algorithm for LMRC based on the concept of linearly mapping CBR to power, the current transmit power can be obtained by adding one step to the power iteration, which can make the power always converge to a suitable value. The algorithm can be explained using the following formula 3.

$$P_{k+1} = P_k + \eta \times (f(U_k) - P_k)$$

$$f(U_k) = \begin{cases} P_{\max} & U_k < U_{\min} \\ P_{\min} + \frac{U_{\max}-U_k}{U_{\max}-U_{\min}}(P_{\max} - P_{\min}) & U_{\min} \leq U_k < U_{\max} \\ P_{\min} & U_k > U_{\max} \end{cases} \quad (3)$$

Where P_k is the latest value of power, and the power range (P_{min}, P_{max}) could be relatively arbitrary set, because the gain step will adjust the power to keep the power value stable. Compared with LMRC, the transmission power in SUPRA is not calculated directly by CBR, but through finding the difference between the target power and latest power P_k, and then adding this different value by the weight η to the latest power value P_k, the algorithm converge to a solution quickly.

3.4 A Heterogeneous Architecture Based on VANET and LTE Cellular Network

Although two algorithms mentioned above are highly robust and no parameters such as propagation model, vehicle density and other vehicles' transmission parameters are needed, the performance in high vehicle density in VANET still cannot meet the reliability requirements of vehicle safety applications, so we propose a heterogeneous network based on VANET and LTE cellular network as Fig. 2 shows. With the assistance of LTE base station to determine the state of SM and the power control algorithms in VANET, we could achieve a better performance (Fig. 3).

The *Simple App* layer in Fig. 2 is the top layer of the heterogeneous network and used to send and transmit vehicle safety messages, and the messages have been divided into two types: DSRC messages and LTE messages, DSRC messages mainly include the vehicle safety messages while LTE messages mainly consist of SM information. Then the *Decision Maker* acts as a decision-making layer to determine whether the message is transmitted through VANET network or the LTE cellular network

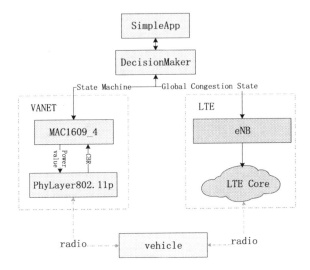

Fig. 2. Heterogeneous architecture

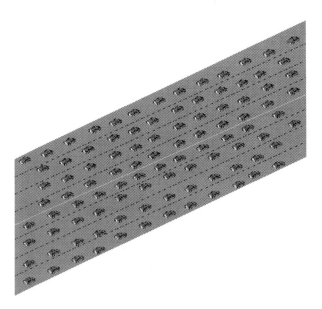

Fig. 3. Simulation scenario

according to the kind of messages. If the message type is DSRC, then *Decision Maker* will send the messages to *MAC1609_4 layer* and broadcast the message to neighbor vehicles through PhyLayer 802.11p; if the message type is LTE, then *Decision Maker* will send the messages to LTE eNB, and broadcast messages to vehicles in the communication range of eNB by LTE core network. The congestion control process in our heterogeneous network is as follows:

- Firstly, in VANET network, each vehicle delivers the CBR value perceived at the PHY layer to the IEEE 1609.4 MAC layer, and then each vehicle will be divided into different congestion state in MAC layer from the perspective of each vehicle.
- Then the vehicle interacts with the base station through *DecisionMaker* layer and sends the congestion status detected by the vehicle itself to the base station.
- Later, the base station will build a vehicle queue to restore the judgement of the congestion state of all the vehicles in the network, and then obtains the global congestion state (GCS) by the following formula:

$$GCS = \frac{R}{R+N+Re} \times \alpha + \frac{N}{R+N+Re} \times \beta + \frac{Re}{R+N+Re} \times (1-\alpha-\beta) \quad (4)$$

Where R refers to the number of vehicles whose congestion state is *Relaxed* at the current moment; N refers to the number of vehicles whose congestion state is *Normal* at this time; Re refers to the number of vehicles whose congestion state is *Restrictive* at this moment. α, β and $1-\alpha-\beta$ respectively represents the gain of these conditions.

- At the end, the base station returns the calculated GSC value to the MAC layer of each vehicle, then we utilize different power adjustment strategies according to the different value of GSC. Not like LMRC and SUPRA in VANET, here we adopt the value of GSC rather than CBR to execute the algorithm, hence we can avoid the misjudgment of the current congestion state of the network to some extent. At the meanwhile, if the value of GSC reaches a threshold value U_{top}, partial vehicle data will be transmitted through LTE cellular network as Eq. 5 shows. Certainly, this scheme only targets at the unforeseen circumstances such as without power control algorithm or the congestion is really serious.

$$P_{k+1}(Heterogeneous) = \begin{cases} P_{k+1}(VANET) = \begin{cases} P_{\max} & U_k < U_{\min} \\ P_{\min} + \frac{U_{\max} - U_k}{U_{\max} - U_{\min}}(P_{\max} - P_{\min}) & U_{\min} \le U_k < U_{\max} \\ P_{\min} & U_{\max} \le U_k < U_{top} \end{cases} \\ P_k(LTE) \quad 45 \text{ mw} \quad U_k > U_{top} \end{cases}$$

$$(5)$$

Our proposed algorithm was evolved from the LMRC and SUPRA, the power in SUPRA could provide faster convergence to a suitable value than LMRC. Compared to LMRC and SUPRA, we used GSC instead of CBR for the CBR could only represent the congestion state by the judgement of each node, the GSC could prevent misjudge of some vehicle node to some extent. At the same time, the value of GSC was a little larger than the value of CBR, then the transmitting power could be lower on the basis of satisfying the requirement of vehicle communication, and the value of CBR in heterogeneous network was also a little lower than in VANET. The simulation results in Sect. 4 could prove the conclusion.

4 Simulation Results

To evaluate performance of our proposed heterogeneous architecture, in this section, we have conducted serval simulation experiments with realistic settings shown as in Table 1 in OMNETPP network simulator. We use Nakagami fading channel model to simulate the actual environment, and use PHY layer in 802.11p working on 5.9 GHz channel and EDCA module in IEEE1609.4 protocol as VANET architecture. Simultaneously, we use LTE-A module as another part of the heterogeneous network to calculate the GSC and transmit partial data.

Table 1. Simulation parameters and values

Parameter	Value
Number of vehicles	10, 20, 40, 60, 80, 120
Vehicle velocity	11.11 m/s, 13.89 m/s
Number of eNB	1 eNB
MAC/PHY protocol	IEEE 802.11p, IEEE 1609.4
Beacon rate	6 Mbps
Sim-time-limit	65 s
Beacon length	300 byte (2400bit)
Receive sensitivity	−89 dbm
Carrier frequency	5.9 GHz
Beacon interval	50 ms

In order to ensure the network congestion will occur in a short period time, we adopt 20 Hz frequency to broadcast the messages. For vehicle dynamics, we use SUMO to generate our traces, the road environment is a two-way and eight-lane straight highway scenario with a length of 1.5 km. The vehicles depart from both sides respectively and then meet in the middle of the road where the LTE base station exists. For the sake of simplicity, we only consider one eNB and assume that all the vehicles in this scenario are in the communication range of the base station. That is, all the vehicles could interact with the base station.

In the simulation, the following parameters are used for our heterogeneous architecture: NDL_minCL = 0.1, NDL_maxCL = 0.3, $P_{\min} = 0.1$mw, $P_{\max} = 100$mw, $\alpha = 0.2$, $\beta = 0.3$, $\eta = 0.5$ in Eqs. 2, 3 and 4, and the threshold value U_{top} is 0.6. Figure 4 shows a typical consecutive loss with the number of vehicles increasing in VANET network and heterogeneous network and different power control algorithm. As we can see, the probability of reception increases when adopting the LMRC and SUPRA power control, especially in high destiny vehicle. But in our proposed heterogeneous network, the probability of reception is clearly higher in comparison with the LMRC and SUPRA in VANET network. And we can observe from Fig. 5 that the changing tendency of CBR is consist with the probability of reception. Also, we could find that the CBR will reach a peak and last for a moment for the sake of the

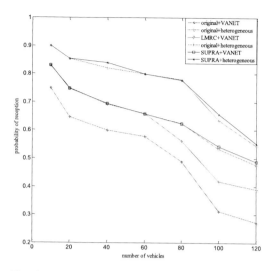

Fig. 4. Probability of reception in different networks

vehicles will meet in the middle of road in our scenario, the information in the network at this time will achieve the largest.

As Figs. 4 and 5 show, the power control algorithm could effectively reduce the value of CBR and sustain CBR in an appropriate range in congestion condition, thus the probability of reception accordingly increases at the same time, and these two figure could verify our proposed architecture could further enhances the performance of the network to meet the requirements of the CVS in high vehicle density.

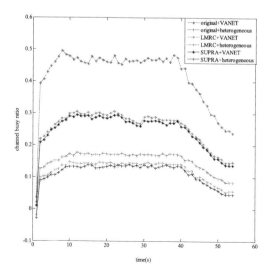

Fig. 5. Channel Busy Ratio in different networks

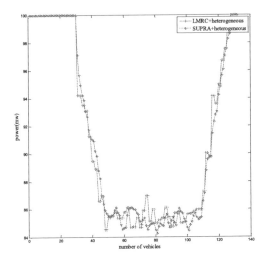

Fig. 6. Power variation by LMRC and SUPRA in heterogeneous network

As we can see in the Figs. 4 and 5, the changing tendency of probability of reception and CBR in LMRC is close to these in SUPRA, because the power in these two conditions are actually very close as Fig. 6 shows. However, as we have analyzed in 3.3, the power in SUPRA converges faster and the value is more stable than in the LMRC, this will assure a reliable performance for CVS applications in different scenarios.

5 Conclusion

In this paper we have proposed a heterogeneous architecture based on LMRC and SUPRA power control algorithm, and presented a detailed analysis of LMRC and SUPRA, which change the power by using channel busy ratio as a feedback measure. Then we used the GSC instead of CBR to adjust the transmitting power and offload the message when the network congestion is extremely severe through the LTE base station. Simulation results demonstrated the effectiveness of our heterogeneous architecture to improve the performance of CVS applications, it is observed that the probability of reception and channel busy ratio have been enhanced greatly in our heterogeneous network.

However, the probability of reception could be higher, meanwhile, the CBR changing trend could be more fluently and the performance of the network can be better if the LTE cellular network could more rational to calculate the GSC and offload the message. The integration between VANET network and LTE cellular network is still not enough, and more complicated enhancements are also possible, therefore, we will do more research about this topic in future work.

Acknowledgments. The authors would like to thank the anonymous reviewers for their careful reviews and insightful comments. This work was supported by the National Natural Science Foundation of China (Grant No. 61331009) and supported by the key project of Science and Technology of Shanghai (Grant No. 15DZ1100801).

References

1. Wireless Access in Vehicular Environments (WAVE) in Standard 802.11, Specific Requirements: IEEE 802.11p/D2.01, March 2007
2. Fallah, Y.P., et al.: Congestion control based on channel occupancy in vehicular broadcast network. In: IEEE Vehicular Technology Conference Fall, pp. 1–5 (2010)
3. Wisitpongphan, N., Tonguz, O.K., Parikh, J.S., Mudalige, P., Bai, F., Sadekar, V.: Broadcast storm mitigation techniques in vehicular ad hoc networks. IEEE Wirel. Commun. **14**(6), 84–94 (2007)
4. Huang, C.L., Fallah, Y.P., Sengupta, R., Krishnan, H.: Adaptive intervehicle communication control for cooperative safety systems. IEEE Netw. **24**(1), 6–13 (2010)
5. Fallah, Y.P., Nasiriani, N., Krishnan, H.: Stable and fair power control in vehicle safety networks. IEEE Trans. Veh. Technol. **65**(3), 1662–1675 (2016)
6. Torrent-Moreno, M., Santi, P., Hartenstein, H.: Fair sharing of bandwidth in VANETs. In: Proceedings of the 2nd ACM International Workshop on Vehicular Ad Hoc Networks, pp. 49–58. ACM (2005)
7. Torrent-Moreno, M., Santi, P., Hartenstein, H.: Distributed fair transmit power adjustment for vehicular ad hoc networks. In: 2006 3rd Annual IEEE Communications Society on Sensor and Ad Hoc Communications and Networks, vol. 2, pp. 479–488. IEEE (2006)
8. Haghani, P., Hu, Y.C.: Power control for fair dynamic channel reservation in VANETs. In: 2012 9th Annual IEEE Communications Society Conference on Sensor, Mesh and Ad Hoc Communications and Networks (SECON), pp. 659–667. IEEE (2012)
9. Torrent-Moreno, M., et al.: Vehicle-to-vehicle communication: fair transmit power control for safety-critical information. IEEE Trans. Veh. Technol. **58**(7), 3684–3703 (2009)
10. Zeeshan, H.M., Filali, F.: On the performance comparison between IEEE 802.11p and LTE-based vehicular networks. In: IEEE Vehicular Technology Conference, pp. 1–5 (2015)
11. Corti, A., Manzoni, V., Savaresi, S.M., Santucci, M.D., Di Tanna, O.: A centralized real-time driver assistance system for road safety based on smartphone. In: Meyer, G. (ed.) Advanced Microsystems for Automotive Applications 2012. Springer, Berlin, Heidelberg (2012). https://doi.org/10.1007/978-3-642-29673-4_20
12. Katsaros, K., Dianati, M., Le, L.: Effective implementation of location services for VANETs in hybrid network infrastructures. In: IEEE International Conference on Communications Workshops, pp. 521–525. IEEE (2013)

Monitoring of the Ground Subsidence in Macao Using the PSI Technique

Shaojing Jiang[1]([✉]), Fenghua Shi[2], Bo Hu[3], Weibo Wang[1], and Qianguo Lin[4]

[1] Research Institute of Yanchang Petroleum (GROUP) Co., Ltd,
Xi'an 710075, China
jshj7010@sina.com, ffslxf@163.com,
wangweibo163@163.com

[2] Urban and Rural Construction Institute, Hebei Agricultural University,
Baoding 071000, China
shifenghua1981@163.com

[3] Department of Surveying and Mapping,
Guangdong University of Technology, Guangzhou 510006, China
358863955@qq.com

[4] Carbon Capture and Storage (Beijing) Technology Co. Ltd,
Beijing 100089, China
lilinshi@hotmail.com

Abstract. In this paper, we investigated the long-term reclamation-induced ground subsidence in Macao, a coastal city of southern China. Persistent Scatterers Interferometry (PSI) technique was applied to retrieve the deformation rate in Macao during the period from April 2003 to August 2010 with a total of 41 scenes of descending ASAR data sets. The PSI-retrieved results showed a relatively stable pattern in Macao Peninsula, Taipa Island and Coloane Island, with an average subsidence velocity of -3 mm/y. In contrast, relatively large subsidence rates were highlighted in Cotai area, a newly reclamation land in 1990s, in which an average subsidence velocity was about -10 mm/y. A consistent relationship between the PSI results and the leveling measurements indicated that this PSI technique is an effective tool to monitor the reclamation-induced ground subsidence with a high accuracy and adequate spatial details. Accordingly the valuable ground subsidence results generated by PSI can be used not only for early detection and remedial activities of potential settlement of buildings, but also for helping the local government to formulate regional sustainable development planning and decision-making in disaster prevention and mitigation.

Keywords: Persistent Scatterers Interferometry (PSI) · Macao
Reclamation land · Ground subsidence

1 Introduction

Land reclamation from sea is regarded as the most common way to resolve the limited land resource in coastal areas of many countries, including China, Japan, Korea and so on [1–5]. Ground subsidence has been a significant geohazard in reclaimed areas, with

© Springer Nature Singapore Pte Ltd. 2018
H. Yuan et al. (Eds.): GSKI 2017, CCIS 848, pp. 250–261, 2018.
https://doi.org/10.1007/978-981-13-0893-2_26

probably large areas of unconsolidated ground material. In particular, the settlement variability is crucial to performance assessment of the reclamation development because this differential settlement can lead to damage of ground constructions and underground facilities.

In recent years, The Differential Interferometry Synthetic Aperture Radar (DInSAR) technique has been proven as an powerful remote sensing tool to map ground tiny deformation, such as volcano dynamics [6, 7], earthquakes [8, 9], groundwater over-exploitation [10, 11], mining [12, 13], coastland reclamation [4, 14–16]. However, this DInSAR technique is limited by the intrinsic problems of temporal and geometrical décor relation as well as atmospheric disturbances [17]. The PSI is a newly developed surface displacement observation technique based on using of a large data set of SAR images over the same area to overcome the limitations of conventional DInSAR, which was first proposed by Ferretti and has been further developed and applied recently [18]. A large number of research projects and applications have demonstrated the remarkable capacity of the PSI technique to detect tiny ground deformation in the literature [19–21]. Particularly in urban areas, for instance that the reclamation-induced ground subsidence [1, 15]. Nevertheless, it is still a challenge to monitor such reclamation settlement due to the complex deformation mechanism relevant to underlying geological conditions and building foundation types.

In this study, we have investigated the surface deformation induced by land reclamation in Macao Special Administrative Region (Macao), a coastal city of China, mostly extended by reclamation since the 17th century. Until now, approximately more than half of the urban area has been built on such reclaimed land and has potential problems of land subsidence. The PSI technique was applied to monitor the reclaimed land deformation based on 41 ASAR images acquired between April 2003 and August 2010. The PSI-retrieved average deformation rates validated by the leveling measurements provided by the Macao Government Cartography and Cadastre Bureau (DSCC) of the Macao, showed that there were significant settlement in reclamation land, especially the new reclamation such as the Cotai area.

2   Study Area and Data Sets

Macao is located in South China, on the western side of the Pearl River Delta as depicted in Fig. 1. It comprises four parts: the Macao Peninsula, the islands of Coloane and Taipa and a newly reclaimed area known as Cotai (Coloane–Taipa). Since Macao has been restricted for the scarce land resource, land reclamation has been a common way to meet the land use demand for growing population and rapid industrial development. Land reclamation from the sea expanded the terrestrial area of the Macao nearly three times, from 11.6 square kilometers in 1912 to 29.9 square kilometers in 2011. The reclaimed land was generally used for commercial, port supporting facilities or simply as landfill sites and residential areas, and approximately half of the urban area in Macao were built on such reclaimed land. The latest large-scale reclamation in Macao has mainly been conducted in the Cotai region since the 1990s. It created a 5.2 square kilometers newly reclaimed land between Taipa and Coloane islands in order to provide a new gambling and tourism area. Numerous large-scale urban

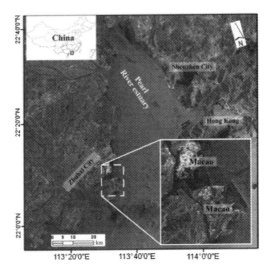

Fig. 1. The geographic location of the study area.

developments have been conducted in the Cotaireclamation area, including the Macao University of Science and Technology, Macao East Asian Games Dome, Cotai Strip, Galaxy World Resort and so on [14]. In solving a scarcity of land at the same time, it brings some related geological problems, causing severe differential ground subsidence in reclamation land.

In the case study, a total of 41 C-band ENVISAT/ASAR scenes over the Macao area were used, acquired between April 2003 and August 2010. Gamma software was employed to process the raw SAR data and interferometric procedure, and IPTA package was used to perform PSI analysis. The ASAR scene on Sep.21, 2008 was used as the master image and 40 interferograms were generated from Single Look Complex (SLC) images. The spatial and temporal baselines of these interferograms are shown in Figs. 2 and 3. The longest spatial baseline is 815 m and the longest temporal baseline is 5.4 years.

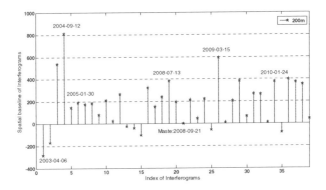

Fig. 2. Spatial baselines of interferograms.

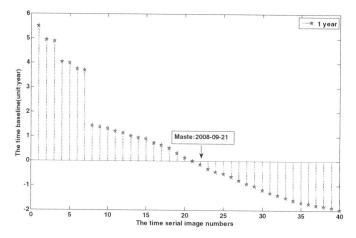

Fig. 3. Temporal baselines of interferograms.

Besides the SAR datasets, a Digital Elevation Model (DEM) data of the study area with a regular grid spacing of 5 m was used to simulate and remove phase component contributed by topography.

3 Methodology

The Persistent Scatterer Interferometry (PSI) is a powerful remote sensing technique able to measure and monitor displacements of the Earth surface over time. Specifically, PSI is a radar-based technique that belongs to the group of differential interferometric Synthetic Aperture Radar (SAR). The PSI technique is quite different from the traditional DInSAR technique. The key steps for the PSI data processing mainly contain the following steps: selection of common master image, identification and selection of Persistent Scatterers (PS) points, formation of differential interferogram, preliminary estimation of the subsidence velocity and the DEM errors, atmospheric phase removing, final estimation of the subsidence velocity and the DEM errors. Accordingly, we focused on the following processing steps in order to monitor and asses the land subsidence in the reclaimed coastal areas of Macao.

3.1 PS Identification

PS identification is one of the key steps for the PSI processing and analysis. Currently there are three available PS detection methods, so-called coherence coefficient threshold, amplitude dispersion threshold and phase deviation threshold respectively [18]. All the above PS detection methods are single threshold detection, which only emphasized some one aspect characteristic of PS. Therefore it's very easy to errors in PS identification. For instance, coherence coefficient threshold is only considering strong scattering characteristics of the PS but ignoring its stability. The amplitude dispersion threshold and the phase deviation threshold only consider properties of PS stability while ignoring the strong scattering properties. In view of the shortcomings of the aforementioned PS selection methods, we proposed in this paper an improved method named three-threshold PS detection method based on the average coherence, amplitude, amplitude dispersion information. This method firstly utilized the PS high SNR echo signals characteristic, combination an average of coherence with amplitude threshold select PS candidates (PSCs), and then considering the stability of PS, further selection of the PS from PSC by the amplitude dispersion threshold. The proposed three-threshold PS detection algorithm details as following:

(1) If M + 1 SLC images are resampled to a common master image, one can make M interferograms. According to coherence coefficient formula, calculate the time series coherence coefficient (γ) of each pixel, so each pixel is to form a coherent factor sequence, the coherence coefficient is defined as

$$\gamma = \frac{\left| \sum_{i=1}^{m} \sum_{j=1}^{n} M(i,j) S^*(i,j) \right|}{\sqrt{\sum_{i=1}^{m} \sum_{j=1}^{n} |M(i,j)|^2 \sum_{i=1}^{m} \sum_{j=1}^{n} |S(i,j)|^2}} \tag{1}$$

where M and S are the master and the slave images, S*is the conjugate of slave images, m is the number of rows, n is the number of columns.

(2) Calculate the average coherence of pixel ($\bar{\gamma}$)) in the time series.

$$\bar{\gamma} = \frac{\sum_{m=1}^{M} \gamma_m}{M} \tag{2}$$

(3) According to the experience, set the coherence threshold (about 0.15–0.25), mainy to filter out water and vegetation areas;
(4) Calculate the time serial amplitude value (mA).
(5) Set the amplitude threshold (TA).

$$T_A = \min\left\{ \frac{1}{mn} \sum_{i=1}^{m} \sum_{i=1}^{n} T_{i,j} \right\} \tag{3}$$

where $T_{i,j}$ is the amplitude threshold of i rows and j columns.

(6) Distinguish the PSC, When the correlation coefficient to meet the threshold condition MA>TA, for the PSC points, or non-PSC points.
(7) Calculate the time series standard deviation of the amplitude (σ_A).
(8) Calculate the PSC amplitude dispersion index (D_A).

$$D_A = \frac{\sigma_A}{m_A} \tag{4}$$

(9) Distinguish the PS, set a reasonable threshold, if meet the condition $D_A \leq T_d$, as PS, or non-PS.

In order to verify the validity of the three-threshold PS detection method, we selected the PS using the aforementioned PS selection methods and the three-threshold respectively. Fig. 4(a) shows the coherence coefficient threshold extracted PS, from the view of PS location distribution, most of the extracted PS points connect into the area, only a few PS points appear alone, we can also find that there are some points in Macao sea. Apparently these points are not the true PS points. Therefore, coherence coefficient threshold method is simple in principle and calculation, but this method still has some shortcomings. Fig. 4(b) shows the amplitude dispersion threshold method extracted PS, the extracted PS points are almost all independent, mostly corresponding to hard targets on the ground, we can also easily observe that many hard targets on the ground were not chosen as PS points, but in fact those hard targets are almost PS points. In addition, some non-PS points were wrongly chosen as PS points, this is because the method only considered the PS stable scattering property, while ignoring the PS strong scattering property, it's very easy to cause wrong justice. Fig. 4(c) shows the three-threshold PS detection method extracted PS, the extracted PS are almost all independent distributed in built-up areas, in line with our actual situation. It was proved that the proposed new method is effective and reliable.

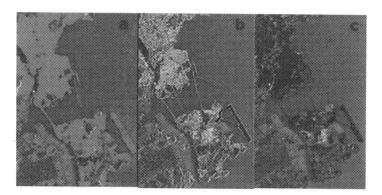

Fig. 4. (a) The coherence coefficient threshold extracted PS. (b) The amplitude dispersion threshold extracted PS. (c) The three-threshold detection method extracted PS

3.2 Differential Interferogram Formation

With $M + 1$ SAR images, precise orbit data and a DEM data, we can obtain differential interferograms with respect to the same master image. For a PS (x) in the interferogram with the temporal baseline of, the differential phase can be written as

$$\Phi(x, t_i) = \phi_{topo}(x, t_i) + \phi_{defo}(x, t_i) + \phi_{atmo}(x, t_i) + \phi_{noise}(x, t_i)$$
$$i = 1 \cdots N \tag{5}$$

where $\phi_{topo}(x, t_i)$ is the phase caused by DEM error, $\phi_{defo}(x, t_i)$ is the phase due to displacement of the point, $\phi_{atmo}(x, t_i)$ is the phase raised by atmospheric delay,

$\phi_{noise}(x, t_i)$ is the decorrelation noise, N is the total number of PS, the topographic phase is a linear function of the perpendicular baseline.

$$\phi_{topo}(x, t_i) = \mu(x, t_i) \cdot \Delta h_x \tag{6}$$

Where $\mu(x, t_i)$ is the height-to-phase conversion factor, and Δh_x is the DEM error at the point. Regarding the deformation phase, it can be separated into two terms, i.e.,

$$\phi_{defo}(x, t_i) = \frac{4\pi}{\lambda} \cdot v(x) \cdot t_i + \phi_{non-linear}(x, t_i) \tag{7}$$

where $v(x)$ is the mean deformation rate of target x, λ is the wavelength of the radar signal, and $\phi_{non-linear}(x, t_i)$ is the phase component due to non-linear motion. The interferometric phase at point can be finally written as

$$\begin{aligned} \Phi(x, t_i) &= \mu(x, t_i) \cdot \Delta h_x + \frac{4\pi}{\lambda} \cdot v(x) \cdot t_i + \omega(x, t_i) \\ i &= 1 \cdots N \end{aligned} \tag{8}$$

where $\omega(x, t_i)$ is the phase sum of three contributions caused by atmospheric delay, noise and non-linear motion respectively. Considering two neighboring PS point, the phase difference between them can be expressed as

$$\Phi(x, y, t_i) = \mu(x, t_i) \cdot \Delta h_{x,y} + \frac{4\pi}{\lambda} \cdot \Delta v(x, y) \cdot t_i + \Delta \omega_i \tag{9}$$

Where is the difference of DEM errors at these two points, is the velocity difference. is the difference of residual phase, which is assumed to be small, since all its components (i.e., atmospheric difference signal, non-linear deformation and random noise) are small.

3.3 Preliminary Estimation of the Subsidence Velocity and the DEM Errors

In PSI technique the estimation of the subsidence velocity and the DEM errors from the observed wrapped phase pairs are performed by a search through the solution space. Under the condition.

$$|\Delta \omega_i| < \pi \tag{10}$$

The absolute value of the complex ensemble coherence $\hat{\gamma}_{x,y}$ can be adopted as a reliable norm.

$$\hat{\gamma}_{x,y} = \left| \frac{1}{N} \sum_{i=1}^{N} e^{i\Delta \omega_i} \right| \tag{11}$$

The value of coherence lies in the interval [0, 1]. High values imply a good estimation of the velocity difference and the difference of DEM errors. In practice the maximum of coherence is found by sampling two-dimensional solution space with a certain resolution and up to certain bounds, each time evaluating the norm.

After obtaining all maximum values of coherence, we need a threshold to remove the unreliable arcs. Unfortunately the determination of this threshold is not practically straightforward. In other words, users have to select the threshold based on experience. As a reference, the value of 0.75 was used in [19], The parameters (the mean deformation rate and the DEM error) at PS points can then be obtained by integrating the rate differences and the DEM error between all pairs of PS points with respect to a reference point.

3.4 Atmospheric Phase Removing and the Final Estimation of the Parameters

After removing the phase components contributed by linear motion and DEM error on arcs, the residual phase at the PS points can be unwrapped by a weighted least-squares integration. The residual phase contains the components due to, atmospheric delay and random noise. Under the assumption that the atmospheric signal behaves randomly in time and is correlated in space, it can be isolated from other components by low-pass filtering in the spatial domain and high-pass filtering in the temporal domain.

3.5 Final Estimation of the Subsidence Velocity and the DEM Errors

After the estimation of atmospheric phase at PS points, the atmospheric component can be determined by Kriging interpolation, which is referred to as "atmospheric phase screen" (APS). From the differential interferograms without APS, the DEM errors and displacement can be estimated on a pixel by pixel basis. The time series deformation can be estimated by the low-pass temporal filtering mentioned earlier.

4 Results and Discussions

A total of 32600 PS points were detected when the ensemble phase coherence threshold was set to be 0.75, which corresponds approximately to 958 PS points per square kilometer. The distribution of the PS points and the corresponding deformation velocity are shown in Fig. 5. Most of the PS points were identified on the ground buildings in the three original islands of Macao, Taipa and Coloane. The surface deformation rates are relatively low, the average subsidence velocity is about -3 mm/y. It can be explained by the interpretation that the geological conditions of the three original islands are dominated by bedrock of fine-grained and fine-to medium-grained granite. In contrast, the relatively strong ground deformation patterns can be observed in the newly reclamation Cotai, the mean deformation velocity is about -10 mm/y. In addition, the differential deformation over a short distance can be found in Cotai area. This differential settlement might be related to numerous large-scale civil constructions, such as the Macao University of Science and Technology, Cotai Strip, Galaxy World

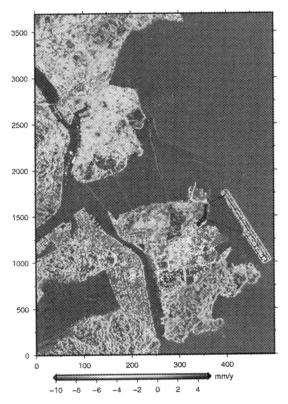

Fig. 5. The deformation rate map estimated by PSI, the redtriangle indicate the ground leveling sites as reference points.

Resort, Macao East Asian Games Dome and so on. Moreover, continuous reclamation of adjacent areas, sand-dominant reclamation material and subterranean structures can result in the differential settlements. The more detailed causes of anomalous phenomenon have still to be investigated by geological engineers.

In order to assess the PSI-obtained results in this study, we conducted a comparison of the PSI deformation velocity with the leveling measurements based on 38 leveling sites provided by DSCC. To enable the comparison, firstly we estimated the mean deformation rates for these sites in the radar line of the sight (LOS) direction based on the leveling measurements by a factor 0.92. Secondly, the location of leveling site is usually not the same as that of the PS, so we searched the PS point nearest from each leveling site and then compared their deformation velocities. The compared results are shown in Fig. 6. For the PSI solution, the PS points G4 and G19 nearest to the corresponding leveling sites were taken as the reference points. The mean values of the velocity difference and the standard deviation of the velocity difference are respectively 1.1 mm/y and 1.9 mm/y for the 38 reference leveling sites, indicating that most of the PSI results are consistent with the leveling results. The validation results are

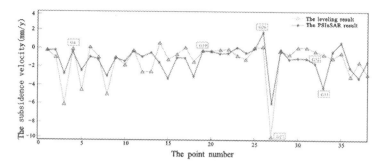

Fig. 6. Comparison between leveling and PSI measurements

comparable with the recent validation experiments available in the scientific literature [14], and demonstrate a reliable achievement in this study.

But large differences do exist at several sites (e.g.G26, G27, G32, G33). The locations of these points are corresponding the Macao East Asian Games Dome in the newly reclaimed Cotaiarea (Fig. 7). The following reasons may be responsible for the large differences between the leveling and the PSI measurements:

(1) The ground deformations are sometimes very localized. The distance between a leveling site and a PS point can cause large difference between the results. For example, the leveling site may measure the ground deformation while InSAR measures the nearby building deformation.

(2) The observation time periods are different between the leveling and the PSI measurements. All of leveling sites with large differences were measured from 2008, much later than some of the SAR data.

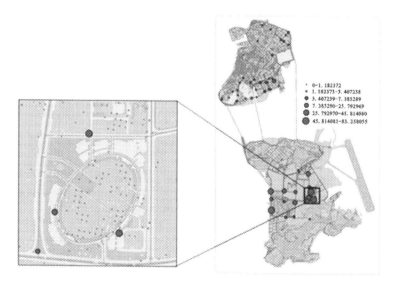

Fig. 7. Sites with large differences between leveling and PSI measurements. The size of red circles indicates the magnitude of the differences.

5 Conclusion Remarks

In this paper, the reclamation-induced ground subsidence of Macao was investigated with the PSI technique utilizing the Envisat ASAR data during the period from April 2003 to August 2010. This study has revealed that some parts of the reclaimed area have been experiencing significant land subsidence during the ASAR data acquisition period. The average subsidence rate was approximately -3 mm/y in the islands of Macao, Coloane, Taipa and -10 mm/y in the newly reclaimed land Cotai. The PSI-retrieved results agreed well with the evolution of land reclamation in Macao. A comparison of the results with leveling measurements indicated that the accuracy of the PSI results was around 1.1 mm/y with 90% confidence (2σ) for most of the points.

For monitoring ground deformation in the future in Macao, there are several possible options to improve our understanding the spatial-temporal varieties of reclamation settlements. One is to use high resolution SAR data, e.g., those acquired by TerraSAR, Cosmo-SkyMedand Radarsat-2. Another option is to use the ALOS/PALSAR L-band data characterized by a radar long-wavelength.

References

1. Jiang, L.M., Lin, H.: Integrated analysis of SAR interferometric and geological data for investigating long-term reclamation settlement of Chek Lap Kok Airport, Hong Kong. Eng. Geol. **110**, 77–92 (2010)
2. Kim, J.S., Kim, D.J., Kim, S.W., Won, J.S.: Monitoring of urban land surface subsidence using PSI. Geosci. J. **11**, 59–73 (2007)
3. Kim, J.: Monitoring of surface deformation in urban areas using PSI technique, M. Sc. thesis, Seoul National University, 109 p. (2007)
4. Liu, G., Ding, X.L., Chen, Y.Q., Li, Z.L.: Ground settlement of Chek Lap Kok Airport, Hong Kong, detected by satellite synthetic aperture radar interferometry. Chin. Sci. Bull. **46**(21), 1778–1782 (2001)
5. Stuyfzand, P.J.: The impact of land reclamation on groundwater quality and future drinking water supply in the Netherlands. Water Sci. Technol. **31**, 47–57 (1995)
6. Fernandez, J., Romero, R., Carrasco, D., Tlampo, K.F., Rodriguez-velasco, G., Aparicio, A., Arana, V., Gonzalez-matesanz, F.J.: Detection of displacements on Tenerife Island, Canaries, using radar interferometry. Geophys. J. Int. **160**, 33–45 (2005)
7. Lu, Z., Fatland, R., Wyss, M., Li, S., Eichelberer, J., Dean, K., Freymueller, J.: Deformation of New Trident volcano measured by ERS-1 SAR interferometry, Katmai National Park. Alask. Geophys. Res. Lett. **24**, 695–698 (1997)
8. Flalko, Y., Sandwell, D., Simous, M., Rosen, P.: Three-dimensional deformation caused by the Bam, Iran, earthquake and the origin of shallow slip deficit. Nature **435**, 295–299 (2005)
9. Yen, J.Y., Chen, K.S., Chang, C.P., Boerner, W.M.: Evaluation of earthquake potential and surface deformation by differential interferometry. Remote Sens. Environ. **112**, 782–795 (2008)
10. Bawden, G.W., Thatcher, W., Stein, R.S., Hudnut, K.W., Peltzer, G.: Tectonic contraction across Los Angeles after removal of groundwater pumping effects. Nature **412**, 812–815 (2001)
11. Hoffmann, J.: The future of satellite remote sensing in hydrogeology. Hydrogeol. J. **13**, 247–250 (2005)

12. Herrera, G., Tomas, R., Lopez-sanchez, J.M., Delgado, J., Mallorqui, J.J., Duque, S., Mulas, J.: Advanced DInSAR analysis on mining areas: La Union case study (Murcia, SE Spain). Eng. Geol. **90**, 148–159 (2007)
13. Jung, H.C., Kim, S.W., Jung, H.S., Min, K.D., Won, J.S.: Satellite observation of coal mining subsidence by persistent scatterer analysis. Eng. Geol. **92**, 1–13 (2007)
14. Jiang, L., Lin, H., Cheng, S.: Monitoring and assessing reclamation settlement of coastal areas with advanced InSAR techniques: Macao city (China) case study. Int. J. Remote Sens. **32**, 3565–3588 (2011)
15. Kim, S.W., Lee, C.W., Song, K.Y., Min, K.D., Won, J.S.: Application of L-band differential SAR interferometry to subsidence rate estimation in reclaimed coastal land. Int. J. Remote Sens. **26**, 1363–1381 (2005)
16. Teatini, P., Strozzi, T., Tosi, L., Wegmuller, U., Werner, C., Carbognin, L.: Assessing short- and long-time displacements in the Venice coastland by synthetic aperture radar interferometric point target analysis. J. Geophys. Res. **112**, 656–664 (2007)
17. Zebker, H.A., Villasenor, J.: Decorrelation in interferometric radar echoes. IEEE Trans. Geosci. Remote Sens. **30**, 950–959 (1992)
18. Ferretti, A., Prati, C., Rocca, F.: Permanent scatterers in SAR interferometry. IEEE Trans. Geosci. Remote Sens. **39**, 8–20 (2001)
19. Ferretti, A., Prati, C., Rocca, F.: Nonlinear subsidence rate estimation using permanent scatterers in differential SAR interferometry. IEEE Trans. Geosci. Remote Sens. **38**, 2202–2212 (2000)
20. Hu, B., Wang, H.: Monitoring ground subsidence with permanent scatters interferometry. J. Geodesy Geodyn. **30**, 14–21 (2010)
21. Kampes, B., Hanssen, R.: Ambiguity resolution for permanent scatterer interferometry. IEEE Trans. Geosci. Remote Sens. **42**, 2446–2453 (2004)

An Application of a Location Algorithm Integrating Beidou and WSN in Agricultural IOT

Tao Chi[1,2(✉)], Lei Wang[1], and Ming Chen[1,2]

[1] College of Information Technology,
Shanghai Ocean University, Shanghai, China
{tchi,mchen}@shou.edu.cn
[2] Key Laboratory of Fisheries Information,
Ministry of Agriculture, Shanghai, China

Abstract. With the development of agricultural IOT technology in Xinjiang plain area, most researchers found it difficult to obtain the real-time position information of all the nodes in the irrigation area because of the restriction of the region. An integrated location algorithm using Beidou and WSN is presented to achieve seamless positioning for all the nodes in the network. This algorithm can calculate the absolute positioning of cluster nodes by configuring the Beidou module on the cluster nodes and then get the relative position of the terminal node through the cluster nodes. Based on the algorithm, a monitoring system is carried out to achieve positioning of the irrigated agricultural area of all the nodes. Simulation results show that the monitoring system based on the integrated algorithm can locate most of the nodes in the network with a lower hardware cost.

Keywords: Agriculture IoT · Integrated location algorithm · Beidou
Seamless location · Wireless sensor network

1 Introduction

With the rapidly development of the Internet of things technology in recent years, farmers can observe the growth of crops in the control room, rather than going to the field. There are many methods to improve GPS' accuracy in the outdoor environment, but the highly-precision positioning is determined by a large number of GPS nodes and the cost is very high. Many researchers have presented different methods, i.e., combining GPS with WiFi and RFID to locate indoor objects [1–5]. In most of GPS system, the received signal strength indicator (RSSI) has been used for fingerprinting localization where RSSI measurements of GPS anchor nodes have been used as landmarks to classify other nodes into one of the GPS nodes classes [6–8, 9]. However, most of the existing monitoring systems are small network systems which can configure the GPS module to achieve the positioning function on each node and the hardware cost is too high.

In order to obtain the real-time, accurate positioning information of Xinjiang plain irrigation area, the paper presents an agricultural monitoring system based on Beidou

H. Yuan et al. (Eds.): GSKI 2017, CCIS 848, pp. 262–267, 2018.
https://doi.org/10.1007/978-981-13-0893-2_27

and Zigbee. The system uses the Beidou module to achieve the absolute positioning of the cluster nodes, and then realize the relative positioning of the terminal node through the Improved Bounding-box algorithm. This monitoring system can reduce the cost of network hardware and expand the network positioning area.

2 Wireless Sensor Network Architecture

According to the difference of the network nodes, the Zigbee protocol divides the network devices into two kinds: the one is called FFDs, which can communicate with all kinds of nodes in the network. It can be used as a sink node or gateway node; the other is called RFDs, which can only communicate with FFDs in the network, and can only be used in the terminal node equipment.

As shown in Fig. 1 irrigation monitoring system designed in the paper, the whole irrigation area is divided into several different monitoring areas during the monitoring process. Each cluster will have a cluster network and each cluster network has a cluster node. The terminal node is to detect the environmental parameters by the semi-sensors, i.e., temperature, humidity, illumination and then to transfer the information to the cluster node by the antenna. The cluster node is to collect and process the information in the cluster network, and send the information to the sink node in the network. The sink node is to upload the collected information to a PC or a handhold terminal through GSM/GPRS or WiFi. Different from the most of the existed agriculture IOT, this irrigation monitoring system only need to configure the Beidou module in the cluster node, and combined with the three-edge-location-algorithm to achieve the entire network positioning. As we can see, this algorithm can save more cost and be used in a wider agricultural area.

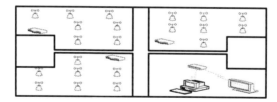

Fig. 1. Our agriculture IoT architecture in Xinjiang irrigation plain.

3 Positioning System and Algorithm

Our positioning system consists of several cluster nodes with Beidou module, which can provide the absolute position of the cluster, and plenty of sensors, which need to calculate their location using localization algorithm.

3.1   Absolute Position of Cluster Node

The hardware part is mainly composed of the Beidou module (UM220), Zigbee module (CC2530) and other components. The received data of the Beidou module will be sent to the micro-controller through the serial port, and then extract a valid information in each 9 s interval. The CC2530 micro-controller serial port uses TTL level to connect directly to the Beidou module, where the 20 pin is used as TX and the 21 pin is used as RX.

The Fig. 2 describes the software part of absolute position of cluster node, used to obtain the UTC time, latitude, longitude, positioning and altitude information. The Beidou module can receive a variety of messages such as $BDGGA, $BDGLL, $BDGSA, but all the useful information that we need is found in $BDGGA and then the effective information can be extracted.

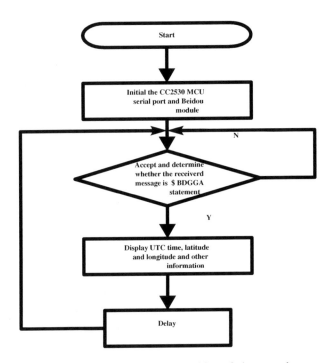

Fig. 2. Flowchart on absolute position of cluster nodes.

3.2   Localization Algorithm

It can be found that the remote control center can not obtain the location information of the terminal node in the edge network position in the irrigation area. The problem reflects the limitations of common Internet of Things technology in a particular environment, so the localization algorithm can improve the application performance of the system.

The existing positioning is divided into the distance based on ranging and non-ranging algorithm, and the non-ranging algorithm is widely used because of its high positioning accuracy and simple algorithm. However, the distribution of nodes in this monitoring system is relatively sparse, especially in the actual positioning process using distance-based localization algorithm. In the monitoring system, the Beidou module is arranged on the cluster node, and the coordinate position of the remaining terminal nodes is positioned by the traditional RSSI (Received Signal Strength Indicator) positioning method. In the application of agriculture IoT, the terminal node is necessary to receive three or more cluster node information when RSSI localization algorithm is used to locate the terminal nodes. If the system can not meet the above conditions as shown in Fig. 2, the problem will happen as follows.

In the Fig. 3, the communication radius of terminal nodes can receive three known location cluster node A, B, C. At the same time, using A, B, C as the center of the circle, D1, D2, D3 as the radius of the circle can not be intersected in a region, and the traditional three edge location algorithm can not locate the terminal node. But at this point, A, B, C points as the center of the circle, D1, D2, D3 radius of the circle can not intersect at the same area, so the traditional weighted three edge positioning algorithm can not locate the terminal node. The terminal node communicates with the cluster nodes A, B of two known coordinate positions. There are only two router nodes in the communication range of the terminal node. The terminal node is located at the intersection of the two nodes with the distance from the router node to the end node. At this time we can only determine the terminal node in the two rounds of the intersection area, but can not accurately determine the actual location of the node.

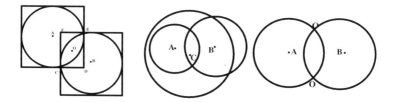

Fig. 3. Two kinds of common problems in the actual location.

When the coordinates of the cluster nodes are determined, we use RSSI distance measurement combined with trilateral positioning algorithm to locate the terminal node so that we can complete the positioning of the entire network. The following is the positioning process of the terminal node.

To solve the above positioning problem, we use the positioning algorithm based on RSSI and boundary box to locate the terminal node. Here the nodes are located through the following steps.

Step 1: Select the RSSI ranging model to reduce the error in the process of node ranging and improve the positioning accuracy of the node. The theoretical transmission model is defined as follows:

$$RSSI = -(A + 10 \cdot n \cdot \lg d) \tag{1}$$

The formula indicates the signal strength received by the terminal node at distance d from the transmitting node. A is the absolute value of the received signal strength at a

Table 1. The parameters with different environment.

Environment parameter	n
Free space	2.0
Greenhouse	2.2
Tree, Crop	1.8
Building, hard partitions	3.0
Building, soft partitions	2.6

distance of 1 m from the transmitting node, n is the path loss factor (as show in Table 1) and d represents the distance from the transmitting node a terminal node.

Step 2: Monitoring area has M nodes, where there are N Compass modules with the same transmission power and the communication radius cluster nodes, each node periodically broadcasts its surrounding like ID and coordinate information;

Step 3: The terminal node receives the information which broadcast by the cluster node and then stops receive the information, records the RSSI value and the absolute coordinates of the cluster nodes;

Step 4: The terminal node uploads the RSSI value and the cluster node coordinates to the pool node through the cluster head;

Step 5: The pool node determines the number of RSSI values in each group firstly. If the number of values is not less than 3, we use the trilateral positioning algorithm to locate the terminal node, else we use the Border -box algorithm.

4   Experiment and Analysis

In this section, we conducted experiments in two parts. The first part of the experiment was used to determine the Eq. 1 in A, n value. The experimental site is located in the irrigation area, we fixed a node as a transmitting node and placed the receiving node at 0.5 m, 1 m, 1.5 m, 2 m, 2.5 m, 3 m, 3.5 m, 4 m, 5 m from the transmitting node. Then we recorded the RSSI values in the receiving nodes, and found the average of RSSI through the record RSSI value. Finally, Last least square curve fitting of RSSI mean value can be calculated using MATLAB tool, compared the fitted with actual values, and obtained the value of A and n in the formula of distance (Table 2).

The second group of experiments is mainly used to compare the loss rate of the network node between the improved before and after the improved network.

Table 2. Different positions of the average RSSI value.

Distance (m)	RSSI mean value (DB/m)	Distance (m)	RSSI mean value (DB/m)
0.5	−38	3	−65
1	−42	3.5	−71
1.5	−48	4	−76
2	−53	4.5	−80
2.5	−59	5	−83

In the irrigation area, two 200 m * 200 m irrigation areas were selected, and the nodes were randomly distributed in two regions. The communication radius of the nodes was 100 m, and there were five cluster nodes in each region, and 20 terminal nodes that need to be tested. Adjust the position of the cluster node and the terminal node in the region 1, so that it satisfied that there are at least three cluster nodes within the communication radius of the terminal node. In the region 2, the cluster node and the terminal node position are adjusted to satisfy two cluster nodes within the communication radius of the terminal node.

5 Conclusion

In this paper, an improved bounding box localization algorithm is proposed, which is applied to solve the problem of missing information in the edge of Xinjiang plain irrigation. This algorithm is applied to the agricultural monitoring system based on Beidou. It is proved that this monitoring system can realize the real-time monitoring of crop in the irrigation area, which reduces the positioning error rate by 16% compared with the traditional boundary box algorithm. The results show that the Beidou-based monitoring system is real-time effective in plain irrigation and thus assist all the nodes for calculating right position. We would like to extend this work by comparing our results using various network metrics such as power consumption, latency and throughput.

Acknowledgments. This work is partly supported by the national natural science fund (61561027) and the shanghai natural science fund (16ZR1415100).

References

1. Liu, Z.P., Yuan, M., Academy, S., et al.: An improved indoor positioning method based on Wi Fi fingerprinting. Comput. Mod. (2016)
2. Chen, L., Li, B., Zhao, K., et al.: An improved algorithm to generate a Wi-Fi fingerprint database for indoor positioning. Sensors **13**(8), 11085 (2013)
3. Yu, F., Jiang, M., Liang, J., et al.: An improved indoor localization of WiFi based on support vector machines. Int. J. Future Gener. Commun. Netw. **7**, 191–206 (2014)
4. Benkic, K., Malajner, M., Planinsic, P., et al.: Using RSSI value for distance estimation in wireless sensor networks based on ZigBee. In: International Conference on Systems, Signals and Image Processing, pp. 303–306. IEEE (2008)
5. Huang, H., Sun, L., Wang, R., et al.: A novel coverage enhancement algorithm for image sensor networks. Int. J. Distrib. Sens. Netw. **8**, 184–195 (2012)
6. Sallouha, H., Chiumento, A., Pollin, S.: Localization in long-range ultra narrow band IoT networks using RSSI (2017)
7. Shen, X., Yang, S., He, J., et al.: Improved localization algorithm based on RSSI in low power Bluetooth network. In: International Conference on Cloud Computing and Internet of Things, pp. 134–137 (2016)
8. Zhang, K.S., Xu, Y.M., Yang, W., et al.: Improved localization algorithm based on proportion of differential RSSI. Appl. Mech. Mater. **192**, 401–405 (2012)

Spatial Data Acquisition Through RS and GIS in Resource Management and Sustainable Ecosystem

A Distinct Approach for Discovering the Relationship of Disasters Using Big Scholar Datasets

Liang Zheng, Fei Wang[(✉)], Xiaocui Zheng, and Binbin Liu

Institute of Safety Science and Technology, Department of Engineering Physics,
Shenzhen Graduate School, Tsinghua University, Shenzhen 518055,
Guangdong Province, China
{zheng116,liubb16}@mails.tsinghua.edu.cn,
{wang.fei,zheng.xiaocui}@sz.tsinghua.edu.cn

Abstract. Natural disasters frequently occur all over the world in recent years. Current researches show that a disaster often causes different kinds of secondary disasters. A good understanding of the chain reaction in disasters can provide guidance for disaster prevention and mitigation. Most of current researches analyze the disaster from the perspective of the disaster mechanism such as the geo-statistical model. This paper proposed an intelligent method of discovering the relationship of disasters using big scholar datasets. This method does not investigate the mechanism of disasters themselves, but analyze the relationship among disasters from the perspective of big data mining. The experiment results show that it is able to get reasonable relationship of disasters without much human interventions. The proposed method will enlighten many other knowledge-discovering applications in geospatial domain.

Keywords: Disaster chain · Co-occurrence analysis · Community division
Complex network · Data mining

1 Introduction

During the past several years, frequent occurrence of a variety of disasters has greatly influenced the development of our society. It is concerned that how to decrease the damages caused by disasters.

A large number of cases show that almost any disaster is a non-independent event. Great amount of secondary and derivative events are always accompanied with the development of the original disaster. The accumulative enlargement of disasters often causes the heavy casualties. Sometimes the damage caused by secondary disasters may be more serious than caused by original disaster [1], for example, the damage caused by explosion, as a secondary disaster of fire, often be more serious than caused by fire. Therefore, disaster researchers should deliberately consider the explicit relationships among disasters. Due to the evolving trend between various disasters, disaster research from the perspective of disaster chain will be helpful for disaster prevention and mitigation.

© Springer Nature Singapore Pte Ltd. 2018
H. Yuan et al. (Eds.): GSKI 2017, CCIS 848, pp. 271–279, 2018.
https://doi.org/10.1007/978-981-13-0893-2_28

Nowadays, there are many researches contributing to find the universal rules of the disaster chain. Ye and Lin tried to find the typhoon disaster chain using Fujian Province datasets [2]. Based on the historical typhoon data, they analyzed the characteristics of disaster-causing factors and the environmental characteristics. Then the different disaster chain characteristics of the typhoon with different paths were achieved, and the scientific basis for the customization of the response plan of typhoon was provided. Han and etc. have compared the earthquake in Wenchuan with the earthquake in Fukushima [3]. They compared the differences of the disaster environment and disaster bearing bodies between the two places, and explained why the disaster chain different in two places.

However, at present, most researches concern about the particular disasters in particular place, which has some limitations. First, the results will only be suitable for those special observed places and may not be helpful for other places with different geospatial or environmental conditions. Second, these methods only take few disaster cases as experiment datasets. The results inevitably depend on expert's experience and prior knowledge, and thus the achieved disaster chain might not be convincing and ubiquitous.

To solve those problems, this paper employs the big data method to build disaster chain from Baidu scholar datasets and Google scholar datasets. Firstly, this paper introduces the current research of disaster chain and analysis the advantages and disadvantages of several methods. Then the complex network model is adopted to construct the big disasters data network. To solve the problem of lacking disasters cases, the co-occurrence analysis method is used to get the relevance of disasters from Baidu scholar datasets and Google scholar datasets. After wards, a network analysis method is carried out to extract a specific disaster chain of a specific disaster.

2 State of the Disaster Chain Research

At present, there are many researches of disaster chain. Four kinds of disaster models are widely used. They are empirical geo-statistical model, disaster simulation model, probability model and complex network model [4].

Empirical geo-statistical model analyzes disaster cases, and then selects some characteristics as bases of judging. This model requires a lot of prior knowledge and expert experience. In addition, this model uses a large number of simplified methods. Some disaster researches in geospatial domain are now using this model [5].

Disaster simulation system will simulate the whole disaster by investigating the disaster mechanism. This model can describe the intermediate state of the evolution process of disaster. However, the existing research of this system is still relatively fewer, and it is difficult to build a complete disaster chain by this system [6].

Probabilistic model can describe the likelihood of a relationship between two disasters. This model needs a large number of cases to analyze and refine to get a reasonable and realistic network [7].

Complex network model can be used to describe the dynamic evolution of disaster chain events. However, it is difficult to find enough disaster cases to build the model.

When the complex network of disaster is built, the structure and topology character-istics of it can be used to analyze the characteristics of disasters [8].

The study of the complex network model is a relatively mature system. Therefore, using complex networks to express the disaster chain can be effective.

3   Establishment of the Complex Network Model of Disasters

This paper chooses complex network model to construct the disaster chain network, and there are some problems need to be solved. The first challenge is data acquisition. The establishment of complex networks is derived summed up from the accident cases, but the number of these practical cases is very limited. The second challenge is to get the disaster chain of a special disaster from disaster chain network.

This paper uses the co-occurrence analysis method to get the relationship between the disasters from a large number of literatures. Then community division method is adopted to get a special disaster chain from the disasters chain network.

3.1   Big Scholar Data Acquisition Approach

Nowadays, there are many literatures about disasters. It is a challenge to find the relationship of disaster from those literatures. This paper adopt co-occurrence method to analysis amount of literatures and find the relationship of disasters.

The co-occurrence analysis method is an effective method to get the relevance of event [9]. In the study of disaster, most of time there is a strong relevance between the two disasters if the two disasters occur in the same literature frequently. Using this method to analyze a large number of literature, the correlation among the disasters can be and the strength of this correlation can be calculated.

To find out the relevance among disasters by co-occurrence analysis, the search key words should be determined first.

Our country divides all emergency into 4 categories: natural disasters, work safety, public health incidents and social security accidents. Each type of emergency can be subdivided while there are more than 300 disasters. It is unnecessary to pay attention to all of those disasters because many disasters occur at very few times, which means that there may be no paper about those disasters. Meanwhile, some different disasters can be seen as one disaster for our research because the secondary disasters of them are quite same. For example, the earthquake has been divided into three disasters: natural earthquake accident, artificial earthquake accident and other earthquake accidents. When it comes to investigating the disaster chain, it is unnecessary to care whether it is natural or artificial and only consider those as earthquake.

All of disasters in "Emergencies Classification and Coding Norms of National Emergency Platform System" have been searched to find the number of literatures about them. There are 73 kinds of disasters whose number of literatures more than 1000. Those disasters have been chosen as search keywords for next work.

3.2   Building the Co-occurrence Matrix

The frequency of co-occurrence among these disasters should be got after the disaster search keywords were identified. Baidu scholar datasets and Google scholar datasets provide a convenient condition for this study. Those two datasets provide a platform with massive Chinese and English literature and give a convenient condition of searching literature.

The number of papers that mention both disasters is called the frequency of co-occurrence between these two disasters, which can quantificational represent the correlation of them. Choose the search method as the accurate search. A crawler is adopted to get the frequency among those 73 disasters. Then a 73 * 73 matrix of frequency has been constructed. Part of the matrix is showed in Table 1.

Table 1. Part of the disaster co-occurrence frequency matrix.

	Flood	Water-logging	Ice flood	Flash floods	Agricultural drought	Typhoon
Flood	364000	740	122	549	12	8750
Water-logging	740	24000	0	19	0	216
Ice flood	122	0	888	3	0	4
Flash floods	549	19	3	10500	2	101
Agricultural drought	12	0	0	2	736	13
Typhoon	8750	216	4	101	13	148000

In Table 1, the number on the diagonal indicates the number of papers that contains the determined keywords. For example, the number '364000' in the first row and first column indicates that there are 364,000 papers mentioned the keyword 'Flood'. The number '740' in the first row and second column indicates that there are 740 papers mentioned both the keyword 'Flood' and 'Water logging'.

It can be seen that the co-occurrence frequency of two disasters is affected by the frequency of each search item. When the number of disasters literatures is large, the frequency of co-occurrence between this disaster and others will be relatively large. Therefore, it is better to use co-occurrence rate to represent the strength of relevance among disasters.

There are many ways to calculate the co-occurrence rate. In the co-occurrence analysis theory, the researchers put forward the inclusion index, similarity index and equivalence index. In later studies, the researchers also proposed the Dice index, Jaccard index, Salton Index and so on [10]. In this paper, the Salton index as shown in (1) is used as the index of the relationship among disasters. The part of Salton matrix table among disasters is showed in Table 2.

$$S_{ij} = \frac{c_{ij}}{\sqrt{c_i \times c_j}} \qquad (1)$$

Table 2. Part of the Salton matrix of disasters

	Flood	Water-logging	Ice flood	Flash floods	Agricultural drought	Typhoon
Flood	1	0.007917	0.006785	0.008880	0.000733	0.037699
Water-logging	0.007917	1	0	0.001197	0	0.003624
Ice flood	0.006785	0	1	0.000982	0	0.000349
Flash floods	0.008880	0.001197	0.000982	1	0.000719	0.002562
Agricultural drought	0.000733	0	0	0.000719	1	0.001246
Typhoon	0.037698	0.003624	0.000348	0.002562	0.001246	1

In (1), S_{ij} represents Salton index of disaster i and disaster j. c_{ij} represents the co-occurrence frequency of disaster i and disaster j. c_i and c_j represents the frequency of disaster i and disaster j respectively.

3.3   Creation of the Disaster Complex Network

The disaster network is constructed with complex network model as shown in Fig. 1. The network has 73 nodes and each node represents a disaster. If the co-occurrence rate of two disasters is greater than 0, a line is established between those two disaster nodes.

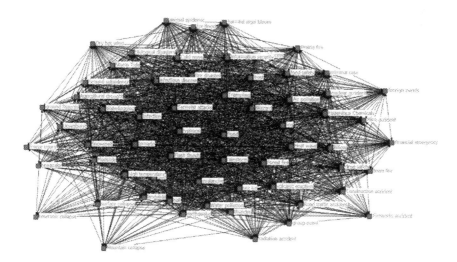

Fig. 1. Complex network of 73 disasters

It can be seen from Fig. 1 that the disaster chain network obtained by this method is too complicated to make the next analysis. If the co-occurrence rate of two disasters is low, it can be seen that the relevance of those two disasters are weak. Therefore, the threshold is used to remove those disturbances and optimize the network. The appropriate threshold can be set to optimize the network. For example, if the threshold

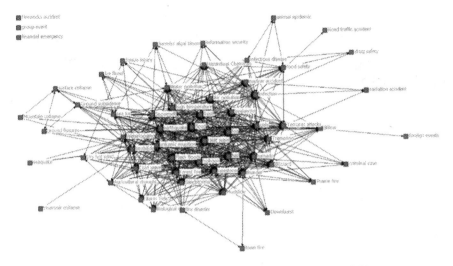

Fig. 2. Complex network of disaster with threshold as 0.01

is set to 0.01, the network shown in Fig. 2 can be obtained. The threshold should be changed to meet the actual demand.

The number of lines from a node to other nodes is called the degree of the node, which can reflect the importance of the node in the whole network. The larger the degree of a disaster node is, the greater the probability of a disaster causing other disasters is. Moreover, it means the relationship between this disaster and other disasters is much closer.

3.4   Extraction of a Specific Disaster Chain Network

The current disaster network contains all 73 disasters. However, most of time a disaster chain of a special disaster is needed. As for the complex network, the whole network can be divided into several communities by using the method of community division. This way can also be adopted to divide the disaster network into several parts to get a disaster chain of a special disaster.

This paper compares the methods of community division, and adopts a community division method that is based on the improvement of the maximum flow [11]. This method can get a few communities with overlapping parts. Using this method to divide the disaster network, the results will be changed with the change of threshold. This paper has test the result with different threshold and selected a disaster chain with a reasonable number of nodes as the result.

4   Experimental Result

Baidu scholar and Google scholar are used as database to build our disaster chain. This paper uses Chinese keywords in Baidu scholar dataset and English keywords in Google scholar dataset to get the different result with different source.

Using community division method to get a disaster chain of a special disaster after getting disaster network. Figure 3 shows the typhoon disaster chain. The rectangle points and circle points from the disaster chain that is built by using Baidu scholar datasets; the rectangle points and triangle points from the disaster chain that is built by using Google scholar datasets.

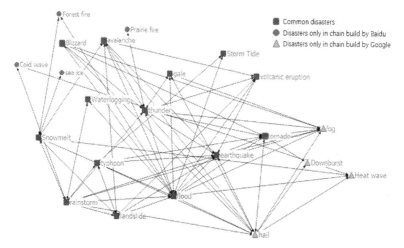

Fig. 3. Thetyphoon disaster chain built by using Baidu scholar datasets and Google scholar datasets. The red points and blue points form the disaster chain that is built by using Baidu scholar datasets; the red points and yellow points form the disaster chain that is built by using Google scholar datasets. (Color figure online)

The typhoon disaster chain constructed by Baidu scholar datasets contains 18 disasters: typhoon, gale, water logging, landslide, avalanche, storm tide, flood, blizzard, volcanic eruption, thunder, snowmelt, rainstorm, earthquake, grassland fire, cold wave, sea ice, prairie fire and forest fire.

It is obvious that most of the disaster in typhoon disaster chain is reasonable. Most of the disasters can be found in some literatures about typhoon disaster chain [2].

The disaster chain built by using Google scholar dataset contains 18 disasters: typhoon, gale, water logging, landslide, avalanche, storm tide, flood, blizzard, volcanic eruption, thunder, snowmelt, rainstorm, earthquake, grassland fire, downburst, hail, heat wave and fog.

We can see from Fig. 3 that the main body of two disaster chains are consistent meanwhile there are still some different between them. It can be found the disasters only appear in one disaster chain is always with low degree.

The proposed method can get similar result with different datasets, which can confirm the method is effective.

5 Conclusion

By using the co-occurrence analysis method, we get the relevance of the disaster from a large number of disaster scholar datasets. This method avoids the dependence on the expert experiences in the process of building the disaster chain. The community division method is employed to get specific disaster chain from the constructed complex network. With comparison of the results between Baidu scholar datasets and Google scholar datasets, it is shown that our proposed method is reasonable and effective.

However, some other research work need to be done in our future study. More efforts need to be paid on the semantic issue in order to avoid the synonyms for one disaster. For example, some of the literature may use "hurricane" rather than "typhoon". Therefore, some literature papers may be lost if only term "typhoon" is searched. Moreover, this paper only considers the scholar datasets. It might be helpful to extensively consider website datasets like the disaster news. In addition, the result is also can be improved. The method we used might not best. It might have a more effective way to divide the disaster network.

Acknowledgments. This paper is funded by National Key Research and Development Program of China (Grant No. 2016YFC0803107 and Grant No. 2016YFB0502601) and Shenzhen Technology Innovation Program (JCYJ20170307152553273).

References

1. Liu, W., Xiao, S., Sui, Y., Zhou, J., Gao, H.: Analysis of natural disarster chain and chain-cutting disarster mitigation mode. Chin. J. Rock Mech. Eng. **25**, 2675–2681 (2006)
2. Ye, J., Ling, G., Zhang, M.: Spatial characteristics of typhoon disaster chains in Fujian Province. J. Fujian Norm. Univ. **30**, 99–106 (2014)
3. Han, J., Wu, S., Wang, H.: Preliminary study on geological hazard chains. J. Earth Sci. Front. **14**, 011–023 (2007)
4. Jianli, L., Jiahong, W., Zhaner, Y., Yu, C., Fei, W.: Review of disaster system simulation techniques and methods. J. Catastrophology **24**, 106–111 (2009)
5. Hongjian, Z., Xi, W., Yi, Y., Dandan, W.: Rapid-assessing methods of loss in extremely heavy rainfall disaster chain in semiarid region. J. Arid Zone Res. **31**(3), 440–445 (2014)
6. Keefer, D.K.: Investigating landslides caused by earthquakes: a historical review. J. Surv. Geophys. **23**(6), 473–510 (2002)
7. Changkun, C., Daoxi, J.: Risk analysis and control for the evolution disaster system of typhoon based on complex network. J. Catastrophology **27**(1), 1–4 (2012)
8. Li, Y., Gong, J.H., Zhu, J., et al.: Spatiotemporal simulation and risk analysis of dam-break flooding based on cellular automata. Int. J. Geograph. Inf. Sci. **27**(10), 2043–2059 (2013)
9. Schedl, M., Pohle, T., Knees, P., Widmer, G.: Assigning and visualizing music genres by web-based co-occurrence analysis. In: Ismir 2006, International Conference on Music Information Retrieval, pp. 260–265 (2006)

10. Egghe, L.: New relations between similarity measures for vectors based on vector norms. J. Am. Soc. Inf. Sci. Technol. **60**(2), 232–239 (2009)
11. Chuanjian, L.: Community Detection and Analytical Application in Complex Networks. Shandong University (2014)
12. Han, Y., Jin-ai, W., Mei, C., Peijun, S.: Progress in the research on the accumulative enlargement of disaster chain disaster. J. Prog. Geogr. **33**(11), 1498–1511 (2014)
13. Ai-hua, L., Chao, W.: Research on risk assessment method of disaster chain based on complex network. J. Syst. Eng. Theory Pract. **35**(2), 466–472 (2015)
14. Lili, R., Yingying, C., Duo, W.: Research on China's incident association based on co-occurrence analysis. J. Syst. Eng. **6**, 1–7 (2011)
15. Li, J., Chen, C.: Modeling the dynamics of disaster evolution along causality networks with cycle chains. J. Phys. Stat. Mech. Appl. **401**, 251–264 (2014)

Design of Sensor System for Air Pollution Monitoring

Hua Fan[1(✉)], Junru Li[1], Yulin Qin[2], Quanyuan Feng[3], Dagang Li[4],
Daqian Hu[4], Yuanjun Cen[4], and Hadi Heidari[5]

[1] State Key Laboratory of Electronic Thin Films and Integrated Devices,
School of Electronic Science and Engineering,
University of Electronic Science and Technology of China, Chengdu, China
fanhua7531@163.com, lijunru@uestc.edu.cn
[2] Chongqing No.11 Middle School, Chongqing, China
qylin0505@sina.com
[3] The School of Information Science and Technology,
Southwest Jiaotong University, Chengdu, China
fengquanyuan@163.com
[4] Chengdu Sino Microelectronics Technology Co., Ltd., Chengdu, China
{dagang, dq_hu, cen}@csmsc.com
[5] Electronics and Nanoscale Engineering Division, School of Engineering,
University of Glasgow, Glasgow G12 8QQ, UK
hadi.heidari@glasgow.ac.uk

Abstract. In this work, we present the design of sensor platform for air pollution monitoring. During the design process, we took into account a lot of problems such as system architecture, power consumption and linearity consideration. ADC plays a vital important role in high-linearity sensor micro system, several practical techniques which can improve the performance and decrease power consumption of ADC are discussed in this paper.

Keywords: Particulate matter (PM) · Analog-to-Digital converter
Successive approximation register (SAR) ADC
Sensor micro system · Linearity

1 Introduction

Airborne Particulate Matter (PM) refers to a mixture of heterogeneous particles suspended in the air having both natural and anthropic origin [1]. The adverse impact on human health of the exposure to airborne particulate matter (PM) is well known [2, 3]. Although optical and gravimetric instruments are available to detect PM, they lack portability, have poor potential for miniaturization, and are not low cost. The objective of this work is to develop a portable nano-sensor micro system which can be applied to detect the airborne magnetite pollution nanoparticles with an aerodynamic diameter of less than 200 nm. Airborne detection system is shown as in Fig. 1, the main functional block of the sensor micro system is a sensor node which consists of sensor, analog front-end, ADC and digital signal processing(DSP). ADC plays a vital important role in

© Springer Nature Singapore Pte Ltd. 2018
H. Yuan et al. (Eds.): GSKI 2017, CCIS 848, pp. 280–288, 2018.
https://doi.org/10.1007/978-981-13-0893-2_29

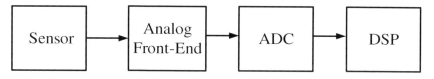

Fig. 1. Basic architectural of sensor

high-linearity sensor micro system, several practical techniques which can improve the performance and decrease power consumption of ADC are discussed in the following sections.

2   Overview of Mainstream Analog-to-Digital Converter Architecture

As well known, all real-world signals are essentially analog signal. Before the middle of the 1970s, almost all signal processing is carried out in the analog domain. However, in the process of storage and transmission of analog signals, the noise and distortion will be accumulated, so the signal processing has a bad effect. Over the past 30 years, very large scale integrated circuits develops, suppression noise capacity of digital signal is much better than the analog signal, and in the digital domain, digital signals can be stored and transmitted without any loss. Therefore, in order to make use of these advantages of digital signal processing, analog signals are often converted into digital signals by Analog-to-digital converter (ADC), then Digital Signal Processors (DSP) take real-world signals like voice, audio, video, temperature, pressure, or position that have been digitized by ADC and then mathematically manipulate them. The digital domain can perform various signal processing functions like "add", "subtract", "multiply" and "divide" in the digital domain with higher accuracy, higher reliability, and lower price than analog domains. In a word, in typical DSP systems, signals need to be processed so that the information that they contain can be displayed, analyzed, or converted to another type of signal that may be of use. In the real-world, analog products detect signals such as sound, light, temperature or pressure and manipulate them. ADC then takes the real-world signal and turns it into the digital format of 1's and 0's. From here, the DSP takes over by capturing the digitized information and processing it. It then feeds the digitized information back for use in the real world. It does this in one of two ways, either digitally or in an analog format by going through a Digital-to-Analog converter (DAC). During this process, the analog to digital conversion involves two processes: the sampling process is to make the signal discrete in time, and the quantization process is to make the signal discrete in amplitude. ADC has two important performance indicators: speed and accuracy. The speed reflects how fast discretization is in time, and the precision reflects how accurate the discretization is in amplitude. Today, digital signal processors process much more data than ADC can provide, in fact, in many digital systems, ADC becomes a bottleneck.

ADC is mainly divided into over-sampling ADC and Nyquist-Rate ADC. Over-sampling ADC has become a practical solution for high precision ADC design, but over-sampling ADC consists of analog modulators and digital parts used to implement decimation and digital filtering, which consumes a lot of chip area and power consumption. Typical Nyquist ADC can be divided into many types according to diverse working principles, for example Flash, Pipelined, Sub-arrangement, successive approximation register (SAR) ADC, etc. They are able to work at a faster rate with much larger bandwidth compared with the over-sampling ADC. Recent works show. As shown in Fig. 2, SAR ADC is simple to implement, mainly including three important sub-blocks: comparator, SAR control logic and digital-to-analog converter (DAC) to implement binary search algorithm in Fig. 3, which leads that power efficiency of SAR ADC is much superior to Flash ADC, Pipeline ADC and $\Sigma\Delta$ADC [4–12]. This work focuses on design considerations of SAR ADC, some important design issues related to comparators in (ADCs) are discussed, and it is appropriate for low power smart sensor application.

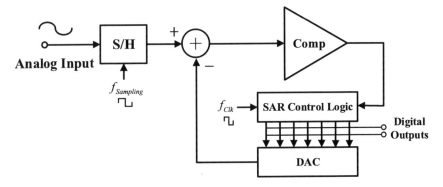

Fig. 2. Basic architectural of SAR ADC

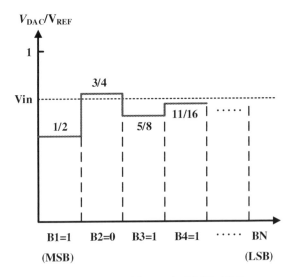

Fig. 3. Basic architectural of SAR ADC.

3   Mainstream Basic Structures of SAR ADC

There are two popular architectures for SAR ADC, voltage SAR ADC and charge redistribution SAR ADC. As shown in Fig. 4, voltage SAR ADC is simple and easy to implement, 2^N resistors divide the reference voltage $0 \sim$ VREF, obviously, monotonicity of ADC can be ensured adequately, however, resistors consume static current all the time, which degrades the power efficiency of ADC.

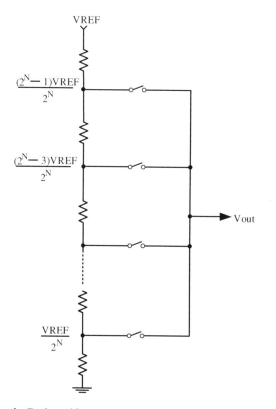

Fig. 4. Basic architectural components of voltage SAR ADC

Charge redistribution SAR ADC is the most popular architecture at present due to its ultra-low power consumption, however, its static nonlinearity error is limited by the capacitive mismatch. The core of the charge redistribution ADC is a capacitor array that redistributes the charge stored in the capacitor array based on a binary digital input, producing an analog output that is less than or equal to the reference voltage. As shown in Fig. 5, a basic structure of the 7-bit SAR ADC, the unit capacitance of the capacitor array is C, from LSB to MSB: 2^0C, $2^1C,...2^{7-1}C$. The DAC is controlled by two non-overlapping clocks $\phi1$ and $\phi2$. When $\phi1$ is active, all the bottom plates of upper capacitors are connected to VINP and all the bottom plates of lower capacitors are connected to VINN, and top plates of all capacitors are connected to VCM

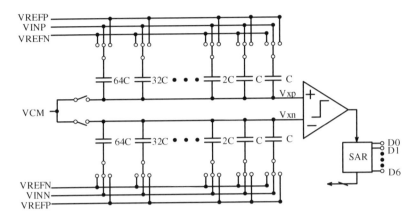

Fig. 5. Basic architectural of charge redistribution SAR ADC

simultaneously; When φ2 is active, the bottom plates of capacitor on the upper side with the corresponding bit "1" is connected to VREFP and the bottom plates of capacitor on the upper side corresponding bit "0" is connected to VREFN, while the bottom plates of capacitor on the lower side with the corresponding bit "1" is connected to VREFN and the bottom plates of capacitor on the lower side corresponding bit "0" is connected to VREFP. The DAC output V_{xp}–V_{xn} is valid. Since there is no loss of charge before and after the conversion, it remains conserved at top plates of capacitors. Finally, Vxp and Vxn converge towards the common mode voltage VCM. The change in Vxp and Vxn can be calculated as follows:

$$V_{xp} = V_{CM} - V_{INP} + \sum_{j=0}^{6} \frac{D_j C_j}{C_{total}} V_{REFP} + \sum_{j=0}^{6} D_j (1 - \frac{C_j}{C_{total}}) V_{REFN}. \qquad (1)$$

$$V_{xn} = V_{CM} - V_{INN} + \sum_{j=0}^{6} \frac{D_j C_j}{C_{total}} V_{REFN} + \sum_{j=0}^{6} D_j (1 - \frac{C_j}{C_{total}}) V_{REFP}. \qquad (2)$$

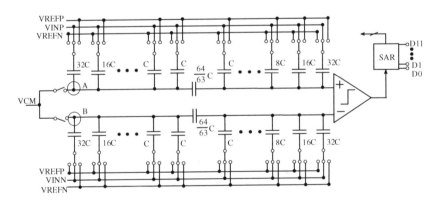

Fig. 6. 10-Bit split SAR ADC

4 Overview of Low Power Charge Redistribution SAR ADC Techniques

4.1 Ultra-low Power SAR ADC Architecture

As shown in Fig. 5, for N-bit binary SAR ADC, $2^N + 1$ unit capacitors are required, for example, for 12-bit binary SAR ADC, 4096 unit capacitors are needed, which limits its application to high resolution and low power consumption sensor system, split ADC in Fig. 6 is applied to break this limit by introducing coupling capacitor. In Fig. 6, 12-bit

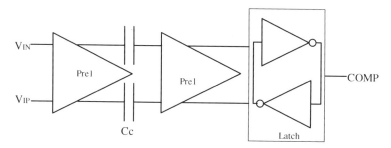

Fig. 7. Time-domain comparator proposed in [13]

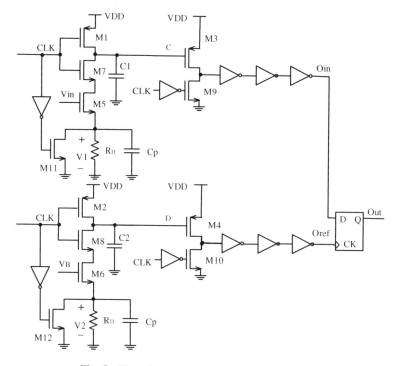

Fig. 8. Time-domain comparator proposed in [13]

split SAR ADC only needs 128 unit capacitors, but parasitic capacitances of float nodes A and B will degrade the linearity of ADC.

4.2 Ultra-low Power Comparator

As well known, conventional voltage comparator applied to SAR ADC consists of two or three preamplifiers and latch. The advantage of voltage comparator lies into the fact that preamplifier always consumes static power consumption, limits its application to low power sensor. Inverter based comparator was invented to decrease the power

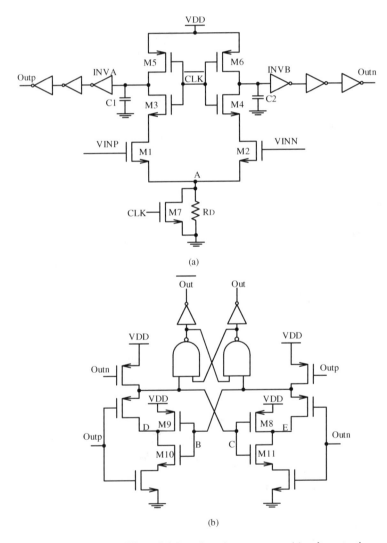

Fig. 9. Schematic of proposed differential time-domain comparator (a) voltage-to-time converter and (b) binary phase detector [14]

consumption and replace the conventional voltage comparator. The time-domain comparator proposed in [13] obviates the need of preamplifier that dissipates static power, but it can only be applied to single-ended SAR ADC, because one of the inputs of the time-domain comparator in Fig. 8 is connected to a fixed voltage, VB, which must be large enough to provide the reference pulse, as a result, differential signal cannot be applied to VB. On the basis of this work, we invented a time-domain comparator which is publish on [14], as shown in Fig. 9. As shown in Fig. 9, it can be applied to both single-ended and differential SAR ADC (Fig. 5).

5   Conclusion

In this work, we present the design of sensor platform for air pollution monitoring. During the design process, we took into account a lot of problems such as system architecture, power consumption and linearity consideration. ADC plays a vital important role in high-linearity sensor micro system, several practical techniques which can improve the performance and decrease power consumption of ADC are discussed in this paper.

6   Acknowledgments

The work of Hua Fan was supported by the National Natural Science Foundation of China (NSFC) under Grant 61771111 and 61401066, as well as supported by China Postdoctoral Science Foundation under grant 2017M612940 and Special Foundation of Sichuan Provincial Postdoctoral Science Foundation.

The work of Quanyuan Feng was supported by the National Natural Science Foundation of China (NSFC) under Grant 61531016, supported by the project of Science and Technology Support Program of Sichuan Province under Grant 2015GZ0103, and in part by the Sichuan Provincial Science and Technology Important Projects under Grant 2017GZ0110.

References

1. Ciccarella, P., Carminati, M., Sampietro, M., Ferrari, G.: Multichannel 65 zF rms resolution CMOS monolithic capacitive sensor for counting single micrometer-sized airborne particles on chip. IEEE J. Solid-State Circuits 51(11), 2545–2553 (2016)
2. Carminati, M., Ferrari, G., Sampietro, M.: Emerging miniaturized technologies for airborne particulate matter pervasive monitoring. Measurement 101, 250–256 (2015)
3. Ciccarella, P., Carminati, M., Sampietro, M., Ferrari, G.: CMOS monolithic airborne-particulate-matter detector based on 32 capacitive sensors with a resolution of 65zF rms. In: 2016 IEEE International Solid-State Circuits Conference (ISSCC), pp. 486–488 (2016)
4. Shim, M., Jeong, S., Myers, P.D., Bang, S., Shen, J., Kim, C., Sylvester, D., Blaauw, D., Jung, W.: Edge-pursuit comparator: an energy-scalable oscillator collapse-based comparator with application in a 74.1 db SNDR and 20 ks/s 15 b SAR ADC. IEEE J. Solid-State Circuits 52, 1077–1090 (2017)

5. Fan, H., Maloberti, F.: High-resolution SAR ADC with enhanced linearity. IEEE Trans. Circuits Syst. II Express Br. **64**(10), 1142–1146 (2017)
6. Fan, H., Hadi, H., Maloberti, F., Li, D., Hu, D., Cen, Y.: High resolution and linearity enhanced SAR ADC for wearable sensing systems. In: IEEE International Symposium on Circuits and Systems (ISCAS), pp. 180–183 (2017)
7. Tang, X., Chen, L., Song, J., Sun, N.: A 10-b 750 μw 200 ms/s fully dynamic single-channel SAR ADC in 40 nm CMOS. In: 42nd European Solid-State Circuits Conference, ESSCIRC Conference 2016, pp. 413–416. IEEE (2016)
8. Chen, Y.-J., Chang, K.-H., Hsieh, C.-C.: A 2.02–5.16 fJ/conversion. step 10-bit hybrid coarse-fine SAR ADC with time-domain quantizer in 90 nm CMOS. IEEE J. Solid-State Circuits **51**(2), 357–364 (2016)
9. Chen, Z., Jiang, Y., Cai, C., Wei, H.-G., Sin, S.-W., Seng-Pan, U., Wang, Z., Martins, R.P.: A 22.4 μW 80 dB SNDR ΣΔ modulator with passive analog adder and SAR quantizer for EMG application. In: IEEE Asian Solid-State Circuits Conference (A-SSCC), pp. 257–260 (2012)
10. Luo, H., Han, Y., Cheung, R.C., Liu, X., Cao, T.: A 0.8-V 230-μw 98-dB DR inverter-based ΣΔ modulator for audio applications. IEEE J. Solid-State Circuits **48**(10), 2430–2441 (2013)
11. Kuo, C.-H., Hsieh, C.-E.: A high energy-efficiency SAR ADC based on partial floating capacitor switching technique. In: European Solid-State Circuits Conference (ESSCIRC), pp. 475–478. IEEE (2011)
12. Yanfei, C., Xiaolei, Z., Tamura, H., Kibune, M., Tomita, Y., Hamada, T., Yoshioka, M., Ishikawa, K., Takayama, T., Ogawa, J., et al.: Split capacitor DAC mismatch calibration in successive approximation ADC. In: Digest of Technical Papers of IEEE Custom Integrated Circuits Conference (CICC), pp. 279–282. IEEE (2009)
13. Agnes, A., Bonizzoni, E., Malcovati, P., Maloberti, F.: A 9.4-ENOB 1 V 3.8 μw 100 ks/s SAR ADC with time-domain comparator. In: Digest of Technical Papers of IEEE International Solid-State Circuits Conference (ISSCC), pp. 246–610. IEEE (2008)
14. Fan, H., Han, X., Wei, Q., Yang, H.: A 12-bit self-calibrating SAR ADC achieving a Nyquist 90.4-dB SFDR. Analog Integr. Circuits Signal Process. **74**(1), 239–254 (2013)

China Crude Oil Purchase Decision Under Considering Disruption Risk

Wei Pan[1,2(✉)] and Cheng Hu[1,2]

[1] Economics and Management School,
Wuhan University, Wuhan 430072, China
`mrpanwei2000@163.com`
[2] Management Science and Data Analytics Research Center,
Wuhan University, Wuhan 430072, China

Abstract. The objective of this article is to study how to avoid crude oil import supply disruption risk. For this purpose, we bring forward two algorithms to crude oil supply order allocation. By finding the solution with minimum percentage of disruption risk and step algorithms, we optimize 2005 china importing crude oil order allocation and gain better result.

Keywords: Multi-supplier · Order allocation · Supply disruption risk
Step algorithm

1 Introduction

With China's economic growth over the past two decades averaging around 8% (following market reforms commencing in the late 1970s), the crude oil demand is increasing rapidly. However, most of the crude oil imports come from the unstable Middle East, of which 80% have to get across the perilous Malacca Strait. Disruptions risk in the crude oil supply have attracted a great deal of attention in recent years. In such environment, we hope to settle this problem by answering why multi-supplier is better than single supplier in avoiding importing risk and optimizing crude oil import order allocation among suppliers.

Pan [1] proposed multiple sourcing for improving the reliability of supply for critical materials, in which more than one supplier is used and the demand is split between them. Pan [2] constructed multi-objective supplier selection model for solving uncertain information, disruption risk and so on. Pan [3] established order allocation model for supplier. Wei [4] provided some valid optimal strategic petroleum reserve in china by empirical analysis. Wei [5] researched china energy strategy and policy by report. Smeltzer and Siferd [6] clearly pointed out that when an organization reduces its supplier base, it relies on fewer suppliers for critical materials, possibly increasing the risk of an interruption of supply. Based on event study method, Liao [7] studied the impact that emergencies and strategic petroleum reserve have on oil price. Monge [8] hold that oil price trend depend on possible events that disturb oil transportation and find that oil price is continuous and interruptible. Armin Jabbarzadeh [9] focuses on exploring the extent to which supply chain design decisions are influenced by factors

© Springer Nature Singapore Pte Ltd. 2018
H. Yuan et al. (Eds.): GSKI 2017, CCIS 848, pp. 289–296, 2018.
https://doi.org/10.1007/978-981-13-0893-2_30

such as facility fortification strategies, demand fluctuations and so on. E. Bompard [10] put an overarching methodology to evaluate energy security which include external and internal dimensions and the methodology is then applied to the Italian case, considering different geopolitical scenarios.

However, the past studies shown above have little literature on crude oil import order allocation. Therefore, in this paper, we try to construct a method that will be used to allocate crude oil orders to the selected supplier to guarantee high steady crude oil supply levels to china. The factors that we use to allocate the order consist of percentage of disruption risk and order price. We seek to examine the interactions between supply disruption mitigation and supply order cost, and to investigate the role of order allocation method in alleviating disruption risk.

2 Materials and Methods

For explanation, the situation (crude oil import need multi-supplier) by a probability model, we make some simplifying assumptions. We presume that there are potential "super-events" that can occur affecting all suppliers simultaneously and its occurring probability is denoted by P. In the same time, we also summarize "unique-event" scenario for each supplier, every scenario is only associated with a particular supplier that puts it down during the supply cycle for simplifying our exposition. We point out this probability as T_i for supplier i (T_i and T_j are independent for $i \neq j$). And, we reasonably assume that T_i and P are independent events. Then, the probability that supplier i is down during the supply period and cannot supply the focal company during this period, is

$$P(1) = P + (1 - P)T_1. \tag{1}$$

And when there are n suppliers, the probability that all are down is

$$P(n) = P + (1 - P)T_1 \cdot \cdot T_n \tag{2}$$

Hence, if we look at the difference between the above two probabilities, we get

$$P(n) - P(1) = (1 - P)T_1(T_2 \cdot \cdot T_n - 1) \leq 0 \tag{3}$$

Thus, while no surprise, (3) illustrates that, having n suppliers is less risky than having only one supplier in unstable crude oil environment.

2.1   Performance Measure

The performance measure in this paper is the disruption risk rate obtained from

$$f_1(X) = \frac{\sum\limits_{i=1}^{n} X_i q_i}{\sum\limits_{i=1}^{n} X_i} \tag{4}$$

Where $f_1(X)$ is the percentage of disruption risk about crude oil import order, X_i is order quantity for i supplier, q_i is disruption risk rate of i supplier.

Consequently, the total purchase cost of crude oil could be obtained by using following equation, CIF (Cost, insurance and freight, $CIF_i = C_i + T_i + I_i$) meaning selling price includes all costs so far plus cost of insurance.

$$f_2(X) = \sum\limits_{j=1}^{n} X_i (C_i + T_i + I_i) = \sum\limits_{j=1}^{n} X_i CIF_i \tag{5}$$

where $f_2(X)$ is the total purchase cost of crude oil in the period, C_i is the unit price of crude oil corresponding to supplier i, T_i is unit crude oil transportation cost for i supplier, I_i represents unit crude oil insurance cost for i supplier.

$$\sum\limits_{i=1}^{n} X_i = X \tag{6}$$

$$H = \sum\limits_{i=1}^{n} \left(\frac{X_i}{X}\right)^2 = \sum\limits_{i=1}^{n} S_i^2 \tag{7}$$

$$f_3(X) = HHA = \sqrt{\sum\limits_{i=1}^{n} S_i^2} \tag{8}$$

$$\text{Amendatory HHA}: f_4(X) = HHA = \sqrt{\sum\limits_{i=1}^{n} w_i^2 S_i^2} \tag{9}$$

Where $f_3(X)$ is the concentration index about crude oil import order and $f_4(X)$ is crude oil import risk index, X_i is order quantity for i supplier, w_i is risk weight coefficient of i supplier. S_i is the proportion of i supplier order in total order.

2.2   Order-Allocation Algorithm

(1) Finding the solution with minimum percentage of disruption risk

Step 1: For each product j, select the supplier with maximum score of disruption risk and give the percentage of ordering of $\alpha\%$ of the annual demand to this supplier.

Step 2: For the remaining suppliers, if there are more than two suppliers left, select the one that contains the second maximum score of disruption risk and assign a% of the annual demand to this supplier.

Step 3: Repeat step 2 until there is only one supplier left. Give the available percentage to this supplier.

Steps 1 until Step 3 are steps to find the total score according to the first policy.

Step 4: (computer simulation.) Vary the value of percentage of order for each supplier to obtain the total score from the maximum value (from step 3) to the minimum feasible total score required.

(2) Linear programming with multiple objective functions: Step method (stem) Benayoun [11] develops a solution technique for Linear Programming problems with multiple objective functions.

Step 1: For every objective $f_j(X)(j = 1\ldots\ldots m)$, we calculate respective maximum value, that is $f_{jmax} = \max f_j(X)\, f_{jmax} = f_j^* = f_j(X_j^*)$

Step 2: Compute performance index table

Step 3: The objective function is: $d_\infty(f(X) - f^*) = \max\{w_j(f_{jmax} - f_j)\}$

$$\min \lambda \quad \lambda \geq w_j \frac{f_{jmax} - f_j}{f_{jmax} - f_{jmin}}$$

$$\varepsilon_i \leq X_i \leq V_i, \quad \sum_{i=1}^{n} X_i = D, \ i = 1, 2, \ldots. \ n. \ X_i \geq 0, \ V_i \geq 0, \ \varepsilon_i \geq 0$$

Where V_i represents capacity of the i supplier, X_i is units of crude oil and its order quantity, ε_{ij} is minimum purchased quantity, D represents total demand.

Hypothesis: $f_j(X) = \sum_{i=1}^{n} c_{ji} X_i$

$$w_j = \frac{\frac{\left| f_j^* - f_j^{min} \right|}{f_j^* \cdot \sqrt{\sum_{i=1}^{n} c_{ji}^2}}}{\sum_{j=1}^{m} \frac{\left| f_j^* - f_j^{min} \right|}{f_j^* \cdot \sqrt{\sum_{i=1}^{n} c_{ji}^2}}} \quad w_j \geq 0 \text{ and } \sum_{j=1}^{m} w_j = 1$$

f_j^{min} is minimum value of X_j^* row in Table 1.

Table 1. Performance index

	f_1	....	f_j	....	f_m
X_1^*	f_1^*	....	f_{1j}^*	....	f_{1m}^*
.	.		.		.
X_m^*	f_{m1}	....	f_{mj}	....	f_m^*

Step 4: If decision maker is not satisfied with this conclusion, we modify corresponding objective value. If $f_l(X)$ is so good that others are very bad, modification criteria as following:

$$\begin{cases} f_l(X) = f_{original-l}(X) - \nabla f_l \\ w_l = 0 \\ f_j(X) \geq f_{original-j}(X) \end{cases}$$

2.3 The Source of Data

The china crude oil CIF, China's crude oil export and import, the world historical information of crude oil for each year are taken from United Nations Commodity Trade Statistics Database BP Statistical Review of World Energy 2006 (BP, 2006); the risk weight coefficient of China crude oil import (Table 2) is taken from China Energy Report (2006)-Strategy and Policy Research.

Table 2. China crude oil import risk weight coefficient

	Russia	Southeast Asia	West Africa	Middle East	Other Area
Weight coefficient	0.051	0.117	0.217	0.537	0.078

3 Results and Discussion

All petroliferous countries (export quantities more than import quantities) are divided into five zone, they are Russia, Southeast Asia, West Africa, Middle East and Other Area. In 2005, their actual crude oil export capacity and unit CIF (Table 3) and China crude oil import risk weight coefficient (Table 1) are shown:

Table 3. 2005 petroliferous five zone crude oil export capacity

Million Ton	Russia	Southeast Asia	West Africa	Middle East	Other Area
import weight	0	24.8	2.9	10.2	88.1
export weight	267.6	49.8	208.7	862.9	411.4
export capacity	267.6	25	205.8	852.7	323.3
China crude oil CIF ($/ton)	388.1	394.49	376.57	371.88	376.31

We have performed a simulation test to find the total purchase average CIF while varying the percentage of order allocation together with the maximum and minimum percentage of disruption risk. The sections below detail the empirical analysis.

The empirical analysis in this paper is based on the following assumptions:

(1) We assume that China's import crude oil disruption risk rate are 0.051, 0.117, 0.217, 0.537, 0.078 respectively, which refers to Table 2. And the estimated (or assumed) value of some parameters in performance measure can be seen in Table 3.
(2) We assume that the impact of the disruption of net crude oil import on the loss is only dependent on loss quantity.
(3) We assumed that export capacity is actual rude oil export net-weight in 2005 (Table 3). In the same time, we ascertain world five zone china import crude oil CIF according to actual CIF in 2005.

① Finding the solution with minimum percentage of disruption risk;

According to this algorithm, we know value of α from 0 to 0.2. When we assume α more than and equal 5%, the optimal order quantity of 2005 will be calculated. We can found the value of unit purchase CIF and HHA under different α value (Table 4).

Table 4. Percentage of disruption risk and value of CIF and HHA in different α

α	The percentage of disruption risk	Corresponding china crude oil purchase CIF ($/ton)	Corresponding china crude oil HHA	Corresponding china crude oil amendatory HHA
5%	0.08825	386.44	0.806226	0.050204
10%	0.1255	384.785	0.632456	0.066998
15%	0.16275	383.13	0.5	0.0917
20%	0.2	381.47	0.447214	0.119638

② Linear programming with multiple objective functions: Step method (stem)

This programming about allocating crude oil orders among five zone is built to minimize supply disruption risk. In this optimization algorithm, two objectives are considered: crude oil import risk index and crude oil import cost (Table 5).

Table 5. performance index

	f_2	f_4
X_2^*	44774.4	46397.27
X_4^*	0.537	0.0394

Objective: $\min\{f_2(X), f_4(X)\}$

Step 1: $\min f_2(X) = 44774.4$ $X_2^* = (0,0,0,120.4,0)$

$$\min f_4(X) = 0.0393$$
$$X_4^* = (71.6141, 13.58876, 3.953524, 0.6444461, 30.59917)$$
$$f_{24} = 46397.27 \quad f_{42} = 0.537$$

Step 2: $f_2^{\min} = 46397.27$ $f_4^{\min} = 0.537$

Step 3: $w_2 = 0.0014$ $w_4 = 0.9986$

Objective: $\min \lambda$

Constrains: $X_i \geq 0, \sum_{i=1}^{n} X_i = 120.4, \lambda \geq w_j \frac{f_j - f_{j\min}}{f_{j\max} - f_{j\min}}$

$$X = (71.58598, 13.60293, 3.954602, 0.6457730, 30.61071)$$
$$f_2 = 46397.19 \ f_4 = 0.077788$$

(Assumes: If decision maker is not satisfied with result, we can adjust objective's value by step 4)

.

4   Conclusions

According to the above-mentioned results, we have analyzed the results as follows: percentage of disruption risk of crude oil is 8.825% and maximum value is 20% as according to the solution with minimum percentage of disruption risk. If we want to decrease the percentage of disruption risk from 20% to 8.825%, it requires only 1.3% of increasing unit rude oil CIF. Therefore, ideal choice should allocate most importing crude oil to supplier with minimum percentage of disruption risk. Importing risk index HHA and Step method yet prove this conclusion.

Acknowledgment. This work is partially supported by grants from the National Natural Science Foundation of China (NSFC nos. 71373188 and U1333115).

References

1. Pan, A.C.: Allocation of order quantity among suppliers. J. Purch. Mater. Manag. **25**(3), 36–39 (1989)
2. Pan, W., Yu, L., Wang, S., et al.: A fuzzy multi-objective model for provider selection in data communication services with different QoS levels. Int. J. Prod. Econ. **147**, 689–696 (2013)

3. Pan, W., Wang, X., Zhong, Y.-g., Lean, Yu., Jie, C., Ran, L., Qiao, H., Wang, S., Xu, X.: A fuzzy multi-objective model for capacity allocation and pricing policy of provider in data communication service with different QoS levels. Int. J. Syst. Sci. **43**(6), 1054–1063 (2012)

4. Wei, Y.-M., Wu, G., Fan, Y., Liu, L.-C.: Empirical analysis of optimal strategic petroleum reserve in China. Energy Econ. **30**, 290–302 (2006)

5. Wei, Y.-M., China Energy Report: Strategy and Policy Research. Science Publishing Company, Beijing (2006)

6. Smeltzer, L.R., Siferd, S.P.: Proactive supply management: the management of risk. Int. J. Purch. Mater. Manag. **34**(1), 38–45 (1998)

7. Liao, S., Wang, F., Ting, W., Pan, W.: Crude oil price decision under considering emergency and release of strategic petroleum reserves. Energy **102**(1), 436–443 (2016)

8. Monge, M., Gil-Alana, L.A.: Fernando Pérez de Gracia. Crude oil price behaviour before and after military conflicts and geopolitical events. Energy **120**(1), 79–91 (2017)

9. Jabbarzadeh, A., Fahimnia, B., Sheu, J.B., et al.: Designing a supply chain resilient to major disruptions and supply/demand interruptions. Transp. Res. Part B Methodol. **94**, 121–149 (2016)

10. Bompard, E., Carpignano, A., Erriquez, M., et al.: National energy security assessment in a geopolitical perspective. Energy **130**, 144–154 (2017)

11. Benayoun, R., de Montgolfier, J., Tergny, J., Laritchev, O.: Linear programming with multiple objective functions: step method (stem). In: Computer Science and Mathematics and Statistics, vol. 1(1), December 1971

Variation of NDVI in Wetland of Nansihu Lake Based on Landsat Images

Fang Dong[✉] and Xiaoying Chi

School of Water Conservancy and Environment, University of Jinan,
Jinan, China
2008smilefang@163.com

Abstract. Normalized difference vegetation index (NDVI) was calculated using data of Landsat-5/8 to study interannual variations of wetland vegetation in spring during 1997–2015 with taking Nansihu Lake wetland as the study area. Also, correlations between NDVI and the concentration of atmospheric pollutants of the same seasons in 2015 were analyzed. The results are as followed: (1) From 1997 to 2005, average NDVI in spring decreased firstly and then increased; (2) From 1997 to 2005, total vegetation coverage decreased firstly and then increased: the proportion of extremely-low vegetation coverage was the largest with a tendency of increasing, and that of high vegetation coverage is the smallest with a tendency of decreasing; (3) R^2 of cubic multinomial regression fit between NDVI and atmospheric pollutants (SO_2, NO_2, PM_{10} and $PM_{2.5}$) were no less than 0.8, all being in negative correlation respectively. The results explain that the wetland vegetation has a function of purifying air.

Keywords: Nansihu Lake · Wetland · NDVI · Vegetation coverage
Atmospheric pollutants · Correlation analysis

1 Introduction

Wetland vegetation plays an important role in study of terrestrial ecosystem in global and regional change. Wetland vegetation cannot only remove harmful substances in wastewater but also filter atmospheric pollutants. Remote sensing has the characteristics of macroscopic, real-time and dynamic in acquiring the information of ground object, so it is an effective tool to investigate wetland vegetation [1, 2]. Since 1980s, remote sensing has become a significant means of wetland research, and has good applied effects and theoretical results [3–5].

The study aims at using NDVI from images of Landsat-5&8 to study the spatio-temporal variations of wetland vegetation coverage, and doing correlation analysis to acquire relations between NDVI and four atmospheric pollutants (SO_2, NO_2, PM_{10} and $PM_{2.5}$) quantitatively, in order to know the function of wetland in filtering atmospheric pollutants, and its significance to the environment.

Nansihu Lake wetland was taken as the study area. Nansihu Lake wetland is located in Weishan County, Jining City, Shandong province. It is composed of Weishan Lake, Zhaoyang Lake, Dushan Lake and Nanyang Lake. Nansihu Lake is located at 116°34'- 117°21'E, 34°27'- 35°20'N, which is the largest natural surface water source in Shandong province.

© Springer Nature Singapore Pte Ltd. 2018
H. Yuan et al. (Eds.): GSKI 2017, CCIS 848, pp. 297–304, 2018.
https://doi.org/10.1007/978-981-13-0893-2_31

2 Data Sources and Technical Route

2.1 Sources of Data

The images of May 1997, April 2000, May 2003, April 2007 and May 2010 were from Landsat-5. The images of January 2015, March 2015, April 2015, July 2015, October 2015, and December 2015 were of Landsat-8. The cloud cover of each image was less than 5%.

The data of atmospheric pollutants was from Jining Environmental Protection Bureau. The concentration of atmospheric pollutants (including SO_2, NO_2, PM_{10} and $PM_{2.5}$) in 2015 were of January, March, April, July, October and December in Weishan County.

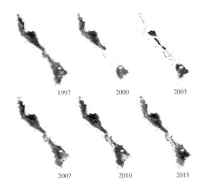

Fig. 1. Nansihu wetland area.

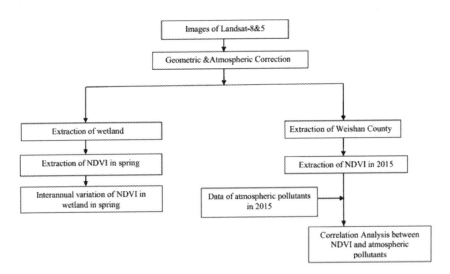

Fig. 2. Technical route.

2.2   Technical Route

Buffer zones with a radius of 5 km were taken in images (Fig. 1) to study the NDVI and vegetation coverage. Correlations between NDVI and atmospheric pollutants were analyzed based on the administrative area of Weishan County. The technical route is shown in Fig. 2.

3   Results and Discussion

3.1   Variation of Average NDVI in Spring

NDVI of 1997, 2000, 2003, 2007, 2010 and 2015 were calculating respectively by using the vegetation index images (Fig. 3). The results are shown in Table 1.

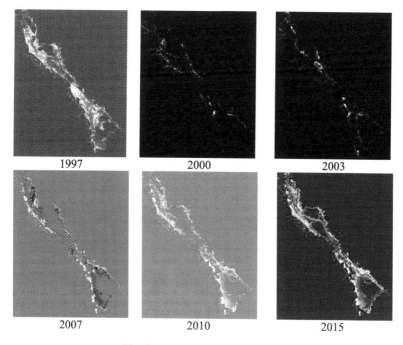

Fig. 3. Vegetation index images.

The results show that the average NDVI in spring varied from 0.05 to 0.20 per year. The minimums are between 0.0001–0.005 with little interannual changes, and the maximums are between 0.2–0.8, only being slightly small in 2000. The average NDVI of spring decreased firstly and then increased from 1997 to 2015, reaching its minimum in 2000 and maximum in 2010, and presented a drop slightly in 2015.

Table 1. Statistics of NDVI in spring.

Time	Minimum	Maximum	Average
1997	0.001157	0.536232	0.1234
2000	0.000470	0.278689	0.0567
2003	0.001961	0.500000	0.0902
2007	0.004801	0.729323	0.1817
2010	0.002758	0.688623	0.1968
2015	0.001283	0.513747	0.1497

3.2 Variation of Vegetation Coverage in Spring

Each of spring NDVI images from 1997–2015 was classified by the means of density slice with the threshold ranges of 0–0.15, 0.15–0.3, 0.3–0.5 and greater than 0.5, which represent extremely-low, low, middle and high vegetation coverage respectively. The results are shown in Fig. 4.

It can be seen that vegetation was mostly distributed in the northwest and the southeast, and little around the center. Extremely-low vegetation coverage with was mostly concentrated around the lake; Low vegetation coverage was mostly

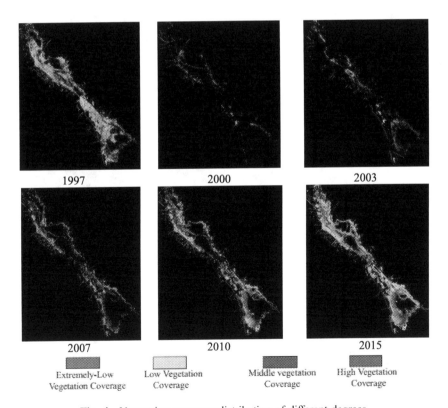

Fig. 4. Vegetation coverage distribution of different degrees.

concentrated around extremely-low vegetation coverage in the southeast; Middle vegetation coverage was also mostly concentrated around extremely-low and low vegetation coverage in the southeast; the proportion of high vegetation coverage was the smallest, which mostly distributed around the middle vegetation coverage in the southeast.

Wide distributions of extremely-low vegetation coverage in 1997 and 2015 were caused by the differentiation in NDVI of aquatic vegetation. NDVI values of floating and emergent plants are bigger, and those of submerged plants are smaller, which mostly vary from 0 to 0.15. The abundant submerged plants in 1997 and 2015 led to the result.

The statistics of wetland vegetation coverage in spring (1997–2015) are shown in Table 2. It can be concluded that the total vegetation coverage decreased firstly and then increased. Among it, the annual area of extremely-low vegetation coverage accounted for more than 50% of the total; Low vegetation coverage accounted for 5%–30% around increasing slowly year by year, reaching the maximum in 2010; Middle vegetation coverage accounted for 5%–20% around, which firstly increased and then decreased, reaching the maximum in 2003; The proportion of high vegetation did not reach 10%, and presented the tendency of decreasing.

Table 2. Statistics of vegetation coverage in spring.

Time	Area & proportion	Total	Extremely-low	Low	Middle	High
1997	Area/km^2	588.6	400.65	155.84	31.6	0.51
	Proportion/%	100	68.06	26.48	5.36	0.1
2000	Area/km^2	33.28	31.37	1.91	0	0
	Proportion/%	100	94.26	5.74	0	0
2003	Area/km^2	96.19	59.25	11.78	25.16	0
	Proportion/%	100	61.6	12.25	26.15	0
2007	Area/km^2	195.75	105.34	52.8	24.43	13.18
	Proportion/%	100	53.81	26.97	12.48	6.74
2010	Area/km^2	393.79	174.78	139	59.28	20.73
	Proportion/%	100	44.38	35.3	15.05	5.27
2015	Area/km^2	656.16	365.68	228.62	60.54	1.32
	Proportion/%	100	55.73	34.84	9.23	0.2

The reason why the coverage of the middle & high vegetation in 2000 and high vegetation in 2003 were quite low, which were almost 0, was that the drought made Nansihu Lake almost run dry, resulting in the breakdown of habitats of some aquatic plants, especially for emergent and floating plants, and plants did not grow to maturity before death.

3.3   Correlation Analysis Between Atmospheric Pollutant and NDVI

The correlation between NDVI in wetland of different time in one year and atmospheric pollutant concentration in Weishan County of the same period was analyzed (shown in Fig. 5), which explained that the variation trend of NDVI and four kinds of atmospheric pollutants (SO_2, NO_2, PM_{10} and $PM_{2.5}$) in one-year time sequence were opposite. The average NDVI reached the minimum in winter and reached the maximum in summer; the concentration of SO_2 decreased significantly from January to March, and decreased slowly from March to April, reaching the minimum in July and the maximum in December; the concentration of NO_2, PM_{10} and $PM_{2.5}$ decreased evenly from January to July and increased evenly from July to December, reaching the minimum in July and the maximum in December.

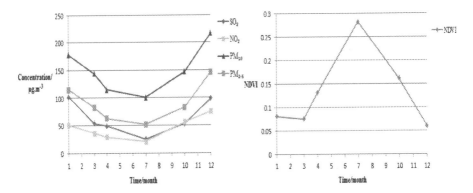

Fig. 5.   Variation of the concentration of atmospheric pollutants and NDVI in 2015.

Cubic multinomial regression fit between average NDVI and atmospheric pollutants concentration of the same period in 2015 was implemented, and the results are shown in Fig. 6. R^2 of fit between SO_2, NO_2, PM_{10}, $PM_{2.5}$ and NDVI are 0.6921, 0.8729, 0.8696 and 0.8469 respectively. R^2 of fitting between three other atmospheric pollutants and NDVI except SO_2 are more than 0.8, which shows that the three atmospheric pollutants are strongly correlated with NDVI, and the regression model is capable of certain explanatory ability; The $R^2 = 0.6921 < 0.8$ of fit between NDVI and SO_2 indicates that the regression model is not quite good for the two variables but also explains correlations in some way.

The results above show that the concentration of atmospheric pollutants is negatively correlated with average NDVI of vegetation in wetland. It can be deduced that vegetation of wetland plays a key role in purifying air, especially for the process of absorption and sedimentation of main atmospheric pollutants, such as NO_2.

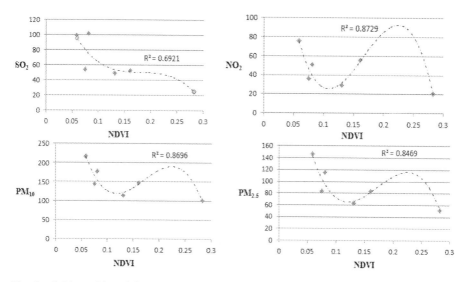

Fig. 6. Cubic multinomial regression fit between average NDVI and atmospheric pollutants concentration. The data was collected in January, March, April, July, October and December in 2015, Weishan County.

4 Conclusion

Based on the Landsat-5/8 data of 1997, 2000, 2003, 2007, 2010 and 2015, the study analyzed the spatio-tempral variation of NDVI and vegetation coverage. Also, data from January, March, April, July, October and December in 2015 was analyzed to study the correlation between atmospheric pollutants and NDVI of wetland vegetation in Weishan County. The following conclusions are obtained:

(1) The inter-annual variation of NDVI in spring firstly decreased and then increased from 1997 to 2015, reaching its minimum in 2000 and maximum is in 2010, decreasing slightly in 2015;

(2) From 1997 to 2015, the total vegetation coverage in spring in Nansihu wetland decreased firstly and then increased, with the largest of the extremely-low vegetation coverage per year; the low vegetation coverage increases year by year; the middle vegetation cover increased firstly and then decreased, except for 2000; the high vegetation coverage accounts for less than 10% of the total per year, and the trend was decreasing year by year.

(3) The concentration of atmospheric pollutants in Weishan County in 2015 are all negatively correlated with NDVI, and R^2 of three air pollutants except SO_2 are more than 0.8 with NDVI's. These three pollutants are highly correlated with NDVI, which means that the higher wetland NDVI is, the smaller the atmospheric pollutant concentration is. In other words, the larger wetland vegetation or the more areas of higher degrees of wetland vegetation are, the less atmospheric pollutants are. This indicates the importance of protecting the wetland to reduction of atmospheric pollutants.

References

1. Harvey, K.R., Hill, G.J.E.: Vegetation mapping of a tropical freshwater swamp in the Northern territory Australia: a comparison of aerial photography, Landsat TM and SPOT satellite imagery. Int. J. Remote Sens. **22**(15), 2911–2925 (2001)
2. Zhang, H., Hong, J.: Functions of plants of constructed wetlands. Wetland Sci. **2**, 146–154 (2006)
3. Han, X., Chen, X., Feng, L.: Four decades of winter wetland changes in poyang lake based on landsat observations between 1973 and 2013. Remote Sens. Environ. **156**, 426–437 (2015)
4. Wang, T.: Vegetation NDVI change and its relationship with climate change and human activities in Yulin, Shanxi Province of China. J. Geosci. Environ. Protect. **4**, 28–40 (2016)
5. Bansal, S., Katyal, D., Garg, J.K.: A novel strategy for wetland area extraction using multispectral MODIS data. Remote Sens. Environ. **200**, 183–205 (2017)

Mapping Heavy Metals in Cultivated Soils Based on Land Use Types and Cokriging

Jinling Zhao[1,2], Chuang Liu[2], Qixiang Song[3], Yan Jiang[2], Qi Hong[1,2], and Linsheng Huang[1,2(✉)]

[1] Key Laboratory of Intelligent Computing and Signal Processing, Ministry of Education, Anhui University, Hefei 230039, China
linsheng0808@163.com
[2] Anhui Engineering Laboratory of Agro-Ecological Big Data, Anhui University, Hefei 230601, China
[3] Information Engineering Institute, Suzhou University, Suzhou 234000, China

Abstract. It is extremely important to explore the heavy metal content and spatial distribution in different cultivated soils. In our study, cokriging (COK) method was used to investigate the relationship between heavy metals and land use types. A total of six heavy metals including Zn, Fe, Cu, Mn, B, S were selected to forecast the heavy metals in cultivated soils. Five types of cultivated land were considered in the study area, including vegetable land, irrigated land, irrigated paddy field, dry land, orchard. Test of normality was firstly carried out to assure that higher prediction accuracy can be obtained, and then correlation analysis and analysis of variance (*ANOVA*) were performed to find out the most sensitive heavy metals for spatial interpolation. The analysis results showed that Zn, Cu and Fe were the primary heavy metals in soil of the study area. It was obvious that the effect of Mn and Fe were much greater caused by land use types, while they were smaller for B and S. Three errors of mean standard (*MS*), root mean square error (*RMSE*), and root mean square standardized error (RMSSE) were derived to assess the prediction accuracy. In comparison with ordinary kriging (OK), the MS of COK approached to 1, the RMSE was much smaller and the RMSSE also approached to 1, which showed that COK can make better predictions than OK.

Keywords: Remote sensing · Soil heavy metal · Spatial interpolation
Land use type · Cokriging

1 Introduction

As a developing and agricultural country, China is striving to feed its people and can basically achieve self-sufficiency in grain through self-reliance. Consequently, the conflict between humans and agricultural croplands has been greatly sharpened, especially in the regions with a well-developed economy [1, 2]. Agricultural pollution (e.g. pesticides, fertilizers, plastic film) has been a leading source of many soil problems in the process of increasing the comprehensive grain production ability [3]. It is highly necessary to monitor and estimate the soil quality for ensuring the food security.

© Springer Nature Singapore Pte Ltd. 2018
H. Yuan et al. (Eds.): GSKI 2017, CCIS 848, pp. 305–311, 2018.
https://doi.org/10.1007/978-981-13-0893-2_32

Heavy metals in soil, as important indicators for assessing soil health, must be accurately monitored and analyzed, especially at a relatively large scale.

Traditionally, monitoring and identification of soil heavy metal content mainly depend on manually collecting site-specific soil samples in the field and measuring the values in the experimental room. There is no doubt that such an on-farm diagnosis method is always labor-intensive and time-consuming. Conversely, the development and innovation of earth observation and spatial analysis techniques, especially with the development of remote sensing (RS) and geographic information system (GIS) technology, have greatly improved the capability of estimating soil pollution and have been extensively used in corresponding studies on cropland landscape, arable land loss, spatial and temporal patterns of farmland, etc. [4–7]. The combination of spatial expansion of GIS and ground-based accurate measurement can be a more suitable solution for identifying and mapping the soil pollution at a regional scale.

Spatial interpolation is usually used to obtain the spatial distribution of soil nutrient status and heavy metals [8, 9]. In comparison with other interpolation methods, kriging has been approved and widely used to derive the values and distribution characteristics of specific indictors from known sample points. In this study, a total of six heavy metals were collected in five typical agricultural croplands and their relationship was also explored. Cokriging was used to predict the soil heavy metals at a regional scale.

2   Materials and Methods

2.1   Experimental Design

In our experiment, five typical agricultural croplands including vegetable land, irrigated land, irrigated paddy field, dry land and orchard, were selected to estimate their soil heavy metal contents. Two different analysis methods were respectively considered. On one hand, different agricultural croplands were used as the variables to estimate a certain soil heavy metal content. On the other hand, a certain agricultural cropland was used for estimating different soil heavy metal. In addition, the planting crop was also considered to find the relationship between agricultural cropland and soil heavy metal. Finally, the soil heavy metals were mapped and quantitatively analyzed.

2.2   Data Collection and Preprocessing

Three types of data sources were collected including Landsat time series, soil sample points and agricultural statistic data. Multi-temporal Landsat imagery were firstly pre-processed for extracting agricultural croplands. Field sampling was also carried out to obtain the ground census data of soil heavy metal. A total of six heavy metals including Zn, Fe, Cu, Mn, B, S were collected. R was used eliminate the abnormal values for making better predictions. Those sampling points could be overlaid on the agricultural croplands for finding the spatial distribution and selecting the suitable interpolation method.

2.3   Sampling Method and Analysis of Variance

Stratifying sampling (80%) was used to estimate the soil heavy metal for a certain agricultural cropland. Analysis of variance (ANOVA) is a collection of statistical models used to analyze the differences among group means and their associated procedures (such as "variation" among and between groups), developed by statistician and evolutionary biologist Ronald Fisher [10]. In our study, five land use types were used as independent variables the and six soil heavy metals were used as the dependent variables. ANOVA was used to investigate the significance effect of heavy metals caused by land use types.

2.4   Cokriging

Cokriging is an enhanced interpolation method which uses information on several variable types [11]. The main variable of interest is Z_1, and both autocorrelation for Z_1 and cross-correlations between Z_1 and all other variable types are used to make better predictions. It is appealing to use information from other variables to help make predictions, but it comes at a price. Let us suppose that there is a total of n measured points $(x_1, x_2, x_3, \ldots, x_n)$, whose spatial estimation value $(Z_*(x_0))$ is jointly determined by $Z_1(x_i)$ and $Z_2(x_j)$. The co variation function is shown in the following equation:

$$\gamma_{12}(h) = E\{[Z_1(x+h) - Z_1(x)][Z_2(x+h) - Z_2(x)]\} \tag{1}$$

The interpolation formula of cokriging is shown in the following equation:

$$Z_*(x_0) = \sum_{i=1}^{n} a_i Z_1(x_i) + \sum_{j=1}^{m} b_j Z_2(x_j) \tag{2}$$

where $Z_*(x_0)$ is the heavy metal content of estimated point, n and m are respectively the number of sample points for primary and secondary variables, $Z_1(x_i)$ and $Z_2(x_j)$ are respectively the heavy metal content, a_i and b_j are respectively the weights, and $\Sigma a_i = 1$ and $\Sigma b_j = 0$.

2.5   Accuracy Evaluation

Cross-validation is a model validation technique for assessing how the results of a statistical analysis will generalize to an independent data set [12]. Three indicators were selected to perform the accuracy evaluation including mean standard (*MS*), root mean square error (*RMSE*), and root mean square standardized error (*RMSSE*).

$$MS = \frac{1}{n} \sum_{i=1}^{n} [Z(x_i) - Z(x_{0i})] \Big/ \sigma(x_i) \tag{3}$$

$$RMSE = \sqrt{\frac{1}{n} \sum_{i=1}^{n} [Z(x_i) - Z(x_{0i})]} \tag{4}$$

$$RMSSE = \sqrt{\sum_{i=1}^{n} \left\{ [Z(x_i) - Z(x_{0i})]/\sigma(x_i) \right\}^2 \Big/ n} \qquad (5)$$

where $Z(x_i)$ is the measured values, $Z(x_{0i})$ is the predicted value, n is the number of validated sampling points, and $\sigma(x_i)$ is the variance square root.

3 Results and Discussion

3.1 Test of Normality

To improve the prediction accuracy, it is an extremely important step to perform a test of normality of sampling points. Four methods in R software were used to achieve such a goal. We found that all the p-values of each heavy metal were less than 2.2e-16 and they could not meet the requirements of normality. When making some changes in R software, all the p-values were greater than 0.05 (Table 1).

Table 1. Test of normality using the four methods in R software.

	Zn	Fe	Cu	Mn
Cramer-von Mises	0.3275	0.9362	0.2985	0.111
AD	0.1932	0.9302	0.2847	0.1039
Pearson	0.4369	0.7205	0.06105	0.262
Lilliefors	0.3708	0.9807	0.1218	0.1133

3.2 Analysis of Correlation

R software was used to carry out the analysis of correlation among six heavy metals (Table 2). It was obvious that they showed positively significant correlation among Zn, Cu and Fe at the probability level of 0.01. Similarly, they showed also significant correlation positively between Cu and Mn. They analysis results showed that Zn, Cu

Table 2. Correlation testing for each soil heavy metal.

	Zn	Fe	Cu	Mn	B	S
Zn	1					
Fe	0.109**	1				
Cu	0.127**	0.333**	1			
Mn	0.0324	0.0316*	0.017**	1		
B	−0.049	−0.0333	0.0245	−0.00917	1	
S	−0.00521	−0.00113	−0.0029	−0.00485	−0.022	1

** indicates significance differences at the probability level of 0.01, and * indicates significance differences at the probability level of 0.05.

and Fe were the primary heavy metals in soil of the study area. The reasons might be that mining activities produced many sulfide-bearing mine tailings. Lots of heavy metals were introduced by much acid during the oxidation process [13].

3.3   Results of ANOVA

The significance effect of each heavy metal caused by land use types was performed in R software (Table 3). We supposed that there was no effect of heavy metal caused by land use types. It was obvious that the effect of Mn and Fe were much greater caused by land use types, while they were smaller for B and S.

Table 3. Significance of six soil heavy metals using five land use types.

	Zn	Fe	Cu	Mn	B	S
P-value	0.0768	0.0005866	0.09113	0.0000008614	0.4263	0.4511

3.4   Spatial Interpolation

According to the results of ANOVA, the spatial interpolation was just performed (Fig. 1).

We could find that the cokriging based interpolation results showed more differences in different sub-regions. For both Mn (Fig. 1a) and Fe (Fig. 1b), the spatial differences were much smaller in the northwestern part. The reason was that little sampling points were collected in the region due to the existence of built-up areas and other non-soil types. It is an alternate solution to eliminate such a phenomenon by masking the non-soil types [14, 15].

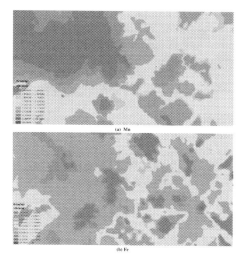

Fig. 1. Spatial interpolation of Mn (a) and Fe (b).

3.5 Validation of Interpolation

80% stratifying sampling was adopted to construct the interpolation models. To validate the prediction accuracy, cross-validation and ordinary kriging were used to compare the accuracies. Cross-validation is assumed that each measured point is not obtained and then is estimated using the n-1 points [16, 17]. The interpolation result is assessed by the rest 20% data. Three errors of MS, $RMSE$ and $RMSSE$ were derived (Table 4). It was obvious that, in comparison with ordinary kriging, the MS of cokriging approached to 1, the $RMSE$ was much smaller and the $RMSSE$ also approached to 1, which showed that COK can make better predictions than OK.

Table 4. Comparison of errors between ordinary kriging (OK) and cokriging (COK).

Heavy metal	MS		RMSE		RMSSE	
	OK	COK	OK	COK	OK	COK
Mn	−0.001957	0.000837	20.81	20.39	1.0725	1.0212
Zn	0.00367	−0.000815	73.01	71.51	0.9516	0.9549
Fe	−0.001	−0.0027	19.00	18.92	1.6593	1.5569

4 Conclusion

Cokriging interpolation is a reliable method to predict soil heavy metals and spatially map the distribution in a region. To get a prediction accuracy, it is a key step to carry out the test of normality and change to normal distribution before using the cokriging method. In addition, the correlation among different heavy metals must be also performed to determine whether COK is suitable for a certain heavy metal. When mapping the heavy metals, some disturbance land use types must be firstly eliminated and masked. For example, the agricultural croplands can be identified using remote sensing based techniques and cokriging is just performed on the masked regions.

Acknowledgements. This work was supported by and Anhui Provincial Major Scientific and Technological Special Project (17030701062), National Key Research and Development Program of China (2016YFD0800904), Fund for "Integration of Cloud Computing and Big Data, Innovation of Science and Education" (2017A10014), and Application Research of Anhui Provincial Public Welfare Technology on Linkage Projects (1704f0704059).

References

1. DeFries, R.S., Foley, J.A., Asner, G.P.: Land-use choices: balancing human needs and ecosystem function. Front. Ecol. Environ. **2**, 249–257 (2004)
2. Eklund, L., Persson, A., Pilesjö, P.: Cropland changes in times of conflict, reconstruction, and economic development in Iraqi Kurdistan. Ambio **45**, 78–88 (2016)
3. Tournebize, J., Chaumont, C., Mander, Ü.: Implications for constructed wetlands to mitigate nitrate and pesticide pollution in agricultural drained watersheds. Ecol. Eng. **103**, 415–425 (2017)

4. Ye, Y., Zhang, H., Liu, K., Wu, Q.: Research on the influence of site factors on the expansion of construction land in the Pearl River Delta, China: by using GIS and remote sensing. Int. J. Appl. Earth Obs. **21**, 366–373 (2013)

5. Kumar, A., Devi, M., Deshmukh, B.: Integrated remote sensing and geographic information system based RUSLE modelling for estimation of soil loss in western Himalaya. India. Water Resour. Manag. **28**, 3307–3317 (2014)

6. Pandey, B., Seto, K.C.: Urbanization and agricultural land loss in India: comparing satellite estimates with census data. J. Environ. Manage. **148**, 53–66 (2015)

7. Gaubi, I., Chaabani, A., Mammou, A.B., Hamza, M.H.: A GIS-based soil erosion prediction using the Revised Universal Soil Loss Equation (RUSLE) (Lebna watershed, Cap Bon, Tunisia). Nat. Hazards **86**, 219–239 (2017)

8. Zhao, J.L., Xue, Y.A., Yang, H., Huang, L.S., Zhang, D.Y.: Evaluating and classifying field-scale soil nutrient status in Beijing using 3S technology. Int. J. Agric. Biol. **14**, 689–696 (2012)

9. Ha, H., Olson, J.R., Bian, L., Rogerson, P.A.: Analysis of heavy metal sources in soil using kriging interpolation on principal components. Environ. Sci. Technol. **48**, 4999–5007 (2014)

10. Shaw, D.J., Vrij, A., Leal, S., Mann, S., Hillman, J., Granhag, P.A., Fisher, R.P.: Expect the unexpected? Variations in question type elicit cues to deception in joint interviewer contexts. Appl. Cogn. Psych. **27**, 336–343 (2013)

11. Yang, Q., Luo, W., Jiang, Z., Li, W., Yuan, D.: Improve the prediction of soil bulk density by cokriging with predicted soil water content as auxiliary variable. J. Soil Sediment. **16**, 77–84 (2016)

12. Braga-Neto, U.M., Dougherty, E.R.: Is cross-validation valid for small-sample microarray classification? Bioinformatics **20**, 374–380 (2004)

13. Boularbah, A., Schwartz, C., Bitton, G., Morel, J.L.: Heavy metal contamination from mining sites in South Morocco: 1. Use of a biotest to assess metal toxicity of tailings and soils. Chemosphere **63**, 802–810 (2006)

14. Stein, A., Hoogerwerf, M., Bouma, J.: Use of soil-map delineations to improve (co-) kriging of point data on moisture deficits. Geoderma **43**, 163–177 (1988)

15. Zhang, C., Li, W., Travis, D.J.: Restoration of clouded pixels in multispectral remotely sensed imagery with cokriging. Int. J. Remote Sens. **30**, 2173–2195 (2009)

16. Wong, T.T., Yang, N.Y.: Dependency analysis of accuracy estimates in k-fold cross validation. IEEE Trans. Knowl. Data Eng. **29**, 2417–2427 (2017)

17. Gu, B., Sheng, V.S., Tay, K.Y., Romano, W., Li, S.: Cross validation through two-dimensional solution surface for cost-sensitive SVM. IEEE Trans. Pattern Anal. **39**, 1103–1121 (2017)

Detection of Redundant Condition Expression for Large Scale Source Code

Dandan Gong[⊠], Wensheng Xu, Chunfang Qiu, and Libei Zhou

Shanghai Institute of Aerospace Information,
Shanghai Academy of Spaceflight Technology, Shanghai 201109, China
gongdandan0418@126.com

Abstract. Redundant condition expression not only causes noise in code debugging which confuses developers, but also correlates with the presence of traditional severe software errors. In this paper, an approach is proposed to detect the redundant condition expression, and the detailed algorithm is provided. The experiments on large scale open source software systems show that our approach can find redundant condition expression efficiently. It is very convenient for developers to detect and correct the defects by our approach, and thereby to further guarantee the software quality.

Keywords: Redundant condition expression · Abstract syntax tree
Lexical analysis

1 Introduction

Redundant condition expression means the branch statements are always true or false, so the state and the control flow of program cannot be affected. Redundant condition expression signals the use of the wrong variables. Otherwise, redundant condition expression always correlate with traditional hard errors, such as an unintentionally lost result and calculations aborted by unexpected control flow.

There have been limited researches about redundant condition expression by now. The first approach uses constraint solving [1, 2] and symbolic execution [3, 4] to detect infeasible paths [5, 6]. This approach can check for "impossible" conditions accurately, but its computational-complexity is very high. So it is not suitable for analyzing large open source projects. The second approach is based on interval arithmetic [7]. Only partial unreachable path defects can be detected when the interval arithmetic is applied in program static analysis, and the detection accuracy is relatively low. The interval operations of nonlinear functions and interval operations of complex conditional expressions can not be solved using interval arithmetic. The above two methods are based on the analysis of control dependency graph [8] and data dependency graph [9], and the complexity of the analysis is not suitable for testing large software.

Totally speaking, existing approaches all have limits in detecting redundant condition expression. A sound redundant condition expression system should has the following characteristic.

(1) It should be industrial strength and applicable to one hundred thousand-line size system within affordable computation time usage.
(2) It should have the ability to report only helpful information for user to examine redundant code. In other words, it needs to produce accurate results.

In this paper, we propose a redundant condition expression detection approach for large scale source code. Firstly, an overview of redundant condition expression detection is proposed. Then, the detailed detection methods are described. Finally, the faults in large scale source code are presented and discussed. The test method based on the abstract syntax tree is widely used for duplicating code detection because of its optimal spatial and temporal efficiency. This method has less time and space overhead, so it is suitable for large-scale program analysis.

2 Redundant Condition Expression Detection Approach

The model of redundant condition expression detection is shown in Fig. 1.

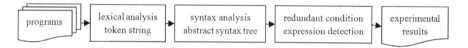

Fig. 1. The model of redundant condition expression detection

(1) Lexical analysis, transform the source code into token string and do struct and typedef identifiers analysis on the token string.
(2) Syntax analysis, generate AST (abstract syntax tree). The syntax tree is a graphical representation of the procedural syntax specification process, not only the complete lexical and grammatical information of the program, but also the corresponding representation of the syntax in each step of the grammar analysis, as shown in Fig. 2.
(3) Detect the redundant condition expression based on AST (as shown in Fig. 2), and display the experimental results.

In this paper, a set is maintained according to analysis of conditional expressions based on AST. Our approach analyzes the assignment statements and conditional branch statements to derive variable-constant bindings, so as to test the conditional expression behind. Then, the conditional expressions are collected which are true along the current path and test the validity of subsequent control predicates.
The type of each node is analyzed by traveling AST.

(1) If it is an assignment subtree or increment or decrement subtree, derive variable-constant bindings and adjust the set.
(2) If it is a selection subtree or iteration subtree, the value of the conditional expression is calculated according to variable-constant information. The redundant conditional expression is reported if the value is true or false. The selection

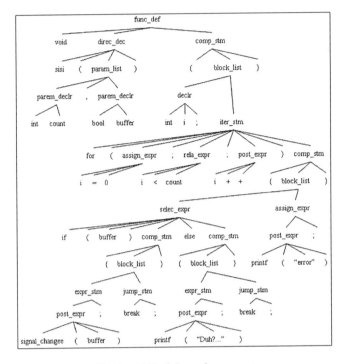

Fig. 2. AST of the code segment

subtree or iteration subtree is further analyzed according to (3) if the conditional expression cannot be calculated.

(3) For selection subtree and iteration subtree which the conditional expression cannot be calculated, first backup the set and add the conditional expression into set. Traverse the subtree using the variable-constant information known. After the analysis of subtree is finished, delete the variable which the value is changed in the subtree from the set, which is used as known information for subsequent program analysis.

3   Experiment and Discussion

Our approach is used to detect the faults in large scale source code. We have analyzed part of the gcc-core-2.95(34045 lines), part of the Linux 1.0 and Linux 2.4.5 (130868 lines) with our approach. The experiment environment is Lenovo T540P (Intel(R) Core (TM) i7-4710MQ CPU @2.50 GHz 2.50 GHz, Memory 16.00 GB). The results show that our approach has a low false positive and a low time-complexity. The false positive is 0% in the 34 thousands lines code. For more than 130 thousands lines code, the false positive is also 0%. The false positive is measured by formula 1. It calculates the ratio of the number of the wrong detection to all detected defects. The experimental result was shown in Table 1.

Table 1. The results in detection of large open source projects.

Open source	Code lines	Total time (s)	Testing results	Redundant conditionals
gcc-core-2.95	34045	6.2	Wrong detection	0
			Real defect	0
Linux 1.0 and Linux 2.4.5	130868	25.5	Wrong detection	0
			Real defect	4

$$\text{false positive} = \frac{\text{wrong detection}}{\text{wrong detection} + \text{real defect}} \times 100\% \qquad (1)$$

```
/*Linux 1.0/drivers/block/mcd.c*/
1 int check_mcd_media_change(int full_dev, int flag)
2 {
3   int retval, target;
4 #if 1
5     return 0;
6 #endif
7   target=MINOR(full_dev);
8   ......
9 }
```

Fig. 3. The statements cannot be executed

```
/*Linux 2.4.5-ac8/fs/fat/inode.c*/
1 error=0;
2 if(!error) {
3   sbi->fat_bits=fat32?32:
4     (fat/fat:
5     (sbi->clusters>MSDOS_FAT12?16:12));
```

Fig. 4. The nonsense programming style

Some real faults are detected by this approach as shown from Figs. 3, 4, 5, and 6.

In Fig. 3, the condition expression is true by the conditional compilation in line 4, and this function always return 0 on line 5, so the statements after line 7 cannot be executed forever.

```
/*Linux 2.4.5-ac8/drivers/net/tokenring/smctr.c*/
1 while((status=tp->rx_fcb_curr[queue] ->frame_status)!=SUCCESS);
2 {
3   err=HARDWARE_FAILED;
4   ... /*large chunk of apparent recovery code, with no updates to
err*/
5   if(err!=SUCCESS)
6         break;
7 }
```

Fig. 5. Redundant conditional that suggests a serious program error

```
/*Linux 2.4.5-ac8/drivers/scsi/qlal280.c*/
1 srb_p=q->q_first;
2 while(srb_p)
3   srb_p=srb_p->s_nest;
4   if(srb_p)
5     sp->s_prev=srb_p->s_prev;
6   if(srb_p->s_prev)
7     rb_p->s_prev ->s_next=sp;
8   else
```

Fig. 6. A serious error in a linked list insertion implementation

In Fig. 4, the value *error* is assignment 0 in line 1, and the conditional expression is always true in line 2. There was no obvious mistake, but the statement was confusing. I don't know what the function of this expression is, and the expression increase the complexity of program understanding.

In Fig. 5, the variable err is not updated before the conditional judgment in line 5, and the value of err is never SUCCESS. The conditional expression for line 5 is always true. After the break statement is executed, the while loop is out of the loop so that the statements in the loop are executed at most once. This is likely to indicate an error: users forget to update the value of err, and such errors are hard to find in debugging.

Figure 6 has a serious error in line 4. When the while loop in line 2 ends, the value of the variable srb_p is false, causing the fourth row to always be false, so all statements in if branch will never be executed.

4   Conclusion

In this paper, a redundant condition expression detection approach is proposed to detect redundant code. This method detects the redundant condition expression based on AST, which can effectively detect the defects in large scale open source software systems.

Introducing set and equivalence class set into path-sensitive analysis is beneficial to calculating values of conditional expression, and it also can be applied to not only software defects detection but also code recognition to make them more powerful and flexible.

Experimental results show that our approach can find redundant condition expression accurately and also has a low time-complexity. It can be applied to software defects detection, as well as to software maintenance and software testing to improve software quality.

Acknowledgments. This research is supported by the Natural Science Foundation of Shanghai (Grant No. 15ZR1421400).

References

1. Jin, J.W., Ma, F.F., Zhang, J.: Brief introduction to SMT solving. J. Front. Comput. Sci. Technol. **9**(7), 769–780 (2015)
2. Li, J., Liu, W.W.: A survey on theoretical combination techniques of SMT solvers. Comput. Eng. Sci. **33**(10), 111–119 (2011)
3. Baluda, M., Denaro, G., Pezze, M.: Bidirectional symbolic analysis for effective branch testing. IEEE Trans. Softw. Eng. **42**(5), 403–426 (2016)
4. Cadar, C., Sen, K.: Symbolic execution for software testing: three decades later. Commun. ACM **56**(2), 82–90 (2013)
5. Guo, X., Wang, P., Wang, J.Y., Zhang, H.G.: Program multiple execution paths verification based on k proximity weakest precondition. Chin. J. Comput. **11**, 2203–2214 (2015)
6. Xiao, X., Zhang, X.S., Li, X.D.: New approach to path explosion problem of symbolic execution. In: 2010 First International Conference on Pervasive Computing, Signal Processing and Applications, pp. 301–304 (2010)
7. Wang, Y.W., Gong, Y.Z., Xiao, Q., Yang, Z.H.: Variable range analysis based on interval computation. J. Beijing Univ. Posts Telecommun. **32**, 36–41 (2009)
8. Dandan, G., Xiaohong, S., Tiantian, W., Peijun, M., Yu, W.: State dependency probabilistic model for fault localization. Inf. Softw. Technol. **57**, 430–445 (2015)
9. Baah, G.K., Podgurski, A., Harrold, M.J.: The probabilistic program dependence graph and its application to fault diagnosis. IEEE Trans. Softw. Eng. **36**(4), 528–545 (2010)

Airplane Fine-Grained Classification in Remote Sensing Images via Transferred CNN-Based Models

Li Yan[1], Shouhong Wan[1,2(✉)], Peiquan Jin[1,2], and Chang Zou[1]

[1] School of Computer Science and Technology,
University of Science and Technology of China, Hefei 230027, China
{yanli15, kkpanda}@mail.ustc.edu.cn,
{wansh, jpq}@ustc.edu.cn
[2] Key Laboratory of Electromagnetic Space Information,
Chinese Academy of Science, Hefei 230027, China

Abstract. Airplane fine-grained classification is a challenging task in the field of remote sensing, because it requires for differentiating varieties of airplanes. Convolutional neural networks (CNNs) have recently achieved remarkable progress, due to their ability to learn high-level feature representations. However, training CNNs requires a large number of data, and there are few mature and public data sets concerned on airplane fine-grained classification in remote sensing images. In this paper, we propose a transferred CNN-based model that focus on airplane fine-grained classification by adopting a pre-trained CNN-based model with a large source data set and fine-tuning the model on a small task-specific data set. For fine-tuning the model, we collect a new data set, 11 Types of Airplanes in Remote Sensing Images (ARSI-11), which consists of 2200 images of 11 types of airplanes. The experimental results demonstrate that our transferred CNN-based model significantly improves the classification performance than the comparative methods.

Keywords: Airplane fine-grained classification · Remote sensing images
Convolutional neural networks · Transferred CNN-based models

1 Introduction

Over the past few decades, a considerable number of remote sensing images now are available with the rapid development of modern remote sensing technology, which facilitates a wide range of civilian and military applications such as land planning, traffic monitoring, disaster prevention, military reconnaissance and military mapping. In these applications, airplane target recognition is one of the research hotspot of remote sensing images interpretation and understanding, in which airplane fine-grained classification has attracted increasing attention due to the abundant visual and contextual information contained in high spatial resolution remote sensing images. However, fine-grained classification of airplane remains a great challenge in the remote sensing field because of the cluttered background, illumination variations, airplane appearance complexity, the variation between each airplane type, and the multiple scale of airplane.

© Springer Nature Singapore Pte Ltd. 2018
H. Yuan et al. (Eds.): GSKI 2017, CCIS 848, pp. 318–326, 2018.
https://doi.org/10.1007/978-981-13-0893-2_34

Note that there have been fewer studies concerning the airplane fine-grained classification task. In contrast to coarse-grained classification, the fine-grained classification of airplane requires for differentiating various types of airplanes, faced for remote sensing images. Li et al. [1] proposed a scheme based on tree classifier for airplane fine-grained classification in remote sensing images. Zhang et al. [2] presented an algorithm based on extraction of closed contour and partial feature matching for airplane fine-grained classification in remote sensing images. Wu et al. [3] determined the types of airplanes by the combination of three features including Multi-Scale Auto-convolutions, Pseudo-Zernike moments and Harris-Laplace features. Although, these works can address the issue, the features they used are low-level and hand-designed which affect the representational ability as well as the performance for airplane fine-grained classification.

Deep learning is becoming an emerging technique with the advent of the era of big data in recent years, its essential is learning powerful and hierarchical feature representations from large collections of data by building multi-layer structural machine learning models and being applied data analysis and prediction. Due to the advances of deep learning theory [4], a great amount of effort has achieved revolutionary performance than traditional approaches in a wide range of domains and in a variety of applications. Nowadays, convolutional neural networks (CNNs), as one of the most representative deep learning models, have made significant achievements in many computer vision fields such as handwritten numeral recognition [5], face recognition [6], scene classification [7], and so on. A large quantity of remarkable CNN models have been proposed to meet ImageNet Large Scale Visual Recognition Challenge (ILSVRC) [8], particularly the work of Krizhevsky et al. [9] which obtained the top-5 error rates of 16.4%, dramatically lower than the previous state-of-the-art result (26.2%). In 2017, the last year of ILSVRC, the WMW team proposed Squeeze-and-Excitation networks and won the first place in the image classification task with the classification error rates of 2.251% [10], which is beyond the human being ability to identify the classification of objects. Compared with traditional human-designed features, the CNN-based model relies on neural networks of deep architecture to extract much more powerful feature representation. Moreover, the feature captured by higher layers of CNN performs more semantic characteristics, which lead to performance improvements on object classification and recognition.

In order to train a CNN model with strong generalization ability and high classification accuracy, large amounts of training data is necessary. Recently, much of the deep learning model dealing with classification of nature scene images has been well studied with a huge volume of training data and achieved outstanding marks. However, in the case of airplane fine-grained classification in remote sensing images, the training data is not large enough, and there are few mature and public data sets. Therefore, it is posing a profound challenge for using CNN-based models to deal with airplane fine-grained classification in remote sensing images.

Due to the above-mentioned issues, in this paper, we firstly propose a transferred CNN-based model involved in airplane fine-grained classification in remote sensing images by adopting a supervised pre-trained CNN-based model with a large source data set like ImageNet [8] and fine-tuning the model on a small task-specific date set. And this model is capable of acquiring more semantic concepts and capturing high-level feature representations. Second, to fine-tune the proposed airplane fine-grained classification model, a new data set, 11 Types of Airplanes in Remote Sensing Images (ARSI-11), is collected from the Google Earth imagery and artificially augmented, which consists of totally 2200 images of 11 types of airplanes. In the experiments, we compare the proposed method with other five methods by carrying out airplane fine-grained classification on ARSI-11 data set. The results indicate that our proposed transferred CNN-based model outperforms the tradition methods.

The rest of this paper is organized as follows. In Sect. 2, we present the proposed transferred CNN-based model. Section 3 gives the details of ARSI-11 data set. Section 4 reports the details of our experiments and results of different methods on our own data set. Finally, conclusion and future work are drawn in Sect. 5.

2   Transferred CNN-Based Model

In this section, we present our proposed transferred CNN-based model for airplane fine-grained classification in remote sensing images. Figure 1 illustrates the overall architecture of the proposed model. Here, we describe the details of components in the model, and discuss two stages in the model, which consists of the pre-training stage and the fine-tuning stage.

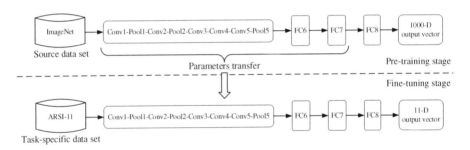

Fig. 1. The overall architecture of the proposed transferred CNN-based model.

2.1   Model Architecture

The proposed transferred model, in this paper, is based on a typical CNN, i.e. AlexNet [9]. It is mainly composed of multiple alternations of convolutional layers and max-pooling layers, followed by several fully-connected layers and a softmax layer. The details of each layer are described as follows.

Convolutional Layer. The input of the convolutional layer is a 3-dimensional vector of size $W \times H \times N$ with N 2-dimensional feature maps $X_i^{l-1}(i = 1, \ldots, N)$, and the output of this layer is also a 3-dimensional vector $W' \times H' \times M$, which is composed of M feature maps $X_j^l(j = 1, \ldots, M)$. The input feature maps are convolved with M learnable kernels k_{ij}^l (also called filters or weights) of size $F \times F \times N$ and put through the non-linear activation function $f(x)$ to form the output feature maps $X_j^l (j = 1, \ldots, M)$. Hence, each feature map of the convolutional layer is computed as

$$X_j^l = f(\sum_{i=1}^{N} X_i^{l-1} * k_{ij}^l + b_j^l), \tag{1}$$

where $*$ is the 2-dimensional discrete convolutional operator, and b_j^l denotes the learnable bias parameter of the j-th output feature map.

With the use of the non-linear activation function, the input and output of the convolutional layer are strongly non-linear mapped, which has more powerful performance. The most common non-linear activation functions are hyperbolic tangent functions, sigmoid functions, and rectified linear units (ReLUs) [11]. Choosing the ReLU as the activation function is a common strategy, due to its advantages in the avoidance of overfitting and the convergence of the training stage. The ReLU function is given by

$$f(x) = \max(0, x). \tag{2}$$

In fact, there are three hyper-parameters control the size of the output feature map: the depth of the output feature map M, stride S and zero-padding P. Specifically, the depth of the output feature map is equal to the number of convolutional kernels, and the stride defines the intervals when sliding the kernels on the input feature map. Moreover, it is convenient for preserving the spatial size of the feature map by padding the border of the input feature map with zeros. Hence, the size of the output can be computed as

$$W' = (W - F + 2P)/S + 1, \tag{3}$$

$$H' = (H - F + 2P)/S + 1. \tag{4}$$

Pooling Layer: The pooling layer involves reducing the amount of parameters and computation in the network and controlling overfitting. It executes a max operation respectively map and outputs the maximum value within a local spatial patch on each feature. To be more specific, given that a pooling layer with the size of $F \times F$, an input with the size of $W \times H \times D$, and the stride S, then the size of the output is $W' \times H' \times D'$, where

$$W' = (W - F)/S + 1, \tag{5}$$

$$H' = (H - F)/S + 1, \tag{6}$$

$$D' = D. \tag{7}$$

Softmax Layer: After the convolutional and pooling layers, a softmax layer is introduced for multi-classification. The goal of this layer is to predict the correct category associated with the input. Note that a softmax normalization is performed in the softmax layer for guaranteeing the output is based on a probability distribution. In other words, the final output of the softmax layer is a K-dimensional vector, where K is the number of classes, and the output vector corresponds to the probabilities $P(y = k|x), k = 1, \ldots, K$. The form of the softmax normalization is as follows:

$$\sigma(z)_i = \frac{\exp(z_i)}{\sum\limits_{k=1}^{K} \exp(z_k)}, \tag{8}$$

where z is an input vector, i.e., the output of the previous fully-connected layer. Let L denotes the loss function, which quantifies the misclassification by comparing the output vector $\hat{y}^i$ and the ground truth vector y^i. The cross-entropy loss function is commonly adopted, and defined as

$$L = -\frac{1}{N} \sum\limits_{n=1}^{N} \sum\limits_{k=1}^{K} y_k^n \log \hat{y}_k^n, \tag{9}$$

where N is the number of training examples. Note that minimizing this loss function can increase the probability of the correct category. In practice, a regularization parameter $\lambda ||w||^2$ is generally introduced into the loss function to avoid overfitting.

2.2 The Pre-training Stage

The typical CNN architecture of the AlexNet consists of approximately 60 million parameters. Directly training such tremendous parameters from only a few thousand training image data with a random parameter initialization can be problematic [12]. Hence, in this work, we carry out a pre-training stage. The goal of this stage is to train the parameters on the source data set like ImageNet and then transfer them to a new model for better suiting the task-specific data set.

In the pre-training stage, we use the network architecture of the AlexNet. It consists of five convolutional layers Conv1, Conv2, Conv3, Conv4, and Conv5, three pooling layers Pool1, Pool2, and Pool5, and three fully-connected layers FC6, FC7, and FC8. Note that local response normalization (LRN) is applied to the output of the first and second convolutional layers [9], and an effective regularization method called Dropout is used in the first two fully-connected layers (FC6 and FC7) to reduce overfitting by randomly setting the output of each fully-connected hidden neuron to 0 with probability 0.5 [13]. We then train the CNN model in pre-training stage on the ImageNet Large Scale Visual Recognition Challenge that has more than 1.2 million images categorized under 1000 object classes.

2.3 The Fine-Tuning Stage

The idea of the fine-tuning stage is to adapt an existing pre-trained CNN model to a different task by fine-tuning the parameters on a new data set. The typical CNNs generally extract the low-level features like edge in the early layers and the top layer contains high-level features related to the specific task. Therefore, the parameter trained in low-level layers can be transferred, while the parameter of higher layers needs to be fine-tuned for task adaptation.

In fine-tuning stage, we first transfer the parameters of the pre-trained CNN model in the previous stage to the CNN model dealing with the specific task. This model has the same architecture with the pre-trained model and the exception is the last fully-connected layer FC8 whose dimension of output vectors depends on the number of categories in the data set. In this work, we replace the last fully-connected layer of the pre-train model with a new fully-connected layer whose dimension of output vector is 11, because the task-specific data set, ARSI-11, has 11 types of airplanes.

3 Data Set

To help facilitate the state of the arts in airplane fine-grained classification of remote sensing images and evaluate our proposed method, we construct ARSI-11, a new data set for airplane fine-grained classification in remote sensing images. The ARSI-11 data set contains 2200 airplane images, which is made up of 11 types of airplanes. And the images are collected from Google Earth imagery with various spatial resolutions ranging from 0.3 to 1.0 m. Some sample images from ARSI-11 data set are shown in Fig. 2.

Fig. 2. Sample images from our ARSI-11 data set. From top left to bottom right: Airliner, KC-10, and E-3.

As known to all, some specific types of airplanes are too scarce to be captured by remote sensing sensors. Hence, this hinders the process of collecting enough airplane images. To tackle this issue, we perform a method of airplane image data simulation for artificially synthesizing the samples of some specific types of airplanes in remote sensing images. Firstly we segment the foreground airplane target from the background in a collected airplane image. Secondly, we randomly select an image that does not contain any airplane targets from background images such as airport runways and landing field. Thirdly, we embed the extracted airplane target image, with rotations and flips, into the background image, and both the airplane and the background are captured by the same remote sensing sensor and with the same spatial resolution. The flowchart of this simulation strategy is illustrated in Fig. 3. After the simulation, there are 200 images for each type of airplane.

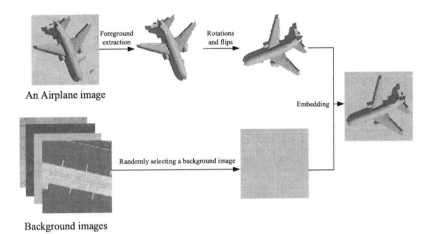

An Airplane image

Background images

Fig. 3. The flowchart of the airplane image simulation strategy

4   Experimental Results and Analysis

In our experiment, we employ the AlexNet CNN model provided in Caffe library [14]. As listed in Table 1, the AlexNet requires inputs of a fixed $227 \times 227 \times 3$ image size. After two alternations of convolutional and pooling layers, 256 feature map with the size of 13×13 is output. The third, fourth, and fifth convolutional layers are connected in turn without pooling layers. The third convolutional layer Conv3 takes the output of the second pooling layer Pool2 as input and filters it with 384 kernels of size $3 \times 3 \times 256$. The fourth convolutional layer contains 384 kernels of size $3 \times 3 \times 384$, and the fifth convolutional layer has 256 kernels of size $3 \times 3 \times 384$. The series of convolutional layers is followed by a pooling layer Pool5 and three fully-connected layers F6, F7 and F8. The output of the last fully-connected layer F8 is a 1000-dimension vector, i.e. a probability distribution over the 1000 class labels.

Table 1. The details of network configurations of the AlexNet used in our experiments.

Layer	Input	Kernel	Stride	Pad	Output
Conv1	227*227*3	11*11	4	0	55*55*96
Pool1	55*55*96	3*3	2	0	27*27*96
Conv2	27*27*96	5*5	1	2	27*27*256
Pool2	27*27*256	3*3	2	0	13*13*256
Conv3	13*13*256	3*3	1	1	13*13*384
Conv4	13*13*384	3*3	1	1	13*13*384
Conv5	13*13*384	3*3	1	1	13*13*256
Pool5	13*13*256	3*3	2	0	6*6*256
FC6	6*6*256	6*6	1	0	4096*1
FC7	4096*1	1*1	1	0	4096*1
FC8	4096*1	1*1	1	0	1000*1

The AlexNet model consists of approximately 5 million parameters in the convolutional layers and about 55 million parameters in its fully-connected layers, and it is trained on ImageNet that contains 1.2 million images with labeled with 1000 semantic classes. In this paper, we adopt the iteration 360,000 snapshot of AlexNet as our pre-trained CNN model. Then, we transfer the pre-trained parameters of Conv1, Conv2, Conv3, Conv4, Conv5, FC6 and FC7 to a new CNN model for airplane fine-grained classification on ARSI-11 data set.

When fine-tuning the new CNN model, we keep the parameters transferred from the pre-trained model fixed, i.e., setting the learning rates of Conv1, Conv2, Conv3, Conv4, Conv5, FC6 and FC7 to zero, and replace the FC8 that outputs 1000-demension vector with a new fully-connected layer that outputs 11-demension vector for fit the ARSI-11 data set. The parameters of the new fully-connected layer is trained with the classic stochastic gradient descent based on the backpropagation algorithm with a learning rate of 0.001, a momentum of 0.9, a weight decay of 0.0005, and a batch size of 64.

To evaluate the proposed transferred CNN-based model, the ARSI-11 data set is divided into 80% for training and 20% for validation. Then, we compare the performance of six methods for airplane fine-grained classification on ARSI-11 data set. Table 2 illustrates that our proposed method significantly enhances the classification performance and outperforms the tradition methods.

Table 2. The performance comparisons of six different methods for airplane fine-grained classification on ARSI-11. For mean average precision (mAP), larger is better. Note that "AlexNet" is to train the AlexNet directly on ARSI-11.

Method	mAP(%)
SIFT [15] + BOVW	63.34
HOG [16] + SVM	66.82
ScSPM [17]	65.09
LLC [18]	70.41
AlexNet [9]	92.68
Ours	97.53

The experiments were run on a PC with an Intel Core i7-7700 CPU at 3.6 GHz, 16 GB memory, and a Nvidia GTX Titan X GPU.

5 Conclusion and Future Work

In this paper, we present a transferred CNN-based method to deal with airplane fine-grained classification. The model includes a pre-training stage and a fine-tuning stage. In the pre-training stage, we adopt the AlexNet and train it on ImageNet. In the fine-tuning stage, we first transfer the parameter of the pre-trained AlexNet to a new CNN model, and fine-tune it on ARSI-11. ARSI-11 is a new data set we proposed in this study for airplane fine-grained classification in remote sensing images. The experimental results indicate that the proposed transferred CNN-based model can achieve better classification precision compared with the tradition methods. In the future, we will enrich and perfect our proposed ARSI-11 data set, and then make it available to the public.

Acknowledgments. This work is supported by the National Natural Science Foundation of China (Grant No. 61272317).

References

1. Li, K., Wang, R.S., Wang, C.: A method of tree classifier for the recognition of airplane types. Comput. Eng. Sci. **28**, 136–139 (2006)
2. Zhang, M.C., Wu, X.Q., Wang, P.W.: Aircraft recognition via extraction of closed contour and partial feature matching. Comput. Simul. **23**, 193–197 (2006)
3. Wu, Z., Zeng, J., Gao, Q.Q.: Aircraft target recognition in remote sensing images based on saliency images and multi-feature combination. J. Image Graph. **22**, 532–541 (2017)
4. LeCun, Y., Bengio, Y., Hinton, G.: Deep learning. Nature **521**, 436–444 (2015)
5. LeCun, Y., Bottou, L., Bengio, Y., Haffner, P.: Gradient-based learning applied to document recognition. Proc. IEEE **86**, 2278–2324 (1998)
6. Sun, Y., Liang, D., Wang, X., Tang, X.: DeepID3: face recognition with very deep neural networks. Comput. Sci. (2015)
7. Zhou, B., Lapedriza, A., Khosla, A., Oliva, A., Torralba, A.: Places: a 10 million image database for scene recognition. IEEE Trans. Pattern Anal. Mach. Intell. (2017)
8. Russakovsky, O., et al.: ImageNet large scale visual recognition challenge. Int. J. Comput. Vis. **115**, 211–252 (2015)
9. Krizhevsky, A., Sutskever, I., Hinton, G.: ImageNet classification with deep convolutional neural networks. In: International Conference on Neural Information Processing System, pp. 1097–1105 (2012)
10. Hu, J., Shen, L., Sun, G.: Squeeze-and-Excitation Networks. arXiv:1709.01507 (2017)
11. Glorot, X., Bordes, A., Bengio, Y.: Deep sparse rectifier neural networks. In: Fourteenth International Conference on Artificial Intelligence and Statistics, pp. 315–323 (2011)
12. Oquab, M., Bottou, L., Laptev, I., Sivic, J.: Learning and transferring mid-level image representations using convolutional neural networks. In: IEEE Computer Society Conference on Computer Vision and Pattern Recognition, pp. 1717–1724 (2014)
13. Hinton, G., Srivastav, N., Krizhevsky, A., Sutskever, I., Salakhutdinov, R.R.: Improving neural networks by preventing co-adaptation of feature detectors. Comput. Sci. **3**, 212–223 (2012)
14. Jia, Y., et al.: Caffe: convolutional architecture for fast feature embedding. In: 22nd ACM International Conference on Multimedia, pp. 675–678 (2014)
15. Lowe, D.G.: Distinctive image features from scale-invariant keypoints. Int. J. Comput. Vis. **60**, 91–110 (2004)
16. Dalal, N., Triggs, B.: Histograms of oriented gradients for human detection. In: IEEE Computer Society Conference on Computer Vision and Pattern Recognition, vol. 1, pp. 886–893 (2005)
17. Yang, J., Yu, K., Gong, Y., Huang, T.: Linear spatial pyramid matching using sparse coding for image classification. In: IEEE Computer Society Conference on Computer Vision and Pattern Recognition, pp. 1794–1801 (2009)
18. Yu, K., Zhang, T., Gong, Y.: Nonlinear learning using local coordinate coding. In: International Conference on Neural Information Processing Systems, pp. 2223–2231 (2009)

Object Detection Based on Deep Feature for Optical Remote Sensing Images

Xujiang Zhao[1], Shouhong Wan[1,2(✉)], Chang Zou[1], Xingyue Li[1], and Li Yan[1]

[1] School of Computer Science and Technology,
University of Science and Technology of China, Hefei, China
{zxj32,kkpanda,yanli15,votelxy}@mail.ustc.edu.cn,
wansh@ustc.edu.cn
[2] Key Laboratory of Electromagnetic Space Information,
Chinese Academy of Science, Hefei, China

Abstract. Automatically detecting ground object from optical remote sensing images has attracted significant attention due to its importance in both military and civilian fields. However, the diversity of configuration for different object and the complex background information makes this task difficult. Moreover, the high-level semantic information is usually ignored. To address these problems, we propose an efficient method that extracts deep feature with high-level semantic information from a classification convolutional neural network, and separates the regions of interested based on deep feature. Then each region of interest will be sent to another convolutional neural network to verify whether they are true objects or not. Our proposed method can adapt different objects. Also, it doesn't need any bounding box information for training. We build two remote sensing datasets, SROD-3 and RSHOA-4, to evaluate our detection method. Experiment result indicates that our detection method performs better than other state of the art methods, including Faster-RCNN and YOLO9000.

Keywords: Object detection · Convolutional neural networks
Remote sensing images · Deep feature

1 Introduction

Optical remote sensing images always contain much details of shape, color, texture and topology of targets. Also, these images include some complex background information. However, it is difficult to detect object automatically from remote sensing images since the diversity of configuration for different object and the complex background contextual information.

A large number of scholars have proposed and researched a variety of methods for ground object detection. There is a deep review on object detection in remote sensing images [1]. Normally, airport, harbor and oil depot are objects of interest. While previous works on object detection concentrated more on airport detection, less on harbor and oil depot. The detection method can be roughly classified into two categories: line segmentation [2, 3], scene segmentation [4, 5]. Line segmentation focuses on the shape

© Springer Nature Singapore Pte Ltd. 2018
H. Yuan et al. (Eds.): GSKI 2017, CCIS 848, pp. 327–335, 2018.
https://doi.org/10.1007/978-981-13-0893-2_35

of airport runways. It is simple and fast, but can easily be influenced by object with line features. The second method concentrates on the texture with image segment. This method only considers about low-level features, but ignores high-level features.

Moreover, most of these methods cannot adapt to other objects, such as harbor and oil depot. Deep leaning method, especially the convolutional neural networks (CNNs) [6], have a great performance on classification task in natural image since CNNs can give a better description of high-level features. In many computer vision fields, CNNs have an excellent performance, such as handwritten numeral recognition [13], face recognition [14] and scene classification [15]. Alex Krizhevsky proposed AlexNet, which was one of the best CNNs models and won the ImageNet Large Scale Visual Recognition Challenge (ILSVRC) [7].

Based on CNNs, some state-of-art methods are proposed for object detection [16–18], such as Faster-RCNN [8], the champion of 2016 object detection challenge, and YOLO9000 [9]. However, these detection methods need large bounding box information to guarantee the accuracy, which spend huge human costs to finish the label work. In this paper, we propose an efficient method that extracts deep features with high-level semantic information from a classification convolutional neural network, and separates the RoI based on strongest region of deep features. Then each RoI will be sent to another convolutional neural network to verify whether they are true objects. Our proposed method can adapt different objects. Moreover, it doesn't need any bounding box information for training.

The rest of this paper is organized as follows. In Sect. 2, we present the object detection method. Section 3 gives the details of RSROD-3 and RSHOA-4 datasets. Section 4 reports the details of our comparative experiments and results of different methods on our own dataset. Finally, conclusion and future work are drawn in Sect. 5.

2   Object Detection Method

In this section, we investigate how to detect the object on optical remote-sensing image based on deep feature without any bounding box information. The main detection framework is show in Fig. 1. First, we use CNNs to train a classification network on high-resolution remote sensing images. When we get the trained classification network, we can use it to detect object on low-resolution remote sensing image. Then we extract deep features with high-level semantic information from classification network since we choose global average pooling layer instead fully connected layer. Then we find all connected regions as RoI, which will be sent to another trained classification network to verify whether they are true objects.

2.1   Classification Network

We design a convolutional neural networks based on AlexNet [7], named C-Net. The C-Net has 12 layers, including 7 convolutional layers, 3 pooling layers, 1 global average pooling layer (GAP) [10] and 1 softmax layer. The structure of C-Net is shown in Fig. 2, and the details of C-Net will be shown in Sect. 4.

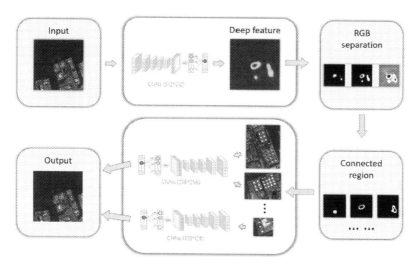

Fig. 1. Object Detection Framework. We extract deep features through CNNs (512*512), and separate the deep feature into RGB channels. Then we consider one channel to generate all connected regions, which will be treated as RoI. For each RoI, we send it to a classification network to verify whether it is the real target.

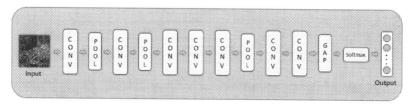

Fig. 2. The overall architecture of the proposed C-Net, a classification convolutional neural networks based on AlexNet.

As shown in Fig. 2, we choose GAP layer as last pooling layer, which replaces the traditional fully connected layer in CNNs. The main idea of GAP is to take average of each feature map from last convolutional layer, and the resulting vector is fed directly into softmax layer. One advantage of global average pooling over fully connected layer is that there are less parameters thus overfitting is avoided at this layer and CNNs model is more efficient. Another advantage is that global average pooling sums out the spatial information, thus it keeps more spatial information of the input.

2.2 Deep Feature

Normally, we pre-trained the classification network with ImageNet dataset [7], then we use our remote sensing dataset to train (fine-tune) the pre-trained network. Once the network is trained, the layer before the softmax layer is used to extract deep feature. Most feature maps [11] in the network have a special visual field, which responds to a specific character, such as color, dog and people in ImageNet dataset. Most visual fields of feature maps from shallow layers responds to simple character, like color, texture and edge. However, visual fields of feature maps from deep layers have a better response to advanced character, such as people, building and cat.

We extract the deep features from the deepest layer by weighted summing all the feature maps from the deepest layer. The detail is shown in Fig. 3 and the calculation method is shown in Eq. (1). Due to the GAP, w can be a proper coefficient to generate the most suitable deep features, which have strong responding correspond every category. For each category, we have different w. So one test image can get m deep feature, m is the number of category, as shown in Fig. 4.

$$D_c(x, y) = \sum_{i=1}^{n} w_i^c f_i(x, y) \tag{1}$$

Hereby D is the deep feature, c is the category, $w = \{w_1, w_2 ... w_n\}$ is weight coefficient from the last two layers, $\mathbf{n}$ is the number of feature maps the same as the dimension of vector, f is the feature map of last convolutional layer.

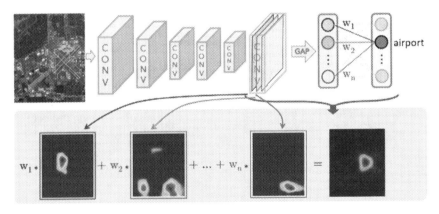

Fig. 3. The method of extracting deep feature from the deepest layer. $w = \{w1, w2...wn\}$ is weight coefficient from the last two layers, $\mathbf{n}$ is the number of feature maps the same as the dimension of vector.

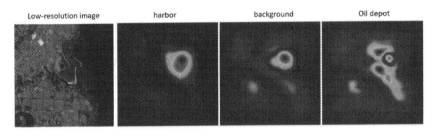

Fig. 4. Deep features corresponding to each category. These deep features contain high-level semantic information.

2.3   Detection Stage

The main detection framework is shown in Fig. 1. When we have trained a CNNs with input size of 512*512 in high-resolution remote sensing dataset, we use it to detect low-resolution remote sensing image. First, we extract deep feature through CNNs (512*512), and separate the deep feature into RGB channels. Then we consider one channel to generate all connected regions, which will be treated as RoI. For each RoI, we send it to a classification network to verify whether it is the real target. Actually, for different size of RoI, we send it to different input size of classification network, including 256*256 and 128*128, as shown in Fig. 1.

The different input sizes of classification network have the same network structure, and trained with the same dataset. The only difference between these classification networks is that the kernel size of global average pooling layer is different. The reason why we use different input size of classification network is that some RoIs are too small to adapt the classification network (with input size of 512*512), which means the quality of classification is not good enough [11].

The key point of our detection algorithm is using a classification network, trained with high-resolution remote sensing image, detecting the low-resolution remote sensing image based on deep features. The reason why we use high-resolution remote sensing image to train the classification network is that CNNs can't learn well with low-resolution remote sensing image since one picture has too much other information except ground truth information. The left part of Fig. 5 shows an example, the deep feature extracted from CNNs, which was trained with low-resolution remote sensing image, cannot describe airport well. In other word, the strongest area of the deep features corresponds to background, not the airport. The deep features contain too much messy semantic information. On the other hand, if we use the classification network (trained with high-resolution remote sensing image) to extract the high-resolution remote sensing image. The result is unsatisfactory since most feature maps from CNNs can only correspond to a local region [11]. For instance, the right part of Fig. 5 shows a deep feature of high-resolution image. The strongest area of the deep feature is not large enough to cover the whole target. In other word, we can't detect object well with this kind of deep feature.

Fig. 5. Deep feature of airport extracted from two classification network, respectively.

3   Dataset

To help improve the state of the art in object detection of optical remote sensing image and evaluated our proposed algorithm, we build a new classification dataset, RSHOA-4, and a new detection dataset, RSROD-3. The RSHOA-4 dataset contains 720 images with various spatial resolutions ranging from 1.0 to 10 m, which include 4 categories, airport, harbor, oil depot and background. And each category includes 180 images. As for RSROD-3, it contains 360 images with 3 categories. The spatial resolution of RSROD-3 dataset ranges from 5.0 to 30 m. All images from these two dataset are collected from Google Earth imagery. Some sample images from RSHOA-4 and RSROD-3 are shown in Fig. 6.

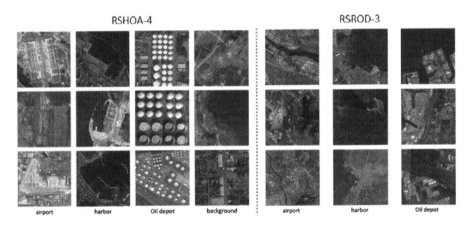

Fig. 6.   Some samples of RSHOA-4 Dataset and RSROD-3 Dataset.

4   Experimental Results and Analysis

This section evaluates the performance of our proposed methods using RSHOA-4 dataset and RSROD-3 dataset for remote sensing object detection.

In our experiment, we designed a classification network based on AlexNet, named C-Net. Table 1 shows the detail of C-Net with input size of 256*256 (227*227 is the crop size of input size). The C-Net has 12 layers, including 7 convolutional layers, 3 pooling layers, 1 global average pooling layer and 1 softmax layer (FC8). The output of the softmax layer is a 1000-dimension vector, i.e. a probability distribution over the 1000 class labels.

Comparing with AlexNet, C-Net removes two fully connected layers and adds another three layers, including two convolutional layers and one global average pooling layer. The parameter size of AlexNet is 233 M, however the parameter size of C-Net is 20 M, much less than the AlexNet.

We pre-trained C-Net in ImageNet dataset [7], then we fine-tuned C-Net with RSHOA-4 dataset. The RSHOA-4 dataset is divided into 66% for training and 34% for validation. The result of classification is shown in Table 2. The result illustrates that

C-Net performance well in RSHOA-4 dataset, which means C-Net can improve the accuracy of object detection. In other word, we can use C-Net to extract deep features for detection.

Table 1. The details of C-Net.

Layer	Input	Kernel	Stride	Pad	Output
Conv1	227*227*3	11*11	4	0	
Pool1	55*55*96	3*3	2	0	
Conv2	27*27*96	5*5	1	2	
Pool2	27*27*256	3*3	2	0	
Conv3	13*13*256	3*3	1	1	
Conv4	13*13*384	3*3	1	1	
Conv5	13*13*384	3*3	1	1	
Pool5	13*13*384	3*3	1	0	
Conv6	11*11*384	3*3	1	1	
Conv7	11*11*512	3*3	11	1	
GAP7	11*11*512	11*11	11	0	
FC8	512*1	1*1	1	0	

Table 2. The result of classification task for C-Net.

Classification Networks	Iterations	Run Time	mAP(%)
C-Net (512*512)	3000	20 min	92.6%
C-Net (256*256)	3000	15 min	91.3%
C-Net (128*128)	3000	12 min	90.8%

55*55*96
27*27*96
27*27*256
13*13*256
13*13*384
13*13*384
13*13*384
11*11*384
11*11*512
11*11*512
512*1
1000*1

For all classification experiments, we use Caffe library [12] to implement training of C-Net.

In our experiment, we use SROD-3 dataset to evaluate our proposed detection algorithm. When C-Nets are trained, we use C-Net (512*512) to extract deep features from SROD-3 dataset. After RGB separation of deep features, we usually choose green channel of deep feature to generated RoI. Then we use C-Net (256*256) and C-Net (128*128) to verify all RoIs whether they are true objects. The whole process of our detection algorithm doesn't use any bounding box information of SROD-3 dataset.

To evaluate our proposed detection algorithm, we choose faster-RCNN [8] and YOLO9000 [9] to detect SROD-3 dataset, which are the state of the art methods of object detection in natural scene image. When we train faster-RCNN and YOLO9000, the SROD-3 dataset is divided into 50% for training and 50% for test. As we know, when training faster-RCNN and YOLO9000, these algorithms will extend training data automatically through methods of mirror, crop, etc. So we use the same extending methods to extend the training data of RSHOA-4 dataset for training C-Net. Table 3 shows the result of detection experiment. The experiments were run on a PC with an Intel Core i7-7700 CPU at 3.6 GHz, 16 GB memory, and an NVidia GTX Titan X GPU.

Table 3. The performance comparisons of two state of the art methods for object detection task.

Method	Train	Test	Bounding Box	Training Time	Test Time	mAP (%)
Faster-RCNN [8]	60% RSHOA-4	50% RSROD-3	√	6 h	5 min	90.2
YOLO9000 [9]	60% RSHOA-4	50% RSROD-3	√	5.5 h	3 min	90.0
Ours	60% RSHOA-4	50% RSROD-3	×	48 min	2 min	**96.0**

The result of detection experiment illustrates that our proposed method outperforms than other methods, especially when we extend training data the same way that Faster-RCNN and YOLO9000 use. As for training data, our method just needs a classification dataset without any bounding box information. On other hand, the efficiency of our method is much better than Faster-RCNN and YOLO9000 since training with bounding box information always need much more time and iteration to convergence.

5   Conclusion

In this paper, we have proposed an efficient object detection method for different resolution remote sensing image with a classification network. And we build two remote sensing datasets, SROD-3 and RSHOA-4, to evaluate our detection method. Meanwhile, our method can adapt to different objects and can be trained without any bounding box information. The experiment results indicate that our detection method performs better than other state of the art methods both on mAP and time.

Acknowledgments. The authors would like to thank all the researchers and community who gladly shared the open source codes and tools used in this paper. And this work is supported by the National Natural Science Foundation of China (Grant No. 61272317).

References

1. Cheng, G., Han, J.: A survey on object detection in optical remote sensing images. ISPRS J. Photogram. Remote Sens. **117**, 11–28 (2016)
2. Wang, X., Lv, Q., Wang, B., et al.: Airport detection in remote sensing images: a method based on saliency map. Cogn. Neurodyn. **7**(2), 143–154 (2013)
3. Qu, Y., Li, C., Zheng, N.: Airport detection base on support vector machine from a single image. In: 2005 Fifth International Conference on Information, Communications and Signal Processing, pp. 546–549. IEEE (2005)
4. Tao, C., Tan, Y., Cai, H., et al.: Airport detection from large IKONOS images using clustered SIFT keypoints and region information. IEEE Geosci. Remote Sens. Lett. **8**(1), 128–132 (2011)
5. Li, Z., Itti, L.: Saliency and gist features for target detection in satellite images. IEEE Trans. Image Process. **20**(7), 2017–2029 (2011)
6. Hinton, G.E., Salakhutdinov, R.R.: Reducing the dimensionality of data with neural networks. Science **313**(5786), 504–507 (2006)
7. Krizhevsky, A., Sutskever, I., Hinton, G.E.: Imagenet classification with deep convolutional neural networks. Adv. Neural Inf. Process. Syst. **2012**, 1097–1105 (2012)
8. Ren, S., He, K., Girshick, R., et al.: Faster R-CNN: Towards real-time object detection with region proposal networks. IEEE Trans. Pattern Anal. Mach. Intell. **39**(6), 1137–1149 (2017)
9. Redmon, J., Farhadi, A.: YOLO9000: better, faster, stronger. arXiv preprint arXiv:1612.08242 (2016)
10. Lin, M., Chen, Q., Yan, S.: Network in network. arXiv preprint arXiv:1312.4400 (2013)
11. Zhou, B., Khosla, A., Lapedriza, A., et al.: Object detectors emerge in deep scene CNNS. arXiv preprint arXiv:1412.6856 (2014)
12. Jia, Y., et al.: Caffe: convolutional architecture for fast feature embedding. In: Proceedings of the 22nd ACM International Conference on Multimedia, pp. 675–678 (2014)
13. LeCun, Y., Bottou, L., Bengio, Y., Haffner, P.: Gradient-based learning applied to document recognition. Proc. IEEE **86**, 2278–2324 (1998)
14. Sun, Y., Liang, D., Wang, X., Tang, X.: DeepID3: Face Recognition with Very Deep Neural Networks. Comput. Sci. (2015)
15. Zhou, B., Lapedriza, A., Khosla, A., Oliva, A., Torralba, A.: Places: a 10 million image database for scene recognition. IEEE Trans. Pattern Anal. Mach. Intell. (2017)
16. Girshick, R., Donahue, J., Darrell, T., et al.: Rich feature hierarchies for accurate object detection and semantic segmentation. Proc. IEEE Conf. Comput. Vis. Pattern Recogn. **2014**, 580–587 (2014)
17. Redmon, J., Divvala, S., Girshick, R., et al.: You only look once: unified, real-time object detection. Proc. IEEE Conf. Comput. Vis. Pattern Recogn. **2016**, 779–788 (2016)
18. Girshick, R.: Fast R-CNN. Proc. IEEE Int. Conf. Comput. Vis. **2015**, 1440–1448 (2015)

Ship Detection from Remote Sensing Images Based on Deep Learning

Ziqiang Yuan, Jing Geng[(⊠)], and Tianru Dai

School of Software, Beijing Institute of Technology, Beijing 100081, China
{2220170718, Janegeng, 2220170633}@bit.edu.cn

Abstract. Due to the complicated maritime climate environment, the detection of marine Ship by using Remote sensing images is faced with many challenges in the field of object detection. In this paper, a ship detection method based on dark channel priority haze removal and Faster RCNN is proposed to solve this problem. We label and experiment with thousands of ships images on the sea. Compared with the using of object detection model directly and some traditional methods, the detection accuracy of the new method is obviously improved.

Keywords: Haze removal · Deep learn · Remote sensing · Faster RCNN

1 Introduction

As unmanned aerial vehicles (UVA) and satellites become increasingly used in the monitoring of natural resources, more and more important data and information can be gained through these advanced technologies. For instance, it can constantly produce ships, the state of the cities and large amounts of data. Compared with other kinds of data like SAR images, the optical images that were used in this paper have many advantages. Optical images have higher resolution and more visualized contents [1]. It is unrealistic to analyze such a large amount of data manually, and it cannot be done in real time. With the continuous emergence of automated object detection methods based on deep learning, such as SSD, YOLO and Faster RCNN. The performance of these algorithms on object detection is much better than the traditional algorithms. Compared with the traditional method that the mAP (mean Average Precision) can only reach about 50%, deep learning can greatly improve the accuracy and increase mAP to more than 70%. It is reasonable to apply these methods to vessel identification.

At the same time, due to the complex climatic conditions at sea, it is also necessary to de-haze and repair the image before the object detection. In this paper, we combine haze removal with object detection and propose a ship detection method on the sea from remote sensing images. The effectiveness of this method are validated in experiments which can achieve better performance and accuracy than direct object detection.

This paper is arranged as follows. The rest of the paper starts from a brief review of related work. Section 3 introduces the methods used in this paper for ship detection and haze removal. Section 4 mainly describes the experimental process and results. Analysis of experiments and conclusion are summarized in Sect. 5.

© Springer Nature Singapore Pte Ltd. 2018
H. Yuan et al. (Eds.): GSKI 2017, CCIS 848, pp. 336–344, 2018.
https://doi.org/10.1007/978-981-13-0893-2_36

2 Related Work

At present, the use of remote sensing images for object detection (include ships) is still an important filed. However, most researches are based on SAR images, inverse synthetic aperture radar (ISAR) images and other traditional methods [2] like CFAR based on the statistical model [3]. Detection algorithm usually contains three parts, the first one is the choice of detection window, the second part is the design of features, and the third part is the design of the classifier. In order to find the object, it is necessary to find the boxes that may contain the object. Move all the possible boxes in the image from left to right and from top to bottom. Getting the image pyramid to multi-scale search by scaling a group of image size. Then, extract the features from these boxes. These features are often defined by people in traditional methods, such as Hog, LBP and so on. Finally, these features are transferred into the classifier to determine whether these boxes contain the target object. Traditional classifiers include SVM, random forest, decision tree and so on.

There are two problems that traditional classifiers cannot solve. (1) The accuracy of identification is difficult to improve due to the use of artificially defined features. (2) It takes a lot of time to get proposal boxes by using traversal methods.

With the release of RCNN after 2014, the first problem is solved by using feature extraction from deep learning. This method improves mean average precision (mAP) by more than 30% [4]. Compared with the traditional method, not only the classifier, but also the parameters in the convolutional layer (like vgg, res) can be trained by the data. This leads to a dramatic increase in detection accuracy. Although RCNN and Fast RCNN after that partially changed the way the proposal boxes were acquired, the speed was still not satisfactory [5].

The speed of object recognition, which is the problem (2), is basically solved until Faster RCNN appears. Faster R-CNN directly uses the RPN (Region Proposal Networks) network to calculate the proposal box. RPN takes a picture of any size as input and outputs a series of rectangular areas, each of which corresponds to a target score and location information. The way people think about detection problems is constantly changing and breaking the old sliding-window framework. This method puts the extracting of the proposal boxes into the network which greatly improves the speed of calculation, making this method even useful for object detection in video. People also find that the same network can perform both scene recognition and object localization in a single forward-pass, without ever having been explicitly taught the notion of objects [6].

At present, deep learning continues to evolve in the field of object detection. From RCNN to Faster RCNN, the accuracy of object detection is constantly increasing. Now, more and more methods focus on the speed of computing, such as YOLO, SSD and so on. While the problem of low accuracy has also appeared.

In the field of image de-fogging, the dark channel prior haze removal method proposed by Kaiming He in 2009 is able to achieve ideals results and is widely used in various fields.

3 Ship Detection Based and Haze Removal

3.1 Haze Removal

The main challenge is due to the fact that climatic conditions at sea are complex. In order to get clear images for the training of ship detection model, we need to implement Haze Removal on the training data, as well as detect the remote sensing images.

In order to get high-quality output images, we chose to use the algorithm from the *Single Image Haze Removal Using Dark Channel Prior* which can remove haze from a single input image. This algorithm was proposed for single image haze removal in 2009 and received the CVPR Best Paper Award of the year due to its ideal results.

Algorithm Principle. In most non-sky partial images, some pixels always have at least one color channel with a low value. In other words, the minimum value of light intensity in this area is a small number. We define a dark channel as a mathematical definition. For any input image J, its dark channel can be expressed as:

$$J^{dark}(x) = \min_{y \in \Omega(x)} \left(\min_{c \in \Omega\{r,g,b\}} J^c(y) \right) \tag{1}$$

In this formula, J^c represents each channel of the color image, and $\Omega(x)$ represents a window centered at pixel X. Dark channel priori theory states [7]:

$$J^{dark} \to 0 \tag{2}$$

First, there is a widely used expression formula for foggy images in the field of computer vision and computer graphics, as follows:

$$I(x) = J(x)t(x) + A(1 - t(x)) \tag{3}$$

In Eq. (3) $I(x)$ is the image to be haze removed, $J(x)$ is the recovered image without haze, A is the global atmospheric light component and $t(x)$ is the transmissivity. $I(x)$ is a known variable and $J(x)$ is an unknown variable. Obviously, Eq. (3) has an infinite number of solutions. This needs to be solved by using the priori mentioned above. Following formula can be derived from formula (3)

$$\frac{I^c(x)}{A^c} = t(x) \frac{J^c(x)}{A^c} + 1 - t(x) \tag{4}$$

The superscript C indicates the meaning of the three channels R/G/B of the image in (4). First, suppose that the transmissivity $t(x)$ in each window is constant, define it as $\tilde{t}(x)$, the value A has been given, and then calculate the minimum value operation twice on both sides of the formula (4), following formula can be deduced.

$$\min_{y \in \Omega(x)} \left(\min_c \frac{I^c(y)}{A^c} \right) = \min_{y \in \Omega(x)} \left(\min_c \frac{J^c(y)}{A^c} \right) + 1 - \tilde{t}(x) \tag{5}$$

According to formula (3):

$$\min_{y \in \Omega(x)} \left(\min_c \frac{J^c(y)}{A^c} \right) = 0 \tag{6}$$

Substituting formula (6) into formula (5)

$$\tilde{t}(x) = 1 - \min_{y \in \Omega(x)} \left(\min_c \frac{J^c(x)}{A^c} \right) \tag{7}$$

In real word, there are some particles in the air even in sunny weather. Therefore, objects in the distance can still feel the influence of haze. In addition, the existence of haze makes people feel the depth of field. Therefore, A certain degree of haze is retained in haze removal, which can be corrected by introducing a factor between [0, 1] in formula (8)

$$\tilde{t}(x) = 1 - w \min_{y \in \Omega(x)} \left(\min_c \frac{J^c(x)}{A^c} \right) \tag{8}$$

The above inferences are all based on the assumption that the global amalgam A is known. In practice, value can be obtained from a foggy image with the aid of a dark channel graph. Specific steps are as follows:

(1) Take the first 0.1% of the pixels from the dark channel map according to the brightness.
(2) In these pixels, we found the point with the highest luminance from the original image as the A.

According to the equation, when the value of t is small, the value of J will be too large; as a result, the image will be too white. To solve this problem, a threshold t_0 can be set to modify and adjust these values. When the value of t is less than t_0, make t = t_0. Therefore, the final recovery formula is as follows:

$$J(x) = \frac{I(x) - A}{\max(t(x), t_0)} + A \tag{9}$$

3.2   Ship Detection

In order to accurately and quickly detect the ships and find out its type and location from the image, we decided to use the Faster-RCNN method which is a quite sophisticated algorithm in the field of region-based target detection.

Faster RCNN. The Faster RCNN algorithm was presented by the Ross Girshick team in 2015. Its speed on Simple network target detection is 17fps and the accuracy rate on PASCAL VOC is 59.9%; the speed on complex network is 5fps, and the accuracy rate is 78.8% [8]. Faster RCNN is used to solve the problem of Object Detection in the field of computer vision (CV). The traditional solution uses SS (selective search) to generate proposals, and then uses classifiers such as SVM to classify and get all possible goals. But one of the salient drawbacks of SS is that it is time-consuming. And using a traditional classifier like SVM has poor performance. In view of the powerful feature extraction of the neural network, the task of detecting the target can be realized by implementing the neural network (Fig. 1).

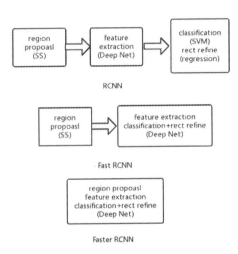

Fig. 1. Development of RCNN to Faster RCNN.

The process of object detection can be divided into four basic steps, including region proposal, feature extraction, classification and react refine. Faster RCNN organized these steps into one deep network framework. All the calculations are completely accomplished in the GPU without any repetition, which greatly improves the speed of computing (Fig. 2).

Conv Layers. As a CNN object detection method, Faster RCNN first uses a set of basic layers in the form of conv + relu + pooling to extract the feature maps from the image. The feature maps are shared with subsequent RPN layers and fully connected layers. All the convolutions in the Faster RCNN's Conv layers are edge-expanded (filled with a circle of 0), resulting in the original image size becoming $(M + 2) \times (N + 2)$. After a 3×3 convolution, the size of output matrices becomes $M \times N$. It is this setting that causes the conv in Conv layers to maintain the size of the input and output matrices.

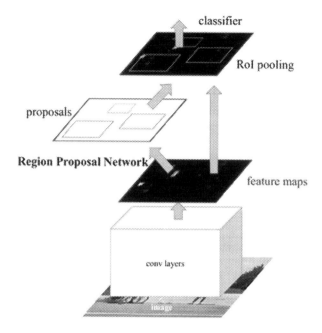

Fig. 2. Faster RCNN structure diagram [9]

Region Proposal Networks. The RPN network is used to generate the region proposals. This layer takes advantage of soft-max to determine whether anchors belong to the foreground or background, and then uses bounding box regression to fix the anchors to get the exact proposals. The RPN network contains two processes. The first one distinguishes the foreground from the background by the soft-max class anchors, and the next one is used to calculate the bounding box regression offset of the anchors for accurate proposal. The final Proposal layer is responsible for synthesizing foreground anchors and bounding box regression offsets, as well as removing proposals that are too small or out of bounds. In fact, the equivalent of the object positioning function has been completed when the calculation process reaches to the Proposal Layer.

Roi Pooling. This layer collects the input feature maps and proposals, synthesizes the information and extracts the proposal feature maps, and then sends them to the subsequent fully connected layer to determine the object category. For the traditional network, because the size of the network input is fixed, the picture needs to be scaled before being put into the network. This led to the inevitable loss of information. Faster RCNN's Roi pooling keeps the size of the output matrix by adjusting the size of the pooling window. This approach reduces the loss of information and improves accuracy.

Classification. Using proposal feature maps to calculate the type of proposal, and repeating bounding box regression to get the final exact position of the bounding box.

4   Experiment

The experiment is divided into three parts, including data and processing, model training and testing. All coding work finished with python 2.7 in the Ubuntu 16.04 system. Third-party tools like TensorFlow, Numpy, OpenCV are used in the experiment.

Data Preprocessing. In order to test the effectiveness of the method, we collected more than 7800 remote sensing images with ships near the harbor. There are four types and more than 10 thousands ships in these images including 6211 images for cargo ships, 2442 images for cruise ships, 4473 images for yachts, and 239 images for fishing boats. All images are labeled and stored as format of pascl voc data sets. (The Pascal Visual Object Classes challenge is a benchmark in visual object category recognition and detection [10]) The size of the image is 1024 × 1024. All these pictures are divided into training set, verification set and testing set in a ratio of 6: 2: 2. Here, we choose to use OpenCV which supports gpu operation and is available on different platforms [11] to deal with the images.

After all the image data is sorted out, the next step is to remove the haze from images. The speed of Dark Channel priority Haze Removal algorithm is 2.83 FPS. By implementing haze removal, the quality of the picture has been significantly improved.

Model Training. In order to enable the comparison of experimental results, two models are trained with two sets of data (original images and images after haze removal). The training of each model costed about 12 h with 70000 iters on GPU (gtx 1080). The model is built on Tensorflow which is a machine learning system that operates at large scale and in heterogeneous environments [12].

Testing and Results. After training, 1581 images are used on the test. (The model without haze removal uses original images, the model with haze removal uses images after haze removal). During the detection, each image consumes only 0.16 s. When the detection is completed, the model generates four files in txt format, representing the results of the four types of ship detection respectively. In these files, each column of data in a row represents the name of the image, the confidence, the vertex coordinates of the bounding box (xmax, ymax, xmin, ymin). To make it easier to understand and analyze the results, the results are visualized (Figs. 3 and 4).

The result of the map calculation is shown in the figure below

(a) Original image

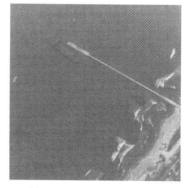
(b) image after haze removal

Fig. 3. Comparison between haze removed image and original images

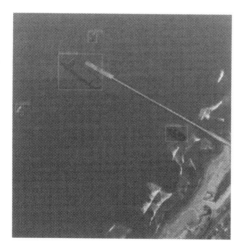

Fig. 4. Result of ship detection

It is not difficult to see from Table 1 that the work of haze removal has obvious improvement on the object detection accuracy. Especially for fishing boats with small data volumes and small size, the accuracy is obviously enhanced.

Table 1. The result of the map calculation

Type of ships	Map with haze removal	Map of original images	Number of ships
cargo ships	0.866	0.851	6211
cruise ships	0.888	0.885	2442
yachts	0.889	0.879	4473
fishing boats	0.762	0.710	239

5 Conclusion

It can be seen from the experimental results that this method can detect ships and identify their location and types by using remote sensing images in complicated weather on the sea. In contrast with the traditional methods which directly use original images as input images, the proposed method in this paper is able to provide the images after haze removal as input images. After applying this novel method, the accuracy and performance of object detection has been improved. However, the large number of data is still hard to process and manage, and some kinds of recognition rate of ships still needs to be improved. In addition, the haze removal algorithm also needs to be optimized. On the one hand, dark channel priority for the sea picture of the fog effect is not ideal. On the other hand, the images after haze removal appears color distortion. It costs more than nearly 0.5 s for a single image (0.35 s for haze removal, 0.16 s for ship detection). Calculation speed of this method also needs to be improved.

Acknowledgements. This work was supported by National Key Research and Development Plan of China (2016YFC0803000, 2016YFB0502604), National Natural Science Fund of China (61472039), and Frontier and Interdisciplinary Innovation Program of Beijing Institute of Technology (2016CX11006), International Scientific and Technological Cooperation and Academic Exchange Program of Beijing Institute of Technology (GZ2016085103).

References

1. Tang, J., Deng, C., Huang, G., Zhao, B.: Compressed-domain ship detection on spaceborne optical image using deep neural network and extreme learning machine. IEEE Transactions on Geoscience and Remote Sensing **53**(3), 11741185 (2015)
2. Xu, C., Zhang, D.: BgCut: automatic ship detection from UAV images. Sci. World J. (2014)
3. Zhao, M., He, J., Fu, Q.: Fast algorithm for SAR image CFAR detection review. J. Autom. **38**(12), 1885–1895 (2012)
4. Girshick, R.B., Donahue, J., Darrell, T., Malik, J.: Rich feature hierarchies for accurate object detection and semantic segmentation. In: Proceedings of the Computer Vision and Pattern Recognition (2014)
5. Girshick, R.B.: Fast R-CNN. In: International Conference on Computer Vision (2015)
6. Bolei, Z., Khosla, A., Lapedriza, A., Oliva, A., Torralba, A.: Object detectors emerge in deep scene CNNs. In: International Conference on Learning Representations (2015)
7. He, K., Sun, J., Tang, X.: Single image haze removal using dark channel prior. In: Computer Vision and Pattern Recognition (2009)
8. RCNN, Fast RCNN, Faster RCNN Technion. https://webcourse.cs.technion.ac.il/236815/Spring2016/ho/WCFiles/RCNN_X3_6pp.pdf
9. Ren, S., He, K., Girshick, R.B., Sun, J.: Faster R-CNN: towards real-time object detection with region proposal networks. IEEE Trans. Pattern Anal. Mach. Intell. **39**(6), 1137–1149 (2017)
10. Everingham, M., Van Gool, L., Williams, C.K.I., Winn, J.M., Zisserman, A.: The pascal visual object classes (VOC) Challenge. Int. J. Comput. Vis. **88**(2), 303–338 (2010)
11. Documentation of OpenCV python. https://docs.opencv.org/3.0-beta/doc/py_tutorials/py_tutorials.html
12. Abadi, M., Barham, P.: TensorFlow: a system for large-scale machine learning. Operating Systems Design And Implementation (2016)

Congestion Analysis Based on Remote Sensing Images

Hanning Yuan[✉], Jiakai Yang, Xiaolei Li, and Shengyu Ma

School of Software, Beijing Institute of Technology, Beijing 100081, China
{yhn6,2220170716,2220170659,2220170675}@bit.edu.cn

Abstract. Most Congestion analysis are based on the urban traffic video surveillance, which depend on the quality of existing surveillance equipments. In this paper, we propose a novel method to perform congestion analysis by utilizing remote sensing images for undeveloped areas or disaster-affected areas where lack of traffic video surveillance. Firstly, the vehicles and extract road area is detected from remote sensing images using objects detection technique. Then the number of Vehicles in the road are counted and mapped into data instances. Finally, density-based clustering algorithm is adopted to find the locations which are probably the Congestion points. The experimental results on real world datasets demonstrate that the proposed method can perform congestion analysis effectively.

Keywords: Congestion analysis · Vehicle detection · Road extraction
Remote sensing image

1 Introduction

With the rapid development of public infrastructure and the growth in human being living standard, vehicles are not unaffordable luxury any more. As a result, the number of vehicles increased dramatically in recent years which makes people spend large amount of time on commuting day after day. Road congestion leads to slower speeds of the traffic stream, longer trip times, and increased vehicular queueing in our daily life. Recognizing congestion and planning the route in time to avoid the jammed roads could save us lots of time. Most Congestion analysis are based on the urban traffic video surveillance, which depend on the quality of existing surveillance equipment. While for undeveloped areas or disaster-affected area, they cannot satisfy the required quality for these equipment.

In order to obtain comprehensive information of the congestion, one of the feasible methods is to analyze the remote sensing image. At present, remote sensing technology has been very effective for image recognition filed. However, there exist many sheltering, overlapping, disordering, interlacing and shadows in remote sensing images which makes it difficult to directly use geometry feature, radiation feature, topology feature and contextual feature to extract objects from image.

In this paper, we propose a novel method for congestion analysis by taking advantage of remote sensing images, which combines object detection and clustering algorithm. Firstly, we detect vehicles with faster-RCNN, along with lane detection with

H. Yuan et al. (Eds.): GSKI 2017, CCIS 848, pp. 345–352, 2018.
https://doi.org/10.1007/978-981-13-0893-2_37

FCN. Then, adding corresponding coordinates into the result. Finally, density based clustering algorithm is used to find the candidate Congestion points.

The rest of the paper starts from a brief review of related work. Then we present the congestion analysis framework based on remote sensing images, followed by conclusion.

2   Related Work

There are quite many literatures on congestion and jams analysis based on remote sensing sensors installed on aircrafts or satellites. However, previous works on this field did not use remote sensing images.

Many researches focus on velocity of vehicles. For example, Palubinskas et al. (2009) used vehicle detection on the road segment just like our method, but their detection was based on the difference between two images with a short time lag. Also, they adopted a priori information such as road data base, vehicle sizes and road parameters and a simple linear traffic model based on a spacing between vehicles [1]. Analogously, Reinartz et al. also take velocity into account, along with vehicle type and distance between vehicles [2].

Instead of detecting velocity of single vehicle, Gintautas Palubinskas and Hartmut Runge model a traffic on the road segment and thus they can derive directly the required traffic parameters from the data. They achieved the traffic congestion detection in along-track two-channel SAR imagery in a different way [3].

Ernst *et al.* showed that special GIS data products are available for simulations or analysis and merge of sociodemographic and socioeconomic structure data (people and pixels). Additionally, the GIS System offers the opportunity to implement and manage the historical traffic flow data generated and derived from all data collecting systems (terrestrial, airborne and space borne sensors) [4].

3   Congestion Analysis Framework Based on Remote Sensing Images

3.1   Vehicle Detection

In this section, we give a brief description on how to detect vehicle. Previous work in this field often extract information about geometry, radiation, topology and contextual features. And then, they use these features to detect objects in the target images. As deep learning became more and more popular, huge amount of excellent algorithms have been generated, which were faster and more accurate comparing to those traditional methods. Among these algorithms we selected Faster R-CNN (faster region-based convolutional neural network) to detect objects in the target images.

Faster R-CNN is the third generation of this series of algorithm proposed by Ren *et al.*, and the first two generations of this series of algorithm are RCNN and Fast R-CNN [5–7]. Compared to the previous algorithms, the biggest improvement is that Faster R-CNN combines four steps of object detection (region proposal, feature

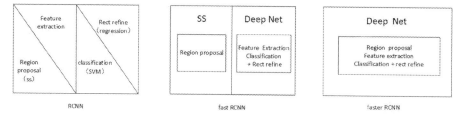

Fig. 1. The difference structure between R-CNN, Fast R-CNN, Faster R-CNN

extraction, classification and rectify refine) into one deep network. Without repeated calculation, the running speed is greatly improved (Fig. 1).

In general, the whole system is consisted of two different modules. The first one is deep fully conventional network which is used to propose regions and another one is Fast R-CNN detector which uses the proposed region. It is a single and unified network for object detection and the RPN module serves as the 'attention' of this unified network (Fig. 2).

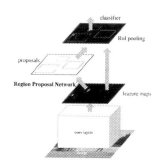

Fig. 2. Faster R-CNN structure.

From Fig. 2, the basic structure of Faster R-CNN is shown.

Convolutional layers, which combines convolutional layer, RELU function and pooling layer together, are used to extract feature maps from image. The feature maps are also shared with the following RPN layer and fully connected layer.

Region Proposal Networks (RPN) are used to generate region proposals. This layer use softmax function to judge whether anchors belong to foreground or background. After that, in order to acquire precise proposal, bounding box regression is used to rectify the anchors.

ROI Pooling. This layer collects the input feature maps and proposal, synthesizes this information and sends them to the following fully connected layer for classification.

Classifier. Classifying the proposal by using feature map. Meanwhile, bounding box regression is manipulated to get the precise position of the detection frame.

As it is shown in Fig. 3, all the vehicles in the image had been detected and labeled using faster R-CNN. In order to get more accurate result, we adopted K-fold cross validation. We cut 12,000 images into 5 batches, in each experiment we use different batch as test, and the rest of batches are regarded as training set. Mean AP (average precision) for each experiment are listed in Table 1.

Fig. 3. Left: The original image. Right: Labelled image

Table 1. Results of mean AP for each experiment of vehicle detection.

Experiment	Mean AP
1	0.903
2	0.918
3	0.879
4	0.899
5	0.932
Average	0.906

3.2   Road Extraction

Pervious road extraction methods mostly focused on radiation, topology, texture features [8], template matching [9] or wavelet transformation [10]. Comparing to those methods, the convolutional neural network (CNN) has shown its effectiveness in object detection in remote sensing images. Furthermore, the fully convolutional network (FCN), as one kind of CNN, has shown outstanding performance in dense semantic labeling of aerial images. In the field of road extraction from remote sensing images, CNN and FCN have also been incorporated to automatically learn features [11].

For its multiple layers, CNN can learn the features automatically. Shallow convolutional layer has small perception domain, while the deep convolutional layer has bigger perception domain to help the network to learn more abstract features. These abstract features are less sensitive to the size, position and direction of the objects, which improves the accuracy of detection results. CNN uses few fully connected layers

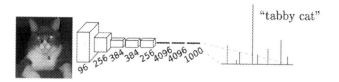

Fig. 4. Result using AlxeNet

after the convolutional layers to reflect the feature map to a fixed-length eigenvector. Classical CNN like AlexNet performs well for classification and regression tasks, as their expected result was a numerical description of the whole input image, just like it is shown in Fig. 4.

However, in order to classify a pixel, CNN uses the image block around the pixels as the input of training and prediction, which brought some disadvantages. Huge consumption of storage and low computation efficiency. While FCN trained in the way of end-to-end, pixels-to-pixels on semantic segmentation to help resolve the above disadvantages. Different from the classical CNN, FCN takes input with arbitrary size of images. Both learning and inference are performed whole-image-at-a-time by dense feedforward computation and backpropagation. In-networkupsampling layers enable pixelwise prediction and learning in nets with subsampled pooling. (Figure 5)

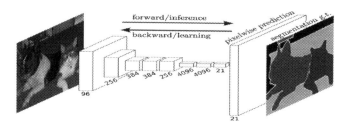

Fig. 5. Fully convolutional networks can efficiently learn to make dense predictions for per-pixel tasks like semantic segmentation.

Cross validation was introduced for obtaining more accurate result. 10,000 images were cut into five batches, each batch was used as test for 5 experiments. The result of Mean AP for each experiment are listed in Table 2. Final results are shown in Fig. 6.

3.3   Congestion Analysis

Density-Based Clustering algorithm is adopted in this paper to find out which part of the roads are congested. It mainly focuses on finding the high-density regions which are separated by low-density area. Differentiating from the distance-based clustering algorithms, the Density-Based Clustering algorithms generates results in arbitrary shape, it is extraordinarily essential for the removal of noisy data points. Compared with traditional clustering algorithm, DBSCAN does not require manually input the

Table 2. Result of mean AP for each experiment of road extraction.

Experiment	Mean AP
1	0.708
2	0.676
3	0.604
4	0.789
5	0.767
Average	0.709

Fig. 6. Left: the original image. Right: the road was labelled with different color (Color figure online).

clustering numbers. Also, it does not have bias over the shape of clusters. Moreover, the input parameters can filter the noise when needed.

DBSCAN requires a pair of global density parameters: MinPts and Eps as input values. MinPts refers to the number of data points of a certain region in the field, and Eps is the radius of this certain region. With the unique pair of global density parameter, DBCSCAN can detect the class and noise points in the dataset. In general, the density of the boundary points is smaller than the inner ones, and the density of the noise points is smaller than those inside the class. There are two types of points in a class, core points inside the class and boundary points on the edge.

Suitable parameters MinPts and Eps can be determined after several trials, which is the number of vehicle in certain region and the radius of this region respectively. After MinPts and Eps are set, we can start traversal from a randomly selected point, and draw a circle with that point as center point and Eps as radius. If the number of points inside this circle is greater than MinPts, keep drawing circle with the center of those points. Repeating traversal process to get a class until there has no new circle can be generated. The rest points are considered as the noise points [12].

In order to get visualized result of congestion, color each point during the process of DBSCAN. If the previous point is also in the same class, draw a line between them. That way, we can get bunch of broken lines that shows the traffic jam. Then mix the result with the road extraction result, the roads marked with red color are the congested area. The final result is shown as in Fig. 7.

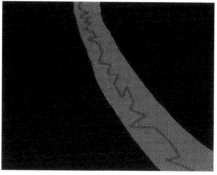

Fig. 7. Left: congested cars marked with broken lines. Right: Final result of the congestion (Color figure online)

4 Conclusion

In this paper, we propose a novel method to analyze congestion from remote sensing image based on objects detection for undeveloped areas or disaster-affected area. Faster R-CNN is chosen to extract vehicles and FCN, which trained end-to-end, pixels-to-pixels on semantic segmentation, is adopted for road extraction. After the off-road vehicles are removed, DBSCAN algorithm is used to find the candidate congestion locations. The experimental results on real world datasets demonstrate that the proposed method can perform congestion analysis effectively.

Acknowledgements. This work was supported by National Key Research and Development Plan of China (2016YFC0803000, 2016YFB0502604), International Scientific and Technological Cooperation and Academic Exchange Program of Beijing Institute of Technology (GZ2016085103), and Frontier and Interdisciplinary Innovation Program of Beijing Institute of Technology(2016CX11006), National Natural Science Fund of China (61472039).

References

1. Palubinskas, G., Kurz, F., Reinartz, P.: Detection of traffic congestion in optical remote sensing imagery. In: 2008 IEEE International Geoscience and Remote Sensing Symposium, IGARSS 2008, pp. II-426–II-429. IEEE (2009)
2. Reinartz, P., Lachaise, M., Schmeer, E., et al.: Traffic monitoring with serial images from airborne cameras. ISPRS J. Photogramm. Remote Sens. **61**(3), 149–158 (2005)
3. Palubinskas, G., Runge, H.: Detection of traffic congestion in SAR imagery. In: European Conference on Synthetic Aperture Radar, pp. 1–4. VDE (2011)
4. Ernst I, Hetscher M, Lehmann S, et al. Use of GIS methodology for online urban traffic monitoring. In: Remote Sensing and Data Fusion Over Urban Areas - Urban. DLR (2005)
5. Girshick, R., Donahue, J., Darrell, T., et al.: Rich feature hierarchies for accurate object detection and semantic segmentation. In: Computer Vision and Pattern Recognition, pp. 580–587. IEEE (2014)
6. Girshick, R.: Fast R-CNN. Comput. Sci. (2015)

7. Ren, S., He, K., Girshick, R., et al.: Faster R-CNN: towards real-time object detection with region proposal networks. IEEE Trans. Pattern Anal. Mach. Intell. **39**(6), 1137–1149 (2015)
8. Xia, W., Hongmei, T., Yang, Y., et al.: Study on road extraction method in remote sensing image. In: International Conference on Industrial Control and Electronics Engineering, pp. 1578–1580. IEEE (2012)
9. Pudaruth, S.: Extraction of roads from remotely sensed images using a multi-angled template matching technique. In: International Symposium on Computer Vision and the Internet, pp. 21–29. ACM (2016)
10. Sghaier, M.O., Lepage, R.: Road extraction from very high resolution remote sensing optical images based on texture analysis and beamlet transform. IEEE J. Sel. Top. Appl. Earth Obs. Remote Sens. **9**(5), 1946–1958 (2016)
11. Zhong, Z., Li, J., Cui, W., et al.: Fully convolutional networks for building and road extraction: preliminary results. In: Geoscience and Remote Sensing Symposium, pp. 1591–1594. IEEE (2016)
12. Bi, F.M., Wang, W.K., Chen, L.: DBSCAN: density-based spatial clustering of applications with noise. J. Nanjing Univ. **48**(4), 491–498 (2012)

Detection of Oil Spill Through Fully Convolutional Network

Yan Li[1], Xiaofei Yang[2(✉)], Yunming Ye[2], Lunan Cui[2], Binfeng Jia[2],
Zhongming Jiang[2], and Shaokai Wang[2]

[1] Shenzhen Polytechnic, Shenzhen, China
liyan@szpt.edu.cn
[2] Department of Computer Science, Shenzhen Graduate School,
Harbin Institute of Technology, Shenzhen, China
yangxiaofei@stu.hit.edu.cn, 1617325767@qq.com,
1468652359@qq.com, 13612844878@163.com,
binfengj@gmail.com, wangshaokai@gmail.com

Abstract. In this paper, a deep learning classification model is proposed for automatically detecting the marine oil spill in Lanset-7 and Lanset-8 images, which can combine fully convolutional network (FCN) with Resnet and Googlenet respectively. The classification algorithms, i.e. FCN-Googlenet and FCN-ResNet are compared to the state-of-the-art Support Vector Machine (SVM) method. The experimental results show that our FCN-Googlenet and FCN-ResNet models outperform other approaches with a significant improvement. Moreover, our methods are more flexible in that no restriction on the size of input image is required in our algorithmic setups, which is more suitable in real applications.

Keywords: Oil spill · Deep learning · Fully convolutional network

1 Introduction

Oil spills are often seen on the ocean, which lead the significant damage to the marine ecological environment [23]. Generally, the detection of oil-spill is to distinguish oil spills from other low-backscatter ocean phenomena. The rapid development of satellite sensors has significantly advanced the imaging techniques, which can deliver images with rich information. And the images enable us to identify the part of Marine oil spill. Due to the advantage of the remote sensing technology has been widely used on Marine environment monitoring.

According to [1], the oil spills and look-alike phenomena would appear as dark formations on SAR images, which has been extensively used for oil spill detection in the marine environment. But, it is impossible for us to discriminate oil spills from look-alikes solely based on SAR intensity values [18]. To address the curse of noise, some studies perform image filtering first and feature extraction for second, then apply the feature to classify for discriminating oil spills from look-likes [1, 23]. Some researchers propose a series of oil spill detection algorithms, such as threshold segmentation, edge detection and zone segmentation [14]. In [10], the horizontal set

© Springer Nature Singapore Pte Ltd. 2018
H. Yuan et al. (Eds.): GSKI 2017, CCIS 848, pp. 353–362, 2018.
https://doi.org/10.1007/978-981-13-0893-2_38

mathematical method is integrated in segmentation method by Ganta et al., namely horizontal set segmentation algorithm. To address the model of identification, many researchers resort to conventional pattern recognition approaches, such as the support vector machine (SVM), linear discriminant analysis (LDA), Bayesian classifiers and nearest neighbor (NN) classifiers. For example, in [7, 22], the author performs the artificial neural network (ANN) approach, which is used to calculate approximate the relation between dark-spot features and the class labels. The support vector machine (SVM) was proposed in [2], the main idea of which is automatic assigning the confidence levels to the slicks. And in [9], linear discriminant analysis (LDA) approach was used based on the Mahalanobis distance. In [17–19], the Bayesian classification scheme was performed with the prior knowledge, Gaussian densities and rule-based density corrections.

Nowadays, many efforts have been conducted in identification of oil spills based on remote sensing. However, these methods constitute only a limited set of popular classification techniques. Other advanced techniques such as Deep Learning and Generative Adversarial Networks (GAN) have not been explored for oil spill classification. Moreover, a systematic, quantitative comparison of the available classifiers is still lacking, although performance differences may be substantial in their application to remote sensing problems (e.g. [3, 4]).

Thanks to the recent development of deep learning, especially the convolutional neural networks (CNN) model, the image object detection has made great breakthroughs. However, in many visual tasks, especially in biomedical image processing, localization should be included in the desired output, i.e., each pixel should be assigned a class label. Moreover, thousands of training images are usually beyond reach in biomedical tasks. Hence, a local region (patch) around that pixel was provided in [5], in which a network was trained in a sliding-window setup to predict the class label of each pixel. In [11], convolutional neural networks (CNNs) end-to-end were trained to classify the proposal regions into object categories or background. Region Convolutional Neural Network (R-CNN) mainly plays as a classifier, and it does not predict object bounds. Its accuracy depends on the performance of the region proposal module. In [16], the authors predicted the box coordinates for the localization task that assumes a single object by training a fully-connected layer. The fully-connected layer is then turned into a convolutional layer for detecting multiple class-specific objects. The MultiBox methods [8, 21] generate region proposals from a network whose last fully-connected layer simultaneously predicts multiple classagnostic boxes, generalizing the single-box fashion of OverFeat. These classagnostic boxes are used as proposals for recurrent convolutional networks. The MultiBox proposal network is applied on a single image crop or multiple large image crops (e.g., 224 × 224), in contrast to our fully convolutional scheme. MultiBox does not share features between the proposal and detection networks. We discuss the Fully convolutional networks (FCN) model [15] on identifying of oil-spill based on remote sensing.

Therefore, this paper aims to detect Marine oil-spill with the state-of-the-art deep learning techniques based on remote sensing, and compares with SVM and DT methods by using the accuracy index. We firstly implement a model of oil spill detection through fully convolutional network. Although the FCN model has got some good results on detection of common images, there is no implementation for the detection of oil-spill based on remote sensing by using FCN model. Second, we present the detection of oil-spill through different FCN models in this paper, which is combined with different deep learning models. We extract the feature maps with different deep learning model as the input data for FCN model, for example the residual network (ResNet) [12] and the GoogLeNet [20], and then the feature maps are send to FCN model as the input data to classify the oil-spill. At last, we compare the results with SVM and DT methods by using the accuracy index.

The paper is organized as follows. Section 2 present our proposed methods. Experimental setup and results are given in Sect. 3. Finally, we conclude the paper in Sect. 4.

2 The Proposed Methods

2.1 A Model of Oil Spill Detection Through Fully Convolutional Network

We build a model of oil spill detection through FCN, which is illustrated in the Fig. 1. In FCN model, each layer of the input data is a three-dimensional array, and its size is h × w × d, where h and w are the spatial dimensions of the data, and d is the feature dimension. As shown in the Fig. 1, the first input data of layer is the image, with the spatial size h × w, and the color channels. Their receptive fields are located in higher layers, which correspond to the locations in the image.

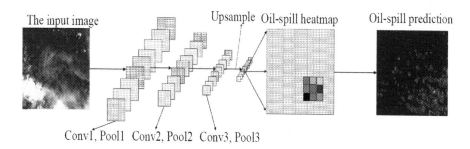

Fig. 1. The FCN model for oil-spill detection

The convolutional networks are built on translation invariance. The FCN model employs the basic components, as convolution, pooling, and activation functions, to operate on local input regions, which is depended only on relative spatial coordinates. Define x_{ij} as the data vector at location (i,j) in a particular layer, and y_{ij} for the following layer, then we can get the output features y_{ij} by

$$y_{ij} = f_{ks}\left(\{x_{sj + \delta i, sj + \delta j}\} 0 \le \delta i, \delta j \le k\right) \tag{1}$$

where k is called the kernel size, s is the stride, and f_{ks} determines the layer type: a matrix multiplication for convolutional network function with different operation, for example the convolution operation, pooling operation, and a spatial max operation an elementwise nonlinearity for an activation). And it's same for other types of layers.

This functional form is maintained under composition, with kernel size and stride obeying the transformation rule

$$f^{\circ}_{ks} g_{k's'} = (f^{\circ} g)_{k' + (k-1)s', ss'} \tag{2}$$

We call a deep filter or fully convolutional network, if a general deep net computes a general nonlinear function, and net with only layers of this form computes a nonlinear filter. The advantage of FCN model is that it naturally operates on an input of any size, and produces an output of corresponding (possibly resampled) spatial dimensions.

With the several operations (convolution operation, and pooling operation), the input data is transferred to as many feature maps of small size. Then, the FCN model upsamples the feature maps into the new data with the same size of the input data. The loss function composed with the FCN defines a task. The final layer loss function is a sum over the spatial dimensions, $\iota(x; \theta) = \sum_{ij} l'(x_{ij}; \theta)$. Its gradient will be a sum over the gradients of each of the spatial components. As a result, the stochastic gradient descent (SGD) on l computed on the whole images will be the same as the SGD on l'. And the final layer receptive fields are token as a minibatch.

When these receptive fields overlap significantly, both feedforward computation and backpropagation are much more efficient when computed layer-by-layer over an entire input data instead of patch-by-patch.

2.2   The FCN-GoogLeNet Dection Model

We combine the FCN model with the GoogLeNet model, namely FCN-GoogLeNet model. In GoogLeNet, a new and deeper model was proposed, namely GoogLeNet. The GoogLeNet employ the average pooling instead of the fully connection. And it adds two additional support sotfmax on the feedforward computation. There have nine inception of the GoogLeNet model, so the receptive fields is bigger than the old model. Due to this advantage, the GoogLeNet model effectively prevents the gradient from disappearing, when the level deepens. And we propose the FCN model with GoogLeNet, as shown in Fig. 2.

2.3   The FCN-ResNets Dection Model

With increasing of the network depth, traditional methods are not as expected to improve accuracy but introduce problems like vanishing gradient and degradation. Now, in [12, 13], the residual network (ResNet) is introduces skip connections that allow the information (from the input or those learned in earlier layers) to flow more into the deeper layers. And the ResNets give better function approximation capabilities as they gain more parameters and successfully contribute to solving vanishing gradient and degradation problems. Deep residual networks with residual units have shown compelling accuracy and nice convergence behaviors on several large-scale image recognition tasks, such as ImageNet [12] and MS COCO [6] competitions. So, we

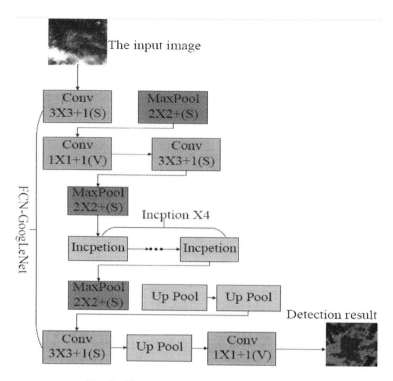

Fig. 2. The proposed FCN-GoogLeNet model

redesigned the FCN model with ResNets, and add more information when we upsampled it. As shown in Fig. 3, we extract the feature maps from the input data by using ResNets, and do upsampling with the FCN model.

3   Experiments

In this section, we first describe the experimental setup and the performance metrics applied to evaluate the proposed models. Then, we report the experimental results of the proposed algorithm based on two benchmark datasets that consist of oil spills.

3.1   Experiment Setup

The model is trained by using the SGD. We use a minibatch size of 20 images and set the learning rates as 10^{-4}, and 10^{-5} for FCN-GoogLeNet, and FCN-ResNet. Respectively, a line search is chosen. We set momentum 0.9, weight decay of 5^{-4} or 2^{-3}, although we found training to be insensitive to these parameters. Besides, we zero-initialize the class scoring convolutional layer. We also employ the dropout in the original classifier nets. We fine-tune all layers by BP algorithm through the whole networks. And we find that fully convolutional training can balance classes by

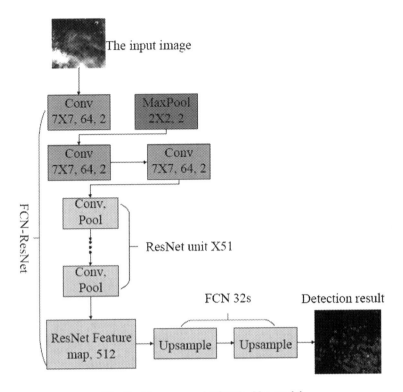

Fig. 3. The proposed FCN-ResNet model

weighting or sampling the loss. At last, all models are trained and test with Tensorflow on two NVIDIA GTX1080Ti GPUs.

3.2   Experiment Results

We test our proposed model with two datasets based on remote sensing. In fact, due to weather conditions and the state of the sensor itself instability, which can lead to the data is not available, so there only have a small data can be used for oil spill information extraction, need to filter the data first. At last, we compare different models with accuracy index.

Yantai dataset is in Yantai, China. And the dataset is obtained from the Lanset-7 satellite. In May 12, 2007, the oil spill events was occurred in the bohai sea waters to yantai "golden rose", there has three days of the original data. We found data of the target area that points on May 12, 2007, 13 and May 13, 2007, 2 PM, but after analysis, the oil spill information is not obvious. So only the information of the oil spill in the target area was significantly enhanced by the data on 13 May 2007. Lanset-7 satellite contains eight bands of the sensor, covered from infrared to visible light different wavelength range. The best contrast effect of oil and water gray value is channel 5. Band larger adjustment is Band5 (0.845–0.885 µ), ruled out 0.825 mum water vapor absorption characteristics. The band Band8 band has a narrow band, which can better distinguish vegetation.

The Table 1 shows state-of-the-art performance on both tasks, which is computed on the standard split into 70% for training and the remaining labeled samples for testing (Fig. 4).

Table 1. Results of the Yantai oil spill based on Lanset-7 remote sensing.

Methods	DT	SVM	FCN-GoogLeNet	FCN-ResNet
AA	77.70 ± 0.3	82.40 ± 0.2	88.25 ± 0.2	89.65 ± 0.4

Bohai bay dataset is in Bohai bay, China, which is obtained from Lanset-8 satellite. In June 2011, oil spill occurred in a oil field of Bohai bay, Cnooc. We employ the bands of 2, 3 and 7 from Lanset-8 as the input date for the models. And we take the same training with the Yantai dataset. The joint representation that simultaneously predicts both types of labels can be learned on the FCN models. Table 2 presents the experimental results of all the methods on the Bohai bay dataset (Fig. 5).

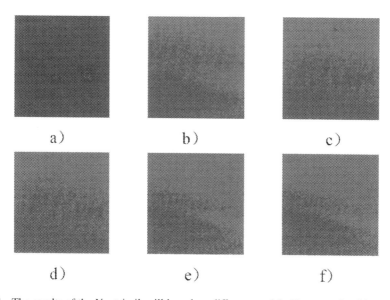

a)   b)   c)

d)   e)   f)

Fig. 4. The results of the Yantai oil spill based on different models (the area of red is polluted): (a) The original data from Lanset-7; (b) The labeled data for truth; (c) The result produced by DT method; (d) The result calculated by SVM method; (e) The result produced by FCN-GoogLeNet method; (f) The result produced by FCN-ResNet method. (Color figure online)

Table 2. Results of the Bohai bay oil spill based on Lanset-8 remote sensing.

Methods	DT	SVM	FCN-GoogLeNet	FCN-ResNet
AA	81.20 ± 0.3	85.20 ± 0.2	90.20 ± 0.2	91.30 ± 0.4

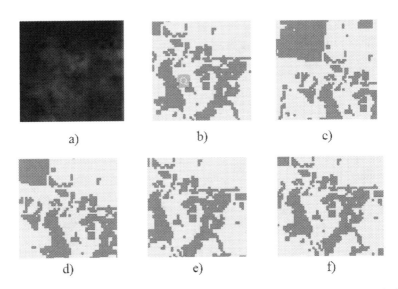

a)   b)   c)

d)   e)   f)

Fig. 5. The results of the Bohai bay oil spill based on different models (the area of plink is polluted): (a) The original data from Lanset-8; (b) The labeled data for truth; (c) The result produced by DT method; (d) The result calculated by SVM method; (e) The result produced by FCN-GoogLeNet method; (f) The result produced by FCN-ResNet method.

4   Conclusion

In this paper, we propose two deep learning models for oil spill detection based on Lanset-7 and Landset-8 remote sensing datasets, of which named FCN-GoogLeNet model and FNC-ResNet model. These two deep learning models can naturally operate on an input of any size. In the original work of FCN, a simple CNN model is used to extract the feature maps in which the calculation of the feature maps is simple. In our work, we use the ResNet model to extract the feature maps with the input data. And we employ the FCN model in oil spill detection.

To demonstrate the FCN-ResNet model training, we conducted experiments on the Yantai dataset and Bohai bay dataset. Our results show that the oil spill detection based on FCN models is feasible. The gains in accuracy observed on the Yantai dataset and Bohai bay dataset are more pronounced.

Acknowledgments. This work has been supported in part by Shenzhen Science and Technology Program under Grant no.JCYJ20160413163534712, J-CYJ20160428092427867, SGG201 50512145714247 and JSGG20160229154017074.

References

1. Brekke, C., Solberg, A.H.: Oil spill detection by satellite remote sensing. Remote Sens. Environ. **95**(1), 1–13 (2005)
2. Brekke, C., Solberg, A.H.: Classifiers and confidence estimation for oil spill detection in ENVISAT ASAR images. IEEE Geosci. Remote Sens. Lett. **5**(1), 65–69 (2008)
3. Brenning, A.: Benchmarking classifiers to optimally integrate terrain analysis and multispectral remote sensing in automatic rock glacier detection. Remote Sens. Environ. **113**(1), 239–247 (2009)
4. Brenning, A.: Spatial cross-validation and bootstrap for the assessment of prediction rules in remote sensing: the r package sperrorest. In: 2012 IEEE International Geoscience and Remote Sensing Symposium (IGARSS), pp. 5372–5375. IEEE (2012)
5. Ciresan, D.C., Meier, U., Masci, J., Maria Gambardella, L., Schmidhuber, J.: Flexible, high performance convolutional neural networks for image classification. In: Proceedings of the International Joint Conference on Artificial Intelligence, IJCAI, Barcelona, Spain, vol. 22, p. 1237 (2011)
6. Dai, J., He, K., Sun, J.: Instance aware semantic segmentation via multi-task network cascades. In: Proceedings of the IEEE Conference on Computer Vision and Pattern Recognition, pp. 3150–3158 (2016)
7. Del Frate, F., Petrocchi, A., Lichtenegger, J., Calabresi, G.: Neural networks for oil spill detection using erssar data. IEEE Trans. Geosci. Remote Sens. **38**(5), 2282–2287 (2000)
8. Erhan, D., Szegedy, C., Toshev, A., Anguelov, D.: Scalable object detection using deep neural networks. In: Proceedings of the IEEE Conference on Computer Vision and Pattern Recognition, pp. 2147–2154 (2014)
9. Fiscella, B., Giancaspro, A., Nirchio, F., Pavese, P., Trivero, P.: Oil spill detection using marine sar images. Int. J. Remote Sens. **21**(18), 3561–3566 (2000)
10. Ganta, R.R., Zaheeruddin, S., Baddiri, N., Rao, R.R.: Segmentation of oil spill images with illumination reflectance based adaptive level set model. IEEE J. Sel. Top. Appl. Earth Obs. Remote Sens. **5**(5), 1394–1402 (2012)
11. Girshick, R., Donahue, J., Darrell, T., Malik, J.: Rich feature hierarchies for accurate object detection and semantic segmentation. In: Proceedings of the IEEE Conference on Computer Vision and Pattern Recognition, pp. 580–587 (2014)
12. He, K., Zhang, X., Ren, S., Sun, J.: Deep residual learning for image recognition. In: Proceedings of the IEEE Conference on Computer Vision and Pattern Recognition, pp. 770–778 (2016)
13. He, K., Zhang, X., Ren, S., Sun, J.: Identity mappings in deep residual networks. In: Leibe, B., Matas, J., Sebe, N., Welling, Max (eds.) ECCV 2016. LNCS, vol. 9908, pp. 630–645. Springer, Cham (2016). https://doi.org/10.1007/978-3-319-46493-0_38
14. Jing, Y., An, J., Liu, Z.: A novel edge detection algorithm based on global minimization active contour model for oil slick infrared aerial image. IEEE Trans. Geosci. Remote Sens. **49**(6), 2005–2013 (2011)
15. Long, J., Shelhamer, E., Darrell, T.: Fully convolutional networks for semantic segmentation. In: Proceedings of the IEEE Conference on Computer Vision and Pattern Recognition, pp. 3431–3440 (2015)
16. Sermanet, P., Eigen, D., Zhang, X., Mathieu, M., Fergus, R., LeCun, Y.: Overfeat: integrated recognition, localization and detection using convolutional networks (2013). arXiv preprint: arXiv:1312.6229
17. Solberg, A.S., Storvik, G., Solberg, R., Volden, E.: Automatic detection of oil spills in ERS SAR images. IEEE Trans. Geosci. Remote Sens. **37**(4), 1916–1924 (1999)

18. Solberg, A.H., Brekke, C., Husoy, P.O.: Oil spill detection in RADARSAT and ENVISAT SAR images. IEEE Trans. Geosci. Remote Sens. **45**(3), 746–755 (2007)
19. Solberg, A.H., Dokken, S.T., Solberg, R.: Automatic detection of oil spills in ENVISAT, RADARSAT and ERS SAR images. In: Proceedings of the 2003 IEEE International Geoscience and Remote Sensing Symposium, IGARSS 2003, vol. 4, pp. 2747–2749. IEEE (2003)
20. Szegedy, C., Liu, W., Jia, Y., Sermanet, P., Reed, S., Anguelov, D., Erhan, D., Vanhoucke, V., Rabinovich, A.: Going deeper with convolutions. In: Proceedings of the IEEE Conference on Computer Vision and Pattern Recognition, pp. 1–9 (2015)
21. Szegedy, C., Reed, S., Erhan, D., Anguelov, D., Ioffe, S.: Scalable, high-quality object detection (2014). arXiv preprint: arXiv:1412.1441
22. Topouzelis, K., Karathanassi, V., Pavlakis, P., Rokos, D.: Detection and discrimination between oil spills and look-alike phenomena through neural networks. ISPRS J. Photogramm. Remote Sens. **62**(4), 264–270 (2007)
23. Topouzelis, K.N.: Oil spill detection by SAR images: dark formation detection, feature extraction and classification algorithms. Sensors **8**(10), 6642–6659 (2008)

A Secure and Energy-Efficient Data Aggregation Protocol Based on Wavelet

Jiana Bi$^{(\boxtimes)}$ and Qiangkui Leng

Department of Information Science and Technology,
Bohai University, Jinzhou, China
bijiana@aliyun.com, qkleng@126.com

Abstract. Directed diffusion is a data dissemination protocol for wireless sensor networks. In directed diffusion, interest and exploratory data are disseminated by flooding, which will bring broadcast storm resulting in substantial energy consumption of networks. Grid-based directed diffusion can improve the energy efficiency where geographic grids are constructed by self-organization of nodes using location information. The flooding of interest and exploratory data is limited in grid head nodes. To save more energy, a scheme of data aggregation based on wavelet sparseness is proposed. At the same time, to adapt to environments with high security requirements, secure schemes based on trust are added. The simulation experiments show that the proposed data aggregation scheme can obtain data aggregation results earlier and effectively extend lifetime of network. And experiments show that the proposed security schemes restrain malicious nodes when network is under attacks.

Keywords: Wireless sensor networks · Wavelet
Data aggregation · Security

1 Introduction

Due to the limited battery capacity, minimizing energy consumption is a key requirement in the design of wireless sensor networks (WSN). Directed diffusion (DD) [1] is a robust, scaled data dissemination protocol for WSN. Although DD provides a reliable and robust data aggregation solution, flooding of interest and exploratory data is its shortcoming. This results in increased channel contention and waste of bandwidth that will take further toll on the scarce energy resource of the nodes.

The problem is resolved by grid-based directed diffusion (GDD) [2]. In GDD, the network area is first divided into fixed grids. In each grid, one grid head node is elected to forward interest and sensing data. Due to rest nodes only receiving interest from grid head and sending data to grid head, broadcast overheads are reduced. To save more energy, in this paper, a scheme of data aggregation based on wavelet sparseness is proposed.

As WSN is usually deployed in open areas, sensor nodes are susceptible to a variety of attacks. A few authentication schemes have been proposed to prevent outside attackers, and they often use message authentication codes and key distribution schemes [3]. But they can't avoid injection of the forged data from malicious

© Springer Nature Singapore Pte Ltd. 2018
H. Yuan et al. (Eds.): GSKI 2017, CCIS 848, pp. 363–371, 2018.
https://doi.org/10.1007/978-981-13-0893-2_39

compromised insider nodes which have already been authenticated as legal ones in the networks. Some insider attack detection schemes based on statistics [4], hidden Markov model [5], data mining [6], game theory [7], and trust management [8] have been proposed. While they need more storage and computing resources of sensor nodes, and extra communications consume more energy. In this paper, a new insider attack detection approach is proposed to revoke the malicious compromised nodes with energy-saving consideration. Different kinds of nodes are monitored by different detection schemes to insure secure data aggregation.

2   Wavelet-Based Data Aggregation

The acquisition and transmission of large amount of sensing data bring heavy burden to the communication of WSN. Distributed data acquisition and processing is one of the most important research topics in WSN. Through distributed data acquisition and processing, data aggregation is realized and data transmission is reduced. It is beneficial to reduce the energy consumption of network transmission and prolong the network lifetime. The topology of WSN can be equated to an undirected graph. The communication links between the sensor nodes correspond to graph edges. In the process of information aggregation, wavelet theory [9] can be used to realize data sparseness and reduce data transmission, which is beneficial to further reduce network energy consumption and prolong network lifetime.

Assuming that $G = (V, E)$ is a connection diagram for topology of WSN. $V = [v_1, v_2 \cdots v_N]$ is the vertex set in the graph. It is the set of sensing nodes. E is the edge set in the graph. It's a set of communication links. The distance between two points in the signal space V is "jump". The extensive quantity and displacement of wavelet function are achieved through "jump".

$\mu(\cdot)$ is simple operation on V. The wavelet function should satisfy that the average value is zero. That is:

$$\int_V \Psi_{j,k}(v)\mu(dv) = 0 \tag{1}$$

In Eq. (1), $k = 1, 2, \ldots, N$. k is the displacement, and j is the extensive quantity. Take the vertex v_k as the center, and the circle of vertices within the range of h jumps is $N_h(v_k)$. The ring of vertices is $N'_h(v_k)(N'_h(v_k) \equiv N_h(v_k)/N_{h-1}(v_k))$.

Assuming that the wavelet function $\Psi_{j,k}$ is fixed value $c_{j,k,h}$, $h = 0, \ldots, j, j \leq J_k$. J_k is the maximum distance of the ring. The Eq. (1) can be rewritten as

$$\int_V \Psi_{j,k}\mu(dv) = \sum_{h=0}^{j} c_{j,k,h} \int_{N'_h(v_k)} \mu(dv)$$

$$= \sum_{h=0}^{j} c_{j,k,h} |N'_h(v_k)| = 0 \tag{2}$$

If $c_{j,k,h}$ has a function set $\varphi_{j,h}$, let it satisfy the Eq. (3):

$$c_{j,k,h} = \varphi_{j,k}/\left|N_h'(v_k)\right| \tag{3}$$

The wavelet function $\Psi_{j,k}$ can be expressed as

$$\Psi_{j,k}(v) = C_{j,k} \sum_{h=0}^{j} \frac{\varphi_{j,h}}{\left|N_h'(v_k)\right|} I_{k,h}(v) \tag{4}$$

And there are

$$\sum_{h=0}^{j} \varphi_{j,h} = 0 \tag{5}$$

$$I_{k,h}(v) = \begin{cases} 1 & v \in N_h'(v_k) \\ 1 & v \notin N_h'(v_k) \end{cases} \tag{6}$$

$$C_{j,k} = \left(\sum_{h=0}^{j} \varphi_{j,h}^2 / \left|N_h'(v_k)\right|\right)^{-0.5} \tag{7}$$

$\Psi_{j,k}$ satisfies the energy normalization:

$$\int v\Psi_{j,k}^2 \mu(dv) = 1 \tag{8}$$

It is known from Eq. (4) that, once topology of WSN is known, the wavelet coefficients can be determined by $\varphi_{j,h}$. $\varphi_{j,h}$ can be obtained by wavelet function piecewise average sampling.

$\varphi(x)$ is a ordinary wavelet function defined in the interval [0, 1]. $\varphi_{j,h}$ value is:

$$\varphi_{j,h} = (j+1) \int_{\Omega_{j,h}} \varphi(x)dx \tag{9}$$

$$\Omega_{j,k} = \left[\frac{h}{j+1}, \frac{h+1}{j+1}\right] \tag{10}$$

Due to $\int_0^1 \varphi(x)dx = 0$, $\varphi_{j,h}$ satisfies the Eq. (5).

The choice of $\varphi(x)$ is not limited. But different $\varphi(x)$ computes different wavelet sparseness and results in different compression performances. This article selects $\varphi(x)$ as the simplest Harr wavelet function, namely:

$$\varphi(x) = \begin{cases} 1 & 0 \leq x \leq 0.5 \\ -1 & 0.5 \leq x < 1 \\ 0 & \text{others} \end{cases} \tag{11}$$

So the value $\varphi_{j,h}$ can be calculated as:

$$\text{if } j \text{ is odd, } \varphi_{j,h} = \begin{cases} 1 & h \in [0, (j-1)/2] \\ -1 & h \in [(j-1)/2, j] \end{cases} \tag{12}$$

$$\text{if } j \text{ is even, } \varphi_{j,h} = \begin{cases} 1 & h \in [0, j/2-1] \\ 0 & h = j/2 \\ -1 & h \in [j/2+1, j] \end{cases} \tag{13}$$

The signal f is transformed by wavelet. So we get the following wavelet coefficients:

$$\langle f, \Psi_{j,k} \rangle = C_{j,k} \sum_{h=0}^{j} \varphi_{j,h} \text{Ave}_{N_h'(v_k)}(f) \tag{14}$$

Ave$(\cdot)$ is the average function.

It is known by the Eq. (14) that, if the central node knows the entire topology of WSN, we can get the wavelet transformation matrix Ψ. The signal sparseness can be obtained by setting the threshold of wavelet coefficients. We can get sparse transformation signals by setting the signal component with lower energy as zero.

By wavelet sparseness, data in WSN can be transmitted according to the wavelet transform matrix. Data traffic is dependent wavelet reduction ratio. When compressed signals are sent to the center processing node of WSN, the central node can obtain the global WSN information by reconstructing signals according to the wavelet transformation matrix.

3   Security Scheme

Since grid members only send exploratory data to grid head which participates with data forwarding, grid heads play more important roles. So electing a secure node to be grid head is important. In order to obtain secure data aggregation, it is necessary to take different monitor methods for grid head and member nodes.

3.1   Trust Evaluation by Neighbors

After setup of grid, the grid head creates a time division schedule and informs each grid member in the same grid. The member nodes are actively transmitting or listening for a period of the time and off the remainder. The member nodes transmit only at their scheduled time. This allows the nodes to listen to the communications in their respective grids. It is through this passive listening that the member nodes are able to develop trust relationship with their neighbor nodes. Nodes that constantly drop packets or which behave in a selective or selfish manner can be easily detected by their neighbors. Each node stores and maintains a trust table and records the trust values of its neighbors. As is shown in Eq. (15–17). T_i is the trust value of its neighbor node i, and it is added by consistency value (C_i) and sensing communication value (S_i). Weights (W_1, W_2) are dynamic and dependent on applications. cs_i means times of collecting the same sensing data with neighbor node i, and is_i means times of collecting different sensing data. ss_i means times of sensing the same event with neighbor node i, and sf_i means times of sensing different event.

$$C_i = \frac{cs_i - is_i}{cs_i + is_i} \quad where \ -1 \leq C_i \leq 1 \tag{15}$$

$$S_i = \frac{ss_i - sf_i}{ss_i + sf_i} \quad where \ -1 \leq S_i \leq 1 \tag{16}$$

$$T_i = W_1 C_i + W_2 S_i \tag{17}$$

3.2 Secure Grid Head Election

When the current grid head's battery power level falls below a predetermined threshold or serves for a predetermined period of time, it broadcasts (within the grid) a new election message. All the nodes then vote for a new grid head by using ballot. This is done by replying to the new election message with its choice of candidate. The top pick from the trust table of its neighbors is selected as the grid's candidate. At the same time, every node sends its remainder of energy to the gird head.

The current grid head then tallies the votes and decides the winner based on Eq. (18). P_j means votes of node j, while B_j means its remainder of energy. Weights (W_3, W_4) are dynamic and dependent on applications. If security is more important, W_3 is designed higher. If lifetime of network is critical, W_4 is designed higher. At the completion of computing, the grid head broadcasts the winner that has the highest value of Z to all the members of the grid.

$$Z = W_3 P_j + W_4 B_j \tag{18}$$

3.3 Monitoring Method for Grid Head

We add a virtual grid head in each grid to monitor grid head. The virtual grid head is elected among neighbors of the grid head. Its work is to listen to grid head's all input and output communications, and record the wrong conclusion counts being drawn by the grid head. Once the wrong counts exceed a threshold, the virtual head sends a broadcast message in its grid to initiate a new round of grid head election, and the former grid head is forbidden to be elected as grid head for ever.

3.4   Monitoring Method for Grid Member

Every gird head maintains an alarm table to record the alarm messages of its grid members. The alarm table consists of two fields. The first field records the identify (ID) of the suspected grid member, and the second one takes down the counts of alarm messages. When detecting misbehavior of a grid member, grid head updates alarm messages. Once a suspected grid member's alarm counts exceed the alarm threshold, the grid head will send a broadcast message in its grid to revoke this abnormal member node, so malicious nodes are restrained.

3.5   Secure Data Aggregation

To combat failures in the reporting nodes, each node is assigned a SI, maintained at the grid head, to indicate its track records in reporting past events correctly. SI is a real number between zero and one, and it is initially set one. For each report a node makes, if that is deemed incorrect by the grid head, the node's SI is decreased. Similarly, for each report a node makes, if that is deemed correct by the grid head, the node's SI is increased, but not beyond one. Thus correctly functioning nodes will have a SI approaching one, while faulty and malicious nodes will have a low SI.

We assume that correct nodes are allowed to make occasional error due to natural causes. The rate of these errors is denoted the natural error rate. Let the natural error rate be f_r (<1). A variable v is maintained for each node at the grid head. Each time a node makes a report deemed faulty by the grid head, then v is increased by the expression $(1 - f_r)$. Each time a node makes a report deemed faulty by the grid head, v is decreased by f_r (if v is larger than zero). The SI is calculated as shown in Eq. (19). Where λ is a proportionality constant that is dependent on applications.

$$SI = e^{-\lambda V} \tag{19}$$

When receiving the first sensing event report, the grid head sets up a timer. When the timer expires, according to whether reporting the sensing event, the grid head divides the nodes into two groups. When the nodes that report the sensing event are more than that do not report, the grid head accepts the sensing event, and verifies the corresponding nodes' value of v. Then the grid head aggregates the sensing data according to Eq. (20). SI_i means the trust value of nodes. SR is the aggregation result. sr_i is the data sent by nodes.

$$SR = \frac{\sum_{i=1}^{m} (SI_i + 1)sr_i}{\sum_{i=1}^{m} (SI_i + 1)} \tag{20}$$

4   Performance Simulation

Our simulation uses the 1.6 Mbps802.11 MAC layer inns-2. The idle-time power dissipation is 35 mW, or nearly 10% of receive power dissipation (395 mW) and about 5% of transmit power dissipation (660 mW). We use vehicle tracking instance as simulation model application. In the application, a number of sensor nodes are randomly deployed in a rectangular sensor field. Each node has a radio range of 40m, and the grid size is 14 m × 14 m. The sources are selected at the top-left corner of the sensor field. Each source generates two events per second. The rate for exploratory events is chosen to be one event in 60 s. Events are modeled as 148-byte packets and interests as 120-bytepackets. Interests are periodically generated every 30 s at each sink. Diffusion is reinforced by default in the lowest delay path, along which exploratory data is first transmitted to the sink. Special grid messages are modeled as 88-byte packets.

4.1   Data Aggregation Result

Figure 1 shows results of average function, when captured node rate is 15%. Normal means normal average aggregation results. WSEDA is our secure data aggregation protocol based on wavelet. TFSDA [10] is another secure data aggregation protocol based on statistics. In Fig. 1, WSEDA obtains aggregation data earlier than TFSDA.

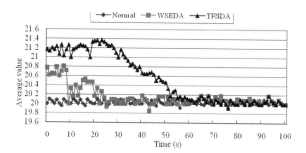

Fig. 1.   Aggregation result of average function

4.2   Network Lifetime

We apply attack to WSEDA and TSFDA. The traffic attack is assumed as that there are ten percent of nodes compromised and these nodes consume the energy of grid heads by sending abnormal sensing data with large size and forwarding redundant and forged data to grid heads. The network lifetime is observed. Network lifetime is defined as the time when the last node depletes its energy. The relationships between the number of total alive nodes and network lifetime are shown in Fig. 2 (without attacks) and Fig. 3 (under attacks). The simulation results show that the network lifetime is obviously decreased when network is under attacks. The network lifetime of WSEDA is much

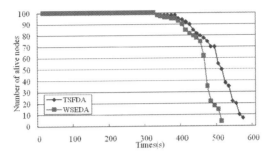

Fig. 2. Without attacks

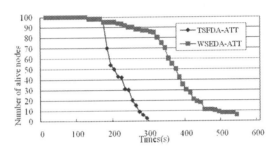

Fig. 3. Under attacks

longer than TSFDA. Because malicious nodes are detected and abnormal sensing data is dropped by the proposed approach.

5 Conclusion

In this paper, in order to save more energy, and adapt to secure applications, data aggregation protocol based on wavelet and secure schemes are added to GDD. By decreasing sensing data via wavelet sparseness, our data aggregation scheme cuts the aggregation time by half. According to different roles played by nodes, different monitor approaches are used. These approaches can detect malicious and compromised sensor nodes, and filter out false sensing data. Under attacks, the network lifetime of WSEDA is 2 times as much as ordinary protocol. Our secure data aggregation scheme does not employ cryptographic approaches or certification schemes, so it is light enough to fit well with WSN without great overheads.

Acknowledgement. This work was supported by the National Natural Science Foundation of China under grant 61602056, the Doctoral Scientific Research Foundation of Liaoning Province under grant 201601348, and the Scientific Research Project of Liaoning Provincial Committee of Education under grant LZ2016005.

References

1. Intanagonwiwat, C., Govindan, R., Estrin, D.: Directed diffusion for wireless sensor networking. IEEE Trans. Netw. **11**, 2–16 (2003)
2. Jiana, B., Zhenzhou, J., Zhiyan, C.: Grid-based directed diffusion for wireless sensor networks. High Technol. Lett. **14**, 342–347 (2008)
3. Tian, B., He, M.: A self-healing key distribution scheme with novel properties. Int. J. Netw. Secur. **7**, 115–120 (2008)
4. Loo, C.E., Ng, M.Y., Leckie, C., Palaniswami, M.: Intrusion detection for routing attacks in sensor networks. Int. J. Distrib. Sens. Netw. **2**, 313–332 (2006)
5. Doumit, S., Agrawal, D.P.: Self-organized criticality and stochastic learning based intrusion detection system for wireless sensor networks. In: IEEE Military Communications Conferences, Boston, USA, pp. 609–614 (2002)
6. Rajasegarar, S., Leckie, C., Palaniswami, M., Bezdek, J.C.: Distributed anomaly detection in wireless sensor networks. In: 10th IEEE Singapore International Conference of Communication System, Singapore, pp. 1–5 (2006)
7. Agah, A., Das, S.K., Basu, K., Asadi, M.: Intrusion detection in sensor networks: a non-cooperative game approach. In: 3rd IEEE International Symposium on Network Computing and Application, Cambridge, USA, pp. 343–346 (2004)
8. Hur, J., Lee, Y., Hong, S.M., Yoon, H.: Trust-based secure aggregation in wireless sensor networks. In: 3rd International Conference on Computing, Communications and Control Technologies, Austin, USA, pp. 491–496 (2005)
9. Crovella, M., Kolaczyk, E.: Graph wavelets for spatial traffic analysis. In: 22nd IEEE INFOCOM, San Francisco, USA, pp. 1848–1857 (2003)
10. Zhang, W., Das, S.K., Liu, Y.: A trust based framework for secure data aggregation in wireless sensor networks. In: 3rd Annual IEEE Communications Society Conference on Sensor and Ad Hoc Communications and Networks, Reston, USA, pp. 60–69 (2006)

Efficient Processing of the SkyEXP
Query Over Big Data

Zhenhua Huang[1(✉)], Chang Yu[1], Yong Tang[2], Yunwen Chen[3],
Shuhua Zhang[4], and Zhonghua Zheng[5]

[1] Tongji University, 4800 Caoan Road, Shanghai 201804, China
huangzhenhua@tongji.edu.cn, ycmels7@163.com
[2] South China Normal University,
55 Zhongshan Avenue West, Guangzhou 510631, China
ytang.scnu@163.com
[3] Datagrand Info. Tech. Co., Ltd., 112 Liangxiu Road, Shanghai 201203, China
dgchenyw@gmail.com
[4] Shanghai Zhongxin Info. Dvpt. Inc., Ltd.,
879 Zhongjiang Road, Shanghai 200333, China
zhangshuhual@gmail.com
[5] Anhui Boryou Info. Tech. Co., Ltd.,
2800 Chuangxin Road, Hefei 230000, Anhui, China
zhzheng.by@gmail.com

Abstract. Skyline query processing has recently received a lot of attention in the big data analysis community. However, in most real applications, the skyline result can not satisfy the needs of users. In this paper, we propose a novel type of skyEXP query to more efficiently analyze and explore the data. The skyEXP query on the subspace V divides the input data M into w separate subsets SE^1 $(M, V),..., SE^w (M, V)$ such that an object p belongs to $SE^i (M, V)$ if it is not dominated by any other objects on V except for those in $SE^1 (M, V),..., SE^{i-1}$ (M, V) where $i \in [1, w]$. In order to fast implement the proposed query over big data, an efficient parallel algorithm SQMRM (the SkyEXP Query using Map-Reduce Model) which utilizes the map-reduce framework is presented. Detailed theoretical analyses and extensive experiments demonstrate that our SQMRM algorithm is both efficient and effective.

Keywords: SkyEXP query · Map-reduce · Big data · Parallel processing

1 Introduction

The skyline operator and its computation have attracted much attention recently. This is mainly due to the importance of skyline results in several applications, such as information recommendation [1], social network analysis [2], and topic discovery [3]. A skyline query over k dimensions selects the objects that are not dominated by any other objects restricted to those dimensions. In fact, the preference function "dominate" can be defined in anyway as long as it is monotone on all these dimensions.

Tan *et al.* [4] presented the first progressive algorithms, namely Bitmap and Index method, which can output the skyline without having to scan the whole dataset. Lee

© Springer Nature Singapore Pte Ltd. 2018
H. Yuan et al. (Eds.): GSKI 2017, CCIS 848, pp. 372–383, 2018.
https://doi.org/10.1007/978-981-13-0893-2_40

et al. [5] developed and presented a novel and efficient processing framework to evaluate skyline queries and their variants, and to support skyline result updates based on Z-order curves. Zhang *et al.* [6] proposed an efficient skyline join algorithm Skyjog, which is applicable for query on two or more relations. Skyjog can quickly identify most of skyline join results with simple calculation. Chen *et al.* [7] designed a novel tree, named the G-tree, to upgrade the performance of a skyline query. The G-tree is based on the Gaussian function and able to overcome the difficulties that R-tree has in the skyline problem. To eliminate the negative effects on massive data processing in IoT (Internet-of-Things), Wang *et al.* [8] presented a novel skyline preference query strategy based on massive and the incomplete data set. And this strategy simply separates and divides massive and incomplete data set into two parts according to dimension importance and executes skyline query, respectively. Bai *et al.* [9] proposed the maintenance methods to process the subspace global skyline (SGS) queries in dynamic databases. Hsueh *et al.* [10] introduced a cache-based framework, called CSS, for reducing the query processing time to support high-responsive skyline query applications. The answered queries are cached with both their results and user preferences such that the query processor can rapidly retrieve the result for a new query only from the result sets of selected queries with compatible user preferences. Kim *et al.* [11] proposed an efficient method for processing multi-skyline queries with MapReduce without any modification of the Hadoop internals. Fu *et al.* [12] studied a new problem of range-based skyline queries (CRSQs) in road networks, and proposed two efficient algorithms: landmark-based (LBA) and index-based (IBA).

Clearly, these above existing works analyze the input dataset only by investigating its skyline result. However, in most real applications, for a k-dimensional dataset M, the cardinality of its skyline result does not exceed $(\ln^{k-1}|M|)/(|M|\cdot(k-1)!)$ [13]. Hence, the skyline result returned by these existing works cannot efficiently assist the users to explore the whole dataset. Motivated by this fact, in this paper, we proposes a novel type of skyEXP query to more efficiently analyze and explore the input data. The skyEXP query on the subspace V ($|V| \leq k$) divides the input dataset M into w separate subsets $SE^1 (M, V),\ldots, SE^w (M, V)$ such that an object p belongs to $SE^i (M, V)$ if and only if it is not dominated by any other objects on V except for those in $SE^1(M, V),\ldots,$ $SE^{i-1}(M, V)$ where $i \in [1, w]$. For example: assume that there exists a set of 2-dimensional objects $M = \{p_1(1.0, 2.9), p_2(2.2, 3.1), p_3(9.7, 2.8), p_4(3.9, 3.3), p_5(5.6, 2.4), p_6(4.9, 2.1), p_7(9.1, 2.8), p_8(3.7, 3.7)\}$. Then the skyEXP query on the full space $F = \{d_1, d_2\}$ returns 4 groups of skyline objects: $SE^1(M, F) = SKYLINE(M, F) = \{p_1, p_6\}$, $SE^2(M, F) = SKYLINE(M, SE^1(M, F), F) = \{p_2, p_5\}$, $SE^3(M, F) = SKYLINE(M-(SE^1(M, F) \cup SE^2(M, F)), F) = \{p_4, p_7, p_8\}$, and $SE^4(M, F) = SKYLINE(M-(SE^1(M, F) \cup SE^2(M, F) \cup SE^3(M, F)), F) = \{p_3\}$. Note that in the above example, $SKYLINE$ (M, F) denotes the set of skyline objects in M on F.

It is not difficult to see that compared with the traditional skyline query [4–11], the skyEXP query has at least two advantages: (*i*) the skyEXP query can provide more opportunities for users to analyze and explore the whole data, since it also consider the non-skyline objects; and (*ii*) since the skyEXP query divides the input dataset into k separate subsets which have the different grades, we can easily identify the feature of each object. Consequently, the skyEXP query is more meaningful in practice than the traditional skyline query.

To handle the skyEXP query on arbitrary subspace V, a straightforward solution is to run the existing approaches on the input dataset M w times, and each time it obtains one subset SE^i (M, V) where $i \in [1, w]$. Obviously, the straightforward solution becomes extremely inefficient as the cardinality of the input dataset increases, which can be seen in our experimental evaluation. In this paper, an efficient parallel algorithm SQMRM (SkyEXP Query using Map-Reduce Model) which utilizes the map-reduce framework is presented to meet the big data challenge. Furthermore, our SQMRM algorithm utilizes the multi-dimensional tensor [14] to organize the basic big data, and reduces the number of comparisons between objects by pruning all the tensor cells which are dominated by any other ones. Based on the map-reduce model [15] and multi-dimensional tensor, our SQMRM algorithm can dramatically decrease the computation cost of the SkyEXP query. The detailed theoretical analyses and extensive experiments demonstrate that our SQMRM algorithm is both efficient and effective.

2   The SkyEXP Query

In order to efficiently assist the users to explore the whole dataset, in this section, we present a new type of SkyEXP query. Give a k-dimensional full space $F = \{d_1, \ldots, d_k\}$, a set of objects $M = \{p_1, \ldots, p_n\}$ is said to be a dataset on F if each object $p_i \in M$ is a k-dimensional object on F. We use $p_i[d_t]$ to denote the t-th dimension value of p_i. For each dimension d_t, we assume that there exists a total order relationship, denoted by $\prec_t$, on its domain values. Here, $\prec_t$ can be '<' (i.e., MIN) or '>' (i.e., MAX) relationship according to the user's preference. For simplicity, in the following definitions, we assume that each pt represents '<'.

Definition 1 (*Dominance relationship*). An object p is said to dominate another object r on the subspace V ($V \subseteq F$) if it satisfies the following two conditions: (1) $\forall d_t \in V, p[d_t] \leq r[d_t]$; and (2) $\exists d_t \in V, p[d_t] < r[d_t]$; For simplicity, we use $r \prec_V p$ ($r \not\prec_V p$) to denote the relationship that p dominates (does not dominate) r on V. Moreover, we regard the full space F as a special subspace.

Definition 2 (*Subspace skyline object*). Let M be the set of k-dimensional objects. An object p is a skyline object in M on V ($V \subseteq F$) if and only if there does not exist any other object $r \in M$ such that $p \not\prec_V r$. We use $SKYLINE(M, V)$ to denote the set of skyline objects in M on V. Specially, $SKYLINE(AD, V)$ is called the skyline set of M on V.

Definition 3 (*Subspace skyline layers*). Let M be the set of k-dimensional objects. Then we can recursively define skyline layers on the subspace V as follows:

$$SE^{i+1}(M, V) = \begin{cases} SKYLINE(M, V) & \text{if } i = 0; \\ SKYLINE(M - \cup_{t=1}^{i}(M, V), V) & \text{if } i > 0. \end{cases}$$

The skyEXP query on V returns w subspace skyline layers SE^1 $(M, V), \ldots, SE^w(M, V)$ which have the different grades. Detailedly speaking, the 1st layer $SE^1(M, V)$ has the highest grade and corresponds to the skyline set of M on V (i.e., $SKYLINE(M, V)$); the

2nd layer $SE^2(M, V)$ has the second grade and corresponds to the skyline set of M-$SE^1(M, V)$ on V (i.e., $SKYLINE(M-SE^1(M, V), V)$); and so on. Thus, the users can evaluate each object in M according to its corresponding grade, and hence the subspace skyline layers returned by the skyEXP query can provide more opportunities for users to analyze and explore the whole dataset. Below, we prove that w is finite.

Theorem 1. Let M be the finite set of k-dimensional objects. Then we can have: $\forall p \in M, (\exists i, (i \geq 1 \land p \in SE^i(M, V)))$.

Proof. We prove the theorem by contradiction. Assume there exist an object $p \in M$ such that $\forall i, (i \geq 1 \land p \notin SE^i(M, V))$. Clearly, there exists an integer l such that $\forall t \geq l, SE^t(M, V) = \varnothing$ and $p \in M - \cup_{z=1}^{l-1} SE^z(M, V)$. Since $p \notin SE^l(M, V)$, there exists an object q such that $p \prec_V q$ and $q \in M - \cup_{z=1}^{l-1} SE^z(M, V)$; otherwise $p \in SE^l(M, V)$, which contradicts with the fact that $p \notin SE^l(M, V)$. Since $q \notin SE^l(M, V)$ and the dominance relationship "$\prec_V$" is a strict partial order relation, we can have that M is infinite. This contradicts with the fact that M is a finite set of k-dimensional objects. Hence, Theorem 1 holds.

3   The SQMRM Algorithm

In this section, we focus on efficient processing of arbitrary subspace skyEXP query.

3.1   Multi-dimensional Tensor Structure

In our SQMRM algorithm, we utilize the multi-dimensional tensor structure [14] to organize the objects, which has three advantages: (1) The multi-dimensional tensor can be efficiently used to implement arbitrary-subspace skyEXP query. Note that the R-tree structure and its variants [16] can be only used to implement fixed-subspace skyEXP query. (2) The multi-dimensional tensor can markedly reduce the cost of arbitrary-subspace skyEXP query by reducing the number of comparisons between objects. (3) Compared with other data structures, the multi-dimensional tensor is more suitable for the map-reduce model.

Example 1 (*Multi-dimensional tensor structure*). Assume there exists a set of 2-dimensional objects $M = \{p_1(1.0, 2.9), p_2(2.2, 3.1), p_3(9.7, 2.8), p_4(3.9, 3.3), p_5(5.6, 2.4), p_6(4.9, 2.1), p_7(9.1, 2.8), p_8(3.7, 3.7)\}$. Figure 1 shows the 2-dimensional tensor over M where the full space $F = \{d_1, d_2\}$. The ranges on d_1 and d_2 are $ranges_{d1} = \{[0, 2), [2, 4), [4, 6), [6, 8), [8, 10)\}$ and $ranges_{d2} = \{[0, 1), [1, 2), [2, 3), [3, 4), [4, 5)\}$. There are 25 tensor cells, $B_0, B_1, \ldots, B_{24}$. Each object is shown inside its converging tensor cell. For instance, $B_8 = <range_{d1}^1, range_{d2}^3> = <[2, 4), [3, 4)>$. It has three objects p_2, p_4 and p_8.

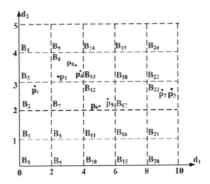

Fig. 1. The example for the multi-dimensional tensor.

3.2 Algorithm Description

In this section, based on the multi-dimensional tensor and map-reduce model, we propose the SQMRM algorithm to efficiently implement arbitrary subspace skyEXP query. For simplicity, in the rest of paper, we let the symbols V and v denote a special subspace and its dimensionality, respectively.

Since the multi-dimensional tensor is built on the full space F, we need to project each tensor cell on the subspace V before implementing the SQMRM algorithm. Let e be a full-space tensor cell. If pe is the projectee of e on the subspace V, then pe is called V-dimensional tensor cell of e and denoted as $e(V)$. In order to efficiently realize the algorithm, we need to distinguish three possibilities about the relationship between any two V-dimensional tensor cells $e_x(V) = <rg_1^{x_1}, \ldots, rg_v^{x_v}>$ and $e_y(V) = <rg_1^{y_1}, \ldots, rg_v^{y_v}>$.

(1) If $e_x(V)$ and $e_y(V)$ satisfy the following condition, then we say "$e_x(V)$ fully dominates $e_y(V)$": $\forall i \in [1, v], x_i < y_i$. We denote this relationship as $e_y(V) \lhd\lhd_V e_x(V)$.

(2) If $e_x(V)$ and $e_y(V)$ satisfy the following condition, then we say "$e_x(V)$ partially dominates $e_y(V)$": $\exists B \subset V, \forall z \in [1, |B|], x_z = y_z, \forall i \in [|B|, v], x_i < y_i$. We denote this relationship as $e_y(V) \lhd_V e_x(V)$.

(3) If $e_x(V)$ and $e_y(V)$ satisfy the following condition, then we say "$e_x(V)$ is incomparable with $e_y(V)$": $\exists i \in [1, v], x_i < y_i, \exists j \in [1, v], x_j > y_j$. We denote this relationship as $e_y(V) \rhd\lhd_V e_x(V)$.

Moreover, in order to efficiently implement our SQMRM algorithm, we need to organize all non-empty V-dimensional tensor cells as a consistent sequence $VSeq = <e_1(V), \ldots, e_\eta(V)>$ which satisfies the following property:

Property 1. For any two V-dimensional tensor cells $e_x(V), e_y(V) \in VSeq, e_x(V) = <rg_1^{x_1}, \ldots, rg_v^{x_v}>$ and $e_y(V) = <rg_1^{y_1}, \ldots, rg_v^{y_v}>$, if $x < y$, then $\Sigma_{i=1}^{v} x_i \leq \Sigma_{i=1}^{v} y_i$.

The main purpose to organize the cells as a consistent sequence $VSeq$ is to guarantee that $e_y(V)$ can not fully or partially dominate $e_x(V)$. Then for each object r inside $e_y(V)$, r can not dominate any object p inside $e_x(V)$ on V. Hence, it can markedly reducing the number of comparisons between objects. Moreover, if $e_y(V)$ is fully dominated by $e_x(V)$, then we can simply remove $e_y(V)$ from $VSeq$ and need not to handle any object inside $e_y(V)$. On the other hand, in order to utilize the map-reduce model, the SQMRM algorithm divides the consistent sequence $Vseq$ into m parts, and parallel processes these parts. In the map step, for each part $Vseq_i$ ($i \in [1, m]$), the SQMRM algorithm obtains its skyline layers on V. And in the reduce step, the SQMRM algorithm synthesizes all sub-skyline layers and produces the final skyline layers.

Based on the above analyses, the complete SQMRM algorithm can be shown below.

Algorithm 1: SQMRM
Input: the set of objects M, the subspace V, and k-dimensional tensor $\exists(M, F)$;
Output: the skyline layers on V;
Begin
1. Obtain all V-dimensional tensor cells which contain at least one object from $\exists(M, F)$;
2. Organize these non-empty tensor cells as a consistent sequence $VSeq=<e_1(V),\ldots, e_{\mathcal{G}}(V)>$ which satisfies: for any two tensor cells $e_x(V)=<rg_1^{x1},\ldots, rg_v^{xv} >$ and $e_y(V)=<rg_1^{y1}$ $,\ldots, rg_v^{yv} >,$

   if $x<y$, then $\Sigma_{i=1}^{v}x_i \leq \Sigma_{i=1}^{v}y_i$;
3. Construct $VSeq$'s corresponding key-value set $KY^{(Vseq)}=$ $\{<\text{'cs'}+i, e_i(V)>|i\in[1, \mathcal{G}]\}$;
4. Divide $KY^{(Vseq)}$ into m parts $KY^{(Vseq)}_1,\ldots, KY^{(Vseq)}_m$;
   /* m is the user parameter */
5. For $i=1$ to m Do
6. $\{<grade^p, p>\}\leftarrow$**map**$(KY^{(Vseq)}_i)$;
      /* p is the object inside $e_i(V)$, $grade^p$ is the grade of p */
7. Let the partition function $\overline{f}$ equal $(i \bmod n)$;
      /* n is the number of computers used to execute the reduce function */
8. For $j=1$ to n Do /* parallel processing */
9. $\{<grade^{SE}, SE>\}\leftarrow$**reduce**$(<grade^p, p>\})$;
      /* SE is the objects set, $grade^{SE}$ is the grade of SE */
10. Return SE in ascending order of $grade^{SE}$.
End
The map and reduce functions can be shown in Algorihm 2 and Algorihm 3.

The map and reduce functions can be shown in Algorithms 2 and 3.

Algorithm 2: the map function

Input: the key-value set $KY^{(Vseq)}=\{<\text{tensor cell ID, tensor cell}>\}$;

Output: the intermediary key-value set $KY^{(int)}$;

Begin

1. Let $p.dn \leftarrow 1$ for each object p;
   /* initialize the grade value of p */

2. For orderly visit each tensor cell $e(V)$ in ascending order of tensor cell ID Do

3. $O \leftarrow$ the set of objects inside $e(V)$;

4.   For each object $p \in O$ Do

5. $p.key \leftarrow \Sigma_{i=1}^{v} \ln(p[i]+1)$;

6. $L \leftarrow$ the object list obtained by sorting all the objects in O in the key ascending order;

7.   For orderly visit each object $p \in L$ Do

8.   For orderly visit each object $r \in L$ that locates before p Do

9.   If $p \prec_V r$ and $p.dn < r.dn+1$ Then

10. $p.dn \leftarrow r.dn+1$;

11.   For orderly visit each tensor cell $e(V)$' whose ID is smaller than $e(V)$ Do

12.   If $e(V) \lhd\lhd_V e(V)$' Then

13.   For each object $p \in L$ Do

14. $p.dn \leftarrow p.dn + \max_{r \in L'}\{r.dn\}$;

15.   If $e(V) \lhd_V e(V)$' Then

16.   For $\forall p \in L, \forall r \in L'$ Do

17.   If $p \prec_V r$ and $p.dn < r.dn+1$ Then

18. $p.dn \leftarrow r.dn+1$;

19. $OS \leftarrow$ the set of objects inside all tensor cells of $KY^{(Vseq)}$;

20. $KY^{(int)} \leftarrow \varnothing$;

21.   For each objects $p \in OS$ Do

22. $KY^{(int)} \leftarrow KY^{(int)} \cup <p.dn, p>$;

23.   Return $KY^{(int)}$;

End

Algorithm 3: the reduce function
Input: the intermediary key-value set $KY^{(int)}$={<the grade of object, the object inside tensor>}
Output: the key-value set KY;
Begin
1. $mg \leftarrow$ the maximal grade value of objects inside tensor;
2. For i=1 to mg Do
3. $S_i \leftarrow \{p|p.dn=i\}$; /* dn is the grade value of p */
4. $KY \leftarrow \varnothing$;
5. For i=1 to mg-1 Do
5.   Obtain the skyline objects set SE_i over S_i;
6. $KY \leftarrow KY \cup \{<i, SE_i>\}$;
7. $S_{i+1} \leftarrow S_{i+1} \cup (S_i - SE_i)$;
8. $KY \leftarrow KY \cup \{<mg, S_{mg}>\}$;
9. Return KY;
End

4   Experimental Evaluation

4.1   Experimental Environment

In our experiments, the experimental architecture consists of 30 PCs, each PC has a quad-core i5-3450 CPU, 4G memory, 500G hard drive, and CentOS Linux 6.4 operating system. One PC is selected as the control computer (Master). These 30 PC constitutes a Hadoop platform whose version number is 1.0.3. Using the data generator [4], we generate two types of synthetic datasets: (1) Independent datasets where the dimension values of the generated objects are uniformly distributed; (2) Anti-correlated datasets where if an object is good in one dimension, it is unlikely to be good in other dimensions. In our experiments, we totally produce 800G data, and each object has 10 dimensions whose data types are 4-byte float.

Since the G-tree algorithm [7] up till now is the best one to process arbitrary subspace skyline query, we extend it to process the skyEXP query, and denote this extended version as G-tree$^+$. The modification policy is straightforward and can be described in Algorithm 4.

Algorithm 4: G-tree⁺

Input: the set of objects M, the subspace V;

Output: the skyline layers on V;

Begin

1. $dn \leftarrow 0$;
2. While there exists an object $p \in M$ which does not belong to any skyline layer Do
3. $dn \leftarrow dn + 1$;
4. $\mathfrak{I} \leftarrow \bigcup_{t=1}^{dn-1} SE^{dn}(M, V)$;
5. $SE^{dn}(M, V) \leftarrow$ G-tree⁺$(M - \mathfrak{I}, V)$;
6. Return dn skyline layers on V: $SE^1(M, V), \ldots, SE^{dn}(M, V)$;

End

4.2   Evaluating the SkyEXP Query

In this subsection, we compare our SQMRM algorithm with the G-tree⁺ algorithm for the skyEXP query. The experimental setting is: (1) the size of every dataset varies in the range [200G, 800G]; (2) the dimensionality of full space is fixed to 10; (3) the dimensionality of subspace varies in the range [2, 10]. Figures 2 and 3 show the results of experiments for independent datasets and anti-correlated datasets, respectively.

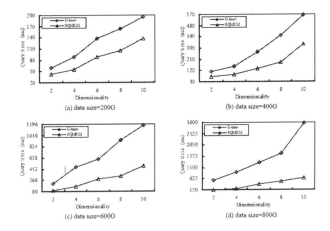

Fig. 2. Independent datasets.

From Fig. 2, we can observe that our SQMRM algorithm evidently outperforms the G-tree⁺ algorithm in all cases. For example, in Fig. 2(a), when the dimensionality of subspace is equal to 10, the query times of the algorithms G-tree⁺ and SQMRM are equal to 194.7 s and 137.2 s, respectively. That is, in this case, the query time of our SQMRM algorithm is about 70.5% of that of the G-tree⁺ algorithm. While in Fig. 2(d), when the dimensionality of subspace is equal to 10, the query times of the algorithms

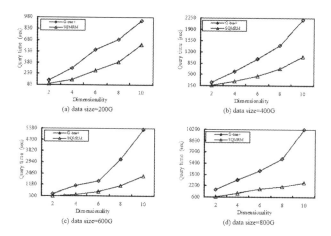

Fig. 3. Anti-correlated datasets.

G-tree$^+$ and SQMRM are equal to 2982.9 s and 653.7 s, respectively. That is, in this case, the query time of our SQMRM algorithm is only about 21.9% of that of the G-tree$^+$ algorithm.

The results of experiments in Fig. 3 are similar with the case where the datasets are independent. Observe however, that each algorithm needs to spend more query time in this case. It is mainly because there are more skyline layers in anti-correlated datasets. We further observe that our SQMRM algorithm can outperforms the G-tree$^+$ algorithm by factors ranging from two for the low dimensionality to more than an order of magnitude for the high dimensionality.

From Figs. 2 and 3, we can further observe that the superiority of our SQMRM algorithm over the G-tree$^+$ algorithm becomes more marked as the size of data increases. The main reasons are: (*i*) when the size of data increases, the number of objects falling inside each tensor cell will increase, and hence the pruning effect of our SQMRM algorithm is more evident; and (*ii*) when the size of data increases, the map-reduce parallel model will be more efficient for skyEXP computation. For more visuality, we draw this observation in Fig. 4. It is easy to see from Fig. 4 that as the size of data increases, the query time ratio of SQMRM to G-tree$^+$ becomes smaller. For example, in Fig. 4(a), when the dimensionality of subspace is equal to 10, the query time ratio of SQMRM to G-tree$^+$ is 70.5%, 58.1%, 43.1% and 21.9%, respectively, for

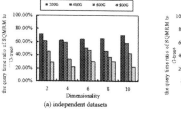
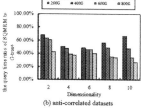

Fig. 4. The query time ratio of SQMRM to G-tree$^+$.

200G, 400G, 600G and 800G. While in Fig. 4(b), when the dimensionality of subspace is equal to 10, the query time ratio of SQMRM to G-tree$^+$ is 66.3%, 47.9%, 34.2% and 26.1%, respectively, for 200G, 400G, 600G and 800G.

5 Conclusions

Skyline query result can not satisfy the needs of users in most real applications because it filters many meaningful objects. In this paper, we present a novel type of skyEXP query to more efficiently analyze and explore the data. To efficiently handle the arbitrary subspace skyEXP query, an efficient parallel algorithm SQMRM which uses the map-reduce framework and the multi-dimensional tensor is presented to meet the big data challenge. The detailed theoretical analyses and extensive experiments demonstrate that our SQMRM algorithm is both efficient and effective.

Acknowledgments. This work is supported by the Shanghai Rising-Star Program (No. 15QA1403900), the Natural Science Foundation of Shanghai (No. 17ZR1445900), the National Natural Science Foundation of China (No. 61772366), the Fok Ying-Tong Education Foundation (142002) and the Fundamental Research Funds for the Central Universities.

References

1. Qin, G., Li, T., Yu, B., et al.: Mining factors affecting taxi drivers' incomes using GPS trajectories. Transp. Res. Part C: Emerg. Technol. **79**, 103–118 (2017)
2. Huang, Z., Shijia, E., Zhang, J., et al.: Pairwise learning to recommend with both users' and items' contextual information. IET Commun. **10**(16), 2084–2090 (2016)
3. Kou, N.M., Yang, Y., Gong, Z.: Travel topic analysis: a mutually reinforcing method for geo-tagged photos. GeoInformatica **19**(4), 693–721 (2015)
4. Tan, K.L., Eng, P.K., Ooi, B.C.: Efficient progressive skyline computation. In: Proceedings of the International Conference on Very Large Data Bases, pp. 301–310. Morgan Kaufmann Publishers Inc. (2001)
5. Lee, K.C., Lee, W.C., Zheng, B., et al.: Z-SKY: an efficient skyline query processing framework based on Z-order. VLDB J. Int. J. Very Large Data Bases **19**(3), 333–362 (2010)
6. Zhang, J., Lin, Z., Li, B., et al.: Efficient skyline query over multiple relations. Procedia Comput. Sci. **80**, 2211–2215 (2016)
7. Chen, Y.C., Liao, H.C., Lee, C.: A novel G-tree for accelerating the time-consuming skyline query. In: Proceedings of the 12th International Conference on Information and Knowledge Engineering, pp. 1–7 (2013)
8. Wang, Y., Shi, Z., Wang, J., et al.: Skyline preference query based on massive and incomplete dataset. IEEE Access **5**, 3183–3192 (2017)
9. Bai, M., Xin, J., Wang, G., et al.: The subspace global skyline query processing over dynamic databases. World Wide Web **20**(2), 291–324 (2017)
10. Hsueh, Y.L., Hascoet, T.: Caching support for skyline query processing with partially ordered domains. IEEE Trans. Knowl. Data Eng. **26**(11), 2649–2661 (2014)
11. Kim, J., Lee, K.H., Kim, M.H.: Simultaneous processing of multi-skyline queries with MapReduce. IEICE Trans. Inf. Syst. **100**(7), 1516–1520 (2017)

12. Fu, X., Miao, X., Xu, J., et al.: Continuous range-based skyline queries in road networks. World Wide Web **20**, 1–25 (2017)
13. Huang, Z., Sun, S., Wang, W.: Efficient mining of skyline objects in subspaces over data streams. Knowl. Inf. Syst. **22**(2), 159–183 (2010)
14. Wu, K., Shin, Y., Xiu, D.: A randomized tensor quadrature method for high dimensional polynomial approximation. SIAM J. Sci. Comput. **39**(5), A1811–A1833 (2017)
15. Peng, C., Zhang, C., Peng, C., et al.: A reinforcement learning approach to map reduce auto-configuration under networked environment. Int. J. Secur. Netw. **12**(3), 135–140 (2017)
16. Jin, P., Xie, X., Wang, N., et al.: Optimizing R-tree for flash memory. Expert Syst. Appl. **42**(10), 4676–4686 (2015)

Research on Comprehensive Benefits of Urban Rail Transit System Based on the Joint Evaluation Methods

Hongjiao Xue[(✉)], Ping Yang, and Hong Zhang

Beijing Polytechnic, No. 9, Street 1 Liangshuihe, Beijing, China
18519339569@126.com, kisssun2016@126.com,
13661165431@126.com, 13436520270@126.com,
chipzhang@126.com

Abstract. In this paper, based on qualitative and quantitative analysis method and the use of theoretical deduction, model building, empirical research and statistical analysis, the comprehensive benefits of urban rail transit system are studied. This paper analyzed the system structure of the comprehensive benefits of urban rail transit system, and described the traffic benefits, economic benefits, social benefits from the angles of causal relationship, then revealed the system correlation and development law of the various benefits of urban rail transit system. In this paper, the analytical hierarchy process and fuzzy comprehensive evaluation method were used to establish a comprehensive evaluation model, which constructed the evaluation process and improved the evaluation system of existing rail transit system. Finally, the author conducted an empirical study, tested the evaluation methods and analyzed the results, then put forward some suggestions on the development strategy of urban rail transit system and provided decision support.

Keywords: Urban rail transit · Comprehensive benefits · Evaluation
Traffic benefits · Economic benefits · Social benefits

1 Introduction

With the rapid economic development and improvement of urbanization in china, the demand for urban transport has soared and the contradiction between supply and demand is prominent. Heavy traffic and pollution have become widespread problems in big cities. The traditional way of road transportation has been unable to adapt to the growing demands of residents, then developing the urban rail transport system has become an effective solution to urban traffic congestion and can also bring comprehensive benefits to urban development at the same time. The urban rail transit system has become the first choice to solve traffic problems in many big cities with the advantages of large freight volume, fast, safety and less environmental pollution.

In recent decades, the rate of public transportation growth has significantly outpaced the growth of highway travel and the growth of the population. Recent trends also indicate ridership on public transit is growing faster than funding levels and

© Springer Nature Singapore Pte Ltd. 2018
H. Yuan et al. (Eds.): GSKI 2017, CCIS 848, pp. 384–396, 2018.
https://doi.org/10.1007/978-981-13-0893-2_41

service provided. The number of trips on the buses, trains and ferries has reached the highest level since 1980.

Urban rail transportation encompasses a broad, interconnected set of modes including subways, light rail, streetcars, commuter rail, and high-performance intercity passenger rail.

As the important infrastructure, urban rail transit system brings obvious economic benefits, social benefits and traffic benefits, the sum of all three of these benefits compose the comprehensive benefits of urban rail transit system. The overall improvement of comprehensive benefits is the goal of the development of the urban rail transit system, and the improvement of the three benefits is an effective way to improve the efficiency of the comprehensive benefits.

The traffic benefits of urban rail transit system refer to the benefits for urban transportation system and other aspects brought by the urban rail transit project. The beneficiary includes two aspects: passenger and urban transport system. When the beneficiary subject is passenger, the traffic benefits of urban rail transit system are reflected by the efficient travel tools, reduced time cost, comfort and traffic safety provided for passengers; When the beneficiary subject is urban transport system, the rail transit projects increased the supply of urban transportation products, so as to improve the public transport structure and spatial structure of the public traffic and relieve the urban ground traffic congestion, improve the supply and demand of urban public transport. At the same time, the characteristic of large volume and convenience of rail transit will trigger the new passenger traffic.

The economic benefits of urban rail transit system refer to the benefits for urban economic development and other aspects brought by urban rail transit projects. The beneficiary includes three aspects: Orbital operation enterprise, indirect enterprise and urban economic system. When the beneficiary subject is a rail project enterprise, the urban rail transit project brings rail operators operating income, the direct economic returns as the ticket revenue, space rental income, and other related services. Due to the construction and operation of urban rail transit projects, the benefits of real estate enterprises, commercial service enterprises and other related enterprises have undergone great changes. Both domestic and foreign experience have proved that urban rail transit projects can greatly enhance the value of real estate along the line. Due to the improvement of traffic environment and the surrounding traffic conditions along the orbit, the urban rail brings more traffic and become a cluster of different passenger flows, the benefits of corresponding commercial service enterprise will be improved. These are the economic benefits of urban rail transit system.

The social benefits of urban rail transit system refer to the benefits that urban rail transit projects bring to urban social development and other aspects. The beneficiary includes two aspects: City or related area, environmental system. When the beneficiary subject is the city, the urban rail transit project will bring about the improvement of urban popularity, the optimization of the investment environment and the provision of more employment and other social benefits. When the beneficiary subject is the urban environment system, the urban environment can be protected and optimized because the urban rail transit project has a larger capacity, lower energy consumption and the advantages of more intensive utilization of land than in buses, cars and other public transportation.

2   Methods

In this evaluation model, there are 14 indicators that constitute the comprehensive evaluation index system of urban rail transit, Marked B1, B12...... et al.

There are 3 primary indicators, namely traffic benefits, economic benefits and social benefits.

A total of 14 secondary indicators, the secondary indicators from traffic benefits are transport capacity alternative benefits, accessibility benefits, safety benefits, travel efficiency benefits and comfort benefits; The secondary indicators of economic benefits have operation benefits, economic growth benefits, value-added benefits of real estate, industrial restructuring and the layout optimization benefits. The secondary indicators of social benefits have energy conservation benefits, pollutant emission reduction benefits, land conservation benefits, employment benefits and urban vitality benefits. As shown in Fig. 1.

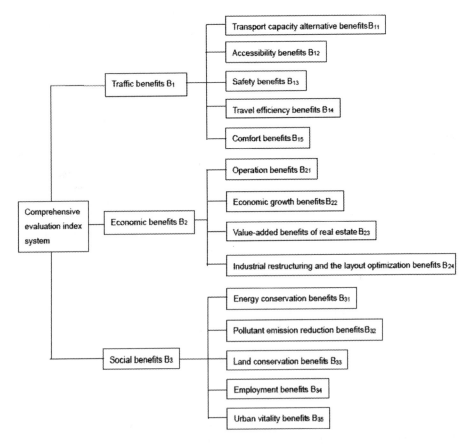

Fig. 1. The composition indicators of the comprehensive benefits of rail transit.

2.1   Traffic Benefits Indicator

Transport capacity alternative benefits: Transport capacity alternative benefits refer in particular to the benefits of the operation of the urban rail transit lines instead of buses, taxis and other public transport resource, including savings in vehicle purchase expense, vehicle operating costs, transport infrastructure construction fee, etc.

Accessibility benefits: Accessibility benefits mainly refer to the benefits brought by the accessibility advantages of urban rail transit under abnormal climate conditions. Abnormal climate conditions mainly refer to the extreme weather such as storm and blizzard. Fully enclosed urban rail transit is less affected by the weather, and it is the best choice to ensure the smooth and normal transport of passengers in bad weather.

Safety benefits: The safety benefits mainly refer to the benefits caused by the decrease of the frequency of accidents and reduction of economic losses by using urban rail traffic compared with the buses, taxis and private cars.

Travel efficiency benefits: The travel efficiency benefits are the benefits of the efficiency by saving the travel time due to choosing to take the urban rail transit instead of the bus on the ground.

Comfort benefits: The comfort benefits mean that urban rail transit is more comfortable than the bus, and because of the short journey time and the decline in the fatigue, it can improve the efficiency of the passenger's labor productivity.

2.2   Economic Benefits Indicator

Operation benefits: Operation benefits refers to the economic benefits brought by the operation of urban rail transit projects, mainly composed of operating costs and investment costs. The operating costs of urban rail transit projects at home and abroad are mostly divided into: operating expenses and operating government subsidies; The cost of investment is divided into construction cost and renovation cost.

Economic growth benefits: The economic growth benefits of urban rail transit mainly refer to the effects of urban rail transit on urban economy, which can be divided into the direct effects and indirect effects. Direct effects refer to the impact of urban rail transit on direct related industries during construction and operation, such as construction, design, supervision, building materials, machinery manufacturing, electronics, metallurgy and other industries. Indirect effects refer to the radiation effects of urban rail transit construction on industry and social groups, the effects on those who are not directly related with the main subject of urban rail transit construction, such as real estate, environmental protection, tourism, entertainment, e-commerce and other industries.

The value-added benefits of real estate: The value-added benefits of real estate refer to the benefits caused by traffic accessibility, convenience, comfort and transformed site conditions which were brought by the urban rail transit development in the area along the urban rail.

Industrial restructuring and the layout optimization benefits: The benefits of industrial restructuring and layout optimization refers to the benefits brought by the adjustment and optimization of different industries in the area caused by urban rail transit development.

2.3 Social Benefits Indicator

Energy conservation benefits: Energy conservation benefits mainly refers to the benefits of reduced energy consumption as a result of the urban rail transit lines running instead of other transportation.

Pollutant emission reduction benefits: The pollutant emission reduction benefits are the benefits of decreased pollution emission due to the use of urban rail transit line compared with other urban modes of transportation.

Land conservation benefits: The land conservation benefits are mainly reflected in the efficiency of the use of the urban rail transit route in lieu of other urban modes of transportation.

Employment benefits: Employment benefit is the result of the construction of urban rail transit line and the increase of employment.

Urban vitality benefits: The urban vitality benefits are the results of the construction of urban rail transit system which enhances the flow of goods and turnover and drives the benefits of the benign development of the city.

2.4 Design of Traffic Benefits Indicator

Transport capacity alternative benefits:
The calculation method is as follows:

$$B_{11} = \sum_{j=1}^{n} \left(\frac{N_i * C_{\text{purchase i}}}{Y_i} + C_{\text{operation i}} * N_i \right) + \sum_{i=1}^{m} \left(\frac{N_{\text{facility i}} * C_{\text{facility i}}}{Y_{\text{facility i}}} \right)$$
$$- C_{\text{operating cost}}$$

B_{11}:	Urban rail transit transport capacity alternative benefits, ten thousand yuan;
N_i:	The number of buses and taxis that urban rail transit replaced, unit;
$N_{\text{facility i}}$:	The area of transport facilities that urban rail transit replaced, m²;
$C_{\text{purchase i}}$:	Unit bus, taxi purchase fee, ten thousand RMB/car;
$C_{\text{operation i}}$:	Unit bus, taxi year operating expenses, ten thousand RMB/car;
$C_{\text{facility i}}$:	Construction cost of unit transportation facilities, Yuan/m²;
Y_i :	Years of depreciation of buses and taxis, years;
$Y_{\text{facility i}}$:	The period of depreciation of transportation facilities that urban rail transit replaced, 10 years;
$C_{\text{operating cost}}$:	Annual operating expenses of urban rail transit lines, Yuan/year

Accessibility benefits:
The calculation method is as follows:

$$B_{12} = D_{\text{extreme}} * T_{\text{congestion}} * F_{\text{line average daily}} * GDP_{person} * 0.5$$

B_{12}:   The accessibility benefits of urban rail transit, ten thousand yuan;
$D_{extreme}$:   The average annual extreme weather occurs, days;
$T_{congestion}$:   Daily traffic congestion time, hours;
$F_{line\ average\ daily}$: Daily passenger flow of urban rail transit line, 000-person-time;
GDP_{person}:   Per capita GDP per unit time, Yuan/Hour. Person

Safety benefits:
The calculation method is as follows:

$$B_{13} = \sum_{i=1}^{n} N_i * L_i$$

B_{13}:   The safety benefits of urban rail transit;
L_i: Annual vehicle accident cost, Ten thousand RMB/car

Travel efficiency benefits:
The calculation method is as follows:

$$B_{14} = F_{line} * T_{rail} * GDP_{person} * 0.5$$

B_{14}:   Travel efficiency benefits of urban rail transit, ten thousand yuan;
F_{line}: Annual passenger volume of urban rail transit, 000 person-time;
T_{rail}: Travel time saved on average of each person by urban rail transit, hours

Comfort benefits:
The calculation method is as follows:

$$B_{15} = \left(F_{line} * CO_{round\ trip} * CO_{work} \right) * \left[\frac{1 - R_{rail}}{1 - R_{others}} - 1 \right] * T_{average\ daily} * GDP_{person}$$

B_{15}:   The comfort benefits of urban rail transit, ten thousand yuan;
$CO_{round\ trip}$:   Passenger flow coefficient;
CO_{work}:   The proportion of passengers who work;
R_{others}:   Reduced productivity by other public transport fatigue;
R_{rail}:   Reduced productivity by urban rail transit fatigue;
$T_{average\ daily}$: Per capita labor time, hours

2.5   Design of Economic Benefits Indicator

Operation benefits:
The calculation method is as follows:

$$B_{21} = I_{ticket} + I_{commerce} - C_{operation} - C_{capitalized\ cost}$$

B_{21}:   The operational benefits of urban rail transit, ten thousand yuan;
I_{ticket}:   Ticket revenue, ten thousand yuan/year;
$I_{commerce}$:   Other commercial income, ten thousand yuan/year;

$C_{operation}$:   Annual operation cost of urban rail transit, ten thousand yuan/year;
$C_{capitalized\ cost}$:   Investment cost of rail transit construction, ten thousand yuan/year

Economic growth benefits:
Economic growth benefits indicator is difficult to quantify, and experts are generally used to rate it.
The value-added benefits of real estate:
The calculation method is as follows:

$$B_{23} = (P_2 - P_1)/P_1$$

B_{23}:   The value-added benefits of real estate in urban rail transit, Percentage increase;
P_2:   The added value of real estate in the area within 2000 m of the urban rail transit line, yuan/m^2;
P_1:   The added value of real estate in the area outside of the urban rail transit line, yuan/m^2

Industrial restructuring and the layout optimization benefits:
Industrial restructuring and the layout optimization benefits indicator is difficult to quantify, and experts are generally used to rate it.

2.6   Design of Social Benefits Indicator

Energy conservation benefits:
The calculation method is as follows:

$$B_{31} = (N_{bus} * E_{bus} + N_{taxi} * E_{taxi}) * V_{gas} - N_{rail} * E_{rail} * V_{electricity}$$

B_{31}:   Energy conservation benefits of urban rail transit, ten thousand yuan;
N_{bus}:   The number of buses replaced by urban rail transit, unit;
N_{taxi}:   The number of taxis replaced by urban rail transit, unit;
E_{bus}:   The annual energy consumption of each bus, Tons/year;
E_{taxi}:   The annual energy consumption of each taxi, Tons/year;
V_{gas}:   The economic value of unit gasoline, Yuan/ton;
N_{rail}:   The number of urban rail vehicles, unit;
E_{rail}:   The annual energy consumption of each urban rail transit, KWH/year;
$V_{electricity}$:   Unit energy economic value, Yuan/KWH

Pollutant emission reduction benefits:
The calculation method is as follows:

$$B_{32} = N_{bus} * P_{bus} + N_{taxi} * P_{taxi}$$

B_{32}:   Pollution reduction benefits from urban rail transit;
P_{bus}:   The air pollution cost per bus, ten thousand yuan/year;
P_{taxi}:   The air pollution cost per taxi, ten thousand yuan/year

Land conservation benefits:
The calculation method is as follows:

$$B_{33} = \left(\sum_{i=1}^{n} S_i - S_{rail} \right) * IV_{opportunity}$$

B_{33}:   Land conservation benefits, ten thousand yuan;
S_i: The area of the saved traffic facilities by urban rail transit, m²;
S_{rail}:   The area of urban rail transit, m²;
$IV_{opportunity}$:   Opportunity cost per unit area, ten thousand yuan/m²

Employment benefits:
The calculation method is as follows:

$$B_{34} = IV_{rail} * 140 * GDP_{per\ capita\ area}$$

B_{34}:   Employment benefits;
IV_{rail}:   Total investment in urban rail transit lines, ten thousand yuan;
$GDP_{per\ capita\ area}$:   Per capita GDP, ten thousand yuan/year

Urban vitality benefits:
Urban vitality benefits indicator is difficult to quantify, and experts are generally used to rate it.

2.7   The Assessment Method of Comprehensive Benefits for Urban Rail Transit

This paper selects a fuzzy comprehensive evaluation model based on hierarchical analysis to evaluate the comprehensive benefit of urban rail transit system. The calculation steps are as follows:
Multiply each row of the matrix by M_{ij}:

$$M_{ij} = \prod_{j=1}^{n} b_{ij}(i - 1, 2, \ldots,)$$

Calculate the n th root Wi of M_{ij}:

$$W_i = \sqrt[n]{m_i}(i = 1, 2, \ldots n)$$

The weight of each index is obtained by normalization of vectors:

$$W_i = \frac{W_i}{\sum_{j=1}^{n} w_j}(i = 1, 2, \ldots n)$$

Calculate the maximum characteristic root of matrix:

$$\lambda_{max} = \sum_{i=1}^{n} \frac{(AW)_j}{nw_i}$$

Determine the index of matrix consistency:

$$CI = \frac{\lambda_{max} - n}{n - 1}$$

Random consistency ratio:

$$CR = \frac{CI}{IR}$$

2.8 The Nondimensionalization of the Comprehensive Benefit Evaluation Indicator

In this paper, the threshold method is proposed to make the evaluation indicator of urban rail transit comprehensive benefit dimensionless. Threshold method is a dimensionless method for evaluating the value of the indicator by comparing the actual value with the threshold value. The algorithm formula is as follows:

$$y_i = \frac{x_i}{\max_{1 \leq i \leq n} x_i}$$

$$y_i = \frac{x_i - \min_{1 \leq i \leq n} x_i}{\max_{1 \leq i \leq n} x_i - \min_{1 \leq i \leq n} x_i}$$

After the dimensionless evaluation of the comprehensive evaluation indicator, the judgment matrix of the comprehensive benefit evaluation of urban rail transit is obtained by V:

$$V = \begin{bmatrix} V_{1,1} & \cdots & V_{1,14} \\ \vdots & \ddots & \vdots \\ V_{n,1} & \cdots & V_{n,14} \end{bmatrix}$$

2.9   The Determination of Index Weight of Comprehensive Benefit Assessment

Through the analysis of different weighting methods, this paper selects the analytic hierarchy process to give weight to the comprehensive evaluation index of urban rail transit. The specific steps are as follows:

Construct the hierarchy of comprehensive benefit evaluation index. Start by grouping all the included indicators, then each group as a hierarchy, arranged in the form from the highest, middle layers to the lowest layers, as is shown in Fig. 1.

Construct two comparison judgment matrix. According to the evaluation indicator system of urban rail transit comprehensive benefits, two comparison judgment matrices is constructed. Five experts were invited to evaluate the relative importance of each indicator in terms of its importance from scale 1 to 9.

Hierarchical order ranking and its consistency check. According to the expert judgment matrix, the weight value of the order of importance of the contact factor as to the upper factors is calculated.

Total ordering. It mainly uses the results of the previous step to calculate the weight value of the importance of all factors in this level, i.e. the total ordering, which is carried out from the highest to the lowest layer. Based on the above four steps, we finally get the weight of evaluation index given by five experts, and the average weight of five experts is used as the weight of the comprehensive benefit evaluation model of urban rail transit system, represented by B. In the calculation of this paper, the weights of the integrated benefit indexes of each line are the same in order to facilitate the comparison of the comprehensive benefit ratio between different lines. B = (b1, b2......b14).

Synthesis algorithm design and comprehensive evaluation. After evaluating each indicator, the weighted average synthesis algorithm is selected in this paper to evaluate the total indicators. The comprehensive benefit evaluation model of urban rail transit system is calculated by:

$$
\begin{bmatrix} z_1 \\ \cdots \\ z_n \end{bmatrix} = V * B = \begin{bmatrix} v_{1,1} & \cdots & v_{1,14} \\ \vdots & \ddots & \vdots \\ v_{n,1} & \cdots & v_{n,14} \end{bmatrix} * \begin{bmatrix} b_1 \\ \cdots \\ b_{14} \end{bmatrix}
$$

2.10   Empirical Analysis of Comprehensive Benefit Assessment of Urban Rail Transit System

Based on the investigation of the subway line 1, line 3, line 4 and line 5 and the related operating and environmental data of Shenzhen urban rail transit railway, we carried out the calculation of the value of the comprehensive benefit evaluation indicators of each line.

Quantifiable urban rail transit benefits:

Based on the simple calculation, the quantifiable benefits of four urban rail transit lines in Shenzhen in 2014 and 2015 are as follows (Table 1 and 2):

Table 1. Quantifiable urban rail transit value

Year	2014				2015			
Line	1	3	4	5	1	3	4	5
Quantifiable benefits	85.1	32.2	75.2	26.9	92.6	40.8	88.7	38.5

Comprehensive benefit evaluation:

Based on the weighted average calculation, the comprehensive benefits evaluation of four urban rail transit lines in Shenzhen in 2014 and 2015 are as follows:

Table 2. Assessed value of urban rail transport comprehensive benefits

Year	2014				2015			
Line	1	3	4	5	1	3	4	5
Comprehensive benefit evaluation	89.3	48.3	84.9	38.9	93.5	45.3	86.2	47.6

As you can see from the result of comprehensive benefit evaluation, the comprehensive benefit evaluation value of line 1 in 2014 and 2015 is respectively 89.3, 93.5, and line 4 in 2014 and 2015 is respectively 84.9, 86.2, mainly due to line 1 and line 4 operating for many years, the completion of all kinds of benefits have been fully revealed and have achieved high steady state. However, line 3 and line 5 are newly built and operated lines, and all kinds of benefits are emerging in the process of rapid growth.

Based on the analysis of quantifiable benefits, comprehensive benefits and the composition of urban rail transit system, we can draw some conclusions:

Firstly, in the case of rapid development of the city, the value of the benefits of four lines above continues to grow. This indicates that the construction of urban rail transit line plays a major role in economic development and development of new areas along the cities, as is shown in Fig. 2.

Secondly, the construction of urban rail transit can realize the extension of the business circle, which plays a big role in improving the economic vitality, the vitality of the real estate economy and the vitality of the commercial economy.

Thirdly, the benefits of urban rail transit system can be significantly affected by the line operation area. We found that the more prosperous the urban areas are, the more quantifiable benefits the urban rail transit line brings, such as the line 3 brought more benefits than that of the line 5.

Fourthly, the development of urban rail transit can bring considerable energy saving benefits and pollutant emission reduction benefits. It can be seen that the

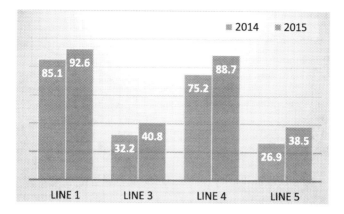

Fig. 2. Constitution of quantifiable benefit of urban rail transport

environmental effect of urban rail transit system is obvious, which provides strong support for urban development of low-carbon transportation mode.

Finally, the value of urban rail transit comprehensive benefits is not necessarily equal to the value of quantifiable benefits, and the composition of comprehensive benefits has compound character. In other words, the greater the absolute value of the quantifiable benefit of urban rail transit is not necessarily the more comprehensive benefit of urban rail transit. This indicates that the development of urban rail transit should not only attach importance to the economically developed and economically efficient regions, but also pay attention to the new urban areas with underdeveloped economy and the areas with potential for development to achieve balanced development.

Acknowledgments. The funds of this paper are provided by the Beijing Polytechnic project of Research on Comprehensive Benefits of Urban Rail Transit System. We very much appreciate the valuable comments of Dongye Sun, Jianghua Gao and Yuan Liu.

References

1. Talley, W.K., Anderson, P.E.: Effectiveness and efficiency in transit performance: a theoretical perspective. Transp. Res. **15**, 431–436 (1981)
2. Christer, A., Lars-Goran, M.: Appraising large-scale investments in a metropolitan transportation system. Transportation **19**, 267–283 (1992)
3. Phillips, J.Y., Rousseau, J.: Systems and Management Science by Extremal Methods. Kluwer Acadmic Publishers, Boston (1992)
4. Fielding, G.J., Glauthier, R.E., Lave, C.A.: Performance indicators for transit management. Transportation **7**, 365–379 (1978)
5. Viver, J.: Methods for assessing urban public transport projects. Public Transp. Int. (1998)
6. Wei, Q.L., Yu, G., Lu, S.: A necessary and sufficient condition for return to scale properties in generalized data envelopment analysis models. Chin. Sci. **45**(5), 503–517 (2002)

7. Tiry, C.: Hong Kong's future guided by transit infrastructure. Jpn. Railw. Transp. Rev. **33**, 28–35 (2003)
8. UMTA: Major urban mass transportation investments. UMTA, Washington (1976)
9. Pawlak, Z.: Rough set. Int. J. Comput. Inf. Sci. **11**, 341–356 (1982)
10. Mette, K.S.B.: Accuracy of traffic forecasts and cost estimates on large transportation projects. Transp. Res. Rec. (1996)
11. Box, P.C.: Curb Parking Findings Revisited. Transportation Research Board, Washington DC (2000)
12. World Bank: Cities on the Move: A World Bank Urban Transport Strategy Review. World Bank, Washington DC (2002)
13. Allport, R.: A Tale of Three Cities: Urban Rail Concessions in Bangkok, Kuala Lumpur, and Manila. Asian Development Bank, Japan Bank for Intonational Cooperation and World Bank, Washington DC (2005)
14. Chris, N., Jeremy, S., Markus, M., et al.: Social cost of railways relative to other modes of transport. Institute for Transport Studies, University of Leeds (2008)

Experimental Analysis of Space Acoustic Field Positioning Characteristics of Plecotus Auritus Pinna Model

Sen Zhang[1], Xin Ma[1(✉)], Yufeng Pan[1], and Hongwang Lu[2]

[1] School of Information Science and Engineering,
Shandong University, Jinan, China
max@sdu.edu.cn
[2] School of Physics, Shandong University, Jinan, China
lu@sdu.edu.cn

Abstract. The purpose of this paper is to simulate a brown long-eared bat (Plecotus auritus) ear model, and analyze the sound field in detail to get specific data on the frequency scanning properties. In this study, through the ultrasonic simulation using the FEM (finite element method) of the bat ear model, we obtained the data of the near-field and far-field acoustic pressure, and extracted and analyzed the data of positioning. The results show that the bat-ear model has obvious linear frequency scanning characteristics within a certain frequency range in the elevation axis of spherical coordinates, and provides evidence for the study of this kind of bat localization mechanism.

Keywords: Beam forming · Biosonar · Antenna · Finite element method
Frequency scanning

1 Introduction

Acoustic positioning is of great significance in engineering applications. As the key technology of wireless transmission signal, antenna technology are not limited to receive and send information. In another applications such as communication, radar, guidance, antenna technology also has fast and great innovation and development [5]. As an important branch of the antenna, the acoustic antenna is an indispensable aspect of acoustic location technology. The echo-location of bats can make the bats have flexible movement under the dark and complex environment. There are many differences of different species of bats between the structure of the ear and nose leaf. Bats ears, a bioacoustics antenna, played a crucial role in acoustic positioning.

According to a document report [1, 6], in addition to using a mechanical method for the ear rotations, some species of bats have evolved the more complex structures. When bat's ear rotate machinery, bats can detect the signal on the different directions according to the change of the frequency. With the continuous development of science and technology, a variety of algorithms have emerged to calculate the distribution of space fields, which makes the field distribution and beam forming of the antenna more effective [2].

© Springer Nature Singapore Pte Ltd. 2018
H. Yuan et al. (Eds.): GSKI 2017, CCIS 848, pp. 397–404, 2018.
https://doi.org/10.1007/978-981-13-0893-2_42

In this study, we calculate the Plecotus auritus ear model using the finite element method in its frequency range and get the sound pressure values at near field of each frequency. The kirchhoff diffraction integral can be used to convert the near field acoustic pressure data into a distant field. From far field sound pressure data, the structure of the bat ears gives the model frequency scanning characteristics in the angular direction of spherical coordinates within a certain frequency range, the frequency scanning characteristic of the bat ear model was obtained, but there is no significant change in the direction of azimuth. This plays an important role in the study of bat localization mechanism.

2   Algorithm Introduction

2.1   Finite Element Method

FEM (Finite Element Method) is a numerical method based on the rapid development of modern computer, and this kind of approximation is used to solve mechanics, mathematics with specific boundary conditions of the partial differential equation (PDE) problem. FEM and computer development constitute the basis of modern Computational Mechanics. The core idea of finite element method is "numerical approximation" and "discretization", so the two points is the center of FEM's development.

According to the generalized hooke law, the spring stiffness coefficient is k, and the force is F, and the shape variable is x

$$F = kx \tag{1}$$

In FEM, the same deformation may be affected by a few common force, and there may be multiple different nodes in an element. Therefore, hooke's law can shift from one dimensional computation for multidimensional operation, and its formula can exist in the form of matrix. The core formula of hooke's law after one dimension to multidimensional computing is

$$KU = F \tag{2}$$

In this formula, K is voxel of element stiffness matrix. U is voxel node displacement matrix, in this article it is the sound pressure matrix in the air. F is voxel node matrix, in this article is the element boundary conditions. The boundary conditions can be set before calculation, and the stiffness matrix can be obtained by the formula of solid mechanics. The near field sound pressure value can be obtained by the finite element formula.

Hooke's law can be extended to any linear system to describe the relationship between force and displacement, and the expression form is invariant. It can be expressed in the general form above, but the force and the displacement can be multi-dimensional. Because of the superposition of the matrix, the relationship matrix of the whole system can be superimposed by the force of the unit and the displacement relation matrix. The coefficient of the displacement matrix is the stiffness matrix of the whole system [3].

2.2   Fresnel-Kirchhoff Diffraction Integral Formula

The theoretical analysis of diffraction is based on the famous huygens Fresnel principle in optics, which is also the theoretical basis of the problem of opening cavity. The cavity needs to be studied is the field from one mirror to the other, and after a more frequent cycle, the self-reproduction mode will be formed. The mathematical representation of this principle is the Fresnel-kirchhoff diffraction integral [4], which can be derived from the universal theory of electromagnetic fields. The integral formula shows that, if you know the amplitude and phase distribution of the electromagnetic field in the reach of any space curved surface, you can work out any other location in the space of the electromagnetic field amplitude and phase distribution.

Let's say that the amplitude and the phase distribution function of the light wave field on any surface S of a given surface is $u(x', y')$, and the (x', y') is the coordinate of the point on S. The following relationships are:

$$u(x,y) = \frac{jk}{4\pi} \iint_S u(x',y') \frac{\exp(-jk\rho)}{\rho} (1 + \cos\theta) ds' \tag{3}$$

In the formula, ρ is the length of the line between the source point (x', y') and the observation point (x, y). θ is the angle between the normal line n of the point (x', y') and the above line. ds' is the area element of the point (x', y') on the surface S. $K = 2\pi/\lambda$ is the magnitude of the wave vector. The integral goes along the entire S plane. Formula (3) is the Fresnel-kirchhoff diffraction integral formula. The significance of this equation can be understood in this way: the field $u(x, y)$ of the observation point P can be regarded as the superposition of the non-uniform spherical waves emitted by the various subsources on the S surface.

3   Data Analysis

According to previous studies, the frequency range of ultrasonic frequencies used by the Plecotus auritus was 22.7 ± 1.7 kHz to 55.7 ± 5.6 kHz [8]. The bat ear model can be obtained from the digital image processing of the Plecotus auritus ear tomography with CT scanning, as shown in the Fig. 1. According to the reciprocity principle of acoustic field, the acoustic field of monopole is only associated with the distance of the sound source to the receiver. The sound field obtained at the receiving point while the sound source is placed at the source point is exactly the same as the sound field obtained at the source point while the sound source is placed in the receiving point [7].

After place the sound source in the inner ear canal of the ear model, we calculate the Plecotus auritus ear model using the finite element method in its frequency range. We can get the sound pressure values at near field of each frequency. For the near field data, the distance field lobe data can be obtained by using the Fresnel-kirchhoff diffraction integral. In this far field calculation, the far field refers to the distance from

Fig. 1. The ear model of the Plecotus auritus obtained by CT scan

the ear model to a distance of 10 m. Using the spherical coordinate, the data for the azimuth Angle from 0° to 360°, pitching Angle is from 0° to 180°, accuracy of 1°.

It can be seen from the far field lobe pattern, as the frequency increases, the first lobe of the orientation graph becomes larger and larger, indicating that the acoustic signals received by the bat when the frequency changes are not limited to the main lobe, but are also received in the other side of the lobe. The distance data obtained from the FEM is expanded from the sphere to the plane, and the Fig. 2 can be obtained. The figure can be seen from the Fig. 2, main lobe of the patten as part of the elevation angle is more than 160°, and the first side lobe pattern flap for the graphic color deep circular in the middle of the figure. With the change of frequency, the size and directivity of the first side have changed in part (Fig. 3).

Fig. 2. The distance field lobe pattern of different frequencies (30.5 kHz, 31.5 kHz, 32.5 kHz) from left to right.

Then we analyze and discuss the far field sound pressure data, and calculate the of HPBW, the numerical ratio of the first side and the main lobe, and the tilt of the elevation and azimuth. As shown in the figure below:

The right figure of the Fig. 4 shows the change curve of the elevation angle and azimuth angle of the sidelobe which have the frequency scan feature with the frequency change. It can be seen from the curve of the lateral lobe elevation that the frequency of the change of the elevation of the side lobe is mainly between 30 to 42 kHz. The wider the width of the antenna, the better the direction, the farther the distance, the stronger the anti-interference ability. For the antenna used in this article, the more concentrated the lobe, the higher the resolution of the signal direction. Due to the large width of the

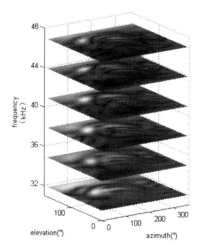

Fig. 3. Shows the raw data of acoustic far field obtained by using kirchhoff integral, and the number of layers from low to high is that the frequency is getting higher and higher, and the deeper the color represents the higher the sound pressure in different frequencies.

HPBW (half power beamwidth) of the 30–32.5 kHz lobe in Fig. 4, the directivity of the lobe is not concentrated, so the high HPBW is not significant to the experiment. In figure right of the Fig. 4, when the frequency is 33 to 42 kHz, the azimuth angle changes little. The left figure shows the relationship between the power ratio of the side lobe and the main lobe of the frequency sweep characteristic. We can see from the figure that the maximum power of the side lobe less than 32.5 kHz is less than the maximum power of the main lobe, indicating that the bat ear model has a higher gain in the main lobe direction and lower gain in the other direction (Figs. 5 and 6).

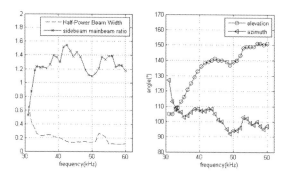

Fig. 4. The azimuth angle of the side lobe, the change curve of the elevation with the change of frequency and the curve of the half-power wave flap with the change of frequency.

It can be concluded from the far field data, as each change 1 kHz frequency, elevation changes about 4°. The graph of the plane far field is divided by the following

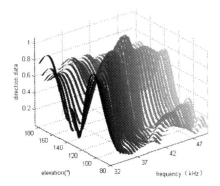

Fig. 5. In the case of the fixed azimuth, the ear model of the large ear bats has the lateral lobe orientation of the frequency scanning characteristic. The X axis is frequency (33–48 kHz, the accuracy is 0.5 kHz), the Y axis is the elevation (80–180°, the accuracy is 1°), Z axis is the normalized direction.

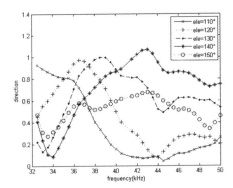

Fig. 6. Take an elevation angle from 110° to 150° every 10°, draw the elevation angle of fixed frequency response curve.

figure, and take the elevation of 70 to 150°, divide it into 20 segments, 4° per paragraph, then the 0 to 360° azimuth angle is divided into 15 segments, 24° each. The data graph is divided into 20 × 15 pieces, and according to the following formula, the average acoustic energy flow or average sound power of each region is calculated.

$$\overline{W} = \varepsilon c_0 S = \frac{p_a^2 S}{2\rho_0 c_0} \tag{4}$$

Among it, ε is the average acoustic energy density, which represents the average acoustic energy in the unit volume. c_0 is sound velocity; pa is the acoustic amplitude of the plane sound field; S is the area of zone; ρ_0 is air density. Make the normalization treatment and get the image below.

The lighter color in the image indicates the higher power, whereas the darker the area indicates the lower power. As it can be seen from the Fig. 7 above, bats can process the echo signal using their ear by sending a series of chirp signals when using similar positioning function. The frequency of the signal of the maximum energy is extracted from the echo signal, and the angle and distance of the target are estimated, thus the accurate positioning is carried out. In reality, the echo-location method of the Plecotus auritus is also treated this way.

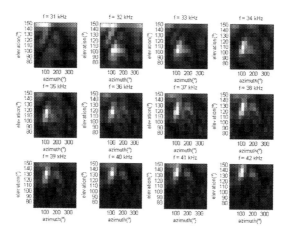

Fig. 7. The distribution of normalized mean acoustic power of frequencies (31–42 kHz).

4   Conclusion

In this study, we used the finite element method to simulate the frequency scanning characteristics in the direction of spherical coordinates. The data of far-field sound pressure is analyzed in detail. It can be seen from the far-field sound pressure data that the ear model of the brown long-eared bat is equivalent to a spatial filter in a certain frequency range. If we change the frequency, the lobe will be in a different direction. In the main direction of this filter, the sound energy is almost not weakened, and in other directions, the acoustic energy received is significantly reduced. We can conduct experiments on the basis of this research of the location mechanism of bat, the transfer function of bat ear and performing structural simulation calculation.

Acknowledgements. This work was supported by the National Natural Science Foundation of China under Grant No. 62171453, the Key Research and Development Program of Shandong Province under Grant No. 2017GGX10113.

References

1. Milligan, T.A.: Modern Antenna Design, 2nd edn. Wiley, Hoboken (2005)
2. Zhou, P.-B.: Numerical Analysis of Electromagnetic Fields. Springer, Heidelberg (1993). https://doi.org/10.1007/978-3-642-50319-1
3. Ceretti, E., Lazzaroni, C., Menegardo, L., et al.: Turning simulations using a three-dimensional FEM code. J. Mater. Process. Technol. **98**(1), 99–103 (2000)
4. Xu, Y., Tan, Q., Erricolo, D., et al.: Experimental verification of a 3D propagation model based on Fresnel-Kirchhoff integral (2004)
5. Lazure, L., Fenton, M.B.: High duty cycle echolocation and prey detection by bats. J. Exp. Biol. **214**(Pt 7), 1131 (2011)
6. Fenton, M.B., Audet, D., Obrist, M.K., et al.: Signal strength, timing, and self-deafening; the evolution of echolocation in bats. Paleobiology **21**(2), 229–242 (1995)
7. Wang, P., Zhuang, Q., et al.: Frequency driven scanning characteristic of a pinna model inspired from the Brown Big-eared bat (Plecotus auritus). Chin. J. Acoust. **30**(2), 181–190 (2011)
8. Obrist, M.K., Boesch, R., Flückiger, P.F.: Variability in echolocation call design of 26 Swiss bat species: consequences, limits and options for automated field identification with a synergetic pattern recognition approach. Mammalia **68**(4), 307–322 (2004)

Spectrum Zoom Processing for Low-Altitude and Slow-Speed Small Target Detection

Xuwang Zhang[1], Jinping Sun[1(✉)], and Songtao Lu[2]

[1] School of Electronic and Information Engineering,
Beihang University, Beijing 100191, China
buaaeezxw@163.com, sunjinping@buaa.edu.cn
[2] Department of Electrical and Computer Engineering,
Iowa State University, Ames, IA 50011, USA
songtao@iastate.edu

Abstract. To detect the low-altitude and slow-speed small (LSS) target in the heavy ground clutter environment, a spectrum zoom processing based target detection algorithm is proposed in this paper. This algorithm firstly performs the coherent accumulation on each frame of range-time image, then concatenates the data from the same low Doppler frequency slot of multiple frames of range-Doppler frequency images, after that performs the spectrum zoom processing on the concatenated data, finally performs the clutter suppression and target detection. Simulation results show that the proposed algorithm has a good LSS target detection performance.

Keywords: Low-altitude · Slow-speed · Small target · Spectrum zoom
Coherent accumulation · Ground clutter

1 Introduction

In recent years, there are various types of aircraft including the paraglider, light helicopter, and rotorcraft emerging quickly in the market. These aircraft are mostly called as the low-altitude and slow-speed small (LSS) targets. The LSS target detection and tracking has become an important task for the radar system. Unfortunately, the traditional radar system is mainly designed for the routine target whose RCS and speed are within a given range. For the LSS target beyond this given range, the detection performance of traditional radar system would be seriously deteriorated. The main reason is that the insufficient energy accumulation and invalid clutter suppression in the signal processing can result that the output signal to clutter ratio (SCR) cannot meet the requirement of effective target detection. Therefore, it is necessary to retrofit the traditional radar system to detect the LSS target effectively.

There have been already many studies in the literatures focusing on the problem of detecting LSS targets in the sea clutter. For example, a short-time fractional Fourier transform based detection algorithm was proposed in [1] through investigating the micro-Doppler effect of targets. An adaptive waveform was designed dynamically in [2], where the expectation-maximization algorithm is used to estimate the time-varying parameters of sea clutter. A time-frequency method was applied to detect the small

© Springer Nature Singapore Pte Ltd. 2018
H. Yuan et al. (Eds.): GSKI 2017, CCIS 848, pp. 405–413, 2018.
https://doi.org/10.1007/978-981-13-0893-2_43

accelerating target in the background of sea clutter [3]. A knowledge-aided non-parametric detector was studied in [4, 5], and a track-before-detect method is proposed in [6]. In fact, it is very significant to study the LSS target detection problem under the background of ground clutter. After all, most LSS targets mainly fly on the ground. However, there are few literatures focusing on the LSS target detection in the ground clutter.

Considering this, a new detection algorithm based on the spectrum zoom processing is proposed in this paper to detect the LSS target in the heavy ground clutter environment. By making some improvements on the basis of traditional detection algorithms, the proposed algorithm can obtain an excellent LSS target detection ability. Meanwhile, the routine target detection ability is still retained. In particular, the main steps of the proposed algorithm are as follows: (1) perform coherent accumulation on each frame of observation data and get the range-Doppler frequency images; (2) take out the data of the same low Doppler frequency slot from all the range-Doppler frequency images and concatenate these data together; (3) perform the spectrum zoom processing on the concatenated data by the discrete Fourier transform (DFT); (4) suppress the ground clutter and detect the target. Simulation experiments with real data show that the proposed algorithm has a good performance of LSS target detection.

2   Basic Theory of Spectrum Zoom Processing

Let $s(t)$, $0 \leq t < MNT_s$ be a continuous time complex signal with a finite length, where M and N are positive integers and $T_s > 0$. Dividing the signal $s(t)$ into M signals $s_0(t), s_1(t), \cdots, s_{M-1}(t)$ with the length of NT_s, we can get

$$s(t) = s_0(t) + s_1(t) + \cdots + s_{M-1}(t), \tag{1}$$

where

$$s_m(t) = \begin{cases} s(t) & mNT_s \leq t < (m+1)NT_s \\ 0 & \text{other} \end{cases}, \quad m = 0, 1, \cdots, M-1.$$

Define

$$x_m(t) = s_m(t + mNT_s). \tag{2}$$

Combining (1) with (2), we can obtain

$$s(t) = x_0(t) + x_1(t - NT_s) + \cdots + x_{M-1}(t - (M-1)NT_s). \tag{3}$$

Taking the Fourier transform on both sides of (3), we arrive at

$$S(\omega) = \sum_{m=0}^{M-1} X_m(\omega) e^{-j\omega mNT_s}, \tag{4}$$

where $S(\omega)$ represents the Fourier transform of $s(t)$, and $X_m(\omega)$ represents the Fourier transform of $x_m(t)$.

After sampling the continuous time signal $s(t)$ and $x_m(t)$ with a period of T_s respectively, the resulting discrete sequences are

$$s[n] = s(nT_s), \ n = 0, 1, \cdots, MN - 1, \tag{5}$$

and

$$x_m[n] = x_m(nT_s), \ n = 0, 1, \cdots, N - 1. \tag{6}$$

The discrete time Fourier transform (DTFT) of sequence $s[n]$ can be written as

$$S(\Omega) = \sum_{n=0}^{MN-1} s[n] e^{-j\Omega n}, \tag{7}$$

and the DFT can be written as

$$S[k] = \sum_{n=0}^{MN-1} s[n] W_{MN}^{kn}, \tag{8}$$

where $k = 0, 1, \cdots, MN - 1$ and $W_{MN} = e^{-j2\pi/(MN)}$. Correspondingly, the DTFT and DFT of sequence $x_m[n]$, $n = 0, 1, \cdots, N - 1$ can be written as $X_m(\Omega)$ and $X_m[k]$, $k = 0, 1, \cdots, N - 1$.

The sequence $S[k]$ can be divided into N subsequences with the length M, and the qth ($q = 0, 1, \cdots, M - 1$) component in the pth ($p = 0, 1, \cdots, N - 1$) subsequence is $S[pM + q]$. Next, we would provide an approximate calculation method of $S[pM + q]$.

Obviously, we have

$$S[k] = S(\Omega)|_{f=k\Delta f}, \tag{9}$$

where $\Delta f = F_s/(MN)$ and $F_s = 1/T_s$. Assume that the sampling process of $s(t)$ obeys Nyquist's law, then we have

$$S[k] = S(\Omega)|_{f=k\Delta f} = S(\omega)|_{f=k\Delta f}. \tag{10}$$

Correspondingly, similar conclusions also apply to $X_m(\omega)$, $X_m(\Omega)$ and $X_m[k]$, $k = 0, 1, \cdots, N - 1$.

For simplicity, define $f_0 \triangleq (pM + q)F_s/MN$ and $\omega_0 \triangleq 2\pi f_0 = 2\pi(pM + q)F_s/MN$. Then, we have

$$S[pM + q] = \sum_{m=0}^{M-1} X_m(\omega_0) e^{-j\omega_0 mNT_s} = \sum_{m=0}^{M-1} X_m(\omega_0) W_M^{qm}, \tag{11}$$

where $W_M = e^{-j2\pi/M}$. It can be seen from (11) that $S[pM + q]$ is just the DFT of $X_0(\omega_0), X_1(\omega_0), \cdots, X_{M-1}(\omega_0)$.

Since ω_0 includes the variable q, we need to calculate a set of $X_0(\omega_0), X_1(\omega_0), \cdots, X_{M-1}(\omega_0)$ for each given value of q, which would result in a high computational load. Therefore, we approximate ω_0 as follows

$$\omega_0 \approx \frac{2\pi pMF_s}{MN} = \frac{2\pi pF_s}{N} \triangleq \hat{\omega}_0. \tag{12}$$

Then, $S[pM + q]$ in (11) can be approximated as

$$S[pM + q] \approx \sum_{m=0}^{M-1} X_m(\hat{\omega}_0) W_M^{qm} = \sum_{m=0}^{M-1} X_m[p] W_M^{qm}. \tag{13}$$

By the approximation in (13), we only need to calculate one set of $X_m(\hat{\omega}_0) = X_m[p]$, $m = 0, 1, \cdots, M - 1$ when q takes $0, 1, \cdots, M - 1$ for a given p. This way can significantly reduce the computational load. In fact, $X_m[p]$ is the sample of $X_m(\Omega)$ with the period of $\Delta f = F_s/N$, while $S[pM + q]$ is the sample of $S(\Omega)$ with the period of $\Delta f = F_s/(MN)$. In (13), the frequency spectrum sample $S[pM + q]$ with a short sampling period can be obtained from the frequency spectrum sample $X_0[p], X_1[p], \cdots, X_{M-1}[p]$ with a relative longer sampling period by DFT, which is the so-called *spectrum zoom processing*.

According to the above analysis, we can summarize the spectrum zoom processing as follows: (1) sample the continuous time complex signal $s(t)$ whose frequency spectrum locates in $[0, F_s]$ with a period of T_s, and obtain M sequences $x_m[n]$, $n = 0, 1, \cdots, N - 1$ with the length N; (2) write the DFT of $x_m[n]$ as $X_m[k]$, $k = 0, 1, \cdots, N - 1$; (3) for a given $p \in \{0, 1, \cdots, N - 1\}$, the DFT of sequence $X_0[p], X_1[p], \cdots, X_{M-1}[p]$ can be approximately regarded as the spectrum sampling result of $s(t)$ in $[pF_s/N, (p+1)F_s/N)$ with a period of $\Delta f = F_s/(MN)$, and can also be equivalently regarded as the DFT of sequence $s[n]$, where $s[n]$ is the sequential arrangement of $x_0[n], x_1[n], \cdots, x_{M-1}[n]$, in the frequency range $[pF_s/N, (p+1)F_s/N)$.

The spectrum zoom processing provides a new method to achieve the refined spectrum information of a long discrete sequence. The advantage of this method is that it can obtain the refined spectrum on a given frequency range. For the applications that only need the refined spectrum information on a partial frequency range, this new method is more targeted and can significantly reduce the computation complexity.

3   Spectrum Zoom Processing for the LSS Target Detection

The radar echo of LSS target is very weak, and its Doppler frequency is very close to the Doppler frequency of ground clutter. Therefore, improving the SCR and separating the target echo and ground clutter are two important issues in the LSS target detection. The spectrum zoom processing introduced in Sect. 2 can refine the spectrum to separate the target echo and ground clutter. Meanwhile, it is essentially a coherent accumulation process, which contributes to improving the SCR.

A typical model of pulse Doppler radar observation data is shown in Fig. 1. The horizontal axis represents the fast time dimension, containing L range gates. The vertical axis represents the slow time dimension, containing MN pulses. Each sequential N pulses are regarded as a frame of observation data, and it contains M frames of observation data in Fig. 1.

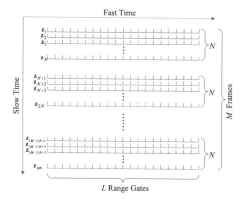

Fig. 1. Typical model of the pulse doppler radar observation data.

The block diagram of the spectrum zoom processing based detection algorithm proposed in this paper is shown in Fig. 2. It mainly contains three steps: (1) perform the coherent accumulation on each frame of observation data separately, and divide the resulting range-Doppler frequency image into the high Doppler frequency (HDF) area and low Doppler frequency (LDF) area; (2) detect the fast speed target in the HDF area of range-Doppler frequency image; (3) concatenate the LDF areas from the sequential M frames of range-Doppler frequency images according to the Doppler frequency, and perform the DFT and slow speed target detection on the concatenated data.

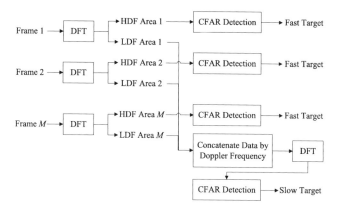

Fig. 2. Block diagram of the spectrum zoom processing based target detection algorithm.

Firstly, perform the coherent accumulation on each frame of the observation data separately, i.e., perform the DFT along the slow time dimension. After the coherent accumulation, M frames of $N \times L$ range-Doppler frequency images are obtained. The horizontal axis represents the range gate, and the vertical axis represents the Doppler frequency slot. Assume that the pulse repetition period is T_s. Then, the interval of two adjacent Doppler frequency slots is $\Delta f = F_s/N = 1/(NT_s)$.

The difference of radial velocities corresponding to two adjacent Doppler frequency slots is $\Delta v = \lambda \Delta f/2$ in the range-Doppler frequency image. In this case, the Doppler frequencies are $-\Delta f$, 0 and Δf when $k = -1, 0, 1$, and the corresponding radial velocities are $-\Delta v$, 0 and Δv. The radial velocities in these Doppler frequency slots are very low. Thus, these Doppler frequency slots are the so-called LDF area where the LSS target and ground clutter are located. On the other hand, the radial velocities are high when $k = -N/2, \cdots, -2, 2, \cdots, N/2 - 1$. Thus, these Doppler frequency slots are assigned to the HDF area.

In the HDF area, the target position can have an obvious movement within a short time because of the fast speed. Thus, the detector needs to output the detection results with a higher rate. Meanwhile, the HDF area is free of ground clutter and has a uniform background noise spectrum in general. Therefore, we only need to perform the classical constant false alarm rate (CFAR) detection in the HDF area of each frame of range-Doppler frequency image to detect the fast speed target. The detector updates the detection result whenever a new frame of observation data is received, which can guarantee an enough high resulting detection output rate.

Next, consider the LDF area. When the coherent accumulation on each frame of observation data is performed, the resulting Doppler frequency resolution is too low. In this case, the ground clutter mainly distributes in the $k = 0$ Doppler frequency slot and spreads to the adjacent $k = \pm 1$ Doppler frequency slots. Meanwhile, the LSS target echo is also distributed in the $k = -1, 0, 1$ Doppler frequency slots. Therefore, the key point is to separate the target echo and ground clutter by the spectrum zoom processing before detecting the LSS target.

After the first coherent accumulation, M frames of range-Doppler frequency images are obtained. Take out the data in the $k = 0$ Doppler frequency slot from these images, and concatenate the data to form a $M \times L$ matrix. Perform the DFT on this matrix along the vertical axis. This is actually the spectrum zoom processing introduced in Sect. 2. Then, a new $M \times L$ matrix is obtained. The horizontal axis represents the range gate, and the vertical axis represents the refined Doppler frequency slot. The range of Doppler frequency is $-\Delta f/2 \sim \Delta f/2$, and the interval of two adjacent Doppler frequency slots becomes $\Delta f/M$. Compared with the result of first coherent accumulation, the spectrum zoom degree improves M times in the new range-Doppler frequency image. The ground clutter is still near the zero Doppler frequency, while the target echo is away from the zero Doppler frequency. The target echo and ground clutter are obviously separated in the frequency domain. Correspondingly, perform the similar process on the $k = -1$ and $k = +1$ Doppler frequency slots. Thus, three new $M \times L$ range-Doppler frequency images are obtained in total. Concatenate the three images to form a $3M \times L$ image. Eliminate several Doppler frequency slots near the zero Doppler frequency to realize the ground clutter suppression. And then detect the LSS target on the remaining area with common CFAR algorithms.

The spectrum zoom processing based target detection algorithm proposed in this paper manages the HDF area and LDF area with different strategies. It can guarantee the high resulting detection output rate required in the fast speed target detection, and also the high spectrum zoom precision required in the slow speed target detection.

4   Simulation Experiments with Real Data

In order to test and verify the effectiveness of the spectrum zoom processing based detection algorithm, we choose some real data from the ground-based radar. The pulse repetition period is $T_p = 18$ µs and the sampling rate is $f_s = 160$ MHz. The real data

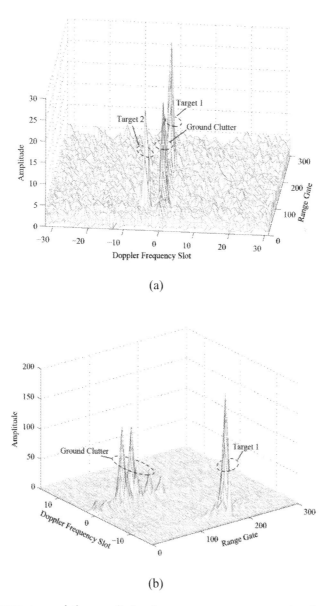

(a)

(b)

Fig. 3. Coherent accumulation result for the spectrum zoom processing based detection algorithm: (a) Result of the first DFT, (b) Result of the second DFT.

contains $M = 32$ frames of observation data, and each frame of observation data contains $N = 64$ pulses and $N_r = 300$ range gates. There are two small targets flying at a low altitude in the observation area. One is a slow target marked as Target 1 which moves away from the radar with a constant velocity $v_1 = 4.35$ m/s. And the other is a fast target marked as Target 2 which moves away from the radar with a constant velocity $v_2 = 50.13$ m/s.

For the spectrum zoom processing based detection algorithm proposed in this paper, we firstly perform the coherent accumulation on each frame of observation data separately, where the result is shown in Fig. 3(a). It can be seen that both the echo of Target 1 and the ground clutter lie in the $k = 0, \pm 1$ Doppler frequency slots. We cannot distinguish them according to their spectrum characteristic in Fig. 3(a). Target 2 lies in the $k = -5$ Doppler frequency slot. Meanwhile, the HDF area is free of ground clutter, which is consistent with the previous analysis. Take out the $k = 0$ Doppler frequency slots from the M frames of range-Doppler frequency images obtained in the first DFT. Concatenate them and perform the second DFT on the concatenated data. The result is shown in Fig. 3(b). After the second DFT, the spectrum zoom precision is enough high such that the echo of Target 1 and the ground clutter are well separated in the frequency domain.

5   Conclusions

For the special characteristics of LSS target detection, a spectrum zoom processing based target detection algorithm was proposed in this paper. This algorithm firstly performs the DFT on each frame of observation data; then concatenates the data from the same low Doppler frequency slot of multiple frames of range-Doppler frequency images together, and performs the second DFT on the concatenated data; finally, perform the LSS target detection on the resulting refined range-Doppler frequency image. Simulation results show that the proposed algorithm has a good performance of LSS target detection.

Acknowledgments. This work was supported in part by the National Natural Science Foundation of China (61471019).

References

1. Chen, X.L., Guan, J., Bao, Z.H., He, Y.: Detection and extraction of target with micromotion in spiky sea clutter via short-time fractional fourier transform. IEEE Trans. Geosci. Remote Sens. **52**(2), 1002–1018 (2014). https://doi.org/10.1109/TGRS.2013.2246574
2. Sira, S.P., Cochran, D., Papandreou-Suppappola, A., et al.: Adaptive waveform design for improved detection of low-RCS targets in heavy sea clutter. IEEE J. Select. Top. Sign. Process. **1**(1), 56–66 (2007). https://doi.org/10.1109/JSTSP.2007.897048
3. Yasotharan, A., Thayaparan, T.: Time-frequency method for detecting an accelerating target in sea clutter. IEEE Trans. Aerosp. Electron. Syst. **42**(4), 1289–1310 (2006). https://doi.org/10.1109/TAES.2006.314573

4. Zhang, X.W., Sun, J.P., Lu, S.T., Wang, G.H.: Non-parametric detector in non-homogeneous clutter environments with knowledge-aided permutation test. IET Radar Sonar Navig. **10**(7), 1310–1318 (2016). https://doi.org/10.1049/iet-rsn.2015.0566
5. Zhang, X.W., Sun, J.P., Fu, J.B., Lu, S.T.: Fast implementation method of permutation test with valid strategy. J. Sign. Process. **31**(10), 1233–1239 (2015). (In Chinese)
6. Zhang, X.W., Sun, J.P., Zhang, Y.X., Lu, S.T., Liu, C.: H-PMHT track-before-detect processing with DP-based track initiation and termination. IET Sign. Process. **10**(9), 1118–1125 (2016). https://doi.org/10.1049/iet-spr.2016.0208

Knowledge-Aided Wald Detector
for Range-Extended Target
in Nonhomogeneous Environments

Nan Wang[✉], Jinping Sun, and Wenguang Wang

School of Electronic and Information Engineering,
Beihang University, Beijing 100191, China
wangnanbeihang@126.com,
{sunjinping,wwenguang}@buaa.edu.cn

Abstract. This paper deals with the problem of detecting the moving range-extended target in the distributed MIMO radar. As the distributed MIMO radar is equipped with multiple transmit and receive antennas, the interference covariance matrices corresponding to different transmit-receive (Tx-Rx) antennas are modeled as random matrices which express nonhomogeneous environments in this paper first. Then a knowledge-aided model which makes these random matrices share a prior covariance matrix structure is built to simulate the characteristics of clutter and noise in nonhomogeneous environments. Finally, we design a new knowledge-aided Wald (KA-Wald) detector to detect the range-extended target for the distributed MIMO radar. Simulation results show that the proposed detector possesses a better detection performance compared with the traditional Wald detector. And relative to the knowledge-aided generalized likelihood ratio test (KA-GLRT) detector, the proposed KA-Wald detector has a similar detection performance but a higher detection efficiency.

Keywords: Wald detector · Distributed MIMO radar · Knowledge-aided
Nonhomogeneous environments · Range-extended target

1 Introduction

MIMO radar has received much attention globally in recent years because of its new work mode. Different with the traditional phased-array radar, MIMO radar is equipped with multiple transmit and receive antennas. These antennas form multiple transmit-receive (Tx-Rx) pairs which are illustrated in Fig. 1. Lots of theories and practices prove that MIMO radar has many potential advantages, such as enhanced detection performance [1], improved angular resolution [2], providing more degrees of freedom and better spatial coverage [3] and so on. There are two kinds of MIMO radar according to configuration. The first one is called the co-located MIMO radar where both transmit and receive antennas are closely distributed. The other one is called the distributed MIMO radar with widely separated antennas. The paper mainly focuses on the distributed MIMO radar.

© Springer Nature Singapore Pte Ltd. 2018
H. Yuan et al. (Eds.): GSKI 2017, CCIS 848, pp. 414–425, 2018.
https://doi.org/10.1007/978-981-13-0893-2_44

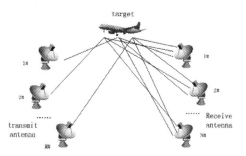

Fig. 1. MIMO radar configuration

As the antennas in the distributed MIMO radar are widely spaced, they provide better spatial diversity which can be used to enhance detection performance [4]. A sample covariance matrix (SCM)-based detector [5] is designed in case with homogeneous environments. Then in [6] the author develops a robust SCM (RSCM) detector to simulate the compound Gaussian model for interferences. Persymmetric covariance structure is exploited in [7] to reduce the amount of training data in the distributed MIMO radar. Most of these studies assume that the interference signal is homogeneous. But in reality, different Tx-Rx pairs have different locations, so the interferences are different from one Tx-Rx pair to another. Hence it is unreasonable to assume the interference to be homogeneous.

On the other hand, the range-extended target detection is always a critical problem in the application of the high range resolution radar system. In [8], the GLRT detector incorporating the target scatter density is derived. In [9], the range-extended target detection in Gaussian environment with an unknown covariance matrix is considered. GLRT and two-step GLRT are proposed to detect the range-extended target, exploiting training data to estimate the covariance matrix. The range-extended target detection is decomposed as multiple subspace target signals detection in [10]. Thought there are lots of researches about the range-extended target detection, there are few studies about the range-extended target detection for the distributed MIMO radar in nonhomogeneous environments.

In this paper, the prior covariance matrix is first built according to the characteristics of the working environments. Then different Tx-Rx pairs share this prior covariance matrix structure to simulate their own interference signal characteristics. Finally a knowledge-aided Wald detector is designed to detect the range-extended target for the distributed MIMO radar in nonhomogeneous environments.

The following notations are used throughout the paper: $(\bullet)^T$ and $(\bullet)^H$ respectively denote the transpose operation and conjugate transpose operation. $etr\{\bullet\}$ denotes $\exp\{tr(\bullet)\}$. $tr(\bullet)$ denotes the trace of a matrix. $\exp\{\bullet\}$ denotes the exponential function. CN denotes the complex Gaussian distribution. CW denotes the complex inverse Wishart distribution.

2 Signal Model

As the detection for the moving range-extended target is discussed in the paper, it is assumed that:

(1) The distributed MIMO radar is equipped with M transmit antennas and N receive antennas.
(2) The transmit antennas transmit orthogonal waveform signals.
(3) Each transmit antenna transmits L pulses.
(4) A target may spread up to $H \geq 1$ range cells.

The signal at the nth receive antenna which is matched to the mth transmit antenna after matched filter can be expressed as

$$\mathbf{X}_{mn} = \left[\mathbf{x}_{mn,1}, \mathbf{x}_{mn,2}, \cdots, \mathbf{x}_{mn,H}\right] \tag{1}$$

Where $\mathbf{X}_{mn} \in \mathbb{C}^{L \times H}, m = 1, 2, \cdots, M, n = 1, 2, \cdots, N$. As the antennas are widely separated in the distributed MIMO radar, each signal $\mathbf{X}_{mn}$ is independent to another.

According to the traditional detection rule, the detection problem can be converted to the following binary hypothesis problem.

$$H_1 : \begin{cases} \mathbf{X}_{mn} = \mathbf{p}_{mn}\boldsymbol{\alpha}_{mn}^T + \mathbf{N}_{mn} \\ \mathbf{X}_{mn}^k = \mathbf{N}_{mn}^k \end{cases} \quad H_0 : \begin{cases} \mathbf{X}_{mn} = \mathbf{N}_{mn} \\ \mathbf{X}_{mn}^k = \mathbf{N}_{mn}^k \end{cases} \tag{2}$$

$$m = 1, 2, \cdots, M \quad n = 1, 2, \cdots, N \quad k = 1, 2, \cdots, K$$

Where $\boldsymbol{\alpha}_{mn} = \left[\alpha_{mn,1}, \alpha_{mn,2}, \cdots, \alpha_{mn,H}\right]^T$ contains the unknown amplitude parameters of the range-extended target. $\mathbf{N}_{mn} = \left[\mathbf{n}_{mn,1}, \mathbf{n}_{mn,2}, \cdots, \mathbf{n}_{mn,H}\right]$ denotes the interference in test data. It is supposed that each column vector of $\mathbf{N}_{mn}$ is independent and identically distributed complex zeros-mean Gaussian vector with covariance matrix $\mathbf{R}_{mn}$, namely

$$\mathbf{n}_{mn,h} \sim CN(0, \mathbf{R}_{mn}) \tag{3}$$

Where $\mathbf{R}_{mn}$ denotes the covariance matrix of the mth Tx-nth Rx pair.

$\mathbf{N}_{mn}^k = \left[\mathbf{n}_{mn,1}^k, \cdots, \mathbf{n}_{mn,H}^k\right]$ denotes the interference in train data. Each column vector of $\mathbf{N}_{mn}^k$ is independent and identically distributed complex zeros-mean Gaussian vector with covariance matrix $\mathbf{R}_{mn}$, namely

$$\mathbf{n}_{mn,h}^k \sim CN(0, \mathbf{R}_{mn}) \tag{4}$$

$\mathbf{p}_{mn} \in \mathbb{C}^{L \times 1}$ is target steering vector which can be expressed as

$$\mathbf{p}_{mn} = \left[1, e^{-j2\pi f_{mn}}, \cdots, e^{-j2\pi(L-1)f_{mn}}\right]^T \tag{5}$$

Where f_{mn} is the Doppler frequency for target relative to the mth Tx- nth Rx pair.

For the distributed MIMO radar, the size of training data will be $M \times N$ times to that for signal radar if covariance matrices for Tx-Rx pairs need to be estimated. It will be a large scale if the distributed MIMO radar system is equipped with many transmit and receive antennas. In addition to this, the size of available training data will reduce in nonhomogeneous environments which results in the descent of detection performance. Hence, in order to keep the detection performance under the small size of training data, it is very essential to build the knowledge-aided model for the distributed MIMO radar system.

Generally speaking, there are two aspects to consider when choosing the prior distribution. First, the prior distribution is able to reflect the prior information for Tx-Rx pairs. Second, the prior distribution should not be too complicated. In order to derive expression easily, it is common to choose the prior distribution which possessed conjugation.

The inverse Wishart distribution has been proved to reflect the prior information around the working environment in recent years. So this paper also applies the inverse Wishart distribution as the prior distribution. Specifically we model $\mathbf{R}_{mn}$ as a complex inverse Wishart random matrix

$$\mathbf{R}_{mn} \sim CW^{-1}\left(\mu, (\mu - L)\sum\right) \tag{6}$$

Where $\mu > L$ denotes the degree of freedom of the inverse Wishart distribution, $\sum$ is a positive semi-definite matrix which contains the prior information for $\mathbf{R}_{mn}$. According to the formula (6), the probability density function (PDF) of $\mathbf{R}_{mn}$ can be expressed as

$$f(\mathbf{R}_{mn}) = \frac{|(\mu - L)\sum|^{\mu}}{c(L, \mu)|\mathbf{R}_{mn}|^{(N+\mu)}} etr\left\{-(\mu - L)\mathbf{R}_{mn}^{-1}\sum\right\} \tag{7}$$

Where

$$c(L, \mu) = \pi^{(L(L-1)/2)}\prod_{k=1}^{\mu}\Gamma(\mu - L + k) \tag{8}$$

$\Gamma(\bullet)$ denotes the Gamma function. According to the statistic characteristic of the inverse Wishart distribution, it can be known that

$$\mathbf{E}[\mathbf{R}_{mn}] = \sum \tag{9}$$

This states that the inverse Wishart distribution reflects the environment information in the distributed MIMO radar.

3   Knowledge-Aided Wald Detection

In order to derive the expression of the KA-Wald detector, we make following assumptions:

(1) $\alpha_{mn,h} = \alpha_{mn,h}^R + j\alpha_{mn,h}^I$, so $\boldsymbol{\theta}_{r_{mn,h}} = \left[\alpha_{mn,h}^R, \alpha_{mn,h}^I\right]^T$.

(2) $\boldsymbol{\theta}_{s_{mn,h}}$ is a real column vector with size of L^2. It is composed of elements in $\mathbf{R}_{mn}$.

(3) $\boldsymbol{\theta}_{mn,h} = \left[\boldsymbol{\theta}_{r_{mn,h}}^T, \boldsymbol{\theta}_{s_{mn,h}}^T\right]^T$.

According to the Wald test rule for point target, the test rule for range-extended target can be expressed as

$$\prod_{m,n}\sum_{h=1}^{H}\left[\left(\hat{\boldsymbol{\theta}}_{r1_{mn,h}} - \hat{\boldsymbol{\theta}}_{r0_{mn,h}}\right)^T\left(\left[\mathbf{J}^{-1}\left(\hat{\boldsymbol{\theta}}_{1_{mn,h}}\right)\right]_{\hat{\boldsymbol{\theta}}_{r_{mn,h}},\hat{\boldsymbol{\theta}}_{r_{mn,h}}}\right)^{-1}\left(\hat{\boldsymbol{\theta}}_{r1_{mn,h}} - \hat{\boldsymbol{\theta}}_{r0_{mn,h}}\right)\right]\begin{array}{c}H_1\\>\\<\\H_0\end{array}T_{W1}$$

$$(10)$$

Where $\hat{\boldsymbol{\theta}}_{1_{mn,h}} = \left[\boldsymbol{\theta}_{r1_{mn,h}}^T, \boldsymbol{\theta}_{s1_{mn,h}}^T\right]^T$ denotes the estimation of $\boldsymbol{\theta}_{mn,h}$ under H_1 condition. Similarly, $\hat{\boldsymbol{\theta}}_{0_{mn,h}}$ denotes the estimation of $\boldsymbol{\theta}_{mn,h}$ under H_0 condition. $\mathbf{J}\left(\boldsymbol{\theta}_{mn,h}\right) = \mathbf{J}\left(\boldsymbol{\theta}_{r_{mn,h}}, \boldsymbol{\theta}_{s_{mn,h}}\right)$ is the Fisher information matrix which can be expressed as

$$\mathbf{J}\left(\boldsymbol{\theta}_{mn,h}\right) = \begin{pmatrix}\mathbf{J}_{\boldsymbol{\theta}_{r_{mn,h}},\boldsymbol{\theta}_{r_{mn,h}}}\left(\boldsymbol{\theta}_{mn,h}\right) & \mathbf{J}_{\boldsymbol{\theta}_{r_{mn,h}},\boldsymbol{\theta}_{s_{mn,h}}}\left(\boldsymbol{\theta}_{mn,h}\right)\\ \mathbf{J}_{\boldsymbol{\theta}_{s_{mn,h}},\boldsymbol{\theta}_{r_{mn,h}}}\left(\boldsymbol{\theta}_{mn,h}\right) & \mathbf{J}_{\boldsymbol{\theta}_{s_{mn,h}},\boldsymbol{\theta}_{s_{mn,h}}}\left(\boldsymbol{\theta}_{mn,h}\right)\end{pmatrix}$$

$$(11)$$

Where

$$\left[\mathbf{J}^{-1}\left(\boldsymbol{\theta}_{mn,h}\right)\right]_{\boldsymbol{\theta}_{r_{mn,h}},\boldsymbol{\theta}_{r_{mn,h}}}$$
$$= \left(\mathbf{J}_{\boldsymbol{\theta}_{r_{mn,h}},\boldsymbol{\theta}_{r_{mn,h}}}\left(\boldsymbol{\theta}_{mn,h}\right) - \mathbf{J}_{\boldsymbol{\theta}_{r_{mn,h}},\boldsymbol{\theta}_{s_{mn,h}}}\left(\boldsymbol{\theta}_{mn,h}\right)\mathbf{J}_{\boldsymbol{\theta}_{s_{mn,h}},\boldsymbol{\theta}_{s_{mn,h}}}^{-1}\left(\boldsymbol{\theta}_{mn,h}\right)\mathbf{J}_{\boldsymbol{\theta}_{s_{mn,h}},\boldsymbol{\theta}_{r_{mn,h}}}\left(\boldsymbol{\theta}_{mn,h}\right)\right)^{-1}$$

$$(12)$$

In our detection problem, it can be known that

$$\mathbf{J}_{\boldsymbol{\theta}_{r_{mn,h}},\boldsymbol{\theta}_{s_{mn,h}}}\left(\boldsymbol{\theta}_{mn,h}\right) = \mathbf{0}_{2,L^2}$$

$$(13)$$

$$\mathbf{J}_{\boldsymbol{\theta}_{r_{mn,h}},\boldsymbol{\theta}_{r_{mn,h}}}\left(\boldsymbol{\theta}_{mn,h}\right) = 2\mathbf{p}_{mn}^H\mathbf{R}_{mn}^{-1}\mathbf{p}_{mn}\mathbf{I}_{2,2}$$

$$(14)$$

So the formula (12) can be simplified as

$$\left[\mathbf{J}^{-1}\left(\boldsymbol{\theta}_{mn,h}\right)\right]_{\boldsymbol{\theta}_{r_{mn,h}},\boldsymbol{\theta}_{r_{mn,h}}} = \mathbf{J}_{\boldsymbol{\theta}_{r_{mn,h}},\boldsymbol{\theta}_{r_{mn,h}}}^{-1}\left(\boldsymbol{\theta}_{mn,h}\right)$$

$$(15)$$

As $\alpha_{mn,h} = 0$ under H_0 condition, $\hat{\boldsymbol{\theta}}_{r0_{mn,h}} = [0,0]^T$. According to the formula (15) and $\hat{\boldsymbol{\theta}}_{r0_{mn,h}} = [0,0]^T$, the formula (10) can be simplified as

$$\prod_{m,n} \sum_{h=1}^{H} \left[\hat{\boldsymbol{\theta}}_{r1_{mn,h}}^T \mathbf{J}_{\hat{\boldsymbol{\theta}}_{r_{mn,h}},\hat{\boldsymbol{\theta}}_{r_{mn,h}}} (\hat{\boldsymbol{\theta}}_{1_{mn,h}}) \hat{\boldsymbol{\theta}}_{r1_{mn,h}} \right] \overset{H_1}{\underset{H_0}{\gtrless}} T_{W1} \tag{16}$$

It can be known from the formula (16) that the expression of the KA-Wald detector will be derived after $\hat{\boldsymbol{\theta}}_{1_{mn,h}}$ is estimated.

There are two steps to get expression of the KA-Wald detector:

Step 1: estimate $\mathbf{R}_{mn}$, derive $\mathbf{J}_{\hat{\boldsymbol{\theta}}_{r_{mn,h}},\hat{\boldsymbol{\theta}}_{r_{mn,h}}} (\hat{\boldsymbol{\theta}}_{1_{mn,h}})$.

The joint probability density function under H_1 condition can be expressed as

$$f\left(\mathbf{x}_{mn,h}, \mathbf{y}_{mn,h} | \mathbf{R}_{mn}, \alpha_{mn,h}\right) = \frac{\pi^{-L(K+1)}}{|\mathbf{R}_{mn}|^{K+1}} etr\left\{ -\mathbf{R}_{mn}^{-1}\mathbf{C}_1 \right\} \tag{17}$$

Where $\mathbf{y}_{mn,h} = \left[\mathbf{x}_{mn,h}^1, \mathbf{x}_{mn,h}^2, \cdots, \mathbf{x}_{mn,h}^K \right]$ is the training data of the hth scattering point.

$$\mathbf{C}_1 = \left(\mathbf{x}_{mn,h} - \alpha_{mn,h}\mathbf{p}_{mn} \right) \left(\mathbf{x}_{mn,h} - \alpha_{mn,h}\mathbf{p}_{mn} \right)^H + \mathbf{S} \tag{18}$$

$$\mathbf{S} = \sum_{k=1}^{K} \mathbf{x}_{mn,h}^k \left(\mathbf{x}_{mn,h}^k \right)^H \tag{19}$$

According to the formula (7) and the formula (17), the likelihood function for $\alpha_{mn,h}$ can be derived as

$$\begin{aligned}
&f\left(\mathbf{x}_{mn,h}, \mathbf{y}_{mn,h} | \alpha_{mn,h}\right) \\
&= \frac{|(\mu - L)\Sigma|^{\mu}}{\pi^{L(K+1)} c(L,\mu)} c(L, K+\mu+1) |\mathbf{C}_1 + (\mu-L)\Sigma|^{-(K+\mu+1)}
\end{aligned} \tag{20}$$

So the PDF of the maximum a posteriori (MAP) about $\mathbf{R}_{mn}$ under H_1 condition can be expressed as

$$\begin{aligned}
f\left(\mathbf{R}_{mn} | \mathbf{x}_{mn,h}, \mathbf{y}_{mn,h}, \alpha_{mn,h}\right) &= \frac{f\left(\mathbf{x}_{mn,h}, \mathbf{y}_{mn,h} | \mathbf{R}_{mn}, \alpha_{mn,h}\right) f\left(\mathbf{R}_{mn}\right)}{f\left(\mathbf{x}_{mn,h}, \mathbf{y}_{mn,h} | \alpha_{mn,h}\right)} \\
&= \frac{|\mathbf{C}_1 + (\mu-L)\Sigma|^{(K+\mu+1)} etr\left\{ -\mathbf{R}_{mn}^{-1}(\mathbf{C}_1 + (\mu-L)\Sigma) \right\}}{|\mathbf{R}_{mn}|^{L+K+\mu+1} c(L, K+\mu+1)}
\end{aligned} \tag{21}$$

The MAP estimation of $\mathbf{R}_{mn}$ can be obtained according to the formula (21).

$$
\begin{aligned}
\hat{\mathbf{R}}_{mn_{MAP}} &= \frac{\mathbf{C}_1 + (\mu - L)\Sigma}{K + L + \mu + 1} \\
&= \frac{\left(\mathbf{x}_{mn,h} - \alpha_{mn,h}\mathbf{p}_{mn}\right)\left(\mathbf{x}_{mn,h} - \alpha_{mn,h}\mathbf{p}_{mn}\right)^H + \mathbf{S} + (\mu - L)\Sigma}{K + L + \mu + 1}
\end{aligned}
\tag{22}
$$

So, the expression of $\mathbf{J}_{\hat{\theta}_{r_{mn,h}},\hat{\theta}_{r_{mn,h}}}\left(\hat{\theta}_{1_{mn,h}}\right)$ can be derived based on the formula (14) and the formula (22).

$$
\begin{aligned}
\mathbf{J}_{\hat{\theta}_{r_{mn,h}},\hat{\theta}_{r_{mn,h}}}\left(\hat{\theta}_{1_{mn,h}}\right) &= 2\mathbf{p}_{mn}^H \hat{\mathbf{R}}_{mn_{MAP}}^{-1} \mathbf{p}_{mn} \\
&= 2\mathbf{p}_{mn}^H \left[\frac{\left(\mathbf{x}_{mn,h} - \alpha_{mn,h}\mathbf{p}_{mn}\right)\left(\mathbf{x}_{mn,h} - \alpha_{mn,h}\mathbf{p}_{mn}\right)^H + \mathbf{S} + (\mu - L)\Sigma}{K + L + \mu + 1}\right]^{-1} \mathbf{p}_{mn}
\end{aligned}
\tag{23}
$$

Step 2: estimate $\alpha_{mn,h}$, derive $\hat{\theta}_{r1_{mn,h}}$.

Substituting the formula (22) into the formula (21), the maximum likelihood estimation (MLE) of $\alpha_{mn,h}$ is

$$
\hat{\alpha}_{mn,h} = \frac{\mathbf{x}_{mn,h}^H (\mathbf{S} + (\mu - L)\Sigma)^{-1} \mathbf{p}_{mn}}{\mathbf{p}_{mn}^H (\mathbf{S} + (\mu - L)\Sigma)^{-1} \mathbf{p}_{mn}}
\tag{24}
$$

So the expression of $\hat{\theta}_{r1_{mn,h}}$ is

$$
\hat{\theta}_{r1_{mn,h}} = \left[\mathrm{Re}\left\{\frac{\mathbf{x}_{mn,h}^H (\mathbf{S} + (\mu - L)\Sigma)^{-1} \mathbf{p}_{mn}}{\mathbf{p}_{mn}^H (\mathbf{S} + (\mu - L)\Sigma)^{-1} \mathbf{p}_{mn}}\right\}, \mathrm{Im}\left\{\frac{\mathbf{x}_{mn,h}^H (\mathbf{S} + (\mu - L)\Sigma)^{-1} \mathbf{p}_{mn}}{\mathbf{p}_{mn}^H (\mathbf{S} + (\mu - L)\Sigma)^{-1} \mathbf{p}_{mn}}\right\}\right]^T
\tag{25}
$$

Substituting the formula (23) and the formula (25) into the formula (16), the KA-Wald detector can be expressed as

$$
\prod_{m,n}\sum_{h=1}^{H} \frac{\left|\mathbf{x}_{mn,h}^H (\mathbf{S} + (\mu - L)\Sigma)^{-1} \mathbf{p}_{mn}\right|^2}{\left[\mathbf{p}_{mn}^H (\mathbf{S} + (\mu - L)\Sigma)^{-1} \mathbf{p}_{mn}\right]^2} \mathbf{p}_{mn}^H [\mathbf{C}_1 + (\mu - L)\Sigma]^{-1}\mathbf{p}_{mn} \underset{H_2}{\overset{H_1}{\underset{<}{>}}} T_{W2}
\tag{26}
$$

According to the matrix inverse theory, the final expression of the KA-Wald detector is given by

$$
\prod_{m,n}\sum_{h=1}^{H} \frac{\left|\mathbf{x}_{mn,h}^H (\mathbf{S} + (\mu - L)\Sigma)^{-1} \mathbf{p}_{mn}\right|^2}{\mathbf{p}_{mn}^H (\mathbf{S} + (\mu - L)\Sigma)^{-1} \mathbf{p}_{mn}} \underset{H_2}{\overset{H_1}{\underset{<}{>}}} T_{W2}
\tag{27}
$$

4 Detector Comparison

For comparison purpose, we consider another knowledge-aided generalized likelihood ratio test (KA-GLRT) [11] detector which is proposed by Yongchan Gao.
The rule for the KA-GLRT detector is

$$\max_{\alpha} \frac{\prod\limits_{m,n} \int f_1\left(\mathbf{X}_{mn}, \mathbf{X}_{mn}^k | \mathbf{R}_{mn}, \alpha_{mn}\right) f(\mathbf{R}_{mn}) d\mathbf{R}_{mn}}{\prod\limits_{m,n} \int f_0\left(\mathbf{X}_{mn}, \mathbf{X}_{mn}^k | \mathbf{R}_{mn}\right) f(\mathbf{R}_{mn}) d\mathbf{R}_{mn}} \overset{H_1}{\underset{H_0}{\gtrless}} T_{G1} \qquad (28)$$

The final expression of the KA-GLRT detector is given by

$$\prod_{m,n} \prod_{h=1}^{H} \left(1 - \frac{\left| \mathbf{x}_{mn,h}^H \hat{\mathbf{R}}_{mn_{MAP}}^{-1} \mathbf{p}_{mn} \right|^2}{\mathbf{p}_{mn}^H \hat{\mathbf{R}}_{mn_{MAP}}^{-1} \mathbf{p}_{mn} \sum\limits_{h=1}^{H} \mathbf{x}_{mn,h}^H \hat{\mathbf{R}}_{mn_{MAP}}^{-1} \mathbf{x}_{mn,h}} \right)^{-L} \overset{H_1}{\underset{H_2}{\gtrless}} T_{G2} \qquad (29)$$

Compared with the KA-GLRT detector, the KA-Wald detector proposed in this paper has the following advantages:

(1) The derivation process of the KA-GLRT detector is more complicated. As the KA-GLRT detector applies GLRT detection rule, the MAP estimation of $\mathbf{R}_{mn}$ and the MLE of $\alpha_{mn,h}$ under H_1 condition and H_0 condition have to be derived. However, the KA-Wald detector only needs to derive the MAP estimation of $\mathbf{R}_{mn}$ and the MLE of $\alpha_{mn,h}$ under H_1 condition. So the KA-Wald has fewer unknown parameters to be estimated than KA-GLRT which results in a relative simple derivation process.
(2) Compare formula (27) and (29), it can be found that the KA-Wald detector has a more concise expression than the KA-GLRT detector. So, the KA-Wald detector has a smaller computational scale and a higher detection efficiency.

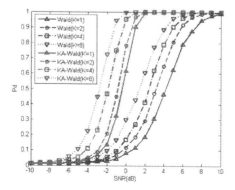

Fig. 2. Probability of detection

5 Simulation

For comparing detection performance and detection efficiency of the Wald detector, the KA-Wald detector and the KA-GLRT detector, the paper carries $10/P_{fa}$ independent simulations.

In all simulations, we set $M = 2, N = 2, L = 20, \mu = 24$. The false alarm rate $P_{fa} = 10^{-2}$. For simplicity, $\alpha_{mn,h}$ is set to the same value among the H range cells, but is different for different Tx-Rx pairs. The PRF of pulses is $500\,Hz$. The carrier frequency $f_c = 1\,GHz$. The velocity of the target is $108\,km/h$. As to prior information

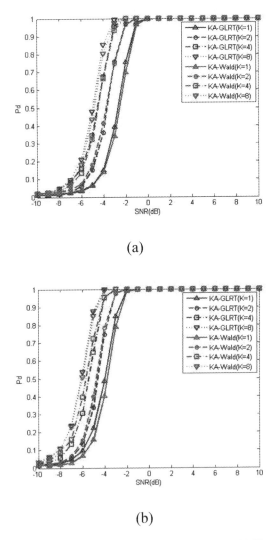

(a)

(b)

Fig. 3. Probability of detection for KA-Wald and KA-GLRT, (a) H = 6, (b) H = 10

matrix $\sum$, we set it an exponentially correlation covariance matrix with one-lag correlation coefficient $\rho = 0.9$, namely, the $(i,j)th$ element of $\sum$ is given by $\rho^{|i-j|}$.

Figure 2 shows the detection performance of the Wald detector and the KA-Wald detector under different numbers of training data. It can be found that the performance of the proposed KA-Wald detector is much better than the Wald detector. That's because the KA-Wald detector exploit the prior information matrix at the beginning which compensates the detection performance loss caused by limited numbers of training data in nonhomogeneous environments. So, compared with the Wald detector, the proposed KA-Wald detector improves the detection performance under small numbers of training data.

Figure 3 shows the detection performance of the KA-GLRT detector and the KA-Wald detector under different numbers of training data while Fig. 4 shows the corresponding detection efficiency.

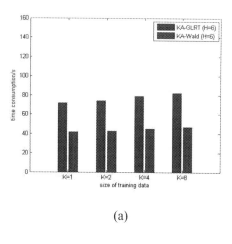

(a)

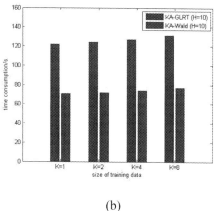

(b)

Fig. 4. Time consumption for KA-Wald and KA-GLRT, (a) H = 6, (b) H = 10

In Fig. 3, we can carry the following conclusions: (1) The detection performance for both two detectors improves with the increasing SNR. (2) The more numbers of training data, the better detection performance both of the two detectors will have. (3) Both two detectors have a brilliance detection under small numbers of training data. (4) Under same detection conditions which include the same SNR, the same number of training data, the same value of H, etc., the proposed KA-Wald detector has a similar probability curve of detection with the KA-GLRT detector which means a similar detection performance.

In all simulations in this paper, we just set $M = 2, N = 2$ which means a small distributed MIMO radar system. The amount of dealing data will be little in the small distributed MIMO radar system. But it's opposite in a large distributed MIMO radar system. So the detection efficiency is very important in the large system. In Fig. 4, it can be found that the propped KA-Wald detector spends less time to calculate the probability of detection than the KA-GLRT detector under same detection conditions (it's calculated to be about 58% of KA-GLRT). Therefore, the proposed KA-Wald detector has a higher detection efficiency than the KA-GLRT detector. The proposed KA-Wald detector can detect a target in a shorter time which makes great sense to the large distributed MIMO radar system.

6   Conclusion

This paper first introduces the signal model in the range-extended target detection for the distributed MIMO radar. In the signal model, the prior information matrix is built to simulate the characteristics of interferences for different Tx-Rx pairs and $\mathbf{R}_{mn}$ is modeled as a complex inverse Wishart random matrix. Then the KA-Wald detector for the distributed MIMO radar is designed based on the signal model in the paper. Finally the simulations on the one hand prove that the proposed KA-Wald detector has a better detection performance than the Wald detector under small numbers of training data, as the KA-Wald detector considers the prior information about nonhomogeneous environments at the beginning. On the other hand, the simulations also state that the proposed KA-Wald detector has a similar detection performance with the KA-GLRT detector. But the proposed KA-Wald detector only spends 58% of time to calculate the probability of detection than the KA-GLRT detector which means the KA-Wald detector has a higher detection efficiency. So the KA-Wald detector is more suitable to be applied in the large distributed MIMO radar system.

Acknowledgments. Part of this work was supported by National Nature Science Foundation of China (Grant No. 61471019, 61673146 and 61771028).

References

1. Tajer, A., Jajamovich, G.H., Wang, X., Moustakides, G.V.: Optimal joint target detection and parameter estimation by MIMO radar. IEEE Trans. Signal Process. **59**(10), 4809–4820 (2011)

2. Li, J., Stoica, P.: MIMO Radar Signal Process. Wiley, New York (2009)
3. Liu, W., Wang, Y., Lin, J., Xie, W., Chen, H., Gu, W.: Adaptive detection without training data in collocated MIMO radar. IEEE Trans. Aerosp. Electron. Syst. **51**(3), 2469–2479 (2015)
4. Xu, L., Li, J., Stoica, P.: Target detection and parameter estimation for MIMO radar system. IEEE Trans. Aerosp. Electron. Syst. **44**(3), 927–939 (2008)
5. Liu, J., Zhang, Z., Cao, Y., Yang, S.: A closed-form expression for false alarm rate of adaptive MIMO-GLRT detector with distributed MIMO radar. Signal Process. **93**(9), 2771–2776 (2013)
6. Chong, C.Y., Pascal, F., Ovarlez, J.P., Lesturgie, M.: MIMO radar detection in non-gaussian and heterogeneous clutter. IEEE J. Sel. Top. Signal Process. **4**(1), 115–126 (2010)
7. Liu, J., Li, H., Himed, B.: Persymmetric adaptive target detection with distributed MIMO radar. IEEE Trans. Aerosp. Electron. Syst. **51**(1), 372–382 (2015)
8. Gerlach, K., Steiner, M., Lin, F.: Detection of a spatially distributed target in white noise. IEEE Signal Process. Lett. **4**(7), 198–200 (1997)
9. Conte, E., De Maio, A., Ricci, G.: GLRT-based adaptive detection algorithms for range-spread targets. IEEE Trans. Signal Process. **49**(7), 1336–1348 (2001)
10. Burgess, K.A., Van Veen, B.D.: Subspace-based adaptive generalized likelihood ratio detection. IEEE Trans. Signal Process. **44**(4), 912–927 (1996)
11. Gao, Y., Li, H., Himed, B.: Knowledge-aided range-spread target detection for distributed MIMO radar in nonhomogeneous environments. IEEE Trans. Signal Process. **65**(3), 617–627 (2017)

Data Deterministic Deletion Scheme Based on DHT Network and Fragmentation Deletion

Yongsheng Zhang[1,2], Nengneng Li[1,2(✉)], Ranran Cui[1,2],
and Yueqin Fan[3]

[1] School of Information Science and Engineering, Shandong Normal University,
Jinan, China
{15666965768, zhangys}@sdnu. edu. cn,
13583189960@163. com, linengneng1992@163. com,
15154119208@qq. com, 851758457@qq. com
[2] Shandong Provincial Key Laboratory
for Distributed Computer Software Novel Technology, Jinan 250358, China
[3] Beijing Key Laboratory of Intelligent Telecommunications Software
and Multimedia, Beijing University of Posts and Telecommunications,
Beijing 100876, China
{13589079087, fanyq}@bupt. edu. cn

Abstract. During the life cycle of the cloud data, the technique of data deterministic deletion is designed to completely destroy the data and ensures that cloud data that is out of date or backed up in the cloud server is completely deleted or will never be decrypted or accessed. However, the existing scheme simply deletes the key or the cipher text. Once the key or the cloud backup of the cipher text is stolen, data privacy will be threatened. For this reason, this paper proposes a data deletion scheme that is dynamic deletion is based on fragmented cipher text and key. The core of this scheme is to use the dynamic characteristics of DHT network to realize the periodic deletion of fragmented cipher text. Using the idea of fragmented cipher text dynamic deletion, in the unauthorized time even if in the case that the key is leaked, illegal user can not get all the cipher text and key, and can not restore the complete data. The theoretical analysis and experimental results show that the scheme can effectively delete some fragmented cipher texts and key, and has low performance cost, which can meet the requirements for deterministic deletion of excessive data or backup files in cloud storage system.

Keywords: Key spanning tree · Cipher text fragmentation
CP-ABE algorithm · Shamir secret sharing algorithm

1 Introduction

The Ephemerizer mechanism proposed in literature [1] requires one or more trusted third parties to store the user's data decryption key and is responsible for destroying the decryption key after a period of time specified by the user, so that no one can decrypt the data. But the program did not get a concrete realization, and the article did not evaluate its performance, there is no strong persuasive. In literature [2], a method of

© Springer Nature Singapore Pte Ltd. 2018
H. Yuan et al. (Eds.): GSKI 2017, CCIS 848, pp. 426–436, 2018.
https://doi.org/10.1007/978-981-13-0893-2_45

database-based deterministic deletion is proposed to realize the deterministic deletion of data and its backup in cloud storage system. The basic idea of this method is to encrypt the data by the data key, and then encrypt the data key by the control key associated with the policy, and delete the control key to confirm the data. However, in this scenario, a control key managed by a third party's key manager is used, which is a centralized management approach. There is a security risk that the key manager is not trusted to delete or leak the control key. Literature [3] thinks that only destroys the key but not destroy the data, there are security risks that attacker's violent crack password algorithm. On the basis of Vanish system, the key and part of the cipher text data distributed to the DHT network, making the attacker violent creak the incomplete cipher text data required to increase the key space, thereby increasing the difficulty and cost of the attack. The program distributes part of the cipher text to the network, increase network communication costs. In literature [4], by improving Shamir secret sharing algorithm, the author extends the length of the key to resist the jump attack in the Vanish system. The resistance to the sniffing attack is achieved by means of public and private key encryption and decryption. Based on the study of the existing privacy protection method, literature [5] proposed a method of cloud data deterministic deletion method ADCSS based on cipher text sampling fragmentation. The idea based on cipher text sampling, fragment storage cipher text; store the simple cipher text in a trusted third-party platform to achieve the deterministic deletion of cloud data. However, the text mentions that the cipher text is stored in a third-party trusted institution. The promise is that the third party is credible, but now many third parties have untrustworthy risks. In the literature [6], the proposed method is based on the key-derived tree and DHT network. According to the characteristics of the cloud storage data, the idea of using structured hierarchical key management, the key generation tree based on the hash function is used to generate and manage the secret key, which effectively reduces the number of keys required to maintain the main data and the number of keys exposed to the external key and through the data block level encryption to provide fine-grained data management and operation. Combined with the proposed scheme, this paper proposes a data deletion scheme that distributes the cipher text and key fragment to the DHT network. On the one hand, it can increase the cost of network communication as little as possible, and on the other hand, protect the data to determine the deletion.

2 Related Works

2.1 Key-Derived Tree

First, the data owner will segment the data to be stored, and segment into different lengths of n data blocks, expressed as d1, d2...dn. Then encrypt the n data blocks by different keys. After encrypting, these different keys are managed and maintained by the data owner or key management module. Considering that the number of keys increases as the number of data blocks increases, and it will increase overhead of the system maintenance key. Therefore, this paper drawing on [7], uses the hierarchical key and key-derived tree to generate and manage the key. The method generates and organizes the key through the binary tree, and the key is expressed as $k_{i,j}$, where i is the

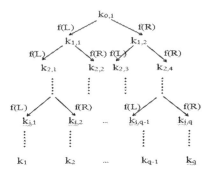

Fig. 1. Key spring tree

level of $k_{i,j}$ in the tree, j is the number of $k_{i,\,j}$ in the i layer. Except for the root key $k_{0,1}$, the other keys are generated by the parent node through the left or right derived rule f (L) or f (R). The specific process shown in Fig. 1.

2.2 DHT Network

DHT network is a major network type in P2P network [8], which uses DHT table [9, 10] to store data and implement node routing. The usability, large scale and wide geographical distribution, and dynamic of the DHT network determine that it can be used in the deterministic deletion of data. The following briefly describes these three characteristics.

Availability, DHT network can provide reliable distributed storage function. DHT network have been applied in many practical systems, this feature can be protected data is available in the authorization time, this feature is the basis that DHT network can be applied to the data deterministic deletion.

Large-scale and widely distributed geographical. There are more than a million active nodes in the Vuze network. This completely decentralized distribution can provide a robust anti-attack capability.

Dynamic. In the DHT network, the nodes continue to join and leave, changing over time, the information stored in them will be regularly cleared. When the data reaching the time limit, it will be deleted. The dynamic and regular removal of the data determines the DHT network can be used to determine the data to delete.

2.3 Shamir Threshold Scheme

Shamir threshold scheme [11], also is known as (k, n) - threshold scheme, where k is called the threshold, n is the threshold value, k/n is the threshold rate. The scheme divides a key into n parts (called n subkeys), which are handed over to n individuals so that the integer k (k < n) is satisfied for:

(1) In this n individuals, any r (r ≥ k) personal collaboration, they can restore the original key;
(2) Any r (r < k) collaboration cannot restore the original key.

With this scheme, the key s and the sampled cipher text are split into n parts, and reconstructing complete key and cipher text needs at least t or more than t s_i. When the part s_i is leaked, if the number of leaks is less than t, it does not affect the reconstruction of the complete key, and the leaked part does not generate a complete key. In the DHT network, due to the dynamic nature of the network, part of the key is easy to lose, Shamir threshold program is an effective solution to this situation.

3 Data Deterministic Deletion Method Based on Fragmentation Cipher Text and Key Dynamic Deletion

First, in the key generation stage, the traditional data encryption and decryption using of CP-ABE algorithm need to go through four steps:

(1) Setup: Generate public key PK and master key MK.
(2) C = Encrypt (PK, D, T), encrypts the plain text D using the public key PK and the access structure T, and generate the cipher text C.
(3) DK = Keygen (MK, A), use MK and user attribute set A to generate the user's private key DK.
(4) D = Decrypt (C, DK), use the private key DK to decrypt the cipher text C to get the data clear D.

After generating the PK and MK using the CP-ABE algorithm, the PK encrypts the data to generate cipher text and then is deleted. The MK is stored in the data owner or key management side. When the user accesses the data, generate the private key DK through the MK and the user attribute set A. If the number of data blocks that want to encrypt increase, the MK that each block corresponds will increase, which undoubtedly increase overhead that the data users store key. For this reason, the data deterministic deletion scheme proposed in this paper combines the key-derived tree with the CP-ABE algorithm in the key generation process. The specific program process is as follows:

(1) Setup: Let G_0 be a multiplicative cyclic group of order p, g is a generator of group G_0, G_1 is a multiplicative cyclic group of order q, e is a bilinear pair G0 × G0 → G1, $e(g, g)^{\alpha}$ is a bilinear mapping. the hash function H: $\{0,1\} * \to$ G0 is as a random oracle, Z_p is an integer field of order p, α and β are the random value in Z_p. Randomly select a value $t_j \in$ Zp, the algorithm outputs the system public key

$$(PK = g, g^{\beta}, y = e(g, g)^{\alpha}, \{g^{t_j}\}_{j=1}^{n}) \tag{1}$$

The master key is calculated as follows

$$MK = (\beta, \{t_j\}_{j=1}^{n}) \tag{2}$$

(2) Generate public key. Produce PK (n, p, PK0, 1, fL, fR, f) → {PKi}

First, according to the formula (1) to generate a public key $PK_{0,1}$ that is as the root of the key spanning tree root, n data blocks correspond to n leaf nodes, tree height p meets $2^{p-1} < n \leq 2^p$ according to the nature of the binary tree. When $PK_{i,j}$ is non-leaf nodes, its left and right children respectively are $PK_{(i+1),(2*j-1)}$ and $PK_{(i+1),(2*j)}$. And $PK_{(i+1),(2*j-1)} = f_L(PK_{i,j})$, $PK_{(i+1),(2*j)} = f_R(PK_{i,j}).f_L(PK_{i,j}) = h$ $(PK_{i,j}\|(2*j-1))$, $f_R(PK_{i,j}) = h(PK_{i,j}\|(2*j))$. h() is the hash function SHA-1, $\|$ means series. By repeating this process, all leaf nodes $PK_{p,i}$ can be calculated by $PK_{0,1}$. Finally, $PK_{p,1}$ to $PK_{p,n}$ are used as the public keys PK_1 to PK_n to encrypt 1 to n block data blocks.

(3) Encrypted data. Encrypt (PK, D, T) → C

Data user encrypts the original data D using of CP-ABE mechanism, generate cipher text C. Algorithm inputs system public key PK, access control structure T, and plain text data D. Firstly, calculate the intermediate variable

$$c_0 = (g^\beta)^\delta \tag{3}$$

$$c_1 = My^\delta = Me(g,g)^{\alpha\delta} \tag{4}$$

$$c_{j,i} = (g^{t_j})^{\delta i} \tag{5}$$

And then calculate the file cipher based on the intermediate variable

$$C = (T, c_0, c_1, \{c_{j,i}\}_{a_{j,i \in T}}) \tag{6}$$

(4) Cipher text fragment. DataSample (C, m, k) → (SD, RD)

In order to protect the privacy of the data, the data owner will not be able to upload the complete cipher text to the cloud service provider after encrypting the data locally. Before that, we need to sample the n-segment data cipher text generated by the n data blocks. The article uses the cipher text sampling method proposed in literature [5], C is the file cipher text, m is the number of bits per sample, and k is the number of samples. Let i = 1,…, k, the algorithm randomly generates integer p_i, it need to meet $0 \leq pi \leq$ Len (C^i) -m, Len (Ci) indicates the length of current file cipher text C^i, the unit is bit. the sampling information is located in the interval $[p_i, p_i + m]$ in the cipher text C^i. Di represents the data obtained by the i-th sample, and C^{i+1} represents the cipher text data after the i-th sample, then $C^1 = C$. The number of bits sampled in this process is represented by the tuple SB = (b_1, L, b_i, L, b_n), and the corresponding sampling position information is represented by tuple SP = (p_1, L, p_i, L, p_n). The complete sampling cipher text SD = (SB, SP), LD is the remaining cipher text after sampling. The concrete description formula is:

$$SD = (SB, SP) \tag{7}$$

$$LD = (C, m, k, SD) \tag{8}$$

(5) Generate private key. ProduceDK (MK, A) → DK

Generate $PK_1 \sim PKn$ using the known $PK_{0,1}$ and key spanning tree managed by data owner. Then, use the inverse operation of the formula (1) to calculate the random values α, β, t_j of each public key, and the randomly select values r from Z_p to prepare for generating n different private key DK_u. First calculate the public value D_0 of the user's private key

$$D_0 = g^{\frac{\alpha + r}{\beta}} \tag{9}$$

Then calculate the attribute value D_j of the user's private key

$$D_j = \{g^{\frac{r}{t_j}}\}_{a_j \in A_u} \tag{10}$$

A_u denotes the attribute set that the data owner assign to the authorized user, $Ur_j \in Z_p$. For each attribute $a_j \in A_u$, choose a random number t_j that is selected as a randomly selected value in Zp, j denotes the subscript of the attribute of the system attribute set Ω. Finally, algorithm outputs the complete private key

$$(DK_u = D_0, D_i) \tag{11}$$

(6) Distribution slices. TrKeyDis (R, {L}, δ, t, m, {SKu} n, {SD} n) → {Node}

With the Random () function as R, take the time of the current system as the random seed Li, a total select $|\{SK_u\}_n|$ times the system's current time to obtain {L} ($|\{X\}|$ represents the number of elements in collection {X}) and the simple cipher text SD uploaded by data owner, then SD is divided into $|\{SK_u\}_n|$ segments to generate {SD}. Make the elements L_i in the {L} and the elements SD_i in {SD} be one to one correspondence by mapping δ: $SK_{ui} \rightarrow (L_i, SD_i)$. Then combine SD_i and SK_{ui} to set {SD, SKu}. Divide each of the elements (SD_i, SK_{ui}) in the {SD, SK_u} and subscript i into m slices by Shamir secret sharing scheme. Li is as the input of R and generates m random values. Then distribute m slices of each element (SD_i, SK_{ui}) in the {SD, SK_u} and subscript i to the m nodes of the DHT network through the m random values.

(7) Restore the cipher text and secret key. TrKeyExtract (R, {L}, t, m) → {SK$_u$} $_n$

L_i is as the input of R, and generates m random values. Then extract the slices of SD_i, SK_{ui} and subscript i from the DHT network according to the m random values. Recover the sampling cipher text SD_i and the private key SK_{ui} according to the Shamir secret sharing scheme. Finally, get the final decryption private key and complete cipher text.

(8) Decrypt cipher text. Decryption ({C_i}, {SK_u}) → {M_i}

Through the CP-ABE scheme, use the {SK_u}$_i$ recovered in step 7) to decrypt for each corresponding cipher text block {C_i} and obtain the plaintext block {M_i}.

(9) Delete the cipher key. Delete ({SD, SK_u})

When the data that arrived deadline needs to be deleted, use the dynamic characteristics of the DHT network to delete the cipher text and private key fragments stored in the DHT network. According to the Shamir secret sharing scheme, if the remaining slices are less than the threshold after the cipher text and private key are deleted, the complete sample cipher text collection {SD} and private key collection {SK$_u$} cannot be generated. Even if there is a backup of the cipher text in the cloud storage, and then obtain private key fragment less than the threshold from the DHT network, user cannot decrypt all the cipher text. Therefore user cannot form a complete cipher text.

4 Experiment Analyses

In this paper, we mainly analyze and verify the scheme of the above-mentioned DHT-based cipher text key fragment deletion. The main test is to test time of the key generation tree generating private key, time of key fragmenting, time of file encryption and decryption etc. time overhead in the CP-ABE algorithm and key deterministic deletion effect in the DHT network. The elements of {SD, SK$_u$} are fragmented to the DHT network one to one correspondence. Therefore, only test the availability and the deletion situation of key after being fragmented the DHT network, we can judge the availability and the deletion situation of cipher text after being fragmented the DHT network. So this article only tests the availability and the deletion situation of key after being fragmented the DHT network in the case of different thresholds and threshold rates.

4.1 Experimental Environment

The experimental environment for this article is Intel (R) Core (TM) 2.20 GHz, memory is 4.00 GB, and the operating system is Windows10. Installed Ubuntu 10.10 VMware Workstation6.5.2, allocated 2 GB of memory. DHT network used Vuze DHT; the validity period of the data is 8 h that DHT network defaults.

4.2 Experimental Results and Analysis

Experiment 1: CP-ABE algorithm encryption and decryption time comparison

Firstly, the data owner encrypt data by using the CP-ABE algorithm. The traditional CP-ABE algorithm generates the private key according to the random number α, β and so on and attribute set after generating the public key PK and encrypting data. The improved CP-ABE algorithm in this paper generated n public key $PK_0 \sim PK_n$ encrypting n data blocks firstly. Then calculate random value α, β according to $PK_0 \sim PK_n$, and generate private key to decrypt the data according to the algorithm and the user attribute set. Figure 2 is comparison the private key generation time of the traditional CP-ABE algorithm with the improved CP-ABE algorithm in this paper.

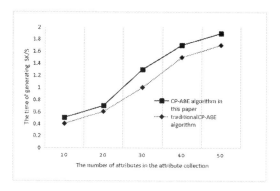

Fig. 2. Comparison between the traditional CP-ABE algorithm and CP-ABE algorithm

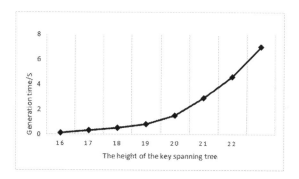

Fig. 3. The relationship between the key generation time and the height of the tree

Experiment 2: The time of the key spanning tree

Experiment 2 tests the relationship between the time of the key generation and the height of the tree in the key spanning tree. As shown in Fig. 3, when the height of the tree is 18, if the size of the data block is 4 KB, there need to generate a 20-layer key spanning tree to encrypt 4 GB of data, the time required is only about 1.5 s. The time overhead is relatively small.

Experiment 3: DHT network key removal effect test

This paper mainly determines the effect of key deterministic deletion by testing the availability of a single key in the DHT network. According to the decision method of key deterministic deletion mentioned in literature [6], the experiment idea is to distribute many times the same key to the network at different thresholds N and different thresholds rate p, after a period of time, extract the key from the network and reconstruct the key. After repeating several times, determine the availability of key in the network according to the reconstruction key. In this experiment, set the value of N to 10, 30, 50, 100, 150, 200, the threshold is set to 50%, 60%, 70%, 80%, 90%, 100%. When N is different, the times that the key is distributed to the network is different. The time for distributing the key once is related to the size of N. When N is 10, the time to distribute a single key is about 30 s, and when N is 30, the time to distribute a single key is about 100 s and N is 50, the time to distribute a single key is about 150 s. The value of N is 100, the time to distribute a single key is about 270 s, the value of N is 150, the time to distribute a single key is about 400 s, the value of N is 200, and the time to distribute a single key is about 600 s. In order for the key to be distributed to the network in one hour, that is an extraction cycle, set a different distribution time when the value of N is different. When N is 10 and 30, generate 20 seeds randomly, and then distribute 20 times the same key to the network at random according to these seeds.

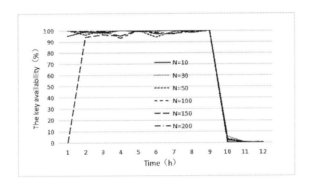

Fig. 4. The key availability when threshold rate is 80% and N is different

When N is 50, generate 15 seeds randomly and distribute 15 times the same key to the network at random. When N is 100, and 150, the distribution time is 10. And when N is 200, the distribution time is 5. After that, starting from the first distribution key, extract and reconstruct the key from the network every hour, and extract 12 times. Figure 4 shows the relationship between the availability of the key in the network and the time when N is different and the threshold is 80%.

As can be seen from the experimental data in Fig. 4, the availability of the key is almost 100% within 9 h after distribution, and the data for the Vuze DHT network is valid for 8 h. The data distributed in the network after 8 h cannot be deleted

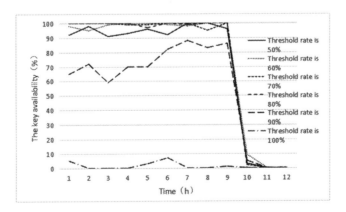

Fig. 5. The key availability when N is 100 and threshold rate is different

immediately, it can keep a few minutes to an hour ranging from time. After that, if the data is not updated, DHT network will completely delete the data. so after 10 h the key availability is almost 0. When N is 150, the key is distributed to the network for a period of time of about 4000 s, exceeding one extraction cycle for one hour, so the key is not distributed completely before 1 h, so the available rate is 0 (Fig. 5).

Based on the above experimental data, we can see that the key availability rate is the highest when N is 50 to 100 and the threshold rate is between 60% and 80%. The system performance cost is low and it ensures system availability. Experiments show that the availability of key recovered from the network is nearly 100% when the key is shared into the DHT network and needs to decrypt. And also show the recoverable rate of the cipher text is 100%. So the program has great feasibility. In the deterministic deletion scheme of the data, the scheme of this paper not only realizes the preservation of the key and some cipher text and protects it from being obtained illegally, but ensures the deterministic deletion of the cipher text and key.

5 Summary

In this paper, based on the study of the traditional data deterministic deletion method and learning from the improvement scheme of data deterministic deletion in the literature. This paper puts forward the cipher text and key deterministic deletion scheme based on DHT network after analyzing the inadequacies of these programs. It solves the problem that the cloud server backs up the data resulting in cipher text is not deleted completely, and the problem that key management side and third party institutions are not credible. Thus ensure the data to determine the deletion. However, in this scenario, the sampling cipher text and the key are distributed together into the DHT network, it adds a certain amount network communication overhead, and follow-up will continue to improve it, and solve the communication overhead problem cause by sampling cipher text is distributed to the DHT network for management and deletion.

Acknowledgments. This research was supported by the Postgraduate Education Innovation Projects of Shandong Province of China under Grant No.SDYC15042. In addition, the authors would like to thank the reviewers for their valuable comments and suggestions.

References

1. Perlman, R.: File system design with assured delete. In: SISW 2005 Proceeding of the Third IEEE International Security in Storage Workshop, pp. 83–88 (2005)
2. Tang, Y., Lee, P.P.C, Lui, J.C.S., et al.: FADE: secure overlay cloud storage with file assured deletion. In: Proceedings of the SecureComm 2010, pp. 380–397. ACM Press, New York (2010)
3. Yue, F., Wang, G., Liu, Q.: A secure self-destruct-ing scheme for electronic data. In: Proceedings of EUC 2010, pp. 651–658. IEEE Press, New York (2010)
4. Zeng, L., Shi, Z., Xu, S., et al.: Safevanish: animproved data self-destruction for protecting data privacy. In: Proceedings of CloudCom 2010, pp. 521–528. IEEE Press, New York (2010)

5. Zhang, K., Yang, C., Ma, J., Zhang, J.: Study on deterministic deletion of cloud data based on cipher text sampling fragmentation. J. Commun. **11**, 108–117 (2015)
6. Wang, Li-na, Ren, Zheng-wei, Yu, Rong-wei, Han, Feng, Dong, Yong-feng: A method for deterministic data removal for cloud storage. Acta Electr. J. **02**, 266–272 (2012)
7. Wang, W., Li, Z., Owens, R., et al.: Secure and efficient access to outsourced data. In: Proceedings of CCSW 2009, pp. 55–65. ACM Press, New York (2009)
8. Wei, A.: DHT Network Measurement and Analysis. University of Electronic Science and Technology (2011)
9. Stoica, I., Morris, R., Karger, D., et al.: Chord: a scalable peer-to-peer lookup service for internet applications. In: Proceedings of the SIGCOMM 2001, pp. 149–160. ACM Press, New York (2001)
10. Dabek, F.: A Distributed Hash Table. Massachusetts Institute of Technology, Massachusetts (2005)
11. Huan-ping, L.I.U., Yi-xian, Y.A.N.G.: Generalized (k, n) - threshold scheme. J. Commun. **08**, 73–78 (1998)

Wavelet Entropy Analysis for Detecting Lying Using Event-Related Potentials

Yijun Xiong[1], Junfeng Gao[2(✉)], and Ran Chen[2]

[1] College of Mechanical and Electrical Engineering, Wuhan Donghu University,
Wuhan 430212, China
[2] Key Laboratory of Cognitive Science of State Ethnic Affairs Commission,
College of Biomedical Engineering, South-Central University for Nationalities,
Wuhan, China
junfengmst@163.com

Abstract. This paper presents a method to identify lying automatically using EEG signals. The wavelet entropy of event-related potentials (ERP) carries information about the degree of order associated with a multi-frequency brain electrophysiological activity. We used wavelet entropy to analyze ERP during a lying task. Ten subjects were divided into guilty and innocent groups randomly. They were instructed to make a truthful or deceptive responses on the stimuli. EEG recordings on Pz channel were collected and the features of wavelet entropy were extracted. Statistical result reveals that there is significantly lower wavelet entropy value for the guilty group than that for the control group. We concluded that guilty subjects showed much high order degree of the brain state than normal persons after about 300 ms after stimulus onset. Hence, wavelet entropy is an effective and reliable approach to detect deception, and can help us to understand cognition processing deeply for lying behaviors.

Keywords: Wavelet Entropy · Deception Detection · EEG

1 Introduction

Deception occurs when one person tries to convince another to accept as correct what the prevaricator believes is incorrect [1]. P300, a kind of event-related potential (ERP), is a positive-going wave with a scalp amplitude distribution in which it is largest parietally (at Pz) and smallest frontally (Fz), taking intermediate values centrally (Cz) [2]. Recently the deception detection (DD) methods based on ERP [3, 4], has attracted considerable research interest [5–8].

For one thing, EEG reflects the activity of ensembles of generators producing spontaneous or ERP oscillations in several frequency ranges. Upon stimulation, functionally activated generators begin to act together in a coherent way. This transition from a disordered to an ordered state can be detected as frequency stabilization, synchronization, and enhancement of the ongoing EEG in the post-stimulus period [9].

For another, linear analysis is the common character for the current LD methods. In fact, brain is composed of a huge amount of neurons that connect each other, and nonlinearity is first introduced at the cellular level because the dynamical behavior of

© Springer Nature Singapore Pte Ltd. 2018
H. Yuan et al. (Eds.): GSKI 2017, CCIS 848, pp. 437–444, 2018.
https://doi.org/10.1007/978-981-13-0893-2_46

individual neuron is governed by threshold and saturation phenomena [10]. For the reason, the EEG appears to be an appropriate area for non-linear analysis [11]. Although much research has been devoted to lie detection, little attention has been done on using non-linear measures to detect deception with EEG.

Entropy, based on the information theory, is a measure of order and disorder in a dynamic system [12]. For analysis of EEG disorder, the spectral entropy has been first introduced in the report [13]. However, because of the low time resolution of the Fourier transform, the spectral entropy cannot follow fast changes of EEG states, especially assess the ERP. To overcome these limitations, a new method based on the time/frequency decomposition of the EEG by means of the wavelet transform (WT) has been recently developed and applied to ERPs [14].

The method is called wavelet entropy (WE). The WT provides for optimal time resolution for each frequency band and can accordingly extract in a reliable way superimposed event-related oscillations from different frequencies. Therefore, WE can precisely follow and measure the time dynamics of order/disorder states for the ERP [9].

In the present study, the WE method is applied to study ERP from two kinds of subjects: the innocent subjects and guilty subjects. The ERP signals were decomposed by WT into four frequency bands: delta, theta, alpha and gamma. Finally, the time-varying WE were calculated and were compared between two groups.

2   Methods

2.1   Subjects and Experimental Protocol

Eighteen subjects (8 males) participated in this study. They were generally undergraduate or postgraduate students and all had normal or corrected vision. After we had explained the nature and possible consequences of the study, the participants signed the informed consent before the beginning of the experiment. The participants were randomly divided into two groups: liar group (4 females, age of 21.3 ± 1.3) and truth-teller (4 females, 21.4 ± 1.5) group. The images of six watches with different characteristics were prepared. Each subject was trained and then asked to perform a mock crime scenario. A box containing two watches was given to the guilty. Then, the guilty were instructed to steal one, which was served as the probe (P) stimuli. The other objects in box are the Target (T) stimulus. The remaining four objects are irrelevant (I) stimuli. For the innocent, they only saw one watch (T stimulus) in the box and stole nothing. The standard three stimuli protocol was employed in this study [15, 16]. When the subjects stole the jewels, all researchers were asked to stay outside of the room.

After being trained, each subject was asked to sit on a chair. A computer screen was placed approximately 70 cm from them, on which the stimulus pictures were presented randomly. Each stimulus remained on the screen for 500 ms, and the inter-stimulus interval varied randomly between 1.6 and 1.7 s. All subjects were instructed to respond to each stimulus as quickly as possible by pressing buttons. The innocent responded honestly to all stimuli, whereas the guilty group was to press the right button when P stimulus was presented in an attempt to hide the stealing act. Each session lasted approximately 5 min, followed by a 3-min rest period. In each session, each stimulus was randomly repeated 30 times, resulting in approximately 30 P, 30 T and 120 I responses. Above session was repeated four times for each subject. Behavioral data (response time and type) were recorded and embedded into the EEG signals using NeuroScan Stim2 software to enable correct segmentation of the EEG data. The guilty group was told that the task bonus would be 100 RMB if they successfully concealed the identity of the P stimuli during the detection task.

2.2   EEG Recording

No subject was excluded because all the clicking error rate were smaller than 5%. Electrodes were placed according to the International 10-20 System. EEG was recorded on Pz channel. The vertical EOG (VEOG) signal was recorded from the right eye (below and above the pupil 2.5 cm), and the horizontal EOG (HEOG) was recorded from the outer canthus. Amplifiers used were Neuroscan Synamps. One earlobe was served as reference. The bandwidths of amplifiers were 0.1–30 Hz and sampling frequency was 500 Hz.

All of the subjects were seated in chairs, facing a video screen that was approximately 1 m away from their eyes. The stimuli pictures were presented randomly at the screen. Each item remained 1.1 s with 30 iterations for one session; each session lasted for about 5 min with 2 min' resting time. The inter-stimulus interval was 1.6 s. Each subject was instructed to perform 3 sessions. One push button was given to each subject and he or she was asked to press "Yes" or "No" button when facing with familiar or unknown items, respectively.

Based on prior experience, only P responses (response wave from P stimuli) were selected for further processing. Afterwards, EEGLAB was used to divide the EEG data into 4500 epoch datasets.

2.3   Preprocessing

The artifact removal criterion was $\pm75\mu v$. Using EEGLAB toolbox, he continuous EEG signals was first segmented into epochs from 0.3 s before to 1.3 s after the stimuli onset. Then, all the P responses (from P stimuli) were baseline-corrected based on the pre-stimulus interval. Each 3 single trials were then averaged within each subject.

2.4   WE Algorithm

A wavelet family $\Psi_{a,b}(t)$ is the set of elementary functions generated by dilations and translations of a mother wavelet $\Psi(t)$:

$$\Psi_{a,b}(t) = \frac{1}{\sqrt{a}} \cdot \Psi\left(\frac{t-b}{a}\right), \tag{1}$$

where a, $b \in \mathbb{R}$, $a \neq 0$. When for the discrete set of parameters, $a = 2^m$ and $b = k2^m$, respectively, wavelet family is changed to be:

$$\Psi_{m,k}(i) = 2^{-\frac{m}{2}}\Psi(2^{-m}i - k), \tag{2}$$

where i is the discrete time and m and k are the new scale and shift parameters, respectively.

Accordingly, the discrete wavelet transform (DWT), which can be interpreted as a measure of correlation between the analyzed signal $S(t)$ and the wavelet family $\Psi_{m,k}(i)$, is defined as follows:

$$A_m(k) = \sum_{i=1}^{M} s(i) \cdot \Psi_{m,k}(i), \tag{3}$$

where M denotes the length of the analyzed signal $S(i)$. In this study, in order to study time-varying WE, the analyzed signals were divided into N_T non-overlapping time windows of length L. The mean wavelet energy is given by:

$$E_m^n = \frac{1}{N_m} \sum_{k=(n-1)L+1}^{nL} |A_m(k)|^2, \ n = 1, 2, \ldots N_T \tag{4}$$

In the above equation, N_m represents the number of wavelet coefficients at a certain level m and n is the index of the windows. Hence, the time-varying wavelet energy is defined as:

$$p_m^n = \frac{E_m^n}{E_{all}^n}, \tag{5}$$

where E_{all}^n denotes the total wavelet energy at all levels.

Hence, the WE can be defined as:

$$W_{WE}^n(p) = -\sum_{m > 0} p_m^n \log_2(p_m^n) \tag{6}$$

2.5   WE Calculation

Using the above algorithm, the WE of each averaged P response was calculated. We then averaged these time-varying WE across the trials in the two groups. The entire calculation procedure was shown in Fig. 1.

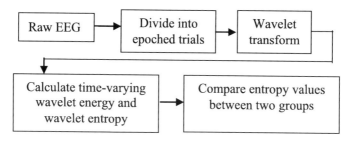

Fig. 1. Block diagram of the main steps of the proposed methods.

3   Results

3.1   ERP Waveforms

We show two ERP waveforms in Fig. 2 by averaging 3 raw P responses. From this figure, one can see that one relatively obvious P300 potential for the guilty (the bottom panel in Fig. 2), compared with the innocent subject (see the top panel in Fig. 2). However, one cannot observe the non-linear characteristics (or the changes of the entropy) for the two waveforms.

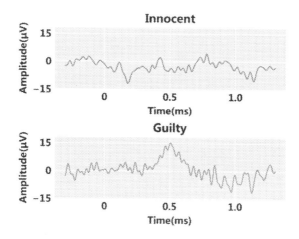

Fig. 2. ERP waveforms from one innocent subject (top) and one guilty subject (bottom).

3.2   Wavelet Energy and Wavelet Entropy

Based on the Eq. (4), we first decomposed the above ERP signals and the results is shown in Fig. 1. After a six octave wavelet decomposition, the following frequency bands were obtained: 0.03–7 Hz, 8–15 Hz, 16–31 Hz, 32–63 Hz, 64–125 Hz and 126–250 Hz. Then we calculated the wavelet energy of the six bands and corresponding wavelet entropy. The average results on group are illustrated in Fig. 3.

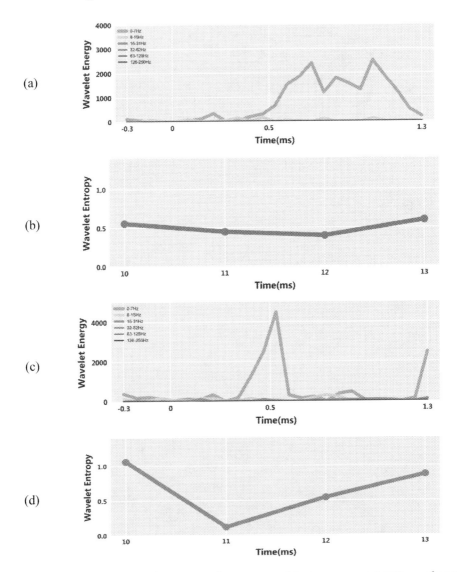

Fig. 3. The time-varying wavelet energy and we entropy of the two averaged (ERP) waveforms for the two groups shown in Fig. 2. (a) Wavelet energy for the innocent group. (b) Wavelet entropy for the innocent group within the time window 10–13. (c) Wavelet energy for the guilty group. (d) Wavelet entropy for the guilty group within the time window 10–13.

Observing the Fig. 3(a), we cannot find a leading energy of a frequency band after stimuli onset. However, an especially bigger energy from the band 0–7 Hz was existed at about 0.6 s after the stimuli onset. Correspondingly, we can obtain especially lower entropy values at 0.4–0.6 s (correspond to the time window 10–13) for the guilty group than that for the innocent group.

Regarding above result, we also analyzed the WE values for each subject. The computation results show that the WE values in each guilty subject significantly decreases in some a time window than that in the other time windows, which was not found in most of innocent subjects.

3.3   Statistical Analysis for Wavelet Entropy

After the computation for the WE in the two groups of subjects, the independent sample t-test was employed to analyze the difference in the mean of the WE values between the two groups of subjects. The results of statistical analysis shows that there is significant difference in WE values at the 11th time window between the two groups of subjects ($p < 0.05$). The WE values in the guilty group was remarkably lower than that in the innocent group. The above results was not found at the other time windows.

4   Discussion

Most of the current DD methods using EEG were based on a hypothesis that EEG/ERP was linearly changed signals. However, increasing number of reports have demonstrated that EEG was of non-linear characteristics. The aim of this study is to assess the possibility of using one of entropy measure, WE, to detect liars. Many studies have successfully applied non-linear analysis methods, such as various measures of entropy or complexity in the study of EEG. The processing of information by the brain results in dynamical changes of its neuronal activities. After the authors in the reports [9] introduced the method of wavelet entropy (WE) into ERP study, many researches have proved the robustness of the method. WE reflects the degree of order–disorder associated with a multi-frequency signal response. To the best of our knowledge, there is no research used WE to analyze the ERP signals.

In this study, based on the non-linear character of ERPs, we combined WT and entropy measure to follow the time-course of spectral entropy for different frequency components. Experimental results show that upon a subject madding a lying responses for the stimuli, wavelet entropy can follow the change of energy of the multi frequency bands, which should be used to differentiate the guilty subjects from the innocent subjects. The classification performance of using WE in DD was not proposed in this study, which is one of the future research contents. Additionally, Clinic or real application of DD need to be in the level of single trials, rather than the level of the ERPs from averaging many stimuli responses. Hence DD using WE need to analyze on the single-trials level, which deserves to study in future.

Acknowledgment. The work was supported by the National Nature Science Foundation of China (No. 81271659 and 61773408), the China Postdoctoral Science Foundation (No. 2014 M552346).

References

1. Spence, S.A., Farrow, T.F., Herford, A.E., Wilkinson, I.D., Zheng, Y., Woodruff, P.W.: Behavioural and functional anatomical correlates of deception in humans. NeuroReport **12**, 2849–2853 (2001). https://doi.org/10.1097/00001756-200109170-00019
2. Rosenfeld, J.P., Ellwanger, J.W., Nolan, K., et al.: P300 scalp amplitude distribution as an index of deception in a simulated cognitive deficit model. Int. J. Psychophysiol. Off. J. Int. Organ. Psychophysiol. **33**, 3–19 (1999). https://doi.org/10.1016/S0167-8760(99)00021-5
3. Allen, J.J.B., Iacono, W.G.: A comparison of methods for the analysis of event-related potentials in deception detection. Psychophysiology **34**, 234–240 (1997). https://doi.org/10.1111/j.1469-8986.1997.tb02137.x
4. Abdulmajeed, A., Alexia, Z., Marco, F., et al.: A new method for detecting deception in event related potentials using individual-specific weight templates. BMC Neurosci. **14**, 34 (2013). https://doi.org/10.1186/1471-2202-14-S1-P34
5. Johnson, M.M., Rosenfeld, J.P.: Oddball-evoked P300-based method of deception detection in the laboratory. II: utilization of non-selective activation of relevant knowledge. Int. J. Psychophysiol. Off. J. Int. Organ. Psychophysiol. **12**, 289–306 (1992). https://doi.org/10.1016/0167-8760(92)90067-L
6. Elaad, E.: Effects of context and state of guilt on the detection of concealed crime information. Int. J. Psychophysiol. **71**, 225–234 (2009). https://doi.org/10.1016/j.ijpsycho.2008.10.001
7. Verschuere, B., Spruyt, A., Meijer, E.H., et al.: The ease of lying. Conscious. Cognit. **20**, 908–911 (2011). https://doi.org/10.1016/j.concog.2010.10.023
8. Sun, D., Lee, T.M.C., Chan, C.C.H.: Unfolding the spatial and temporal neural processing of lying about face familiarity. Cereb. Cortex **25**, 927–936 (2015). https://doi.org/10.1093/cercor/bht284
9. Quiroga, R.Q., Rosso, O.A., Başar, E., et al.: Wavelet entropy in event-related potentials: a new method shows ordering of EEG oscillations. Biol. Cybern. **84**, 291–299 (2001). https://doi.org/10.1007/s004220000212
10. Abásolo, D., Hornero, R., Espino, P., et al.: Entropy analysis of the EEG background activity in Alzheimer's disease patients. Physiol. Meas. **27**, 241–253 (2006). https://doi.org/10.1088/0967-3334/27/3/003
11. Kantz, H., Schreiber, T.: Nonlinear Time Series Analysis. Cambridge University Press, Cambridge (2004)
12. Shannon, C.E.: A mathematical theory of communication. ACM SIGMOBILE Mob. Comput. Commun. Rev. **5**, 3–55 (2001)
13. Inouye, T., Shinosaki, K., Sakamoto, H., et al.: Quantification of EEG irregularity by use of the entropy of the power spectrum. Electroencephalogr. Clin. Neurophysiol. **79**, 204–210 (1991). https://doi.org/10.1016/0013-4694(91)90138-T
14. Rosso, O.A., Yordanova, J., Kolev, V., et al.: Time-frequency analysis of sensorial brain activity. Suppl. Clin. Neurophysiol. **54**, 443–450 (2002). https://doi.org/10.1016/s1567-424X(09)70485-4
15. Phan, K.L., Magalhaes, A., Ziemlewicz, T.J., et al.: Neural correlates of telling lies: a functional magnetic resonance imaging study at 4 Tesla. Acad. Radiol. **12**, 164–172 (2005). https://doi.org/10.1016/j.acra.2004.11.023
16. Gao, J.F., Wang, Z., Yang, Y., et al.: A novel approach for lie detection based on F-score and extreme learning machine. PLoS ONE **8**, e64704 (2013). https://doi.org/10.1371/journal.pone.0064704

Improved CRC for Single Training Sample on Face Recognition

Wei Huang$^{(\boxtimes)}$ and Liming Miao

School of Computer and Information Engineering, Hanshan Normal University,
Dongshan Road XiangqiaoQu, Chaozhou, Guangdong, China
weihuang.china@qq.com, miaolmcz@126.com

Abstract. Lack of training samples is the primary cause of low accuracy in the face recognition problem. Especially when only one labeled sample per person is available, many algorithms suffer a slump on performance or even fail to work. In order to increase the accuracy in single training samples **recognition** problem, virtual samples are generated to enlarge the training set. In this paper, we generate the virtual sample by subtracting the test sample from each training sample and proposed the improved CRC for single training sample face recognition. The experiment results on ORL and FERET face database are provided to validate the effectiveness and robustness of the proposed method.

Keywords: Collaborative representation · Virtual sample
Single training sample · Face recognition

1 Introduction

Representation based face recognition methods become more and more attractive in recent years [1–3]. In these methods, the representation of the test sample will be obtained by all or some of the training samples. Then the reconstructive error between the representation of each class and the test sample will be taken as the classification criteria. Recently, there are many important works about representation based face recognition. Linear regression classification (LRC) [1] assumes that samples from a specific object class lie on a linear subspace. The basic idea of sparse representation based classification (SRC) [2] is to represent the test sample using all the training samples with sparsity constraint, and then classify it based on the representation coefficients. The difference between LRC and SRC is that LRC combines each class's training sample to represent the test sample, but SRC obtain an optimal linear combination of the training samples with 1 norm restriction on the coefficients. So 1 regularization is taken as the most significant core of SRC. But 1 regularization causes the high time complexity. Many researchers proposed SRC with 2.1 regularization [4] or 2 regularization [5–7] to improve the performance of the face recognition. Recently, Zhang and etc. revealed it was the collaborative representation but not 1 regularization that caused the robustness of the SRC and then proposed Collaborative Representation based Classification (CRC) [3]. The good robustness and the low time consumption of CRC have attracted many researchers' interest. Weighted SRC [8], two-phase test sample sparse representation (TPTSR) [9] and Adaptive Weighted Collaborative

© Springer Nature Singapore Pte Ltd. 2018
H. Yuan et al. (Eds.): GSKI 2017, CCIS 848, pp. 445–451, 2018.
https://doi.org/10.1007/978-981-13-0893-2_47

Representations Classification (AWCRC) [10] are proposed to increase the performance of CRC further more.

One drawback of representation based face recognition is the lack of training samples. It is well known that face recognition is a special small sample problem and the training set is always under-complete. The representation residual will be large when the training samples are not enough. If the representation residual caused by lack training samples is larger than that by intra-class information, the accuracy of face recognition will be reduced.

In some particular application such as law enforcement, driver license, passport card identification and entrance control, only one labeled sample per person is available usually. We call this special application as single training sample per person face recognition [11]. In this special case, many famous face recognition methods such as PCA, LDA and so on will suffer a slump on performance or even fail to work. Similarly, LRC will degenerate into the nearest neighbor classification. The single sample per person will aggravate the lack of the training samples for SRC and CRC. So the performance and robustness will drop severely. An alternative and natural way to deal with this problem is to generate more virtual samples for training. The mirror face image [12], the symmetry face image [9, 10, 13] and inverse representation [14] are the effective visual sample generation methods for face recognition. In these methods, the virtual samples look similar to the training samples which have been labeled class information. In order words, the virtual samples enlarge the training set so the representation residual will reduce and the accuracy rate will improved. In this paper, we proposed a different virtual generation methods to improve the performance on CRC for single training sample per person.

The rest of the paper is organized as follows: Sect. 2 introduce the proposed method. Section 3 shows the experiment results and Sect. 4 concludes the paper.

2   The Proposed Method

As mentions above, the test sample cannot be accurately expressed by a linear combination of all training samples in general. In this section we will present the improvement method for single training sample face recognition based on CRC. Intuitively, the virtual samples which look similar to the original samples are generated to enlarge the training set. In this paper, a new idea is put forward for the generation of virtual samples. We try to generate the virtual samples which look far from all the original training samples. Then the test sample will be represented by the new training set. As for classification period, the coefficients of virtual samples will be ignored and the similar classification criteria of CRC will be done for classification. In our experiments, we generate the virtual sample by subtracting the test sample from each training sample. The virtual samples are the difference between the test sample and the training samples. When the test sample is expressed by a linear combination of the new training set, the virtual samples can effectively reduce the reconstructive residuals. It is worthwhile to note that the virtual samples don't belong to any class on the training set. So we do not consider the contributions of the virtual samples on classification.

In summary, the virtual samples reduce the disturbance of the information which cannot express by a linear combination on original training set.

We assume that there are c classes, each class has n training samples and y is the test sample. Let $x_1, \ldots, x_c$, be all the N training samples and $X_0 = [x_1, x_2, \ldots, x_c]$ denotes the original training set.

The virtual samples $x_i (i = 1, 2, \ldots, c)$ for the test samples y can be gotten by

$$x_i = x_i - y \tag{1}$$

We denote the new training set as $X = [X_0, X] = [x_1, x_2, \ldots, x_c, x_1, x_2, \ldots, x_c]$. Then the coefficients vectors X can be estimated by:

$$\Phi = \left(X^T X + \lambda I\right)^{-1} X^T y \tag{2}$$

where λ is a positive small constant and we set $\lambda = 0.01$ in this paper.

Equation (2) estimates the coefficients which can represent the test samples collaboratively using the original and virtual training set.

The representation residual d_l can be calculated as follows:

$$d_i = \|y - \varphi_i x_i\|^2 \qquad i = 1, 2, \ldots, c \tag{3}$$

The rule in favor of the class with minimum distance can be calculated by:

$$identity(y) = argimin\{d_i\} \tag{4}$$

From Eq. (3) we can see that the coefficients of virtual samples are ignored when we calculate the representation residual. When we estimate the coefficients, all the training samples including the virtual samples are used to represent the test sample collaboratively. Because the virtual samples are generated by subtracting the test sample from training samples, the virtual training samples only include the residual error between test sample and each training samples. If the distractive information is all ignored when classifies the test sample, the decrease of distraction will improve the performance of CRC.

3   Experiment Results

In this section we will represent the experiment results on ORL and FERET face databases. The contrastive methods include SRC and CRC. On each face database, the $t^{th}(t = 1, 2, \ldots)$ sample per person will form the training set and the remaining samples for test.

Experiment on ORL face database.

The ORL [15] face database contains images from 40 individuals, each providing 10 different images. For some individuals the images are taken at different times. The facial expressions (open or closed eyes, smiling or no smiling) and facial detail (glasses or no glasses) also vary. The images are taken with a tolerance for some titling and rotation of the face of up to 20°. Moreover, there is also some variation in the scale of up to about 10%. In our experiments, all the images were normalized to 32 × 32 pixels. Figure 1 shows all samples of two individuals on the ORL face database.

Fig. 1. All samples of one individual randomly chosen from the ORL database.

Figure 1 All samples of one individual randomly chosen from the ORL database. The experiment results compared with SRC and CRC are shown in Fig. 2.

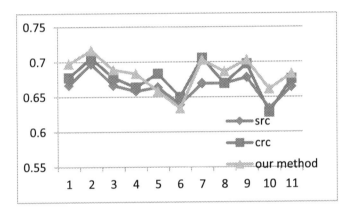

Fig. 2. The accuracy rate of different training sample on ORL face database.

The experiment results compared with SRC and CRC are shown in Fig. 2.

We can observe from Fig. 2 that the proposed method outperforms SRC and CRC in most cases. In order to estimate the overall performance, we calculate the average accuracy rate of each method and show them in Table 1.

Table 1. The average accuracy rates on ORL face database.

Method	Average accuracy rate
SRC	0.66416
CRC	0.67584
Our method	0.68305

4   Experiment on FERET Face Database

The FETET [16] face database includes 1400 images from 200 distinct subjects. Each subject has 7 images. The variations of images include facial expression, illumination and post. The FERET face database has become a standard database for testing and evaluating state-of-the-art face recognition algorithm. In our experiments, all the images were normalized to 32×32 pixels. Figure 3 shows all the images of one subject.

Fig. 3. All the images of one subject on FERET face image database.

In this section, the t^{th}(t = 1, 2,..., 7) sample per person will form the training set and the remaining samples for test. The experiment results are shown in Fig. 4.

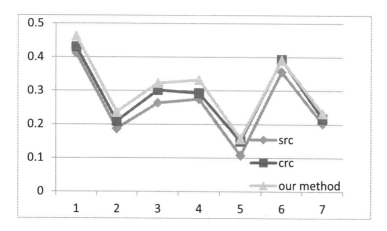

Fig. 4. The experiment results on FERET face database

We can observe from Fig. 4 that our method outperforms the other two state-of-the-art face recognition algorithms SRC and CRC in any case. And the average accuracy rates are shown in Table 2.

Table 2. The average accuracy rates on FERET face database.

Method	Average accuracy rate
SRC	0.257614
CRC	0.284886
Our method	0.305243

From Table 2 we can learn that our method have increased by 18.5% and 7.1% compared with SRC and CRC respectively.

The experiment results of this section reveals that the average accuracy rate of the proposed method is higher than that of SRC and CRC in ORL and FERET face databases. Especially, the accuracy rate has a big increment in FERET face database.

5 Conclusion

In this paper, we proposed a novel virtual training sample generation method for CRC to improve the performance on single training sample face recognition. In general, the virtual samples are generated to enlarge the training set which can reduce the representation residual and improve the accuracy recognition. So the virtual samples are always looked similar to the original samples. In this paper we try to generate the virtual samples by subtracting the test sample from each training sample. The virtual training set includes the residual error between test sample and each training samples. When classifies the test sample all the distractive information is ignored. Our method gives another new resolution to generate the virtual sample on face recognition. The experiment results on ORL and FERET face database show the proposed method is outperform SRC and CRC on single training sample face recognition.

Acknowledgments. This work is partially supported by the Natural Science Foundation of Guangdong Province (No. 2016A030307050), the Special Foundation of Public Research of Guangdong Province (No. 2016A020225008, No. 2017A040405062).

References

1. Togneri, R.: Linear regression for face recognition. IEEE Trans. Pattern Anal. Mach. Intell. **32**(11), 2106–2112 (2010)
2. Wright, J., Yang, Y., Sastry, S.S., Ma, Y.: Robust face recognition via sparse representation. IEEE Trans. Pattern Anal. Mach. Intell. **31**(2), 210–227 (2009)
3. Zhang, L., et al.: Sparse representation or collaborative representation: which helps face recognition? In: ICCV 2011 (2011)
4. Ren, C., Dai, D., Yan, H.: Robust classification using $\ell2,1$-norm based regression model. Pattern Recogn. **45**, 2708–2718 (2012)
5. Xu, Y., Zhu, Q., Fan, Z., Zhang, D., et al.: Using the idea of the sparse representation to perform coarse to fine face recognition. Inf. Sci. **238**, 138–148 (2013)
6. Liu, Z., Pu, J., Xu, M., Qiu, Y.: Face recognition via weighted two phase test sample sparse representation. Neural Process. Lett. http://link.springer.com/article/10.1007%2Fs11063-013-9333-6#
7. Xu, Y., Zhang, D., Yang, J., Yang, J.Y.: A two-phase test sample sparse representation method for use with face recognition. IEEE Trans. Circ. Syst. Video Technol. **25**, 1255–1262 (2011)
8. Lu, C.-Y., Min, H., Gui, J., Zhu, L., Lei, Y.: Face recognition via weighted sparse representation. J. Vis. Commun. Image R **24**, 111–116 (2013)

9. Xu, Y., Zhang, D., Yang, J., Yang, J.-Y.: A two-phase test sample sparse representation method for use with face recognition. IEEE Trans. Circ. Syst. Video Technol. **21**(9), 1255–1262 (2011)

10. Timofte, R., Van Gool, L.: Adaptive and weighted collaborative representations for image classification. Pattern Recogn. Lett. **43**, 127–135 (2014)

11. Tan, X.Y., Chen, S.C., Zhou, Z.H., Zhang, F.Y.: Face recognition from a single image per person: a survey. Pattern Recogn. **39**(9), 1725–1745 (2006)

12. Xu, Y., Zhu, X., Li, Z., Liu, G., Lu, Y., Liu, H.: Using the original and 'symmetrical face' training samples to perform representation based two-step face recognition. Pattern Recogn. **46**, 1151–1158 (2013)

13. Singh, A.K., Nandi, G.C.: Face recognition using facial symmetry. In: CCSEIT 2012, pp. 550–554 (2012)

14. Xu, Y., Li, X., Yang, J., Lai, Z., Zhang, D.: Integrating conventional and inverse representation for face recognition. IEEE Trans. Cybern. (2013). https://doi.org/10.1109/TCYB.2013.2293391

15. Samaria, F., Harter, A.: Parameterisation of a stochastic model for human face identification. In: Proceedings of Second IEEE Workshop Applications of Computer Vision, December 1994

16. Phillips, P.J., Wechsler, H., Huang, J.S., Rauss, P.J.: The FERET database and evaluation procedure for face-recognition algorithms. Image Vis. Comput. **16**(5), 295–306 (1998)

Combating Malicious Eavesdropper in Wireless Full-Duplex Relay Networks: Cooperative Jamming and Power Allocation

Ronghua Luo[1]([⊠]), Jun Lei[2], and Guobing Hu[3]

[1] School of Networks and Telecommunications Engineering,
Jinling Institute of Technology,
Hongjing Road Jiangning District of Nanjing No. 99, Nanjing, China
luoronghua@sohu.com
[2] Nanjing Panda Handa Technology Company Limited, Nanjing, China
thunder76@163.com
[3] School of Electronical and Information Engineering,
Jinling Institute of Technology,
Hongjing Road Jiangning District of Nanjing No. 99, Nanjing, China
njcithgb@163.com

Abstract. In this paper, the physical layer security in decode-and-forward wireless full-duplex relay network was investigated. In this scenario, an eavesdropper was present. For improving the physical layer security, the source and relay not only transmitted message signal but also transmitted jamming signal to interference with the untrusted eavesdropper, which needed not external friendly jammers. How to allocate the power to transmit message signal and jamming signal was a problem. Furthermore, the constrained optimization problem was formulated and the optimal power allocation solution was derived. Compared with other cooperative jamming schemes, our proposed scheme will effectively improve physical layer security of the legitimate user. And simulation results verify the properties.

Keywords: Physical layer security · Decode-and-forward · Full-duplex
Power allocation · Cooperative jamming

1 Introduction

In recent years, more and more research interests focus on the security issue in wireless communication networks. Because of broadcast nature in wireless medium, wireless networks are vulnerable to malicious attacks. Especially when malicious eavesdroppers are present, how to ensure secure communication of legitimate users is particularly important. Traditionally, cryptographic algorithms are usually used to improve the security of legitimate users [1]. However, there are some challenges in cryptographic algorithms, such as complexity of private key management, obstacles of key distribution, and security issues of key transmission. Towards these issues, based on the time-varying properties of fading channels, physical layer based security attracts more and more attention. The concept of wiretap channel is first proposed in [2]. However,

© Springer Nature Singapore Pte Ltd. 2018
H. Yuan et al. (Eds.): GSKI 2017, CCIS 848, pp. 452–463, 2018.
https://doi.org/10.1007/978-981-13-0893-2_48

it has been proved that if the main channel condition is worse than the wiretap channel, the secrecy capacity will be zero [3], in order to overcoming this limitation, cooperative relaying and cooperative jamming has been proposed.

In addition, due to the ability of providing cooperative diversity against the fading channel, the cooperative relaying for enhancing physical layer security have attracted much attention. Early works mainly focus on half-duplex (HD) cooperative relaying [4–6]. In order to further improve spectral efficiency of wireless networks, full-duplex (FD) technology is proposed [7, 8]. Compared with half-duplex relaying, full-duplex relaying has double spectral efficiency. But at the same time, the self-interference was introduced. And so, in order to reduce the self-interference, interference cancellation and suppression techniques are proposed, which makes the loop interference levels (LI) close to noise levels. Obviously, if the self-interference is well controlled, the physical layer security can be more effectively improved by deploying FD mode than HD mode.

In [9], the physical layer security is enhanced by the FD receiver transmitting the jamming signal to the eavesdropper, and the relay also deploys FD mode. Furthermore, this paper derives the expressions for secrecy outage probability of the system. In [10], a full-duplex friendly jammer is utilized to enhance the physical layer security in the presence of malicious eavesdropper, and in which the jammer employs accumulate-and-jam scheme. In [11], in order to improve the secrecy rate, an energy harvesting-based cooperative jamming scheme is proposed and FD mode is deployed by the relay. In [12], the relay is untrusted, the destination-based cooperative jamming scheme is proposed. Moreover, the optimal power allocation strategy is discussed in this paper. However, in the above proposed cooperative jamming schemes, FD relay, FD destination or friendly jammer is deployed to send jamming signal respectively. Where, the FD relay either sends jamming signal or forwards the message signal. When the FD relay is only utilized to forward the message signal, the external friendly jammer is required to confuse the eavesdropper, which needs more overheads. For further enhancing the physical layer security with a few overheads, the source can also be utilized to send jamming signal to the eavesdropper. To the best of our knowledge, the strategy of transmitting message signal and jamming signal simultaneously by the source and FD relay has not be discussed. So, in this paper, we will discuss the scenario in which the source and FD relay are both deployed for cooperative jamming. And then, the important problem is needed to discuss that how to allocate the power to send the message signal and jamming signal. Furthermore, the power allocation problem is discussed, and the optimal power allocation solution is derived. For comparison, the two benchmark schemes without cooperative jamming are proposed, and the power allocation problems are also conducted. In addition to this, the physical layer security of our proposed cooperative jamming scheme in this paper is compared with the proposed scheme with HD mode in [13].

This paper is organized as follows. In Sect. 2, the system model is formed. In Sect. 3, the constrained optimization power allocation problem is presented. In Sect. 3, the optimal power allocation solution is discussed. Furthermore, the two benchmark schemes are analyzed. The simulation results are presented in Sect. 4. And main conclusions are drawn in Sect. 5.

2 System Model

In this system model, the four-node one-way wireless relay network consists of one source, one trusted relay, one destination and one malicious eavesdropper, which is shown in Fig. 1. Where, the relay uses full-duplex mode for improving spectral efficiency. The source, the relay, the destination and the eavesdropper are denoted by S, R, D and E respectively. It is assumed that there is no direct link between the source and destination, and the relay must be utilized to deliver the message from the source to destination. The relay employs decode-and-forward (DF) protocol. The source with one omnidirectional antenna transmits message signal X_S with αp_S and jamming signal X_Z with $(1-\alpha)p_S$ to interrupt the eavesdropper simultaneously. The relay is equipped with two antennas, one antenna is used to receive signal and the other antenna is used to transmit signal. The transmit antenna sends message signal X_S' with βp_R and new jamming signal X_Z' with $(1-\beta)p_R$, where, X_S' is the re-encoded message signal. It is assumed that the jamming signal X_Z and X_Z' are known to the relay and destination respectively. All of the message signals and jamming signals are unit-power. We define the received signal at the relay as XR, and it is expressed as

$$
\begin{aligned}
X_R = &\sqrt{\alpha p_S} h_{SR} X_S + \sqrt{(1-\alpha)p_S} h_{SR} X_Z + \sqrt{\beta p_R} h_{LI} X_S' \\
&+ \sqrt{(1-\beta)p_R} h_{LI} X_Z' + Z_1
\end{aligned}
\tag{1}
$$

Where $Z_1[i]$ is an additive white gaussian noise(AWGN), the mean is zero and variance is σ^2. Meanwhile, the residual self-interference h_{LI} is introduced at the relay

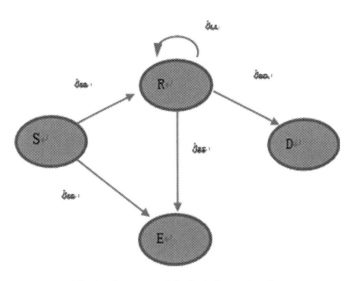

Fig. 1. System model of wireless networks.

resulting from the full-duplex mode. The signal to interference plus noise ratio (SINR) at the relay can be expressed as

$$\gamma_{\text{SR}} = \frac{\alpha p_S h_{\text{SR}}^2}{p_R h_{\text{LI}}^2 + \sigma^2} \tag{2}$$

The achievable rate at the relay can be defined as

$$R_R = \log_2(1 + \gamma_{\text{SR}}) \tag{3}$$

We assume that the FD relay can completely identify the jamming signal with a few overheads and remove it from the received Signal. And then, the relay decodes X_S and re-encodes it. So, the received signal at the destination is defined as

$$X_D = \sqrt{\beta p_R} h_{\text{RD}} X_S' + Z_2 \tag{4}$$

Where, $Z_2[i]$ is also AWGN with mean of 0 and variance of σ^2. The SINR at the destination can be expressed as

$$\gamma_{\text{RD}} = \frac{\beta p_R h_{\text{RD}}^2}{\sigma^2} \tag{5}$$

So, the achievable rate at the destination can be defined as

$$R_D = \log_2(1 + \gamma_{\text{RD}}) \tag{6}$$

As is well known, if $R_R \geq R_D$, the relay can successfully decode the signal sent from the source. And so, the following condition must be met

$$\alpha \geq \frac{\beta p_R h_{\text{RD}}^2 (p_R h_{\text{LI}}^2 + \sigma^2)}{\sigma^2 p_S h_{\text{SR}}^2} \tag{7}$$

For the eavesdropper, the accumulated signal is followed as

$$X_E = \sqrt{\alpha p_S} h_{\text{SE}} X_S + \sqrt{(1 - \alpha)p_S} h_{\text{SE}} X_Z + \sqrt{\beta p_R} h_{\text{RE}} X_S' \\ + \sqrt{(1 - \beta)p_R} h_{\text{RE}} X_Z' + Z_3 \tag{8}$$

Where, just the same as Z_1 and Z_2, Z_3 is AWGN with mean of 0 and variance of σ^2. The received SINR at the eavesdropper can be expressed as

$$\gamma_E = \frac{\alpha p_S h_{\text{SE}}^2 + \beta p_R h_{\text{RE}}^2}{(1 - \alpha)p_S h_{\text{SE}}^2 + (1 - \beta)p_R h_{\text{RE}}^2 + \sigma^2} \tag{9}$$

So, the achievable rate at the eavesdropper is defined as

$$R_E = \log_2(1 + \gamma_E) \tag{10}$$

And then, the received secrecy rate at the destination is calculated as

$$
\begin{aligned}
R_{sec} &= R_D - R_E \\
&= \log_2(1 + \gamma_{RD}) - \log_2(1 + \gamma_E) \\
&= \log_2\left(1 + \frac{\beta p_R h_{RD}^2}{\sigma^2}\right) - \log_2\left(1 + \frac{\alpha p_S h_{SE}^2 + \beta p_R h_{RE}^2}{(1 - \alpha)p_S h_{SE}^2 + (1 - \beta)p_R h_{RE}^2 + \sigma^2}\right)
\end{aligned} \tag{11}
$$

As we have known, when $\alpha = \frac{\beta p_R h_{RD}^2 (p_R h_{LI}^2 + \sigma^2)}{\sigma^2 p_S h_{SR}^2}$, the secrecy rate can be maximized, so α is substituted into (11), we can derive the following formula

$$R_{sec} = \log_2\left(\frac{(\sigma^2 + \beta p_R h_{RD}^2)\left(p_S h_{SE}^2 - \frac{\beta p_R h_{RD}^2 h_{SE}^2 (p_R h_{LI}^2 + \sigma^2)}{h_{SR}^2 \sigma^2} + (1 - \beta)p_R h_{RE}^2 + \sigma^2\right)}{\sigma^2 (p_S h_{SE}^2 + p_R h_{RE}^2 + \sigma^2)}\right) \tag{12}$$

In above equations, all channel gains h_{ij} are non-selective flat Rayleigh fading. In the next section, we will focus on how to allocate the power of p_S and p_R to make the secrecy rate R_{sec} maximized.

3 Physical Layer Security with Power Allocation

From (12), it indicates that the secrecy rate R_{sec} is a function of β. And $2^{R_{sec}}$ is can be expressed as

$$2^{R_{sec}} = \frac{(\sigma^2 + \beta p_R h_{RD}^2)\left(p_S h_{SE}^2 - \frac{\beta p_R h_{RD}^2 h_{SE}^2 (p_R h_{LI}^2 + \sigma^2)}{h_{SR}^2 \sigma^2} + (1 - \beta)p_R h_{RE}^2 + \sigma^2\right)}{\sigma^2 (p_S h_{SE}^2 + p_R h_{RE}^2 + \sigma^2)} \tag{13}$$

In order to facilitate the discussion, the constrained optimization problem can be formed as

$$\max \frac{(\sigma^2 + \beta p_R h_{RD}^2)\left(p_S h_{SE}^2 - \frac{\beta p_R h_{RD}^2 h_{SE}^2 (p_R h_{LI}^2 + \sigma^2)}{h_{SR}^2 \sigma^2} + (1 - \beta)p_R h_{RE}^2 + \sigma^2\right)}{\sigma^2 (p_S h_{SE}^2 + p_R h_{RE}^2 + \sigma^2)} \tag{14}$$

$$st \quad 0 \le \beta \le 1$$

After calculation, we can obtain that $\frac{\partial^2 2^{R_{sec}}}{\partial \beta^2} < 0$, which denotes that $2^{R_{sec}}$ is a convex function. When the first order derivative of $2^{R_{sec}}$ is calculated and $\frac{\partial^2 2^{R_{sec}}}{\partial \beta} = 0$ is assumed, the following lemma can be derived:

Lemma 1: the optimal power allocation ratio β for transmitting message signal at the relay can be given by

$$\beta^{\text{opt}} = [\tilde{\beta}]_0^1 \tag{15}$$

where $[x]_0^1 = \min(1, \max(0, x))$, $\tilde{\beta} = \frac{A-C}{2B}$, where

$$
\begin{aligned}
A &= p_R h_{\text{RD}}^2 (p_S h_{\text{SE}}^2 + p_R h_{\text{RE}}^2 + \sigma^2) \\
B &= p_R h_{\text{RD}}^2 \left(\frac{p_R h_{\text{RD}}^2 h_{\text{SE}}^2 (p_R h_{\text{LI}}^2 + \sigma^2)}{h_{\text{SR}}^2 \sigma^2} + p_R h_{\text{RE}}^2 \right) \\
C &= \sigma^2 \left(\frac{p_R h_{\text{RD}}^2 h_{\text{SE}}^2 (p_R h_{\text{LI}}^2 + \sigma^2)}{h_{\text{SR}}^2 \sigma^2} + p_R h_{\text{RE}}^2 \right)
\end{aligned}
\tag{16}
$$

According to above conclusions, if $\tilde{\beta} \leq \frac{\sigma^2 p_S h_{\text{SR}}^2}{p_R h_{\text{RD}}^2 (p_R h_{\text{LI}}^2 + \sigma^2)}$, $\tilde{\alpha} = \frac{\tilde{\beta} p_R h_{\text{RD}}^2 (p_R h_{\text{LI}}^2 + \sigma^2)}{\sigma^2 p_S h_{\text{SR}}^2}$ can be selected as the optimal solution of α. If $\tilde{\beta} > \frac{\sigma^2 p_S h_{\text{SR}}^2}{p_R h_{\text{RD}}^2 (p_R h_{\text{LI}}^2 + \sigma^2)}$, $\tilde{\alpha}$ can be selected as 1.

Then, the optimal power allocation of the relay and destination can be summarized as

$$
\left(\tilde{\alpha}, \tilde{\beta} \right) =
\begin{cases}
\left(\frac{\tilde{\beta} p_R h_{\text{RD}}^2 (p_R h_{\text{LI}}^2 + \sigma^2)}{\sigma^2 p_S h_{\text{SR}}^2}, \tilde{\beta} \right) & \text{if } \tilde{\beta} \leq \frac{\sigma^2 p_S h_{\text{SR}}^2}{p_R h_{\text{RD}}^2 (p_R h_{\text{LI}}^2 + \sigma^2)} \\
\left(1, \frac{\tilde{\alpha} \sigma^2 p_S h_{\text{SR}}^2}{p_R h_{\text{RD}}^2 (p_R h_{\text{LI}}^2 + \sigma^2)} \right) & \text{elsewhere}
\end{cases}
\tag{17}
$$

According to above results, it is important to note that even under the optimal power allocation solution, the secrecy rate is not always positive.

Remarks

1. Compared with the traditional cooperative jamming schemes, our proposed strategy only utilizes the source and relay itself to transmit jamming signal for interfering the eavesdropper, which eliminates the need for additional jammer. Generally, in the traditional cooperative jamming schemes, the legitimate user needs to pay cost to the jammer. In addition to this, how to coordinate between the source and jammer is a problem, which needs additional overheads. Moreover, if the jamming signal is unknown to the legitimate receiver, the interference will be introduced and the cooperative jamming is not necessarily beneficial. However, in our proposed cooperative jamming scheme, it is always beneficial for the legitimate user, because that the jamming signals sent from the source and relay are known. The cost we need to pay is that the jamming signals are known to the relay and destination of legitimate user, which requires a few overheads.

2. From (17), the global channel state information (CSI) including h_{RD}^2, h_{SR}^2, h_{SE}^2 and h_{RE}^2 needs to be known in the optimal power allocation solution. When implementing power allocation, the relay can collect the CSI and the noise term expressed as $p_R^2 h_{\text{LI}}^2 + \sigma^2$ then compute the optimal power allocation solution α and β, α is sent to the source via a secure control channel. In addition to this, the channels are

assumed to be non-selective flat fading in the above content, which means the channel state changes very slowly and can be tractable. Thus, we always update the results of power allocation periodically depending on the rate of channel state changes.

For comparison, the two benchmark schemes are analyzed in the following content.

Benchmark 1: It is assumed that both the source and relay do not transmit jamming signals and the eavesdropper is present, which is proposed in [13]. Meanwhile, not all available power is used by the source and relay. And then, XR is defined as follows

$$X_R = \sqrt{\alpha p_S} X_S h_{SR} + \sqrt{\beta p_R} X_S' h_{LI} + Z_1 \tag{18}$$

The received SINR is expressed as

$$\gamma_{SR} = \frac{\alpha p_S h_{SR}^2}{\beta p_R h_{LI}^2 + \sigma^2} \tag{19}$$

In order to decode the received signal correctly, $\gamma_{SR} > \gamma_{RD}$ must be satisfied, so the following condition must be met

$$\alpha \geq \frac{\beta p_R h_{RD}^2 (\beta p_R h_{LI}^2 + \sigma^2)}{p_S h_{SR}^2 \sigma^2} \tag{20}$$

The received signal at the eavesdropper is

$$X_E = \sqrt{\alpha p_S} X_S h_{SE} + \sqrt{\beta p_R} X_S' h_{RE} + Z_3 \tag{21}$$

And the secrecy rate is presented as

$$R_{sec} = \log_2\left(1 + \frac{\beta p_R h_{RD}^2}{\sigma^2}\right) - \log_2\left(1 + \frac{\alpha p_S h_{SE}^2 + \beta p_R h_{RE}^2}{\sigma^2}\right) \tag{22}$$

After $\alpha = \frac{\beta p_R h_{RD}^2 (\beta p_R h_{LI}^2 + \sigma^2)}{p_S h_{SR}^2 \sigma^2}$ is substituted into (22), $2^{R_{sec}}$ is expressed as

$$2^{R_{sec}} = \frac{\sigma^2 + \beta p_R h_{RD}^2}{\sigma^2 + \frac{\beta p_R h_{RD}^2 h_{SE}^2 (\beta p_R h_{LI}^2 + \sigma^2)}{h_{SR}^2 \sigma^2} + \beta p_R h_{RE}^2} \tag{23}$$

For convenience, the optimization problem can be formed as

$$\max \frac{\sigma^2 + \beta p_R h_{RD}^2}{\sigma^2 + \frac{\beta p_R h_{RD}^2 h_{SE}^2 (\beta p_R h_{LI}^2 + \sigma^2)}{h_{SR}^2 \sigma^2} + \beta p_R h_{RE}^2} \tag{24}$$

$$st \quad 0 \leq \beta \leq 1$$

We take the first derivative of $2^{R_{sec}}$ with respect β, and set $\frac{\partial 2^{R_{sec}}}{\partial \beta} = 0$, the following solution is obtained

$$\tilde{\beta} = \sqrt{A_1/B_1} - C_1 \tag{25}$$

Where

$$
\begin{aligned}
A_1 &= \sigma^4 h_{SR}^2 - \sigma^4 h_{SE}^2 - \frac{\sigma^4 h_{RE}^2 h_{SR}^2}{h_{RD}^2} + \frac{\sigma^4 h_{LI}^2 h_{SE}^2}{h_{RD}^2} \\
B_1 &= p_R^2 h_{LI}^2 h_{SE}^2 h_{RD}^2 \\
C_1 &= \frac{\sigma^2}{p_R h_{RD}^2}
\end{aligned}
\tag{26}
$$

The optimal solution is $\beta^{opt} = [\tilde{\beta}]_0^1$.

Benchmark 2: It is assumed that the source and relay do not transmit jamming signals and the eavesdropper's presence is not considered, which is proposed in [13]. Just the same as benchmark 1, the source and relay only use αp_S and βp_R to transmit their message signals respectively. Thus, only constraint (20) must be satisfied, the received secrecy rate of the destination is defined as

$$R_{sec} = \log_2 \left(1 + \frac{\beta p_R h_{RD}^2}{\sigma^2} \right) \tag{27}$$

After calculation, we can obtain that $\frac{\partial 2^{R_{sec}}}{\partial \beta} > 0$, which indicates that $2^{R_{sec}}$ monotonically increases with β. And so, if $\frac{p_R h_{RD}^2 (p_R h_{LI}^2 + \sigma^2)}{p_S h_{SR}^2 \sigma^2} \leq 1$, the optimal power allocation is $\tilde{\beta} = 1$ and $\tilde{\alpha} = \frac{p_R h_{RD}^2 (p_R h_{LI}^2 + \sigma^2)}{p_S h_{SR}^2 \sigma^2}$, but if $\frac{p_R h_{RD}^2 (p_R h_{LI}^2 + \sigma^2)}{p_S h_{SR}^2 \sigma^2} > 1$, the optimal power allocation is $\tilde{\alpha} = 1$ and $\tilde{\beta} = \sqrt{\frac{\sigma^4}{4 p_R^2 h_{LI}^4} + \frac{p_S h_{SR}^2 \sigma^2}{p_R^2 h_{RD}^2 h_{LI}^2}} - \frac{\sigma^2}{2 p_R h_{LI}^2}$.

4   Simulation Results

The proposed scheme has been simulated numerically by using MATLAB software. In the simulation, the source, relay and destination are located at $(-1, 0)$, $(0, 0)$ and $(1, 0)$ respectively. Therefore, the channel h_{ij} between different nodes can be modeled as $h_{ij} \sim \mathcal{CN}(0, d^{-l})$, where d is distance and $l = 2$ is the path loss factor. The other parameters are defined as: $p_S = p_R = 1$, the AWGN variance $\sigma^2 = 0.1$. Monte-Carlo experiments are implemented 10^5 trials, and the dependent simulation results are averaged.

In Fig. 2, our proposed cooperative jamming scheme is compared with Benchmark 1 and Benchmark 2. The received average secrecy rates of legitimate user versus the location of eavesdropper moving from $(-3, -1)$ to $(3, -1)$ are showed. We can see that the physical layer security of our proposed scheme is always better than Benchmark 1 and 2. The closer the distance between the eavesdropper and source and relay, the lower the secrecy rates obtained by the three schemes. When the location of eavesdropper is located in $(-1, -1)$, the secrecy rates are minimal because h_{SE} and h_{RE} are strong. This indicates that the physical layer security of legitimate user is related to the location of eavesdropper. At the same time, compared to Benchmark 2, Benchmark 1 receives more secrecy rate because of considering the presence of eavesdropper.

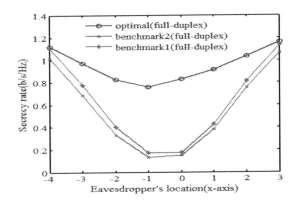

Fig. 2. Secrecy rate versus eavesdropper's location (in different power allocation schemes).

In Figs. 3 and 4, the average parameter values of α and β are shown. We can see that α and β in our proposed scheme and Benchmark 1 decrease with the decreasing distance between the eavesdropper and source and relay. Since for ensuring the physical layer security, the legitimate user will decrease the transmit power of message signal along with the eavesdropper getting closer to the source and relay. However, α and β always remain unchanged in Benchmark 2, because it doesn't consider the presence of the eavesdropper.

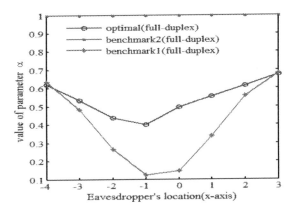

Fig. 3. The value of parameter α versus eavesdropper's location.

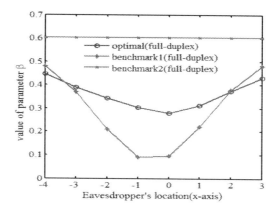

Fig. 4. The value of parameter β versus eavesdropper's location.

In Fig. 5, the curve of secrecy rate versus the residual self-interference is shown. It is seen that the secrecy rate of the legitimate user decreasing with the increasing residual self-interference. The reason is that the relay will suffer more and more interference from the increasing residual self-interference. If the self-interference is well controlled, the spectral efficiency of FD can be effectively improved compared with HD.

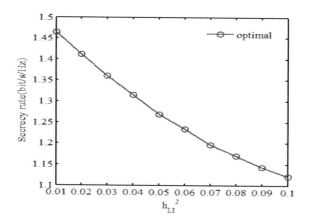

Fig. 5. Secrecy rate versus the residual self-interference h_{LI}^2.

In Fig. 6, the physical layer security of FD relaying and HD relaying is compared. It indicates that the secrecy rate received by the legitimate user using FD relaying is significantly higher than using HD relaying. The reason is that FD is inherently able to achieve higher spectral efficiency. And so, FD relaying is deployed by our proposed cooperative jamming scheme.

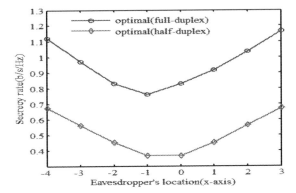

Fig. 6. Secrecy rate under different duplex modes.

5   Conclusions

In this paper, we have investigated the power allocation problem with cooperative jamming scheme in decode-and-forward wireless FD relay network considering the presence of an eavesdropper. For improving physical layer security of the legitimate user, the message signals and the jamming signals are transmitted simultaneously by the source and FD relay. Based on this, the constrained optimization power allocation problem is formed, where the objective is maximizing the secrecy rate of the legitimate user and the constrained conditions are available power of the source and relay. Furthermore, the optimal power allocation solution is derived and depends on the CSI. At last, the power allocation problem of two benchmarks without jamming are analyzed for comparison. Simulation results show that the physical layer security can be significantly improved in our proposed jamming scheme.

Acknowledgments. This work was supported by the Natural Science Foundation of Jiangsu Province (Grants No. BK20161104), The Scientific Research Fund Project of JIT (2016 incentive program, jit-2016-jlxm-24), the Doctoral Scientific Research Foundation of JIT (jit-b-201409, jit-b-201408, jit-b-201633) and Incubation Project of Science Foundation of JIT (jit-fhxm-201605).

References

1. Liang, Y., Poor, H.V., Shamai, S.P.: Information Theoretic Security. Now Publishers Inc., Delft (2009)
2. Wyner, A.D.G.: The wire-tap channel. Bell Syst. Tech. J. **54**, 1355–1387 (1975)
3. Csiszar, I., Korner, J.L.: Broadcast channels with confidential messages. IEEE Trans. Inf. Theor. **24**, 339–348 (1978)
4. Zou, Y., Wang, X., Shen, W., Hanzo, L.L.: Security versus reliability analysis of opportunistic relaying. IEEE Trans. Veh. Technol. **63**, 2653–2661 (2014)
5. Deng, H., Wang, H., Guo, W., Wang, W.L.: Secrecy transmission with a helper: to relay or to jam. IEEE Trans. Inf. Forensics Secur. **10**, 4005–4019 (2015)

6. Lv, L., Chen, J., Yang, L., Kuo, Y.: Improving physical layer security in untrusted relay networks: cooperative jamming and power allocation. IET Commun. **11**, 393–399 (2017)
7. Krikidis, I., Suraweera, H.A., Yuen, L.: Full-duplex relay selection for amplify-and-forward cooperative networks. IEEE Trans. Wirel. Commun. **11**, 4381–4393 (2012)
8. Zhang, Z., Long, K., Vasilakos, A.V., Hanzo, C.: Full-duplex wireless communications: challenges, solutions and future research directions. Proc. IEEE **104**, 1369–1409 (2016)
9. Zhou, W., Gao, R., Ji, X., Bao. Z.: A cooperative jamming protocol for full-duplex relaying with full-duplex receiver. In: 8th International Conference on Wireless Communications & Signal Processing, WCSP 2016, Yangzhou, China, 13–15 October 2016, pp. 1–5. IEEE Press (2016)
10. Bi, Y., Chen, H.G.: Accumulate and jam: towards secure communication via a wireless-powered full-duplex jammer. IEEE J. Sel. Top. Signal Process. **10**, 1538–1550 (2016)
11. Mobini, Z., Mohammadali, M., Tellambura, C.: Security enhancement of wireless networks with wireless-powered full-duplex relay and friendly jammer nodes. In: IEEE International Conference on Communications Workshops, ICC Workshops, Paris, France, 21–25 May 2017, pp. 1329–1334. IEEE Press (2017)
12. Kuhestani, A., Mohammadi, A.L.: Destination-based cooperative jamming in untrusted amplify-and-forward relay networks: resource allocation and performance study. IET Commun. **10**, 17–23 (2016)
13. Dong, L., Yousefi'zadeh, H., Jafarkhani, H.: Cooperative jamming and power allocation for wireless relay networks in presence of eavesdropper. In: Proceedings of the IEEE ICC, Kyoto, Japan, 5–9 June 2011, pp. 1–5. IEEE Press (2011)

Short-Term Subway Passenger Flow Prediction Based on ARIMA

Danfeng Yan[1], Junwen Zhou[1(✉)], Yao Zhao[1], and Bin Wu[2]

[1] State Key Laboratory of Networking and Switching Technology,
Beijing University of Posts and Telecommunications, Beijing, China
{yandf,zhaoyao}@bupt.edu.cn, zhoujunwen1992@126.com
[2] School of Computer Science, Beijing University of Posts
and Telecommunications, Beijing, China
wubin@bupt.edu.cn

Abstract. Traffic flow prediction has become a hot spot in the intelligent transportation system study and is attracting more and more researchers. Short-term traffic flow prediction is an important issue of Traffic flow prediction. In this paper, ARIMA (Auto-Regressive Integrated Moving Average) model is used to predict short-term traffic flow of subway. We focus on selecting the most appropriate parameters - p and q of ARIMA model through Stationarity Test, Model Recognition, Parameter Estimation, Model Diagnosis and Prediction except a single AIC (Akaike Information Criterion) estimation or single SACF (Sample Auto-Correlation Function) plots. And then, we predict passenger flow of five subway stations of Guangzhou Metro using presented method and SVM (Support Vector Machine). The experiments' results show that ARIMA model performs better than SVM, AIC or SACF&SPACF (Sample partial Auto-Correlation Function) in short-term traffic flow prediction.

Keywords: Transportation data analysis · Prediction model · ARIMA
Passenger flow prediction

1 Introduction

Citizen transportation system has become a convenient way for people to travel. The movement characteristics included in the passenger's travelling has attracted many researchers.

Traffic flow prediction could be classified as railway passenger prediction, urban traffic passenger prediction, etc. As an important part of urban traffic, subway which has become part of citizen's first choice to travel has its own characteristic. For instance, subway must draw up at stations on time and can carry numerous passengers every day. Guangzhou has representative passenger flow which has become a city with powerful traffic. And more than eight million passengers per day travel by subway in Guangzhou [1]. So intelligent traffic transport technology needs to be focus to meet traffic jam and other severe traffic problems. For example, transportation data analysis and accurate short-term subway passenger flow prediction play key roles in intelligent traffic system for transforming it more passive to active reaction.

© Springer Nature Singapore Pte Ltd. 2018
H. Yuan et al. (Eds.): GSKI 2017, CCIS 848, pp. 464–479, 2018.
https://doi.org/10.1007/978-981-13-0893-2_49

Because of large passenger flow and green environment, the subway has a good trend of development in the future. It's passenger flow analysis is valuable especially. Effective subway passenger flow prediction can be used to optimize traffic-control system. More turnstiles should be turned on if passenger flow volume is predicted to increase in next period. Staff can also guide passengers travel through un-crowded line for reducing accidents and stagger peak suggestion is informed to passenger based on traffic flow prediction. Traffic operators can take appropriate and timely responses for coming passenger flow peak by modeling history records. In addition, an accurate prediction can assist the administrative department such as Ministry of Transport to perfect current transportation routes or plan new ones.

And if it is classified by different purpose, subway passenger flow investigation could be classified into the period before urban rail construction and after it's completed. When subway station is completed, researchers investigate passenger records for analyzing and forecasting passenger flow. Statistical and machine learning methods such as ARIMA, SVM, and neural network are useful tools for predicting passenger flow. So investigating subway passenger flow has become a hot challenge [2]. In our work, we focus on characteristic of passenger flow after subway station is completed.

Auto-Regressive Integrated Moving Average model (ARIMA(p, d, q)), a tool for understanding and predicting future values of time series whose dependent variable has correlation with lagged values. Since passenger flow can be represented as time series and has correlation with history records, ARIMA (p, d, q) is appropriate to fit and predict passenger flow. Researchers have used it in predicting motorway traffic flow, railway passenger volume, GDP of a country, etc.

Through ARIMA (p, d, q) has been used successfully across many sectors, researchers only use AIC or BIC (Bayesian Information Criterion) or SACF to estimate ARIMA (p, d, q) parameters when forecasting subway passenger flow. But the estimated methods of parameters are not so persuasive because they are chosen by convenient way [3, 4]. Many researchers focus on novel methods and compare their methods with ARIMA (p, d, q) for proving their improvement, but their methods to generate ARIMA (p, d, q) is unpersuasive.

In fact, the quality of ARIMA model depends greatly on parameters. In this paper, we will not only use AIC or SACF plots to estimate p and q of ARIMA (p, d, q) but also use Stationary Test, Model Recognition, Model Diagnosis and Prediction in test set to screen alternative models and prove that when estimate ARIMA's p and q, AIC and SACF plots are all should be considered in different data sets repeatedly.

2   Related Work

ARIMA is a tool to understand and predict future values of time series and is already used in many sectors such as econometrics, intelligent traffic system [5], workload prediction [6, 7], examining the evolution of software clone components [3], etc.

In Jayadeep's [3] work, they consider prior information regarding the software clone evolution will be valuable information which will reduce the maintenance effort. So they predict cloned software components' evolution by ARIMA. In their experiments, they used SACF plots to test series stationary and estimate ARIMA's p and q.

In intelligent transportation system, subway passenger flow has similarities with railway passenger flow and freeway traffic flow. For example, they are all affected by some accidents like bad weather and holiday [8]. In the past research, ARIMA is appropriate to model traffic flow because of their lag-correlation. So ARIMA is also an appropriate method to model subway passenger flow. In previous research, researchers have investigated subway passenger behavior such as passenger flow attribution algorithms [9], crowding degree in transfer station [10], which is based on question-naires or manual measurement.

Short-term forecasting has become interest of researchers in many practical fields such as controlling highway traffic based on minute-based highway traffic forecasting, making power policies based on hour-based load forecasting, and implementing seat allocation based on daily-based passenger demand forecasting.

Wei Xu [11] used multiple method including ARIMA, Liner Regression and Neural Network to predict railway station passenger flow during Spring Festival. He used ARIMA's prediction as a part of result and use Neural Network to predict stations' passenger volume which is close in map. Finally, he combined these two predictions with SVM. Reference [12] also use neural network to forecast demand of passengers. In his work, he designs two novel neural network, multiple temporal units neural for dealing with distinctive input information and parallel ensemble neural network for dealing with distinctive input information in several individual models and then he proves they can upgrade predictive performance in comparison with conventional MLP. With development of High-Speed Railway in China, it has become one of most popular way for long journey. Reference [4] use SVM model to predict travel choice of High-Speed Railway passengers and investigate their travel behavior. His experiment shows that price, speed, environment, safety and overall satisfaction are most important factors for passengers choosing High-Speed Railway. And he proved result of SVM is more accurate than result of logical models. But Because of the difference between railway and subway, for example, passenger of a railway station is influenced by travel distance which is not so important in subway. Railway passenger flow prediction algorithms may not be suitable in subway passenger flow prediction.

Reference [13] makes a comparison of ARIMA, SARIMA (seasonal ARIMA) and ARIMA-GARCH (General Auto-Regressive Conditional Heteroskedasticity) and find out ARIMA-GARCH is the most accurate model to predict traffic volume of different roads. SACF and SPACF plots are used to find out p, d, q parameters in their research.

Reference [14] defines series stationarity and use 1-week lag difference to yield the most nearly stationary transformation of the series. And they proposed novel ARIMA to predict freeway traffic flow which consider correlation between up-stream and down-stream and seasonal factors within traffic flow.

Most experiments in their works focus on novel methods and compare their results with ARIMA which only consider result of AIC or SACF for proving their improvement. But [15] shows residual analysis, stationarity test, prediction analysis is also important for testing p and q of AIC and SACF&SPACF results. And there is no evidence which method is more appropriate in most cases. A more complete and high-quality process of AIC and SACF&SPACF is needed. So in this paper, we will focus on estimating p and q of ARIMA with more complete and high-quality experiments which consider both AIC and SACF&SPACF repeatedly to forecast subway passenger flow.

3 Definition of ARIMA

ARMA (p, q) can be transformed from ARIMA (p, d, q) by initial and limited differencing steps. So firstly, definition of ARMA (p, q) model is assumed a time series can be represented as a random process Y_t and a weakly stationary stochastic process can be described as two polynomials, one is the auto-regression part and another is the moving average part. So ARMA model is written:

$$Y_t = Y_{t1} + Y_{t2} \tag{1}$$

$$Y_{t1} = \Phi_1 Y_{t-1} + \Phi_2 Y_{t-2} + \ldots + \Phi_p Y_{t-p} + e_t \tag{2}$$

$$Y_{t2} = -\theta_1 e_{t-1} - \theta_2 e_{t-2} - \ldots - \theta_q e_{t-q} \tag{3}$$

This model consists of two parts, Y_{t1} is the AR(p) part, Y_{t2} is the MA(q) part. "d" corresponding to the "integrated" times and e_t is noise which is a hypothetical normal distribution. A time series Y_t is weakly stationary if the following two conditions hold:

- The expectation of Y_t is the almost same within all t.
- The covariance between any two observations in the series is dependent only on the lag between the observations.

If limited and initial differencing steps can transform original series to stationary one, we can use ARIMA (p, d, q) model to fit this original series.

Common methods to test stationary area SACF plot which shows the relationships between values and lagged ones. In this paper, we will use SACF plots and Dickey-Fuller test which is more persuasive. Because of dependent variables are "independent", "normal distribution" and "identically distributed" with noise, autocorrelation of MA(q) is zero when lag is larger than q. So if q is smaller than infinity, MA (q) series is stationary. For testing Stationarity of AR (p) which doesn't have this characteristic, we use another AR (p) characteristic equation which is written:

$$\phi(x) = 1 - \phi_1 x - \phi_2 x^2 - \ldots - \phi_p x^p \tag{4}$$

If no matter what value the ϕ_i is, all results of $\phi(x) = 0$ is greater than 0. The AR (p) model will be stationary [16]. Dickey-Fuller test is a tool to estimate result of $\phi(x) = 0$ and estimate the probability to accept original hypothesis: "series isn't stationary". The smaller the probability is, the hypothesis of "series is stationary" is more acceptable.

4   Data and Algorithm

4.1   Passenger Flow Data

In our work, we use online subway ticket records of five stations from September 1 to October 31 which contains 244048 samples after data cleaning. Every piece of ticket records contains all information of this purchase including time of payment, picking, order time, origin station, terminal station and number of tickets. Because we focus on time characteristic of passenger flow, we transform these records into passenger flow series of every day. To translating ticket records into passenger flow, we map picking time into passenger arriving time and select records using following criterion:

- Origin station must be five subway stations we choose.
- Picking time must be available which means passengers have already picked up tickets.
- Picking time must be during service time of subway stations.

After selecting available records, we divide records into 61 days and calculate sums of each day's records which show in Fig. 1. Passenger prediction work flow is shown in Figs. 2 and 3 proposes basic steps for modeling ARIMA. Table 1 shows that ticket records with online payment have randomness and high volatility. Even though the numbers of records are less than real values because most passengers prefer to use cash or smart card. But it has much passenger flow regulation than questionnaires do.

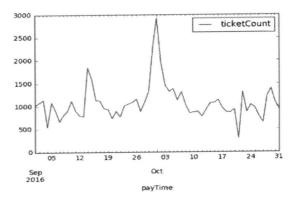

Fig. 1. Records of tickets

Fig. 2. Process Steps which contains three kinds of data (origin ticket records, passenger flow and prediction) and two kinds of data operation (data transformation and modeling). This shows the fundamental work flow.

Fig. 3. ARIMA modeling steps which is the detail of "Modeling" part in Fig. 1 and will be stated in next subsection

Table 1. Passenger Flow Overview

Guangzhou east station			
Min	Max	Mean	Std
295.00	2919.00	1075.56	398.56
25%	50%	75%	
867.00	1013.00	1130.00	

4.2 Short-Term Passenger Flow Prediction

In this paper, we propose six steps to fit and predict short-term subway passenger flow which shows in Fig. 3:

- Stationarity Test. Dickey-Fuller test is appropriate to test the stationarity of passenger flow.
- Model Recognition. Use methods of SACF, SPACF, AIC to estimate p and q of ARIMA.
- Parameter Estimation. Use maximum likelihood function to estimate parameters of these alternative models.
- Model Diagnosis. SACF and Ljung-Box will be applied to test residual of these alternative models. Models selected from all those alternative models will be used to predict.
- Prediction. Use these selected models to predict passenger volume of five stations in Guangzhou.
- Comparison. Make a comparison with SVM model and show the results.

4.3 Estimate p and q of ARIMA

SACF plots, SPACF plots and AIC are common methods to estimate p and q of ARIMA (p, d, q).

Because subway passenger flow sequence is an unknown distribution, we can't calculate its auto-correlation like known distributions do. So we used SACF method to investigate its auto-correlation between values and lagged ones. It has ACF-like pattern and is written as:

$$\gamma_k = \Sigma(Y_t - Y')(Y_{t-k} - Y')/\Sigma(Y_t - Y')^2, \; k = 1, 2 \ldots \tag{5}$$

It has been proved that, when n is large enough, γ_k can be recognized as normal distribution. Considering the characteristics of normal distribution and white noise, we could use SACF and twice the standard deviation to estimate q of MA (q). If SACF's result in k-order lag is smaller than twice the standard deviation, it could be considering as zero and series doesn't have correlation in k-order lag.

It has also been proved that MA (q) model doesn't have autocorrelation when lag is larger than q. So q of MA (q) can be estimated using this method. For MA (q) model, the variance of γ_k could change because it relieson γ_k:

$$\mathrm{Var}(\gamma_k) = [1 + 2\Sigma\gamma_j^2], \ k > q \tag{6}$$

Because AR (p) model can be transformed into MA (∞.) model, we can't use SACF to estimate p of AR (p) model. The reason is Y_t is affected by Y_{t-1}, Y_{t-2}..., Y_{t-p+1}. So we use SPACF to eliminate these correlations. SPACF is written as:

$$\begin{aligned} \varphi_k &= \mathrm{Corr}(Y_t, Y_{t-k}|Y_{t-1}, Y_{t-2}, \ldots, Y_{t-k+1}) \\ &= (\gamma_k - \Sigma\varphi_{k-1,j}\,\gamma_{k-j})/(1 - \Sigma\varphi_{k-1,j}\,\gamma_j) \end{aligned} \tag{7}$$

Quenoulle (1949) has proved that SPACF of AR (p) model satisfies a normal distribution when lag is larger than q-order. So when k is larger than q, we use 2/sqrt(n) as critical value. Table 2 demonstrates characteristics of AR (p) and MA (q).

Table 2. Characteristics of AR (p) and MA (q)

	AR(p)	MA(q)
SACF	sinusoidal oscillation, damped exponential law	zero after q-order lag
SPACF	zero after p-order lag	sinusoidal oscillation, damped exponential law

AIC, BIC use maximum likelihood function for appropriate p and q of ARIMA (p, d, q). But recommendation of maximum likelihood function could be much complex and over-fitting. AIC and BIC use penalty factor to reduce models' complexity:

$$\mathrm{AIC} = -2\ln(L) + 2k \tag{8}$$

$$\mathrm{BIC} = -2\ln(L) + \ln(n) * k \tag{9}$$

L is maximum likelihood function, k is the number of parameters (k is p + q of ARIMA (p, d, q)) and n is number of samples. Because of penalty factor, AIC and BIC could return better recommendations than orthodox maximum likelihood function.

4.4   Parameter Estimating

For pages other than the first page, start at the top of the page, and continue in double-column format. The two columns on the last page should be as close to equal length as possible.

After estimate p and q, next step is to estimate all parameters. Normal methods for estimation are moment estimation, maximum likelihood estimation and least square estimation. Considering about accuracy of these method, we choose maximum likelihood estimation. Residual analysis methods are used to diagnose models after estimating alternative models' parameters. If ARMA (p, q) model is represented as:

$$Y_t = \pi_1 Y_{t-1} + \pi_2 Y_{t-2} + \pi_3 Y_{t-3} + \ldots + \varepsilon_t \qquad (10)$$

and use next formulation to predict records in next period:

$$Y'_t = \pi'_1 Y'_{t-1} + \pi'_2 Y'_{t-2} + \pi'_3 Y'_{t-3} + \ldots \qquad (11)$$

residual will be defined as below:

$$e'_t = Y'_t - \pi'_1 Y'_{t-1} - \pi'_2 Y'_{t-2} - \pi'_3 Y'_{t-3} - \ldots \qquad (12)$$

If ARIMA (p, d, q) is recognized correctly, and the estimated parameters are close enough to the true fraction, residual will has characteristics of independent identically normal distribution.

Model Diagnose is to investigate independence and other characteristics of residual to prove it's similar with white noise. Because of characteristic of normal distribution, SACF which is used in Model Recognition could be applied to test its independence since it can investigate auto-correlation between values.

4.5   Prediction and Evaluation

One of characteristics of stationary sequence prediction is, as time goes by, prediction of ARIMA (p, d, q) will be closer and closer to a constant. If time series isn't a stationary sequence, prediction of ARIMA (p, d, q) will be more and more close to infinity. For example, AR (1) is written:

$$Y_t - \mu = \phi(Y_{t-1} - \mu) + e_t \qquad (13)$$

If to predict Y_{t+1} of next period. It can be written:

$$Y_{t+1} - \mu = \phi(Y_t - \mu) + e_{t+1} \qquad (14)$$

And if $Y_1, Y_2, \ldots, Y_t$ is given, we can use next formula to calculate expectance of Y_{t+1} which is the prediction in next period:

Because of characteristics of conditional expectation and white noise:

$$E(Y_t | Y_1, Y_2, \ldots, Y_t) = Y_t \qquad (15)$$

And

$$E(e_{t+1}|Y_1, Y_2, \ldots, Y_t) = 0 \qquad (16)$$

Then

$$Y'_t(1) = \mu + \phi(Y'_t - \mu) \qquad (17)$$

So

$$Y'_t(L) = \mu + \phi(Y_t(L-1) - \mu) = \mu + \phi^L(Y_t - \mu) \qquad (18)$$

If series is stationary, $|\phi| < 1$, prediction will be more and more close to constant. And finally we use MAPE (mean absolute percentage error) to evaluate the prediction:

$$R = \Sigma|(tf - tv)/tv|/t \qquad (19)$$

Symbol of tf is prediction, tv is the real passenger flow and t is interval of prediction. Mean absolute percentage error measures the average of trend deviation between error and truth values. And it will be applied to compare predictions of different models.

5   Experiment and Discussion

5.1   Experiment Settings

In experiment, we divide data set into training set which contains passenger flow from September 1 to October 23 and test set from October 24 to 31. And experiment is proposed in Windows system with Python2.7.

In this paper, we investigated differences between SACF&SPACF plots, AIC and SVM in predictive performance based on five stations records of Guangzhou East station, Renhe Station, Guangzhou Tower Station, Tianhe Coach Terminal Station and Airport South Station. And we will focus on describing every step in experiment with Guangzhou East Station records and use five stations records to compare predictive performance between ARIMA and SVM.

In the last period, we have proved that stationary series is necessary because if the series isn't stationary, the variance of prediction will become larger and larger. So before experiments, we should be sure that all series we use are stationary.

The acceptable probability of Dickey-Fuller test is around 0.7674% which means the original series could be consider as a stationary series. For a more persuasive comparison, we take a difference step on original series. And the acceptable probability of difference series is around $0.3208 * 10^{-11}$% which means ticket records with one difference step is more stationary than original series. So the original series and difference one will be used in follow steps.

5.2   Experiment with Guangzhou East Station Records

Original ticket records mean and variance which uses every 12 days' records of Guangzhou East station are shown in Fig. 4. And Fig. 5 shows the difference ticket records, mean and variance.

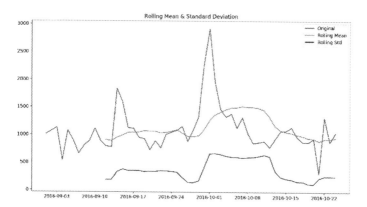

Fig. 4. Original Records, Mean and Variance. Mean and variance is over time span of seven days, so their first points are lagged for seven days

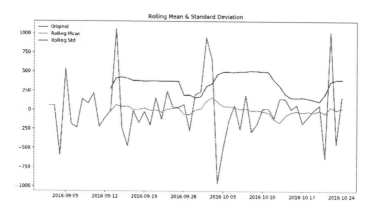

Fig. 5. Difference Series, Means and Variances

Figures 6 and 7 demonstrate SACF and SPACF of original and difference passenger flow. First part is SCAF plot which shows original series has relationship between 1-order lag values. When $k \geq 2$, relationship between k-order lag values isn't larger than twice the standard deviation, which should be consider as zero. So original ticket records don't have relationship when order is larger than or equal to 2. Considering the characteristics of SACF and AR(p) model, AR(1), AR(2) and MA(1) are alternative models. According to Fig. 7 and characteristics of SPACF, ARIMA(1, 1, 1) is another alternative model.

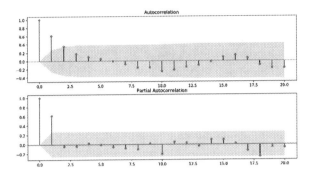

Fig. 6. SACF & SPACF of Origin Series

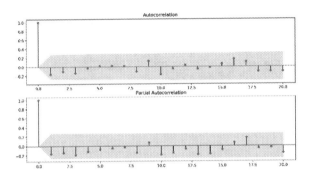

Fig. 7. SACF & SPACF of Difference Series

AIC could also estimate p and q of ARIMA (p, d, q) model, in our experiment, recommendation of AIC are ARIMA (1, 0, 0) and ARIMA (4, 0, 1). Above all, ARIMA (4, 0, 1), ARIMA (1, 0, 0), ARIMA (2, 0, 0), ARIMA (0, 0, 1), ARIMA (1, 1, 1) will become alternative models.

Table 3 contains estimation of all parameters. Because two parameters of ARIMA (4, 0, 1) are not so significant, we add ARIMA (2, 0, 1) to alternative models.

Table 3. Parameters Estimation

ARIMA(p, d, q)	Const	Ar.L1	Ar.L2	Ar.L3	Ar.L4	Ma.L1
(4,0,1)	1079.514	0.412	0.123	−0.076	0.040	0.210
(2,0,1)	1116.855	1.568	−0.622	0.000	0.000	−1.000
(1,0,0)	1081.886	0.948	0.000	0.000	0.000	0.000
(2,0,0)	1082.406	0.622	−0.037	0.000	0.000	0.000
(0,0,1)	1087.402	0.000	0.000	0.000	0.000	0.510
(1,1,1)	0.661	0.629	0.000	0.000	0.000	−0.999

Figure 8 demonstrates residual of ARIMA (1, 0, 0) model, there are five outliers which are on September 14, 2016, September 30, 2016, October 1, 2016, October 21, 2016 and October 22, 2016. The reason for first catastrophe point is that September 14, 2016 is Chinese mid-autumn festival. Second and third ones are corresponding to Chinese National Day. Because of typhoon, Guangzhou East railway station stopped 81 trains on October 21, 2016. So subway passenger flow on October 21, 2016 and October 22, 2016 become outliers.

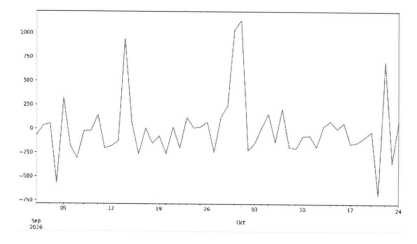

Fig. 8. Residual Series of ARIMA (1, 0, 0)

Residual's randomness and independence are important evidence to prove that this model fit series well because the part which the model doesn't fit is similar with white noise. For testing residual's randomness and independence, we proposed investigating SACF of ARIMA (1, 0, 0) residual series. Result is shown in Fig. 9. In Fig. 9 we are sure that every piece of residual series of ARIMA (1, 0, 0) is independent. In our experiment, ARIMA (1, 0, 0) and ARIMA (1, 1, 1) are acceptable based on their SACF plots.

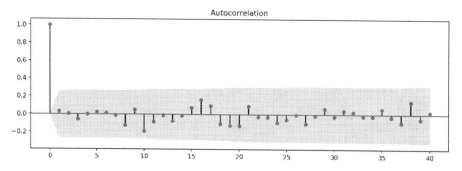

Fig. 9. SACF of ARIMA (1, 0, 0)'s Residual Series

The prediction of ARIMA (1, 0, 0) and ARIMA (1, 1, 1) show in Table 4 which illustrate that ARIMA (1, 1, 1) performs better in test set.

Table 4. Prediction of two selected models which are ARIMA (1, 0, 0) and ARIMA (1, 1, 1)

Model	Prediction	MAPE
ARIMA (1, 0, 0)	797.3889, 908.2414, 855.4138, 880.5891, 868.5917, 874.3092, 871.5844	0.2357
ARIMA (1, 1, 1)	694.4706, 791.3768, 751.1642, 767.8510, 760.9266, 763.7999, 762.6076	0.2023

5.3 Experiment with Other Stations' Records

We use four other subway stations records whose training set contains 155333 samples and test set contains 23106 samples. The result shows in Fig. 10 which proves that AIC and SACF&SPACF have different performance in different stations' records.

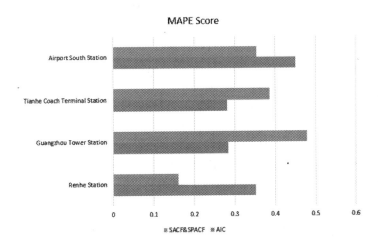

Fig. 10. Comparison of Selection Methods

5.4 Comparison with SVM

For investigating differences between ARIMA and other models, in this section, we predict passenger flow using SVM and compare its predictive performance with ARIMA. SVM can handle linear and nonlinear relationships between dependent variable and features while ARIMA can find out linear relationship between passenger flow and lagged values.

In our experiments, we also proposed SVM to find out relationships between passenger flow and lagged values for a reasonable comparison with ARIMA. So we use lagged passenger flow as features and current value as dependent variable. Numbers of lag order are set from 2 to 5.

Result is shown in Fig. 11 which shows that selected ARIMA model (which is "Best ARIMA Score" in Fig. 11) can have better performance than SVM (Fig. 11 only shows best SVM score for demonstration) and a complete selection process can estimate more appropriate p and q and leads ARIMA be better than SVM.

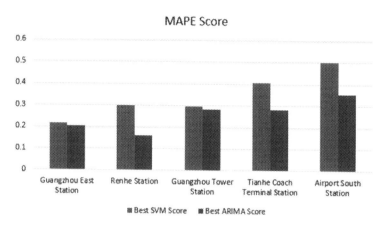

Fig. 11. Comparison of ARIMA and SVM

5.5   Conclusion and Discussion

In the first experiment, ARIMA (1, 0, 0) have predicted around a constant. So second and fourth predictions in first result series are considered as extreme points. Comparing MAPE of these prediction, ARIMA (1, 1, 1) which is the recommended by SACF plot is more acceptable than AIC's recommendation, ARIMA (1, 0, 0). And result of BIC, ARIMA (4, 0, 1) doesn't match residual independence. In second experiment, recommendation of SACF plot or AIC or BIC may not be the most accurate method when to predict passenger flow in different stations.

Summarizing the description in the first experiment, the investigation of subway passenger flow consists of five steps. First step is to use Dickey-Fuller test to verify whether all results of AR (p) characteristic equation is greater than 0 for proving passenger flow series is stationary. Dickey-Fuller test, SACF and SPACF plots show original and one-step differencing passenger flow of five subway stations are stationary. Second step is to use SACF, SPACF, AIC, BIC to estimate p and q of ARIMA (p, d, q), and they recommend five alternative models. And then, maximum likelihood function is used to estimate parameters of all alternative models and Table 2 presents all these models' parameters. After using SACF to investigate independence of their residual, ARIMA (1, 0, 0) and ARIMA (1, 1, 1) are selected to predict the test set. Through comparing MAPE, ARIMA (1, 1, 1) is more appropriate and persuasive in all alternate models.

For proving a more complete selection progress could estimate better p and q of ARIMA, we propose experiments with other four subway stations' records to investigate whether AIC or SACF plot is better than the other method, but results show that in different cases, AIC and SACF has different predictive performance.

In the last experiment, a comparison between ARIMA and SVM proves a more complete ARIMA selection progress could predict better than SVM do in these five stations.

So progress in this paper could perform better than single AIC and BIC and SACF&SPACF methods and more appropriate in more cases. And if we follow a complete selecting progress, we could have a high probability to estimate ARIMA model which has better predictive performance than SVM does.

Short-term subway passenger flow prediction is a challenge because of its massive factors such as weather, land-used beside subway stations. Because of data limitation, we only select ticket records of Guangzhou subway stations from September to October which means we couldn't investigate seasonal regulation and used seasonal ARIMA model. But the stationarity test, model selection and residual analysis methods are also appropriate to investigate and predict subway passenger flow for months.

In our experiment, we found reasons for four outliers are typhoon or mid-autumn festival which means passenger flow are also affected by catastrophes or festivals. So investigation of outliers in subway passenger flow will be another intelligent.

Acknowledgments. This paper is supported by "National 863 project (No. 2015AA050204)" and "State Grid Corporation project (No. 520626170011)". We would like to thank Guangzhou Metro Operation Department.

References

1. Official Statistics of GuangZhou Passenger. http://www.gzmtr.com/ygwm/xwzx/gsxw/
2. Yan, M.: Study and application of time series similarity and forecasting algorithm. Doctoral thesis. Beijing Jiaotong University (2014)
3. Pati, J., Kumar, B., Manjhi, D., Shukla, K.K.: A comparison among ARIMA, BP-NN and MOGA-NN for software clone evolution prediction. IEEE Access **5**, 11841–11851 (2017)
4. Shu, K., Jing, L., Mei, L., Xin, Z.: Prediction based on support vector machine for travel choice of high-speed railway passenger in China. In: International Conference on Management Science and Engineering, pp. 28–33 (2011)
5. Cao, C.: High-speed rail passenger flow forecasting based on EMD-BPN method. Lanzhou Jiaotong University (2015)
6. Dhib, E., Zangar, N., Tabbane, N., Boussetta, K.: Impact of seasonal ARIMA workload prediction model on QoE for massively multiplayers online gaming. In: 2016 5th International Conference on Multimedia Computing and Systems (ICMCS), pp. 737–741 (2016). http://dx.doi.org/10.1109/ICMCS.2016.7905664
7. Calheiros, R.N., Masoumi, E., Ranjan, R., Buyya, R.: Workload prediction using ARIMA model and its impact on cloud applications' QoS. Cloud Comput. IEEE Trans. **3**(4), 449–458 (2014)
8. Ni, M., He, Q., Gao, J.: Forecasting the subway passenger flow under event occurrences with social media. In: Proceedings of IEEE Transactions on Intelligent Transportation Systems, pp. 1–10 (2017)
9. Si, B., Fu, L., Liu, J., Shiravi, S.: A multi-class traffic assignment model for predicting transit passenger flows - a case study of beijing subway network. In: Transportation Research Board 93rd Annual Meeting (2014)

10. Zhou, J.B., Chen, H., Yan, B., Zhang, W., Feng, W.: Identification of pedestrian crowding degree in metro transfer hub based on normal cloud model. J. Jilin Univ. Eng. Technol. Ed. **46**(1), 100–107 (2016)
11. Xu, W., Qin, Y., Huang, H.: A new method of railway passenger ow forecasting based on spatio-temporal datamining. In: The International IEEE Conference on Intelligent Transportation Systems, Proceedings, pp. 402–405 (2004)
12. Tsai, T., Lee, C.K., Wei, C.H.: Neural network based temporal feature models for short-term railway passenger demand forecasting. Expert Syst. Appl. **36**(2), 3728–3736 (2009)
13. Gavirangaswamy, V.B., Gupta, G., Gupta, A., Agrawal, R.: Assessment of ARIMA-based prediction techniques for road-traffic volume. In: Fifth International Conference on Management of Emergent Digital EcoSystems, pp. 246–251 (2013)
14. Williams, B.: Multivariate vehicular traffic flow prediction: evaluation of ARIMAX modeling. Transp. Res. Rec. J. Transp. Res. Board **1**, 194–200 (2001)
15. Pemberton, J.: Time Series Analysis with Applications in R, 2nd edn. Springer, New York (1999). https://doi.org/10.1007/978-0-387-75959-3
16. Box, G.E.P.: Time Series Analysis: Forecasting and Control, 4th edn. Wiley, Canada (2008)

Bounded Correctness Checking
for Knowledge with eCTLK

Fei Pu$^{(\boxtimes)}$

College of Computer and Information Engineering,
Zhejiang Gongshang University, Hangzhou, China
pufei@zjgsu.edu.cn

Abstract. Bounded semantics of LTL and that of CTL, and the characterization of these properties have been widely studied and used as the theoretical basis for SAT-based bounded model checking. This has led to a lot of successful applications with respect to error detection in the checking of LTL and CTL properties by satisfiability testing. In this paper, we further investigate bounded semantics for the extended computational tree logic with epistemic components ($eCTLK$) which can be applied to verification of multi-agent systems (MAS). On the theoretical aspect, we propose a bounded correctness checking algorithm for $eCTLK$ properties that can handle both verification and falsification problems with bounded models. On the practical aspect, we apply the bounded semantics of $eCTLK$ to derive a QBF-based characterization of $eCTLK$ properties which is more succinct to encode symbolic model checking problems than SAT formulas.

Keywords: eCTLK · Bounded semantics · Multi-agent systems
Bounded correctness checking · Epistemic logic

1 Introduction

Within the past decade, push-button verification techniques (e.g. model checking [1]) have become commonplace in the development of hardware and software systems. An integration of model checking methods with software development is highly required by the manufacturers of critical and embedded software (avionics, telecom, public transport, etc.). Model checking is maturing into an effective technique for verifying and validating properties of complex systems. Bounded model checking (BMC) as a complementary approach to BDD based symbolic model checking [12,13] applies satisfiability checking to the verification of temporal properties, especially, for efficient error detection. Given a temporal logic property ϕ to be verified on a finite transition system M, the essential idea of BMC is to search for counterexamples to ϕ in the space of all executions of M whose length is bounded by some integer k. This problem is translated into a Boolean formula which is satisfiable if and only if a counterexample exists for the given value of k. The basic idea of the bounded semantics for temporal logics

© Springer Nature Singapore Pte Ltd. 2018
H. Yuan et al. (Eds.): GSKI 2017, CCIS 848, pp. 480–491, 2018.
https://doi.org/10.1007/978-981-13-0893-2_50

(or fragments of such logics) is to consider bounded paths (possibly with loops) instead of all of the infinite ones. Such a bounded semantics need to be sound and complete in general.

The successes of bounded model checking have led to extensive research on bounded semantics for various (fragments of) temporal logics such as LTL, $ACTL$, $ECTL$, and $ACTL^*$ [2–10, 16–28]. Rotem Oshman and Orna Grumberg [6] proposed a new approach to bounded model checking for universal branching-time logic in which they encode an arbitrary graph and allow the SAT solver to choose both the states and edges of the graph that could significantly reduce the size of the counter-example produced by BMC. Omar Inverso et al. [8] applied BMC to sequentially consistent C programs. They first translated a multi-threaded C program into a non deterministic sequential C program and then used existing high-performance BMC tools as backends for the sequential verification problem. Ralf Wimmer et al. [25] applied bounded model checking to generate counterexamples when invariant properties of Markov chains are violated. By returning not simply flat paths, but paths which are annotated with loops, they make not only the algorithm more efficient, but also the counterexamples more useful for the designer.

Zhang [16] proposed a bounded semantics for the extended computation tree logic which allows some sort of fairness, and developed a QBF encoding of the temporal logic from the definition of the bounded semantic. Zhang [17] also presented characteristics of bounded semantics for clarifying the concept of bounded semantics and provided a QBF-based bounded correctness checking algorithm for CTL under the given bounded semantics. As reported in [17], there is no bounded semantics which is sound and complete for CTL^* and $ACTL^*$ properties. For CTL (the Computation Tree Logic) and extended CTL [14], QBF (Quantified Boolean formula)-based bounded correctness checking [15] has been studied. QBF allows an exponentially more succinct representation of the checked formulas than SAT [2, 13]. Xu and Zhang [18] further studied $ACTL$ formulas which have linear counterexamples using bounded semantics, and applied them to SAT-based verification, in particular, bounded correctness checking of $ACTL$ properties. There are many advantages over the existing approaches at both semantic and algorithmic levels, in particular, at the semantic level, it may gain at least a polynomial factor on the size of bounded models for verifying a property in certain cases and at the algorithmic level, the approach can be exponentially better than the existing one in certain cases. Duan et al. [28] presented a bounded model checking approach for propositional projection temporal logic ($PPTL$). $PPTL$ is an extension of interval temporal logic which allows us to verify full regular properties and time duration related properties of systems in a convenient way.

BMC was initially developed for the verification of reactive systems, and now extended for multi-agent system. Lomuscio et al. [23] presented $TECTLK$, a logic to specify knowledge and real time in multi-agent systems and also proposed an algorithm for bounded model checking based on a discretisation method. Their algorithm can solve the difficulty of dense time problem. Armando et al.

[9] presented a notion of stuttering equivalence, and proved the semantical equivalence of stuttering-equivalent traces with respect to $LTLK\text{-}X$, a linear temporal logic for knowledge without the next operator. They gave an algorithm to reduce the size of the models before the model checking step and showed that it preserves $LTLK\text{-}X$ properties. Huang et al. [4] presented a symbolic BDD-based model checking algorithm for an epistemic strategy logic with observational semantics. The logic has been shown to be more expressive than several variants of ATEL and therefore the algorithm can also be used for ATEL model checking.

In this paper, we are interested in extending CTL formulas to $eCTL$ with epistemic components($eCTLK$), after presenting a sound and complete bounded semantics we develop a QBF encoding of $eCTLK$ from the definition of the bounded semantics and then propose an algorithm for bounded correctness checking of $eCTLK$ properties. Bounded correctness checking [17] can be seen as an extension of bounded model checking in such a way that given a universally quantified property, it not only tries to identify whether the property does not hold within a bound, but also tries to identify whether it holds within the bound by applying the bounded semantics instead of the standard semantics.

The rest of this paper is organized as follows. Section 2 introduces the definitions of relevant logics and concepts. Section 3 discusses properties of $eCTLK$, and a bounded semantics for $eCTLK$ is given. In Sect. 4, the bounded correctness checking approach for $eCTLK$ is developed, and Sect. 5 presents the QBF-based characterization of $eCTLK$ properties. Section 6 is concluding remarks.

2   Preliminaries

We introduce the definition of transition system models and that of the extended computation tree logic with epistemic components.

2.1   Kripke Structure Model

Let AP be a set of atomic propositions and A a set of agents. A Kripke structure is a tuple $M =< S, T, I, k_1, ..., k_n, L >$, where S is a finite set of states, $T \subseteq S \times S$ is a transition relation which is total (i.e., for every $s \in S$, there is $s' \in S$ such that $(s, s') \in T$). $I \subseteq S$ is a set of initial states and $L : S \rightarrow 2^{AP}$ is a labeling function that maps each state to a subset of propositions of AP. $k_i \subseteq S \times S$ ($i \in A$) is an equivalence relation on S, that is, a set of pairs of states of S. A Kripke structure is also called a model.

Paths and computations. An infinite path of M an infinite sequence $s_0 s_1 \ldots$ such that $(s_i, s_{i+1}) \in T$ for $i \geq 0$. A computation of M is an infinite path $s_0 s_1 \ldots$ of M such that $s_0 \in I$. A finite path is a finite prefix of an infinite path. Given a path $\pi = \pi_0 \pi_1 \ldots$, we use π^i to denote the subpath of π starting at π_i, use $\pi(s)$ to denote a path with $\pi_0 = s$. Then $\exists \pi(s).\varphi$ means that there is a path π with $\pi_0 = s$ such that φ holds, and $\forall \pi(s).\varphi$ means that for all path π with $\pi_0 = s$, φ holds.

2.2   Extended Computation Tree Logic of Knowledge (eCTLK)

Properties of a Kripke structure may be represented by temporal logic formulas. Extended computation tree logic [15] is a propositional branching time logic that extends the computation tree logic (CTL) with possibility to express fairness constraints. For brevity, the extended computation tree logic is hereafter denoted $eCTL$. Extended Computation Tree Logic of Knowledge $(eCTLK)$ is a temporal logic added epistemic logic operators.

Syntax.   Let AP be a set of propositional symbols and A a set of agents. Let p range over AP. Let ϕ be state formula and ψ be the path formula. The set of $eCTLK$ formulas over AP is defined as follows:

$$\phi ::= p \mid \neg\phi \mid \phi \wedge \phi \mid \phi \vee \phi \mid A\psi \mid E\psi$$
$$K_i\phi \mid E_\Gamma\phi \mid C_\Gamma\phi \mid D_\Gamma\phi \mid \overline{K}_i\phi \mid \overline{E}_\Gamma\phi \mid \overline{C}_\Gamma\phi \mid \overline{D}_\Gamma\phi$$
$$\psi ::= X\phi \mid F\phi \mid G\phi \mid F^\infty\,\phi \mid G^\infty\,\phi \mid \phi\,U\,\phi \mid \phi\,R\,\phi$$

where $i \in A$ and $\Gamma \subseteq A$.

Negation Normal Form.   A $eCTLK$ formula is in negation normal form, if the negation $\neg$ is applied only to atomic propositions. Each $eCTLK$ formulas can be transformed into an equivalent formula in NNF. Without loss of generality, we only consider formulas in NNF, formulas not in NNF are considered as an abbreviation of the equivalent one in NNF.

Definition 1. *(Semantics of eCTLK) Let p denote a propositional symbol, ϕ_0, ϕ_1 denote state formulas, ψ_0, ψ_1 denote path formulas. Let s be a state and π be a path of M. The relation $\models$ is defined as follows:*

Definition 2. *Let φ be a eCTLK formula. $M \models \varphi$ iff $M, s \models \varphi$ for all $s \in I$.*

3   Bounded Semantics

To define the bounded semantics one needs to represent infinite paths in a model in a special way. To this aim, we define the notions of k-paths and loops.

k-paths.   Let M be a model, $k \geq 0$, and $0 \leq n \leq k$. A k-path of M is a path $\pi(k) = (s_0, s_1, ..., s_k)$ (also denoted by π) with length $k + 1$. A k-path may start at any state of M in the model. A k-path π is a loop $\pi_{rs}(k, n)$ if $n < k$ and $\pi_k = \pi_n$. As in the definition of bounded semantics, we need to define the satisfiability relation on suffixes of k-paths, we denote $\pi^m(k)$ by the k-path $\pi(k)$ starting at point π_m, where $0 \leq m \leq k$. We denote k-path $\pi(k)$ starting at s by $\pi(k)(s)$.

Bounded models.   The k-model of M is a structure $M_k = < S, ph_k, I, k_1, ..., k_n, L >$, where Ph_k is the set of all different k-paths of M. M_k can be considered as an approximation of M. The k-model M_k is a special unique (k, n)-model of M with $n = |Ph_k|$.

$M, s \models p$	iff	$p \in L(s)$
$M, s \models \neg p$	iff	$M, s \not\models p$
$M, s \models \phi_0 \wedge \phi_1$	iff	$(M, s \models \phi_0)$ and $(M, s \models \phi_1)$
$M, s \models \phi_0 \vee \phi_1$	iff	$(M, s \models \phi_0)$ or $(M, s \models \phi_1)$
$M, s \models A\psi_0$	iff	$\forall \pi(s).(M, \pi \models \psi_0)$
$M, s \models E\psi_0$	iff	$\exists \pi(s).(M, \pi \models \psi_0)$
$M, \pi^m \models \phi_0$	iff	$M, \pi_m \models \phi_0$
$M, \pi^m \models \psi_0 \wedge \psi_1$	iff	$M, \pi^m \models \psi_0 \wedge M, \pi \models \psi_1$
$M, \pi^m \models \psi_0 \vee \psi_1$	iff	$M, \pi^m \models \psi_0 \vee M, \pi \models \psi_1$
$M, \pi^m \models X\psi_0$	iff	$M, \pi^{m+1} \models \psi_0$
$M, \pi^m \models G\psi_0$	iff	$\forall i \geq 0.(M, \pi^i \models \psi_0)$
$M, \pi^m \models F\psi_0$	iff	$\exists i \geq m.(M, \pi^i \models \psi_0)$
$M, \pi^m \models G^\infty \psi_0$	iff	$\exists i \geq m.\forall k \geq i.(M, \pi^k \models \psi_0)$
$M, \pi^m \models F^\infty \psi_0$	iff	$\forall i \geq m.\exists k \geq i.(M, \pi^k \models \psi_0)$
$M, \pi^m \models \psi_0 U \psi_1$	iff	$\exists j \geq m.(M, \pi^j \models \psi_1$ and $\forall m \leq i < j.(M, \pi^i \models \psi_0))$
$M, \pi^m \models \psi_0 R \psi_1$	iff	$(\exists j \geq m.(M, \pi^j \models \psi_0$ and $\forall 0 \leq i \leq j.(M, \pi^i \models \psi_1))$ or $\forall j \geq m.(M, \pi^j \models \psi_1)$
$M, s \models K_i \phi_0$	iff	$\forall s' \in S.((s, s') \in k_i \to (M, s' \models \phi_0))$
$M, s \models D_\Gamma \phi_0$	iff	$\forall s' \in S.((s, s') \in \cap_{i \in \Gamma} k_i \to (M, s' \models \phi_0))$
$M, s \models E_\Gamma \phi_0$	iff	$\forall s' \in S.((s, s') \in \cup_{i \in \Gamma} k_i \to (M, s' \models \phi_0))$
$M, s \models C_\Gamma \phi_0$	iff	$\forall s' \in S.((s, s') \in (\cup_{i \in \Gamma} k_i)^+ \to (M, s' \models \phi_0))$
$M, s \models \overline{K}_i \phi_0$	iff	$\exists s' \in S.((s, s') \in k_i \wedge (M, s' \models \phi_0))$
$M, s \models \overline{D}_\Gamma \phi_0$	iff	$\exists s' \in S.((s, s') \in \cap_{i \in \Gamma} k_i \wedge (M, s' \models \phi_0))$
$M, s \models \overline{E}_\Gamma \phi_0$	iff	$\exists s' \in S.((s, s') \in \cup_{i \in \Gamma} k_i \wedge (M, s' \models \phi_0))$
$M, s \models \overline{C}_\Gamma \phi_0$	iff	$\exists s' \in S.((s, s') \in (\cup_{i \in \Gamma} k_i)^+ \wedge (M, s' \models \phi_0))$

The encoding of the BMC problem for $eCTLK$ when the bounded path has no loop is fairly straightforward. The case when loops are allowed in bounded paths becomes more complicated.

Definition 3. *(Bounded Semantics of eCTLK) Let p denote a propositional symbol, ϕ_0, ϕ_1 denote state formulas, and ψ_0, ψ_1 denote path formulas. Let s be a state of M and π be a k-path of ph_k. Let $M, s \models_k \varphi$ denote the relation that φ holds on s of M_k. The relation $\models_k$ is defined inductively as follows.*

Definition 4. *Let ϕ be $eCTLK$, $M \models_k \phi$ iff $M_k, s \models_k \phi$ for all $s \in I$.*

$M, s \models_k p$	iff	$p \in L(s)$
$M, s \models_k \neg p$	iff	$M, s \not\models_k p$
$M, s \models_k \phi_0 \wedge \phi_1$	iff	$(M, s \models_k \phi_0)$ and $(M, s \models_k \phi_1)$
$M, s \models_k \phi_0 \vee \phi_1$	iff	$(M, s \models_k \phi_0)$ or $(M, s \models_k \phi_1)$
$M, s \models_k A\psi_0$	iff	$\forall \pi(k)(s).(M, \pi \models \psi_0)$
$M, s \models_k E\psi_0$	iff	$\exists \pi(k)(s).(M, \pi \models \psi_0)$

$M, \pi^m \models_k \phi_0$	iff	$M, \pi_m \models_k \phi_0$
$M, \pi^m \models_k \psi_0 \wedge \psi_1$	iff	$M, \pi^m \models_k \psi_0 \wedge M, \pi^m \models_k \psi_1$
$M, \pi^m \models_k \psi_0 \vee \psi_1$	iff	$M, \pi^m \models_k \psi_0 \vee M, \pi^m \models_k \psi_1$
$M, \pi^m \models_k X\psi_0$	iff	$(m < k$ and $M, \pi^{m+1} \models_k \psi_0)$ or $(m = k$ and $\pi_{rs}(k, n)$ and $M, \pi^{n+1} \models_k \psi_0)$
$M, \pi^m \models_k G\psi_0$	iff	$n < k$, $\pi_{rs}(k, n)$ and $(\forall \min(m,n) \leq j \leq k$ and $M, \pi^j \models_k \psi_0)$
$M, \pi^m \models_k F\psi_0$	iff	$(\exists m \leq j \leq k, M, \pi^j \models_k \psi_0)$ or $(n < m$ and $\pi_{rs}(k, n)$ and $(\exists n < j < m, M, \pi^j \models_k \psi_0))$
$M, \pi^m \models_k G^\infty \psi_0$	iff	$\exists i \geq m, \forall i \leq l \leq k.(n < k, \pi_{rs}(k, n)$ and $(\forall \min(l,n) \leq j \leq k, M, \pi^j \models_k \psi_0))$
$M, \pi^m \models_k F^\infty \psi_0$	iff	$\forall i \geq m, \exists i \leq l \leq k.((\exists l \leq j \leq k, M, \pi^j \models_k \psi_0)$ or $(n < l$ and $\pi_{rs}(k, n)$ and $(\exists n < j < l, M, \pi^j \models_k \psi_0)))$
$M, \pi^m \models_k \psi_0 U\psi_1$	iff	$(\exists m \leq j \leq k, M, \pi^j \models_k \psi_1$ and $(\forall m \leq i < j, M, \pi^j \models_k \psi_0))$ or $(n < m$ and $\pi_{rs}(k, n)$ and $(\exists l \leq j \leq m, M, \pi^j \models_k \psi_1)$ and $(\forall l < i < j, M, \pi^i \models_k \psi_0)$ and $(\forall m \leq i \leq k, M, \pi^i \models_k \psi_0))$
$M, \pi^m \models_k \psi_0 R\psi_1$	iff	$(\forall m \leq j \leq k, M, \pi^j \models_k \psi_1$ or $(\exists m \leq i \leq j, M, \pi^j \models_k \psi_0))$ or $(n < m$ and $\pi_{rs}(k, n)$ and $(\exists n < j < m, M, \pi^j \models_k \psi_0)$ and $(\forall n < i \leq j, M, \pi^i \models_k \psi_1)$ and $(\forall m \leq i \leq k, M, \pi^i \models_k \psi_1))$ or $(n < k$ and $\pi_{rs}(k, n)$ and $(\forall \min(m,n) \leq j \leq k, M, \pi^j \models_k \psi_1))$

$M, s \models_k K_i\phi_0$	iff	$\forall \pi(k)(s).(\pi_{rs} \wedge \forall m \leq k.((s, m) \in k_i \rightarrow (M, \pi_m \models_k \phi_0)))$
$M, s \models_k D_\Gamma\phi_0$	iff	$\forall \pi(k)(s).(\pi_{rs} \wedge \forall m \leq k.((s, m) \in \cap_{i \in \Gamma} k_i \rightarrow (M, \pi_m \models_k \phi_0)))$
$M, s \models_k E_\Gamma\phi_0$	iff	$\forall \pi(k)(s).(\pi_{rs} \wedge \forall m \leq k.((s, m) \in \cup_{i \in \Gamma} k_i \rightarrow (M, \pi_m \models_k \phi_0)))$
$M, s \models_k C_\Gamma\phi_0$	iff	$\forall \pi(k)(s).(\pi_{rs} \wedge \forall m \leq k.((s, m) \in (\cup_{i \in \Gamma} k_i)^+ \rightarrow (M, \pi_m \models_k \phi_0)))$
$M, s \models_k \overline{K}_i\phi_0$	iff	$\exists \pi(k)(s).(\pi_{rs} \wedge \exists m \leq k.((s, m) \in k_i \wedge (M, \pi_m \models_k \phi_0)))$
$M, s \models_k \overline{D}_\Gamma\phi_0$	iff	$\exists \pi(k)(s).(\pi_{rs} \wedge \exists m \leq k.((s, m) \in \cap_{i \in \Gamma} k_i \wedge (M, \pi_m \models_k \phi_0)))$
$M, s \models_k \overline{E}_\Gamma\phi_0$	iff	$\exists \pi(k)(s).(\pi_{rs} \wedge \exists m \leq k.((s, m) \in \cup_{i \in \Gamma} k_i \wedge (M, \pi_m \models_k \phi_0)))$
$M, s \models_k \overline{C}_\Gamma\phi_0$	iff	$\exists \pi(k)(s).(\pi_{rs} \wedge \exists m \leq k.((s, m) \in (\cup_{i \in \Gamma} k_i)^+ \wedge (M, \pi_m \models_k \phi_0)))$

4 Bounded Correctness Checking of eCTLK

In this section, we will apply bounded semantics ($M \models_k \phi$) to model checking problem ($M \models \phi$).

Lemma 1. *Let ϕ be an eCTLK formula, if $M, s \models_k \phi$, then $M, s \models_{k+1} \phi$.*

Proof. The proof of all properties other than $K_i\phi$, $D_\Gamma\phi$, $E_\Gamma\phi$ and $C_\Gamma\phi$ are similar to the proofs in [16]. We then omit it here and only prove properties of the forms $K_i\phi$, $D_\Gamma\phi$, $E_\Gamma\phi$ and $C_\Gamma\phi$. Let $\psi = K_i\phi \mid D_\Gamma\phi \mid E_\Gamma\phi \mid C_\Gamma\phi$. Let $equalS = k_i \mid \cap_{i \in \Gamma} k_i \mid \cup_{i \in \Gamma} k_i \mid (\cup_{i \in \Gamma} k_i)^+$ corresponding to ψ. Suppose that $M, s \models_k \psi$ holds and $M, s \models_{k+1} \psi$ dose not hold. Then there is $(k+1)$-path π with $\pi_0 \in I$ such that $\pi_{rs} \wedge \forall m \leq (k+1).((s,m) \in equalS \rightarrow (M, \pi_m \models_{k+1} \phi))$ does not hold. Taking the k-prefix of path π, we get a k-path $\pi(k) = \pi_0...\pi_{k-1}$. Since $M, s \models_k \phi$ holds, we then have that $\pi(k)_{rs} \wedge \forall m \leq k.((s,m) \in equalS \rightarrow (M, (\pi(k))_m \models_k \phi))$ which implies $\pi_{rs} \wedge \forall m \leq k.((s,m) \in equalS \rightarrow (M, \pi_m \models_{k+1} \phi)$. Then, we have that $M, \pi_k \models_{k+1} \phi$ doesn't hold. On the other hand, there exist i and j such that $\pi_i = \pi_j$ because of π_{rs}. We could construct a k-path π' with prefix $\pi_0...\pi_i, \pi_{j+1}...\pi_k$, from the fact of $M, s \models_k \phi$, we obtain $M, \pi_k \models_k \phi$ which implies $M, \pi_k \models_{k+1} \phi$. Therefore, we have the contradiction.

Lemma 2. *Let ϕ be an eCTLK formula, if $M, s \models_k \phi$ for some $k \geq 0$, then $M, s \models \phi$.*

Lemma 3. *Let ϕ be an eCTLK formula, if $M, s \models \phi$, then $M, s \models_k \phi$ for some $k \geq 0$.*

Theorem 1 (Soundness and Completeness). $M, s \models \phi$ iff $M, s \models_k \phi$ *for some $k \geq 0$.*

Since the number of k-paths in the k-model is large, to verify more efficiently, we focus on using submodels with smaller size of the k-model M_k. A (k, n)-model of M is a structure $N =< S, ph'_k, I, k_1, ..., k_n, L >$, where ph'_k is a multi-set with the size $|ph'_k| = n$ and all paths of ph'_k are in Ph_k. A (k, n)-model is then considered as a submodel of M_k. The k-model M_k is a special unique (k, n)-model of M with $n = |ph_k|$. Let $N' =< S, ph''_k, I, k_1, ..., k_n, L >$, if $ph'_k \subseteq ph''_k$, then $N \leq N'$.

Definition 5 (Sufficient Number of k-path for Checking an eCTLK Formula). *Let ϕ be an AeCTLK formula, ψ be an EeCTLK formula and φ be an eCTLK formula over the set of atomic propositions AP respectively, f_k is defined as follows.*

$f_k(p) = f_k(\neg p) = 0$ if $p \in AP$	
$f_k(\phi_0 \wedge \phi_1)$	$= \max(f_k(\phi_0), f_k(\phi_1))$
$f_k(\phi_0 \vee \phi_1)$	$= f_k(\phi_0) + f_k(\phi_1)$
$f_k(AX\phi)$	$= f_k(\phi) + 1$
$f_k(AF\phi)$	$= (k+1)f_k(\phi) + 1$
$f_k(AG\phi)$	$= f_k(\phi) + 1$
$f_k(AG^{\infty}\phi)$	$= f_k(\phi) + 1$
$f_k(AF^{\infty}\phi)$	$= (k+1)f_k(\phi) + 1$
$f_k(A(\phi_0 R \phi_1))$	$= (k+1)\max(f_k(\phi_0), f_k(\phi_1)) + f_k(\phi_1) + 1$
$f_k(A(\phi_0 U \phi_1))$	$= f_k(\phi_1) + k \cdot \max(f_k(\phi_0), f_k(\phi_1)) + 1$
$f_k(\psi_0 \wedge \psi_1)$	$= f_k(\psi_0) + f_k(\psi_1)$
$f_k(\psi_0 \vee \psi_1)$	$= \max(f_k(\psi_0), f_k(\psi_1))$
$f_k(EX\psi)$	$= f_k(\psi) + 1$
$f_k(EG\psi)$	$= (k+1)f_k(\psi) + 1$
$f_k(EG^{\infty}\psi)$	$= (k+1)f_k(\psi) + 1$
$f_k(EF^{\infty}\psi)$	$= f_k(\psi) + 1$
$f_k(E(\psi_0 U \psi_1))$	$= kf_k(\psi_0) + f_k(\psi_1) + 1$
$f_k(E(\psi_0 R \psi_1))$	$= (k+1)f_k(\psi_1) + f_k(\psi_0) + 1$
$f_k(K_i\varphi)$	$= f_k(\varphi) + 1$
$f_k(D_\Gamma\varphi)$	$= f_k(\varphi) + 1$
$f_k(E_\Gamma\varphi)$	$= f_k(\varphi) + 1$
$f_k(C_\Gamma\varphi)$	$= f_k(\varphi) + k$
$f_k(\overline{K}_i\varphi)$	$= f_k(\varphi) + 1$
$f_k(\overline{D}_\Gamma\varphi)$	$= f_k(\varphi) + 1$
$f_k(\overline{C}_\Gamma\varphi)$	$= f_k(\varphi) + k$

Theorem 2. ϕ be an AeCTLK formula, $n = f_k^a(\phi)$. $M, s \models_k \phi$ iff there is a (k,n)-model N such that $N, s \models_k \phi$. (2). Let φ be an EeCTLK formula, $n = f_k^e(\varphi)$. $M, s \models_k \varphi$ iff there is a (k,n)-model N such that $N, s \models_k \varphi$.

5 QBF Characterization of eCTLK

From the bounded semantics, a QBF-based characterization of eCTLK formulas can be developed as follows.

Let $k \geq 0$. Let $u_0, \ldots, u_k$ be a finite sequence of state variables. The sequence $u_0, \ldots, u_k$ (denoted by $\overrightarrow{u}$) is intended to be used as a representation of a k-path of M.

Definition 6. Let $k \geq 0$.

$$P_k(\overrightarrow{u}) := \bigwedge_{j=0}^{k-1} T(u_j, u_{j+1})$$

Every assignment to the set of state variables $u_0, \ldots, u_k$ satisfying $P_k(\overrightarrow{u})$ represents a valid k-path of M. The (k,n)-model of M can be encoded as $[[M]]_k^n := \bigwedge_{i=1}^{n} P_k(\overrightarrow{u_i})$. Let $rs_k(\overrightarrow{u})$ denote that there are same states appearing in different positions in k-path $\overrightarrow{u}$. Formally,

$$\pi_{rs}^k(\overrightarrow{u}) := \bigvee_{x=0}^{k-1} \bigvee_{y=x+1}^{k} u_x = u_y$$

From the above definition, $\pi_{rs}^k(\overrightarrow{u}, n)$ is the same as $\pi_{rs}(k, n)$ $(n < k)$. Let $p \in AP$ be a proposition symbol and $p(v)$ be the propositional formula such that $p(v)$ is true whenever v is assigned the truth value representing a state s in which p holds.

Definition 7. *(Translation of eCTLK formulas). Let $k \geq 0$. Let v be a state variable and φ_0, φ_1 be state formulas and ψ_0, ψ_1 be path formulas. The encoding $[[\phi, v]]_k^m$ is defined as follows.*

$[[p, v]]_k$	$= p(v)$
$[[\neg p, v]]_k$	$= \neg p(v)$
$[[\varphi_0 \vee \varphi_1, v]]_k$	$= [[\varphi_0, v]]_k \vee [[\varphi_1, v]]_k$
$[[\varphi_0 \wedge \varphi_1, v]]_k$	$= [[\varphi_0, v]]_k \wedge [[\varphi_1, v]]_k$
$[[A\psi_0, v]]_k$	$= \forall \overrightarrow{u}.(P(\overrightarrow{u}) \wedge v = u_0 \wedge [[\psi_0, \overrightarrow{u}]]_k)$
$[[E\psi_0, v]]_k$	$= \exists \overrightarrow{u}.(P(\overrightarrow{u}) \wedge v = u_0 \wedge [[\psi_0, \overrightarrow{u}]]_k)$
$[[X\varphi_0, \overrightarrow{u}]]_k^m$	$= ((m < k) \wedge [[\varphi_0, u_{m+1}]]_k) \vee (m = k \wedge \pi_{rs}^k(\overrightarrow{u}, n) \wedge [[\varphi_0, u_{n+1}]]_k))$
$[[F\psi_0, \overrightarrow{u}]]_k^m$	$= (\bigvee_{j=m}^{k} [[\psi_0, u_j]]_k) \vee ((n < m) \wedge \pi_{rs}^k(\overrightarrow{u}, n) \wedge (\bigvee_{j=n+1}^{m-1} [[\psi_0, u_j]]_k))$
$[[G\psi_0, \overrightarrow{u}]]_k^m$	$= (n < k) \wedge \pi_{rs}^k(\overrightarrow{u}, n) \wedge (\bigwedge_{j=min(m,n)}^{k} [[\psi_0, u_j]]_k)$
$[[F^\infty \psi_0, \overrightarrow{u}]]_k^m$	$= \bigwedge_{i=m}^{k} \bigvee_{l=i}^{k} ((\bigvee_{j=l}^{k} [[\psi_0, u_j]]_k) \vee ((n < l) \wedge \pi_{rs}^k(\overrightarrow{u}, n) \wedge$ $(\bigvee_{j=n+1}^{l-1} [[\psi_0, u_j]]_k)))$
$[[G^\infty \psi_0, \overrightarrow{u}]]_k^m$	$= \bigvee_{i=m}^{k} \bigwedge_{l=i}^{k} ((n < k) \wedge \pi_{rs}^k(\overrightarrow{u}, n) \wedge (\bigwedge_{j=min(l,n)}^{k} [[\psi_0, u_j]]_k))$
$[[\psi_0 U \psi_1, \overrightarrow{u}]]_k^m$	$= (\bigvee_{j=m}^{k} [[\psi_1, u_j]]_k \wedge \bigwedge_{i=m}^{j-1} [[\psi_0, u_j]]_k) \vee ((n < m) \wedge \pi_{rs}^k(\overrightarrow{u}, n) \wedge$ $(\bigvee_{j=l}^{m} [[\psi_1, u_j]]_k) \wedge (\bigwedge_{i=l+1}^{j-1} [[\psi_0, u_i]]_k) \wedge (\bigwedge_{i=m}^{k} [[\psi_0, u_i]]_k))$
$[[\psi_0 R \psi_1, \overrightarrow{u}]]_k^m$	$= (\bigvee_{j=m}^{k} [[\psi_0, u_j]]_k \wedge (\bigwedge_{i=m}^{j} [[\psi_1, u_j]]_k)) \vee ((n < m) \wedge \pi_{rs}^k(\overrightarrow{u}, n)$ $\wedge (\bigvee_{j=l+1}^{m-1} [[\psi_0, u_j]]_k) \wedge (\bigwedge_{i=l+1}^{j} [[\psi_1, u_i]]_k) \wedge (\bigwedge_{i=m}^{k} [[\psi_1, u_i]]_k))$ $\vee ((n < k) \wedge \pi_{rs}^k(\overrightarrow{u}, n) \wedge (\bigwedge_{j=min(m,n)}^{k} [[\psi_1, u_j]]_k))$
$[[K_i \varphi, v]]_k$	$= \pi_{rs}^k \wedge \bigwedge_{m=0}^{k} ((s, m) \in k_i \rightarrow [[\varphi, \pi_m]]_k)$
$[[D_\Gamma \varphi, v]]_k$	$= \pi_{rs}^k \wedge \bigwedge_{m=0}^{k} ((s, m) \in \cap_{i \in \Gamma} k_i \rightarrow [[\varphi, \pi_m]]_k)$
$[[E_\Gamma \varphi, v]]_k$	$= \pi_{rs}^k \wedge \bigwedge_{m=0}^{k} ((s, m) \in \cup_{i \in \Gamma} k_i \rightarrow [[\varphi, \pi_m]]_k)$
$[[C_\Gamma \varphi, v]]_k$	$= \pi_{rs}^k \wedge \bigwedge_{m=0}^{k} ((s, m) \in (\cup_{i \in \Gamma} k_i)^+ \rightarrow [[\varphi, \pi_m]]_k)$
$[[\overline{K}_i \varphi, v]]_k$	$= \pi_{rs}^k \wedge \bigvee_{m=0}^{k} ((s, m) \in k_i \wedge [[\varphi, \pi_m]]_k)$
$[[\overline{D}_\Gamma \varphi, v]]_k$	$= \pi_{rs}^k \wedge \bigvee_{m=0}^{k} ((s, m) \in \cap_{i \in \Gamma} k_i \wedge [[\varphi, \pi_m]]_k)$
$[[\overline{E}_\Gamma \varphi, v]]_k$	$= \pi_{rs}^k \wedge \bigvee_{m=0}^{k} ((s, m) \in \cup_{i \in \Gamma} k_i \wedge [[\varphi, \pi_m]]_k)$
$[[\overline{C}_\Gamma \varphi, v]]_k$	$= \pi_{rs}^k \wedge \bigvee_{m=0}^{k} ((s, m) \in (\cup_{i \in \Gamma} k_i)^+ \wedge [[\varphi, \pi_m]]_k)$

Remark. $v(s)$ denotes that the state variable v has been assigned a value corresponding to the state s.

Definition 8. *Let ϕ be an eCTLK formula. $[[M, \phi, v]]_k = [[M]]_k \wedge [[\phi, v]]_k$*

Lemma 4. *Let ϕ be an eCTLK formula. $[[M, \phi, v(s)]]_k^n$ is satisfiable iff there is a (k, n)-model N such that $N, s \models_k \phi$.*

Theorem 3. *Let ϕ be an eCTLK formula. $M_k, s \models \phi$ iff $[[M, \phi, v(s)]]_k$ is satisfiable.*

Theorem 4. *Let ϕ be an eCTLK formula. $M, s \models_k \phi$ iff $[[M, \phi, v(s)]]_k^{f_k(\phi)}$ is satisfiable.*

6 Conclusions

Many bounded model checking algorithms have mainly been applied to the area of error detection of various universal properties such as LTL and the universal fragments of CTL. In this paper, we apply a QBF-based bounded correctness checking to the set of $eCTLK$ properties (the extended computational tree logic with the epistemic components) that may be specified with both universal and existential path quantifiers, and can handle verification and falsification problems with bounded models.

Our translation from $eCTLK$ to QBF can reduce the size of the submodels submitted to the QBF solver while testing satisfiability of the formula to be verified. On the other hand, $eCTLK$ properties not only support some sort of fairness that are not handled by some well known model checkers such as Spin and NuSMV, but also support knowledge reasoning by its epistemic components. Our bounded semantics based approach has advantage when a small k is sufficient for verification or error detection of given $eCTLK$ properties. From the practical point of view, combining abstract technique with bounded semantics may be a promising direction.

Acknowledgements. This work is supported by Zhejiang Provincial Natural Science Foundation of China under Grant No.LY13F020009 and State Key Laboratory of Computer Science, Institute of Software, Chinese Academy of Sciences under Grant No.SYSKF1011.

References

1. Baier, C., Katoen, J.P.: Principles of Model Checking. MIT Press, Cambridge (2008)
2. Dershowitz, N., Hanna, Z., Katz, J.: Bounded model checking with QBF. In: Bacchus, F., Walsh, T. (eds.) SAT 2005. LNCS, vol. 3569, pp. 408–414. Springer, Heidelberg (2005). https://doi.org/10.1007/11499107_32
3. Biere, A., Cimmatti, A., Clarke, E., Strichman, O., Zhu, Y.: Bounded Model Checking. Advances in Computers, vol. 58. Academic Press, Massachusetts (2003)
4. Huang, X., van der Meyden, R.: Symbolic Model Checking Epistemic Strategy Logic, pp. 1426–1432, AAAI (2014)
5. Penczek, W., Wozna, B., Zbrzezny, A.: Bounded model checking for the universal fragment of CTL. Fundamenta Informaticae **51**, 135–156 (2002)
6. Oshman, R., Grumberg, O.: A new approach to bounded model checking for branching time logics. In: Namjoshi, K.S., Yoneda, T., Higashino, T., Okamura, Y. (eds.) ATVA 2007. LNCS, vol. 4762, pp. 410–424. Springer, Heidelberg (2007). https://doi.org/10.1007/978-3-540-75596-8_29

7. Laroussinie, F., Schnoebelen, P.: Specification in CTL past for verification in CTL. Inf. Comput. **156**, 236–263 (2000)
8. Inverso, O., Tomasco, E., Fischer, B., La Torre, S., Parlato, G.: Bounded model checking of multi-threaded C programs via lazy sequentialization. In: Biere, A., Bloem, R. (eds.) CAV 2014. LNCS, vol. 8559, pp. 585–602. Springer, Cham (2014). https://doi.org/10.1007/978-3-319-08867-9_39
9. Lomuscio, A., Penczek, W., Qu, H.: Partial order reduction for model checking interleaved multi-agent systems, pp. 659–666. AAMAS (2010)
10. Armando, A., Carbone, R., Compagna, L.: SATMC: A SAT-Based model checker for security-critical systems. In: Ábrahám, E., Havelund, K. (eds.) TACAS 2014. LNCS, vol. 8413, pp. 31–45. Springer, Heidelberg (2014). https://doi.org/10.1007/978-3-642-54862-8_3
11. Kroening, D., Tautschnig, M.: CBMC – C bounded model checker. In: Ábrahám, E., Havelund, K. (eds.) TACAS 2014. LNCS, vol. 8413, pp. 389–391. Springer, Heidelberg (2014). https://doi.org/10.1007/978-3-642-54862-8_26
12. McMillan, K.L.: Symbolic Model Checking. Kluwer Academic Publisher, Dordrecht (1993)
13. Bryant, R.E.: Binary decision diagrams and beyond: enabling technologies for formal verification, pp. 236–243 ICCAD (1995)
14. Jussila, T., Biere, A.: Compressing BMC Encodings with QBF. Electron. Notes Theoret. Comput. Sci. BMC **174**(3), 45–56 (2006)
15. Emerson, E.A., Halpern, J.Y.: "Sometimes" and "Not Never" revisited: on branching versus linear time temporal logic. J. ACM **33**(1), 151–178 (1986)
16. Zhang, W.: QBF encoding of temporal properties and QBF-based verification. In: Demri, S., Kapur, D., Weidenbach, C. (eds.) IJCAR 2014. LNCS (LNAI), vol. 8562, pp. 224–239. Springer, Cham (2014). https://doi.org/10.1007/978-3-319-08587-6_16
17. Zhang, W.: Bounded semantics. Theoret. Comput. Sci. **564**, 1–29 (2015)
18. Xu, Z., Zhang, W.: Linear templates of ACTL formulas with an application to SAT-based verification. Inf. Process. Lett. **127**, 6–16 (2017)
19. Zhang, W.: Bounded semantics of CTL and SAT-Based verification. In: Breitman, K., Cavalcanti, A. (eds.) ICFEM 2009. LNCS, vol. 5885, pp. 286–305. Springer, Heidelberg (2009). https://doi.org/10.1007/978-3-642-10373-5_15
20. Clarke, E., Kroening, D., Ouaknine, J., Strichman, O.: Computational challenges in bounded model checking. Int. J. Softw. Tools Technol. Transf. **7**, 174–183 (2005)
21. Ganai, M.K., Gupta, A.: Accelerating high-level bounded model checking. ICCAD, pp. 794–801 (2006)
22. Wang, B.-Y.: Proving ∀µ-Calculus properties with SAT-based model checking. In: Wang, F. (ed.) FORTE 2005. LNCS, vol. 3731, pp. 113–127. Springer, Heidelberg (2005). https://doi.org/10.1007/11562436_10
23. Lomuscio, A., Penczek, W., Wozna, B.: Bounded model checking for knowledge and real time. Artificial Intelligence **171**, 1011–1038 (2007)
24. Ji, K.: CTL model checking in deduction modulo. In: Felty, A.P., Middeldorp, A. (eds.) CADE 2015. LNCS (LNAI), vol. 9195, pp. 295–310. Springer, Cham (2015). https://doi.org/10.1007/978-3-319-21401-6_20
25. Kemper, S.: SAT-based verification for timed component connectors. Sci. Comput. Program. **77**(7–8), 779–798 (2012)
26. Wimmer, R., Braitling, B., Becker, B.: Counterexample generation for discrete-time markov chains using bounded model checking. In: Jones, N.D., Müller-Olm, M. (eds.) VMCAI 2009. LNCS, vol. 5403, pp. 366–380. Springer, Heidelberg (2008). https://doi.org/10.1007/978-3-540-93900-9_29

27. Hoffmann, J., Gomes, C.P., Selman, B., Kautz, H.A.: SAT Encodings of State-Space Reachability Problems in Numeric Domains. IJCAI, pp. 1918–1923 (2007)
28. Duan, Z., Tian, C., Yang, M., He, J.: Bounded model checking for propositional projection temporal logic. In: Du, D.-Z., Zhang, G. (eds.) COCOON 2013. LNCS, vol. 7936, pp. 591–602. Springer, Heidelberg (2013). https://doi.org/10.1007/978-3-642-38768-5_52

Ecological and Environmental Data Processing and Management

AHP-Based Susceptibility Assessment on Debris Flows in Semiarid Mountainous Region: A Case of Benzilan-Changbo Segment in the Upper Jinsha River, China

Jian Chen[1(✉)], Yan Li[1], Wendy Zhou[2], Chong Xu[3], Saier Wu[1], and Wen Yue[1]

[1] School of Engineering and Technology,
China University of Geosciences, Beijing 100083, China
`jianchen@cugb.edu.cn`
[2] Department of Geology and Geological Engineering,
Colorado School of Mines, Colorado 80401, USA
[3] Institute of Geology, China Earthquake Administration, Beijing 100029, China

Abstract. The semiarid mountainous region is characterized by sparse vegetation and rich source of loose deposits, which is favorable for the formation of debris flows. Benzilan-Changbo segment in the upper reaches of Jinsha River is selected in this study. Based on field investigation and interpretation of remote sensing images, the development characteristics of regional debris flows in the semiarid area are studied. Six assessment indices are selected, including lithology, structural fault, slope gradient, relative height of the watershed, annual average rainfall and normalized vegetation index. Based on GIS, the assessment model of debris flow susceptibility for semiarid region was built using AHP (analytical hierarchy process) method, so as to obtain the grid map of debris-flow susceptibility zoning in the study area. The study area is divided into small watershed as one unit for regional statistical analysis and classification. Finally, the debris-flow susceptibility assessment map based on small watershed analysis can be obtained. The assessment results show that the very high susceptibility area and high susceptibility area of debris flow are mainly distributed in the northeast, central and southwest banks of Jinsha River, with an area of about 1040.9 km^2, accounting for 35.7% of the study area. The area of low susceptibility and very low susceptibility for debris flow covers about 1341.7 km^2, accounting for 46.0% of the study area, mainly distributed in the high altitudes of western and southeastern study area. Through examination, the prediction successful rate of debris flow susceptibility is 62.2%. The present actual areas of debris flow with extremely high and high susceptibility are about 651.4 km^2, accounting for 51.1% of the total assessed debris-flow area, indicating the favorable comparative test results of susceptibility assessment against real debris flow occurrence.

Keywords: Dry valley · Debris flow · Susceptibility assessment
Analytic hierarchy process · Upper Jinsha River

© Springer Nature Singapore Pte Ltd. 2018
H. Yuan et al. (Eds.): GSKI 2017, CCIS 848, pp. 495–509, 2018.
https://doi.org/10.1007/978-981-13-0893-2_51

1 Introduction

Debris flow is a kind of common mass movement involving water and sediments occurring on steep slopes in the mountainous areas. China is one of the countries the most affected by debris flow disasters in the world. Debris flows are widely distributed in 26 provinces and cities in China, causing a direct economic loss of RMB 1 billion yuan on average and nearly one thousand deaths per year (Luo 2000). In recent years, in the semiarid southwest mountainous area and northwest regions of China, many large and super large debris flows occurred, such as plenty of debris flows induced by continuous rainfall in Beichuan County, Sichuan province after Wenchuan Earthquake on May 20, 2008; the catastrophic debris flow in Zhouqu, Gansu province on August 8, 2010 with 1463 deaths and 302 missing. Lots of research has been reported concering the formation conditions, sedimentary characteristics, influence factors and susceptibility assessment methods of debris flows (Coussot and Meunier 1996; Dai et al. 1999; 2001; Liu 2002; Li and Tang 2007; Nandi and Shakoor 2009; Blahut et al. 2010; Liu et al. 2010; Liu and Chen 2010; Xue et al. 2012; Pourghasemi et al. 2014).

GIS technology has the advantages of processing mass data and cartographic visualization function to become an efficient and convenient technology for assessment on the susceptibility and risk of debris flow and landslide disasters (Dai and Li 1994; Chen and Xie 1999; Zong et al. 2006; Li et al. 2008; Tang and Yang 2012; Li 2011; Popit et al. 2013; Yue et al. 2014). In the vast semiarid regions in the southwest China, because of unique geographical and geological environment, debris flow disasters are very frequent. To establish reasonable evaluation index based on GIS analysis is of great significance to improve the accuracy of assessment on the susceptibility and risk of regional debris flows.

Benzilan – Changbo segment in the upper reaches of Jinsha River is a typical semiarid region with annual precipitation in 300–400 mm (Zhang 1998; Chen et al. 2013), where is one of the most important regions for Chinese southwest hydropower development. At present, the research reports of the assessment on the susceptibility of semiarid debris flows in the upper reaches of Jinsha River is in a great lack. In this paper, based on GIS platform, the analytic hierarchy process (AHP) is used to establish index system for assessing debris-flow susceptibility in Benzilan-Changbo segment, which provides the basis for prevention and control work of debris flows in semiarid mountainous areas.

2 Regional Geologic and Geomorphologic Settings

Benzilan-Changbo segment is located in the upper reaches of Jinsha River at the junction of Sichuan, Yunnan and Tibet with the coordinates of 98° 55′–98° 25′ E, 28° 00′–29° 20′ N. In terms of geomorphic unit, this region is at the SE margin of Qinghai-Tibe Plateau and the middle of Hengduan Mountains (Fig. 1), belonging to the dry-hot valley of Hengduan Mountains (Zhang 1998; Chen et al. 2008). The precipitation mainly comes from the impact of southwest monsoon and southeast warm moist air flows. The mountains with an altitude of 4000 m a.s.l. and above are distributed on both sides of the valley in the study area, where rivers are incised deeply and the mountains on both sides have a relative relief of 1500–2000 m and above. Due to the high mountains on both sides, water vapor is difficult to access the valley, so as to form the so-called "rain shadow region" with the most sparse populated rainfall in Hengduan Mountains. The annual rainfall is only about 300 mm from Benzilan of Jinsha River valley to Sichuan Derong, and that is less than 400 mm from Batang to Derong (Chen et al. 2008, 2013). In the meantime, seasonal distribution of precipitation is uneven, and there is an obvious rainy and dry seasons. The rainy season starts from June to September, when the rainfall is very concentrated, general accounting for more than

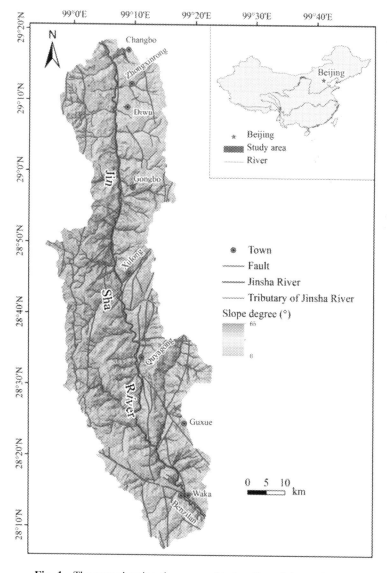

Fig. 1. The map showing the geographic location of the study area

80% of annual rainfall. The temperature changes greatly with days, years and vertical level varying. Due to strong physical weathering, the surface vegetation is sparse, and soil erosion is very serious.

The lithology in the study area are divided into five types (Fig. 2): (1) the Quaternry deposits, i.e. alluvium, taluvium and residual deposits; (2) Strongly weathered Mesozoic and Paleozoic slate and schist petrofabric; (3) Moderately weathered Mesozoic limestone and sandstone petrofabric; (4) Weakly weathered Mesozoic slate and volcanic rock petrofabric; (5) Intact intrusive rock and dike including granite, diorite and diabase etc.

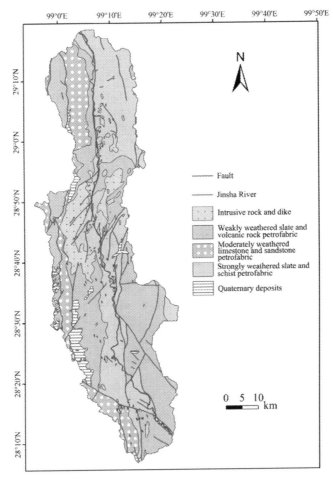

Fig. 2. Geological map of the Benzilan-Changbo reach of the upper Jinsha River

Four groups of faults have developed in the study area (Fig. 2), of which the trend is in the N-S, NW, NE and E-W direction, respectively. There are three major faults, namely the Jinshajiang Fault (F3), Zengdatong Fault (F14) and Nixi Fault (F19). The overall trend of the Jinshajiang Fault is in the N-S direction and it was a strike-thrust fault. The fault fracture zone is about 200 m in width. Several small faults have developed in the north section of the Jinshajiang Fault. The faulted landform and chronology show that the Jinshajiang Fault is still active (Xu et al. 2005; Wang et al. 2014). The Zengdatong Fault is also in the N-S direction and dips into W with a dip angle 60°. The width of the fault breccia is more than 50 m in the south section. A dozen of small faults have developed in the east side of the Zengdatong Fault. The Nixi Fault is located in the south part of the study area and trends in NW direction. Distinct fault fracture zone is distributed along the fault trend with a width of about tens of metres. According to the existing historical earthquake records, seismicity is relatively weak in the study area, and the historical earthquake magnitudes are all less than Ms. 5 (Chen et al. 2011).

3   Distribution Characteristics of Debris Flows

By field investigation and remote sensing image interpretation, there are a total of 91 debris flows into the main valley and tributaries of Jinsha River in the study area (Fig. 3), involving the watershed area of 1274 km^2, and accounting for 44% of total area. Among them, a total of 66 gully-type debris flows are widely developed, accounting for 73% of total number of debris flows, involving a great watershed area of 1242 km^2 with the average river basin area of 18.8 km^2 and average valley length of 6.14 km. A total of 25 slope-type debris flows are developed in the slope zone of Jinsha River, accounting for 27% of total number of debris flows, involving a small watershed area of 32 km^2 with average watershed area of 1.28 km^2 and average valley length of 1.94 km (Table 1).

A great deal of loose source materials favorable for the formation of debris flows are broadly developed, including three main types, i.e., slide deposits, collapse deposits and toppling landslide deposits. The major source materials is totaled at 84 positions with the total volume of 113 million m^3, including 11 positions of slide deposits with total volume of 58.01 million m^3, 55 positions of collapse deposits with total volume of 47.86 million m^3 and 18 positions of toppling landslide deposits with total volume of 7.15 million m^3 (Table 2). Combined with sparse vegetation, intense surface rock weathering and frequent mass movement or fault activity, the debris flow disasters are induced frequently in this region.

The development of debris flows in the study area were dominantly affected by the topography, lithology, fault structure, hydrologic conditions and other factors. Through statistical analysis on the debris flows occurring in the study area, it can be found that in the slope gradient range of 25°–35°, the area proportion of debris flow watershed is 40.4%, while in the slope gradient range less than 15° and greater than 45°, the area proportion of debris flow basin is only 12% (Fig. 4). Within the relative height difference of 250–700 m, the area proportion of debris flow watershed is 89%, while with relative height difference less than 250 m and greater than 700 m, the area proportion of debris flow watershed is only 11% (Fig. 5). The strong weathered slates and schist and rich fault fractured clasts in the study area provides very abundant loose solid matters for the development of debris flows.

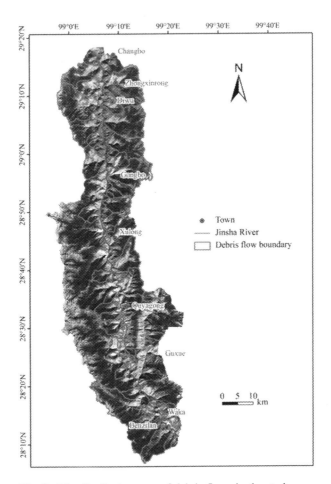

Fig. 3. The distribution map of debris flows in the study area

Table 1. Development characteristics of debris-flows in the study area

Types	No. of gullies	Percentage of debris flow (%)	Channel length (km)	Average area watershed (km^2)	Sum of area (km^2)
Gully type	66	73%	6.14	18.8	1242
Slope type	25	27%	1.94	1.28	32

Table 2. The types, quantities and volume of source materials for debris flows

Types	Quantities	Volume (m³)
Slide deposits	11	58,010,000
Collapse deposits	55	47,860,000
Toppling landslide deposits	18	7,150,000
Total	84	120,170,000

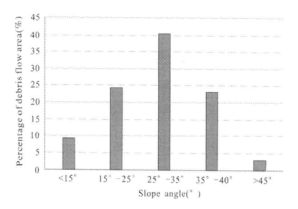

Fig. 4. Distribution of slope gradient of the debris flows

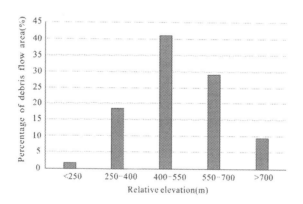

Fig. 5. Relative height difference of the debri-flow watersheds

4   Assessment on Debris-Flow Susceptibility

4.1   Selection of Assessment Indices

The grid with 30 m × 30 m is taken as an assessment unit. Based on analysis on the distribution of debris flows and its impact factors in the study area, six assessment indices are selected, including lithology, fault structure, slope gradient, relative relief of the watershed, annual average rainfall and normalized vegetation index. By

ArcGIS10.0 software, the high-precision DEM, topographic map, rainfall and other data are used to obtain layers of five indices, i.e., rock types, fault structure, slope gradient, relative relief of the watershed and annual average rainfall. The Landsat8 images are used to get the NDVI layer of normalized vegetation index. The Level-5 quantitative standard is used for normalized processing on assessment indices. The level with maximum impact on the formation of debris flow is assigned to 5, while that with the smallest impact is assigned to 1. Finally, the gradation table of assessment indices of debris flow susceptibility is obtained (Table 3).

Table 3. The classification and valuation of assessment indexes

Assignment susceptibility level	5 Very high	4 High	3 Moderate	2 Low	1 Very low
Lithology	I	II	III	IV	V
Fault structure	0–100 m	100–200 m	200–500 m	500–800 m	>800 m
Slope gradient	25°–35°	35°–45°	15°–25°	<15°	>45°
Relative elevation	400–550 m	550–700 m	250–400 m	>700 m	<250 m
Annual average rainfall (from June to September)	>400 mm	400–300 mm	300–200 mm	200–100 mm	<100 mm
NDVI value	0–0.1	0.1–0.3	0.3–0.5	0.5–0.6	0.6–1

Notes: I—Quaternary deposits; II—Strongly weathered slate and schist petrofabric; III—Moderately weathered limestone and sandstone petrofabric; IV—Weakly weathered slate and volcanic rock petrofabric; V—Intrusive rock and dike

4.2 Weighting Calculation of Assessment Indices

The AHP (analytic hierarchy process) method is used to determine the weight value of each index with the following steps (Saaty 1980):

(1) To establish a hierarchy model (Fig. 6);
(2) To establish the judgment matrix;

The values in the judgment matrix are the judgments of relative importance between different factors at all levels. In order to make quantitative judgment, 1–9 scaling method is used to give quantitative scaling for different situations in AHP. The elements at the same level are compared in importance, and the compared results are indicated by values to get the judgment matrix of this level (Eq. 1):

$$B = (b_{ij})_{n \times n}, b_{ij} > 0, b_{ij} = \frac{1}{b_{ji}}, (i,j = 1,2,3\ldots n) \tag{1}$$

where b_{ij} is the ratio of relative importance between element B_i and B_j.

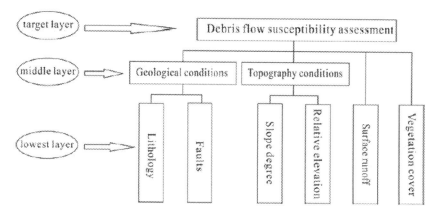

Fig. 6. The hierarchical model of the grade assessment indexes for debris flows

(3) Consistency test of AHP.

Matlab software is used to calculate the maximum characteristic root $\lambda_{\max}$ of judgment matrix and its corresponding eigenvector, and then the eigenvector is normalized to W. The element value of W is the weight of relative importance ranking for the index at the same level relative to a certain index. Usually, CI value is used to check the consistency of judgment matrix (Eq. 2):

$$CI = \frac{\lambda_{\max} - n}{n - 1} \tag{2}$$

where n is the order number of judgment matrix.

Because consistency deviation is likely due to random reason, CI is required to compare with average random consistency RI, so as to obtain the test coefficient CR. Average random consistency index RI is associated with the order of judgment matrix, and their relationship is shown in Table 4:

Table 4. The values of average consistency index RI

n	1	2	3	4	5	6	7	8	9	10	11	12	13	14
RI	0	0	0.52	0.89	1.12	1.26	1.36	1.41	1.46	1.49	1.52	1.54	1.56	1.58

The judgment standard of test coefficient CR = CI/RI is shown as below:

CR < 0.1: judgment matrix has a good consistency with reasonable judgment;
CR = 0.1: judgment matrix has a good consistency with relatively reasonable judgment;
CR > 0.1: judgment matrix is not in conformity with the consistency principle, and the judgment matrix value should be readjusted until satisfied.

According to the principle of AHP, the weight value of single-level index is calculated first, and then the total weight value of assessment indices is calculated to obtain the final total weight value of assessment index, shown in Table 5.

Table 5. The weighted values of the grade assessment indexes for debris-flow susceptibility

Weight of the first hierarchy index	The second hierarchy indexes	Relative weight of the second hierarchy indexes	Total weight of the second hierarchy indexes
Geological conditions 0.2896	Lithology	0.7500	0.2172
	Fault	0.2500	0.0724
Topography conditions 0.4783	Slope degree	0.5455	0.2609
	Relative elevation	0.4545	0.2174
Hydrogeological conditions 0.1448	Annual average rainfall	1	0.1448
Vegetation cover 0.0873	NDVI value	1	0.0873

4.3 Debris-Flow Susceptibility Zoning

On GIS platform, the grid computing tool of spatial analysis module is used for weighted superposition of grading assignment layer of each assessment index, so as to obtain the assessment grid map of debris-flow susceptibility in the study area. The susceptibility index of debris flow is calculated according to the following equation:

$$R = \sum_{i=1}^{n} C_i \cdot W_i \tag{3}$$

where R is the R susceptibility index of debris flow, W_i is the weight of assessment index, and C_i is the grading assignment layer of assessment index.

The hydrological analysis module of ArcGIS10.0 software is used to extract small watersheds in the study area. The water threshold of 5000, 8000, 10000 and 15000 is based to extract the water system. When water threshold is 10000, the extracted water system is consistent with actual water system, so the water threshold of 10000 is selected for watershed division in the study area. The watershed extraction results are compared with remote sensing images to check whether the ridge lines, valley lines and river network lines are consistent with remote sensing images or not. Then, the unreasonable divisions are further revised. Finally, the study area is divided into 217 small watersheds.

The divided small watershed units are superposed on the assessment grid map of debris-flow susceptibility. With the aid of regional statistical tools, the average value of susceptibility index of all grids within the scope of watershed units is taken as the susceptibility value of this watershed to obtain the regional statistical map of debris-flow susceptibility in the study area. Then, the grid re-classification tool of GIS spatial analysis is adopted to divide the statistical map of debris-flow susceptibility into five levels, i.e., very low, low, moderate, high and very high susceptibility area. Finally, the assessment map of debris-flow susceptibility based on small watershed unit in Benzilan-Changbo segment along the upper reaches of Jinsha River is obtained (Fig. 7).

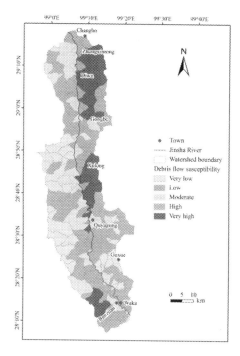

Fig. 7. Debris-flow susceptibility map of the Benzilan-Changbo reach in the upper Jinsha River

5 Assessment Results Analysis and Test

The classification results of debris-flow suceptibility are shown in Table 6. The results show that in the study **area**, the very high susceptibility area of debris flow is mainly distributed in the Nibulong – Gongbo segment on the northeast, Xulong – Niwu segment in the middle and the southwest Shusong surrounding areas. The very high susceptibility area covers 485.7 km^2, accounting for 16.7% of total study area, where the developed debris flows have an area of 327.9 km^2, accounting for 67.5% of the very high susceptibility area. In this area, the mainly exposed schist and slates show serious weathering and a number of fault fractured zones are well develped, where the collapse and slide deposits are widely distributed. Combined with scarce vegetation coverage and concentrated rainfall in summer seasons, the debris flows are prone to occur frequently in the area. The high susceptibility area presents scattered distribution along the Jinsha River valley, accounting for 19.0% of total study area, where the developed debris flows has an area of 323.5 km^2, accounting for 58.3% of high susceptibility area. In this area, debris flows occurrs where the strong weathered schist and slates exposed. The moderate susceptibility area accounts for 18.3% of total study area, where the developed debris flows has an area of 387.0 km^2, accounting for 50.6% of middle susceptibility area. In this area, the lithology mainly consists of slates, fine-grained sandstones, schist and volcanic rock with medium weathering. The low susceptibility area and very low susceptibility area cover about 1341.7 km^2, accounting for 46.0% of total study area, mainly distributed in the west and southeast high altitude areas of the study area. In these areas, the lithology mainly consists of relatively hard slates, limestone and intrusive rocks and the vegetation is well developed, where the ground surface erosion is relatively weak.

Table 6. Statistical results of debris-flow susceptibility zoning

Assessment results	Susceptibility region (km²)	Percentage of Susceptibility region (%)	Actual debris flow area (km²)	Percentage of actual debris flow area (%)	Percentage of actual debris flow area in Susceptibility region (%)
Very high	485.7	16.7%	327.9	25.7%	67.5%
High	555.2	19.0%	323.5	25.4%	58.3%
Moderate	533.8	18.3%	387.0	21.2%	50.6%
Low	851.4	29.2%	158.9	23.9%	35.7%
Very low	490.3	16.8%	55.0	3.8%	9.9%

In order to test the assessment results of debris-flow susceptibility, the relation between the cumulative percentage of predicted debris-flow area and the cumulative percentage of actual debris flow area is used to construct the test curve (Fig. 8). According to test results, the very high susceptibility area and high susceptibility area cover about 1040.9 km², accounting for 35.7% of total study area. In these two areas, the area of actually developed debris flow is 651.4 km², accounting for 51.1% of total debris-flow area and 62.6% of the total area of very high susceptibility area and high susceptibility area, respectively. It indicates that the susceptibility assessment results have favorable test effects compared with the actual developed debris flows.

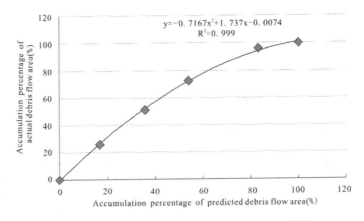

Fig. 8. Success rate graph for debris-flow susceptibility

The test curve is shaped as "convex", suggesting the good assessment result of debris-flow susceptibility (Kamp et al. 2008; Zezere et al. 2008; Xu et al. 2009). The area beneath the test curve can be used to quantitatively denote the success rate of susceptibility prediction. After integral, the area beneath the curve is 62.2%, showing that the assessment result of debris-flow susceptibility has not yet reached the very ideal effect. The reasons may be as follows: on one hand, during the preparation of grading quantitative map of six indices for susceptibility assessment, the grid of 30 m × 30 m is used as an assessment unit and the watershed characteristics of debris flow are possibly ignored; on the other hand, the precision may be not sufficient to select the average annual rainfall as one of the quantitative index of hydraulic geological condition for debris-flow suceptibility.

6 Conclusion

Benzilan – Changbo segment in the upper reaches of Jinsha River is located in the arid-hot valley of Henduan Mountains with annual rainfall of 300 mm–400 mm, belonging to the typical semiarid area. This study area belongs to the mountainous valley area with the slope generally above 30°; the lithology is commonly weak, mainly consisting of schist and slates. In the meantime, the temperature difference is bigger, rock physical weathering is strong, and the slope deformation and failure is more severe, leading to abundant loose source materials along the slope (dominated by collapse, slide and toppling landslide deposits). Under the condition of short-duration heavy rainfall, it is easy to stimulate the formation of debris flows.

Combined with field investigation in detail and remote sensing image interpretation of debris flows in the study area, six indices, i.e., lithology, structural fault, slope gradient, relative relief of the basin, annual average rainfall and normalized vegetation index, are taken as the assessment indices of debris-flow susceptibility.

Using the advantage of AHP method able to deal with complex problems, the qualitative and quantitative combination analysis is conducted to determine the weight of assessment index, which not only reduces the influence of human subjective factors, but also improves the reliability of susceptibility assessment results. According to the susceptibility degree of debris flow, the study area is divided into five levels. Among them, the very high susceptibility area and high susceptibility area cover 1040.9 km^2, accounting for 35.7% of total study area. Considering among 9 countrysides in the study area, there are 4 countrysides distributed in the very high susceptibility area of debris flows, severely threatened by the possible debris flow disasters, it is suggested that monitoring and forecasting of debris flows should be necessary to strengthen so as to prevent and mitigate the potential debris-flow disasters.

Acknowledgements. The study was supported by the National Natural Science Foundation of China (grants nos. 41571012 and 41230743) and the Fundamental Research Funds for the Central Universities (Grant grant no. 2652015060). We sincerely thank the anonymous reviewers for their time and effort devoted to improving the manuscript.

References

Blahut, J., van Westen, C.J., Sterlacchini, S.: Analysis of landslide inventories for accurate prediction of debris-flow source areas. Geomorphology **119**, 36–51 (2010)

Chen, J., Dai, F.C., Lv, T.Y., Cui, Z.J.: Holocene landslide-dammed lake deposits in the Upper Jinsha River, SE Tibetan Plateau and their ages. Quatern. Int. **298**, 107–113 (2013)

Chen, J., Dai, F.C., Yao, X.: Holocene debris-flow deposits and their implications on climate in the upper Jinsha River valley. China. Geomorphology **93**, 493–500 (2008)

Chen, J., Cui, Z.J., Dai, F.C., Xu, C.: Genetic mechanism of the major debris-flow deposits at Benzilan-Dari segment, the upper Jinsha River. J. Mount. Sci. **29**(3), 312–319 (2011). (in Chinese with English abstract)

Chen, X.Q., Xie, H.: Study on Regionalization of debris flow danger degree under GIS support—taking the reservoir area of Xiangjiaba, Xiluodu water-pow er engineering as an example. J. Soil Eros. Soil Water Conserv. **5**(6), 46–50 (1999). (in Chinese with English abstract)

Coussot, P., Meunier, M.: Recognition, classification and mechanical description of debris flows. Earth Sci. Rev. **40**, 209–227 (1996)

Dai, F.C., Lee, C.F., Wang, S.J.: Analysis of slide-debris flows on Lantau Island. Hong Kong Eng. Geol. **51**(4), 279–290 (1999)

Dai, F.C., Lee, C.F., Li, J., Xu, Z.W.: Assessment of landslide susceptibility on the natural terrain of Lantau Island. Hong Kong Environ. Geol. **40**(3), 381–391 (2001)

Dai, F.C., Li, J.: Applications of geographical information systems in landslide studies. Geol. Sci. Technol. Inform. **12**(2), 65–70 (1994). (in Chinese with English abstract)

Kamp, U., Growley, B.J., Khattak, G.A., Owen, L.A.: GIS-based landslide susceptibility mapping for the 2005 Kashmir earthquake region. Geomorphology **101**(4), 631–642 (2008)

Li, K., Tang, C.: Progress in research on debris flow hazard assessment. J. Catastrophology **22** (1), 106–110 (2007). (in Chinese with English abstract)

Liu, J.F., Huang, J.C., Ou, G.Q., Lv, J., Fan, J.R.: Susceptibility evaluation of debris flow in the Wudu District, Longnan City, Gansu province. Chin. J. Geol. Hazard Control **21**(4), 8–12 (2010). (in Chinese with English abstract)

Liu, X.L.: Debris flow assessment in China: a review and perspective. J. Natural Disaster **11**(4), 1–8 (2002). (in Chinese with English abstract)

Liu, X.L., Chen, Y.J.: Application of debris flow risk zonation: an example of West Sichuan. Sci. Geogr. Sin. **30**(4), 558–565 (2010). (in Chinese with English abstract)

Li, W.L., Tang, C., Yang, W.N., Yuan, P.X.: Research on application of GIS and RS in debris flow hazard zonation at county level—a case study in Luding County of Sichuan province. J. Catastrophology **23**(2), 71–75 (2008). (in Chinese with English abstract)

Li, Y.H.: The Assessment of debris flow based on watershed scale: a case study in Wenchuan county of Minjiang River Valley. Chengdu University of Technology, pp. 21–45 (2011). (in Chinese with English abstract)

Luo, Y.H.: Assessment of danger degree of mudrock flow. China Min. Mag. **9**(6), 70–72 (2000)

Nandi, A., Shakoor, A.: A GIS-based landslide susceptibility evaluation using bivariate and multivariate statistical analyses. Eng. Geol. **110**, 11–20 (2009)

Popit, T., Rožič, B., Šmuc, A., Kokalj, Ž., Verbovšek, T., Košir, A.: A lidar, GIS and basic spatial statistic application for the study of ravine and palaeo-ravine evolution in the upper Vipava valley. SW Slovenia. Geomorphol. **204**, 1–8 (2013)

Pourghasemi, H.R., Moradi, H.R., Fatemi Aghda, S.M., Gokceoglu, C., Pradhan, B.: GIS-based landslide susceptibility mapping with probabilistic likelihood ratio and spatial multi-criteria evaluation models (North of Tehran, Iran). Arab. J. Geosci. **7**(5), 1857–1878 (2014)

Saaty, T.L.: The Analytical Hierarchy Process. Mcgraw-Hill Inc., New York (1980)

Tang, Y., Yang, WN.: GIS-based hazard assessment for potential debris flows in Wenchuan county after M 8.0 earthquake. Shanghai Land Resour. **33**(3), 57–60 (2012). (in Chinese with English abstract)

Wang, P.F., Chen, J., Dai, F.C., Long, W., Xu, C., Sun, J.M., Cui, Z.J.: Chronology of relict lake deposits around the Suwalong paleolandslide in the upper Jinsha River, SE Tibetan Plateau: Implications to Holocene tectonic perturbations. Geomorphology **217**, 193–203 (2014)

Xu, C., Dai, F.C., Dai, X., Tu, X.F., Sun, Y., Wang, Z.Y.: GIS-based landslide susceptibility assessment using analytical hierarchy process in Wenchuan earthquake region. Chin. J. Rock Mech. Eng. **28**(Suppl. 2), 3981–3998 (2009)

Xu, X.W., Zhang, P.Z., Wen, X.Z., Qin, Z.L., Chen, G.H., Zhu, A.L.: Features of active tectonics and recurrence behaviors of strong earthquakes in the western Sichuan Province and its adjacent regions. Seism. Geol. **27**(3), 446–461 (2005). (in Chinese with English abstracts)

Xue, D.J., He, Z.W., Fu, Q.: Application of analytic hierarchy process in evaluating the easy eruption of debris flow disaster in Luhuo county. Geospatial Inf. **10**(6), 139–141 (2012). (in Chinese with English abstract)

Yue, X.L., Huang, M., Quan, B., Wang, Z.S., Gu, X.P.: Debris-flow hazard assessment in Bijie district, Guizhou province. Chin. J. Geol. Hazard Control **25**(1), 12–15 (2014). (in Chinese with English abstract)

Zezere, J.L., Garcia, R.A.C., Oliveira, S.C., Reis, E.: Probabilistic landslide risk analysis considering direct costs in the area north of Lisbon (Portugal). Geomorphology **94**(3/4), 467–495 (2008)

Zhang, R.Z.: The dry valley of Hengduan Mountain Area, pp. 1–13. Science Press, Beijing (1998). (in Chinese with English abstract)

Zong, W.Q., Pan, M., Li, T.F., Wu, Z.X., Lv, G.X.: Research on the key problems of landslide, debris flow hazard zonation based on GIS. Earth Sci. Front. **13**(2), 185–190 (2006)

Influence of Index Weights on Land Ecological Security Evaluation: The Case Study of Chengdu Plain Economic Zone, China

Ruoheng Tian[1], Chengyi Huang[1,2(✉)], Liangji Deng[3],
Conggang Fang[4], Weizhong Zeng[1], Yongjiang Lei[5], Lianxin Yang[5],
and Chao Xue[5]

[1] College of Management, Sichuan Agricultural University,
Chengdu 611130, China
chengyihuang@sicau.edu.cn
[2] College of Water Conservancy and Hydropower Engineering,
Sichuan Agricultural University, Yaan 625014, China
[3] College of Resources, Sichuan Agricultural University,
Chengdu 611130, China
[4] Chengdu Land and Resources Information Center, Chengdu 610072, China
[5] College of Economics, Sichuan Agricultural University,
Chengdu 611130, China

Abstract. Land ecological security (LES) evaluation is an essential process for land-use planning in China. Analyzing the LES status of rapid urbanization areas has a significant impact on decision-making of urban development. Based on the integration of ordered weighted averaging (OWA) and sensitivity analysis, this paper focuses on hightening the understanding of indictor weights's influences to LES evaluation and assisting in making a suitable assignment of weights in Chengdu Plain Economic Zone. The results highlight how the statu of LES, in 2014, is closely linked to the administrator's attitude and corresponding indictor weights. Particularly, compared the initial results with situations of the focus on key indicators (like population densit, Chemical fertilizer dosage and et al.) or non-key indicators (such as energy consumption and sewage treatment), There are at least 62.5% differences in the evaluation results of ecological safety level. Meanwhile, the sensitivity analysis confirms that the indictor weights of population density, Grain yield per hectare and agricultural mechanization level are sensitive parameters for LES results. Decision makers should focus on the effects and rationality, brought by weight changes of there indictors. These methodologies can reduce the uncertainty of results caused by weight assignment, and provide for formulating LES evaluation standards in this region.

Keywords: Land use · Ecological security · Ordered weighted averaging
Sensitivity analysis · Chengdu Plain Economic Zone

© Springer Nature Singapore Pte Ltd. 2018
H. Yuan et al. (Eds.): GSKI 2017, CCIS 848, pp. 510–519, 2018.
https://doi.org/10.1007/978-981-13-0893-2_52

1   Introduction

With the rapid industrialization and urbanization, land use change in land ecosystem leads to a collection of land ecological issues, especially the degradation of soil quality and the reduction of ecosystem service value [1, 2]. Therefore, to mitigate these problems, more and more researchers pay attention to the study of land ecological security (LES). The objective of LES is to maintain land ecosystems at an unthreatened statu while satisfy the demands of the development and survival, aiming at reaching to the synergetic state between land ecosystem, social and economical development [3].

At present, research on LES mainly has been focused on the aspects of basic theory definition [4], application framework design [5], selection of evaluation indictors [6] and innovation of evaluation methods [7]. In view of evaluation methodologies, catastrophe theory, ecosystem service value, and matter-element analysis have been widely used [8–10], which expand the system of methods.

The weight assignment of indictors is an unrobustness processes in the afore-mentioned method of LES [11]. It should be recognized that traditional method of weight assignment, such as the Analytical Hierarchy Process (AHP) or entropy weight process, is lack of consideration about the uncertainty change of policy orientations and land ecology status. Thus, as for spatial scales, some studies using the ordered weighted averaging (OWA) show that different weight assignment, reflecting distinct policy guidances and cognitive attitudes, have a significant impact on the evaluation results [12]. For temporal scales, variable weight model is adopted to simulate the attribution of dynamic change in land ecosystem [13].

A few studies have applied to combine variable weight and sensitivity analysis for LES. In other research areas, Chen et al. [14] presented a sensitivity analysis method for land suitability evaluation, identifying the sensitive indicators whose weight changes have a intense influence on results. Then, Romano et al. [15] employed the OWA and sensitive analysis procedure to represent great detail results and generate a series of decision strategies. Therefore, the objective of this study is to adopt OWA and sensitive analysis procedure, identifying the sensitivity of indictor's weight change to LES results and providing more decision situation information to support for land and agricultural management departments.

2   Study Area and Data Source

2.1   Study Area

Chengdu Plain Economic Zone is located in the middle part of Sichuan Province, China between 101°51′ and 108°31′ E, 25°51′ and 33°03′ N. It encompasses 78 thousand km². It governs 8 prefecture-level cities which belong to subtropical semi-humid climate and subtropical monsoon climate. The annual average temperature is 17–22 °C and the annual average precipitation is about 800–1,100 mm. This economic zone is the area where population and economy are highly centralized in Sichuan Province. Since Chengdu has become a national central city, rapid economic development has been gained in this region during recent years. In 2014, the zone had about 37.29 million inhabitants, taking up 45.81% of the total population in the whole province. Its GDP reached 1.78 trillion Yuan, occupying 59.10% of total GDP in Sichuan Province.

2.2 Data Source

The data needed by this paper come from Statistical Yearbook of Sichuan Province 2015, China City Statistical Yearbook 2015, territorial resources bulletins of Sichuan Province, and statistical bulletins of national economy and social development in various prefecture-level cities.

3 Methodology

3.1 Evaluation Creteria Selection

In this paper, domestic and overseas scholars' relevant researches are summarized [16]. According to various experts' opinions, 15 indexes were retained to establish the land ecological security evaluation system of Chengdu Plain Economic Zone (Table 1).

Table 1. Evaluation index system of land ecological security in Chengdu Plain

Factors	Indictors	weight
Resource	Per capita cultivated land area/(hm$^2 \cdot$person^{-1}) $v1$	0.068
	Grain yield per hectare/(t$\cdot$hm^{-2}) $v2$	0.073
	Annual decrease rate of cultivated land/(%) $v3$	0.059
	Water and soil coordination degree/(%) $v4$	0.070
Environment	Forest coverage rate/(%) $v5$	0.058
	Fertilizer dosage per unit area of cultivated land/(kg$\cdot$hm^{-2}) $v6$	0.074
	Energy consumption per unit GDP/(t standard coal$\cdot$10,000 Yuan^{-1}) $v7$	0.058
	Sewage treatment rate (%)	0.055
Economy	GDP per area/(100 million Yuan$\cdot$km^{-2})	0.061
	Proportion of tertiary industry output value in GDP/(%)	0.072
	Per capita net income of rural families/Yuan	0.069
Society	Natural population growth rate/(%)	0.064
	Population density/(person$\cdot$km^{-2})	0.078
	Urbanization rate/(%)	0.071
	Agricultural mechanization level per unit area of cultivated land/ (kW$\cdot$hm^{-2})	0.070

3.2 Indictors Weight and Results Classification

In order to eliminate the influence of dimensions between indexes on the evaluation, this paper conducts standardization treatment for original data via the maximum difference normalization method [8]. The weights are determined by the AHP method

(Table 1). As for the division of security levels, natural break points are classified in ArcGIS10.1 according to the initial result. Land ecological security evaluation of the research area is divided into 5 levels (Table 2).

Table 2. Classification of land ecological security

Level	Harshness	Risk	Critica security	General security	Security
Evaluation score	0–0.36	0.36–0.46	0.46–0.55	0.55–0.70	0.70–1.00

3.3   Ordered Weighted Averaging (OWA)

The OWA evaluation method was proposed in 1998. In this method, index weights and ordered weights are integrated into combination weights. The ordered weight is changed by adjusting the risk level coefficient α, so as to realize the change of weight assignment methods. The change of decision-making risk coefficient α has reflected the transformation of decision makers' focus on evaluation indexes of decision-making and weight assignment issues. When $\alpha = 1$ (decision makers' attitudes have no preference), the ordered weights are equal and the evaluation result is decided by initial weights and data values of the indexes. When $\alpha < 1$, decision makers pay attention to the importance degrees of key indexes in the rating system within the region. On the contrary, if $\alpha > 1$, decision makers will pay close attention to information reflected by indexes seeming to have a general importance degree and unimportant indexes. The OWA algorithm has many forms, and this paper will choose a frequently-used one, as described in the following [17]:

To sum up, the OWA evaluation result about land ecological security evaluation of the ith city is:

$$OWA_i = \sum_{j=1}^{n} \left(\frac{u_j v_j}{\sum\limits_{j=1}^{n} u_j v_j} \right) Z_{ij} \tag{1}$$

In the above formula, Z_{ij} means the standardized data about jth index of the ith city; u_j represents the initial index weight of jth index (Table 1); v_j denotes the ordered weight of this index. The calculation formula is as follows:

$$v_j = \left(\sum_{k=1}^{j} w_k \right)^{\alpha} - \left(\sum_{k=1}^{j-1} w_k \right)^{\alpha} \tag{2}$$

α signifies the risk level coefficient, reflecting evaluators' strategies and preferences in the evaluation system. See Table 3 for common α coefficients and relevant

Table 3. The ordered weight of land ecological security indexes

Risk coefficient α	α → 0	α = 0.1	α = 0.5	α = 1	α = 2	α = 10	α → ∞
Preference and attitude	Attention to key indexes			Neutral	Attention to non-key indexes		
Population density v_1	1.000	0.812	0.354	0.067	0.016	0.000	0.000
Fertilizer dosage per unit area of cultivated land v_2	0.000	0.055	0.138	0.067	0.043	0.000	0.000
Grain yield per hectare v_3	0.000	0.033	0.100	0.067	0.064	0.000	0.000
Proportion of tertiary industry output value in GDP v_4	0.000	0.023	0.079	0.067	0.080	0.000	0.000
Urbanization rate v_5	0.000	0.017	0.065	0.067	0.091	0.002	0.000
Agricultural mechanization level per unit area of cultivated land v_6	0.000	0.014	0.055	0.067	0.097	0.007	0.000
Water and soil coordination degree v_7	0.000	0.011	0.046	0.067	0.099	0.019	0.000
Per capita net income of rural families v_8	0.000	0.009	0.039	0.067	0.098	0.042	0.000
Per capita cultivated land area v_9	0.000	0.007	0.033	0.067	0.093	0.076	0.000
Natural population growth rate v_{10}	0.000	0.006	0.027	0.067	0.085	0.117	0.000
GDP per area forecast v_{11}	0.000	0.005	0.022	0.067	0.075	0.156	0.000
Annual decrease rate of cultivated land v_{12}	0.000	0.004	0.017	0.067	0.062	0.180	0.000
Forest coverage rate v_{13}	0.000	0.003	0.013	0.067	0.048	0.178	0.000
Regional GDP energy consumption v_{14}	0.000	0.002	0.008	0.067	0.033	0.143	0.000
Sewage treatment rate v_{15}	0.000	0.001	0.004	0.067	0.017	0.080	1.000

connotations. w_k refers to the importance degree of kth indexes, and the calculation method is as follows:

$$w_k = \frac{n - r_k + 1}{\sum_{l=1}^{k}(n - r_l + 1)} \qquad (k = 1, 2, \cdots n) \qquad (3)$$

In the above formula, n means the number of evaluation indexes; r_k is the importance degree of kth index. And the value of r_k is decided according to rank the standardized data $Z_{i1}, Z_{i2}, \ldots, Z_{in}$ in descending order. r_k is equal to 1 means that the kth index is the most important; 2 indicates the secondary importance degree, and n signifies the lowest importance degree.

However, the aforementioned ordering method for r_k makes the different city have different weight arrangements, which is not conducive to the provincial department to consider the impact of weight arrangements on the assessment results of cities. Hence, the index ranking method in this paper is changed into ranking according to initial index weights (Table 1) in descending order, which will guarantee consistent ranking results in various regions.

3.4   One-at-a-Time (OAT) Sensitivity Analysis

The OAT method is to explore the influence of variation on evaluation results by changing the single index weight. In this paper, OAT weight sensitivity analysis is mainly conducted to determine which index weight changes are predominant factors and have a great effect on model output. The specific process is as follows [18]:

(1)   The weight of index j is changed into:

$$\overline{W}_j(\mathrm{cr}) = (1 + cr) \times W_j \tag{4}$$

In the above formula, $\overline{W}_j$ means the weight of index j after the change; cr indicates the change rate of the index; W_j represents the original index weight.

$$\overline{W}_k(\mathrm{cr}) = \left(\frac{1 - \overline{W}_j}{1 - W_j}\right) \times W_k \tag{5}$$

In the above formula, $\overline{W}_k(\mathrm{cr})$ means the weight of index k after the adjustment; W_k indicates the original weight of this index, $j \neq k$.

(3)   The comprehensive evaluation result of the evaluation object after the weight of index j is changed is calculated:

$$R_i\left(W_j, cr\right) = \overline{W}_j \times Z_{ij} + \sum_{k=1}^{n} \overline{W}_k \times Z_{ik} \tag{6}$$

In the above formula, Ri(Wj, cr) means the evaluation result of object i after Wj is changed according to the change rate cr; Zij indicates the standardized data of index j in region i; Zik represents the standardized data of index k, $j \neq k$.

(4)   The result change rate (CR) triggered by weight change is calculated.

$$\mathrm{CR}_i\left(W_j, cr\right) = \frac{R_i(W_j, cr) - R_0}{R_0} \times 100\% \tag{7}$$

In the above formula, $\mathrm{CR}_i\left(W_j, cr\right)$ means the change rate of the evaluation result about object i after W_j is changed according to the change rate cr. R0 represents the initial evaluation result before weight change.

(5) The mean absolute change rate (MACR) of the result triggered by weight change
is calculated.

$$\text{MACR}(W_j, cr) = \sum_{i=1}^{N} \frac{1}{N} \times \left| \frac{R_i(W_j, cr) - R_0}{R_0} \right| \times 100\% \qquad (8)$$

In the above formula, $\text{MACR}(W_j, cr)$ means the absolute value of the mean result
change rate of evaluation results about N objects after the weight of index j is changed
according to the change rate cr.

4 Result and Analysis

4.1   Influence of Different Preferences and Attitudes on Results

According to the principle of OWA algorithm, spatial visualization expression is
realized for the result after the information valued by decision makers is transformed
from key indexes into non-critical indexes. The ultimate results are shown in Fig. 1.

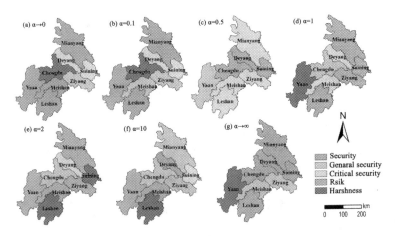

Fig. 1. The evaluation result of land ecological security obtained with changing risk-taking

When $\alpha = 1$ is changed into $\alpha \rightarrow 0$, decision makers pay attention to key indexes
like population density, fertilizer dosage per unit area of cultivated land and grain yield
per hectare only, but ignore the influences of other factors (Table 3). Finally, only
population density is considered. The situation of Fig. 1(a) will be neglected as an
extreme case. According to Fig. 1(d), (c) and (b), Chengdu undergoes a great pressure
in the aspects of grain yield and population density, so it presents a diametrically
opposite state in security change when compared with other cities. With the increase of
the emphasis on population density factor, the situation of ecological security ecological deteriorates gradually. In Deyang City, the evaluation result decreases at first

and then increases. Deyang City involves relatively higher population density, greater fertilizer consumption for cultivated land and lower tertiary industry output value than most regions. Meanwhile, compared with the situation where $\alpha = 0.1$, when $\alpha = 0.5$, decision makers will pay more attention to fertilizer consumption for cultivated land and tertiary industry output value. Therefore, the ecological security in Deyang City shows a deterioration trend. This is indirectly consistent with the situation in which the heavy metal content in farm lands exceeds the standard and the economic growth is mainly promoted by industrial development in Deyang City during recent years.

When $\alpha = 1$ is changed into $\alpha \to 0$, decision makers' major methods to know about LES are transformed from comprehensive consideration for resource, economy and society into emphasis on environment as well as development factors of resource, economy and society. According to Fig. 1(d), (e) and (f), with the weakening of the importance of economic indexes, the ecological security evaluation results in various regions have taken a turn for the better gradually. However, the situations in Meishan and Leshan are just opposite. As for the major reasons, Meishan and Leshan are treated as the key industry planning area of Sichuan Tianfu New Area and an important responsible region of industrial transfer for Chengdu City respectively. When modern industries are developed vigorously, great energy consumption is caused. Meanwhile, associated industries of urban environmental protection covering sewage treatment are still at a relatively low level in the region, remaining to be improved.

4.2   Sensitive Analysis About Weight Changes of Indictors

The variable weight simulation analysis on land ecological security evaluation in Chengdu Plain Economic Zone has quantitatively shown that the uncertainty of decision maker's policy preference and attitude will influence the results. Whereas, Which indexes are important factors resulting in the change of results in the process of concern change? Which factors should decision makers pay attention to in the process of further modifying the index weights for the weight assignment scheme proposed? To solve these problems, we assign the step size at 2% and weight range at $\pm 40\%$, using the OAT analysis.

As shown in Fig. 2(a), there are some differences in the sensitivity level of the evaluation results in Chengdu Plain Economic Zone to the change of various index weights. By taking the situation where the change rate of a single index weight is -40% as an example, the evaluation result is the most sensitive to the weight change of population density, grain yield per hectare and agricultural mechanization level per unit area of cultivated land. When the weight of population density decreases by 40%, the mean of absolute change rate of result (MACR) in the research area is 2.64%. The weights of various indexes decline by 40% respectively, and the corresponding value of MACR is 1.73%. The result change caused by the decrease of the weight of energy consumption per unit GDP is the smallest, and the value of MACR is 1.42%. Overall, the evaluation result is most sensitive to the weight change of social indexes (Fig. 2 (b)), and the mean value of MACR is 2.20%. The sensibility degrees of result changes triggered by index weight changes are as follows: society factor > resource factor > economy factor > environment factor.

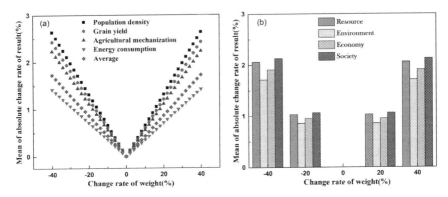

Fig. 2. The result of weight sensitivity analysis simulation runs in study area

5   Conclusion and Discussion

In this study, the OAT results show that the indictor of energy consumption, which is allocated low weight, has a low-sensitivity influence. This conclusion is consistent with Erqi Xu et al. [18]. Meanwhile, the indictor of population density, having a high weight and sensitivity influence, should be considered seriously. Compared with the OWA results of Romano et al. [15], the evaluation results of OWA don't present the homogeneity results at the situation of $\alpha \rightarrow 0$ or $\alpha \rightarrow \infty$. This is because this study changes the ordering method of Eq. (3). And this change provides a spatial visualization to trade-off the results in of preferences and strategies on LES results.

The above methods can be used to moderately reduce errors caused by weight uncertainties in the evaluation of LES. It should be clearly pointed out that this paper does not rely on analysis, comparison and weight sensitivity analysis under various situations to compare or select the optimum assignment scheme. It aims to describe the influences on the spatial pattern of land ecological security in the region brought about by administrators' different subjective cognitions about the importance of resource, environmental, economic and social development as well as their different policy preferences. As for evaluation of land ecological security, the optimum assignment scheme should be decided after trading off various situations according to the development ideas of local administrators.

Restricted to the availability of data sources, this paper does not consider the aspects of land utilization, soil quality and land ecological landscape in the evaluation system, so there is still a perfection and improvement space. Meanwhile, the OAT weight sensitivity analysis method has ignored the influence of the mutual effect between evaluation indexes on the evaluation result, and it cannot explain the influence of the combined action of multiple factors on the result. This is the effort direction of further studies.

Acknowledgments. This research was supported by Social sciences special research funds of Sichuan provincial human resources and social security department (2014) and "Study on regional cultivated land resource multi-source information intelligent management and sharing key techniques of application service platform" research program.

References

1. Pulido, M., Schnarl, S., Contador, J.F.L.: Selecting indicators for assessing soil quality and degradation in rangelands of Extremadura (SW Spain). Ecol. Ind. **74**, 49–61 (2017)
2. Song, W., Deng, X., Yuan, Y.: Impacts of land-use change on valued ecosystem service in rapidly urbanized North China Plain. Ecol. Model. **318**, 245–253 (2015)
3. Huang, H., Luo, W., Wu, C.: Evaluation of land eco-security based on matter element analysis. Trans. CSAE **26**(3), 316–322 (2010)
4. Liu, Y.: Strategies to guarantee land resources safety in China. Bull. Chin. Acad. Sci. **21**(5), 379–384 (2006)
5. Jeroen, C.J.M., van den Bergh, Verbruggen, H.: Spatial sustainability, trade and indicators: an evaluation of the 'ecological footprint'. Ecological Econ. **29**(1), 61–72 (1999)
6. Wang, Z., Zhou, J., Loaiciga, H.: A DPSIR model for ecological security assessment through indicator screening: a case study at Dianchi Lake in China. PLoS ONE **10**(6), e131732 (2015)
7. Huang, C.: Sysergetic Analysis and Adjustment Mechanisms Study on Chengdu Plain Cultivated Land Resource System. Doctor's Degree thesis of Sichuan Agricultural, p. 6 (2011)
8. Su, S., Li, D., Yu, X.: Assessing land ecological security in Shanghai (China) based on catastrophe theory. Stoch. Env. Res. Risk Assess. **25**(6), 737–746 (2011)
9. Chang, X., Zhao, W., Li, X.: Ecological security assessment based on the ecosystem service value in Zhangye Oasis. J. Natural Resour. **25**(3), 396–406 (2010)
10. Yu, D., Chen, W.: Land ecological safety in Poyang Lake Eco-economic Zone: an evaluation based on matter-element model. Chin. J. Appl. Ecol. **22**(10), 2681–2685 (2011)
11. Cariboni, J., Gatelli, D., Liska, R.: The role of sensitivity analysis in ecological modelling. Ecol. Model. **203**(1), 167–182 (2007)
12. Liu, Y., Wang, Y., Peng, J., Zhang, T.: Urban landscape ecological risk assessment based on the 3D framework of adaptive cycle. Acta Graph. Sinica **70**(7), 1052–1067 (2015)
13. Wu, G., Niu, X.: Application of an evaluation model based on punishing variable weight for early warning of land ecological security. Resour. Sci. **32**(5), 992–999 (2010)
14. Chen, Y., Khan, S.: Spatial sensitivity analysis of multi-criteria weights in GIS-based land suitability evaluation. Environ. Model. Softw. **25**(12), 1582–1591 (2010)
15. Romano, G., Dal, S.P., Trisorio, L.G.: Multi-criteria decision analysis for land suitability mapping in a rural area of Southern Italy. Land Use Policy **48**, 131–143 (2015)
16. Sun, P., Yang, H., Liu, Q.: Study on dynamic security of land ecology in water source area of South-to-North Water diversion project: a case study of Shangluo City, Shaanxi Province. J. Nature Resour. **27**(9), 1520–1530 (2015)
17. Eldrandaly, Y.K.A.: Exploring multi-criteria decision strategies in GIS with linguistic quantifiers: an extension of the analytical network process using ordered weighted averaging operators. Int. J. Geogr. Inf. Sci. **27**(12), 2455–2482 (2013)
18. Xu, E., Zhang, H.: Spatially-explicit sensitivity analysis for land suitability evaluation. Appl. Geogr. **45**(5), 1–9 (2013)

An Empirical Study on the Effect of Eco Agriculture Policy in Erhai River Basin

Xiaoyan Yan and Youde Wu[✉]

School of Tourism and Geographical Sciences,
Yunnan Normal University, Kunming, China
missing303@126.com

Abstract. This paper conducts difference-in-difference analysis on the production mode and hydro-environment of the within-policy area and outside-policy areas of Erhai basin by using DID model. The results show that: the impact of agricultural production mode on hydro-environment pollution is −12.59 under the policy, and ecological agriculture policies on agricultural production adjustment and optimization is of a significant effect, including agricultural working population, meat and milk production variables negatively correlated with water pollution index; chemical fertilizer, pesticide application is positively correlated with the amount of water pollution index. Conclusion of analysis: after ecological agriculture policy is implemented, the negative effect of optimization of agricultural production mode on river-related pollution has been eased within the policy-area, and agricultural output has increased. The five towns of 'North Three River' are more actively responded to the policy, compared to the eight towns around the river. Policy recommendations: "Culture + methane cycle of agriculture," harmless agricultural cultivation, "soil testing + balanced fertilization", returning farmland to forest ecology lake ecological agricultural policy - a significant economic effect for the whole basin area.

Keywords: Energy taxation · Erhai basin · DID model
Agricultural production · Ecological agricultural policy

1 Introduction

Globally, the shortage of water pollution and clean water are growing. Currently recognized as point source pollution caused by agricultural water pollution is one of the biggest problems. Especially with the gradual strengthening of the point source pollution control, water pollution in the proportion of agricultural sources increased. U.S. EPA 2003a findings show that agricultural nonpoint source pollution is the largest source of pollution of rivers and lakes polluted U.S., resulting in approximately 40% of the water quality of rivers and lakes failure [1]. In European countries, the agricultural non-point source pollution is also caused by the primary source of water, particularly nitrate contamination of groundwater, surface water is caused by the most important reason of phosphorus enrichment by agricultural sources of phosphorus discharged to surface water pollution load of 24 total 70%–71% [3]. Developed across different types of pollution sources, such as urban non-point source, the agricultural fields, livestock

© Springer Nature Singapore Pte Ltd. 2018
H. Yuan et al. (Eds.): GSKI 2017, CCIS 848, pp. 520–526, 2018.
https://doi.org/10.1007/978-981-13-0893-2_53

scenes were also classify source control [4]. Leshan Jin's study of regional water resources when carrying agricultural production limits to agriculture, and discussed ways to control agricultural pollution [5]. In recent years, scholars have studied the agricultural structure adjustment and optimization problem of water ecological constraints analysis, the impact of the mechanism, structural optimization path and specific measures and so on. Zhao Qing Zhen and other rural industrial structure and layout optimization mathematical model and its stability analysis [6]. Agricultural structure adjustment path Peng and other ecologically fragile areas of research [7]. Yang and other agricultural nonpoint source pollution in our country the situation for the overall estimate, and proposed control measures [8]. Xie analysis model was constructed decoupling of economic growth and state-intensive industries between different environments [9]. Qi Gong in Erhai basin as evidence discussed the point source pollution control targets under the agricultural structure optimization mechanism [10].

Evaluate the effectiveness of policy implementation and agricultural production response, and then adjust the policy, with some theoretical and practical significance. By comparing before and after the implementation of the policy, the policy changes in the area of implementation of key indicators, the overall effect can be estimated with the effective implementation of the policy measures, to adjust and improve the policy system for reference. In this paper, fold difference method (Difference-In-Difference) study design, the use of the study area 2000–2012 years of large sample data to compare changes in policy and non-policy areas interval indicators, identification of agricultural production activities in response to the policy.

2 Structural Basin Pollution

In recent years, with the strengthening of river basin water environment protection efforts, industrial and urban point source pollution has been relatively effective control. However, accounting for the river basin, 70% of the total pollution loads lakes agricultural non-point source pollution becomes a key part of Erhai ecological civilization construction [10]. As shown in Fig. 1, through three indicators of water quality sampling 2011a Erhai basin of rural and agricultural sources, urban sewage, industrial wastewater, tourism, soil erosion and other sources of governance and emissions TN, TP, ammonia and other comparison the main sources are derived basin: agricultural non-point source pollution, manure, rural sewage, urban sewage.

Comprehensive protection and create a new situation of ecological civilization construction Erhai basin, Dali Prefecture established ecological civilization construction leading group, the Erhai lake management extensions to protect the entire Erhai basin, agricultural nonpoint source pollution is one of Erhai lake Area policy focus area. Ecological agriculture policy summed up as "Paul yield, ensure quality, the environment" as the goal, the implementation of watershed agricultural production adjustments, crop structure optimization, and actively promote, mountains of fruit, dam facilities of suburban horticultural, aquaculture standardization, specific measures include: the ability to ecological elements based on the relative influence of water, soil, etc., select the construction of rice, corn, beans, barley four pollution-free production bases, cultivate beans, aquatic seaweed, buckwheat -based Premium newly planted

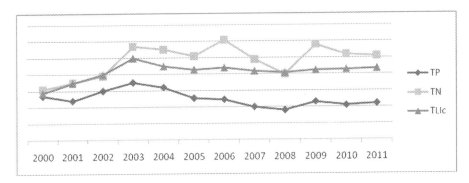

Fig. 1. The water quality index value trends of Erhai Lake

District; promotion of "livestock - biogas - planting" as the focus of resources, environmental protection, product, consumption, renewable resources, recycling development model to enhance the level of standardization of aquaculture; to "reduce chemical pesticides, reduce fertilizer" as the goal, from the variety, medication, fertilization, cultivation techniques and other aspects of improving and strengthening sound agricultural cultivation; Grain as an opportunity to promote the advantages of fruits, nuts, prosperous forest economy. According to Fig. 2, according to the water quality index value trends Erhai Lake water body, before and after implementation of the policy for the effects of comparison, the paper select TP, TN, TLIc trend of convergence in 2003 relative to policy implementation time node.

3   DID Analysis

As used herein, the data derived from the "national pollution census manual", "Dali City Statistical Yearbook," "Eryuan County Statistical Yearbook" and Dali Prefecture EPA survey, obtained from 2000 to 2012 the water environment and agricultural production two sets of data. Water environmental data include: Erhai and "North River" water of COD, TP, TN, TLIc indicators; agricultural production index select agricultural working population, at the end of arable land, of chemical fertilizers, pesticides fertilizer, meat and milk production, forest under fruit production data (Table 1).

Table 1. Comparison of the main features of the agricultural production value

Index	1			2			3		
	Maximum	Minimum	Std.	Maximum	Minimum	Std.	Maximum	Minimum	Std.
Environment Index	82	27	13	52	27	6	82	32	11
Agricultural population	53678	1987	16650	41937	1987	14926	53678	10876	13056
Arable land	59836	4642	14475	32847	4642	7821	59836	9127	15498
Chemical Fertilizers	5568	23	1121	2351	23	513	5568	427	1187
pesticides	127	11	20	97	15	18	127	11	22
Fruit production	56220	222	12609	33548	222	6361	56220	3547	9887
Meat and milk production	33864	674	7489	30657	674	7489	33864	3975	5821

A simple comparison of different years Erhai Lake Water Quality and agricultural production data, can not effectively reflect the true impact of ecological protection policies. First, changes in agricultural production data of different years may reflect systematic differences in the overall ecological protection policies, and the impact can not be fully classified as a policy. Second, the policy area there is an overlap with the traditional administrative divisions and cross space exists between the different administrative policy design, the gap between strength, implementation effect of the implementation of the conventional statistical methods which recognize regional differences in the effectiveness of policies. In addition, the actual purpose and effect evaluation of ecological protection policy is Erhai WECC, but the effect is the change in the path of agricultural production activities, intergenerational effects exist between humans and living activities were compared before and after implementation of the policy to discriminate effects of different policy measures.

Study design idea is the use of policy change area (Lake Area) before and after the implementation of the policy year in agricultural production activities obtained by subtracting the non-policy area ("North River" Area) before and after the implementation of the policy changes in the year acquired agricultural production activities, to identify effects of ecological protection policy Erhai basin and response mode of agricultural production.

A general description of the model are as follows:

$$Y_{it} = \beta_0 + \beta_0 D_{it} + \beta_1 T_{it} + \beta_3 D_{it} T_{it} + \beta_4 X_{it} + \varepsilon_{it} \tag{1}$$

In the above formula, Y_{it} of individual i at time t result values, D_{it} dummy variable for the group, if the individual i belong policy group $D_{it} = 1$, is a non-policy group $D_{it} = 0$; T_{it} for the period dummy variables, $T_{it} = 1$ shows the experimental period, $T_{it} = 0$ represents a non-experimental period; impact D_{it} it for the interaction coefficients is DID estimate the level of the river basin water environment of agricultural production changes; X_{it} as control variables, including water environment index, the number of practitioners in agriculture arable land, chemical fertilizer, pesticide use, fruit production, milk production; β parameters to be estimated; ε_{it} random disturbance. In order to eliminate the possible impact of heteroscedasticity, the number of variables to do treatment on, get on the number of sequences of each variable.

Table 2 shows the changes in the water environment for agricultural production basin regression results. Model 1 estimates the group, time, and their cross-term impact on the water environment index. Add two control variables model estimation result, D * T is −12.77. Model 3 Excluding arable land, gardens fruit production both on the water pollution index is not significant variables after the estimation results, D * T is −12.59. Regression results show that all three models of the cross coefficients are negative, and are in the 1% significance level, indicating that increased agricultural output under the policy environment does not bring rising water pollution index. Model 3 showed that in 2003, the implementation of the policy impact of agricultural production under the effect of water pollution index is −12.59.

Table 2. The estimation results of ecological agriculture policy by DID

	Model 1	Model 2	Model 3
β_0	57.65***	37.01***	36.27***
	(1.57)	(10.57)	(9.19)
D	−15.77***	−10.33***	−9.70***
	(1.99)	(2.09)	(1.72)
T	9.51***	9.07***	9.11***
	(1.89)	(1.54)	(1.53)
D*T	−7.68***	−12.77***	−12.59***
	(2.39)	(2.01)	(1.98)
Agricultural population	–	−3.37***	−2.85***
		(1.21)	(0.89)
Arable land	–	0.53	–
		(1.27)	
Chemical Fertilizers	–	3.92***	4.02***
		(0.90)	(0.88)
pesticides	–	10.36***	10.22***
		(1.11)	(1.09)
Fruit production	–	−0.38	–
		(0.66)	
Meat and milk production	–	−1.74	−2.08**
		(1.21)	(1.00)
Sample size	208	130	78
R^2	0.66	0.79	0.79

Note: Robust standard errors in parentheses; ***, **, * denote the 1%, 5%, 10% significance level.

4   Conclusions

Ecological Agriculture Development of the study area is typical. Erhai basin is considered one of the earliest development of the southwest frontier region of China, is the western Yunnan region's political, economic and cultural center. In recent years, the extensive mode of economic development, especially in aquaculture and farming brought about non-point source pollution, a major factor in the threat of Erhai ecology. 2003 Class IV water level in agricultural non-point source pollution COD, TN, 76% TP total drainage into the lake volume, 58%, 77%, of which agricultural production brought about the loss of fertilizer and manure pollution has become a watershed The main source of pollution. Based on a comprehensive analysis of non-point source pollution characteristics Erhai basin, the implementation of ecological agriculture policy, farmers shift production concept of life, optimizing agricultural planting structure, the development cycle aquaculture, and comprehensively promote the comprehensive prevention and control of agricultural non-point source pollution is significant.

The ecological effects of agricultural policy significantly. DID estimates show that under the policy implementation Lake Area of agricultural production on the Effects of water pollution index is -12.59 that enhance agricultural production index did not bring the deterioration of Erhai basin water pollution, and optimizing agricultural production through restructuring, to "protect the yield and quality of security, environmental security " policy objectives. DID four indicators of the agricultural working population, chemical fertilizer, pesticide use, such as meat and milk production estimation results significantly. ① ecological agriculture policy for farmers to produce environmental awareness, employment structure, the positive impact of the mode of production, per capita agricultural production and reduce pollution levels; ② ecological agricultural policy on agricultural planting structure, green pollution-free agricultural production had adjusted and optimized, leading to agriculture chemical fertilizer, pesticide use and the total decline in the strength of the units to use, reducing the nutrient-rich water into the lake level; ③ ecological agriculture policies to promote agro-industry aquaculture harmless construction, farming industry chain through recycling, farming techniques standardized, intensive mode of operation, etc., to achieve the aquaculture industry to increase production, fell into the lake water eutrophication level.

Erhai ecological agriculture model has promotional value. 2003a, the government put forward "clear Erhai Lake, Dali Xing" the goal, the introduction of "governance Erhai Watershed Protection Plan (2003–2020)", the implementation of structural adjustment for the cultivation of agricultural nonpoint source pollution, aquaculture standardization, sound construction, development of forest economic, scientific fertilization medication and other ecological agriculture policy. Currently, the country has become one of Erhai Lake City suburb of the best-preserved lakes. 2008a, Environmental Protection Minister Zhou said: "Xunfa natural, scientific planning, comprehensive source control, administrative accountability, public participation" Erhai protection experience is worth promoting. Among them, the farmers shift production concept living, optimizing agricultural planting structure, the development cycle aquaculture development model of ecological agriculture and other agricultural nonpoint source pollution prevention and control for the highland lakes, and the wider basin with policy reference value.

Acknowledgments. This paper was funded by National Natural Science Foundation of China (71463067; 41301180).

References

1. Wolfe, M.L.: Hydrology. In: Ritter, W.F., Shirmohammadi, A. (eds.) Agricultural Nonpoint Source Pollution, pp. 1–28. LEWIS Publishers, London (2000)
2. Magette, W.L.: Monotoring. In: Ritter, W.F., Shirmohammadi, A. (eds.) Agricultural Nonpoint Source Pollution, pp. 205–328. LEWIS Publishers, London (2000)
3. Mostaghimi, S.: Best management practices for nonpoint source pollution control: selection and assessment. In: Ritter, W.F., Shirmohammadi, A. (eds.) Agricultural Non-Point Source Pollution, pp. 257–304. LEWIS Publishers, London (2000)

4. Sharpley, A.N., Chapra, S.C.R., Wedepohl, R., Sims, J.T., Daniel, T.C., Reddy, K.R.: Managing agricultural phosphorus for protection of surface waters. Issues Options J. Environ. Qual. **23**, 427–451 (1994)

5. Jin, L.: warren Young, Water use in agriculture in China: importance, challenges, and implications for Policy. Water Policy **3**, 38–47 (2001)

6. Yun-Yun, H.U., Wang, Y.D., Ting-Xuan, L.I., et al.: Characteristics analysis of agricultural nonpoint source pollution on Tuojiang River Basin. Scientia Agricultura Sinica (2015)

7. Yang, Q., Liu, J., Zhang, Y.: Decoupling agricultural nonpoint source pollution from crop production: a case study of Heilongjiang Land Reclamation Area, China. Sustainability **9**(6), 1024 (2017)

8. Peng, W., Xianjin, H., Zhaogan, Z., et al.: Agricultural industrial structure adjustment and farm households' land use change in fragile ecological area: taking Shangrao County of Jiangxi Province as a case. J. Nanjing Univ. Fragile Ecological **39**(6), 814–821 (2003). (NATURAL SCIENCE EDITION)

9. Xie, C.Y., Feng, J.C., Zhang, K., et al.: The Governance Effect of Agricultural Nonpoint Source Pollution on 'Internet+' Strategy–Based on Geographical Spatial Perspective. Soft Sci. (2017)

10. Hu, Y., Peng, J., Liu, Y., et al.: Integrating ecosystem services trade-offs with paddy land-to-dry land decisions: a scenario approach in Erhai Lake Basin, southwest China. Sci. Total Environ. **625**, 849–860 (2018)

Study on the Evolution of Industrial Division of Labor and Structure in Central Yunnan Urban Agglomeration

Yan Li[⊠] and Xiaoyan Yan

Pan-Asia Business School, Yunnan Normal University, Kunming, China
Ly_fdj@126.com

Abstract. The industrial division of labor and the degree of convergence of the industrial structure directly affect the core competitiveness of the urban agglomeration, and it is of great practical significance to measure the industrial division of labor and the degree of structural convergence of the urban agglomeration scientifically and rationally. The similarity coefficient method and grey correlative analysis method more detailed classification based on the study of 22 urban agglomerations in the city in 2007 and 2012 in Yunnan, the whole city and urban agglomeration between the convergence of industrial structure and regional division of different industries and the evolution of city. The results show that: Yunnan city group 22 inter city assimilation degree has obvious upward trend; the industrial structure of Kunming and Yunnan city group of the overall industrial structure is the most similar, belong to the comprehensive development, Yuxi, Chuxiong and Qujing belong to the traditional agricultural and mineral resource type structure, and Yuxi is the agricultural and mineral resource type structure to the integrated development from the industrial transformation; Yunnan city group regional division, the first and the second industry and the third industry in the circulation department and production and Living Services Department of city industrial division of labor between the strengthening of the degree of specialization of the third industry of social public service between the City declined. As a whole, the industrial structure of the central Yunnan Urban Agglomeration tends to be higher and higher, while the industrial division of labor among cities is still not obvious, but it has begun to take shape.

Keywords: City clusters · Convergence of industrial structure
Industrial division · Similar coefficient method

1 Introduction

At present, one of the important goals of China's overall regional development strategy is to achieve regional coordinated development, and an important symbol of achieving regional coordinated development is the formation of a reasonable regional division of labor. [1] urban agglomeration is the main form to promote the rapid development of urbanization, as well as the main form of regional key development and regional coordinated development [2], the key to the formation of urban agglomeration lies in

H. Yuan et al. (Eds.): GSKI 2017, CCIS 848, pp. 527–533, 2018.
https://doi.org/10.1007/978-981-13-0893-2_54

the optimization of its internal industrial structure, the complementarity of urban functions and the enhancement of division of labor and cooperation in economic relations, and the degree of economic integration resulting from it. [3] therefore, scientific and rational research on the evolution of industrial division of labor and structural convergence of urban agglomerations is of great significance for the study of the overall division of labor and collaboration of urban agglomerations.

Many scholars of industrial division of labor and the structure of city group, Shandong City Liaoning peninsula city group, central city group, Guanzhong City Group, Jianghuai city group, Ningbo city economic circle, Xiangtan city group, Chengdu Chongqing region, nzy region or regions of convergence are discussed and analyzed in this study using the method of [4]. The more common is the location entropy method and similarity coefficient method. The similarity coefficient method was proposed in 1979 by the United Nations Industrial Development Organization, to measure the degree of the industrial structure convergence between the two regions, but most of the scholars in the measure when using this method, is the use of three time industry classification method proposed by Fisher, but the classification of industrial structure must have a high degree of similarity to [5], take the industry more detailed classification in using similarity coefficient method, can obtain more reasonable results [6–8]. At the same time, the degree of similarity between the industrial structure similarity coefficient method can measure 22, but not more reflect the internal structure of industry specific; although the location entropy method can measure the internal structure of industry in different regions of specific, but not on the whole measure the similarity of different regions. In view of this situation, Li Xuexin, Miao and Changhong put forward the location entropy grey incidence analysis method, which can measure the similarity degree of multi regional industries and the similarity of different industries in different regions [9]. But the grey relational analysis is a measure of similarity between sequences and reference sequences, similar degree of industrial structure can not directly measure the 22 inter city, therefore need to combine the similarity coefficient method can better reflect the city industrial structure convergence degree [10].

On the basis of previous studies, this paper will object to Yunnan city group, analysis method of grey correlative coefficient method based on similarity and finer industrial classification in combination of the vertical and horizontal comparative study of Yunnan city group 22 city, each city and urban agglomeration overall industrial structure difference and the city of different industry region division, with a greater awareness of the industrial division of labor and the structure of the degree of convergence of the city group in Central Yunnan and its evolution, and provide reference for the adjustment of the industrial structure of the city group in central yunnan.

2   Data Sources and Research Methods

2.1   Figures

The urban agglomeration in Yunnan Province consists of 4 cities: Kunming, Qujing, Yuxi and Chuxiong. In the choice of cross sections, data from 2007 and 2012 are selected to study. In order to overcome the problem of the 3 industrial classification accuracy of similarity coefficient that is not high, the similarity coefficient and location entropy calculation on the grey relational degree, the classification of the 19 industries, the 19 industries are agriculture, forestry, animal husbandry and fishery (referred to as agriculture, mining industry, (with) mining, electricity, gas) and water production and supply industry (electric fuel water), transportation, warehousing and postal industry (warehouse post), manufacturing (Manufacturing), information transmission, computer services and software industry (letter meter soft), construction (building), wholesale and retail (wholesale and retail), the real estate industry (real estate), Finance (financial), leasing and business services (business), accommodation, food and beverage industry (live meal), education (Education), scientific research, technical services and geological prospecting, water conservancy (Science and Technology), environment and public facilities management industry (water), resident services and other services (residents), culture, education and entertainment (Culture), Wei Sheng, social security and social welfare (Wei Sheng), public administration and social organizations (public), industry classification standard in 2013 "Chinese City Statistical Yearbook" prevail. In addition to Chuxiong in 2007 and 2012 industry data from the 2008 "Chuxiong Statistical Yearbook", 2013 "Chuxiong Statistical Yearbook", the other 3 city and national industry data are derived from the "2008 China City Statistical Yearbook" and "2012 China City Statistical Yearbook". All data are the city's 4 city (state) data, including the counties under the jurisdiction of the city and county (District), it is better to consider the city (state) to consider the evolution of urbanization and the overall structure of industrial division of labor.

2.2 Model

The similarity coefficient of industrial structure refers to the approximate degree of industrial structure of the same kind, which is used to compare the degree of difference of industrial structure between two cities or the degree of assimilation. Similarity coefficient between 0–1, the greater the value of similarity coefficient, indicated that the industrial structure between the two city of the city is similar to the division of labor between the low level of economic complementarity is weak; when the similarity coefficient is small, show that industrial structure difference between the two big city, the division of labor between the higher level and more strong economic complementarity. In particular, when the similarity coefficient equals 0, the industrial structure between the two cities is completely different. When the similarity coefficient equals 1, the industrial structure between the two cities is exactly the same. [6] its specific formula is as follows:

$$S_{ij} = \frac{\sum\limits_{k=1}^{n} X_{ik} X_{jk}}{\sqrt{\sum\limits_{k=1}^{n} X_{ik}^2 \sum\limits_{k=1}^{n} X_{jk}^2}} \tag{1}$$

S_{ij} For the urban and urban industrial structure similarity coefficient; X_{ik} for the sector in the city's industrial structure in proportion.

The location entropy grey incidence analysis method is based on the location entropy, and the curve similarity is analyzed by the location entropy of different regions and industries. The main steps of the method of location entropy grey correlation analysis are as follows:

$$LQ_{ik} = \frac{l_{ik}/\sum_{k=1}^{n} l_{ik}}{L_k/\sum_{k=1}^{n} L_k} \tag{2}$$

LQ_{ij} represents the locational entropy of industries in cities; l_{ik} represents the number of employees in urban industries; L_k represents the number of employees in the national industry; $i = 1, 2, 3, \cdots, m$; $k = 1, 2, 3 \cdots, n$.

From the above, we can get the location entropy matrix of the cities and industries in Yunnan and central cities in 2007 and 2012, as shown in Table 1.

Table 1. Location entropy matrix of cities in Yunnan Urban Agglomeration

	KM		YX		QJ		CX	
	2007	2012	2007	2012	2007	2012	2007	2012
X1	0.350	0.142	0.711	0.432	0.794	0.446	1.485	0.745
X2	0.376	0.581	3.280	4.588	1.313	1.042	1.427	1.394
X3	0.770	0.626	0.818	0.682	1.083	1.105	0.461	0.548
X4	0.673	0.618	1.603	1.433	1.209	1.109	1.124	1.120
X5	1.906	1.771	1.098	1.263	0.702	0.967	0.343	1.263
X6	1.828	1.771	0.440	0.249	0.487	0.366	0.564	0.513
X7	1.728	0.912	0.623	0.361	0.361	0.508	1.324	0.906
X8	1.383	1.410	0.803	1.187	2.131	1.808	1.023	0.709
X9	1.955	1.444	0.466	0.676	1.093	0.653	0.509	0.520
X10	0.843	0.796	0.698	0.528	1.174	0.873	1.194	0.901
X11	1.385	1.424	0.338	0.588	0.090	0.885	0.114	0.355
X12	1.626	1.639	0.217	0.131	0.660	0.398	0.240	0.394
X13	1.805	1.527	0.463	0.304	0.483	0.445	0.716	0.840
X14	0.741	0.629	0.994	0.732	0.822	0.849	1.101	1.737
X15	0.874	0.405	0.302	0.020	0.131	0.075	0.085	0.260
X16	0.790	0.875	1.938	1.455	1.406	1.070	1.845	1.612
X17	0.937	0.932	0.997	0.573	1.277	1.022	1.474	1.494
X18	1.345	1.394	0.716	0.359	0.933	0.656	0.939	0.695
X19	0.633	0.806	0.272	1.024	0.409	1.160	2.114	1.792

3 Analysis

3.1 Structural Convergence Evolution

According to the similarity coefficient method of 19 industries, the assimilation degree of urban industrial structure between cities in Yunnan Province can be obtained. In 2007, the industry convergence between Kunming and Chuxiong was lower in the Middle Yunnan Urban Agglomeration, and the industry convergence between Qujing and Yuxi was higher. In 2012, the industrial assimilation between Yuxi and Chuxiong was low among the middle cities of Yunnan Province, and the industry assimilation between Qujing and Yuxi was higher. Moreover, in 2012, the similarity coefficients of industrial structure between 22 cities in the central Yunnan urban agglomeration were above 0.8. From the evolution of industrial structure convergence, the similarity coefficient increased most is between Kunming and Chuxiong, the similarity coefficient between the two cities increased from 0.689 in 2007 to 0.888 in 2012; the similarity coefficient is the largest decline between Qujing and Yuxi, the similarity coefficient between the two cities dropped from 0.925 in 2007 to 0.867 in 2012. In general, the similarity coefficient between 2012 and 2007 in Yunnan urban agglomerations has increased. From the above analysis, it can be preliminarily explained that the convergence degree of industrial structure of Yunnan Urban Agglomeration shows an upward trend, and the level of division of labor of urban agglomeration decreases, and the economic complementarity between cities tends to weaken.

3.2 Structural Convergence Type

Taking the urban agglomerations in Central Yunnan as the frame of reference, we can get the order of the similarity of the overall industrial structure with the urban agglomerations in Central Yunnan province. In 2007, the order from big to small was Kunming, Yuxi, Qujing and Chuxiong. In 2012, the order from large to small was Kunming, Yuxi, Chuxiong and Qujing. Kunming and Yuxi always occupy the top two. From the cross section, Kunming is the capital city of Yunnan Province, because the proportion of each industry in the whole urban agglomeration is higher, so it is similar to the whole industrial structure of the urban agglomeration. From the evolution of the industrial structure of the city, Chuxiong, Qujing and Yunnan city group of the overall industrial structure similarity degree by nearly 0.8 in 2007 rose to nearly 0.7 in 2012, the overall structure of the two industry shows similarity between city and city group to further improve. As a whole, the similarity of the industrial structure between the cities and the urban agglomeration in Yunnan Province has increased in different degrees.

From the type of the industrial structure, combined with the analysis of Table 1 in the 2007 data, the location entropy of Chuxiong agriculture (1.485), the location entropy of the mining industry (1.427), (1.845) the location entropy of education and public management and social organization of the location entropy (2.114) were significantly higher than the national level of the mining industry; location entropy of Qujing (3.280), the production and supply of electric power, industry location entropy of gas and water (1.603) and Education (1.938) is higher than the national level; location entropy of Yuxi's mining industry (1.312), location entropy of wholesale and retail trade (2.131), the location entropy of Education (1.406) is higher than the national level. From 2012 data, the location entropy of Chuxiong's mining industry (1.394), the location entropy of water conservancy, environment and public facilities management industry (1.737), education (1.612), public management and social organization of the location entropy (1.792) is higher than the national level; Qujing mining industry location entropy (4.588), production and supply industry location entropy power, gas and water (1.433) and Education (1.454) is higher than the national level; location entropy Yuxi wholesale and retail industry (1.808) is higher than the national level. It also makes the difference between the industrial structure of the 3 cities and the overall industrial structure of the central Yunnan city group, which belongs to the traditional agricultural and mineral resources structure. But it is worth noting that Yuxi is changing from an agricultural and mineral resources structure to a comprehensive development pattern. The industrial structure in Kunming City, from 2007 data, in addition to the location entropy of traditional agriculture and mining industry are below 0.4, the remaining 17 of the industrial location entropy in more than 0.63, there are 9 industrial location entropy is greater than 1; from 2012 data, in addition to the agricultural industry location entropy the mining industry, as well as resident services and other services are lower than 0.6, the rest of the industrial location entropy is greater than 0.6, indicating that Kunming belongs to the comprehensive development of type structure. The above results are also in line with the economic status of the cities in the region.

4   Conclusions

In this paper, by using the similarity coefficient method and grey correlative analysis showed that the research on the industrial division of labor and the structure evolution of Yunnan city group: (1) the method of similarity coefficient and location entropy grey correlation analysis method are used, which can measure the degree of convergence of industrial structure of the city group in 22 city, each city can also measure the whole city and industrial structure among different industries and the difference between each city geographical distribution, so the similarity coefficient method combined with grey correlative method can comprehensively reflect the degree of convergence of industrial structure of the city group. (2) from the industrial structure of the city group in Central Yunnan 22 inter city assimilation degree, between Yunnan 4 city high degree of industrial structure, and the 22 inter city assimilation degree has obvious upward trend. (3) from the differences of the industrial structure between the cities and the whole urban agglomeration, the industrial structure of Kunming is the most similar to that of the urban agglomeration in Yunnan Province, followed by Yuxi. According to the type of industrial structure, Kunming belongs to comprehensive development type, while the other 3 cities belong to traditional agriculture and mineral resources structure, while Yuxi is changing from agricultural and mineral resources structure to comprehensive development type. (4) from the industry of Yunnan city group regional division, the first industry and the second industry and the third industry in the circulation department and the production and life of Service Department of city to strengthen the industrial division of labor between the third industry, the degree of division of social public service between the city declined. On the whole, the industrial division of labor among cities in Central Yunnan is not obvious yet, but it has begun to take shape.

Acknowledgments. This paper was funded by National Natural Science Foundation of China (71463067; 41301180), Social Philosophy Foundation of Yunnan Province (YB201504D).

References

1. Zhu, R.B.: Value modularity integration and industry convergence. China Ind. Econ. (2003)
2. Guo, L., Zhang, X.J.: A study of value modularity integration and compatibility selection based on network externalities. China Ind. Econ., 103–110 (2005)
3. Bröring, S., Cloutier, L.M., Leker, J.: The front end of innovation in an era of industry convergence: evidence from nutraceuticals and functional foods. R&D Manag. **36**, 487–498 (2006)
4. Bjerregaard, T.: Industry and academia in convergence: micro-institutional dimensions of R&D collaboration. Technovation **30**(2), 100–108 (2010)
5. Dai, S.X.: Industry convergence and promotion of industry competitiveness **107**(3), 259–266 (2004)
6. Lee, S.H., Lee, D.W.: A study on review and consideration of medical industry convergence based on U-healthcare. Phys. Rev. E Stat. Nonlinear Soft Matter Phys. **76**(1), 55–86 (2013)
7. Shuhui, X.U.: Evolution of spatial agglomeration of manufacturing industry and regional division of labor driven in Guangdong Province under the industrial transfer: based on the analysis of statistical data during 2005–2014. Trop. Geogr. **37**, 347–355 (2017)
8. Li, L., Ma, Y.: Spatial-temporal pattern evolution of manufacturing geographical agglomeration and influencing factors of old industrial base: a case of Jilin Province, China. Chin. Geogr. Sci. **25**(4), 486–497 (2015)
9. Nakamaru, M., Shimura, H., Kitakaji, Y., et al.: The effect of sanctions on the evolution of cooperation in linear division of labor. J. Theor. Biol. **437**, 79–91 (2017)
10. Ohdaira, T.: Study of the evolution of cooperation based on an alternative notion of punishment "Sanction with Jealousy". J. Inf. Process. **24**(3), 534–539 (2016)

The Transition Probabilities from Captive Animal's Behavior by Non-invasive Sensing Method Using Stochastic Multilevel State Model

Phudinan Singkahmfu[1,2(✉)], Pruet Boonma[3], Wijak Srisujjalertwaja[1],
Anurak Panyanuwat[4], and Natapot Warrit[5]

[1] Computer Science Department, Faculty of Science,
Chiang Mai University, Chiang Mai, Thailand
phudinan_s@cmu.ac.th, mr_pu@hotmail.com
[2] Software Engineering Department, College of Arts Media and Technology,
Chiang Mai University, Chiang Mai, Thailand
[3] Department of Computer Engineer, Engineering Faculty,
Chiang Mai Univerity, Chiang Mai, Thailand
[4] College of Arts Media and Technology,
Chiang Mai University, Chiang Mai, Thailand
[5] Department of Biology, Faculty of Sciences,
Chulalongkorn University, Bangkok, Thailand

Abstract. This article proposes a stochastic multilevel-state framework to model the animal's behavior. The motivation of this article is the variety behavior influenced by several factors, which can lead to the state explosion. The proposed framework processes data from an automated sensing system and constructs the model. The data gathered from captive Antelope goral (Naemorhedusgriseus) in Chiang Mai Night Safari, Thailand. The data is gathered from the activity and the environmental factors in the cage by none invasive method. The model separated observed data into two main classes: the upper-level data and the lower-level data. The upper-level data represents the environment data such as temperature, humidity, and light density. Moreover, the landscape of the captivity area also takes into consideration. On the other hand, the lower-level represents the location of the animal of interested in the captivity area. The working strategy of this work is to cluster the each type of data and link them together by a stochastic approach. Both layers of data will be handled independently in clustering algorithm and determine probabilistic of state transaction. From the data observed from the sensor, the Probabilistic Automaton (PA) function is constructed. It is a function of producing the next stage based on the previous behavior states. The initial state of the framework is in the lower-level data (the current location of the animal). Then, the PA using the current lower stage and the current upper stage generates the next stage, location of the animal. Both the lower stage and the upper stage are traverse along the constructed automaton. The result can suggest computing methods, which can utilize to zoo research, which performs behavior monitoring, and in the other studies area, or subject of study, such as, air pollution dispersion that tracks the movement of pollutant according to the environment. The benefits of

© Springer Nature Singapore Pte Ltd. 2018
H. Yuan et al. (Eds.): GSKI 2017, CCIS 848, pp. 534–542, 2018.
https://doi.org/10.1007/978-981-13-0893-2_55

the proposed methods also can be used to create the application to attract the tourist to the area, which animally is likely to display themselves.

Keywords: Behavior monitoring · Zoo monitoring · Pattern gathering Data from sensor · Sensor data cleaning · Antelope goral · Stochastic multilevel

1 Introduction

Based on animal's activity (field of biology that examines cyclic phenomena in living organisms known as biological rhythms), the short-term and long-term data collection will be detected by the sensor.

Animal activity can assess by studying the animal condition, and then provide relevant information such as their emotional condition in a particular environment. When combined with an automating computing system, it can record the status of the particular animal without interfering its daily cycle; the data of which can subsequently be modeled to classify emotional conditions of the animal being studied.

Data processing is the part that the process will perform after data gathered from the sensor. Due to animal behavior in the captive environment is occurs in repeating state. Also for most real world, data processing concerns many problems one of major is defining the state, and contains the number of states to comprehend and optimize for processing method. The automation non-invasive sensing method produces an immense amount of data and state, so the result hardy to apply in probabilistic tools for state prediction process. Inconsequent, the multilevel will be appropriate to use along with stochastic method.

2 Background

Since a difference of local, political and institutional statutes and laws protect rare animal species against thorough research such as tagging or other physical methods, some studies have suggested non-invasive methods detect the emotional state of an animal. For instance, Manteuffel and Schön (2004) introduced vocalizations of animals as an indicator of the animal's emotion. In their study, they combined Linear Prediction Coding (LPC) with an artificial neural network to investigate continuous analog time signal. They assumed that changing emotional states can be the cause of the effect of physiological and behavioral reactions, and the dependence of animal vocalization on psycho-physiological conditions makes this sound analysis a well-suited tool for non-invasive judgments of welfare and stress of the animal.

Chandrashekaran (1998) demands that the conceptual base of the field of biological rhythm research in this century were largely yielded by Aschoff, Bunning, and Pittendrigh. Aschoff (1965), one of the noticeable biologists who discovered the model of physiological mechanisms in birds, mammals and humans, suggested that an easy technique for following the rhythmic behavior of an animal without disturbing it is to measure its locomotor activity, especially when investigating its changing conditions in a temporally programmed or artificial world, for example, caged finches. In an in-depth analysis of animal chronobiology, Berger (2002) suggest the stress and welfare of the animals being studied can be accessed from the caged environment. Body growth, food consumption, and other environmental factors such as temperature, light intensity, humid, habitat also play a significant role in the analysis, and the number of available studies is still limited.

Location-based sensor, or GPS-based tracking system, is a technology currently used to detect the action and attitude patterns of wildlife species (Hunter 2007). Just after an implant tagging event, animals are then left alone to behave naturally without further disruption, so one major benefit of remote sensing over direct observation is its ability to monitor the behavior of individual animals with minimal observer interference (Pinter-Wollman and Mabry 2010).

However, animals must be caught and anesthetized to recognize the attachment of a tag. This can be considered a disadvantage unless handled in careful consultation with experts as the anesthetization can be hazardous for the animal, not to mention when done with rare species as antelopes. Besides the tags can also adversely affect the animal if left on for too long (Pinter-Wollman and Mabry 2010). Coyne and Godley (2005) proposed Satellite Tracking and Analysis Tool (STAT) as an integrated system for archiving, analyzing and mapping animal tracking data. This is especially useful in monitoring marine animals (Wilson et al. 2002).

The significant studied area in data mining analysis is data clustering. Depending on purpose, there are numerous aims of clustering such as to identify the most probable values of the model parameters (Dempster et al. 1977) (Gaussian mixture's mean), to decrease a particular cost function (the total within-cluster squared distance to centroid (MacQueen 1967)), or to identify high-density connected regions (Ester et al. 1996) (high data density area) (Fig. 1).

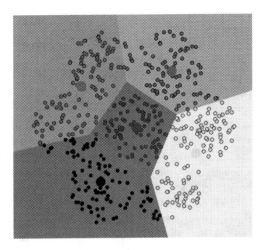

Fig. 1. K-means clustering result as 5 data clusters with centroids

K-Means clustering purposes to separation n objects into k clusters in which each object refers to the cluster with the neighboring mean. The approach offers exactly k different clusters of highest possible diagnosis. The optimal quantity of clusters k provides the proper division (distance) it is must be processed from the data set. The purpose of K-Means clustering is to decrease absolute intra-cluster diversity.

2.1   Framework

The research examines two main data segments, as display in Fig. 2. The figure displays research data model the data section has separated into two layers. The top layer expresses animal behavior stage and transition, which calls biological rhythm (basic manner of animal) and second describes environment factor, as mentioned before the animal behavior can describe as repeated stage by a driven environment. Apparently, some part of behavior data can define stage from expert and caretaker.

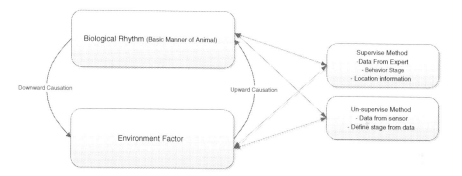

Fig. 2. Data relational flow between two sections

Biological rhythm is living manner of animal in contained environment. Such as feeding, location during the daytime, living location living during night time, defecating, and resting. This part mainly acquires information from the expert and called the Supervise method. The approach is to define role-base state from available research data, and expert interview then display as probabilistic transaction stage. This approach, is recognizes as already known from the expert.

The other approach is called Un-supervise method; the approach will concentrate on the data that gather from automating non-invasive sensor method. Location base designed as symmetric grid base, one location stage in will depend on a single grid. There are the numbers of the factor in each grid that will present different relational output to the behavior, for the instant, ground type (rock, or soil), and ground sloping, ground temperature.

On the other hand, the bottom layer calls Environment factor. The layer represents core relation of an environment in a cage, such as sunrise, sunset, spot climate, ground temperature, light intensity, and humidity. Also, the downward causation will appear to influence the bottom layer by the animal behavior can control environments such as the defecating environment (spot) will select following by group leader including seasonal condition, and daytime living environment will be adjusted depend on the animal life condition (pregnancy, young age, adult, old). Moreover, the upward causation will make bottom layer influence the top layer, for the instant, sunlight will control living spot. The temperature will be directly control feeding habit.

Table 1 shows various kind of sensors which selected to measure contained living factor of the animal. All sensors are control by microcontroller, and link with wireless network to transfer data to server. Each sensor aimed to observation in each particular factor as shows in table. Obviously, temperature monitoring is most significant factor that can identify case condition also is direct influence to emotion condition of the animal; however, there is more aspect needs to be concern.

Table 1. Sensor and measurement

Sensor	Measurement
Temperature	Case environment
Light intensity	Case environment
Water level	Water consumption
Area detection	Habituation

2.2   Data Analysis

Approximately 3,200 of generated data record has been use for this study and evaluates the current results. Data from the sensor will gathered and divide into upper group and lower group. Although after the data successfully stored via wireless upload to the database. There are the practical ways to store data such as, locally store on the site in secondary storage card, or directly upload them to the internet. However, the major drawback for the uploading immediately is noise cleaning process due to all data need to upload via the network before getting through the data filtering process (Fig. 3).

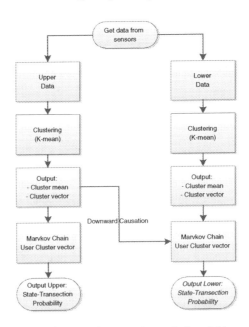

Fig. 3. Data processing framework, to produce rule based (downward causation)

The second step, use both cluster vector of upper and lower data group to apply with Markov chain process to create transition matrix to represent the environment changing state at the particular clustered point. The Markov chain is known as a stochastic or random process, which is determine as a set of random variables. Consequently, the behavior of the process in the future is stochastically independent of its behavior in the past, given the current state of the process (Serfozo 2009).

Output of Markov process provides the transition matrix, which determines a probability of state. Figure 4 shows output transition matrix of upper data group, according to the figure five states is a result from optimal cluster groups then processed and illustrated with Markov chain result.

```
> plot(mcFitLower$estimate)
> mcFitUpper$estimate
MLE Fit
A  5 - dimensional discrete Markov Chain defined by the following states:
1, 2, 3, 4, 5
The transition matrix  (by rows)  is defined as follows:
             1          2          3          4          5
1 0.2133550 0.1840391 0.2117264 0.1970684 0.1938111
2 0.2000000 0.1721311 0.2262295 0.1836066 0.2180328
3 0.2106870 0.2152672 0.1877863 0.1877863 0.1984733
4 0.2136752 0.2188034 0.2256410 0.1897436 0.1521368
5 0.1669506 0.2078365 0.2248722 0.2027257 0.1976150
```

Fig. 4. Marhov chain result the upper transition matrix of five crusted states

After competed for all these steps using upper data group, then all steps will repeat by using lower group data combining with clustered result of upper data as the downward causation from the upper layer to the lower layer, as shown in Fig. 5.

```
> mcFitLower
$estimate
           1          2          3          4          5
1 0.1448413 0.1329365 0.2341270 0.3353175 0.1527778
2 0.1570439 0.1200924 0.2494226 0.3348730 0.1385681
3 0.1673699 0.1603376 0.2236287 0.2897328 0.1589311
4 0.1794595 0.1394595 0.2281081 0.2886486 0.1643243
5 0.1631799 0.1485356 0.2405858 0.2866109 0.1610879
```

Fig. 5. Marhov chain result the lower transition matrix of five crusted states

Therefore, the behavioural state of the animal has to be discovered through the gathered data. Consequently, with the approach converted these two data group into the state. Formally, the problem is to create a function:

$$f : X_1 \times X_2 \to Y$$

The f function will be defined by factor analysis method for investigating variable relationships for complex concepts such as socioeconomic status, dietary patterns, or psychological scales.

Concept of factor analysis is that multiple observed variables have similar patterns of responses because they are all associated with a hidden variable.

The Y is stated with probabilistic value which provided by the Markov chain process. Figure 6 illustrates state space, there are 14 possible transitions of both upper and lower. Every state in the state space is covered once as a row and again as a column, and each cell in the matrix shows the probability of transitioning from row state to column state. Moreover, in the matrix, the cells do the equivalent role that the arrows indicate in the diagram.

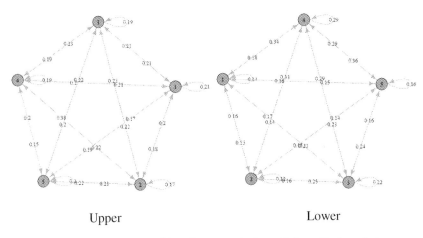

Upper   Lower

Fig. 6. State space transition diagram, which result from Markov chain

The probability of the state Y_j consecutively following Y_i denoted by the Probabilistic Automaton (PA) function:

$$p\big(\big(Y_i, Y_j, Y_k \ldots Y_p\big), Y_q\big)$$

The approach can define the transaction from a state Y_j to Y_i. The Markov chain method shows whether and how strongly pairs (value) of variables (state) are related. For example, eating state and resting state are linked during the hot day is tending to be rest near shade than stayed outside. The animal is influence by history, and their behavior states can show whether and how strongly pairs of variables are related.

2.3   Output Discussion

The test process two output variables were divided as sample 1 and sample 2 there is called independent data. The Chi-square test is used to determine, and there is a significant relationship between the two variables. Due to the generated data is uniform distribution the result produces P-Value is 0 in case of big sampling (3052 Occurrences) as shown in Table 2.

Table 2. Chi-square test result

Output	Value
Chisq statistic	5606.23
Degree of Freedom	99
P-Value	0

The earlier result is illustrated that out model can catch generated a pattern of the uniform distribution.

3   Conclusion

This article has investigated the most common behavior of captive animal based on analysis of animal living behavior, to provide study tools for zoologist. It is verify that the computing automate system is the solution to help the researcher archives better result and enable another way of animal study and monitoring technique. The common behavior can have a pattern in many ways, depending on external factor such as season, temperature, or food quantity. The result of the model is creating a pattern the trained from again software then the pattern recognized as rule base algorithm to define the animal's emotional condition. The common behavior can have a pattern in many ways, depending on external factors such as season, temperature, or food quantity. However, this article is describe only downward causation process and the data processing requires further work for upward causation part and final data process which, analyzed from both upward, and downward causation to complete all of the proposed workflow of this research.

Acknowledgments. This research has been supported partially by Chiang Mai University graduation school's research scholarship and Chiang Mai University International College ASEAN+3 co-research grant.

References

Chandrashekaran, M.K.: Biological rhythms research: a personal account in the perspective, pp. 546–555 (1998)

Aschoff, J.: Cireadian rhythms in man. Science **148**, 1427–1432 (1965)

Berger, A.: Activity patterns, chronobiology and the assessment of stress and welfare in zoo and wild animals. Int. Zoo Yb. **45**, 80–90 (2002). 2011

Hunter, A.: Sensor base animal tracking. Geometric Engineering UCGE Report number 20258 (2007)

Pinter-Wollman, N., Mabry, K.E.: Remote-sensing of behavior. In: Encyclopedia of Animal Behavior, pp. 33–40 (2010)

Coyne, M.S., Godley, B.J.: Satellite Tracking and Analysis Tool (STAT): an integrated system or archiving, analyzing and mapping animal tracking data. Marine Ecology Progress Series Published, 11 October 2005

Manteuffel, G., Schön, P.C.: Measuring pig welfare by automatic monitoring of stress calls. Bornimer Agrartechnische Berichte (2004)

Dempster, A.P., Laird, N.M., Rubin, D.B.: Maximum likelihood for incomplete data via the EM algorithm. J. R. Stat. Soc. Ser. B **39**, 1–38 (1977)

MacQueen, J.B.: Some methods for classification and analysis of multivariate observation. In: 5th Berkeley Symposium on Mathematical Statistics and Probability (1967)

Ester, M., Kriegel, H.-P., Sander, J., Xu, X.: A density-based algorithm for discovering clusters in large spatial databases with noise. In: Proceedings of ACM SIGKDD Conference (1996)

Serfozo, R.: Basics of Applied Stochastic Processes, p. 2. Springer, Heidelberg (2009). https://doi.org/10.1007/978-3-540-89332-5. ISBN 978-3-540-89332-5

Wilson, R.P., Grémillet, D., Syder, J., Kierspel, M.A.M., et al.: Remote-sensing systems and seabirds: their use, abuse and potential for measuring marine environmental variables. Mar. Ecol. Prog. Ser. **228**, 241–261 (2002)

The Temporal Precipitation in the Rainy Season of Koxkar Glacier Based on Observation Over Tianshan Mountain in Northwest of China

Chuancheng Zhao[1,3], Shuxia Yao[1(✉)], Jian Wang[2],
and Haidong Han[3]

[1] Lanzhou City University, Lanzhou 730070, China
yaoshuxia@163.com
[2] Urban and Planning School,
Yancheng Teachers University, Yancheng 224007, China
wjshuigong@lzb.ac.cn
[3] State Key Laboratory of Cryospheric Science,
Cold and Arid Regions of Environmental and Engineering Research Institute,
Chinese Academy of Sciences,
320 Donggang West Road, Lanzhou 730000, China

Abstract. Precipitation, as one of important input variable for land surface hydrologic and ecological models, shows a high spatial and temporal variation. The daily precipitation by manual measurement is collected in Koxkar glacier catchment in rainy season during the period of 2009–2016, and hourly precipitation by standard tipping rain gauge is collected from May 19 to August 22 in 2016. Comparing the manual and standard tipping rain gauge, the performance of standard tipping rain gauge is suited in Koxkar glacier catchment in rainy season. The distribution of hourly precipitation is analyzed. The results have shown that precipitation is occurred more in daytime than in night, and frequency is concentrated at 15:00 to 17:00. The trend of precipitation and precipitation days are consistent at night, but obvious inconsistency in the daytime. These characteristics of precipitation have important role for further understanding of glacier changes with climate change.

Keywords: Precipitation · Koxkar glacier catchment · Precipitation days
Rainy season

1 Introduction

Precipitation is a critical component of the water budget and exploration of its spatiotemporal characteristics at various scales is an important step toward a better understanding and modeling of the hydrological cycle as well as regional climate change (Kyriakidis et al. 2004; Crochet et al. 2007; Michaelides et al. 2009). Due to the influence of orographic and resources limited, precipitation is became one of the most difficult meteorological data to measure accurately (Guan et al. 2005; Zhao et al. 2015). In

© Springer Nature Singapore Pte Ltd. 2018
H. Yuan et al. (Eds.): GSKI 2017, CCIS 848, pp. 543–549, 2018.
https://doi.org/10.1007/978-981-13-0893-2_56

general, precipitation data has been obtained by ground observation, satellite and radar derived, numerical modeling (Michaelides et al. 2009). Although the ground observation suffered from various problems, precipitation measurement is the most reliable source directly by rain guage (Ye et al. 2003). Satellite and radar derived by indirection have proved the high temporal and spatial resolutions, accuracy of estimation need to be calibrated or verified using the rain guage (New et al. 2001; Xie et al. 2003).

Because of the low precipitation and high evaporation, water scarcity is one of the core issues in arid regions of the world (Wang et al. 2013; Modarres and Vdeprda 2007). The variability of spatial and temporal precipitation is a central characteristic of arid and semi-arid regions. With the climate changes, these patterns are likely increase in many arid and semi-arid regions of the world. For example, Xinjiang is belong to the arid and semi-arid region of northwest of China. Due to lies in the Eurasian hinterland and far away the sea, Xinjiang has distributed a large number of deserts and Gobi as well as one of scarce precipitation. Detection the variability of precipitation in needed to help vulnerable dryland agriculturalists and policymakers address current climate variation and future climate change (Batisani and Yarnal 2010).

With the economic and technique limitation, precipitation observation is too sparse in remote mountainous to capture the spatial and temporal distribution. Furthermore, moisture is one of the most influential factors not only determination the total amount of precipitation, but also the distribution of precipitation in mountainous (Bayraktar et al. 2005; Shrestha et al. 2015). Because of complex topography and orographic of mountain, orographic alter the flow of air, moisture forced to rise by the topographic elevation, releasing moisture as precipitation on the windward, and more precipitation at higher elevations, while the air descends and warms, drying as precipitation dissipates on the leeward. As the origination of numerous rivers, the understanding of spatio temporal characteristics of precipitation in mountainous is of course of paramount important role for water resource management and assessment the regional impacts of climate change (Westerberg et al. 2010; Kyriakidis et al. 2004).

In this paper, the aim was to describe the temporal characteristics of precipitation in glacial area of Koxkar. Due to the lack of observation station, the data is only used the daily precipitation by manual and hourly precipitation by standard tipping rain gauges near the glacier terminus. The reliability of standard tipping rain gauge is verified by compared with manual observation, and analyzed the characteristics of different periods precipitation.

2 Materials and Methods

Study Area
The Koxkar Glacier catchment (41°42′ N-41°53′ N and 79°59′E-80°10′ E) is located in southern slope of Tianshan mountains, Wensu County in Xinjiang Province, China. The whole glacier catchment covers an area of 116.5 km², out of which 62.8% is glacierized area. The Koxkar glacier is one of the large dendritic valley glaciers in Tianshan Mountains which extends 25.1 km in length and covers an area of 83.56 km²

covered a layer of moraine. The valley wind is well developed in the ablation zone and is weaker over the upper glacier (Han et al. 2008). The mean annual air temperature observed near the terminus of the glacier is 0.778 °C, while the mean temperature of summer is as high as 7.748 °C. The mean annual precipitation near the terminus is 608 mm, of which >80% occurs during the ablation period (Han et al. 2008). In recent years, the observation is shown a lower belt of rainfall near approximately 3700 m, with precipitation being greater in the terminus and accumulation zones of the glacier (Wang et al. 2012).

Data

There are seven observation stations in Koxkar Glacier catchment, one is manual observation near the glacier terminus, while others are automatic weather stations in glacier. Because of strong ablation and valley wind effect, the precipitation data is missed serious in glacier. Therefore, we collected daily precipitation for manual measurement near the glacier terminus at an elevation of 3009 m from 2009 to 2016 in rainy season, and hourly precipitation for standard tipping rain gauge period from May 19 to August 22 in 2016. The manual observation carried out at GMT 8:00 am and 8:00 pm in every day respectively. The amount of daily precipitation by manual is recorded. The amount of daily precipitation by standard tipping rain gauge is also accumulates from GMT 20:00 to 20:00 of next day.

3   Results

3.1   Comparison of Precipitation

In general, manual observation is considered more accurate and consistent than other ways. However, the shortcoming of manual observation is provided the precipitation at daily time scale. In high mountainous, the precipitation is liquid, solid or mixture. In order to verification of the performance of standard tipping rain gauge, the accuracy of precipitation by standard tipping rain gauge is verified by comparing with the manual observation during May 19 to August 22 in 2016 in rainy season.

The result of comparison is shown in Fig. 1. The two amount of precipitation appear to have same consistency between manual and standard tipping rain gauge. During the measurement period, the amount of precipitation by manual is 303.9 mm, while the amount of precipitation by standard tipping rain gauge is 336.1 mm that the error is less than 10%. The correlation coefficient R^2 is as high as 0.99 (Fig. 2). Both heavy precipitation and small precipitation, the amount of precipitation by standard tipping rain gauge is higher than the manual observation. This phenomenon is more obvious with the increase of daily precipitation. Consequently, the accuracy of precipitation by standard tipping rain gauge is high than by manual observation. It is good illustration of the applicability of standard tipping rain gauge in rainy season over Koxkar Glacier catchment.

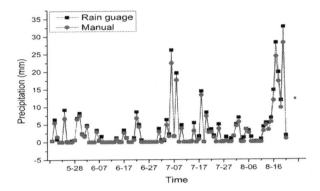

Fig. 1. Comparison of precipitation between manual and standard tipping rain gauge

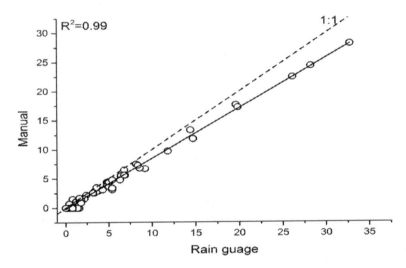

Fig. 2. The correlation coefficient of precipitation between manual and standard tipping rain gauge

3.2 Hourly Precipitation Distribution

The characteristics of hourly precipitation are shown in Figs. 3 and 4 using the precipitation by standard tipping rain gauge. The frequency of precipitation occurrence is counted per hour over whole observation. The distribution of frequency is presented that occurred more during day than night (Fig. 3). The precipitation is mainly occurred from 13:00 to 19:00 accounting for 45%, but less precipitation from 23:00 to 4:00 of next day in whole observation. The maximum of precipitation frequency is 21 times at 17:00, while the minimum of precipitation frequency is only 4 times at 4:00.

Overall, the distribution of amount of hourly precipitation is roughly same as the frequency of hourly precipitation (Fig. 4). There is a certain difference in the distribution of amount and the frequency hourly precipitation. In night, the distribution of

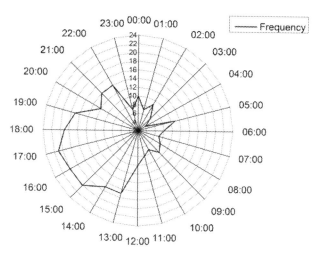

Fig. 3. The frequency of hourly precipitation during May 19 to August 22 in 2016

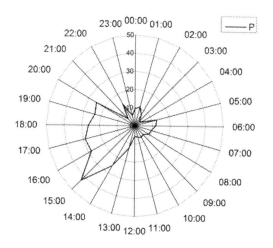

Fig. 4. The amount of hourly precipitation during May 19 to August 22 in 2016

amount and the frequency of hourly precipitation have good consistency. In daytime, the amount of precipitation has increased with the increasing of frequency from 10:00 to 15:00. The amount of precipitation has decreased with the decreasing of frequency from 17:00 to 20:00. The maximum of amount is occurred at 15:00, while the maximum of frequency is occurred at 17:00. It is indicated that precipitation intensity is relatively small after 15:00.

3.3 Precipitation Days Distribution

The amount and days of precipitation is calculated during rainy season from 2009 to 2016 shown in Fig. 5. It is illustrated that the amount of precipitation fluctuated seriously. The maximum of precipitation is 546.4 mm while the minimum is 335.8 mm, the difference exceed 200 mm in rainy season. The amount of precipitation is exhibited slightly increasing trends, but not passed the significance test. The minimum of amount and days of precipitation is occurred in 2014. However, the maximum of amount of precipitation is occurred in 2013, the precipitation days is not consistent with amount of precipitation. The precipitation days is exhibited significant increase trends with increasing 1.5 day/rainy season, the correlation coefficient R is up 0.7.

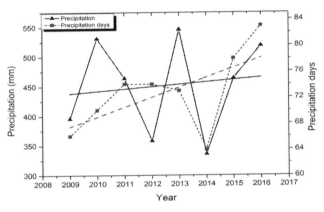

Fig. 5. The distribution of amount and days of precipitation in rainy season during 2008 to 2016 (black solid line: amount of precipitation; blue dotted line: days of precipitation) (Color figure online)

4 Conclusion

(1) By comparing manual and standard tipping rain gauge observation, the performance and suitability of standard tipping rain gauge has been verified, and high temporal resolution of precipitation can be improved in rainy season in Koxkar Glacier catchment.

(2) The occurrence of precipitation is more in daytime than in night. The amount and frequency of precipitation is concentrated at 15: 00–17: 00 in rainy season.

(3) The trend of precipitation is slight increase, while the trend of precipitation days is significant increase.

Acknowledgments. This study was supported by the National Natural Science Foundation of China (No. 41771087; No. 41361013; No. 41471060). The authors would like to express their gratitude to Dr. Q. D. Zhao, S. H. Guo, State Key Laboratory of Cryospheric Science, Cold and Arid Regions of Environmental and Engineering Research Institute, Chinese Academy of Sciences, for their valuable suggestions and cooperation.

References

Batisani, N., Yarnal, B.: Rainfall variability and trends in semi-arid Botswana: implications for climate change adaptation policy. Appl. Geogr. **30**(4), 483–489 (2010)

Bayraktar, H., Turalioglu, F.S., Şen, Z.: The estimation of average areal rainfall by percentage weighting polygon method in Southeastern Anatolia region, Turkey. Atmos. Res. **73**(1), 149–160 (2005)

Crochet, P., Jóhannesson, T., Jónsson, T., Sigurðsson, O., Björnsson, H., Pálsson, F., Idar, B.: Estimating the spatial distribution of precipitation in iceland using a linear model of orographic precipitation. J. Hydrometeorol. **8**(6), 1285–1306 (2007)

Guan, H., Wilson, J.L., Makhnin, O.: Geostatistical mapping of mountain precipitation incorporating autosearched effects of terrain and climatic characteristics. J. Hydrometeorol. **6**(6), 1018 (2005)

Han, H.D., Liu, S.Y., Ding, Y.J., Deng, X.F., Wang, Q., Xie, C.W., Wang, J., Zhang, Y., Li, J., Shangguan, D., Zhang, P., Zhao, J., Niu, L., Cheng, C.: Near-surface meteorological characteristics on the Koxkar baxi glacier, Tianshan. J. Glaciol. Geocryol. **30**(6), 967–975 (2008)

Kyriakidis, P.C., Miller, N.L., Kim, J.: A spatial time series framework for simulating daily precipitation at regional scales. J. Hydrol. **297**(1–4), 236–255 (2004)

Michaelides, S., Levizzani, V., Anagnostou, E., Bauer, P., Kasparis, T., Lane, J.E.: Precipitation: measurement, remote sensing climatology and modeling. Atmos. Res. **94**(4), 512–533 (2009)

Modarres, R., Vdeprda, S.: Rainfall trends in arid and semi-arid regions of Iran. J. Arid Environ. **70**(2), 344–355 (2007)

New, M., Todd, M., Hulme, M., Jones, P.: Precipitation measurements and trends in the twentieth century. Int. J. Climatol. **21**(15), 1889–1922 (2001)

Shrestha, D., Deshar, R., Nakamura, K.: Characteristics of summer precipitation around the Western Ghats and the Myanmar West Coast. Int. J. Atmos. Sci. **2015**, 1–10 (2015)

Wang, S., Zhang, M., Sun, M., Wang, B., Li, X.: Changes in precipitation extremes in Alpine areas of the Chinese Tianshan mountains, Central Asia, 1961–2011. Quat. Int. **311**, 97–107 (2013)

Wang, X., Liu, S., Han, H., Wang, J., Liu, Q.: Thermal regime of a supraglacial lake on the debris-covered Koxkar glacier, Southwest Tianshan, China. Environ. Earth Sci. **67**(1), 175–183 (2012)

Westerberg, I., Walther, A., Guerrero, J.L., Coello, Z., Halldin, S., Xu, C.Y., Chen, D., Lundin, L.C.: Precipitation data in a mountainous catchment in Honduras: quality assessment and spatiotemporal characteristics. Theor. Appl. Climatol. **101**(3–4), 381–396 (2010)

Xie, P., Janowiak, J.E., Arkin, P.A., Adler, R., Gruber, A., Ferraro, R., Huffman, G.J., Curtis, S.: GPCP pentad precipitation analyses: an experimental dataset based on gauge observations and satellite estimates. J. Clim. **16**(16), 2197–2214 (2003)

Ye, B., Yang, D., Ding, Y., Han, T., Koike, T.: A bias-corrected precipitation climatology for China. J. Hydrometeorol. **5**(6), 1147–1159 (2003)

Zhao, C., Yao, S., Zhang, S., Han, H., Zhao, Q., Yi, S.: Validation of the accuracy of different precipitation datasets over Tianshan mountainous area. Adv. Meteorol. **2015**(3), 1–10 (2015)

Graph-Based Tracklet Stitching with Feature Information for Ground Target Tracking

Jinbin Fu, Jinping Sun[⊠], and Peng Lei

School of Electronic and Information Engineering,
Beihang University, Beijing 100191, China
{fujinbin, sunjinping, peng.lei}@buaa.edu.cn

Abstract. Based on the approximation that tracklet kinematic association likelihoods satisfy the Markov or path-independence assumption, several polynomial-time bipartite matching algorithms were proposed to stitch track segments for their effectiveness. However, with target density increasing, their stitching performance would degrade inevitably. Despite the help of feature information, it is remarkable that the aforementioned approximation is no longer valid since the feature information is usually sporadic. In order to solve this problem, track graph is utilized and the feature information is passed through the graph to calculate the tracklet feature association likelihood under path-dependence assumption. It makes bipartite matching algorithms valid again. Finally, simulation results demonstrate that the proposed algorithm out-performs previous algorithms based on path-independence assumption in the dense target situation.

Keywords: Tracklet stitching · Graph-based model · Feature information
Bipartite matching

1 Introduction

In the field of ground target tracking, target tracks usually break into several segments because of low visibility, high clutter, and high target density. One available solution is to do some corresponding treatments during tracking such that the unbroken tracks can be obtained directly. By introducing a move-stop-move model, an interacting multiple model estimator with state-dependent mode transition probabilities (IMM-SDP) solves the track segmentation problem caused by evasive move-stop-move maneuvering [1]. However, since the track segmentation reasons are commonly diverse in practice, it greatly limits the application of such algorithms. The other available solution is to receive all tracklets first and then stitch them. Similarly, IMM-SDP is utilized to stitch the tracklets segmented by evasive move-stop-move maneuvering in the stitching level [2]. Considering the generalization and effectiveness, this paper will focus on the latter solution.

As mentioned above, the commonly used tracklet stitching solution contains two levels. In the lower level, several tracklets are reported by the tracker based on the sensor measurements. Then a track-stitcher associates these tracklets to identify a set of targets in the higher level. A data structure called track graph [3] has been widely used

© Springer Nature Singapore Pte Ltd. 2018
H. Yuan et al. (Eds.): GSKI 2017, CCIS 848, pp. 550–557, 2018.
https://doi.org/10.1007/978-981-13-0893-2_57

in representing the association relationship between tracklets. In such track graph, nodes represent tracklets and edges represent possible association among tracklets. Under above definitions, the stitched tracks are exactly some paths in the track graph. Theoretically, tracklet stitching solves the same data association problem as target tracking, except tracklets replace measurements. However, the tracklets are different from measurements, which usually satisfy the Markov or path-independence assumption. It means the tracklet kinematic likelihood can be calculated as the product of the pairwise association likelihoods defined between consecutive pairs in each path. Therefore, the tracklet stitching can be solved by maximum weight bipartite matching or minimum cost network flow algorithm [4, 5].

However, the stitching performance of such bipartite matching algorithms is usually unperfected in dense target scene. Although the feature information could be used in such situations to aid stitching, the path-independence assumption no longer holds since feature information is usually sporadic. To solve this problem, a graph-based feature-aided (GB-FA) tracklet stitching algorithm is proposed in this paper. By means of passing the feature information in the track graph, the GB-FA tracklet stitching algorithm obtains the feature association likelihood of all edges in the track graph under the path-dependence assumption. Therefore, the tracklets with feature information could be stitched by bipartite matching algorithms again. The algorithm of calculating feature association likelihood under the path-dependence assumption is also the main contribution of this paper.

2 Track Graph Representation and Feature Aided Tracklet Stitching

In order to emphasize the data association of tracklets distributed in time and space, this paper concentrates on the single-sensor situation. Let the input of the track-stitcher be $Y = \{y_1, \ldots, y_N\}$, where y_i, $i = 1, 2, \cdots, N$, denotes the i-th tracklet reported by the tracker. Although it is unnecessary, it is convenient to assume that the graph is directed and the ordering is consistent of the tracklet time, where nodes represent the tracklets and edges represent the association of corresponding tracklets. The weight of an edge represents the association likelihood of the two tracklets. From above definitions, it can be seen that a directed path in the track graph corresponds to a stitched track. Therefore, the problem of tracklet stitching can be interpreted as that of finding a global hypothesis, i.e., a set of compatible paths, for guaranteeing that the selected paths have the maximum posteriori probability.

Let $\tau = \{y_1, \ldots, y_k\}$ be a stitched track, which is a subset of Y. The likelihood of τ can be calculated by

$$
\begin{aligned}
L(\tau) &= v(y_1)P^s(y_1, \ldots, y_k)P^f(y_1, \ldots, y_k)P_E(y_k) \\
&= \gamma_s(y_1)P_E(y_k)\prod_{i=1}^{k-1}P^s(y_{i+1}|y_1, \ldots, y_i)\prod_{i=1}^{k-1}P^f(y_{i+1}|y_1, \ldots, y_i),
\end{aligned}
\tag{1}
$$

where $v(y_1)$ is the expected number of new targets in y_1, $P_E(y_k)$ is the probability of track ending after y_k, and $\gamma_s(y_1)=v(y_1)P^s(y_1)P^f(y_1)$ is the density of the new tracklet y_1. $P^s(y_1,\ldots,y_k)$ and $P^f(y_1,\ldots,y_k)$ are kinematic association likelihood and feature association likelihood, respectively.

If we assume that the kinematic estimation of each tracklet is approximately convergent at the end of the tracklet and each tracklet could obtain precious feature information, the tracklets with feature information would satisfy the Markovian property [6]. Such that, Eq. (1) can be simplified as

$$L(\tau) = \gamma_s(y_1)P_E(y_k)\prod_{i=1}^{k-1}P^s(y_{i+1}|y_i)\prod_{i=1}^{k-1}P^f(y_{i+1}|y_i), \qquad (2)$$

In this way, the likelihood of stitched track is just the product of pairwise association likelihoods $L^s(y_i,y_{i+1})$ and $L^f(y_i,y_{i+1})$.

Furthermore, a hypothesis λ in track graph can be represented by $x_{ij} \in \{0,1\}$, where $i,j = 1,\cdots,N$. If the directed edge $<y_i,y_j>$ belongs to the hypothesis λ, x_{ij} is set as $x_{ij} = 1$. Otherwise, $x_{ij} = 0$. The constraint that each node can just be associated with no more than one node in hypothesis λ can be represented by

$$\sum_{<i,j>\, \in E} x_{ij} \le 1 \quad \text{for all } i,j \in \{1,\ldots,N\}, \qquad (3)$$

where E is the set of all edges in the track graph. Then, the probability of hypothesis λ can be calculated as

$$P(\lambda|Y) = C'^{-1}\prod_{i=1}^{N}\prod_{j=1}^{N}l(y_i,y_j)x_{ij}, \qquad (4)$$

where C' is the normalization constant, and $l(y_i,y_j)$ is the likelihood of associating y_i with a successor y_j as follows

$$l(y_i,y_j) = \frac{L^s(y_i,y_j)L^f(y_i,y_j)}{\gamma_s(y_j)P_E(y_i)}. \qquad (5)$$

Taking the negative logarithm of (4) and ignoring the normalization constant, the objective function becomes

$$J(x) = \sum_{(i,j)\in E} c_{ij}x_{ij}, \qquad (6)$$

where $c_{ij} = -\ln l(y_i,y_j)$ is the cost of associating y_i with y_j. When subject to the constraint of (3), the best hypothesis can be obtained by finding $x_{ij} \in \{0,1\}$ which minimizes $J(x)$ in Eq. (6). If every node y_i in the track graph is split into a head node u_i and a tail node v_i, the tracklet stitching can be regarded as a bipartite matching problem. Furthermore, with adding a source node s and a sink node e, and setting the cost and the capacity of all new edges (s, u_i), (u_i, v_i) and (v_i, e) to be 0 and 1, the bipartite matching problem would be converted into the minimum cost network flow problem.

3   Graph-Based Feature Aided Tracklet Stitching

However, the tracklets with feature information would not satisfy the Markovian property, since the feature information is usually sporadic [6]. Nevertheless, if the target feature association likelihood can be obtained under the path-dependence assumption, the Markovian property would be satisfied again. The algorithm of calculating the feature association likelihood under the path-dependence assumption is described as follow.

Taking Fig. 1 as an example, the sketch map shows a part of three vehicles' tracklets reported by a tracker.

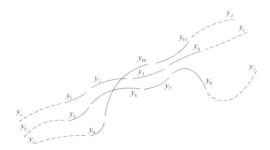

Fig. 1. The tracklets of three vehicles.

According to [3], it supposes that the feature information will be obtained at intervals and the tracker will get the feature information of tracklets only if they are being tracked when the feature information can be obtained. The corresponding track graph of Fig. 1 is shown in Fig. 2, where square nodes, namely feature nodes, indicate that these tracklets have feature information, and circular nodes, namely non-feature nodes, indicate that these tracklets only have the kinematic information.

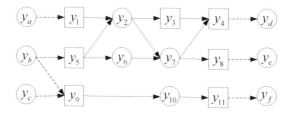

Fig. 2. The track graph corresponding to the tracklets in Fig. 1.

If the Markov assumption is utilized, all feature information in this track graph will be lost except that in y_3 and y_4. Besides, the feature information in y_3 and y_4 can only be used to judge whether or not the edge $<y_3, y_4>$ should be deleted. Besides, if we want to obtain the feature association likelihood of all edges, all association hypotheses in the track graph have to be taken into consideration. However, since the feature information is commonly precious [3], the mutual influence among the feature information can be viewed as partitioned by the feature nodes based on bipartite matching algorithm. Hence, some subgraphs can be extracted from the track graph to reduce the computational burden. Based on the mentioned above, each subgraph must satisfy following conditions: (1) the subgraph should be a connected graph with two or more nodes; (2) if a non-feature node is contained in the subgraph, all direct successors and predecessors of this non-feature node and the directed edges between them should be contained; (3) if a directed edge is contained in the subgraph, all direct successors of the directed edge's head node, all direct predecessors of the directed edge's tail node and the directed edges between them should be contained; (4) each non-feature node contained in the subgraph should have at least one directed edge coming from it and going toward it; (5) the subgraph don't contain any subgraphs which meet above conditions. It can be proofed that the extracting subgraphs are unique and the feature association likelihoods can be calculated independently in these subgraphs. Figure 3 shows the extracted subgraphs.

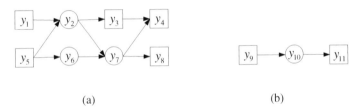

(a)   (b)

Fig. 3. The subgraphs extracted from the track graph in Fig. 2: (a) Subgraph 1, (b) Subgraph 2.

As shown in Fig. 3, some edges may not be contained in any such subgraphs. The feature association likelihood of these edges like the edge $<y_3, y_d>$ actually cannot be calculated because of lack of feature information. However, the feature association likelihood of these edges will not affect the edge selection in extracted subgraphs, and thus the feature association likelihood of these edges can just be set to 1. It means that only kinematic association likelihoods play a role in deciding which edges should be selected among these ages.

After getting subgraphs, the feature association likelihood of each edge in track graph can be calculated as follow. First, the subgraph is travelled to find every feature node. Then, as to each found feature node like y_1, a feature path should be established, such as $y_1 \rightarrow y_2 \rightarrow y_3$. At this time, the feature association likelihood between y_1 and y_3 is calculated. Then, the path returns to $y_1 \rightarrow y_2$ and the feature association likelihood of the edge $<y_2, y_3>$ is set to equal the feature association likelihood between y_1 and y_3. Then, based on the current path, another adjacent node is found, i.e. y_7.

Repeating the previous operation, the feature association likelihoods of edge $<y_7, y_4>$ and edge $<y_7, y_8>$ are calculated. At this moment, since there are no other nodes associated with y_7, the path returns to y_2 and the feature association likelihood of edge $<y_2, y_7>$ is set to be that with bigger product of kinematic association likelihood and feature association likelihood between edges $<y_7, y_4>$ and $<y_7, y_8>$. This is because we cannot judge which edge is correct right now and can just believe the edge with bigger association likelihood is more likely to be the correct one. After that, the path returns to y_1 with the feature association likelihood of edge $<y_1, y_2>$ calculated as above. At present, the processing for the feature node y_1 is completed. Note that the feature association likelihood of all edges is initialized as zero at the beginning and will be updated with the bigger value during the processing for each feature node to get the final results. Furthermore, in order to reduce the repeated calculation, when a newly found node has been visited before, the feature association likelihood of the ending edge in the path can be obtained directly. For example, when the path is $y_5 \rightarrow y_6 \rightarrow y_7$, since the node y_7 has been visited in the path $y_5 \rightarrow y_2 \rightarrow y_7$, the feature association likelihood of edge $<y_6, y_7>$ can be directly set to be that of the edge $<y_2, y_7>$.

This paper adapts the direction of recursion following the direction of the track graph. In fact, it is equivalent for the reverse recursion direction. So far, the feature association likelihoods of all edges have been calculated under the path-dependence assumption. At last, Eq. (5) is utilized in the minimum cost network flow algorithm to perform tracklet stitching. The procedure of the whole algorithm is described as follows:

Step 1: Calculate kinematic association likelihood of all edges in track graph.
Step 2: Calculate feature association likelihood of the edges linking two feature nodes and delete the impossible ones.
Step 3: Initialize all edges' feature association likelihood.
Step 4: Extract all satisfied subgraphs from the track graph.
Step 5: Set the feature association likelihood of the edges no within the subgraphs to 1.
Step 6: Calculate and update the feature association likelihood of the edges in subgraphs.
Step 7: Use minimum cost network flow algorithm with edge weight as the product of kinematic and feature association likelihood.

Since each step can be implemented by polynomial-time algorithm, the total algorithm is still polynomial-time complexity.

4   Simulations

First, in order to generate fragmented tracklets, the visible situation of targets is transformed based on transformation probabilities

$$P(V|V) = 0.8, P(O|V) = 0.2, P(V|O) = 0.4, P(O|O) = 0.6, \tag{7}$$

where V indicates that the sensor can get the measurement from the target, and O indicates that the sensor cannot get the measurement. Meanwhile, the value of feature information is set between 0 and 100 obeying the uniform distribution with the constant standard deviation σ_0. Here, σ_0 is set to 1.

At the lower level of the tracker, the MHT is utilized to generate the tracklets [7]. However, in order to exclude other factors and just analyze the tracklet stitching performance, multiple targets are tracked sequentially in this paper to make sure that each tracklet reported by the tracker is a pure true track.

The simulation time is 200s with the measurement interval of 2s. There are totally 30 targets in the scenario. The x coordinate start positions of all targets are set to $x_0 = 25km$, while corresponding y coordinate start positions are uniformly distributed between 25 km and 27 km. The initial speeds of all targets are identically set to be $v_{x_0} = 10m/s$ and $v_{y_0} = 20m/s$. Besides, each target performs random maneuver during motion and the accelerations in x and y coordinates follow a zero-mean Gaussian distribution with standard deviation of $2m/s^2$. The path-independence-based feature-aided (PIB-FA) tracklet stitching algorithm in [6] is used herein for comparison with the proposed GB-FA tracklet stitching algorithm in this paper.

In order to compare the stitching performance of these both algorithms objectively, two performance metrics in [6] are selected as follows.

(1) Rate of False Association: This is defined as the rate of the selected edges which link two nodes coming from different targets on all selected edges.
(2) Target Fragmentation: The fragmentation of each target is defined as the number of stitched tracks in an association hypothesis that contain tracklets originating from the target, minus one. The target fragmentation is defined as the average fragmentation over all targets.

The simulation is done with different feature measurement intervals. The results of 500 Monte Carlo simulations are shown in Fig. 4.

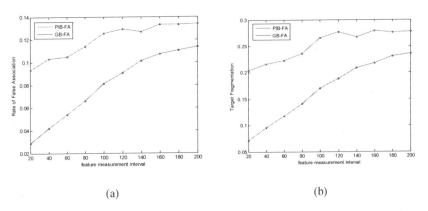

(a)   (b)

Fig. 4. Simulation with different feature measurement intervals: (a) Rate of false association, (b) Target fragmentation.

We can observe that since the target feature information is fully utilized, the tracklet stitching performance of GB-FA is much better than that of PIB-FA. Meanwhile, both of their performance degrades with the increase of feature measurement interval. This is because the probability of adjacent nodes both having feature information decreases and the obtained feature information decreases when the feature measurement interval increases.

5 Conclusions

As to the degradation of tracklet stitching performance of existing approaches in dense target situation, this paper proposes a graph-based feature-aided tracklet stitching algorithm. By means of passing the feature information in the track graph, the feature association likelihood of all edges is calculated under the path-dependence assumption. It makes the tracklets with feature information satisfying the path-independence approximation again. At last, the minimum cost network flow algorithm is utilized to perform tracklet stitching. Simulation results indicate that the algorithm proposed in this paper can achieve better tracklet stitching performance than traditional feature-aided algorithm.

Acknowledgments. This work was supported in part by the National Natural Science Foundation of China (61471019).

References

1. Zhang, S., Bar-Shalom, Y.: Tracking move-stop-move targets with state-dependent mode transition probabilities. IEEE Trans. Aerosp. Electron. Syst. **47**(3), 2037–2054 (2011). https://doi.org/10.1109/taes.2011.5937281
2. Zhang, S., Bar-Shalom, Y.: Track segment association for gmti tracks of evasive move-stop-move maneuvering targets. IEEE Trans. Aerosp. Electron. Syst. **47**(3), 1899–1914 (2011). https://doi.org/10.1109/TAES.2011.5937272
3. Chong, C.Y., Castanon, G., Cooprider, N., Mori, S., Ravichandran, R., Macior, R.: Efficient multiple hypothesis tracking by track segment graph. In Proceedings of the 12th International Conference on Information Fusion IF '09, Seattle, July 06–09, 2009. IC, New York, pp. 2177-2184. ISBN13 = 9780982443804
4. Castanon, G., Finn, L.: Multi-target tracklet stitching through network flows. In: Proceedings of the 2011 IEEE Aerospace Conference AC '11 (Big Sky, MT, USA, March 05–12, 2011). IEEE, New York, pp. 1–7 (2011) https://doi.org/10.1109/AERO.2011.5747436
5. Chong, C.Y.: Graph approaches for data association. In: Proceedings of the 15th International Conference on Information Fusion IF '12 (Singapore, Singapore, July 9–12, 2012), IC, New York, pp. 1578-1585 (2012). ISBN-13 = 9780982443859
6. Mori, S., Chong, C.Y.: Performance Analysis of graph-based track stitching. In: Proceedings of the 16th International Conference on Information Fusion IF '13 (Istanbul, Turkey, July 9–12, 2013). IC, New York, pp. 196–203 (2013)
7. Fu, J.B., Sun, J.P., Lu, S.T., Zhang, Y.J.: Multiple hypothesis tracking based on the Shiryayev sequential probability ratio test. Sci. China. Inf. Sci. **59**(12), 1–11 (2016)

Study In-band & Out-of-band in Monopole Antennas and the Effect of Curved Ground Surface

Mabrook Masoud A$^{(\boxtimes)}$, Donglin Su, and Junjun Wang

School of Electronic and Information Engineering,
Beihang University, Beijing 100191, China
mabrook2006@yahoo.com, {sdl,wangjunjun}@buaa.edu.cn

Abstract. Out-of-band response of an antenna is an important factor that determines the susceptibility of a communication system to its surrounding environment. The aim of this paper was to study the effect of different plane ground on the Input impedance, S-parameter, and radiations pattern of the monopole antenna. Several simulations have been performed, the monopole antenna with wavelength λ/4 was placed on top of the curved and rectangular ground plane surface and then different antenna parameters were obtained in terms of directivity, electric field and gain. Finding the right place of put the antennas in specific location still the big problem. By understanding the out-of-band performances and predictions system designers can better handle and avoid problems caused by electromagnetic compatibility and susceptibility issues. Finally the results were analyzed and concluded that curved ground surface with specific degree can be outperformed the flat ground surface in normal condition at different aspects.

Keywords: Out-of-band · Monopole antenna · S-parameter · Input impedance
Radiation pattern · Curved ground surface

1 Introduction

The quickly improvement in number of Radio Electronic Signals (RES), prompts the rise of different sorts of obstruction that block the typical operation of these methods. One of the fundamental components of the RES is antenna. Thusly, in the examination of Electro-Magnetic Compatibility (EMC) conditions required learning of the essential attributes of the accepting and transmitting radio wires are in the working band, as well as outside it. With the rapid growth of technology, radar systems, satellite and more advanced communication set into a similar region of the military platform. These have brought about a savage rivalry for space which can possibly bring about expanding Radio Frequency Interference (RFI) or Electro-Magnetic Interference (EMI).From this concept, any RFI or EMI platforms are equipped with numerous antennas to give high data rate transmission, reliable signal coverage, and different functionalities [1–3]. As frequently just restricted space is accessible to oblige multiple antennas on such platforms, high mutual coupling of on-board antennas turns into a major concern, and various endeavors are dedicated to lessen conceivable interferences [4, 5].

© Springer Nature Singapore Pte Ltd. 2018
H. Yuan et al. (Eds.): GSKI 2017, CCIS 848, pp. 558–568, 2018.
https://doi.org/10.1007/978-981-13-0893-2_58

Multiple antennas applied in same frequency band can improve the transmission data rate, as realized in the multiple-input multiple-output (MIMO) scheme [6]. Out-of-band response of an antenna is an important factor that determines the susceptibility of a communication system to its surrounding environment. Several strategies have been proposed to reduce the out-of-band interference, such as novel designs of band pass filters [7], receiver architectures [8], and signal forms [9] used in wireless systems. This paper concerned in modeling the out of band performance of the antenna based on its in-band performance and the physical dimension of the antenna. Just an antenna is applied, the more specifications such as impedance, pattern, gain, radiation, voltage standing wave ratio (VSWR) are always appears. It is possible to reduce the out-of-band interference through antenna design [1]. This method is straightforward and requires no change to the architecture of wireless systems. In order to predict the out-of-band performance of the antenna, "Monopole antennas" design and parameters are selected to be the objects of this paper. Based on the study of the in-band and out-of-band performances (based on their S-parameters) and other parameters such as their gain and Radiation of these antennas, the purpose is to predict the out-of-band characteristics of these antennas and of similar antennas from their known in-band characteristics. The relationships between the parameters and the out-of-band performances such as gain, beam width and directivity will be analyzed and formulated into relevant prediction functions. This will enable the effective prediction of the antennas' out-of-band performance. Our aim is to find the right place to put the antennas to help to improve communication systems through the understanding and prediction of possible electromagnetic compatibility (EMC) issues. By understanding their out-of-band performances, system designers can better handle and avoid problems caused by electromagnetic compatibility and susceptibility.

2   The Characteristics of Monopole Antenna

The main parameters of antenna can be described by following formulas:

$$E = A(r)f(\theta, \varphi) \tag{1}$$

The radiation of the antenna is g directional, that is, the intensity of electromagnetic power density radiated by antenna is related to the angle between the antenna and the direction of radiation [5]. In Eq. (1), $A(r)$ is the amplitude factor, and $f(\theta, \varphi)$ is the direction factor, called antenna directivity function. The pattern established in various coordinate systems referred to antenna directivity function is called the antenna pattern. Antenna pattern is an important graphic to describe performance of the antenna [6].

$$G(\theta, \varphi) = \frac{E^2(\theta, \varphi)}{E_0^2} \tag{2}$$

In Eq. (2), $G(\theta, \varphi)$ is the antenna gain, $E(\theta, \varphi)$ is the electric field strength of antenna at a point in space, and E_0 is the electric field strength of an ideal point source non-directional antenna at the same point and with the same input power.

$$G = \frac{P_{in0}}{P_{in}} \qquad (3)$$

Antenna gain also can be defined as Eq. (3). P_{in0} is the input power of a non-directional antenna at a point, and P_{in} is the total input power of the antenna.

For matching of the impedance of antenna and feed line outside the operating frequency band, where there is a change of the input impedance of the antenna, the power supplied to the antenna can be represented in the next form [3]:

$$P_s(f) = P_i(f) + P_r(f) \qquad (4)$$

Where $P_i(f)$ is the power, received by the antenna; and $P_r(f)$ is the power reflected from antenna input. This is loss due to antenna mismatch with supply line $P_i(f) = P_s(f)\left(1 - |\Gamma|^2\right)$, $P_r(f) = P_s(f)\left(1 - |\Gamma|^2\right)$ respectively. When we neglect the thermal losses in the antenna the total efficiency will be

$$\eta(f) = 1 - |\Gamma(f)|^2 \qquad (5)$$

Where $|\Gamma(f)|$ is the modulus of reflection of the antenna; which can be calculated from this formula.

$$|\Gamma(f)| = \frac{|Z_f - Z_a(f)|}{|Z_f + Z_a(f)|} \qquad (6)$$

Where $Z_a(f)$ is the input impedance of antenna; Z_f is the input impedance of the feed line [10].

3   Antenna Design

To study of the out-of-band characteristics, the electrodynamics model of the linear array antenna consisting of two elements constructed. Orientation of the antenna coordinate system and its geometrical parameters are shown in Fig. 1 two monopoles antenna 1 and 2 made from thin strip line with width of w1 and w2 which equal to 2 mm and length of antenna 1 is L1 = 95 mm to operates at frequency 0.9 GHz and the length of antenna 2 is L2 = 30 mm will be operates at 2.3 GHz, the two monopoles fixed in finite sized ground plane in parallel with length and width equal to 40 mm (W = L), connected with feed line 1 mm above the ground to avoid the complex surface junctions. Electromagnetic simulation carried out using the moment method, implemented in the frequency domain. In this case, the determination of the input impedance and the radiation field of the antenna are based on the numerical solution of the problem of finding the amplitude-phase distribution of currents on its elements. During the sampling, the conductive surface of the antenna is divided into segments and calculates the distribution density of the surface currents in these segments [11]. This allows defining the characteristics of the antenna such as the frequency dependence of the input impedance, directivity, antenna gain, and reflection coefficient of frequency. The number of segments per unit design equal to $\lambda/4$, which ensured the convergence of the solution, even on the upper frequency of the range.

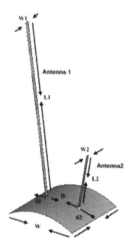

Fig. 1. Two antennas placed in curved surface

4   Proposed Scenarios

The gain characteristics, maximum gain direction, radiation pattern and S-parameter of the monopole antennas are studied for both in-band and out-of-band frequencies, in order to understand the out-of-band performance and characteristic of the monopole antennas the relationship between the dimensions of the antennas are examined. The antennas were simulated to examine the effects of each dimension parameter on both the in-band and out-of-band performance of the antenna. Then, the simulation results obtained, synthesized and analyzed using the FEKO curve fitting tool and surface fitting tool. Regression models relating the dimension parameters, and the in-band and out-of-band resonant frequencies were constructed. Smoothing techniques and interpolation techniques are used in the regression analysis to find the best fit functions. A general prediction function is derived for airborne antennas. However, the main problem in airborne antenna systems is to finding the right place to put the antennas on the surface. there are two scenarios used in that research, first is two antennas putted in curved surface and second scenario is two antennas putted in flat surface the both scenarios are studied and their parameters are calculated. The performance of all of these scenarios and functions derived are able to describe the variation of the in-band and out-of-band resonant frequencies with varied dimensional parameter values.

4.1   Scenario I

In this Scenario, (as shown in Fig. 1) first antenna work as transmit 0.9 GHz with out-of-band emission 2.3 GHz and the second antenna working as receiver with 2.3 GHz. To study the effect out-of-band of the first antenna on the in-band of the second antenna through measuring, input impedance, S-parameter, and radiation. The two antennas putted in curved ground surface. The distance of curved surface is 40 mm.

4.2   Scenario II

As shown in Fig. 2, the same case like first scenario but the difference here is the surface condition, this case performed on flat surface just for compare our work and to show the effect of curved and flat surface on the antenna and also to see the differences between each other.

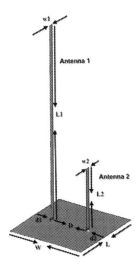

Fig. 2. Two antennas placed in flat surface

5   Results and Discussion

In this section, we introduce some simulation results, using FEKO software, related to the previous work. The effect of input impedance, S-parameter and radiation on performance of monopole antenna is studied. For first scenario the effect of curved ground is shown in Fig. 1. The distance between two antenna is D = 20 mm, d1and d2 is the distance between the antenna and the end of surface edge is 10 mm. the input impedance evaluated is shown in Fig. 3, the mean Real impedance increasing and mean imaginary impedance decreasing due to the effect of bending of the ground between the two antenna and sometimes from the out-of-band radiation resistance of antenna 1 will be effects on the in-band of antenna 2, although decreasing the Peak real impedance at

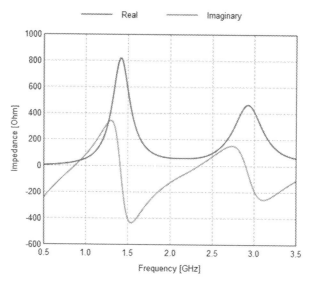

Fig. 3. The real (Blue) and imaginary (Green) of the input impedance in curved ground (Color figure online)

antenna 2 to 450 Ω, the real impedance equal 61.2 Ω at the band of antenna 2 and imaginary impedance equal to −13.4 Ω at 2.3 Ghz.

The s-parameter were discussed in details in Fig. 4 the effect of S-parameter in case of curved ground. is shown as s11 (input impedance) is -12.2 dB at the center frequency of antenna 1 (900 MHz) and s11 for antenna 2 (2.3 GHz) = −21.5 dB. Although for the center frequency of antenna 1 (900 MHz) s21 = −16.01 db and the

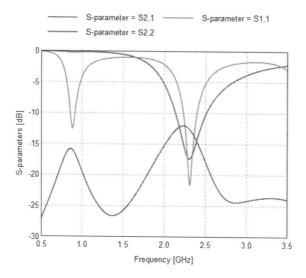

Fig. 4. S-parameter of curved surface.

s21 parameter of antenna 2 (2.3 GHz) is −12.63 db and s22 (output impedance) is equal −17.8 db at the center frequency antenna 2.

The antenna radiation pattern was discussed in details in Figs. 5 and 6, the effect of radiation pattern in case of curved ground is shown as E-plane at φ = 0° and φ = 90° we find the peak gain angle frequency at φ = 90° equal to 1.906 dBi at φ = 70° and main 3 db beam width equal to 85.942° but when the peak gain angle frequency at φ = 0° equal to 1.847 dBi at θ = −90° and main 3 db beam width equal to 90.968° due the effect of curved ground at 0.9 GHz.and we find at frequency 2.3 GHz the peak gain angle frequency at φ = 90° equal to 3.102 dBi at θ = −55° and main 3 db beam width equal to 52.047° but when the peak gain angle frequency at φ = 0° equal to 1.958 dBi at θ = −130° and main 3 db beam width equal to 51.972° due the effect of curved ground at 2.3 GHz.

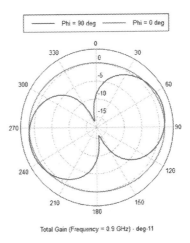

Total Gain (Frequency = 0.9 GHz) - deg-11

Fig. 5. Total gain in E-plane radiation pattern for curved surface is shown for 0.9 GHz

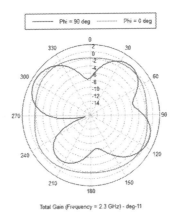

Total Gain (Frequency = 2.3 GHz) - deg-11

Fig. 6. The E-plane radiation pattern for curved surface in 2.3 GHz.

For second scenario the effect of flat ground which appear before in Fig. 2 the input impedance of flat surface is shown in Fig. 7, flat ground plane to see the effect of flat ground plane on performance of input impedance at antenna (1) in this case the impedance of the antennas from simulation result is shown you can see in case (flat ground plane) the mean Real impedance decreasing equal 24.2 Ω at 0.9 GHz and mean imaginary impedance increasing −14.9 O at the band of antenna1 when comparing with curved ground due the effect of flat ground plane at antenna1 band and the out of band radiation resistance of antenna 1 will be effects the in-band of antenna 2 will be increasing the Peak real impedance at the antenna 2 to 482 Ω in flat ground plane and the real impedance equal 72.4 Ω at 2.3Ghz and the imaginary impedance equal to −25.5 Ω at 2.3 Ghz which mean at the band of antenna 2.

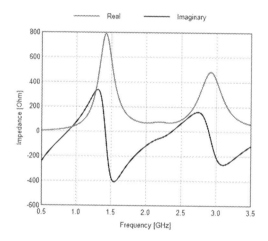

Fig. 7. The real input impedance (Red) and imaginary input impedance (Black) for two antennas in same flat surface. (Color figure online)

Also the s-parameter for flat surface in shown in details in Fig. 8. The s-parameter were discussed in details in Fig. 7 the effect of S-parameter in case of flat ground. is shown as s11 (input impedance) is −11.34 dB at the center frequency of antenna 1 (900 MHz) and s11 for antenna 2 (2.3 GHz) = −19.25 dB. Although for the center frequency of antenna 1 (900 MHz) s21 = −15.25 db and the s21 parameter of antenna2 is −19.25 db at (2.3 GHz) and s22 (output impedance) is equal −16 db at the center frequency antenna 2.

The radiation pattern of flat ground surface was discussed in details in Figs. 9 and 10, the effect of radiation pattern is shown as E-plane at φ = 0° and φ = 90° we find the peak gain angle frequency at φ = 90° equal to 1.898 dBi at θ = 80° and main 3 db beam width equal to 86.296° at 0.9 GHz but when the peak gain angle frequency at φ = 0° equal to 1.862 dBi at θ = 90° and main 3 db beam width equal to 87.529° due the effect of curved ground at 0.9 GHz. and the radiation founded at frequency 2.3 GHz the peak gain angle frequency at φ = 90° equal to 3.434 dBi at θ = 120° and main 3db beam width equal to 57.300° but when the peak gain angle frequency at

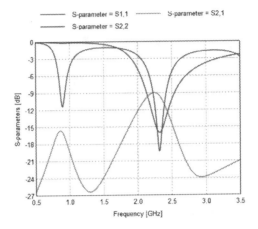

Fig. 8. The s-parameter for the two antennas in same flat surface

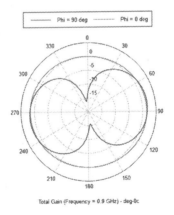

Fig. 9. Total gain in E-plane radiation pattern for flat surface is shown for 0.9 GHz

$\varphi = 0°$ equal to 1.909 dBi at $\theta = 125°$ and main 3 db beam width equal to 52.577° due the effect of curved ground at 2.3 GHz.

The qualitative and quantitative measures were conducted in our work. Table 1 expressed the performance of two scenarios and evaluates the different effect of the different surface.

Table 1. The two scenario performance and effects of different surface

Surface types	Real input impedance @2.3 Ghz	Imaginary input impedance @2.3 Ghz	S-parameter @0.900 GHz	S-parameter @2.3 GHz
Curved	61.2 Ω	−13.4 Ω	−12.20 db	−21.50 db
Flat	72.4 Ω	−25.5 Ωm	−11.34 db	−19.25 db

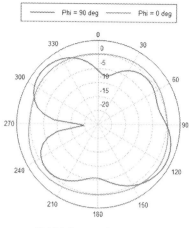

Fig. 10. Total gain in E-plane radiation pattern for flat surface is shown for 2.3 GHz

From above table the main result we can get from it that curved ground surface with specific degree can be outperformed the flat ground surface input impedance, s-parameter and radiation pattern in respectively.

6   Conclusion and Future Work

Out-of-band response of an antenna is an important factor that determines the susceptibility of a communication system to its surrounding environment. Several strategies have been proposed to reduce the out-of-band interference. This paper concerned in modeling the out-of-band performance of the antenna based on its in-band performance and the physical dimension of the antenna. Just an antenna is applied, the more specifications such as Input impedance, S-parameter, and radiations pattern of the monopole antenna were studied and discussed. The results appeared that curved ground surface with specific degree can be outperformed the flat ground surface in normal condition at different aspects. Our future work is to apply the same condition but in the large ground plane to see the effect of large ground surface can reduce the input impedance, s-parameter and radiation pattern more than small ground surface.

Acknowledgments. Our thanks to the department of Circuit and system in BUAA University.

References

1. Wu, Q., Su, W., Li, Z., Su, D.: Reduction in out-of-band antenna coupling using characteristic mode analysis. IEEE Trans. Antennas Propag. **64**(7), 2732–2742 (2016)
2. Jensen, M.A., Wallace, J.W.: A review of antennas and propagation for MIMO wireless communications. IEEE Trans. Antennas Propag. **52**(11), 2810–2824 (2004)

3. Tavik, G.C., Hilterbrick, C.L., Evins, J.B., Alter, J.J.: The advanced multifunction RF concept. IEEE Trans. Microw. Theo. Techn. **53**(3), 1009–1020 (2005)
4. Chiu, C.-Y., Cheng, C.-H., Murch, R.D., Rowell, C.R.: Reduction of mutual coupling between closely-packed antenna elements. IEEE Trans. Antennas Propag. **55**(6), 1732–1738 (2007)
5. Henault, S., Podilchak, S.K., Mikki, S.M., Antar, Y.M.M.: A methodology for mutual coupling estimation and compensation in antennas. IEEE Trans. Antennas Propag. **61**(3), 1119–1131 (2013)
6. Diallo, A., Luxey, C., Thuc, P.L., Staraj, R., Kossiavas, G.: Study and reduction of the mutual coupling between two mobile phone FIPAs operation in the DCS1800 and UMTS bands. IEEE Trans. Antennas Propag. **54**(11), 3063–3074 (2006)
7. Quendo, C., Rius, E., Person, C., Ney, M.: Integration of optimized low-pass filters in a bandpass filter for out-of-band improvement. IEEE Trans. Microw. Theo. Techn. **49**(12), 2376–2383 (2001)
8. Borresmans, J., Mandal, G., Giannini, V., Debaillie, B., Ingels, M., Sano, T., Verbruggen, B., Craninckx, J.: A 40 nm CMOS 0.4-6 GHz receiver resilient to out-of-band blockers. IEEE J. Solid-State Circ. **47**(7), 1659–1671 (2011)
9. Brandes, S., Cosovic, I., Schnell, M.: Reduction of out-of-band radiation in OFDM systems by insertion of cancellation carriers. IEEE Commun. Lett. **10**(6), 420–422 (2006)
10. Siden, S.V.: Out-of-band characteristics of the panel antenna. In: 2016 II International Young Scientists Forum on Applied Physics and Engineering (YSF), Kharkiv, pp. 65–68 (2016)
11. Bankov, S.E., Kurushin, A.A.: Calculation of the radiated structures using FEKO. ZAO «NPP RODNIK», Moscow (2008). (in Russian)

Multi-scale Feature Based Automatic Screen Character Integrity Detection

Chenhong Sui[⊠], Nan Zhu, and Xu Qiao

School of Opto-electronic Information Science and Technology,
Yantai University, Yantai, China
Tsui6662008@163.com

Abstract. Screen character integrity detection is an indispensable part for smart meter production. Compared with manual detection, automatic detection has evident advantage in terms of efficiency and cost. However, current automatic detection methods heavily depend on the preciseness of character segmentation. In this case, the image quality, e.g., inclination, noise, and non-uniform intensity of the screen, tends to highly influence the detection accuracy. To alleviate this problem, this paper proposes a multi-scale feature based automatic detection method. The main idea of this method is to search for the characters in the screen image based on the multi-scale features matching of each character. Therefore, we can determine the character integrity without segmentation. Moreover, the impact of screen image quality is effectively avoided. Experiments on real meter screen image show the effectiveness of the proposed method.

Keywords: Character integrity detection · Smart meter · Multi-Scale feature

1 Introduction

Smart meter is a multi-functional intelligent terminal with real-time monitoring and information interaction. It employs the digital display to show the digital reading. While due to the problem of welding technology, the screen can fail to provide perfect and calibration clear number. Thus, detecting the integrity of screen character is a vital link to ensure the quality of meter.

Since manual detection is inefficient and highly expensive, automatic detection has become a hot topic. Machine vision is becoming a popular automatic detection technique [1, 2], which includes the image acquisition and image analysis. The image acquisition implies utilizing the industrial CCD camera to capture the image of detected objects. Meanwhile, the image analysis involves image pre-process, object detection or recognition. In specific, image pre-process mainly aims to improve the image quality, e.g., de-noising, filtering, and image sharpening, etc. For object detection, the edge detection algorithms are usually emphasized. For example, Ding et al. [3] propose a Circular Hough Transform based defect detection method in Laser Welding. In this method, the canny operator is first used for edge detection, and Circular Hough Transform is further utilized to locate the weld seam position. To avoid the impact of background on edge detection, Yang et al. [4] first apply the threshold segmentation

© Springer Nature Singapore Pte Ltd. 2018
H. Yuan et al. (Eds.): GSKI 2017, CCIS 848, pp. 569–577, 2018.
https://doi.org/10.1007/978-981-13-0893-2_59

to separate target and background. Then, the edges are extracted through the edge detection. After that, the vial bottle mouth defect detection is finished. Additionally, Li et al. propose a principal components analysis (PCA) [5] based defect inspection and extraction method for mobile phone cover glass [6]. While these methods are useful for defect detection on high quality image, they heavily rely on the performance of the edge detection or segmentation process [7]. For instance, the noisy image requires smoothing to reduce noise interference. However, over-smoothing tends to the loss of information, and further leads to missed alarm. In addition, illumination changes in image may cause the over-segmentation or under-segmentation, which may also lead to performance deterioration of object detection.

To alleviate these problems, we propose a multi-scale features based character integrity detection algorithm for smart meter. In the method, multi-scale features are first extracted to provide both global and local information about the character via different scales. Therefore, the characters can be described with more information. This is helpful to avoid the sensitivity to image quality, e.g., noise, non-uniform intensity of the screen, etc. Moreover, the segmentation process is effectively avoided. Then, to detect the character, we utilize the fast normalized cross correlation [8] for matching the character template with the detected screen image. Experiments on real smart meter images show that the proposed method is robust to image quality and can provide high detection accuracy.

The rest of the paper is organized as follows. In Sect. 2, we mainly introduce the proposed automatic screen character integrity detection method, which includes the multi-scale feature extraction and fast normalized cross correlation based matching. To evaluate the effectiveness of the proposed method, experimental results and analysis on real data are presented in Sect. 3.

2 Multi-scale Feature Based Automatic Detection Method

2.1 The Main Framework of the Proposed Method

Assume I_0 is the screen image of fine meter, which is used as the trained image. Meanwhile, I is the screen image of detected meter, which is the test image N_0 and N represent the number of characters in I_0 and I, respectively. Then, if $N < N_0$, the meter corresponding to I is taken as a defective meter, and vice versa. Therefore, we can change the problem of screen characters integrity detection to detecting the charactering in screen image.

In terms of character detection, the multi-scale features corresponding to each character are first extracted in this paper, which can be seen as the template of each character. Second, we employ the fast normalized cross correlation for template matching. Then, characters are found by comparing the template with the screen image. Finally, based on the number of detected characters, we can determine whether the screen is defective or not. The flow chart of the proposed method is shown in Fig. 1.

In the following subsection, the multi-scale gray value based features is introduced.

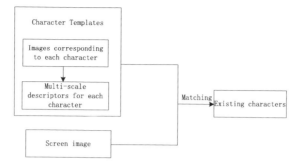

Fig. 1. Flowchart of the proposed method

2.2 Multi-scale Gray Value Based Descriptors

Scale Invariant Feature Transform (SIFT) is a famous multi-scale feature [9]. By providing multi-scale and multi-direction descriptors, it has the advantages of scale invariant, rotation invariant and even affine transformation invariant. Therefore, SIFT descriptor is widely used for image classification or object detection [10]. Since PCA is capable of transforming the high dimensional feature into a lower dimensional feature space, PCA-SIFT is proposed to significantly reduce the SIFT feature dimension [11]. However, locating the key points in SIFT or PCA-SIFT is computational complex. Comparatively speaking, Histograms of Oriented Gradient (HOG) descriptors can avoid locating the key points and provide multi-directional edge or structural information [12]. Nevertheless, HOG is very sensitive to noise or illumination changes when computing the gradient information, not to mention the large amount of calculation.

To alleviate the problem, this paper proposes to use multi-scale gray value based descriptor. This descriptor is generated by repeated Gaussian filtering and down-sampling steps. Compared with HOG of SIFT, this descriptor is more efficient to obtain. In addition, due to the multi-scale information, this descriptor also exhibits robustness to noise or illumination changes. This is helpful to reduce the reliance on image quality.

Suppose $I_c^{(0)}$ is an image corresponding to a character. Then, after repeating Gaussian filtering and down sampling for n times, we can obtain a series of lower resolution images called the image pyramid $\left\{ I_c^{(0)}, I_c^{(1)}, I_c^{(2)}, \ldots, I_c^{(n)}, \right\}$.

From the character image pyramid, we can extract the intensity values. These intensity values can be stacked to multi-scale features with respect to the character, i.e., template of the character. Then, character integrity detection is simplified into employing the template to search for the character in the detected screen image. It is worth noting that fast normalized cross correlation is an efficient and effective algorithm for template matching. Therefore, in the next subsection, we will introduce the fast normalized cross correlation used for character detection.

2.3   Fast Normalized Cross Correlation Based Matching

Pattern matching is a popular means of object detection and recognition. The main idea of pattern matching is to take the features extracted from standard image as template. By sliding the window pixel by pixel in the detected image, we can compare the similarity between the template and the formed sub-images. If the similarity is high, this usually means that there exists the object in the detected image. Then, the object is detected and located in the image. From this point of view we can find that besides template, the similarity metrics is also an important factor for template matching.

There are mainly two kinds of metrics used to measure the consistency between two objects: distance based metrics, e.g., Euclidean distance, Mahalanobis distance, etc. and similarity based metrics, e.g., cosine similarity, Pearson Coefficient, etc. Let S denote the template with size $r \times c$. The detected image I has R rows and C columns. When the top left corner of S has been moved to point (i,j), $1 \leq i \leq R - r + 1, 1 \leq j \leq C - c + 1$, the similarity between I and template S of the above mentioned metrics can be respectively computed as follows.

Euclidean distance

$$d(I,S) = \sqrt{\sum_{x=1}^{r} \sum_{y=1}^{c} [I(i+x,j+y) - S(x,y)]^2} \qquad (1)$$

Euclidean distance is a simple way to measure the similarity between two data objects. However, for sake of effectiveness, it requires the data to be normalized. While different from Euclidean distance, Mahalanobis distance takes the distribution characteristics of variables into consideration. Therefore, normalization is not needed for computing Mahalanobis distance, as shown in Eq. (2).

Mahalanobis distance

$$MD(I,S) = \sqrt{\frac{\sum_{x=1}^{r} \sum_{y=1}^{c} [I(i+x,j+y) - S(x,y)]^2}{\sum_{x=1}^{r} \sum_{y=1}^{c} [I(i+x,j+y) - \bar{I}(i,j)][S(x,y) - \bar{S}]}} \qquad (2)$$

Where $\bar{I}(i,j)$ is the mean of I in the template window, i.e., $\bar{I}(i,j) = \sum_{x=0}^{r-1} \sum_{y=0}^{c-1} I(i+x,j+y)$. $\bar{S}$ denotes the mean of S, i.e., $\bar{S} = \sum_{x=1}^{r} \sum_{y=1}^{c} S(x,y)$. The denominator is actually the covariance between I and template.

Cosine similarity

By measuring the angel between two vectors, Cosine similarity can reflect the similarity between them.

$$Cos\langle I, S\rangle = \frac{\sum\limits_{x=1}^{r}\sum\limits_{y=1}^{c}[I(i+x,j+y) \cdot S(x,y)]}{\sqrt{\sum\limits_{x=1}^{r}\sum\limits_{y=1}^{c}[I(i+x,j+y)]^2} \cdot \sqrt{\sum\limits_{x=1}^{r}\sum\limits_{y=1}^{c}[S(x,y)]^2}} \tag{3}$$

Pearson Coefficient

The Pearson Coefficient between two variables is also called the cross correlation. It is also capable of overcoming the effect of data distribution, as given by Eq. (4).

$$\rho_{I,S} = \frac{\sum\limits_{x=1}^{r}\sum\limits_{y=1}^{c}[I(i+x,j+y) - \bar{I}(i,j)][S(x,y) - \bar{S}]}{\sqrt{\sum\limits_{x=1}^{r}\sum\limits_{y=1}^{c}[I(i+x,j+y) - \bar{I}(i,j)]^2}\sqrt{\sum\limits_{x=1}^{r}\sum\limits_{y=1}^{c}[S(x,y) - \bar{S}]^2}} \tag{4}$$

From Eq. (4) we can see that $\rho_{I,S}$ is limited to $[-1, 1]$, which is effective in quantifying the similarity degree. Therefore, $\rho_{I,S}$ is widely used for pattern matching. However, since calculating $\rho_{I,S}$ is time-consuming, it is advantageous to real-time detection. Considering the redundancy in computing $\bar{I}(i,j)$, the fast normalized cross correlation is used [13]. The main idea of fast normalized cross correlation is to calculate the integral image in advance. Let G denote the integral image of I. Then, for any point (i,j) we have $G(i,j) = \sum\limits_{u=1}^{i}\sum\limits_{v=1}^{j}I(u,v)$. With the pre-calculated integral image G, for any sub-image in I, we can compute its mean $\bar{I}(i,j)$, as given by Eq. (5). Figure 2 depicts the calculation of $\bar{I}(i,j)$ using integral image.

$$\bar{I}(i,j) = G(i+r-1,j+c-1) - G(i,j+c-1) - G(i+r-1,j) + G(i,j) \tag{5}$$

It is evident from Fig. 2 that the redundant computation can be effectively avoided via integral image. In addition, the calculation of $\sum\limits_{x=1}^{r}\sum\limits_{y=1}^{c}[I(i+x,j+y) - \bar{I}(i,j)]^2$ in denominator can be simplified to

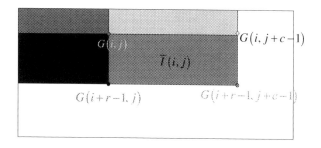

Fig. 2. Calculation of $\bar{I}(i,j)$ using integral image

$$\sum_{x=1}^{r}\sum_{y=1}^{c}[I(i+x,j+y) - \bar{I}(i,j)]^2$$

$$= \sum_{x=1}^{r}\sum_{y=1}^{c}[I(i+x,j+y)]^2 - \frac{1}{r \cdot c}\left[\sum_{x=1}^{r}\sum_{y=1}^{c}I(i+x,j+y)\right]^2 \qquad (6)$$

$$= \sum_{x=1}^{r}\sum_{y=1}^{c}[I(i+x,j+y)]^2 - \frac{1}{r \cdot c}\bar{I}^2(i,j)$$

From Eq. (6) we can see that constructing the integral image of I^2 can further reduce the redundant computation in Eq. (6). Therefore, the efficiency of normalized cross correlation can be greatly improved through integral image.

The main process multi-scale feature based automatic Screen character integrity detection can be described as follows. First, through recursive Gaussian filtering and down-sampling, we can get the multi-scale feature set $\left\{I_c^{(0)}, I_c^{(1)}, I_c^{(2)}, \ldots, I_c^{(n)}\right\}, c = 1, 2, 3, \ldots, M$ of characters, where M represents the number of categories for characters existed in the standard meter screen image. Second, by sliding the template pixel by pixel in I, we can compare template $\left\{I_c^{(0)}, I_c^{(1)}, I_c^{(2)}, \ldots, I_c^{(n)}\right\}, c = 1, 2, 3, \ldots, M$ with the corresponding sub-image through Eq. (4). Then, by counting the actual detected number of the $c^{th}(c = 1, 2, \ldots, M)$ category character, we can determine whether the meter screen is integral or not. The pseudo-code of our method is depicted as follows:

Algorithm1: Multi-scale feature based automatic Screen character integrity detection
Input:

Multi-scale feature set of characters $\left\{I_c^{(0)}, I_c^{(1)}, I_c^{(2)}, \ldots, I_c^{(n)}\right\}, c = 1, 2, 3, \ldots, M$;
     The true number of the $c^{th}(c = 1, 2, \ldots, M)$ category character
     TN_c
     For the $c^{th}(c = 1, 2, \ldots, M)$ category character ,the actual detected
     number N_c
     Image to be detected I ;
     Threshold τ

Output: Detection result

1 for $c = 1 : M$
 2   Calculate the normalized cross correlation $\rho_{I,T}$ between I and
     $\left\{I_c^{(0)}, I_c^{(1)}, I_c^{(2)}, \ldots, I_c^{(n)}\right\}$ according to Eq. (4);
 3   Counting the actual number N_c of characters with $\rho_{I,T} \geq \tau$;
 4   If $N_c == TN_c$, the cth category character in I is complete, else
       exit.
 5 end
 Return Detection result

From Algorithm 1 we can see that the proposed method can locate the first incomplete character.

3   Experiments

To evaluate the effectiveness of the proposed method, real smart meter screen images are utilized. In the following sub-sections, the experimental data are first shown. Then we give the detection results with the proposed method.

3.1   Experimental Data

Figure 4, (a) – (e) depict the detected meter screen images, and (f) is the standard screen image.

It is obvious from Fig. 3 that, due to the impact of backlight, there exist uneven brightness and strip in (a) – (e). In the next sub-section, we will give the detection results in Fig. 3 (a) – (e).

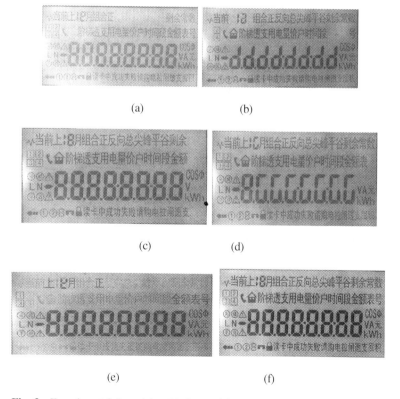

(a)   (b)

(c)   (d)

(e)   (f)

Fig. 3. Experimental data: (a) – (e) detected images, (f) standard screen image

3.2   Experimental Results

For sake of investigating the performance of the proposed method, detection results in Fig. (4) (a) – (e) are be presented in Fig. 4.

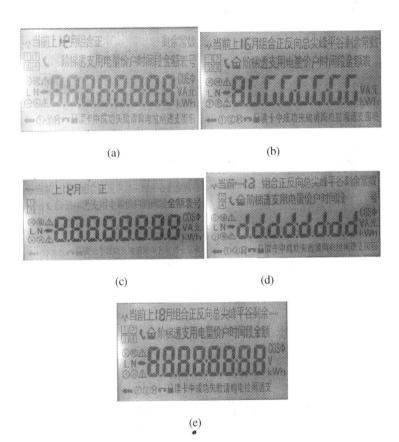

Fig. 4. Experimental results for the defects detection on the smart meter

It is obvious from Fig. 4 that although each screen image has different degree of defection, contrast, and noise, the first defected character can be found. This demonstrates the robustness of the proposed method to image quality.

Acknowledgement. This work was supported by the National Natural Science Foundation of China under Grant 61601397.

References

1. Zhou, J., Ren, K., Shuai, Y.Q., et al.: Machine vision based defect detection on magnetic steel sheet. J. Mech. Electr. Eng., 31(12), 2014
2. Deng, S., Cai, W., Xu, Q., et al.: Defect detection of bearing surfaces based on machine vision technique. In: International Conference on Computer Application and System Modeling. vol. 4, pp. V4-548, IEEE (2010)
3. Ding, Q., Ji, J., Gao, F., et al.: Machine-vision-based defect detection using circular hough transform in laser welding. In: International Conference on Machinery, Materials and Computing Technology. Atlantis Press (2016)
4. Yang, Z.F., Bai, J.Y.: Vial bottle mouth defect detection based on machine vision. In: IEEE International Conference on Information and Automation, pp. 2638–2642 IEEE (2015)
5. Martinez, A.M., Kak, A.C.: PCA versus LDA. IEEE Trans. Pattern Anal. Mach. Intell. **23** (2), 228–233 (2002)
6. Li, D., Liang, L.Q., Zhang, W.J.: Defect inspection and extraction of the mobile phone Cover glass based on the principal components analysis. Int. J. Adv. Manuf. Technol. **73**(9–12), 1605–1614 (2014)
7. Wang, C.C., Jiang, B.C., Lin, J.Y., et al.: Machine vision-based defect detection in IC images using the partial information correlation coefficient. IEEE Trans. Semicond. Manuf. **26**(3), 378–384 (2013)
8. Lewis, J.P.: (Industrial light & magic). fast normalized cross-correlation template matching by cross-Correlation. Circuits Syst. Sign. Process. **82**(2), 144–156 (1995)
9. Lowe, D.G.: Object recognition from local scale-invariant features. In: ICCV. IEEE Computer Society, p. 1150 (1999)
10. Liu, C., Yuen, J., Torralba, A.: SIFT flow: dense correspondence across scenes and its applications. IEEE Trans. Pattern Anal. Mach. Intell. **33**(5), 978 (2011)
11. Ke, Y., Sukthankar, R.: PCA-SIFT: a more distinctive representation for local image descriptors. In: IEEE Computer Society Conference on Computer Vision and Pattern Recognition. IEEE Computer Society, pp. 506–513 (2004)
12. Dalal, N., Triggs, B., Triggs, B.: Histograms of oriented gradients for human detection. CVPR **1**(12), 886–893 (2005)
13. Hanebeck, U.D.: Template matching using fast normalized cross correlation. In: Proceedings of SPIE - The International Society for Optical Engineering, vol. 4387, pp. 95–103 (2001)

An Algorithm Towards Energy-Efficient Scheduling for Real-Time Tasks Under Cloud Computing Environment

Tongtong Sun[1], Ye Tao[2], and Ruichun Tang[1(✉)]

[1] College of Information Science and Engineering,
No. 238 Songling Road, Laoshan District, Qingdao, Shandong, China
18306485730@163.com, tangruichun@126.com
[2] School of Information and Technology, Qingdao University of Science
and Technology, No. 99 Songling Road, Qingdao, China
ye.tao@qust.edu.cn

Abstract. This paper proposes a task scheduling algorithm called AKAM (Adaptive KNN and Adaptive Min-min), which can improve the real-time performance and energy consumption of cloud resource scheduling and allocation. The proposed AKAM based on Min-min task scheduling algorithm and KNN algorithm. Firstly, the Qos requirements contained in the user request task are applied to the KNN algorithm to select the appropriate resources for the task. Secondly, based on Min-min algorithm, we establish task slack and virtual machine threshold to complete task scheduling. Simulation results show the efficiency of AKAM.

Keywords: Cloud computing · Energy-efficient scheduling
MIN-min algorithm · KNN algorithm

1 Introduction

With the development of Internet, cloud computing has been widely used to store, manage and analyze data. However, the problem of low energy efficiency has become increasingly prominent, hindering the development of green cloud computing. Therefore, how to configure and operate the cloud data center in the process of reducing energy consumption has become a huge challenge in the development of cloud computing.

Around the issue of resource scheduling, the literature [6–10] carry on the relevant research. [6] proposed a progressive optimal energy-saving scheduling algorithm, which through DVFS technology to scale the CPU frequency to minimize energy consumption and maximize the benefits. [7] proposed a DVFS-based relaxation iterative rounding algorithm, the algorithm can minimize energy consumption at the task cut-off time. Although DVFS technology can reduce energy consumption, it can only be used in the host processor level, and the level of energy consumed by the total system energy consumption of only one-third. Therefore, the virtualization technology has been widely used to further reduce energy consumption.

© Springer Nature Singapore Pte Ltd. 2018
H. Yuan et al. (Eds.): GSKI 2017, CCIS 848, pp. 578–591, 2018.
https://doi.org/10.1007/978-981-13-0893-2_60

In recent years, most of the energy-saving scheduling algorithm research has focused on merging VMs according to system workloads to minimize the number of active hosts and reducing energy consumption. [8] calculated the cost of migrating VM, and proposed a resource manager called Entropy. This resource manager is dedicated to heterogeneous clusters, enabling to dynamically migrate VMs based on program constraints with the consideration of migration costs. [9] studied how to combine tasks dynamically to improve resource utilization and reduce energy consumption, it proposed an energy-efficient task consolidation method that optimizes energy consumption in cloud systems.

In this paper, we based on the existing research on how to complete the task of energy-efficient scheduling to do a further study. The AKAM algorithm proposed by this article is based on the KNN algorithm and the Min-min algorithm. First, the Qos requirements contained in the user request task are applied to the KNN algorithm to select the appropriate resources for the task. Second, based on Min-min algorithm, we establish task slack and virtual machine threshold to complete task scheduling. Simulation results show the efficiency of proposed algorithm.

2 Tasks Scheduling System Model

In this section, we first introduce the physical machine model and task model in task scheduling respectively. Then introduce the system architecture and formulate the scheduling problem studied in this paper.

2.1 Normal or Body Text

Suppose there are np physical machines in the cloud, denoted by $P = \{p_1, p_2, \ldots, p_{np}\}$, $p_i = \{c_i, m_i, s_i, b_i\}$, where c_i, m_i, s_i, b_i represent the physical processing Capacity, storage space, disk I/O, and network bandwidth respectively. The percentage of free CPU capacity, storage space, disk I/O, and network bandwidth of a physical machine at time t is $fc_i(t)$, $fm_i(t)$, $fs_i(t)$ and $fb_i(t)$ respectively.

Let $T = \{t_1, t_2, \ldots, t_{nt(t)}\}$ be the set of tasks at time t, where $nt(t)$ is the total number of tasks arriving from 0 to t. And $t_j = \{wt_j, ad_j, st_j, L_j\}(1 \leq j \leq nt(t))$, where wt_j, ad_j, st_j and L_j represent the waiting time, the last allocation period, the service time and the slack. The waiting time is the time from the task to the final allocation to the physical machine.

In addition, different tasks may require different operating environment, in order to deal with task t_j, you need to create the corresponding virtual machine v_j and deployed on the physical machine. We use the matrix A (t) of $np \times nt(t)$ to represent the task assignment at time t, where the element $a_{ij}(t)$ in A (t) is binomial: $a_{ij}(t) = 1$ indicates that the virtual machine v_i is allocated to the physical machine p_j for processing, and $a_{ij}(t) = 0$ indicates that the virtual machine v_i is not allocated to the physical machine p_j. The rm_{ij}, rc_{ij}, rs_{ij}, and rb_{ij} represent the resource requirement of the virtual machine v_i for the physical machine p_j storage space, CPU strength, disk I/O, and network bandwidth, respectively. Assuming that the creation and maintenance of virtual machines is also included in the resource requirements, then rc_{ij}, rm_{ij}, rs_{ij}, and rb_{ij} represent all the resources that v_i needs to run on p_j. During the implementation, these resource requirements are derived from user-supplied experimental data, benchmarks, and configuration files for the application. If we want to assign v_i to p_j, the following inequality need to be satisfied:

$$rc_{ij} \leq fc_i(t-1) \tag{1}$$

Similarly, rs_{ij}, rm_{ij}, and rb_{ij} all satisfy this inequality.

Any task assignment that does not meet the resource requirements might result in the increase of completion time, resulting in a task that can not be completed on time. After assigning v_i to p_j, the idle resources as follows:

$$fc_i(t-1) \leftarrow fc_i(t-1) - rc_{ij} \tag{2}$$

Before the end of the time slice, the resource is updated as follows:

$$fc_i(t) \leftarrow fc_i(t-1) \tag{3}$$

Meanwhile, the other resources do similar updated.

2.2   Scheduling System Structure

Task scheduling architecture shown in Fig. 1. Similar to the traditional multiprocessor system, the scheduling model in the cloud environment also includes three levels: the user layer, the scheduling layer and the resource layer. The difference is that the resource layer is further divided into two levels: the host layer and the virtual machine layer, according to the cloud datacenter workload to adjust the number of hosts.

In this paper, we consider the resource scheduling issue in cloud environment as task allocation issue based on the time slot. In each time slice, we use the matrix A (t) to represent the task allocation results. In the distribution process priority assigned to the large tasks, and the urgent tasks need to be allocated immediately. In order to save the long-term cost, we propose a threshold variable $\varphi(t)$ for online assignment and adjust the value of $\varphi(t)$ by PID controller at the end of each time slot.

Because of the uncertainty of task, we use the interval number and degree of relaxation. We express the execution time and deadline of the task by the number of intervals, and use the size of task slack to decide the scheduling order of tasks.

In addition, virtual machine migration is triggered when the server is overloaded or under-loaded. The goal of this process is still to save on long-term costs.

2.3   Scheduling Problem Formulation

In the process of processing large data tasks in the cloud environment, how to reduce energy consumption under the premise of ensuring real-time performance is an important issue.

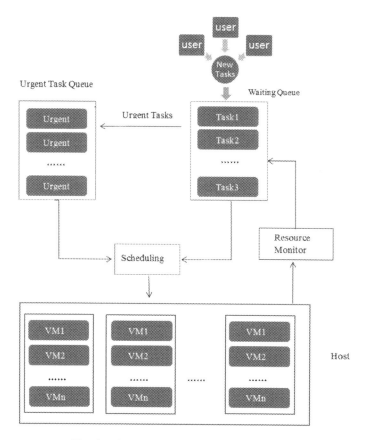

Fig. 1. The task scheduling system architecture

In the cloud environment, the cost is directly related to the utilization of the physical machine, therefore, we define the long-run cost as the total running time of all physical machines (assuming different energy consumption rates for different physical machines are different). The long-term cost can be expressed as:

$$\overline{C} = \lim_{t \to \infty} \frac{1}{t} \sum_{i=1}^{np} \sum_{\tau=0}^{t-1} y_i(\tau) \qquad (4)$$

where $y_i(t)$ is a binomial variable, $y_i(t) = 1$ indicates that the physical machine p_i is running at time t, and $y_i(t) = 0$ indicates that the physical machine p_i is idle at time t.

Obviously, the waste of resources leads to an increase in long-term costs. Assuming that the physical machines and virtual machines are same, the long-term costs $\overline{RW}$ can defined as follows:

$$\overline{RW} = \lim_{t \to \infty} \frac{1}{t} \sum_{i=1}^{np} \sum_{\tau=0}^{t-1} (fc_i(\tau) + fm_i(\tau) + fs_i(\tau) + fb_i(\tau)) \times y_i(\tau) \qquad (5)$$

It is easy to see that $\overline{RW}$ and $\overline{C}$ of any task set $T(t)$ are positively related. Therefore, in order to improve resource utilization, we establish the following objectives:

$$\min_{A(t),t=0,1,2,\dots} \overline{C} = \frac{1}{t}\sum_{i=1}^{np}\sum_{\tau=0}^{t-1} y_i(\tau) \tag{6}$$

$$fc_i(t), fm_i(t), fs_i(t), fb_i(t) \geq 0 \quad \forall t, i \tag{7}$$

$\exists p_i$:

$$fc_i(t) \geq rc_{ij} \quad \forall t, j \tag{8}$$

Similarly, $fm_i(t), fs_i(t), fb_i(t)$ also meet formula (8).

$$t \leq adj_j|j, \sum_{i=1}^{np} a_{ij}(t) = 0 \quad \forall t \tag{9}$$

Formula (4) ensure that a single physical machine and the entire cloud have sufficient resources to use. Equation (5) indicates that all tasks must be allocated before the deadline. Under the premise of satisfying formula (1), we can use the following optimization goal:

$$\min_{A(t),t=0,1,2,\dots} \overline{RW} \tag{10}$$

Note that in this paper we assume that the formulas (9), and (13) are usually feasible.

The computational complexity of the online allocation algorithm is also an important factor. We have adopted a feasible workload pattern, that is, the assignment of tasks at any time t has no link with the previous distribution, and then the complexity of the problem is analyzed.

In addition, the assignment of task at time t is independent, it has no relation with the previous assignments and future assignments. Therefore, the task assignment problem at time t can be simplified as:

$$\min \sum_{i=1}^{np} y_i(t) \tag{11}$$

The above problem can be mapped to multi-dimensional packing problem. The goal of this problem is to map some items to as few boxes as possible, each of which represents a tuple containing dimensions. Since the multidimensional packing problem is a well-known NP-complete problem, the distribution problem at any time tin this paper is also an NP-complete problem. More specifically, the size of the NP-complete problem depends on the number of tasks arriving at time $t - 1$ to t, and the number of arrivaltasks can be expressed as $nt(t) - nt(t - 1)$.

From the formula (6) and formula (7), we can know that long-term service cost is relevant with overall resource utilization. So we can define some parameters to represent the overall resource utilization of the physical machine. Given a physical machine p_i, then:

Resource usage $\mu_i(t)$. The resource usage at time t can be expressed as follows:

$$\mu_i(t) = \frac{fc_i(t) + fm_i(t) + fs_i(t) + fb_i(t)}{4} \tag{12}$$

From $\mu_i(t)$ can be intuitive to see the p_i resource usage at time t.

Resource balance $\sigma_i(t)$. The resource balance at time t can be expressed as follows:

$$temp_1 = (\mu_i(t) - fs_i(t))^2 \tag{13}$$

Similarly, We can calculate $temp_2$, $temp_3$, $temp_4$.

$$\sigma_i(t) = \frac{\sqrt{temp_1 + temp_2 + temp_3 + temp_4}}{2}$$

$\sigma_i(t)$ indirectly represents the overall resource usage.

It is easy to see that the larger the $\mu_i(t)$ and $\sigma_i(t)$ is, the better the overall resource usage will be. Therefore, we combine these two parameters into a simple parameter $cv_i(t)$, which is defined as follows:

$$cv_i(t) = \sigma_i(t) \times \mu_i(t) \tag{14}$$

The actual value of $cv_i(t)$ is obtained by independent measurement, so it may be used for different or inconsistent physical machines. We can evaluate the resource usage of the algorithm by computing the value of $cv_i(t)$.

3 The Proposed Algorithm: AKAM

In order to meet the real-time task scheduling in the cloud, while minimizing the consumption of energy, this paper presents the AKAM algorithm. AKAM is divided into two parts: AKNN algorithm and improved Min-min algorithm. The role of the AKNN is assigning task to the appropriate data center, and improved Min-min's role is scheduling task.

3.1 Task Assignment

First, we need to select the appropriate data center according to the available resources, network throughput and Qos parameters of the data center, and then assign the task to the datacenter. The algorithm used in this process is the adaptive K-nearest neighbor algorithm.

3.1.1   AKNN Algorithm

Algorithm 1

AKNN(Adaptive K Nearest Neighbor)

Input: V, U, current_free, user_load

Output: D

Step 1: k = 1, U = (u_1, u_2)

Step 2:foreach user request

Compute the distance between user request parameters $U = (u_1, u_2)$ and every datacenter parameters $V = (v_1, v_2)$

$$d(U, V) = |U - V|$$
$$= \sqrt{(u_1 - v_1)^2 + (u_2 - v_2)^2}$$

Step 3: Select V_i, the set of k closest points to U arranged in a sequence.

Step 4: For eachk^{th} nearest datacenter selected
           calculate current free resources.

Step 5: **If**(current-free <user_load)
           Allocate U to selected datacenter D

Else
           k = k + 1 and goto Step 4.

Step 6:END

KNN algorithm is a mature machine learning algorithm, which has the advantages of simple thought, easy implementation and short training time. Because the KNN algorithm is only applicable to fixed-point in n-dimensional space, and the load in the data center is dynamic and cannot be represented by points, we propose an adaptive KNN algorithm, which named AKNN algorithm. AKNN calculates the distance between the user and the resource dynamically by using the Qos parameter of the user request and the actual resource of the data center as the parameter to complete the dynamic resource selection. Specific steps see Algorithm 1.

Among them:

(1)   U is the vector to storage the two required values of the physical distance and network throughput required in the task;
(2)   V is the vector to storage the physical distance between datacenters and user distance and the network throughput;
(3)   D refers to the data center, which is used to complete tasks;
(4)   k is the number of datacenters that are ordered for the task;
(5)   current_free refers to the number of idle resources in the data center during the selection process;
(6)   user_load refers to the number of resources required for scheduling tasks.

3.2   Task Scheduling

Please use a 9-point Linux Libertine, or other Roman font with serifs, as close as possible in appearance to Times Roman in which these guidelines have been set. The goal is to have a 9-point text, as you see here. Please use sans-serif or non-proportional fonts only for special purposes, such as distinguishing source code text. If Times Roman is not available, try the font named Computer Modern Roman. On a Macintosh, use the font named Times. Right margins should be justified, not ragged.

3.2.1   Improved Min-min Algorithm

Min-min algorithm is a classic traditional task scheduling algorithm, the main idea is using the shortest possible time to allocate and process the task, and it takes time as a single weight to design task scheduling algorithm. Min-min assigns the task to the virtual machine with the shortest task time to ensure the shortest time to complete the task. At the same time, the virtual machine with strong processing capacity is always in working state, and the virtual machine with weak processing capacity is idle for a long time, thus it has a drawback of high energy consumption. In order to combine the real-time and energy-saving features, we improved Min-min real-time performance and optimized the energy performance.

We use $[cv]\_i$ (t) as a parameter to measure the resource utilization of the algorithm and set a dynamic threshold $\varphi(t)$. In order to achieve energy-saving task scheduling, based on the Min-min algorithm, we divide the time into many time slices, and then use $\varphi(t)$ as the number of virtual machine in the next time slice, the threshold $\varphi(t)$ is adjusted by PID controller to complete the dynamic adjustment. In addition, in each time slice, emergency tasks are prioritized, and a large task with a long processing time is assigned with second priority to ensure that all tasks can be completed at the end of the time slice.

The main allocation process is as follows:

Algorithm 2

Input: A set T of tasks, a set M of machines, a set U of urgent tasks, and
the $\mu_i(J)$ for all $J \in T, i \in M$

Output: A schedule $S = \{List_i\}_{i \in M}$, $t = 0$, $T = \emptyset$, long period $\varphi(t) = +\infty$
   repeat
        For eachp_i
        $fc_i(0) = fm_i(t) = fs_i(0) = fb_i(t) = 100\%$
        For each$i \in M$ do
        Set $List_i = \emptyset$, $t_i = 0$
        CalculateL_i and d_i
        if$(d_i \leq \omega)$
        $U = U \cup t_i$
        end
        while$U \neq \emptyset$ do
            allocate big tasks first
            Let$(i, j) = \arg\min_{(i,j)}\{t_i + \mu_i(J): i \in M, J \in U\}$.
            Set $L_i = L_i \cup \{J\}$, $t_i = t_i + \mu_i(J)$, $U = U\setminus\{J\}$.
            repeat
            until the long period end

According to the system load, the improved Min-min algorithm can turn off the idle host in time so as to achieve the purpose of energy-saving.

4   Performance Evaluation

To test the performance of the AKAM algorithm, we compare the AKAM with Min-min algorithm, MCT algorithm [10], CRS algorithm [11] and EDF algorithm [12]. In order to compare the efficiency of these algorithms, we use the following performance criteria to evaluate the performance of these algorithm:

(1) Success rate: The ratio of tasks completed before the deadline.
(2) Resource utilization: the average utilization of host, it can be calculated as:

$$\text{RU} = \left(\sum_{i=1}^{m} \sum_{j=1}^{n} \sum_{k=1}^{|VM_j|} l_i^r \cdot o_{ijk} \right) \bigg/ \left(\sum_{j=1}^{n} c_j \cdot wt_j \right) \qquad (15)$$

(3) Total energy consumption rate: The total energy consumption of a host performing a task set T.
(4) Stability: The sum of the weighted absolute deviations between the predicted start time of the task and their actual start time in the actual scheduling process.

4.1   Simulation Experiment

The simulation tool used in this experiment is CloudSimtoolkit, we build a kernel-based virtual machine cluster (KVM cluster) in the experiment. The entire experiment was performed in a 1 Gbps Ethernet. In addition, some similar settings have been made for the experimental environment with reference to [14].

Although the average utilization of the host is lower than the peak period, many of the data centers can still handle the task scheduling in the peak period. Suppose the number of hosts in the cloud data center is infinite, and is divided into three types, these host CPU performance are 1000MIPS, 2000MIPS and 3000MIPS, respectively, and their storage space is 8G, RAM are 1 TB, peak power is 250 W, 300 W and 400 W, respectively. The virtual machine is divided into four types, these four virtual machine CPU performance are 250 MIPS, 500 MIPS, 750 MIPS and 1000 MIPS, respectively, and their storage space is 1 GB, RAM are 128 MB. Each task has a CPU demand variable that is assigned to the virtual machine only if its upper and lower bounds do not exceed the CPU performance of the virtual machine. Besides, the start-up time of the host is 90 s, VM creation time is 15 s, the transfer time depends on the performance of RAM and system bandwidth [8].

In addition, the deadline d_i of task t_i satisfies:

$$d_i = a_i + U[deadlineBase, a \times deadlineBase] \qquad (16)$$

where U[deadlineBase, a × deadlineBase] is a arbitrary number between deadlineBase and a × deadlineBase, deadlineBase determines whether the deadline of task is loose or not, and the value of variable a is set 4.

The parameter interval Time determines the time interval between two consecutive tasks, assuming the value of the interval Time is between 0 and 5. While task Uncertainty and VM Uncertainty represent the maximum values of tasks and VM uncertainties in the system, respectively. The mathematical formula are:

$$l_i^- = U\left[1 \times 10^5, 2 \times 10^5\right];$$
$$l_i^+ = l_i^- \times (1 + U[0, \text{taskUncertainty}]); \qquad (17)$$
$$c_{jk}^- = c_{jk}^+ \times (1 - U[0, \text{vmUncertainty}])$$

where c_{jk}^+ represent the CPU performance requirement of vm_{jk}.

The actual completion time is calculated by the following formula:

$$ft_{ijk}^r = ft_{ijk}^- + \left(f_{ijk}^+ - f_{ijk}^-\right) \times U[0, 1] \qquad (18)$$

Note that the parameter ft_{ijk}^r is not available until the task is scheduled except for CRS algorithm. The values of these parameters are shown in Table 1.

Table 1. Parameters for simulation studies

Parameters	Value(fixed)-(varied)
task count(10^4)	(2)-(1,2,3,4,5,6,7,8)
dealline Base(s)	(200)-(100,150,200,250,300,350,400)
interval Time(s)	([0,5])
task Length(10^5 MI)	([1, 2])
task Uncertainty	(0.2)-(0.0,0.05,0.10,0.15,0.20,0.25,0.30,0.35,0.40)
vm Uncertainty	(0.2)-(0.0,0.05,0.10,0.15,0.20,0.25,0.30,0.35,0.40)

4.2   Result Analysis

In the experiment, we conducted the system performance test on the task quantity, the deadline and the uncertainty of the task respectively.

4.2.1   Number of Tasks

In this group of experiments, we tested the effect of the number of tasks on system performance. Figure 2 shows the experimental results of each test algorithm when the number of tasks increases from 1×10^4 to 8×10^4.

And from Fig. 2, we can see that with the increase of the number of tasks, the success rate, resource utilization, system stability and energy efficiency of AKAM algorithm are better than other algorithms.

4.2.2   Task Deadline

In this experiment, we tested the impact of task deadline on system performance. Figure 3 shows the results of test algorithm when task deadline from 100 s to 400 s.

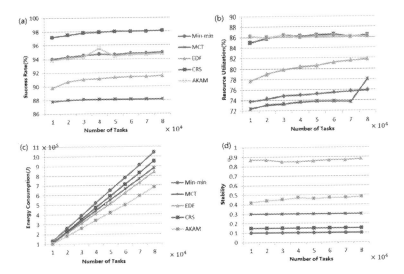

Fig. 2. Performance impact of number of tasks

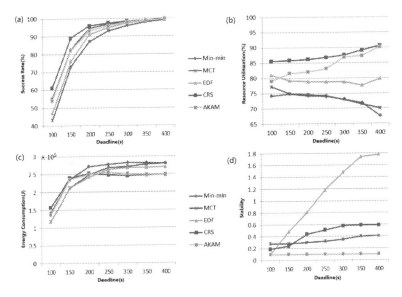

Fig. 3. Performance impact of tasks' deadline

Figure 3 shows the mission success rate, resource utilization rate, energy consumption rate and system stability of the algorithm with the task deadline changes. It can be seen that the AKAM algorithm can balance the energy saving and meet the real-time requirement of the task, and reduce the energy consumption on the basis of real-time.

4.2.3 Task Uncertainty

In this experiment, we tested the effect of task uncertainty on system performance. Figure 4 shows the experimental results of each test algorithm when the task uncertainty increases from 0 to 0.4.

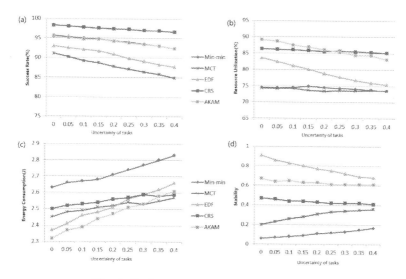

Fig. 4. Performance impact of task uncertainty

It can be seen from Fig. 4 that the AKAM algorithm has a higher success rate and higher resource utilization than other algorithms, as task uncertainty increases.

It can be seen from the above experimental results that the AKAM algorithm is not optimal in terms of success rate, resource utilization, and energy consumption, compared to other algorithms, but it can achieve equalization in these respects, not only taking into account the uncertainty of task and meeting the time constraints to ensure the success rate of the task, but also adjust the number of hosts under the circumstances to save power.

5 Conclusion

In this paper, we focus on how to meet the time constraints in cloud and reduce the energy consumption of the system. We propose an uncertain task scheduling architecture and a new task scheduling algorithm, AKAM algorithm. AKAM can do a good trade-off about task success rate, system resource utilization, system stability and energy consumption rate. Compared with Min-min algorithm, EDF algorithm, MCT algorithm and CRS algorithm, the simulation results show that the AKAM algorithm is effective.

Acknowledgments. This research is supported by the National Key Research and Development Program of China (No. 2015BAF28B01), and Shandong Province Key Research and Development Program (No. 2016GGX103006).

References

1. Barroso, L.A.: The price of performance. Obstet. Gynecol. Surv. **3**(7), 48–53 (2005)
2. Brown, R.E., Masanet, E., Nordman, B., et al.: Report to Congress on Server and Data Center Energy Efficiency: Public Law 109–431: Appendices. Lawrence Berkeley National Laboratory (2007)
3. Wang, L., Khan, S.U., Chen, D., et al.: Energy-aware parallel task scheduling in a cluster. Future Gener. Comput. Syst. **29**(7), 1661–1670 (2013)
4. Barroso, L.A., Holzle, U.: The case for energy-proportional computing. Computer **40**(12), 33–37 (2007)
5. Beloglazov, A., Buyya, R., Lee, Y.C., et al.: Chapter 3–A taxonomy and survey of energy-efficient data centers and cloud computing systems. Adv. Comput. **82**, 47–111 (2011)
6. Ding, Y., Qin, X., Liu, L., et al.: Energy efficient scheduling of virtual machines in cloud with deadline constraint. Future Gener. Comput. Syst. **50**, 62–74 (2015)
7. Li, D., Wu, J.: Energy-aware scheduling for frame-based tasks on heterogeneous multiprocessor platforms. In: 2012 41st International Conference on Parallel Processing (ICPP), pp. 430–439. IEEE (2012)
8. Hermenier, F., Lorca, X., Menaud, J.M., et al.: Entropy: a consolidation manager for clusters. In: ACM SIGPLAN/SIGOPS International Conference on Virtual Execution Environments VEE 2009, pp. 41–50 (2009)
9. Hsu, C.H., Slagter, K.D., Chen, S.C., et al.: Optimizing energy consumption with task consolidation in clouds. Inf. Sci. **258**(3), 452–462 (2014)
10. Li, J., Ming, Z., Qiu, M., et al.: Resource allocation robustness in multi-core embedded systems with inaccurate information. J. Syst. Architect. **57**(9), 840–849 (2011)
11. Vonder, S.V.D., Demeulemeester, E., Herroelen, W.: A classification of predictive-reactive project scheduling procedures. J. Sched. **10**(3), 195–207 (2007)
12. Mills, A.F., Anderson, J.H.: A stochastic framework for multiprocessor soft real-time scheduling. 311–320 (2010)
13. Herroelen, W., Leus, R.: Project scheduling under uncertainty: survey and research potentials. Eur. J. Oper. Res. **165**(2), 289–306 (2005)
14. Beloglazov, A., Buyya, R.: Optimal online deterministic algorithms and adaptive heuristics for energy and performance efficient dynamic consolidation of virtual machines in cloud data centers. Concurr. Comput. Pract. Exp. **24**(13), 1397–1420 (2012)
15. Hu, M., Veeravalli, B.: Requirement-aware strategies for scheduling real-time divisible loads on clusters. J. Parallel Distrib. Comput. **73**(8), 1083–1091 (2013)
16. Beloglazov, A., Buyya, R.: Managing overloaded hosts for dynamic consolidation of virtual machines in cloud data centers under quality of service constraints. IEEE Trans. Parallel Distrib. Syst. **24**(7), 1366–1379 (2013)
17. Abdelmaboud, A., Jawawi, D.N.A., Ghani, I., et al.: Quality of service approaches in cloud computing. J. Syst. Softw. **101**(C), 159–179 (2015)
18. Ardagna, D., Casale, G., Ciavotta, M., et al.: Quality-of-service in cloud computing: modeling techniques and their applications. J. Internet Serv. Appl. **5**(1), 1–17 (2014)

19. Panda, S.K., Nag, S., Jana, P.K.: A smoothing based task scheduling algorithm for heterogeneous multi-cloud environment. In: IEEE International Conference on Parallel, Distributed and Grid Computing, pp. 62–67 (2014)
20. Panda, S.K., Jana, P.K.: Efficient task scheduling algorithms for heterogeneous multi-cloud environment. J. Supercomput. 71(4), 1505–1533 (2015)
21. Ergu, D., Kou, G., Peng, Y., et al.: The analytic hierarchy process: task scheduling and resource allocation in cloud computing environment. J. Supercomput. 64(3), 835–848 (2013)

Execution Time Forecasting of Automatic Test Case Generation Based on Genetic Algorithm and BP Neural Network

Ershun Luo[✉], Dahai Jin, Bo Zhang, and Mingnan Zhou

Beijing University of Posts and Telecommunications, Beijing 100876, China
luoershun@163.com, {jindh,2012213182}@bupt.edu.cn,
zhangwenbo@buput.edu.cn

Abstract. The time spent on automatic test case generation is an important parameter in the code defect detection technology. The accurate forecast of the time spent on automatic test case generation is critical to the efficiency of code defect detection. This paper applied the BP neural network to the forecast of the time spent on automatic test case generation is to consider the factors of the number of constraint variables, the number of function calls, the number of constraint expressions and so on as the input unit of BP neural network. The results show that compared with the traditional BP neural network, the BP neural network optimized by genetic algorithm can speed up the convergence rate of the network and improve the forecasted accuracy of the time spent on automatic test case generation.

Keywords: BP neural network · Genetic algorithm · Software test
Automatic test case generation · Forecast

1 Introduction

Code defect detection technology is becoming more and more important in software testing. However, the problem of the large amount of the alarms and high false positive rate are widespread. The efficiency and difficulty of identification by human have seriously hindered the development of this technology. As an important technology in automated software testing, automatic test case generation based on path can greatly reduce the cost of software defect detection and shorten the development cycle. A test that can cause a runtime exception or error is called a suspect fault. The process that can automatically generate the data and trigger the fault is called automatic verification. In the process of automatic verification, it is of great significance to select a path which spent less time in automatic test case generation when faced with a large number of path that can reach the fault point.

The time spent on automatic test case generation has many influencing factors, and it is dependent on a complex nonlinear system. It is difficult for the general mathematical model to accurately forecast the time spent on automatic test case generation. Neural network has a strong nonlinear, self-organizing and self-learning ability, and can handle nonlinear information well. In recent years, neural networks have been

© Springer Nature Singapore Pte Ltd. 2018
H. Yuan et al. (Eds.): GSKI 2017, CCIS 848, pp. 592–600, 2018.
https://doi.org/10.1007/978-981-13-0893-2_61

widely used in all aspects of software testing [1–5]. However, there is still little research on the application of neural networks to forecast the time spent on automatic test case generation. This paper selects three large projects aa200c, de118i-2, qlib [6], and uses the best-first branch and bound (BFS-BB) test case generation framework of code testing system (CTS) [7–10] to generate the experimental data. Then, the traditional BP neural network and the BP neural network optimized by genetic algorithm are used to train and forecast respectively.

2   Basic Principles of Genetic Algorithm and BP Neural Network

2.1   Genetic Algorithm

Genetic algorithm (GA) is a computational model for the genetic selection and natural elimination of biological evolution in the evolution of organisms [11]. It is an algorithm with strong global search capability and global optimization performance. GA's process mainly includes selection, crossover and mutation operations. Its main advantage is that it is robust, simple and common, and can be used for the parallel-distributed processing. Therefore, GA and BP neural network are combined to train the network. GA is used to optimize the weights and thresholds of the neural network. After narrowing the search range, the BP neural network is used to solve the problem.

2.2   BP Neural Network

BP neural network is the abbreviation of error back-propagation multilayer feedforward neural network. The BP neural network includes input layer, hidden layer and output layer. Neurons are connected between adjacent layers, and there are no connections between the neurons in the same layer [12]. The structure is shown in Fig. 1. BP neural network learns and is trained through the guidance of learning methods. The standard BP learning algorithm uses the error gradient descent method to learn, and adjusts the weights and thresholds of the internal connection through the error back propagation, so as to reduce the error.

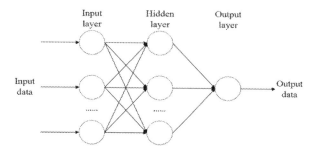

Fig. 1. Structure of BP neural network

The learning process of the network is mainly composed of input forward propagation and error back propagation. For each training data, the BP algorithm performs the following operations: firstly, supply the input data to the input layer neurons and forward transmit the signal layer by layer until the result of the output layer is generated; and then calculate the error of the output layer, and back propagate the error to hidden layer of neurons, and finally adjust the thresholds and weights according to the error of the hidden layer. The iterative process is cycled until the training error reaches a small value.

3 Traditional BP Network

3.1 Preparation of Experimental Data

The selection of the experimental data has great influence on the forecasted results of the neural network, so the selected sample data reflect the change rule of the time spent on automatic test case generation as realistic as possible. The factors that affect the automatic test case generation are not only reasonable but also representative. And it is unrealistic to analyze all the factors that affect the time spent on automatic test case generation. The key part of path-based automatic generation of test cases is constraint solving, and the key factors affecting constraint solving are the types of constraints, the composition of constraints and the number of constraints. This paper selects seven representative factors that influence the time spent on automatic test case generation, including the number of constraint variables (NCV), the number of function calls (NFC), the number of constraint expressions (NCE), the number of branch constraints (NBC), the number of cyclic constraints (NCC), the maximum depth of the cycle (MDC), the maximum number of variables in single constraint expression (MNVSCE). And three large projects are selected for the BFS-BB test case generation framework of CTS to generate the experimental data. Those projects which come from astronomy and mathematics are aa200c, de118i-2 and qlib. Some experimental data are shown in Table 1.

Table 1. Some experimental data of three large projects

NCE	NBC	NCC	MDC	NCV	NFC	MNVSCE	Time (ms)
5	5	1	1	5	0	2	128
2	1	1	1	3	1	2	78
5	3	2	2	6	0	2	121
10	8	2	1	9	0	1	225
1	1	0	0	1	0	1	63
7	3	5	1	8	0	2	173
6	1	5	1	6	0	1	156
3	2	1	1	2	0	1	98
12	8	4	1	7	0	1	259
6	5	1	1	5	0	2	158

3.2 Data Preprocessing

Due to the difference in the size of the selected raw data samples, it is necessary to normalize the data in order to avoid the fact that the smaller data is flooded with larger data. In this paper, the mapminmax method is used to normalize the input and output of the original data samples so that the normalized data will be distributed in the range of [−1, 1]. The conversion formula is:

$$y1 = \frac{(ymax - ymin) * (x1 - x1min)}{x1max - x1min} + ymin. \tag{1}$$

$$y2 = \frac{(ymax - ymin) * (x2 - x2min)}{x2max - x2min} + ymin. \tag{2}$$

Among them, the default $ymax$ and $ymin$ values are 1 and −1; $x1$ and $x2$ are the input samples and the output samples of the original data, respectively. $x1min$ and $x1max$ are the minimum and maximum values of $x1$, respectively. $x2min$ and $x2max$ are the minimum and maximum values of $x2$, respectively. $y1$ and $y2$ are the input samples and the output samples after the function normalization respectively. When the training of BP neural network is finished, the forecasted result is still normalized data, and then the mapminmax method is used to process the inverse normalization and restore the forecasted result to normal value.

3.3 The Design of BP Neural Network

3.3.1 The Design of BP Neural Network

The BP neural network of this paper adopts the gradient descent BP algorithm with momentum back propagation as the training method of the network, and its training function is traingdm function. The performance function is the MSE function. The learning rate is 0.1, the maximum numbr of training is 100 times and the error goal is 0.00004. The initial weights and thresholds are the default values of the system.

3.3.2 Set the Number of Hidden Layer Nodes

In this paper, BP neural network with 3-layer structure is selected to establish the forecasted model. The quantity of the neurons in the hidden layer influences the performance of the neural network, which has direct relationship with the requirement of the problem being solved as well as the quantities of the neurons in the input layer and the output layer. Fewer neurons in the hidden layer are of weak fault-tolerance, and unable to recognize the samples which have not been learned. By contrast, more neurons will cause the training process time-consuming [13]. And this paper empirically adopts Eq. (3) to design the hidden layer

$$m = \sqrt{n + l} + a. \tag{3}$$

Among them, m is the number of hidden layer nodes; n is the number of input layer nodes; l is the number of output layer nodes; a is the integer between 1–10. According to the above analysis, the number of input neurons in BP neural network is 7, and the number of neurons in the output layer is one. According to the empirical formula, the number of neurons in the hidden layer should be 4–13. In the experiment, the number of hidden layer nodes is determined by comparing the mean square error with the same samples and the same times of training. When the time of training is 1000, the mean square error for different hidden layer nodes after network training is shown in Table 2.

Table 2. Mean square error after network training for different hidden layer nodes

The nodes of hidden layer	Mean square error
4	0.016 335 92
5	0.007 356 15
6	0.005 775 32
7	0.007 818 96
8	0.007 662 08
9	0.009 619 01
10	0.004 636 91
11	0.009 250 19
12	0.002 649 12
13	0.007 980 49

As can be seen from Table 2, when the number of hidden layer nodes is 12, its mean square error is minimal. Therefore, the number of hidden layer nodes of BP neural network designed in this paper is 12.

3.3.3 Set the Transfer Function

In the BP neural network designed in this paper, the transfer function of the hidden layer is the tansig function in the Sigmoid function, and the transfer function of the output layer is also the tansig function. The formula for the tansig function is

$$y = \frac{2}{1 + e^{-2x}} - 1. \tag{4}$$

3.3.4 Model Training and Forecasting Results

This paper takes MATLAB R2017a as the software platform, and use Neural network toolbox function programming to realize the construction, training and prediction of BP neural network model. Mix up most of the data in aa200c, de118i-2, and qlib as the input data, and leave fifteen sets of data as the target output. The forecasted value and the actual value of the comparison are shown in Table 3, and the forecasted results are shown in Fig. 2. As can be seen from Table 3 and Fig. 2, the errors in the forecast of the aa200c, de118i-2 and qlib are fluctuating, whose fluctuation range can be controlled less than 11%.

Table 3. BP neural network forecasted results analysis

Test case number	Real execution time (ms)	Forecasted execution time (ms)	Absolute error (ms)	Relative error (%)
1	259	247.21	11.79	4.55
2	129	97.37	31.63	24.52
3	62	68.51	6.51	10.50
4	78	72.49	5.51	7.06
5	94	94.91	0.91	0.97
6	142	146.19	4.19	2.95
7	78	89.02	11.02	14.13
8	109	109.92	0.92	0.84
9	156	117.30	38.7	24.81
10	94	74.82	19.18	20.40
11	195	220.08	25.08	12.86
12	166	157.60	8.4	5.060
13	175	168.25	6.75	3.857
14	89	114.42	25.42	28.56
15	78	73.44	4.56	5.85
Total	1904	1851.53	200.57	10.53

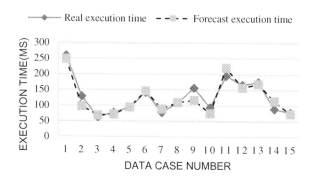

Fig. 2. BP neural network test case automatic generation time forecast

4 BP Improved by GA

Although BP neural network has a strong nonlinear mapping ability, there is some problem such as slow convergence of learning, a great possibility to fall into local minimum, and unstable network topology. GA has a good global search ability, and is helpful to get the global optimal solution. Therefore, GA is used to optimize the BP neural network (GA + BP) [13], which can accelerate the convergence of the network and improve the forecasted accuracy of the model. In this paper, the parts that are optimized by GA in BP neural network are the weights and thresholds.

4.1   GA Optimization Process

Figure 3 shows the specific optimization process.

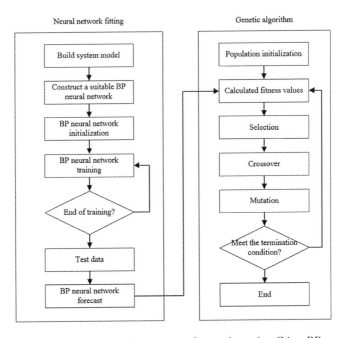

Fig. 3. The process of time spent forecasting using GA + BP

Step 1: Set the initial value. The initial population size of the GA is 30, the number of evolution is 100, the crossover probability is 0.3, and the mutation probability is 0.1.

Step 2: Individual coding and population initialization. The individual contains the entire BP neural network of the ownership and threshold. In this paper, the number of individuals uses the real number code. The encoding length is:

$$S = n \times m + m \times l + m + l. \tag{5}$$

Among them, m is the number of hidden layer nodes, n is the number of input layer nodes, and l is the number of output layer nodes.

Step 3: Set the fitness function. The fitness function uses the forecasted output of the trained BP neural network as the fitness value of the individual.

Step 4: The operation of selection, crossover and mutation. The optimal individual has no crossover operation, but directly copied to the next generation. For other individuals, two individuals are crossed using a crossover probability to produce another two new individuals. Similarly, the optimal individual has no mutation operation, but directly copied to the next generation. For other individuals, mutation probabilities are used to generate new individuals.

Step 5: Cyclic operation. Cycle the above steps 2–4 until the training target reaches the set requirement or the number of iterations reaches the set target.

4.2   Model Training and Forecasting Results

The weights and thresholds obtained by GA are used to retrain BP neural network. This paper uses the neural network toolbox function programming to achieve the GA-BP neural network model, and forecasts the data of 15 sets of the three projects of aa200c, de118i-2 and qlib. The comparison result between the forecasted execution time and the real execution time is shown in Table 4, and the forecast results are shown in Fig. 4. It can be seen from Table 4 and Fig. 4 that the error rate of single data forecasted of aa200c, de118i-2 and qlib is controlled within 15% and the overall fluctuation range can be controlled less than 7%.

Table 4. GA + BP neural network forecasted results analysis

Test case number	Real execution time (ms)	Forecasted execution time (ms)	Absolute error (ms)	Relative error (%)
1	228	229.38	1.38	0.61
2	224	220.74	3.26	1.46
3	87	76.02	10.98	12.62
4	71	81.48	10.48	14.76
5	183	164.88	18.12	9.90
6	110	93.90	16.10	14.64
7	216	188.63	27.37	12.67
8	121	133.57	12.57	10.39
9	62	65.34	3.34	5.39
10	173	156.70	16.30	9.42
11	62	62.23	0.23	0.37
12	259	258.60	0.40	0.15
13	78	86.48	8.48	10.87
14	140	128.12	11.88	8.49
15	202	209.20	7.20	3.56
Total	2216	2155.27	148.09	6.68

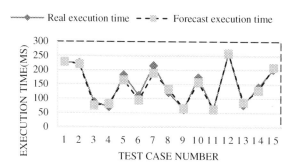

Fig. 4. GA + BP neural network test case automatic generation time forecast

5 Conclusion

The traditional BP neural network has many shortcomings, such as slow convergence speed and a great possibility to fall into local minimum. In order to improve this defect, this paper introduces a way to improve the effect by using the GA to optimize the weights and thresholds of BP neural network. The time spent on automatic test case generation for aa200c, de118i-2 and qlib projects is forecasted by BP neural network and GA + BP neural network respectively. The experimental results show that the GA + BP neural network has achieved better results in forecasting the automatic generation of test cases. The GA + BP neural network not only greatly reduces the relative error of single data, but also improves the overall forecasted accuracy rate.

References

1. Vanmali, M., Last, M., Kandel, A.: Using a neural network in the software testing process. Int. J. Intell. Syst. **17**(1), 45–62 (2002)
2. Zheng, J.: Predicting software reliability with neural network ensembles. Exper. Syst. Appl. **36**(2), 2116–2122 (2009)
3. Neumann, D.E.: An enhanced neural network technique for software risk analysis. IEEE Trans. Softw. Eng. **28**(9), 904–912 (2002)
4. Arar, Ö.F., Ayan, K.: Software defect prediction using cost-sensitive neural network. Appl. Soft Comput. **33**, 263–277 (2015)
5. Roy, P., Mahapatra, G.S., Rani, P., et al.: Robust feedforward and recurrent neural network based dynamic weighted combination models for software reliability prediction. Appl. Soft Comput. **22**, 629–637 (2014)
6. Astronomy and numerical software source codes. http://www.moshier.net
7. Jin, D., Gong, Y., Yang, C., et al.: The application of constraint-procedure information in software static testing. J. Comput. Aided Des. Comput. Graph. **23**(3), 534–542 (2011)
8. Xing, Y., Gong, Y., Wang, Y., et al.: Branch and bound framework for automatic test case generation. Sci. Chin. Press: Sci. Sinica Inf. **44**(10), 1345–1360 (2014)
9. Xing, Y., Gong, Y., Wang, Y., et al.: Path-wise test data generation based on heuristic look-ahead methods. Math. Prob. Eng. **2014**, 19 (2014). Article ID 642630
10. Xing, Y., Gong, Y., Wang, Y., et al.: A hybrid intelligent search algorithm for automatic test data generation. Math. Prob. Eng. **2015**, 15 (2015). Article ID 617685
11. Chen, G., Wang, X., Zhuang, Z.: Genetic algorithm and its application. People's Posts and Telecommunications Press, Beijing (2001)
12. Zhou, Z.: Machine learning. Tsinghua University Press, Beijing (2016)
13. Xing, Y., You, Z., Zhang, B., et al.: City water demand forecasting based on improved BP neural network. J. Residuals Sci. Technol. **14**, S111–S117 (2017)

An Improved Interconnection Network for Data Center Based on BCube Structure

Jianfei Zhang[1(✉)], Weiwu Ren[1], and Guannan Qu[2]

[1] School of Computer Science and Technology,
Changchun University of Science and Technology,
Weixing Road No. 7089, Changchun, People's Republic of China
jfzhang@cust.edu.cn, renww339@163.com
[2] College of Computer Science and Technology,
Jilin University, Qianjin Street No. 2699, Changchun
People's Republic of China
gnqu@jlu.edu.cn

Abstract. BCube has been proposed as a high-performance interconnection networks of modular data center. It is usually deployed in shipping-containers, thus a BCube can be easily deployed any place and be relocated as need. The regular structure of BCube network supports various traffic patterns. A BCube network, however, has to install massive switches to realize all these advantages, which increases the constructing cost and operation overhead. In this paper, we present a folded BCube network, short as FBCube, and it cuts down almost half amount of switches with connecting same amount of servers as BCube. And we show that, although the diameter of FBCube increases, the increment is acceptable.

Keywords: Data center network · FBCube

1 Introduction

Shipping-container based data center [1–6] is a kind of Modular Data Center(MDC), which provides a new way of building and deploying the data center. A MDC usually organizes a few thousands of servers to adapt the size of a shipping-container. Those servers connect to each other via switches to form the interconnection network. Hence, the owners of a MDC can place it anywhere they want, or relocate it if they need. Thus a MDC can be deployed rapidly, and it could run with a higher system and power density, and a lower cooling and manufacturing cost.

Commonly, the network of a MDC is a tree-like structure. And then the BCube [7] structure was proposed, which is a high-performance and robust network architecture. The BCube aims at the data intensive computing which is the requirement trends recently. Meanwhile, a BCube also can well support various traffic patterns including unicast, multicast [8], broadcast, and all-to-all communication [9]. A BCube structure achieves all these benefits only using low-end switches.

The scale of a MDC is not only suitable for shipping-container based data center, but also acceptable for organizations who need a middle scale of data centers.

© Springer Nature Singapore Pte Ltd. 2018
H. Yuan et al. (Eds.): GSKI 2017, CCIS 848, pp. 601–607, 2018.
https://doi.org/10.1007/978-981-13-0893-2_62

Especially, with the development of big data and cloud computing, an organization needs to build their own data center to process sensitively commercial data. A data center with thousand or tens of thousands of servers is appropriate.

Some typical interconnection network of data center include fat-tree [10, 11], DCell [12], HyperCube [13], and other networks [14] based on graph theory. The BCube structure is excellent, but it is designed to deploy in a shipping container whose space is finite. Considering the other devices like wires, power and especially a large amount of switches, a BCube can only include a few thousands of servers, which may not satisfy the demand of extending in the future. Hence several improvements based on BCube network were proposed. Hyper-BCube [15] was proposed by D. Lin et al. Hyper-BCube is designed by combining DCell and BCube network. The routing algorithms [16, 17] deployed in BCube are also studied.

In this paper, we propose an interconnection network called folded BCube (FBCube), which is based on original BCube structure and is improved. Our FBCube structure significantly decreases the amount of switches and wires. At the same time, FBCube can keep the existing advantages.

The rest of this paper is organized as follow. Section 2 describes the original BCube structure briefly. Section 3 introduces our improve structure. And we investigate the properties of our solutions and compare it with the original BCube in Sect. 4. In the last section we conclude our works and discuss the next step works.

2 The Brief of Bcube Structure

In a BCube structure, servers are deployed multiple ports, and uniform switches are used to connect servers to form the network infrastructure. A BCube is defined recursively, thus the lower level structure BCubei is considered as the basic unit to build BCubei+1 structure.

Firstly, a BCube0 is constructed by connecting n servers with an n-port switch. And then a BCube1 is built by n BCube0s and n n-port switches. Further, a BCubek is constructed from n BCubek-1s and nk n-port switches. Hence, a server in a BCubek has k + 1 network ports, which correspond to k + 1 switches in different levels respectively.

The rules of build BCubek is as follow. Each BCubek-1 is assigned a number from 0 to n−1, the servers in BCubek-1 is assigned from 0 to nk−1. Then BCube connect the level-k port of the ith server, where $i \in [0, n^k - 1]$, in the jth BCubek-1, where $j \in [0, n - 1]$, to the jth port of the ith level-k switch.

Figure 1 illustrates an instance of BCube1 with n = 4. Each server has k + 1 = 2 network ports, which connected to switches in different level respectively. The level-0 link of a server connects to level-0 switch to construct the BCube0. And the level-1 links connect to level-1 switches to construct BCube1. Servers in the same BCube0 link to distinct switches in each level. More generically, a BCubek is constructed in the same way, shown in Fig. 2. Each server in BCubek-1 let its level-k link connect with the corresponding switch.

With the above definitions of BCubek, we can see that a BCube structure scale out with the increasing of k. But there is a significant shortcoming that the total number of

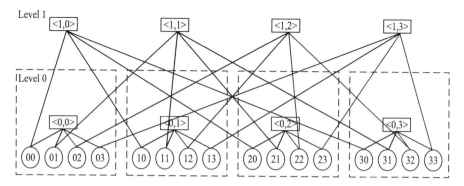

Fig. 1. The structure of a BCube$_1$ with n = 4.

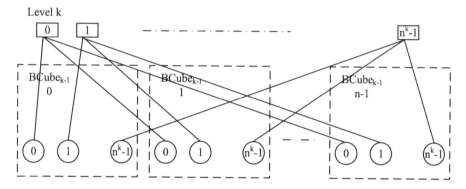

Fig. 2. The structure of BCubek.

switches increasing even faster. Our FBCube structure can resolve this problem and keep the other advantages at the same time.

3   Fbcube, an Improved Structure of Bcube

The structure we proposed in this paper is construct via folding the network of BCube. Different from the original BCube structure, the servers in FBCube do not connect to switches in every level.

Let k denote the number of level of FBCube, the FBCubek is constructed as follow.

Case I: k = 0, every server has one link with level-0 switch to construct the FBCube0. Thus n servers and one switch form a level-0 structure directly, just like BCube0.

Case II: k = 1, using n FBCube0s to construct oneFBCube1, and we select half of total servers from each FBCube0 to connect with the level-1 switches. Hence n × $\frac{n}{2}$ servers connect to $\frac{n}{2}$ n-port switches.

Case III: k ≥ 2, the servers in every FBCubek-2 are split into two parts evenly. We select only one part of servers from each of n FBCubek-2s to connect to the level-(k − 1) switches forming the FBCubek-1 structure. And another part of servers from all of n FBCubek-1s will connect to level-k switches to forming the FBCubek.

We represents every server and switch in FBCubek with an address. The definition of the address space is very like the one in BCube. An address of server is an (k + 1) tuple as [ak ak − 1...a0], where $a_i \in [0, n-1], i \in [0, k]$. Obviously, the (k + 1) tuple can be convert to a single integer by equation $\sum_{i=0}^{k} a_i n^i$. An address of switch can be denoted as [l, sk − 1 sk − 2...s0], where $s_j \in [0, n-1], j \in [0, k-1]$. And the l is the level of switch, where $0 \le l \le k$. The address of switches has similar case that sk − 1 sk − 2...s0 can be convert to a integer number by $\sum_{i=0}^{k-1} s_i n^i$. Each address of switch should satisfy the value of $\sum_{i=0}^{k-1} s_i n^i < n^l$, and the value has the same parity with l. We can see that a level-k switch [l, sk − 1 sk − 2...s0] connects to the port of server isk − 1 sk − 2...s0 (i $\in$ [0, n − 1]).

Figure 3 shows a part of the structure of FBCube2, which is actual a half of the whole network. There are still 2 level-1 units and 4 level-2 switches which is not drew in the Fig. 3. The existing 4 level-2 switches has another two links to the omitted part.

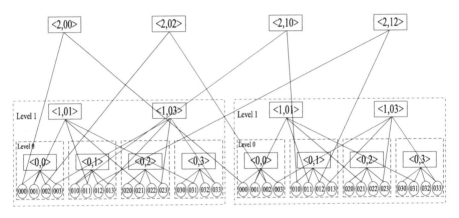

Fig. 3. Part of the structure of FBCube2.

Each server has a sequence of numbers as its address. The number could be even or odd, especially the last one of the sequence. As the definition of FBCube, we have to separate the servers into two sets. Thus we simply partition the servers according to the parity of the last number in a sequence. The set of servers with odd (even) tail number at their addresses link their network port with switches at odd (even) levels. The method is not only easy to realize but also propitious to distributing the communication flows.

4 The Investigations and Analysis

Our FBCube network shrinks the amount of switches that are used, because when level $k > 0$, FBCube cuts half amount of switches in each level. In contrast with that a

BCubek includes n^{k+1} servers via $(k+1)n^k$ switches, an FBCubek includes the same number of servers via nearly half amount of switches.

Case I: k = 0, apparently, the amount of switches in BCube0 and FBCube0 are the same value of 1.

Case II: $k \geq 1$, during the process of constructing a FBCubek structure, we split all servers in every FBCubek-1 into two parts, and only pick up one of them to use. For all switches in level k, there are only $n^{k+1}/2$ servers who are responsible for connecting to them. The size of each switch is n, so the amount of level switches in k-level is $n^k/2$. At the same time there are $n^{k+1}/n = n^k$ switches in level0. Hence the total number of switches in a FBCubek is $n^k + kn^k/2 = \left(1 + \frac{k}{2}\right)n^k$. Comparing to $(k+1)n^k$ switches in BCubek, the FBCube cuts down almost half of switches to connect the same number of servers.

The much intuitive comparison is shown in Table 1. To connect the same amount of servers, the FBCube network uses less switches, meanwhile the number of network ports deployed by a server is also reduced. When $k \geq 1$, the number of links on each server is $\frac{k}{2} + 1$.

Table 1. The amount of switches in BCube and FBCube with n = 8.

k	BCube	FBCube	Amount of servers
2	192	128	512
3	2048	1280	4096
4	20480	12288	32768

In this way, FBCube could decrease the cost on equipment purchase and save the energy as well. In another words, using the same scale of switch network, the FBCube can include much more servers. It provides a better scalability.

The diameter of network is the maximum length among all shortest path of each pair of servers. The diameter measures the average delay between two servers.

For BCubek network, we suppose that server Ss and server Sd are include in different BCubei, $0 \leq i \leq k$. So the length of shortest path between Ss and Sd is the value of diameter. Because each server has k links, apparently the diameter of BCubek is k + 1.

For FBCubek network, we use the same hypothesis. Thus the shortest path of Ss and Sd has 2 cases as follow.

Case I: the value of k is even. If the address of Ss and Sd are all even, and a packet is going to transport from Ss to Sd. the Ss firstly sends the packet to the server Sp which locates in the same FBCubek-1 with Sd. Especially, the k − 1 is odd, so the server Sp cannot directly forwards the packet to the FBCubek-2 of server Sd. So Sp forwards the packet to server Sm whose address is odd. A simply choice of Sm is a neighbor in the same FBCube0 of Sp. Then the packet could be transmitted from Sm to a server Sn which is in the same FBCubek-2 of Sd, but Sn also has to select a neighbor Sq with even address in its FBCube0. Now k − 2 is even, both Sq and Sd have even address. Hence Sq and Sd could route in the same way in FBCubek-2. Finally compare to

BCube, the shortest path of Ss and Sd need additional two steps in each odd level. The length of shortest path is $(k+1) + \frac{k}{2} \times 2 = 2k + 1$.

Further, if one of the Ss and Sd servers has an odd address, the odd server need one more step with its neighbor whose address is even. Then the length of shortest path has to be added one. If both of Ss and Sd have odd address, we can process two of them in the same way. Thus the length has to be added two. In this case, the diameter is 2k + 3.

Case II, the value of k is odd. If the address of Ss and Sd are all odd, similarly with case I, the shortest path need additional two steps in each even level. Hence the length of shortest path is $(k+1) + \frac{k-1}{2} \times 2 = 2k$.

Further, if one or two of the Ss and Sd servers have even address, we deal with it as we do in case I. And it results in additional one or two steps. In this case, the diameter is 2k + 2.

From above analysis, a FBCube network double its diameter than BCube network. In Table 1, we can see that FBCube4 can connect tens of thousands of servers, which means FBCube network with small value of k includes enough servers. Hence the increasing of diameter is acceptable.

Actually, our improvement is a tradeoff between amount of switches and diameter. The increasing of diameter is just because of the reducing amount of switches. But the result is excellent. We cut down nearly half amount of switches, where the number is thousands even tens of thousands. The diameter is only added by a value of single digit.

5   Conclusion

In this paper, we proposed an improved BCube structure, called FBCube. The FBCube structure fold the switch network, so that it reduces almost half amount of switches in contrast to BCube structure. Although the diameter of FBCube increases, but the raise is acceptable. Because FBCube use fewer switches, a data center using FBCube as its underlying interconnection network could be built with a large scales and in an economy way. And the energy for daily operating is also saves.

The communications on data center is various. A data center has to support various traffic patterns. In next step works, we are going to investigating the routing algorithm in FBCube networks.

Acknowledgments. This paper is supported by the project "Research and Realization on Virtualization Technology of Internet Content Delivery Oriented Networks" (20150204082GX), which is financially supported by Jilin Provincial Science and Technology Agency

References

1. Hamilton, J.: An architecture for modular data centers. In: 3rd CIDR, January 2007
2. IBM. Scalable Modular Data Center. http://www-935.ibm.com/services/us/its/pdf/smdc-eb-sfe03001-usen-00-022708.pdf
3. Wu, H., Lu, G., et al.: MDCube: a high performance network structure for modular data center interconnection. In: CoNEXT 2009, pp. 25–36 (2009)

4. Lu, F., Zhu, G., et al.: MDCent: a modular data center interconnection with high scalability and high performance. J. Comput. Res. Dev. **52**(5), 1127–1136 (2015)
5. Sato, M., Matsunaga, A., et al.: Seeking an energy-efficient modular data center: impact of pressure loss on the server fan power. In: IEEE ICEP-IAAC, pp. 617–622 (2015)
6. Waldrop, M.: Data center in a box. Sci. Am. **297**(2), 90–93 (2007)
7. Guo, C., Li, G., et al.: BCube: a high performance, server-centric network architecture for modular data centers. In: SIGCOMM 2009, vol. 39, no 4, pp. 63–74, August 2009
8. Ghemawat, S., Gobioff, H., Leung, S.: The Google file system. In: SOSP, vol. 37, no 5, pp. 29–43 (2003)
9. Dean, J., Ghemawat, S.: MapReduce: simplified data processing on large clusters. In: OSDI, vol. 6, p. 10 (2004)
10. Duato, J., Yalamanchili, S., Ni, L.: Interconnection networks: an engineering approach. IEEE Computer Society, Washington, D.C. (1997)
11. Leiserson, C.: Fat-trees: universal networks for hardware-efficient super computing. IEEE Trans. Comput. **34**(10), 892–901 (1985)
12. Guo, C., Wu, H., et al.: DCell: a scalable and fault-tolerant network structure for data centers. In: SIGCOMM 2008, vol. 38, no 4, pp. 75–86, August 2008
13. Saad, Y., Schultz, M.H.: Topological properties of hypercubes. IEEE Trans. Comput. **37**(7), 867–872 (1988)
14. Loguinov, D., Kumar, A., Rai, V., Ganesh, S.: Graph-theoretic analysis of structured peer-to-peer systems: routing distances and fault resilience. IEEE/ACM Trans. Netw. **13**(5), 1107–1120 (2005)
15. Lin, D., Liu, Y., et al.: Hyper-BCube: a scalable data center network. In: IEEE International Conference on Communications, vol. 11, no 18, pp. 2918–2923 (2012)
16. Xie, J., Guo, D., et al.: Efficient multicast routing on BCube-based data centers. KSII Trans. Internet Inf. Syst. **8**(12), 4343–4355 (2014)
17. Guo, D.: Aggregating uncertain incast transfers in BCube-like data centers. IEEE Trans. Parallel Distrib. Syst. **28**(4), 934–946 (2017)

Message Passing Algorithm Based on Cut-Node Tree

Huanming Zhang[(✉)]

Electronics and Information Engineering Institute, Foshan University,
Foshan 528000, Guangdong, China
511106085@qq.com

Abstract. An LDPC (Low Density Parity Check) code can be described by Tanner graph [1]. In this paper, loop structure in LDPC codes are studied carefully based on Tanner graph, a new notion, cut-node tree, is proposed to describe LDPC codes. Cut-node tree has full information of Tanner graph. So all loop features in LDPCs can be calculated aided by computer. Also a new decoding scheme for LDPC codes is proposed to avoid repeating iteration of information in traditional decoding algorithms. The results help to give further research on related field.

Keywords: LDPC · Iterative decoding · Loop

1 Introduction

In coding theory, Tanner graph, named after Michael Tanner, is a bipartite graph used to state constraints or equations which specify error correcting codes [2] (Fig. 1). They are used to construct longer codes from smaller ones. Both encoders and decoders employ these graphs extensively [3, 4].

In communication system, the transmitted random vector $x = \{x_1, \cdots, x_N\}$ is not observed; instead received noisy vector $y = \{y_1, \cdots, y_N\}$. N is the length of codeword, Parity check equation vector is $c = \{c_1, c_2, \cdots, c_M\}$, M is the number of equations.$f = \{f_1^a, \cdots, f_N^a\}$ represents initial information about transmitted codeword. Where v_i is the ith variable node, and c_j is the jth check equation.

The belief propagation (BP) of LDPC code states as follows [5–7]:

R_{ji}^a is check information from check node c_j to variable node v_i, and Q_{ij}^a variable information from v_i to check node c_j.

$$R_{ji}^0(t+1) = \frac{1}{2}\left(1 + \prod_{j' \in N(i) \backslash j}\left(1 - 2Q_{ij'}^1(t)\right)\right) \tag{1}$$

$$R_{ji}^1(t+1) = 1 - R_{ji}^0(t+1) \tag{2}$$

$$Q_{ij}^0(t+1) = \alpha_{ij}(1 - P_i) \prod_{i' \in M(j) \backslash i} R_{ji}^0(t+1) \tag{3}$$

© Springer Nature Singapore Pte Ltd. 2018
H. Yuan et al. (Eds.): GSKI 2017, CCIS 848, pp. 608–614, 2018.
https://doi.org/10.1007/978-981-13-0893-2_63

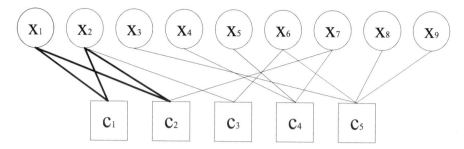

Fig. 1. Tanner graph of an LDPC code

$$Q_{ij}^1(t+1) = \alpha_{ij} P_i \prod_{i' \in M(j) \setminus i} R_{ji}^1(t+1) \tag{4}$$

Where α_{ij} denotes a normalization constant, $Q_{ij}^0(t+1) + Q_{ij}^1(t+1) = 1$.

2 Cut-Node Tree

In order to solve loops of LDPC code, avoiding redundant information iteration. Tanner graph is redrawn as following principle: Choosing an element '1' in H, its variable (or check) node considered root node, check (or variable) nodes connected to the variable (or check) node as 1st order child-nodes, a current node, if once appearing in ancestor node or sibling node, will be cut and forbidden to grow and become an end node like a leaf, but not a leaf actually, it is a cut node. Repeating this process until all end nodes are either cut-nodes or leaf nodes. And so forth, at last a cut-node tree can be got. If all nodes are connected, a single cut-node tree can be got, otherwise it is a forest. See Fig. 2:

HH is mark matrix, when a node appears in graph, the element in HH changes to zero; every element in HH is zero represents end of algorithm.

3 Principle and Results

First, a node (variable node or check node), for instance, variable node $v_i, h_{ij} = 1$, should be chosen as root node, its son nodes are those check nodes which connect to it, according to this principle, all child-nodes can be obtained. This process can be implemented by computer simulation in matlab's cell array, and express H by means of cut-node tree [6].

For example, an LDPC code with check matrix:

$$H = \begin{bmatrix} 1 & 0 & 1 & 0 & 1 & 0 & 1 & 0 \\ 1 & 0 & 0 & 1 & 0 & 1 & 0 & 1 \\ 0 & 1 & 1 & 0 & 0 & 1 & 1 & 0 \\ 0 & 1 & 0 & 1 & 1 & 0 & 0 & 1 \end{bmatrix} \tag{5}$$

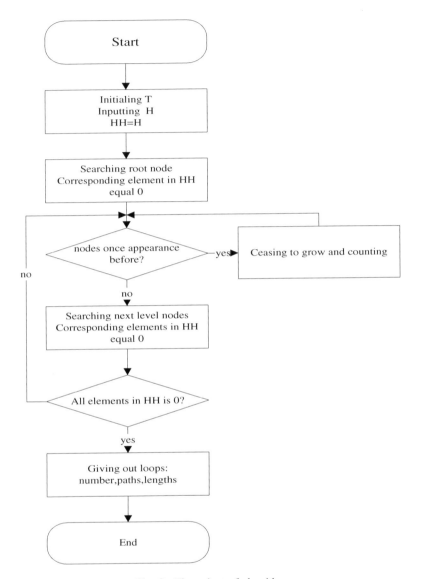

Fig. 2. Flow chart of algorithm

It has the following cut-node tree graph (Fig. 3):
For another instance, an LDPC code with check matrix H:

$$H = \begin{bmatrix} 1 & 1 & 1 & 1 & 0 & 0 & 0 & 0 & 0 & 0 \\ 1 & 0 & 0 & 0 & 1 & 1 & 1 & 0 & 0 & 0 \\ 0 & 1 & 0 & 0 & 1 & 0 & 0 & 1 & 1 & 0 \\ 0 & 0 & 1 & 0 & 0 & 1 & 0 & 1 & 0 & 1 \\ 0 & 0 & 0 & 1 & 0 & 0 & 1 & 1 & 0 & 1 \end{bmatrix} \tag{6}$$

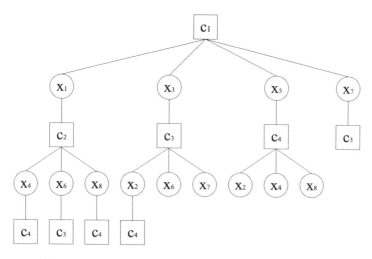

Fig. 3. Cut-node tree Graph of LDPC codes for H of Eq. 5

Following tree matrix expressed by matlab can be get, In fact, tree matrix matches along with Tree of Graph, [i j k l m], [i j] states current node, [k l] states father node, m states times being cut.

Root node: [1 1 0 0]
Level1: [2 1 1 1]
Level2: [2 5 2 1] [2 6 2 1] [2 7 2 1]
Level3: [3 5 2 5] [4 6 2 6] [5 7 2 7]
Level4: [3 2 3 5] [3 8 3 5] [3 9 3 5] [4 3 6 3] [4 8 6 8] [4 10 4 6] [5 4 5 7] [5 9 5 7] [5 10 5 7]
Level5: [1 2 3 2] [4 8 3 8 1] [5 9 3 9 1] [1 3 4 3] [3 8 4 8 1] [5 10 4 10 1] [1 4 5 4] [3 9 5 9 1] [4 10 5 10 1]
Level6: [1 1 1 2 1] [1 3 1 2 1] [1 4 1 2 1] [1 1 1 3 2] [1 2 1 3 1] [1 4 1 3 2] [1 1 1 4 3] [1 2 1 4 2] [1 3 1 4 3]

So, searched by a computer, all loops and features of Eq. 5 can be get by this algorithm. See Table 1.

Loop 1: [4 8]-[3 8]-[3 5]-[2 5]-[2 6]-[4 6]-[4 8]
Loop 2: [5 9]-[3 9]-[3 5]-[2 5]-[2 7]-[5 7]-[5 10]
Loop 3: [5 10]-[4 10]-[4 6]-[2 6]-[2 7]-[5 7]-[5 10]
Loop 4: [1 1]-[1 2]-[3 2]-[3 5]-[2 5]-[2 1]-[1 1]
Loop 5: [1 3]-[1 2]-[3 2]-[3 5]-[2 5]-[2 6]-[4 6]-[4 3]-[1 3]
Loop 6: [1 4]-[1 2]-[3 2]-[3 5]-[2 5]-[2 7]-[5 7]-[5 4]-[1 4]
Loop 7: [1 1]-[1 3]-[4 3]-[4 6]-[2 6]-[2 1]-[1 1]
Loop 8: [1 1]-[1 3]-[4 3]-[4 6]-[2 6]-[2 5]-[3 5]-[3 2]-[1 2]-[1 1]
Loop 9: [1 4]-[1 3]-[4 3]-[4 6]-[2 6]-[2 5]-[3 5]-[3 2]-[1 2]-[1 4]
Loop 10: [1 4]-[1 3]-[4 3]-[4 6]-[2 6]-[2 7]-[5 7]-[5 4]-[1 4]
Loop 11: [1 1]-[1 4]-[5 4]-[5 7]-[2 7]-[2 1]-[1 1]

Table 1. Features of loops about above example

Parameters	Values
Sparsity	0.4
Loops	16
Total length of loops	108
Average length	6.75
Girth	6
Maximum length	10
Loop relativity	3.18

Loop 12: [1 1]-[1 4]-[5 4]-[5 7]-[2 7]-[2 5]-[3 5]-[3 2]-[1 2]-[1 1]
Loop 13: [1 1]-[1 4]-[5 4]-[5 7]-[2 7]-[2 6]-[4 6]-[4 3]-[1 3]-[1 1]
Loop 14: [1 2]-[1 4]-[5 4]-[5 7]-[2 7]-[2 5]-[3 5]-[3 2]-[1 2]
Loop 15: [1 2]-[1 4]-[5 4]-[5 7]-[2 7]-[2 6]-[4 6]-[4 3]-[1 3]-[1 2]
Loop 16: [1 3]-[1 4]-[5 4]-[5 7]-[2 7]-[2 5]-[3 5]-[3 2]-[1 2]-[1 3]

Here, H is just a situation of single tree, with 15 cut-nodes, no leaf node and 16 loops.

In a graph with cycle, Cut-node tree graph can be got by cutting all loops, See Fig. 5.

Cut-node tree has all characters of Tanner graph.

Further, Message-passing form for cut-node tree abides by following rule:

In a tree, Message flows in two form, first passing upwards from end node to a node designated as the root (Fig. 4).

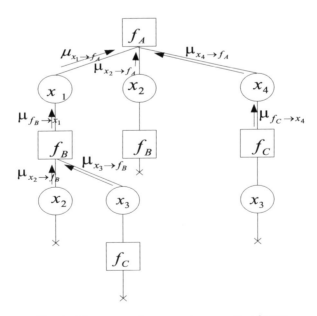

Fig. 4. Message passing upwards over cut-node tree

And then downwards from the root node to end node (See Fig. 5).

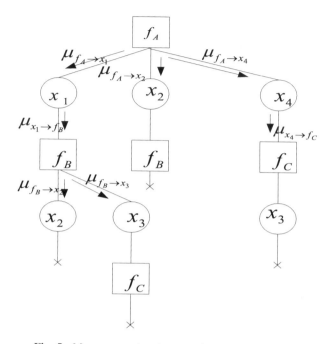

Fig. 5. Message passing downwards over cut-node tree

4 Conclusion

A new method to describe graph of LDPC codes is provided in this paper, it aims to solve loops of LDPC codes and message passing algorithm over cut-node tree. For a large matrix H, it is difficult to solve all loops and their features, because loops can convolve each other. Features of loops have certain relationship with performances. In this paper, cut-node tree can be expressed to a certain matrix through cell array in MATLAB. By computer simulation, cut-node tree can get right results and gives out method to calculate loops of LDPC codes and cut-node tree graph, and message passing algorithm can avoid repeating iteration of information. The results assist to further research on related field.

References

1. Gallager, R.G.: Low-Density Parity Check Codes. MIT Press, Cambridge (1963)
2. Mackay, D.J.C.: Good error-correcting codes based on very sparse matrices. IEEE Trans. Inf. Theory **45**, 399–431 (1999)
3. Tanner, R.M.: A recursive approach to low complexity codes. IEEE Trans. Inf. Theory **27** (5), 533–547 (1981)

4. Kschischang, R., Frey, B.J., Loeliger, H.A.: Factor graphs and the sum-product algorithm. IEEE Trans. Inf. Theory **47**(2), 498–519 (2001)
5. Wiberg, N.: Codes and decoding on general graphs, Linkoping Studies in Science and Technology. Ph.D. dissertation No. 440, University in Linkoping, Sweden (1996)
6. Reinhard, D.: Graph Theory. Springer, New York (1997)
7. Wainwright, M.J.: Sparse graph codes for side information and binning. IEEE Sig. Process. Mag. **24**, 47–57 (2007)
8. Wainwright, M., Jaakkola, T., Willsky, A.: Tree-based reparameterization analysis of belief propagation and related algorithms for approximate inference on graphs with cycles. In: ISIT 2002, Lausanne, Switzerland, 30 June–5 July 2002
9. Polyanskiy, Y., Poor, H., Verdu, S.: Channel coding rate in the finite blocklength regime. IEEE Trans. Inf. Theory **56**(5), 2307–2359 (2010)
10. Kovalev, A.A., Dumer, I., Pryadko, L.P.: Phys. Rev. A, **84**, 062319 (2011)

Energy Efficiency Optimization in SFR-Based Power Telecommunication Networks

Honghao Zhao[1(✉)], Siwen Zhao[2], Rimin Jiang[3], Haiyang Huang[3], Xiangdong Jiang[4], and Ling Wang[4]

[1] State Grid Liaoning Electric Power Company Limited,
Shenyang 110006, China
merry_99@sina.com
[2] China Resources Power Investment Co., Ltd.,
Northeast Branch, Shenyang 110043, China
[3] Liaoning Planning and Designing Institute of Post and Telecommunication
Company Limited, Shenyang 110011, China
[4] State Grid Benxi Electric Power Supply Company, Benxi 117000, China

Abstract. Soft Frequency Reuse (SFR) can coordinate the inter-cell interference (ICI) by control the carriers and transmitting power. It will be used in the 5G. With the energy consumption increasing in the wireless network, the energy efficiency is an important index to evaluate the network performance in 5G. In this paper, we investigates the global energy efficiency optimization problem in SFR-based cellular networks. We formulate the global energy efficiency optimization as a fractional program model. It is very hard to solve directly the optimization model. To find the optimal solution of this model, we utilize the Lagrange function and KKT condition to attain the optimal transmitting power allocations. Then, we utilize the simulated annealing method to find the transmitting power allocations and sub-channel assignments. Finally, we make a numerical simulation to validate the algorithm proposed. The simulation results show that our algorithm proposed is feasible.

Keywords: Soft frequency reuse · Energy efficient · Lagrange function
KKT condition · Simulated annealing method

1 Introduction

With the increasing demand of wireless mobile services demand, the wireless network provide high throughput and multi-users access at the same time. The scale of the system is becoming more complexity than before, then the energy consumption of the wireless network increasing rapidly. The energy efficient (EE) has been regarded as one of the evaluation metrics in future 5G system [1]. Along with moving terminals increasing, the frequency resource is limited, the Orthogonal Frequency Division Multiplexing (OFDM) which could enhance the system capacity and spectrum utilization has been identified as the key technology in the physical layer [2]. But for the OFDM in the full frequency reuse in cellular network, there are more inter-cell interference between neighboring cells, especially more serious for the users who at the

© Springer Nature Singapore Pte Ltd. 2018
H. Yuan et al. (Eds.): GSKI 2017, CCIS 848, pp. 615–628, 2018.
https://doi.org/10.1007/978-981-13-0893-2_64

cell-edge, in order to coordinate the inter-cell interference, Fractional frequency reuse (FFR) [3] and Soft frequency reuse (SFR) [4] scheme are introduced, both of them utilize the frequency reuse rate between 1/3 and 1 by controlling the transmitting power level of BS. For the energy efficiency of the network, it is also affected by the base station transmitting power. So with the optimal resource allocation scheme could obtain the optimal system energy efficient and coordinate inter-cell interference.

There are a lot of literatures about resource allocation scheme with optimal energy efficiency in network. In [5], Ren et al. investigated fair resource allocation with the energy efficiency maximum in the downlink OFDM-based mobile communication system. They proposed a bisection-based optimal power allocation (BOPA) to obtain the maximum EE, under subcarriers assignment given. In [6], Al-Zahrani et al. investigated energy-efficient resource allocation and inter-cell interference management in the heterogeneous networks. In [7], Yang et al. investigated the resource allocation problem for the downlink in heterogeneous networks with the optimal energy efficient. The author has demonstrated that EE is an increasing function in channel gain continuously differentiable and strictly quasi-concave in transmit power associated with each resource block. In [8], Wang et al. investigated maximum energy-efficient resource allocation problem in coordinated downlink multi-cell OFDMA systems based on imperfect channel state information.

The literatures mentioned above mainly considered in downlink OFDMA systems, in recent years, some research has focused on the SFR-based and FFR-based OFDMA systems [9–11]. Mahmud et al. [9] investigated the energy efficient and energy efficient on per channel per cell for both the static FFR and SFR systems, they think that energy efficient for both static FFR and SFR is affected by the power amplification factor. Xie et al. [10] investigated the area spectral efficiency and area energy efficiency in a wireless heterogeneous network with inter-tier FFR and the proportional fairness resource allocation are considered to balance the spectral efficiency and user fairness within each cell. Qi et al. [11] investigated throughput and power efficiency in FFR-based network, and they also propose variable sub-carriers distribution method to improve users' fairness with throughput.

By summarizing the literatures, we find that the energy efficiency maximization mainly formulate as a fractional programming (FP) [12–14] in OFDMA system network. And there are also another form to study the energy efficient maximum. In [15], Bu et al. focus on the Heterogeneous OFMDA network, and propose a game theoretical scheme for energy-efficient resource allocations with interference pricing.

Most researchers investigated the maximum energy efficiency with Lagrange dual decomposition and convex optimization in [16, 17], to obtain the optimal EE by searching for the optimal resource allocation scheme. However, the algorithm which based on the Lagrange consume much time and space for many users network in the practical [18]. So, heuristic algorithm has been proposed to reduce the computation complexity and obtain a globally optimal solution, such as the hybrid genetic, simulated annealing algorithm [19], particle swarm optimization [20].

The energy efficiency optimization in previous is mainly in single cell or Heterogeneous Network enhancing the energy efficiency. Jiang et al. [24–29] studied the problem in their work. For the SFR, there are few literatures research about its energy efficient. In this paper, we mainly research about the global EE optimization to improve the performance of SFR-based OFDMA cellular network. We construct a global optimal EE function and make an analysis with it. Then, we utilized simulated annealing method to obtain the energy efficient maximum. There are three optimal goals in our global EE optimization process:

(1) We formulate the global energy efficient as a fractional function, and introduce a fairness term for each cell.
(2) We utilize Lagrange function to relax the constraint of the user quality of service, then with the KKT condition derivate the optimal power allocation.
(3) We can utilize simulated annealing to find the optimal transmitting power allocation and sub-channel assignment for BSs and decrease the inter-cell interference at the same time.

The rest of this paper is organized as follows: Sect. 2 presents the system assumptions and the system model; Sect. 3 makes an analysis about the GEE of the SFR-based OFDM cellular network, and describes the simulated annealing algorithm. Section 4 describes the simulation parameters, then shows and analyzes the simulation results. Finally, Sect. 5 is a conclusion.

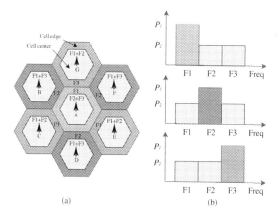

Fig. 1. Frequency allocation for SFR.

2 Problem Statement

In this section, we are mainly talking about a downlink SFR-based OFDMA cellular network scenario. It consists of some base stations (BS) with a number of active users in each BS, as Fig. 1(a) show. All the cells in the full coverage cellular system are regular hexagon. There are some assumptions about the SFR-based cellular network model, the detail as follow:

(1) The physical resource block (PRB) is the unit which allocated to users for transmitting signal, in each cell SFR-based cell the PRB consist of frequency, space, and time slot.

(2) There are total I regular hexagon cells which wrapped each other in the cellular network, and each cell is divided into two parts with the inner radius, cell edge and cell center, as Fig. 1(a) shows.

(3) There are M users which are uniformly randomly distributed in each cell, the user set denotes as $m \in \{1, 2, \ldots, M\}$. All the users in each cell is randomly distributed, e.g. cell-edge users (Ue) who at the cell-edge region and cell-central users (Uc) who at the cell-center region.

(4) The bandwidth is B (MHz) and it is divided into N sub-channels, the sub-channel set is $n \in \{1, 2, \ldots, N\}$. The PRB SFR-based scheme in each cell, the carriers are assigned as two categories by the transmission power levels, namely the major and minor sub-carriers, as Fig. 1(b) shows; all the BSs exchange their user's information of transmitting power and interference with each other through the air interface X2.

(5) The users in cell-edge mainly utilize major sub-carriers, and the users in cell-center can utilize all the carriers, but it mainly use the minor sub-carriers. In order to coordinate inter-cell interference, the transmitting power is limited by all the BS, the transmitting power of the cell-edge users and cell-center users are no more than P_1 and P_2, respectively, as Fig. 1(b) shows.

In the downlink cellular network scenario, we assume that user m receive downlink data from cell i on channel n with the transmitting power p_{imn}, and p_{jmn} is the co-channel transmit power of the BS j who has interference to the user m in cell i. In the multi-cell network, the instantaneous signal-to-interference-plus-noise ratio (SINR) of the m-th user in cell i can be written as follows

$$\gamma_{imn} = \frac{p_{imn} g_{imn}}{B_0 N_0 + \sum\limits_{j \neq i} p_{jmn} g_{jmn}}, \forall i, m, n \tag{1}$$

where B_0 is the sub-channel bandwidth and N_0 is the power spectral density of the additive Gaussian white noise. The term g_{imn} donate the channel gain of user m received power from BS i on sub-channel n; the term g_{jmn} instead of the channel interference gain for user m which come from the neighboring BS j on sub-channel n. The transmitting rate for the m-th user on sub-channel n can be expressed as

$$r_{imn}(p_{imn}) = B_0 \log_2(1 + \gamma_{imn}) \tag{2}$$

then, the total transmitting rate of user m in the cell i is

$$R_{im}(a_{imn}, p_{imn}) = \sum_{n=1}^{N} a_{imn} r_{imn}(p_{imn}) \tag{3}$$

where a_{imn} is channel allocation indicator means whether the PRB of sub-channel n allocated to user m or not. a_{imn} is 1 when the PRB allocated to user m or 0 is otherwise. The total power consumption of BS i is composed of transmit power and circuit power, it can be expressed as:

$$P_i(a_{imn}, p_{imn}) = \sum_{m=1}^{M} \sum_{n=1}^{N} a_{imn} p_{imn} + P_{c_i} \tag{4}$$

where P_{c_i} is the circuit power consumption of BS i.

In this model, we use term η donate the efficient (EE). As the defined about the transmitting rate of each user and the transmitting power, then the energy efficient optimization problem can be expressed as

$$\max \eta \tag{5}$$

subject to

$$\sum_{n=1}^{N} a_{imn} \leq 1, a_{imn} \in \{0, 1\}, \forall i, m, n \tag{5a}$$

$$\sum_{n=1}^{N} a_{imn} R_{imn} \geq R_{\min}, \forall m, i \tag{5b}$$

$$\sum_{m=1}^{M} \sum_{n=1}^{N} a_{imn} p_{imn} \leq P_{\max}, \forall i \tag{5c}$$

where (5a) denotes the PRB can be allocated to one user at most at the same time to utilize; (5b) is the minimum transmit rate constrained for each user; (5c) is the transmission power constraint for each BS.

In general, the energy efficient is defined as ratio of the achieved throughput over the total power consumption, which can be mathematically expressed as [21]. So, in the considered multi-carrier SFR-based network system, EE of BS i can be written as

$$\eta_i = \frac{R_i(a, p)}{P_i(a, p)} \tag{6}$$

and the global energy efficiency (GEE) of the network, defined as the ratio of global throughput to total transmitting power consumed by the system, is written as

$$\eta = \frac{\sum_{i=1}^{I} R_i(a, p)}{\sum_{i=1}^{I} P_i(a, p)} \tag{7}$$

For the GEE, from a global point of view, the GEE (7) is a good choice as the objective to optimal the system energy efficient, but there are also some drawbacks. When maximize the objective (7), there might lead to unfair power allocations for some cells. Then in order to obtain a fair resource allocation, we introduce another indicator β_i, the following new object be considered as:

$$\eta = \frac{\sum_{i=1}^{I} \beta_i R_i(a, p)}{\sum_{i=1}^{I} P_i(a, p)} \tag{8}$$

so the global energy efficient optimization objective of (6) can be written as

$$\max \eta = \max_{\{a,p\}} \frac{\sum_{i=1}^{I} \beta_i R_i(a, p)}{\sum_{i=1}^{I} P_i(a, p)} \tag{9}$$

subject to

$$\sum_{n=1}^{N} a_{imn} \leq 1, a_{imn} \in \{0, 1\}, \forall i, m, n \tag{9a}$$

$$\sum_{n=1}^{N} a_{imn} R_{imn} \geq R_{\min}, \forall m, i \tag{9b}$$

$$\sum_{m=1}^{M} \sum_{n=1}^{N} a_{imn} p_{imn} \leq P_{\max}, \forall i \tag{9c}$$

$$p_{imne} \leq P_1, \forall i, m \in \{Ue_i\} \tag{9d}$$

$$p_{imnc} \leq P_2, \forall i, m \in \{Uc_i\} \tag{9e}$$

$$\beta_i \geq 0, \forall i \tag{9f}$$

The process of solving the GEE objective function of (9) is to obtain the optimal resource allocation scheme about PRB.

3   Problem Transformation and Optimal Algorithm

3.1   Problem Transformation

We note that the objective function (9) is a fractional program, which is usually not feasible for the NP hard problem with the convex optimization method. However, with the non-linear fractional programming theory [22], we transform it as a tractable one with the Lagrange function.

Proposition 1: If η^* is the feasible solution of the objective function (9) and satisfies the constraints (9a)–(9f), so the equation $R_i(a_i^*, p_i^*) - \eta_i^* P(a_i^*, p_i^*) = 0$ is true, where $\{a_i^*, p_i^*\}$ is the optimal PRB and transmitting power allocation scheme.

Then we introduce an auxiliary function as follow:

$$F(a, p) = \sum_{i=1}^{I} \beta_i R_i(a, p) - \eta \sum_{i=1}^{I} P_i(a, p) \tag{10}$$

For (10), when $F(a, p) = 0$, the set $\{\eta_i^*, a_i^*, p_i^*\}$ is the optimal solution. Then we transform it as a Lagrange function to relax the constraints (9a)–(9f), the new form expressed as follow:

$$
\begin{aligned}
L(a_i, p_i, \tau, \mu, \lambda) = & \sum_{i=1}^{I} \beta_i R_i(a_i, p_i) - \eta \sum_{i=1}^{I} P_i(a_i, p_i) \\
& + \sum_{m=1}^{M} \tau_i \left(\sum_{n=1}^{N} a_{imn} R_{imn}(a_{imn}, p_{imn}) - R_{\min} \right) \\
& + \mu \left(P_{\max} - \sum_{m=1}^{M} \sum_{n=1}^{N} a_{imn} p_{imn} \right) \\
& + \sum_{n=1}^{N} \left(\lambda_{ie}(P_1 - p_{imne}) + \lambda_{ic}(P_2 - p_{imnc}) \right)
\end{aligned}
\tag{11}
$$

where τ, μ and λ are both the Lagrange-multiplier vector associated with constraints and satisfy $\tau \geq 0$, $\mu \geq 0$ and $\lambda \geq 0$.

For the integer variable a_{imn}, we can use the Hungarian algorithm to allocate PRB for each user, the variable can be regarded as $a_{imn} = 1$, so Lagrange function can be rewritten as

$$
\begin{aligned}
L(p_i, \tau, \mu, \lambda) = & \sum_{i=1}^{I} \beta_i R_i(a_i, p_i) - \eta \sum_{i=1}^{I} P_i(a_i, p_i) \\
& + \sum_{m=1}^{M} \tau_i \left(\sum_{n=1}^{N} R_{imn}(p_{imn}) - R_{\min} \right) \\
& + \mu \left(P_{\max} - \sum_{m=1}^{M} \sum_{n=1}^{N} p_{imn} \right) \\
& + \sum_{n=1}^{N} \left(\lambda_{ie}(P_1 - p_{imne}) + \lambda_{ic}(P_2 - p_{imnc}) \right)
\end{aligned}
\tag{12}
$$

Then the Karush-Kuhn-Tucker (KKT) [22] conditions for (12) can be written as

$$\frac{\partial L(p_i, \tau, \mu, \lambda)}{p_i} = 0 \tag{13}$$

$$\tau_i \left(\sum_{n=1}^{N} R_{imn} - R_{\min} \right) \geq 0 \tag{14}$$

$$\mu \left(P_{\max} - \sum_{m=1}^{M} \sum_{n=1}^{N} p_{imn} \right) \geq 0 \tag{15}$$

$$\lambda_{ie}(P_1 - p_{imne}) \geq 0 \tag{16}$$

$$\lambda_{ic}(P_2 - p_{imnc}) \geq 0 \tag{17}$$

From (12) the optimal power allocation can be formulated as

$$p_{imne} = \left[\frac{(\beta_i + \tau_i)}{(\eta_i + \mu + \lambda_{ie})} - \frac{\sigma^2 + I}{g_{imne}} \right]^+ \tag{18}$$

and

$$p_{imnc} = \left[\frac{(\beta_i + \tau_i)}{(\eta_i + \mu + \lambda_{ic})} - \frac{\sigma^2 + I}{g_{imnc}} \right]^+ \tag{19}$$

where $[x]^+ = \max(0, x)$, p_{imne} and p_{imnc} are the optimal power allocation for each user in cell-edge and cell-center respectively.

Then, the gradient method can be utilized to solve the dual problem, and the changing gradient can be written as

$$\tau_{imn}(t+1) = \left[\tau_{imn}(t) - len * \left(\sum_{n=1}^{N} R_{imn} - R_{\min} \right) \right]^+, \forall i, m, n \tag{20}$$

$$\mu_{imn}(t+1) = \left[\mu_{imn}(t) - len * \left(P_{\max} - \sum_{m=1}^{M} \sum_{n=1}^{N} p_{imn} \right) \right]^+, \forall i, m, n \tag{21}$$

$$\lambda_{imn}(t+1) = \left[\lambda_{imn}(t) - len * (P_1 - p_{imne}) \right]^+, \forall i, m \in \{Ue_i\} \tag{22}$$

$$\lambda_{imn}(t+1) = \left[\lambda_{imn}(t) - len * (P_2 - p_{imnc}) \right]^+, \forall i, m \in \{Uc_i\} \tag{23}$$

where *len* is a length of each step gradient.

3.2   Simulated Annealing Algorithm

For the optimal transmitting power allocation scheme (18) and (19) if there are many users and PRBs, it is a huge work to find the optimal allocation scheme, then we use the heuristic algorithm to find the optimal solution quickly.

Simulated Annealing (SA) is a reliable and flexible heuristic algorithm, can be used to obtain the global optimization solution [23]. The annealing is a heat treatment by changing the material physical properties to obtain the performance which people need. There are two steps in the process of the annealing. First, heating a material to above its milt temperature and maintaining a suitable temperature; second, cooling down slowly by control until solid back. The cooling speed has a significant impact on the performance of the material. So the temperature controlling is the key parameter of the annealing process.

For the Simulated Annealing method, we make a control about the head parameter. The procedure works as follow.

Step 1: Setting an initial condition L;

Step 2: Making a small perturbation disturbs about the state and brings the system into a new state L^*. If L^* is smaller than L, we accept the change and the new state; if L^* is greater than L, it does not mean worse, and maybe jump out the local optimal to the global optimal, so we accept it with a critical probability, namely

$$\theta = \begin{cases} 1 & \text{if } L > L^* \\ \exp(-(L*-L)/KT) & \text{if } L \leq L^* \end{cases} \tag{24}$$

where T is the current temperature after the state changes and K is a certain constant.

Step 3: The new states change with the T decreases and the accepting probability over iterations, until reached the limit of the temperature changes or the maximum iterations. When the temperature T is higher, it means that the new state is higher accepted probability.

Making an analogy with global energy efficient, the physical states are replaced by power allocation and sub-channel assignment. Although it cannot be proven that simulated annealing guarantees an optimal solution, the practice shows that an appropriate decreasing of the freezing parameter could reach the optimal solution.

In the simulated annealing algorithm, we use temperature parameter function (25) as the cooling schedule.

$$T(t) = T_0/\log_2(2+t) \tag{25}$$

where t is the iteration times and T_0 is the initial temperature.

We utilize the simulated annealing algorithm to search the optimal power allocation, and the process as the Table 1 shows.

Table 1. The simulated annealing algorithm

Algorithm 1. The simulated annealing algorithm
1   Initial the temperature T_0, Num, $\eta^{(0)} = 0$, $\varepsilon = 0.001$;
2   for t = 1:Num
3       $T(t) = T_0 / \log_2(2+t)$
4   for i=1:cells
5   Update the transmit power and channel assignment in each cell with (17) and (18) by (19)-(22).
6   end for
7   Calculate the throughput and energy efficient with (6);
8   Calculate the accepted probability with (23)
9   if the $\left|\eta^{(t+1)} - \eta^{(t)}\right| < \varepsilon$
10   break;
11   end if
12   update the temperature with (24)
13   end for

4   Simulation Result and Analysis

To validate the global EE optimization with simulated annealing algorithm, we make a numerical simulation. We consider a SFR-based OFDM cellular network with 19 cells, the coverage radius of each BS is 500 m, and the inner cell radius is 350 m. The system bandwidth is 10 MHz and each sub-channel bandwidth is 180 kHz. In each cells, there are 36 users randomly distributed. The Maximum transmit power and the Circuit power consumption of each BS is 46 dBm and 43 dBm respectively. The thermal noise power is -174 dBm/Hz, and the path loss function is

$$PL = 135 + 38 * \log_{10}(d) \tag{26}$$

where d is the distance of user to its serving BS, its unit is meter.

We also consider that the downlink load for each user is 500 Kbps in each cell. In the follow, Fig. 2 shows the BSs and users distribution in the simulation scenario. In this paper, for simplicity, we assume the fairness factor $\beta_1 = \beta_2 = \ldots = \beta_I$. When we want to research the fairness for each cell in the network, we can set different fairness factors for each cell.

With the simulated annealing algorithm, as the Fig. 3 shows, the Global energy efficient of the network is convergence, it does not change any more after 8 iterations.

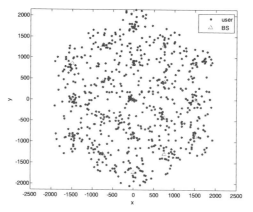

Fig. 2. BSs and users distribution in the simulation scenario.

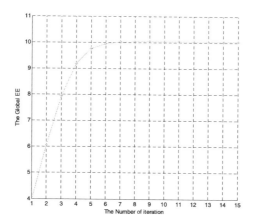

Fig. 3. The Global EE versus the number of iteration.

Figure 4 shows the total transmitting power consumption in the process of Global energy efficient optimization, and we also make a comparison with the single-cell energy efficient (SEE) optimization. From Fig. 4, we note that the total energy consumption of the single-cell EE optimization algorithm is much more than the algorithm with Global EE optimization.

In SFR-based cells, the inner radius which use the category the users has an effect with the frequency reuse efficient and the inter-cell interference, then from Fig. 5 we also note that the Global energy efficient is also affected by the normalized radius. The Global energy efficient of the network for the GEE algorithm is better than the SEE algorithm.

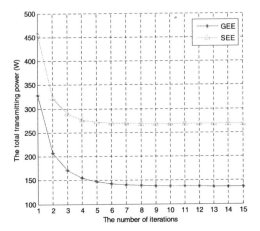

Fig. 4. The total transmitting power consumption versus the number of iteration.

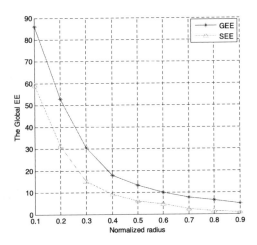

Fig. 5. The energy efficient versus the normalized radius in the SFR-based cellular network.

5   Conclusions

We have researched the global energy-efficient optimization of the SFR-based OFDM cellular network. We formulated a global energy-efficient optimization with and utilizing the simulated annealing algorithm to obtain the optimal scheme of the transmitting power allocation and sub-channel assignment in each cell. The simulation results show that the maximum global energy efficient can be achieved and the total power consumption is low under the quality of serve constraints with the SA algorithm.

References

1. Wu, G.: Recent advances in energy-efficient networks and their application in 5G systems. IEEE Wirel. Commun. **22**(2), 145–151 (2015)
2. Yang, C.: An efficient hybrid spectrum access algorithm in OFDM-based wideband cognitive radio networks. Neurocomputing **125**, 33–40 (2014)
3. Elayoubil, S.E.: Performance evaluation of frequency planning schemes in OFDMA-based networks. IEEE Trans. Wirel. Commun. **7**(5), 1623–1633 (2008)
4. R1-050841, Huawei, Further Analysis of Soft Frequency Reuse Scheme, 3GPP TSG RAN WG1#42, 29 August–2 September (2005)
5. Ren, Z.: Energy-efficient resource allocation in downlink OFDM wireless systems with proportional rate constraints. IEEE Trans. Veh. Technol. **63**(5), 2139–2150 (2014)
6. Al-Zahrani, A.Y., Yu, F.R.: An energy-efficient resource allocation and interference management scheme in green heterogeneous networks using game theory. IEEE Trans. Veh. Technol. **65**(7), 5384–5396 (2016)
7. Yang, K.: Energy-efficient downlink resource allocation in heterogeneous OFDMA networks. IEEE Trans. Veh. Technol. **66**(6), 5086–5098 (2016)
8. Wang, X.: Energy-efficient resource allocation in coordinated downlink multicell OFDMA systems. IEEE Trans. Veh. Technol. **65**(3), 1395–1408 (2016)
9. Mahmud, A.: On the energy efficiency of fractional frequency reuse techniques. In: IEEE Wireless Communications and Networking Conference, pp. 2348–2353 (2014)
10. Xie, B.: Joint spectral efficiency and energy efficiency in FFR based wireless heterogeneous networks. IEEE Trans. Veh. Technol. **PP**(99), 1 (2017)
11. Qi, Z.: Analytical evaluation of throughput and power efficiency using fractional frequency reuse. In: IEEE Vehicular Technology Conference, pp. 1–5. IEEE (2016)
12. Dinkelbach, W.: On nonlinear fractional programming. Manag. Sci. **13**(7), 492–498 (1967)
13. Ng, D.W.K.: Energy-efficient resource allocation in multi-cell OFDMA systems with limited backhaul capacity. IEEE Trans. Wirel. Commun. **11**(10), 3618–3631 (2012)
14. He, S.: Coordinated beam-forming for energy efficient transmission in multicell multiuser systems. IEEE Trans. Commun. **61**(12), 4961–4971 (2013)
15. Bu, S.: Interference-aware energy-efficient resource allocation for OFDMA-based heterogeneous networks with incomplete channel state information. IEEE Trans. Veh. Technol. **64**(3), 1036–1050 (2015)
16. Wang, Y.: Energy-efficient resource allocation for different QoS requirements in heterogeneous networks. In: 2016 IEEE 83rd Vehicular Technology Conference (VTC Spring). IEEE (2016)
17. Masoudi, M.: Energy efficient resource allocation in two-tier OFDMA networks with QoS guarantees. Wirel. Netw. 1–15 (2017)
18. Danish, E.: Content-aware resource allocation in OFDM systems for energy-efficient video transmission. IEEE Trans. Consum. Electron. **60**(3), 320–328 (2014)
19. Xu, L.: Energy-efficient resource allocation for multiuser OFDMA system based on hybrid genetic simulated annealing. Soft Comput. **21**(14), 1–8 (2016)
20. Tang, M., Xin, Y.: Energy efficient power allocation in cognitive radio network using coevolution chaotic particle swarm optimization. Comput. Netw. **100**, 1–11 (2016)
21. Feng, D.: A survey of energy-efficient wireless communications. IEEE Commun. Surv. Tutor. **15**(1), 167–178 (2013)
22. Dinkelbach, W.: On nonlinear fractional programming. Manag. Sci. **13**, 492–498 (1967)
23. Bertsimas, D., Tsitsiklis, J.: Simulated annealing. Stat. Sci. **8**(1), 10–15 (1993)

24. Jiang, D., Li, W., Lv, H.: An energy-efficient cooperative multicast routing in multi-hop wireless networks for smart medical applications. Neurocomputing **220**(2017), 160–169 (2017)
25. Jiang, D., Wang, Y., Han, Y., et al.: Maximum connectivity-based channel allocation algorithm in cognitive wireless networks for medical applications. Neurocomputing **220** (2017), 41–51 (2017)
26. Jiang, D., Xu, Z., Li, W., et al.: An energy-efficient multicast algorithm with maximum network throughput in multi-hop wireless networks. J. Commun. Netw. **18**(5), 713–724 (2016)
27. Jiang, D., Zhang, P., Lv, Z., et al.: Energy-efficient multi-constraint routing algorithm with load balancing for smart city applications. IEEE Internet Things J. **3**(6), 1437–1447 (2016)
28. Jiang, D., Nie, L., Lv, Z., et al.: Spatio-temporal Kronecker compressive sensing for traffic matrix recovery. IEEE Access **4**, 3046–3053 (2016)
29. Jiang, D., Liu, J., Lv, Z., et al.: A robust energy-efficient routing algorithm to cloud computing networks for learning. J. Intell. Fuzzy Syst. **31**(5), 2483–2495 (2016)

Constructing Algorithm of MLMS
Data Center Network

Jianfei Zhang[1(✉)], Weiwu Ren[1], and Guannan Qu[2]

[1] School of Computer Science and Technology,
Changchun University of Science and Technology, Weixing Road No. 7089,
Changchun, People's Republic of China
jfzhang@cust.edu.cn, renww339@163.com
[2] College of Computer Science and Technology, Jilin University,
Qianjin Street No. 2699, Changchun, People's Republic of China
gnqu@jlu.edu.cn

Abstract. As the infrastructure, the interconnection network structure of a data center plays an important role on the performance of a DC, such as its scalability, reliability, robustness, and so on. Recently, we proposed a novel data center interconnection networks structure, which is called Multi-layer MSR structure (MLMS for short). The MLMS structure is defined basing on MSR graph, and we proved that it has good features. In this paper, we will define the address space of the MLMS, and design an algorithm to constructing MLMS. Basing on the definitions of address space and connection rules, we propose a constructing algorithm of MLMS. The algorithm makes that it is better realizability for building a MLMS.

Keywords: Data center network · MSR

1 Introduction

In recent years, many massive data centers are being built to support various of applications, such as search engine, on-line game, on-line shopping, enterprise website, etc. In addition, data center has to host cloud services, including file system like GFS [1], big data storage like BigTable [2], parallel computing like MapReduce [3], etc.

In order to operate all these services, huge volumes of hardware, software and data resources have to be hosted in data center. Meanwhile, with the increasing work load and additional new features of services, the scale of the data center has to extend dynamically, and the communication between servers has to be efficient and safety. The cost of implementing and operating a data center, however, is hoped to be as low as possible. Interconnection network, as the skeleton of a data center, all the factors have to be considered during the process of designing it.

Lots of studies resulted in various interconnection networks in decade of years. Fat-tree [4] is one of the well-known structures, which is based on a tree structure and conquered weakness that the root node of tree is a bottleneck point. But the Fat-tree has limitation of number of nodes. BCube [5] is a novel structure, which can be scaled and shipping in a container. Hence a BCube data center is able to be deployed flexibly.

© Springer Nature Singapore Pte Ltd. 2018
H. Yuan et al. (Eds.): GSKI 2017, CCIS 848, pp. 629–636, 2018.
https://doi.org/10.1007/978-981-13-0893-2_65

But the number of servers in a BCube is also restricted by the space of a container. DCell [6] is another distinctive structure, which has excellent extendibility. Meanwhile, some solutions were proposed based on the traditional interconnection networks, such as HyperCube, Butterfly [7], Banyan, and so on. Recently, S.Q. Zheng [8–10], et al. proposed a series of methods on constructing interconnection network using combinatorial design.

MSR [11] (Modified Shift Register) graph is improved over De Bruijn [12] graph. We proposed a novel interconnection network using MSR as the underlying topology [13]. The network is a multi-layers MSR structure, shorted as MLMS. Basing on the previous work, in this paper, we will give the definitions of the address space for servers in MLMS, and design its constructing algorithm.

The rest of this paper is organized as follow. Section 2 describes our previous work which includes the structure of Multi-layer MSR. Section 3 introduces the constructing algorithm of the MLMS. And the algorithm is designed basing on the address space of servers in MLMS and the connecting rules between units, which are also introduced in this section.In the last section we conclude our works.

2   Previous Work

De Bruijn graph is an-dimensional and directed graph. It has m^n vertices, and each vertex is labeled by an-length sequences. Every element in the sequence is one of the special set of m symbols, and the same symbol may appear multiple times in a sequence. If one of the vertices can be expressed as another vertex by shifting all its symbols by one place to the left and adding a new symbol at the end of this vertex, then the latter has a directed edge to the former vertex. Based on above definitions, a De Bruijn graph has an even degree d = 2m, m ≥ 2, and diameter n. Figure 1 is a De Bruijn graph with parameters of m = 2, n = 3.

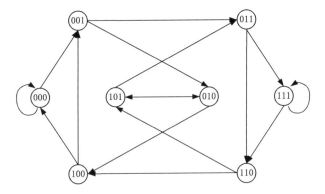

Fig. 1. A De Bruijn graph with m = 2, n = 3.

Kumar and Reddy [11] proposed a family of regular and undirected graphs, which improved De Buijin graphs with optimal connectivity. They are called Modified Shift

Register (MSR) graph. A MSR graph, like the De Bruijn graph, is defined for even degree, but has more nodes than De Bruijn graphs with the same degree and diameter.

Let Δ be a finite set of symbols. We use integer to denote different symbols, hence $\Delta = \{0, 1, \ldots, \delta\}$. Each node in MSR graph has a label of $\{i_0, i_1, \cdots, i_{n-2}, i_{n-1}\}$, where $i_j \in \Delta$ and $i_j \neq i_{j+1}, 1 \leq j \leq n$.

Each node I with label $\{i_0, i_1, \cdots, i_{n-2}, i_{n-1}\}$ has two relevant set of nodes which are:

$$L_j(I) = \{i_1, i_2, \cdots, i_{n-2}, i_{n-1}, (i_{n-1}+j)\}$$

$$R_k(I) = \{(i_0 - k), i_0, i_1, \cdots, i_{n-2}\}$$

where $j, k \in [1, \delta]$, the additions and subtractions are modulo $(\delta + 1)$. A MSR graph draws an edge between I and $L_j(I)$ and an edge between I and $R_k(I)$. Nodes $L_j(I)$ are called left-shift neighbors, nodes $R_k(I)$ are called right-shiftneighbors. Obviously, the shift neighbor nodes are obtained by shifting the label of I left and right respectively, and by adding an elements in the vacated position. The element being placed in belongs to the symbol set Δ except the original one in that position.

Until now, most of nodes in MSR graph have degree 2δ,but the node with label abab...ab(or abab... aba) and the node with label baba ...ba (or baba...bab) are a left or right shift neighbor, and the degree of such node is $2\delta - 1$ as an exception. MSR graph has number of $\delta(\delta + 1)$ such nodes which are called R-nodes. Correspondingly, a node other thana R-nodes is called G-nodes. To keep the MSR graph regular, it is possible to adding $\delta(\delta + 1)/2$ edges for connecting all the R-nodes into a circle.

A MSR graph can be create by algorithm ConRNodes and algorithm CreatMSR, which pseudo-code are as follow:

```
ConRNodes
Begin
 For each node (a, b)ⁿ, b > a do
      if (b ≠ δ) then
            Draw an edge from (a, b)ⁿ to (b + 1, a)ⁿ
      else if (b = δ)
            if (a ≠ δ − 1 ) then
                  Draw an edge from (a, b)ⁿ to (a + 2, a + 1)ⁿ
      else if (a = δ − 1)
            Draw an edge from (a, b)ⁿ to (1, 0)ⁿ
 End
```

CreatMSR(I, flag)/*Without loss of the generality, let the initial node $I = (1, 0)^n$, and flag equals to true*/

```
Begin
    for each L(I) do
        if (I and Lⱼ(I) do not have a links) then
            Draw an edge between I and Lⱼ(I)
    for each L(I) do
        CreatMSR(L(I),false);
    if (flag = true) then
        ConRNodes;
End
```

In CreatMSR, it starts from a random node. For one special node, it draws an edge to each left-shift neighbor node of the starting node. And then the CreatMSR executes recursively, and draws edges for every L(I) node. At last it draws all edges between R-nodes. A MSR graph with $d = 2$, n = 3 is shown in Fig. 2.

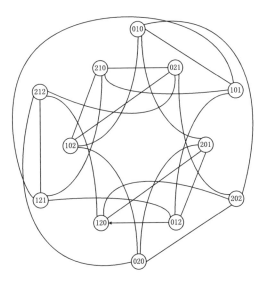

Fig. 2. AMSR graph with $d = 2$, n = 3.

Recently, we proposed a multi-layer data center interconnection network called MLMS structure which is based on MSR graph [13]. Using the graph to convert a data center interconnection network, we let nodes of the graph denote the servers and let edges in graph denote the links. The MLMS structure is defined recursively as follow:

The level 0 structure of MLMS, M_0, is constructed by servers directly. These servers connect to each other via wires according to the topology of a $MSR[\delta_0, n]$ graph. Thus a M_0 includes $N_0 = \delta_0^n + \delta_0^n$ servers, each server has degree $2\delta_0$. Level 1 structure, M_1, uses $\tilde{N}_1 M_0 s$ as its basic block. It means that M_1 connects M_0 according to the topology of a $MSR[\delta_1, n]$ graph by adding one more link to each physical server in every M_0. Hence every logic unit M_0 has degree $2\delta_1 = N_0$ and $\widetilde{N_1} = \delta_1^n + \delta_1^n$. N1 the number of servers in M_1, is equals to $\tilde{N}_1 \times N_0$.

For higher levels, a M_k structure is consisted by $\delta_k M_{k-1}s$, where $M_{k-1}s$ are processed as logic units and connected to each other according to the topology of a $MSR[\delta_k, n]$ graph. During we construct the MLMS M_k with $k \geq 2$, each M_{k-1} is a logic unit with degree $\delta_k = (N_{k-1})/2$. It means that every server in M_{k-1} has to deploy exactly one more link to a server in other different M_{k-1}. Hence, each server in a k level MLMS has $2\delta_0 + k$ links, where $2\delta_0$ links are for M_0 and each one of k links is for a higher level connection.

MLMS has three advantages. (i) High extendibility. The proposed structure has multiple layers. With the increasing number of layers, the number of servers in the structure rises at a double exponential speed. (ii) High performance of routing. Because our structure has a small diameter, the shortest path between a pair of servers is bounded by diameter. Hence a message travels less hops from source to destination. (iii) Low energy cost. Our structure is built without any switch, thus it cuts down the energy cost.

3   Constructing Algorithm of the MLMS

3.1   The Address Space of Servers in MLMS

As we introduced in last section, the MLMS structure is designed with MSR graph theory as its underlying principle. Every vertex in a MSR graph has a label as $[l_0, l_1, \ldots, l_{n-1}]$, where $l_i \in \Delta$ and $i \in \{0, 1, \ldots n - 1\}$. The topology of MLMS structure is hierarchical. Each logic unit in different layers has a label with the same pattern above. Thus every server in a k-level MLMS structure has an address as $Addr_k = \left\{ [l_0, l_1, \ldots, l_{n-1}]^k, [l_0, l_1, \ldots, l_{n-1}]^{k-1}, \ldots, [l_0, l_1, \ldots, l_{n-1}]^0 \right\}$. For $0 \leq i \leq k$, $[l_0, l_1, \ldots, l_{n-1}]^i$ indicates that the server belongs to a ith-level logic unit with label $[l_0, l_1, \ldots, l_{n-1}]$. Obviously, each sub-label in $Addr_k$ has the same length of k, but is consisted by different set of symbols Δ_k. The reason is that the MLMS is constructed iteratively and a logic unit M_i within different level has different dimensions of servers.

The sub-label can be converted to a single number, such that we can simplify the address of each server. Let N denote a sub-label $[l_0, l_1, \ldots, l_{n-1}]$, and they can convert to each other by following method. Since each symbol of l_i has the value belonging to the set of $\Delta = \{0, 1, \cdots, \delta\}$, a label as $[l_0, l_1, \ldots, l_{n-1}]$ can be considered as a δ-base number. The only difference is that the value of this "number" is not consecutive, because every pairs of adjacent symbols are not the same. The transformation between N and a label of $[l_0, l_1, \ldots, l_{n-1}]$ is similar to converting numbers with different radices. In addition, we have to deal with the trouble of discontinuousness.

3.2   The Rules of Connecting Different Units

As the definition of the MLMS, its underlying structure of each level is a $MSR[\delta, n]$ graph, and the physical links of MLMS are deployed on the servers. Thus the connections between the logic units in higher level are realized by the links between the servers. Here is a problem should be considered, which is how to select the servers in two different logic units to build the connections.

Without loss of generality, S and D are two logic units with level i + 1, and S has label $[l_0, l_1, \ldots, l_{n-1}]^{i+1}$. Since S has a connection with D, the unit D has label $[l_1, l_2, \ldots, l_{n-1}, x]^{i+1}$ or $[y, l_0, l_1, \ldots, l_{n-2}]^{i+1}$. We select the level i unit P with label $[l_0, l_1, \ldots, l_{n-1}]^i$ in S and Q with label $[l'_0, l'_1, \ldots, l'_{n-1}]^i$ in D to construct the connection.

Case I: D has label of $[l_1, l_2, \ldots, l_{n-1}, x]^{i+1}$. The label $[l_0, l_1, \ldots, l_{n-1}]^i$ of P can be calculated from x. Because a label and a corresponding integer number can convert to each other, we get the label of P. In the same way, the label of Q can be calculated from $(l_0^{i+1} + \delta_{i+1})$, that l_0^{i+1} is the head symbol of S's label and δ_{i+1} is the value of level-(i + 1) δ.

Case II: D has label of $[y, l_0, l_1, \ldots, l_{n-2}]^{i+1}$. Thus a parameter N can be got from $y + 1 + \delta_{i+1}$ or $y + \delta_{i+1}$, depending on whether y is bigger than l_0. Then, the label P and Q can be gotten in the same way in case I. This N, however, equals to l_{n-1} or $l_{n-1} + 1$, depending on whether l_{n-1} is bigger than l_{n-2} or not, where l_{n-1} is the tail symbol of S's label.

For case I, if we change the roles of S and D to each other, we will get a pair of units within case II. The reason is that a node is also a right-shift node of its left-shift neighbor node. Thus we can define just one rule to deal with both of the two cases.

Without loss of generality, we supposed that S and D are two level i + 1 units. S and D have label $[y, l_0, l_1, \ldots, l_{n-2}]^{i+1}$ and $[l_1, l_2, \ldots, l_{n-1}, x]^{i+1}$, respectively. To connect S and D, we can select a pair of level i units P and Q which belong to S and D respectively. The label of P can be obtained with x as its parameter and the label of Q can be obtained with $y + \delta_{i+1}$ as its parameter.

3.3   The Constructing Algorithm of MLMS

Basing on the definition of address space we proposed above, the construction algorithm can be designed as follow. To build a $MLMS_k$, the address of each server is represented as a (k + 1)-tuple $[a_k, a_{k-1}, \ldots, a_1, a_0]$, where a_i indicates which $MLMS_i$ this server is included in and a_i actually is converted from the label $[l_0, l_1, \ldots, l_{n-1}]^i$ of the complete address. A prefix $[a_k, a_{k-1}, \ldots, a_{i+1}]$ is a part of a (k + 1)-tuple address. Obviously, the prefix can denote an $MLMS_i$ a server belongs to.

The constructing algorithm firstly checks whether it is constructing the level-0 structure. If so, it connects all the servers according to the special MSR graph. If not, it recursively constructs the $MLMS_{l-1}$. At last, all these $MLMS_{l-1}$ are connected according to a $level_{l-i}$ MSR graph.

Each server in $aMLMS_k$ has $(k + 2\delta)$ links. 2δ links are used to connect with other servers in $MLMS_0$, thus they are called level-0 links. Meanwhile, the link, called level-1 link, connects to a server in the same $MLMS_1$, but in a different $MLMS_0$. Similarly, a level-i link connects to a server in different $MLMS_{i-1}$, but in the same $MLMS_i$. The pseudo-code of the MLMS is as follow:

```
BuildMLMS (n , l)
    Begin
        /*building level-0*/
        if(l == 0) then
        Run CreatMSR(I, true) to connect servers;
        return;
    /*building level-(l-1)*/
    for i = 0; i ≤ Ñₗ; i + + do
        BuildMLMS(n, l-1);
    for i = 0; i ≤ Ñₗ; i + + do
        Connect MLMSl-i to each other according the rules;
    return;
    End
```

Figure 3 illustrates a part of M_1 structure of MLMS which is constructed by the constructing algorithm. It proves the correctness of the algorithm.

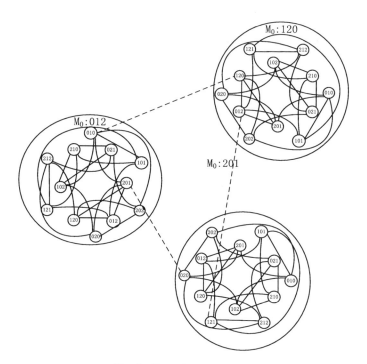

Fig. 3. Part of M_1 structure.

4 Conclusion

Recently, we proposed a novel data center network structure named MLMS, which is defined iteratively using MSR as its underling structure. And we also proved that it has good scalability, multiple paths between two server pair and short network diameter. In this paper, we designed the address space of servers in a MLMS, and the rules of unit connections. Based on these, we design the construction algorithm on how to implement a MLMS network.

Acknowledgments. This paper is supported by the project "Research and Realization on Virtualization Technology of Internet Content Delivery Oriented Networks" (20150204082GX), which is financially supported by Jilin Provincial Science and Technology Agency.

References

1. Ghemawat, S., Gobioff, H., Leung, S.: The Google file system. In: ACM SOSP 2003 (2003)
2. Chang, F., et al.: Bigtable: a distributed storage system for structured data. In: OSDI 2006 (2006)
3. Dean, J., Ghemawat, S.: MapReduce: simplified data processing on large clusters. In: OSDI 2004 (2004)
4. Duato, J., Yalamanchili, S., Ni, L.: Interconnection Networks: An Engineering Approach, vol. 413. IEEE Computer Society, Los Alamitos (1997)
5. Guo, C., Lu, G., Li, D., Wu, H., Zhang, X.: BCube: a high performance server-centric network architecture for modular data centers. In: ACM SIGCOMM Computer Communication Review (2009)
6. Guo, C., Wu, H., Tan, K., Shi, L., Zhang, Y., Liu, S.: DCell: a scalable and fault-tolerant network structure for data centers. In: Proceedings of the ACM SIGCOMM 2008 Conference on Data Communication (2008)
7. Saad, Y., Schultz, M.H.: Topological properties of hypercubes. IEEE Trans. Comput. **37**, 867–872 (1988)
8. Zheng, S.Q.: An abstract model for optical interconnection networks. In: Li, K., Pan, Y., Zheng, S.Q. (eds.) Parallel Computing Using Optical Interconnections, vol. 468, pp. 139–162. Springer, Boston (1998). https://doi.org/10.1007/978-0-585-27268-9_7
9. Zheng, S.Q., Wu, J.: Dual of complete graph as an interconnection networks. In: IEEE Symposium on Parallel & Distributed Processing (1996)
10. Li, Y., Wu, J., Zheng, S.Q.: An optical interconnection structure based on the dual of a hypercube. Informatica (1998)
11. Kumar, V.P., Reddy, S.M.: A class of graphs for fault-tolerant processor interconnections. In: IEEE International Conference on Distributed Computing Systems (1984)
12. Loguinov, D., Kumar, A., Rai, V., Ganesh, S.: Graph-theoretic analysis of structured peer-to-peer systems: routing distances and fault resilience. IEEE/ACM Trans. Netw. **13**, 1107–1120 (2005)
13. Zhang, J.F.: A data center network structure based on multiple layers MSR graph. In: Proceedings of the 7th International Symposium on Computational Intelligence and Industrial Applications (2016)

Research on Election of Distributed Wireless Multi-hop Self-organized Network

Xiaodong Shang$^{(\boxtimes)}$, Xu Li, and Xin Tong

School of Electronic and Information Engineering, Beijing Jiaotong University,
Beijing 100044, China
{15120127,xli,17111029}@bjtu.edu.cn

Abstract. Distributed wireless multi-hop self-organized network has the advantages of flexible networking, powerful extensibility and low costs of operation and maintenance. It has bright prospects in Ultra-Dense Network of 5G (5th Generation Wireless Communication), distributed D2D (Device to Device) communication. An election can avoid excessive signaling overhead caused by repeated reservations and achieve low collision probability of signal transmission, so the election plays an important role in distributed wireless multi-hop self-organized network with its fairness and robustness. However, the study of election has not attracted enough attention, previous studies have focused on election in two-hop range and the performance degradation caused by cumulative interference is never to be considered. Maintaining three-hop neighbors' information can effectively reduce cumulative interference. In this paper, we research the crucial election parameters, different neighbor maintaining ranges and election efficiency. The numerical simulation results show the impacts of different nodes and election parameters on system performance. Simulation is conducted on based on NS2 platform to verify the impact of election consistency on election performance efficiency. The optimization strategies of election parameters and election consistency issues are further obtained.

Keywords: Multi-hop · Distributed election · Consistency · Election efficiency

1 Introduction

Distributed wireless multi-hop self-organized network has the advantages of flexible networking, powerful extensibility and low costs of operation and maintenance. This network only needs partial information, which can reduce signaling transmission costs compared with centralized multi-hop network. In current public cellular network and industrial wireless sensor field, the centralized single-hop or multi-hop network mode are widely used under the requirement of QoS. But with the increase of network's size and hops, the centralized network scheduling mechanism will bring more operation and maintenance costs. Signaling overhead increases dramatically, routing is difficult to optimize and other problems [1]. The distributed network can effectively solve problems above. With the progress of 5G ultra density network, the distributed D2D network and interconnection technology, the research and development of distributed network model are imperative [2]. However, compared with the centralized network,

© Springer Nature Singapore Pte Ltd. 2018
H. Yuan et al. (Eds.): GSKI 2017, CCIS 848, pp. 637–651, 2018.
https://doi.org/10.1007/978-981-13-0893-2_66

the distributed network lacks unified coordination of central controller, and only can rely on neighbors' maintenance to schedule resources or reduce interference. So the key and the difficult point are how to ensure effective transmission of control signaling.

The election mechanism directly affects access of control signaling. By maintaining neighbors' information, nodes are at the same level. It can be adapted to different network scenarios, and can avoid large amount of costs caused by repetitive interaction in reservation mode. Compared with traditional random access mechanism, low transmission collision probability of control signaling can be realized at the same time when the nodes density is large, which can improve the channel utilization rate. So the election mechanism can both reduce the costs and reduce the collision probability.

However, almost existing election mechanism researches only maintain two-hop neighbors' scheduling information. These results showed that there was badly cumulative interference beyond two-hop. With increasing nodes, the link interference was more serious. It led to decrease of network capacity and even interruption, which made actual election performance inefficient. Expanding the scope of election to three-hop will dramatically help to reduce the cumulative interference, but bring about election consistency. This topic has drown little attention of researchers in this field.

In view of above problems, influence of network parameters, key parameters of election, maintenance scope on election performance efficiency and consistency are taken into account in this paper. The effects of different network parameters, backoff parameters and maintenance hops on election performance are given. Finally, the optimization method of core parameters in election mechanism and the feasible strategy of solving the election consistency issue are put forward.

2 Related Work

At present, most scholars at home and abroad have studied channel access mode adopted by wireless multi-hop self-organized network. The CSMA/CA mechanism based on random access is widely adapted [3, 4]. Most multi-hop self-organized network researches which use TDD mechanism are based on fixed multiple accesses such as point-to-point or centralized mode [5]. In contrast, there are few studies on election mechanism proposed by the distributed multi-hop self-organized network. The influence of election parameters and cumulative interference beyond two-hop range are not taken into account which can decrease the election performance. Furthermore, there are little researches on coherence of expanding election scope.

In [6], an enhanced election-based transmission timing mechanism was proposed to improve the collision that may occur in protocol by extending the sending interval of two-hop neighbors' information. However, this approach was only for two-hop neighbors, it also reduced the efficiency of election and may make increasing wastes of slot. In [7], an intelligent distributed search protocol was proposed to improve the election performance by dynamically changing the election parameters, but this method was more complicated and it was difficult to modify the election parameters dynamically in practical application. In [8], a local election mechanism of multi-hop ad-hoc network was used to derive the number of timeslots spent on a slot election, but only for two-hop election. In [9], a dynamic adjustment of back off time algorithm was proposed to improve the network performance when the network density changes, but this literature mainly focused on the influence of back off parameters instead of other parameters affects the network performance. In [10], the authors put forward an improved mesh election algorithm to guarantee the fairness of the election, but it's just for a specific network scene. In [11], a method of competition ranking estimation based on node caching utilization is proposed, and it is proved that the method can effectively reduce end to end delay in a specific network scenario; however, the assumption is too ideal.

3 Analysis of Election Mechanism

3.1 Introduction of Election Mechanism

In [12], a mesh election algorithm was proposed. The sending of MSH-DSCH (Mesh Distributed Scheduling) message is based on the election algorithm. The node elects next transmission opportunity when the control messages are sent. The elected nodes are from the neighbors which meet the election conditions within two-hop. Using this algorithm can realize collision-free transmission within two-hop.

To realize this distributed election mechanism, the nodes need to broadcast the next transmission time of the MSH-DSCH in present sending. In Fig. 1, CXT (Current Xmt Time) stands for the current sending time. After CXT, the nodes hold off for a certain number ($H = 2^{Basic + \exp}$) of control slots to start mesh election. Where, H is the time of backing off, *Basic* is the dynamic back off exponent. *Basic* denotes the fixed back off exponent which is usually suggested to be 4.

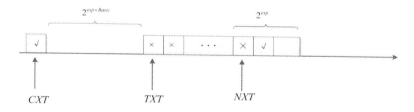

Fig. 1. Process of mesh election

Figure 1 shows the election process. The node waits for its sending time to send MSH-DSCH message, selects the first idle slot after retreating and sets the current slot as TXT (Temp Xmt Time). The node competes with the eligible two-hop neighbors by using the Mesh election algorithm to determine whether this election is successful or not. If it wins, the node will set the NXT (Next Time Xmt) as TXT, otherwise, the node elects for the next slot and add 1 to TXT. If this node fails in election process (marked as ×), it will keep electing the next slot until it succeeds (marked as √).

From (1), we can learn that in order to save network resources, the election result interval of next sending control message is represented by two parameters, *NextXmtMx* & *exp*. That is to say, when the node competes with his neighbors, it is not only focusing on the transmission slot for next sending opportunity of neighbors, but extending to an interval range about 2^{exp} transmission slots.

$$2^{exp} \times NextXmtMx \leq NextXmtTime \leq 2^{exp} \times (NextXmtMx + 1) \qquad (1)$$

We need to determine the next sending time of neighbors through parameters, as well as the third transmission cycle of neighbors from

$$ESXS = NXS + H \qquad (2)$$

3.2 Problems in Election Mechanism

The election mechanism above has following problems. Firstly, the election mechanism is for two-hop range, it does not consider nodes beyond two-hop which can bring the cumulative interference problems. Secondly, the election mechanism is based on complete consistency, but there may exist deviation between nodes' interaction.

3.2.1 Cumulative Interference

The distributed network lacks of unified coordination from central controller, and its resource scheduling is relied on local information which should try to avoid interference. Current protocols maintain neighbor information only one or two hops. The transmission failure probability caused by neighbor cumulative interference is highly as 20%, which dramatically restricts the system's utility of channel reuse to meet practical requirements [13]. The conclusions of [14] showed that when the network's nodes density becomes larger, the success rate of maintenance for two-hop neighbor information will reduce to 82%, and the success rate can be maintained to more than 90% when the nodes maintain three-hop neighbor information.

It can be seen that the maintenance of two-hop neighbor election has a high demand for nodes density, which seriously restricts the expansion of distributed wireless multi-hop ad hoc network. The three-hop election has a significant effect on solving cumulative interference problem, but it will bring election consistency issue. Besides, there are rare researches on the issue of election consistency and its impact on election performance. Therefore, this paper focuses on the key parameters of election mechanism and the relationship between maintenance scope and election performance efficiency, as well as consistency. They can provide a trade-off between election success rate and election efficiency.

3.2.2 Election Consistency Issues

Election mechanism does not give a way to let each node obtain neighbors' election information timely, and the inconsistency of the possible message is not considered. As shown in Fig. 2, node B and node D are one-hop neighbors of node A, node C and E are two-hop neighbors of node A. In time slot t, node A starts election. At the same time, the election set of node A is {B, C, D, E}. From mechanism above, node A can obtained election interval of node B and D by formula (1). However, this is not the exact time of the node B and node D. Thus, the election scope is expanded at node A. Node A can only obtain election information of its two-hop neighbors—node C and E, through the transmission of node B and node D. But it's a long delay from the time of its sending, the two-hop neighbor election information obtained by node A may be hysteretic.

Fig. 2. Chain topology

We define that election is invalid when election consistency lose. The probability of election message consistency is P_{in} and the failure probability is P_{out}. The probability of election message failure is analyzed within three-hop election. For easy description, the nodes in this range are described as local nodes, one-hop nodes, two-hop nodes, three-hop nodes by the hop number. Where S_{hop-k} represents the nodes of $hop(0 \leq hop \leq 3)$ are elected successfully in the k time slot, $S_{hop-i-j}$ represents the nodes of $hop(0 \leq hop \leq 3)$ are elected successfully in the $(i - j)$ time slot.

For one-hop transmission, nodes can send control signal message between two signal intervals of their neighbors when the node selected reasonable election parameters. Therefore, the election information of one-hop transmission is considered to be consistent.

For two-hop transmission, there exists failure of election information. As shown in Fig. 2, recording the current sending time of local sending node is $CXT0$, the next sending time is $NXT0$, the 3rd sending time is $ESXT0$ ($ESXT0 = NXT0 + H$). The sending time of one-hop receiving node is recorded as $XMT1$, two-hop node is $XMT2$. The next election time is $TXT2$. From this Fig. 3, we can see that when $XMT2$ meets the condition of $NXT0 < XMT2 < XMT1$, it can meet the failure condition of $TXT2 > ESXT0$. That is to say, the election information about the local node obtained by two hop nodes loses consistency.

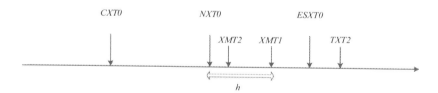

Fig. 3. Election time plan

We presume that one-hop node sends its information after h time slots of source node. The election failure probability can be described as after h time slots of local node's transmission one-hop node send its information, two-hop nodes win the election in the $h < k < H$ time slot. The probability of consistent election information is given by

$$P_{in} = \sum_{k=h+1}^{H-1} P(S_{2-k}) \times P(S_{1-h}) \tag{3}$$

When the back off exponent is fixed. For a certain control time slot, all two-hop nodes have the same probability P_s to elect the same time slot [8]. We can deprive P_s from $P_s = 1/M_s$, where M_s is the number of election nodes. Local node has the election probability $P'_s = 1/(M_s - 1)$ after source node's transmission. The probability of one-hop node's transmission after h time slots of the local node is given by

$$P(S_{1-h}) = (1 - P'_s)^{h-1} P'_s \tag{4}$$

The failure probability for election information can be expressed as

$$P_{out} = (1 - P_{in}) \tag{5}$$

For three-hop transmission, when the source node's election information obtained by two hop nodes is invalid, the source node election information obtained by three-hop nodes must be invalidated. When two-hop nodes obtain information timely, the probability of consistency message for three-hop nodes can be expressed as

$$P'_{in} = \sum_{h=2}^{H} P(S_{1-h}) \times \left\{ \sum_{i=h+1}^{H-1} \left[P(S_{2-i}) \times \sum_{j=i+1}^{H-1} P(S_{3-j}) \right] \right\} \tag{6}$$

The probability of failure is written as

$$P'_{out} = (1 - P'_{in}) \tag{7}$$

It is known that consistency of election information will have a direct impact on election efficiency. At the same time, our laboratory has established relevant models to study and analyze. Literature [14] indicates that the successful number of control slots in election obeys geometric distribution. It defined that access delay as the number of successful control time slots for node election, and measured election efficiency according to that. The expected values of controlling slots in the election process is equal to $1/p$, p is the probability of success for any time slot [8]. Adding the back off time H, the expected value of time delay is obtained by

$$E = H + 2\pi r^2 \rho - 2^{\exp + 3} + \frac{}{\sqrt{(2^{\exp + 3} - 2\pi r^2 \rho)^2 + 2^{\exp}(4\pi r^2 \rho + 15)}} \tag{8}$$

Where ρ is the nodes density? The expectation of election access delay is closely related to core parameters and nodes density in the election. While maintaining different range of election will result in different densities of nodes. There are four election mechanisms when we expand the election range of three-hop. Do not maintain information within two-hop, it means all nodes within two-hop is included in the election collection. To maintain one-hop neighbor information within two-hop, it means all the one-hop and two-hop nodes are included in the election collection.

To maintain the information within two-hop, that is to say, we put all neighbors which meet the selection condition into election collection. To maintain all neighbors' information within three-hop, all neighbors eligible for election are in this collection. When considering with election consistency, the effect of the access delay on two-hop election and three-hop election mechanism are regarded as two-hop election correction access delay and three-hop election correction access delay. The access delay which does not consider the consistency problem is regarded as theoretical access delay. In this paper, we will combine core parameters of election and consistency problem together to calculate the expectation of election access delay for four different kinds of mechanisms.

4   Numerical Calculation and Analysis

Based on the election information consistency probability and access delay expectation formula. This section analyzes the influence of key parameters and hops on the election efficiency and consistency through numerical calculation method. The probability of failure election is P, the election access delay is D, the number of nodes is N, the number of election maintenance hop is hop. P, D are affected by exp, hop, $Basic$ and N. The default value of $Basic$ is 4, which takes from $0 \leq exp \leq 4$. The number of nodes N obeys uniform distribution. The efficacy probability of election information is $P(hop = i)$ when the number of hops is $i(i = 2, 3)$, and $D(hop = j, theoretical)$ is the theoretical time delay of the election when hops is $i(i = 0, 1, 2, 3)$, $D(hop = j, revised)$ is value of election access delay correction when hops is $j(j = 2, 3)$.

4.1   Election Message Failure Probability

Figure 4 shows the relationship of election failure probability P with hop, exp and N. We can learn that, when exp is fixed, $P(hop = 2)$ and $P(hop = 3)$ share the same increase with N, and $P(hop = 3)$ is greater than $P(hop = 2)$. It indicates that the greater A is, the fewer opportunities for each node to succeed in the election gets. Therefore, the information obtained of other nodes when this node is in the process of election has higher probability in losing consistency. It's practically that when hop is fixed, if exp is smaller, the number of election time increases, as well as P. When $hop = 2$, the minimum P for different exp is still around 60%. When $hop = 3$, the minimum P with different exp is about 80%, and it can reach around 95% when $exp = 0$.

In summary, there are message consistencies issues exist if we maintain two-hop or three-hop election. Compare the results of $hop = 2$ and $hop = 3$, we can learn that for different exp values, the failure probability of maintaining three-hop election message is always greater than the maintenance of two-hop election, it's about 15%. It indicates that maintaining the consistency of the three-hop election is even more serious.

4.2   Election Access Delay

The relationship between D and hop, exp and N are shown in Fig. 5. We can learn from Fig. 5(a), (b) and (c) that if we fix N or exp, as the amplify of exp, D increases. That is to say, the larger exp is, the longer back off time to succeed in sending is required. When we fix exp, and $D(hop = 2, theoretical)$ is the smallest, $D(hop = 3, revised)$ is the largest. If N is smaller with the gap about 10 slots, and the difference enlarge with the increases of N.

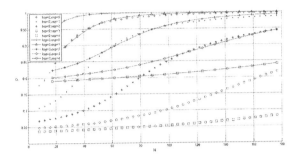

Fig. 4. Failure probability of mesh election message

$D(hop = 2, revised)$ is higher than $D(hop = 2, theoretical)$, but less than $D(hop = 1, theoretical)$. $D(hop = 1, theoretical)$ is less than $D(hop = 0, theoretical)$, and the difference among them is small. It indicates that the election consistency problem led to the actual performance of two-hop election is close to no maintenance or maintenance of one-hop. The relative relationship between $D(hop = 3, theoretical)$ and other schemes have changed a lot. As shown in Fig. 5(a), when $exp = 0$ and $N > 20$, $D(hop = 3, theoretical)$ is better than other three schemes. From Fig. 5(b), we can learn that when $exp = 1$ and $N < 30$, $D(hop = 3, theoretical)$ is worse than $D(hop = 2, revised)$. But when $N > 46$, $D(hop = 3, theoretical)$ is better than other schemes. When $exp = 2$ and $N > 60$, $D(hop = 3, theoretical)$ is better than $D(hop = 2, revised)$, but worse than any other schemes. We can conclude from Fig. 5(c) that when $exp = 3$ and $exp = 4$, $D(hop = 3, theoretical)$ is a better than $D(hop = 2, theoretical)$. The difference is less than 1–2 slots when N is smaller, it can be seen that the performance of $D(hop = 3, theoretical)$ is close to $D(hop = 2, theoretical)$ when exp is larger and N is in a certain range.

Let's focus on the impact of election consistency on two-hop and three-hop election. When N is smaller, $D(hop = 2, revised)$ is better than $D(hop = 2, theoretical)$ about five time slots. With the increase of N, the gap is getting bigger even more than ten slots. When N is smaller, $D(hop = 3, revised)$ wins $D(hop = 3, theoretical)$ about ten time slots. With the increase of N, the gap is getting bigger. It is known that election consistency has great influence on practical performance of two-hop and three-hop election, and the impact on the maintenance of the three-hop election is bigger than two-hop election. Therefore, election consistency has a crucial impact on election performance efficiency.

4.3   Channel Utilization

For four different election mechanisms, channel utilization η can be expressed as

$$\eta = \frac{L_D}{L_M + L_O + L_D} \tag{9}$$

Where L_M donates the cost of the neighbors' information in control message, L_O donates the remaining overhead of control signal. Known by protocol, MSH-DSCH

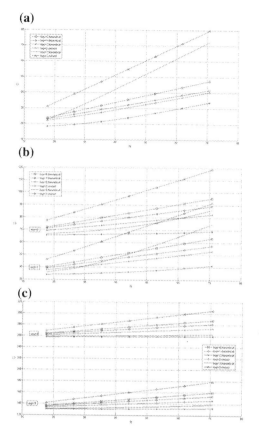

Fig. 5. Relationship between access delay of election with hop, exp and N. (a) exp = 0, (b) exp = 1, exp = 2, (c) exp = 3, exp = 4

carries the node number (16 bits) and the election information necessary (8 bits) for each neighbor. That is to say, the MSH-DSCH carries a neighbor's election information will consume 24 bits. Where L_D donates the length of data transmitted within a data slot. Formula (9) measures channel utilization with overhead, but in fact, the channel utilization rate is affected by the success rate of channel transmission. The relationship between the success probability of transmission and the number of maintenance hops [14] is given by

$$
p_s = \int\limits_{0}^{+\infty} f_{SIR}(x)dx =
$$

$$
\exp\left(-\pi d^2 \frac{1 - e^{-\lambda_p \pi (hop)^2 R^2}}{\pi (hop)^2 R^2} \theta^{\frac{2}{\alpha}} \Gamma\left(1 + \frac{2}{\alpha}\right)\Gamma\left(1 - \frac{2}{\alpha}\right)\right)
$$

(10)

Which $f_{SIR}(x)$ donates the probability density function of signal to interference ratio, R donates the effective distance of signal transmission, *hop* donates the number of maintenance range, d donates the distance between receiving node and sending node, α donates the path loss index, θ donates the threshold of receiving signal to interference ratio. In [14], it was assumed that the cumulative interference of two-hop election is large, which leads to the channel of two-hop election cannot be multiplexed. The three-hop election can solve the cumulative interference problem, and use channel multiplexing. It also gave the best proportion of L_D & L_M. According to this, we give the relationship between the channel utilization and the number of nodes under different maintenance hops. Figure 6 shows that channel utilization with different maintenance hops is inversely proportional to the number of nodes. The greater number of nodes involved, the lower channel utilization gets. With the increase of nodes, maintenance of three-hop election channel can be multiplexed, which leads to the highest channel utilization. The channel utilization rate of two-hop election maintenance is around 90%, one-hop election is around 80%, and non-maintenance neighbor information decreases from 70% to 0.

It can be concluded that considering the influence of channel overhead and cumulative interference, the three-hop election mechanism is used to achieve the highest channel utilization after channel multiplexing. The two-hop neighbor and one-hop neighbor maintenance election mechanism is the second choice. None neighbor maintenance is seriously affected by cumulative interference.

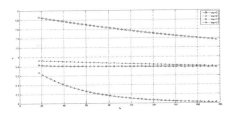

Fig. 6. Channel utilization for different mechanisms

4.4   Mechanism Comparison

This paper accounts for the factors of cumulative interference, and analyzes the influence on efficiency with three-hop election. Table 1 describes the overall comparison of channel utilization, election efficiency, and the impact of election consistency and cumulative interference in four different election mechanisms.

Table 1 shows that the overhead is small when there is no neighbor maintenance within two-hop, as well as one-hop. It is not affected by the election consistency problem, but its election efficiency is lower than three-hop, with serious cumulative interference and low channel utilization rate. Maintenance of two-hop election theory has the smallest access delay, the highest efficiency, but election consistency problem still exists. The channel utilization is affected by the cumulative interference and cannot be used for channel multiplexing. Compared with other mechanisms, the three-hop election theory has bigger access delay; the correction access delay is always the

Table 1. Comparison of different mechanisms

Scheme	Channel utilization	Election efficiency	Effect of consistency	Cumulative interference
No maintenance	Lowest	Lower	None	Large
One-hop maintenance	Lower	Lower	None	Large
Two-hop maintenance	Higher	Highest	Little	Large
Two-hop correction	–	Higher	–	–
Three-hop maintenance	Highest	Changing	Large	Little
Three-hop correction	–	Lowest	–	–

biggest. That is to say, it has poorer actual election performance, highest cost. But it can effectively solve the problem of cumulative interference, with the highest channel utilization rate.

To sum up, for narrowband network, no neighbor maintenance or one-hop election mechanisms can be used when lower overhead, low efficiency and channel utilization are required. When channel utilization and election efficiency are required, maintenance of two-hop election can be used. For large scale network with high density nodes, the cumulative interference is higher, the cost is in lower requirement, and the three-hop election mechanism can be adapted to ensure effective channel reuse.

4.5   Simulation Results

This section is based on the NS2 simulation platform to verify the impact of election consistency on the efficiency of the election. This article gives only four sets of data for node size of 10, 20, 30, and 40 due to the limited memory of the NS2 simulation platform. Figure 7 shows a 40 node simulation scenario topology.

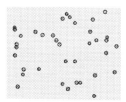

Fig. 7. Network topology of simulation

Taking a smaller value for exp is more reasonable when the number of nodes is small, so we set exp to 1. Table 2 shows the parameters configuration of this paper.

The test methodology we used is to record the number of MSH-DSCH sent by a node in the network, then we can get the average transmission period of MSH-DSCH.

Table 2. Parameter configuration

Parameter	Value
Control time slot	9
Data time slot	14
Basic	4
Exp	1
Frame length	19.76 ms
Communication radius	250 m
Simulation time	120 s

$D(hop = j, experimental)$ is the experimental value of election access delay when hops is $j (j = 0, 1, 2, 3)$. The election access delay of different hops is shown in Fig. 8. We can learn from Fig. 8(a) and (b) that the experimental value of election access delay is worse than the theoretical value. $D(hop = 3, experimental)$ is the largest, $D(hop = 1, experimental)$ is smaller than $D(hop = 0, experimental)$, and $D(hop = 2, experimental)$ is smallest. $D(hop = 2, experimental)$ is better than $D(hop = 3, experimental)$ about five time slots when N is ten. However, the gap increased to 20 when N is forty, which corresponds to the theoretical value. Meanwhile, it is noted that the experimental values of the scheme for maintaining four kinds of hops are all larger than the theoretical values. The reason is that the theoretical calculation usually does not take into account the control time slot occupied by other control messages, which leads to the smaller theoretical estimation. Let's focus $D(hop = 2, experimental)$ and $D(hop = 3, experimental)$, the experimental access delay in the simulation is closer to

(a)

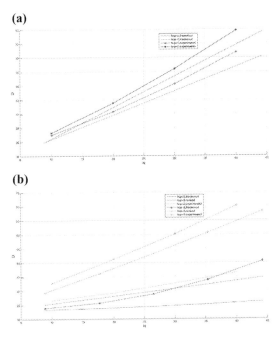

(b)

Fig. 8. Election access delay of different hops. (a) Hop = 0, hop = 1. (b) Hop = 2, hop = 3

the value of election access delay correction. Therefore, we can get the conclusion that the election consistency does have the impact on the efficiency of the election.

5 Election Consistency Improvement Strategy

Through the analysis, the core parameters and maintenance scope of election mechanism produce a great impact on the performance. Under the circumstances of high density nodes, it can avoid cumulative interference by expanding the scope of maintenance, but bring consistency issue which affects the election efficiency greatly. For two-hop and three-hop election, it has bigger gap between the actual performance and the theoretical performance. In this paper, we proposed three kinds of improved strategies to promote the efficiency of election.

First, we design a rational and non-collision election mechanism. Reduce the election information which is not in time caused by the expansion of useless election scope and election collision. For existing protocols, the information each node gets about its one-hop neighbors is an interval, not the accurate value of next sending time. Despite it may decrease a certain amount of network overhead, but the information are not the exact time of neighbors. So there are neighbors may be do not meet the requirements for election, and the node still needs another election, which will cause the waste of slot. This section depends on which will amplify with the increase of nodes, the problems above are more obvious. It may lead to poor election efficiency and excessive waste of slot. The next sending opportunity is determined by this section, which means this opportunity is within this section. If current election time exceeds this section, these slots will become the back off section; this node is excluded from election, which may cause collision. The collision probability will increase when is small, so it is practically useful when turn the election section into accurate information. It can avoid waste above and make the nodes acquire neighbors' accurate information. This can make the nodes delete information of other nodes which are not eligible for election. It can reduce the scope of election and promote its efficiency.

Second, we design a fast and flexible neighbor maintenance mechanism. When the neighbor nodes are invalid, it can be deleted quickly to avoid meaningless expansion of election. When the distributed multi-hop self-organized network is in practical application, it often becomes difficult for nodes to delete their neighbors when they are out of contact. Because mobility and information interference may make it difficult for nodes to verify that whether their neighbors are missing. It will impair the performance of TDD based network when neighbors lost and delete them. Because TDD system requires strict synchronization among nodes, the nodes will restart after deletion. The impact is not just the election process. If we do not remove the neighbor, the election efficiency will decrease. Therefore, it is very important to design a reasonable neighbor maintenance cycle so that the nodes can delete the neighbors' information timely in network, which is also important for election efficiency and network stability.

Third, we extend the opportunity of delivery in the same election. In one election, we will select the next transmission opportunity and the pre-selected third transmission opportunity. According to the analysis of the election consistency, the invalidation of election information is limited by one election information at each election.

For two-hop or three-hop election, the failure probability of election is higher. If two transmission opportunities can be selected at one election process, the node can effectively acquire the transmission time of two or three hop nodes from starting up. Because hash algorithm is adapted in election mechanism, the collision probability is small, so the pre-selected election information has a greater reference value. Therefore, nodes can have one reasonable election at each node at least, thus to improve the election efficiency. Even though this approach increases overhead, it is foreseeable that the problem of consistency in election will be greatly improved in case that sufficient band is available.

6 Conclusion

In this paper, we focus on the election mechanism of the distributed multi-hop self-organized network, and the cumulative interference and the consistency of it. We give the relationship between the key parameters of election mechanism and the consistency between maintenance range and election performance efficiency. Furthermore, the results show that the problem of cumulative interference can be solved by extending the election range to three-hop when the nodes density is large and the cumulative interference is serious. However, extending the scope of the election will bring more serious election coherence issues, and the election consistency issue will have a greater impact on the election performance efficiency. Therefore, for practical application, the conclusion of this paper will provide an important reference for flexible selection of different hops election mechanisms.

References

1. Takita, D.: Centralized scheduling for wireless mesh networks with contention-reduced media access. In: International Symposium on Intelligent Signal Processing and Communications Systems, Japan, pp. 493–496 (2014)
2. Nithys, B., Mala, C., Sivasankar, E.: A novel cross layer approach to enhance QoS performance in multihop adhoc networks. In: International Conference on Network-Based Information Systems, Italy, pp. 229–236 (2014)
3. Christina, V., Albert, B., Pablo, S., et al.: Analysis and enhancement of CSMA/CA with deferral in power-line communications. IEEE J. Sel. Areas Commun. 34(7), 1978–1991 (2016)
4. Gao, L.: PSO based MAC protocol for 802.11 wireless mesh network. Xi'an Electronic and Science University, Xi'an (2013)
5. Gobikannan, S., Rajinikanth, E.: An efficient centralized scheduling handover scheme for IEEE 802.16 networks. Int. J. Appl. Eng. Res. 10(20), 19218–19223 (2015)
6. Lee, B., Chen, C.: An enhanced election-based transmission timing mechanism in IEEE 802.16 mesh networks. In: Asia-Pacific Conference on Communications, APCC 2008, Japan, pp. 1–5 (2008)
7. Sandip, C., Debarshi, K., Abhijnan, C., et al.: Tuning hold-off exponents for performance optimization in IEEE 802.16 mesh distributed coordinated scheduler. In: The 2nd International Conference on Computer and Automation Engineering (ICCAE), Singapore, pp. 256–260 (2010)

8. Min, C.A.O., Wenchao, M.A., Qian, Z.H.A.N.G., et al.: Analysis of IEEE 802.16 mesh mode scheduler performances. IEEE Trans. Wirel. Commun. **6**(4), 1455–1464 (2007)
9. Piyanon, K., Phongsak, K.: An adaptive hold off exponent approach for coordinated distributed scheduling in WiMAX mesh networks. In: International Symposium on Intelligent Signal Processing and Communications Systems, Thailand, pp. 1–5 (2011)
10. Peng, J., Li, X., Liu, T., et al.: Research and optimization for the competition mechanism of distributed multi-hop cooperative networks. In: IEEE Advanced Information Technology, Electronic and Automation Control Conference, pp. 1704–1708. IEEE (2017)
11. Wang, B.: Research on Scheduling Mechanism for IEEE 802.16 Mesh Networks. Tianjin University, Tianjin (2013)
12. Xie, Y.: Research on Resource Scheduling Mechanism and Optimized MAC Protocol of Distributed Multi-hop Self-organizing Networks. Beijing Jiaotong University, Beijing (2014)
13. Zhu, H., Lu, K.: On the interference modeling issues for coordinated distributed scheduling in IEEE 802.16 mesh networks. In: International Conference on Broadband Communications, Networks and Systems, USA, pp. 1–10 (2007)
14. Li, X., Gao, H., Liang, Y., et al.: Performance modeling and analysis of distributed multi-hop wireless ad hoc networks. In: IEEE International Conference on Communications (ICC), Malaysia, pp. 1–6 (2016)

Application of CO_2 Gas Monitoring System in the CO_2 Geological Storage Project

Shaojing Jiang[1], Xufeng Li[2,3(✉)], Weibo Wang[1], Lisha Hu[2,3], and Qianguo Lin[4]

[1] Research Institute of Yanchang Petroleum (GROUP) Co., Ltd., Xi'an 710075, China
jshj7010@sina.com, wangweibo163@163.com
[2] Center for Hydrogeology and Environmental Geology Survey, China Geological Survey, Baoding 071051, China
ffslxf@163.com, lisahu1986@163.com
[3] Key Laboratory of Carbon Dioxide Geological Storage, China Geological Survey, Baoding 071051, China
[4] Carbon Capture and Storage (Beijing) Technology Co. Ltd., Beijing 100089, China
lilinshi@hotmail.com

Abstract. In this paper, we designed a set of CO_2 gas monitoring system in the CO_2 Geological Storage Project which was used in Ordos Basin of western China. The change of CO_2 concentration in atmosphere and soil was effected by environmental factors, for example atmospheric temperature, atmospheric pressure, Atmospheric humidity, wind power, soil temperature, soil moisture, etc. The CO_2 gas monitoring system was designed to monitor CO_2 concentration and key environmental factors. Data transmission technologies were used general packet radio service (GPRS), peanut shell DDNS. The CO_2 gas monitoring system in the CO_2 geological storage project had a series of capacities to monitoring CO_2 gas and environmental parameters. And could been widely used in geological storage projects.

Keywords: CO_2 geological storage · CO_2 gas monitoring · GPRS
Wireless sensor networks

1 Introduction

Wirelessly communicating instruments have fundamentally changed our lives and also play an increasingly important role in industrial environments. It was exactly in this area where the enormous potential of wireless technology was opening up completely new horizons.

General packet radio service (GPRS) was a packet-based wireless data communication service designed to replace the current circuit-switched services available on the second-generation global system for mobile communications (GSM) and time division multiple access (TDMA) IS-136 networks. GPRS communication was designed to complement but not replace current circuit-switched networks, being used solely as an extra means of data communication.

© Springer Nature Singapore Pte Ltd. 2018
H. Yuan et al. (Eds.): GSKI 2017, CCIS 848, pp. 652–659, 2018.
https://doi.org/10.1007/978-981-13-0893-2_67

2 Wireless Data Transmission Technology

Wireless data transmission technology was one of wireless transmission technologies used to transfer various kinds physical quantity from industrial site. Compared with traditional wire data transmission, advantages of wireless data transmission technology included short installation period, less cost, simple preserve, fast move, wide application and so on [1].

Supporting technologies of wireless data transmission include Wi-Fi, cellular data service, mobile satellite communications and wireless sensor networks. Wi-Fi was a wireless local area network that enables portable computing devices to connect easily to the Internet, which had become the de facto standard for access in private homes, within offices, and at public hotspots. Cellular data service offers coverage within a range of 10miles to 15miles from the nearest cell site. Speeds have increased as technologies have evolved, from earlier technologies such as GSM, CDMA and GPRS, to 3G networks such as W-CDMA, EDGE or CDMA2000. Mobile Satellite Communications might be used where other wireless connections were unavailable, such as in largely rural areas or remote locations [2]. Wireless Sensor Networks were responsible for sensing noise, interference, and activity in data collection networks [3].

3 General Packet Radio Service

General Packet Radio Service (GPRS) was a packet-based wireless data communication service designed to replace the current circuit-switched services available on the second-generation global system for mobile communications (GSM) and time division multiple access (TDMA) IS-136 networks. GPRS communication is designed to complement but not replace current circuit-switched networks, being used solely as an extra means of data communication.

There were a lot of advantages of GPRS. Firstly, GPRS users could confirm and install monitor sites without worry about line maintenance or communication outage; secondly, terminal equipment were cheaper; thirdly, Cost of GPRS was low; fourthly, GPRS could well support frequent and little burst data traffic; fifthly, speed of network access was fast and can seamless connection; the last, signal widely covers [4].

4 Data Processing and Transmission

4.1 Data Processing and Transmission: INTERNET Combine with DDNS

Through Internet computer could manage the central data, but could not have a fixed IP address, which leaded to the IP address of the computer keeps changing when router restarted because of power down each time. In this situation, we could apply for the dynamic DNS. The client software of DDNS would run in the center computer, which could send a dynamic IP address to the dynamic DNS server to receive the on-site data capture and transmitted the data to the central computer via the GPRS network.

Then date transfer unit, the GPRS DTU which was wireless data transmitting terminal of GPRS and embedded with High reliable ARM7 CPU, would establish a communication connection for data transmission by accessing dynamic domain name sever to gets the corresponding IP address automatically. And for the DTU, we needed insert an available GPRS/CDMA GSM/SIM card. As shown in the Fig. 1.

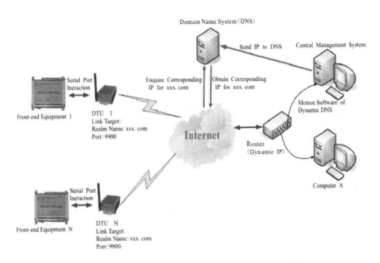

Fig. 1. Data processing and transmission system diagram.

4.2   Hardware and Software Configuration

4.2.1   Hardware

The configuration of CO_2 gas monitoring system needed not very high, which included two GPRS/CDMA GSM/SIM cards and one computer.

The best cards were Easy own or M-Zone of China Mobile. One was used for DTU data transmission, which was better to open the GPRS stream service (monthly, annual or packet streams would be fine) due to the large data and access point needs CMENT; another one was used for sending messages from center platform to field site platform, and only had smaller streams.

The computer was unnecessary for much more requirements, but better configuration would be good for the monitoring system; at least could access to the Internet, preferably via the Internet router instead of 3G Internet access (due to the network environment of Internet via 3G card was unstable, and IP addresses would change frequently). And HUB or the computer itself had two network cards were also necessary.

4.2.2   Software

Software was DDNS of Peanut shell, virtual serial port software VSPM and environmental parameters monitoring system software.

(1) Apply for DDNS

DDNS of Peanut Shell was two types, which were free and fees. The free software could not fulfill the guaranteed online rate, and the pay fee card had many good results than free, the price was also justified.

(2) Virtual serial port software VSPM

VSPM was used for opening port with the DTU communications.

(3) Environmental parameters monitoring system software

In this equipment owned monitoring function on air temperature, press, rainfall, wind speed, wind power, wind direction, soil temperature and soil humidity.

4.3   Processing of Normal Data Communications

First open peanut shell DDNS client software, and then enter a valid user name and password, after normal login, IP address of the machine will be determined. Next opening VSPM virtual serial port software, we could set the appropriate serial port.

Powered DTU on-site and wait a minute until the yellow of the WAN port constant light, it was indicated that DTU had been able to properly access the specified IP address, and the data had been linked successfully in the system.

Powered the other equipment on-site, and the whole system started to work, then to start the software of environment parameter monitoring system and choose the appropriate parameters, it could be communicated normally.

4.4   Explanation for Use of Relevant Software

4.4.1   Peanut Shell DDNS Client Software

After the login user name and password, dynamic domain name had been activated and pointed to the right. And then the IP address had been fixed, as long as the network connection was normal, paid version of Peanut shell DDNS could basically ensure the stability of the basic dynamic domain IP address (Figs. 2, 3, 4, 5, 6, 8, 9 and 10).

Fig. 2. Peanut shell DDNS client software.

Fig. 3. Domain diagnosis.

4.4.2   Router Settings: Opening Port Number

(1) Enter the router's IP address in IE (about IP address of the router, please see the instructions, for example: 192.168.1.1), and then get into the following interface.

Fig. 4. Router setting.

(2) Click on "Advanced Settings" to enter the following interface

Fig. 5. Advanced settings (1).

(3) Select individual IP address belongs to the host computer, click on the text edit box, and enter the following interface.

Fig. 6. Advanced settings (2)

(4) Separately set the private and public server port, and ensure the port number was the same as the remote port number of DTU meanwhile, click "Run" to open successfully. The Fig. 7 showed the other routers settings.

Fig. 7. Virtual server settings.

Corresponding to the IP address of PC, we must enter the consistent service ports like DTU, such as 6020.

If one single computer tapped into the Internet through 3G cards or ADSL without router, all ports will be open by default on the server.

4.4.3 VSPM-Virtual Serial Port

Select the mode of VSPM running in Server, and the device supports running in Client mode.

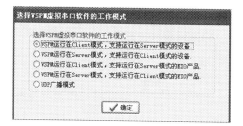

Fig. 8. Operating mode of VSPM-virtual serial port

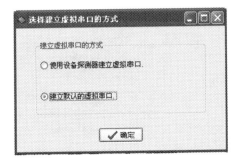

Fig. 9. Select one mode to create a virtual serial port

Create the default virtual serial port, then select the serial port which was corresponding to the open ports 6020, for example COM2. And this serial port would be used to data communicate for the Environmental Parameters Monitoring System later.

4.4.4 Environmental Parameters Monitoring System

For the monitors this system was very simple and practical. After they entered the user interface, they should select the serial port firstly that has been set mentioned earlier for VSPM. And then click [start transferring data] button, it would be able to display the data collected at the scene on the screen according to the boot sequence mentioned earlier, and the system status bar would displays the status of field devices. If the SMS platform was connected properly, the data would be recorded in the database after a group of data collected completely, and screen on the right was also increase the database record at the same time; meanwhile the mobile phone number which has been specified to receive a corresponding data.

On the screen of left, buttons of [Import Parameters], [Input Parameters], [Import System Time], [Input system time] only be valid in the case of system standby.

Buttons of [System Standby], [System Reset] which at the bottom left of the screen, was the mandatory instruction. Under the normal system acquisition mode, they could force the system into standby mode, or reset to re-run the scene.

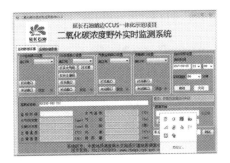

Fig. 10. Environmental parameters monitoring system (Wireless)

There were a series of commands such as [upload all recorded to EXCEL], [Clear the current record], [Clear All Records] at right side of the screen were for database operations. And the database named as data.mdb which had been saved under the currently installation directory. Monitors could open, modify, delete, query, report or print database through Microsoft Access.

5 Conclusions

Abnormal change of CO$_2$ concentration in atmosphere and soil was one of most important and direct factors to verificate a leakage for CO$_2$ geological storage project. The usage showed that CO$_2$ gas monitoring system had a series of capacities to monitoring CO$_2$ gas and the environmental parameters.

(1) The CO$_2$ gas monitoring system was an economical and effective technology to monitor CO$_2$ concentration and main environmental factors.
(2) The CO$_2$ gas monitoring system was easy to run with hardware and software configuration. Hardware was GPRS card and computer. The software was peanut shell DDNS, Virtual serial port software VSPM and environmental parameters monitoring system software
(3) The CO$_2$ gas monitoring system in the CO$_2$ geological storage project had a series of capacities to monitoring CO$_2$ gas and the environmental parameters, which could been widely used in geological storage projects.

References

1. Cai, P., Tan, Y., Dong, Z., Yang, Q., Chen, C.: Application and prospect of wireless data transmission technologies used in petroleum industry. Technol. Superv. Pet. Ind. **28**(6), 1–4 (2012)
2. Ilcev, S.D.: Global Mobile Satellite Communications: For Maritime, Land and Aeronautical Applications. Springer, Heidelberg (2005). https://doi.org/10.1007/1-4020-2784-2
3. Lewis, F.L.: Wireless sensor networks. In: Cook, D.J., Das, S.K. (eds.) Smart Environments: Technologies, Protocols, and Applications. Wiley, New York (2004). Automation and Robotics Research Institute, October 2013
4. Ji, Z., Zhao, H., Liu, Y., Ji, G., Song, B., Wang, S.: Application of GPRS wireless data transmission technique in electric power dispatching system. Hebei Electr. Power **30**(5), 31–32 (2011)

Key Technologies of Comprehensive Monitoring of Safety Production in Networked Coal Mine

Jie Tian[✉], Hongyao Wang, Louyue Zhang, Pufan Zhu,
Yaosong Hu, and Shan Song

School of Mechanical Electronic and Information Engineering, China University
of Mining and Technology (Beijing), 100083 Beijing, China
jessicatianj@163.com

Abstract. Digital mining and unmanned mining have become the development trend of the coal industry at present. Aiming at the deficiency of the existing safety monitoring technology in coal mine in the aspects of progressiveness, reliability and real-time, this paper puts forward the key technology of networked coal mine safety production monitoring. The structure of the communication mode based on "one network one station" is discussed in this study, and the design method of the specific network is analyzed. The accurate locating method of mine moving target based on TOF is studied. The technology of mine fire monitoring system based on wireless self-networking is studied. This paper is of theoretical and practical value to improve the development of coal mine safety monitoring technology and the level of mine safety control.

Keywords: Interoperability · One network one station
Precise positioning of moving target · Digital mine monitoring

1 Introduction

The safety of coal mine is the important factor of the healthy and stable development of the national economy, the social harmony and stability, constantly improving the technical level of safe production of coal mines has been the goal of the party and government, the *Plan Outline of National Medium and Long Term Science and Technology Development (2006–2020)* considers "Public security" as one of 11 key areas, and takes "Major production accident early warning and rescue "as a priority theme in this field. Coal mine safety monitoring system is the main means of early warning and safety management of major disasters in coal mine, only by raising the technology and level of coal mine safety monitoring, can we find out the hidden trouble in time, improve the early warning ability of coal mine safety production, and effectively manage the safe production of coal mine [1].

Most of the coal mines in our country have already completed six big system construction work, has promoted the mine automation and the information technical level, has reduced the gas, the coal dust explosion, the fire, the roof, the water disaster and so on big malignant accident occurrence probability, has promoted the work

© Springer Nature Singapore Pte Ltd. 2018
H. Yuan et al. (Eds.): GSKI 2017, CCIS 848, pp. 660–669, 2018.
https://doi.org/10.1007/978-981-13-0893-2_68

efficiency, has provided the powerful guarantee for the coal. The underground information system of coal mine has made great progress through the deep development in recent years, and is in a preliminary and temporary position in the domestic coal industry. However, in the actual monitoring work, the existing monitoring and control system for coal mine safety monitoring still lags behind in terms of advanced technology, reliability and real-time performance, and there is still a certain gap compared with foreign advanced technologies, displays in:

(1) Monitoring system network structure reliability: with the automation and information of mines, the deployment of chimneys brought excessive number of cables, difficult management and maintenance. Especially when there is a fire and other accidents, resulting in optical cable interruption, it is difficult to distinguish between optical cable and business system of the corresponding relationship, the resumption of the connection to waste a lot of manpower and time, to the mine production accident recovery brings more difficulties. There are many monitoring subsystems under the mine, which are independent of each other and lack of effective data fusion and communication among the subsystems [2].

(2) Personnel positioning technology: at present, most coal mines have installed personnel management system, with personnel regional positioning and attendance management function, in coal mine safety production and mine disaster emergency rescue played an important role. However, the existing personnel positioning system is based on the location of the card reader region positioning, only to determine the down hole staff in a certain card reader's perceptual area, only to support the underground personnel and equipment in the area of the range of inquiries and statistics, area coverage radius between 15–300 m, positioning accuracy is low, It cannot meet the needs of site safety management and rescue personnel. In addition, improving the positioning accuracy must increase the density of the inquiry device (such as card reader), which will increase the cost of the positioning system, so the positioning of the existing personnel positioning system is the double limit of technology and cost.

(3) Fire monitoring technology in mining and control area: Spontaneous combustion of coal mine seriously threatens the production safety of coal mine and restricts the production of coal mine, and coal spontaneous combustion in goaf occupies is a main part in the whole coal spontaneous combustion. At present, the method of mine fire monitoring is mostly fire piping system, it takes a long gas path to pump down hole gases to the sensor to analyze the prediction, not intuitive and real-time performance is poor, cannot play a good fire timely response, and there are monitoring points intermittent, alarm lag, difficult to accurate real-time measurement and other difficult problems, often lead to untimely emergency rescue causing greater loss of personnel and property.

Therefore, how to increase research in the next stage, following the industry technology development trend and the leading, available, continuous security monitoring new technology applied to the coal mine is an effective way to build the modernized new model mining area of domestic coal industry and the world's first-class coal mining industry, it is also the effective way to lead the development direction of world coal enterprises and enhance the core competitiveness of coal plate.

Digital mining and unmanned mining have become the development trend of the coal industry today. The research and development of networked coal mine Safety production monitoring system based on IoT technology is the foundation of realizing this goal, also is the foundation of the application of digital mine at all levels system, and also is the important content of building world first-class digital mine, it solves the key problems in use through technical means, promotes standardization, digitization and intellectualization of monitoring system, and lays a foundation for realizing the leading management goal of coal mine industry. Therefore, it is very important and urgent to research on the key technology of comprehensive monitoring system for safety production in coal mine.

2 "One Network One Station" the Whole Frame of Communication Mode Thought

Through the construction of "High speed Ring network" in the underground to unified access to multiple systems of mine production, safety and communication, flatten the chimney-type vertical system, and solve the problem of too much cable in the underground. The stability and reliability of the unified high speed ring network require high, and to ensure that in a variety of business running on the same high-speed network while being able to provide differentiated QOS (quality of service) according to business requirements. For example, the existing video lagging problem and the QOS of the technology has a greater relationship. In this scheme, we introduce a telecom-grade enhanced switch to meet the bandwidth, reliability, and QOS issues of high-speed ring networks.

Through the construction of "three-in-one integrated substation", it can merge the wireless communication base stations, personnel positioning stations and radio stations into one station, and integrate into an explosion-proof shell, use common power and common transmission interfaces externally, to reduce equipment costs and maintenance costs. The overall structure of the "One network one station" scheme is shown in Fig. 1 [3, 4].

2.1 "One Network "Scheme and the Method of Networking

(1) According to the characteristics of underground roadway planning unified load-carrying network, simplify underground transmission, construction of underground highways:

   (1) In the main roadway deployment unified digital ring network, access to the main lane business system, "One network" switch equipment installed in the flameproof cabinet, and then placed in the underground substation;

   (2) For the branch roadway is not built ring network, other ways to access to the branch lane business system, and then connected to the main roadway on the ring network.

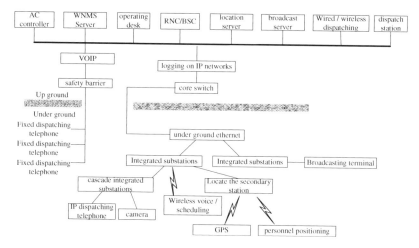

Fig. 1. "One network one station" overall framework

(2) Integrated service access scheme
  (1) Integrated substation provides 4G wireless communication base station access, location base station access and broadcast substation access, but also provide IP video surveillance camera access and IP telephone access, to achieve a unified transmission access to the ring network switch and reduce the number of optical cables;
  (2) Ring network switch provides GE/FE optical interface access IP video surveillance camera;
  (3) Ring network switch also provides industrial automation system and security monitoring system access capacity, through the QOS mechanism to ensure the forwarding of high priority services, to achieve the unified business load and quality assurance;
  (4) It can also be based on the importance of business isolation requirements, industrial automation systems and security monitoring system to build separate switch ring network.
(3) Features and advantages of the programmer
  (1) Programmer features:

  • "One network" switch equipment uplink provides 2 GE interfaces, Downlink provides a number of FE opto-Electronic Composite Interface (By the way 10GE ring network scheme have 2 uplink interface-10GE interface, downlink multiple GE/FE Adaptive Photoelectric combination interface), while supporting 485/232/CAN Low-speed interface, access to a large number of sensors, Camera, positioning system, CDMA base station and other system equipment;
  • Support 1588 v2 to provide 4G wireless system accuracy, the security station switch between the calls uninterrupted
  • Provide reliable loop redundancy protection, protect switching delay < 50 ms, and ensure the continuity of business

(2) The advantage of "One net"

- Greatly reduce the number of optical cable, reduce maintenance workload and maintenance difficulty;□
- Low cost million trillion network, build digital mine highway, business expansion strong;
- Hawaii Switch QoS technology can solve industrial TV video of cotton and the flower screen problem;
- Multi-Protocol protection, rapid convergence of failure, can ensure the continuity of the business;
- Large number of interfaces are photoelectric interface mixed configuration, which can meet the needs of different access methods.

2.2 "One-Station" Scheme and Networking

As shown in Fig. 2, the integrated substation integrates 4G wireless base stations (including WiFi), accurate positioning of the base station, switch function, wireless communication, WiFi access, personnel positioning, landline, scheduling, broadcasting and other functions, through the built-in switch, we can not only meet the integration of the integrated substation demand, but also to provide 4*RS-485 The RS-232 interface and the free FE port realize the integrated access function to reduce the access pressure on the backbone fiber ring network.

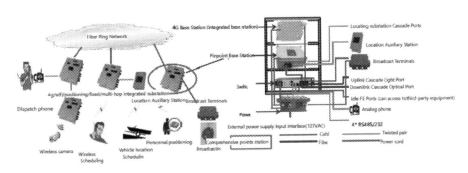

Fig. 2. "One-station" scheme and networking

Integrated substation integrates 4G, WIFI, and accurate location base station, because the three coverage distances are different, so the deployment needs considering the use of separate WIFI base station and location base station to do supplemental coverage:

As shown in Fig. 3, the coverage of 4G station ≈ the coverage of Locating base Station ≈ 3 * the coverage of WIFI, so that when both Personnel positioning and WIFI need full coverage, one Integrated Base Station needs two WIFI base stations' Supplemental coverage on average. The number of stations can be change according to business needs.

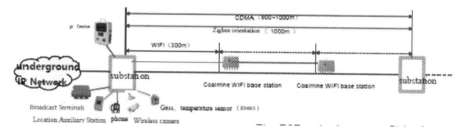

Fig. 3. Locating base Station distribution map

What needs to be stressed is that we use the Precise locating base station based on Zigbee TOF(flying time) technology whose Positioning accuracy up to 10 m even up to 3 m at uncomplicated environment. One Locating base Station/assistant station could cover 1000 m roadway. This technology is much better than RFID which widely used at coal mine at present.

The broadcasting system of "one-station" use IP, so the comprehensive station only should provide FE port to link the broadcasting terminal. The broadcasting system based on IP can not only complete traditional broadcasting, but also link dispatch station to achieve the fusion of broadcasting and dispatch station.

3   Precise Positioning and Management System of Mining Moving Target Based on TOF

3.1   The Precise Positioning Technology Based on TOF and Main/Deputy Reader

The TOF technology uses flight time to obtain distance data which can Basically eliminates the impact of signal strength and obtain precise positioning data at many environment.

As shown in Fig. 4, local nodes send Prime command to remote nodes to initialize the test, then repeat the test mentioned above. At last, local nodes send data request to remote nodes to get distance data. In reverse distance test, the direction of poll and ask is opposite.

The underground electromagnetic environment is complicated, Multipath, non-line-of-sight and other factors will all have a great impact on the results of the distance test so that need to study location algorithm that is suitable for underground environment to reduce the effect of environment on positioning effect. This paper uses RSSI ranging technique as compensation for TOF distance measurement.

The experiment found that the effect of distance measurement based on RSSI is more accurate than that based on TOF distance measurement in the proximity distance of the reader. Therefore, we can use the distance measurement based on RSSI in this interval. Besides, the value of RSSI distance measurement can also be used as a reference supplement in areas where TOF distance measurement is used to correct measurement errors caused by multipath or non-line-of-sight.

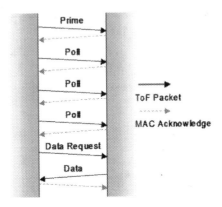

Fig. 4. Diagram of distance principle

Considering the actual environment of underground, Choosing logarithmic-Normal distribution model is more reasonable.

Logarithmic-normal distribution model expressions such as type (1), $P_L(d)$ is for the loss of passing distance d [5].

$$P_L(d) = P_L(d_0) + 10\delta \lg(d/d_0) + X_\sigma \tag{1}$$

δ is Path attenuation factor, whose value depends on the propagation environment of the wireless signal and it is an experience value. d_0 is the distance between the transmitting node and the reference node which is always set up to 1 m. X_σ is the random variable of normal distribution whose mean is zero and standard deviation is σ. $P_L(d_0)$ can be derived from free space model.

Using the method that primary and secondary card reader joint positioning: For effective identification card in front or rear of reader, we need to set up a secondary card reader near the card reader to study on the identification of direction by using the information interaction of the primary and secondary reader. In the meanwhile, the additional of the auxiliary card reader provides more reference information of positioning.

3.2 Underground Communication Networking Technology Based on IEEE 802.15.4

IEEE 802.15.4 is a basic protocol of Zigbee which defines the communication standard of physical layer and the link layer. According to the characteristics of underground positioning, IEEE 802.15.4 is more suitable for locating devices than ZigBee.

This paper studies the characteristics of IEEE 802.15.4 network, and uses the topological structure of star networks. We set the card reader to coordinator, set the identification card to end device, make the devices belong to a network to complete the network, as shown in Fig. 5.

High-efficiency uniqueness identification technology. There is a card system at the wellhead, using iris recognition technology and RFID technology to identify the

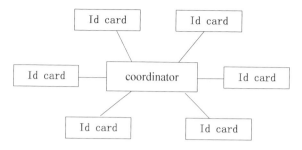

Fig. 5. Star network topology

personnel and equipment in the well. The personnel and equipment under the well must pass the card system before they get down. Checking card machine is coordinator, every person and equipment has a identification card, when they get through the checking card machine which is networked, their uniqueness is confirmed.

4 Mine Fire Monitoring System Based on Wireless AD-Network

4.1 Research on Topological Topology of Wireless Sensor Networks

The traditional wireless sensor network technology uses the "End-to-end" edge theory, emphasizing that all functions related to the endpoint of the network, the intermediate node is only responsible for data transport. This is not absolutely a reasonable choice for the actual situation of coal mines. According to the actual situation of coal mines, we adopt the wireless network structure shown in Fig. 6.

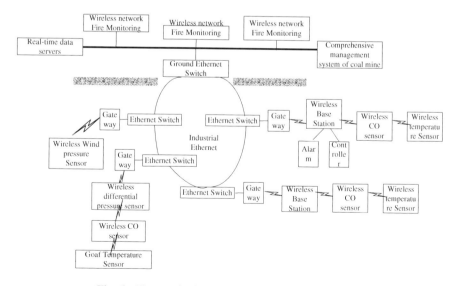

Fig. 6. Fire monitoring system of wireless AD-network

From the practical application of theoretical research and monitoring system in coal mine, the topological structure of wireless sensor network fire monitoring system is tree-like (cluster-tree) network structure [6].

4.2 ZigBee Protocol Core Routing Algorithm

Based on the characteristics of the network topology of the underground WSN, the network layer routing algorithm is one of the key technologies in this paper, and the CLUSTER-TREE+AODVJR routing algorithm is adopted by studying the network layer routing algorithm. The algorithm could improve the efficiency of network communication, and it is suitable for the tree-like network structure under coal mines. Besides, it has the advantages of saving battery energy and convenient application.

4.3 System Communication Mode

Combined with the characteristics of data collection in the fire monitoring and the requirements of each sensor network monitoring point, the terminal node and the network node adopt the sudden communication mode, the wireless base station and the Monitoring Center computer software use the master-slave communication mode.

The sudden communication means that the communication between the network nodes would happen when data changed in a certain time interval, and the datasending is abrupt, so the end-node burst-wake communication mechanism is used in the processing of this technology. Each WSN node consumes energy when it is sending data, the biggest advantage of burst communication is saving battery energy, which could prolong the life cycle of the node, and has practicability.

5 Conclusion

This study could significantly improve the level of coal mines' safety equipment, enhance the ability of disaster and disaster prevention, effectively control the occurrence of heavy accidents, reduce casualties, maintain the occupational health of coal workers. It has great significance on guaranteeing the national coal stable supply, the healthy and stable development of mines, accelerating the transformation of the development of coal industry and building a harmonious mining area. This paper is an important demand of digital mine construction in coal mines and fills the application gap of mine material networking technology in coal mines, and do some significant work for the development of technical equipment suitable for coal mine underground characteristics. The application and popularization of these equipment could guarantee the safe of production of coal mines, like establishing intelligent control and communication transmission network of coal mine, it can realize the interrelation of human, machine and ring in coal mines' wells. Through sensors' sensing technology, collecting personnel, equipment and environment parameters, it could achieve the precise positioning of downhole moving target, the comprehensive coverage of safety information and on-line monitoring and early warning of the running state of key equipment, and achieve the interaction of equipment information and data synchronization. The research results of this paper could produce greater output value and inestimable economic benefit.

Acknowledgments. The authors would like to thank the National Training Program of Innovation and Entrepreneurship for Undergraduates for the direct support to facilitate research and development, and members of the China Coal Research Institute safety and equipment research team for their vital contributions to this work. National Natural Science Foundation of China (51774293, 51404276); National key research and development program (2016YFC0600907); National Training Program of Innovation and Entrepreneurship for Undergraduates (201711413037); Supported by the Yue Qi Young Scholar Project and Yue Qi Distinguished Scholar Project, China University of Mining &Technology, Beijing.

References

1. Sun, J.: New technology and new equipment of coal mine monitoring. Min. Autom. **1**, 1–5 (2015)
2. Sun, J.: "Internet plus coal" and coal mine informatization. Coal Econ. Res. **35**(10), 16–19 (2015)
3. Huo, Z., Wu, X.: Development tendency of internet plus intelligent mine. Coal Sci. Technol. **44**(7), 28–33 (2016)
4. Chen, W.: Design of "One Network and One Station" communication mode in coal mine. Colliery Mech. Electr. Technol. **1**, 60–63 (2017)
5. Li, Z., Li, Q., Wen, L., Meng, Q.: Underground joint localization method based on electromagnetic wave and ultrasonic. Ind. Mine Autom. **42**(7), 30–33 (2016)
6. Ye, J.: Coal mine gas patrol inspection management system based on wireless sensor networks. (3), 63–65 (2012)

Author Index

Ahmad, Zeeshan II-117
Aimer, Y. II-611
Akbar, Arslan II-273

Bachir, S. II-611
Bai, Xiaoming II-263
Bi, Jiana I-363
Boonma, Pruet I-534
Bouazza, B. S. II-611

Cai, Xiahong I-221
Cao, Dong II-284
Cao, Lina II-31
Cao, Zhi I-55
Cen, Yuanjun I-280
Chang, Xixi I-188
Chen, Changchang II-3
Chen, Donglin II-725
Chen, Guoqiang I-168
Chen, Hongmei II-43
Chen, Jian I-495
Chen, Ming I-262
Chen, Ran I-437
Chen, Shaohui I-229
Chen, Shuang II-622
Chen, Weiyun I-106
Chen, Yan I-158
Chen, Yixiang I-83
Chen, Yunwen I-372
Cheng, Quan II-531
Cheng, Ruqi I-229
Cheng, Wen II-161
Chi, Tao I-262
Chi, Xiaoying I-297
Crispino, Ferdinando II-152
Cui, Hongyan I-146
Cui, Juanmin II-88
Cui, Longfei II-127
Cui, Lunan I-353
Cui, Ranran I-426

Dai, Tianru I-336, II-56
de Souza, Jose Mauricio Scovino II-152

Deng, Chuhong I-126
Deng, Lelai II-218
Deng, Liangji I-510
Ding, Heng II-392
Ding, Yingying II-746
Ding, Yuanming I-198
Dong, Fang I-297
Dong, Huazhen II-513
Dong, Huizhu II-670
Dong, Peng II-243
Dong, Yuning I-134
Du, Xiaobing II-466
Du, Xiaoping II-218
Du, Yu'e II-178
Du, Yusong II-650
Duan, Shuiqiang II-178
Duvanaud, C. II-611

Fan, Hua I-280
Fan, Yueqin I-426
Fang, Conggang I-510
Fang, Meng II-284
Feng, Quanyuan I-280
Fu, Jinbin I-550
Fu, Liguo II-414
Fu, Meijun II-513
Fukuoka, Shingo I-83

Gao, Junfeng I-437
Gao, Kang II-662
Ge, Jingjing II-98
Geng, Jing I-336
Geng, Yujie II-364
Gong, Dandan I-312
Gou, Xiaodong II-294
Gu, Lichuan II-350
Guan, Hangjian II-662
Guangming I-168
Guo, Jing II-79
Guo, Zhonghua II-13

Han, Haidong I-543
Han, Xiangyu II-69, II-143

Hao, Gang   II-746
Hao, Xianwei   II-170
He, Ling   II-588
He, Mingyuan   II-98
He, Weiguo   II-178
Heidari, Hadi   I-280
Hong, Qi   I-305
Hou, Shengli   II-79
Hu, Bin   II-725
Hu, Bo   I-250
Hu, Cheng   I-289
Hu, Daqian   I-280
Hu, Guobing   I-452
Hu, Lisha   I-652
Hu, Qiangxin   I-67
Hu, Wei   II-500
Hu, Yaosong   I-660
Hu, Yuping   II-232
Huang, Chengyi   I-510
Huang, Chunhui   II-717
Huang, Haiyang   I-615
Huang, Linsheng   I-305
Huang, Lucheng   II-695
Huang, Wei   I-445
Huang, Xiaobo   II-31, II-375
Huang, Xiaoping   II-662
Huang, Zhenhua   I-372

Iltaf, Adnan   II-117

Jardini, José Antonio   II-152
Jardini, Mauricio G. M.   II-152
Ji, Changming   II-107
Ji, Ling   II-695
Ji, Peng   I-75
Ji, Wenguang   II-88
Ji, Xin   I-67
Ji, Yunjie   II-588
Jia, Binfeng   I-353
Jia, Yijun   II-622
Jiang, Jiaolong   I-176
Jiang, Rimin   I-615
Jiang, Shaojing   I-250, I-652
Jiang, Weijia   II-736
Jiang, Xiangdong   I-615
Jiang, Yan   I-305
Jiang, Yao   II-588
Jiang, Zhengtao   II-313
Jiang, Zhongming   I-353
Jiao, Jun   II-350

Jin, Dahai   I-592
Jin, Fusheng   II-21, II-69, II-143
Jin, Guiping   I-126
Jin, Peiquan   I-318
Jin, Sunmei   II-447
Ju, Yi   II-364

Lee, Yang Jae   II-88
Lei, Jun   I-452
Lei, Peng   I-550
Lei, Yongjiang   I-510
Lei, Zhenjiang   I-55
Leng, Qiangkui   I-363
Li, Bojia   I-67
Li, Dagang   I-280
Li, Danyang   II-684
Li, Daosheng   II-31
Li, Dapeng   II-161
Li, Dengyuhui   II-670
Li, Dong   II-127
Li, Duo   II-170
Li, Guangli   II-531
Li, Guangshun   II-392
Li, Guohe   II-254
Li, Junru   I-280
Li, Nana   I-198
Li, Nengneng   I-426
Li, Wei   I-3
Li, Wenjing   I-75
Li, Xiaolei   I-345
Li, Xingyue   I-327
Li, Xu   I-637
Li, Xufeng   I-652
Li, Yan   I-353, I-495, I-527, II-21
Li, Yangyang   I-229
Li, Yuanzhang   I-115
Li, Yuanzhou   II-544
Li, Zhao   I-55
Liang, Tiangang   II-178
Liang, Wanjuan   I-3
Lin, Qianguo   I-250, I-652
Liu, Baokang   II-178
Liu, Binbin   I-271
Liu, Chuancai   II-117
Liu, Chuang   I-305
Liu, Chuanlu   I-40
Liu, Fang   I-198, II-305
Liu, Fuqiang   I-238
Liu, Lei   II-437
Liu, Lu   II-313

Liu, Shaoru   I-115
Liu, Shaoying   I-83
Liu, Shuang   II-31
Liu, Shuguang   II-135
Liu, Wenjing   II-294
Liu, Xianjing   I-75
Liu, Xiaofeng   II-492
Lu, Hongwang   I-397
Lü, Shuai   II-531
Lu, Songtao   I-405
Luo, Ershun   I-592
Luo, Jialiang   I-96
Luo, Ronghua   I-452

Ma, Guoguang   II-429
Ma, Shengyu   I-345
Ma, Tengteng   II-383
Ma, Xiao   II-650
Ma, Xin   I-397
Malang, Kanokwan   II-56
Masoud A, Mabrook   I-558
Mei, Zijie   II-322
Mekonen, Messaykabew   I-106
Meng, Fanbo   II-375
Miao, Liming   I-445
Milis, Koen   II-596

Nematullakyzy, Ulsara Zhantore   I-48
Ning, Weixun   II-343
Nouri, K.   II-611

Ou, Qinghai   I-75
Ouyang, Zhuang   II-662

Pan, Wei   I-289
Pan, Wenlin   II-513
Pan, Yufeng   I-397
Pang, Jianmin   II-414
Panyanuwat, Anurak   I-534
Pei, Zhongmin   II-709
Peng, Jun   II-192
Peng, Tu   II-21
Peng, Xiaoyong   II-500
Perrine, C.   II-611
Pu, Fei   I-480, II-563

Qi, Wenbo   II-334
Qi, Yuhua   I-168
Qiao, Xu   I-569

Qin, Tuanfa   I-106
Qin, Yulin   I-280
Qiu, Chunfang   I-312
Qiu, Le   I-75
Qiu, Weijiang   II-13
Qu, Guannan   I-601, I-629

Ramay, Waheed Yousuf   II-273
Ren, Weiwu   I-601, I-629

Sajjad, Muhammad   II-273
Shan, Zheng   II-414
Shang, Xiaodong   I-637
Shao, Jiejing   II-531
Shen, Jiaji   II-670
Shen, Junling   II-117
Shi, Fenghua   I-250
Shi, Haoqian   I-212
Shi, Tianyun   II-161
Shi, Wenxiu   I-32
Simões, Augustinho José Menin   II-152
Singkahmfu, Phudinan   I-534
Song, Li   II-375
Song, Qixiang   I-305
Song, Shan   I-660
Srisujjalertwaja, Wijak   I-534
Su, Donglin   I-558
Su, Yiran   II-670
Su, Zhulin   II-472
Sui, Chenhong   I-569
Sun, Jinping   I-405, I-414, I-550
Sun, Qing   II-746
Sun, Tongtong   I-578
Sun, Yongfeng   II-13
Surapunt, Tisinee   I-40

Tang, Bin   II-574
Tang, Ruichun   I-578
Tang, Yong   I-372
Tao, Ye   I-578
Tian, Haibo   II-650
Tian, Jie   I-660
Tian, Li   II-404
Tian, Ruoheng   I-510
Tian, Shuangliang   I-221
Tong, Xin   I-637

Ullah, Matee   II-117

Van, Nguyen Ngoc   I-238

Wan, Shouhong   I-318, I-327
Wang, Chengzhang   II-263
Wang, Chunmei   II-232
Wang, Fei   I-55, I-271
Wang, Hongyao   I-660
Wang, Huizan   II-437
Wang, Jian   I-543
Wang, Jun   II-414
Wang, Junjun   I-558
Wang, Kewen   II-243
Wang, Lei   I-262
Wang, Lina   II-596
Wang, Ling   I-615
Wang, Lizhen   II-43, II-472
Wang, Ludi   II-524
Wang, Moshi   II-350
Wang, Nan   I-414
Wang, Runan   II-69, II-143
Wang, Shaokai   I-353
Wang, Shuliang   I-40, II-56, II-437
Wang, Tao   I-146
Wang, Wei   II-79
Wang, Weibo   I-250, I-652
Wang, Wenguang   I-414, II-284
Wang, Xin   I-23
Wang, Xue   I-198
Wang, Yale   I-55
Wang, Yao   I-115
Wang, Yi   II-98
Wang, Ying   II-170
Wang, Yue   I-23, I-32
Wang, Yuxia   II-69
Wang, Zhijie   II-662
Wang, Ziqiang   II-544
Warrit, Natapot   I-534
Wei, Baodian   II-650
Wei, Chengyang   II-662
Wei, Mingkun   II-684
Wu, Bin   I-464
Wu, Jiajie   II-107
Wu, Jianping   II-192
Wu, Junhua   II-392
Wu, Pingping   II-472
Wu, Saier   I-495
Wu, Xijuan   II-650
Wu, Youde   I-520
Wu, Yun   II-552
Wu, Zebin   II-117

Xia, Fei   II-31, II-375
Xia, Zongguo   I-146
Xia, Zongze   II-375
Xiao, Aiqun   II-170
Xiao, Hang   II-232
Xiao, Xiaoqiang   II-343
Xie, Pulong   I-238
Xing, Ying   II-524
Xiong, Wanan   II-574
Xiong, Yijun   I-437
Xu, Changjun   I-13, II-447
Xu, Chong   I-495
Xu, Juan   I-176
Xu, Junkui   II-127
Xu, Shuzhen   II-392
Xu, Wen   I-75
Xu, Wensheng   I-312
Xu, Xiaomin   II-695
Xu, Yanwei   II-205
Xue, Chao   I-510
Xue, Hongjiao   I-384
Xue, Tianyun   I-13, II-447

Yan, Danfeng   I-464, II-364
Yan, Gongda   II-243
Yan, Hengqian   II-437
Yan, Li   I-318, I-327
Yan, Qiong   I-3
Yan, Xiaoyan   I-520, I-527
Yan, Yongdun   II-305
Yang, Faquan   II-457
Yang, Hongyu   I-158
Yang, Hua   II-513
Yang, Huadong   II-305
Yang, Huan   I-221
Yang, Jiakai   I-345
Yang, Jinhui   II-192
Yang, Junwei   I-67
Yang, Li   II-143
Yang, Lianxin   I-510
Yang, Ling   II-457
Yang, Lulu   I-96
Yang, Peizhong   II-43
Yang, Ping   I-384
Yang, Qinghong   II-218
Yang, Wenjing   II-472
Yang, Wenwei   I-106
Yang, Xiaofei   I-353
Yang, Xiaoxin   II-135
Yang, Yahui   II-641

Yang, Yi   II-364
Yang, Yicheng   II-205
Yang, Yichuan   II-161
Yao, Shuxia   I-543
Ye, Yunming   I-353
Yi, Xiaodong   II-631
Yin, Fukang   II-192
Yin, Xiaohua   I-55
You, Jinjun   II-107
Yu, Boyang   II-531
Yu, Chang   I-372
Yu, Hang   II-531
Yu, Liang   II-725
Yu, Lingfei   I-188
Yu, Peng   II-243
Yu, Qing   II-524
Yu, Tao   I-146
Yuan, Hanning   I-345, II-161
Yuan, Ziqiang   I-336
Yue, Feng   II-414
Yue, Fuzhan   II-404
Yue, Wen   I-495

Zeng, Fuping   II-294
Zeng, Guangde   I-126
Zeng, Weizhong   I-510
Zhang, Bo   I-592, II-631
Zhang, Chunsheng   II-457
Zhang, Gebin   II-760
Zhang, Guanqi   I-96
Zhang, Guoping   I-146
Zhang, Haiyang   II-98
Zhang, Han   II-135
Zhang, Hong   I-384
Zhang, Hongyu   I-75
Zhang, Huanming   I-608
Zhang, Jiahao   II-414
Zhang, Jianfei   I-601, I-629
Zhang, Jianmin   II-760
Zhang, Jun   II-334
Zhang, Louyue   I-660
Zhang, Mi   I-134
Zhang, Mingchao   I-3
Zhang, Mingyi   I-3
Zhang, Quanxin   I-115
Zhang, Ren   II-437
Zhang, Sen   I-397, II-232
Zhang, Shuangna   II-404

Zhang, Shuhua   I-372
Zhang, Wanbin   II-343
Zhang, Wenjie   II-254
Zhang, Xing   II-127
Zhang, Xingzhi   II-218
Zhang, Xinyan   I-96
Zhang, Xuwang   I-405
Zhang, Yanke   II-107
Zhang, Yanqi   II-631
Zhang, Ying   I-229
Zhang, Yong   II-383
Zhang, Yongsheng   I-426
Zhang, Yuan   II-500
Zhang, Yuexia   II-622
Zhang, Zhigang   II-670
Zhang, Zhixiong   II-552
Zhao, Chuancheng   I-543
Zhao, Hai   II-334
Zhao, Haifeng   II-736
Zhao, Honghao   I-615
Zhao, Jiasong   II-43
Zhao, Jinling   I-305
Zhao, Jun   I-23, I-32
Zhao, Rongying   II-684
Zhao, Siwen   I-615, II-31
Zhao, Xuan   II-364
Zhao, Xujiang   I-327
Zhao, Yakun   I-176
Zhao, Yao   I-464
Zheng, Huajing   II-3
Zheng, Liang   I-271
Zheng, Lili   I-146
Zheng, Xiaocui   I-271
Zheng, Yifeng   II-254
Zheng, Zhonghua   I-372
Zhou, Hongbo   II-641
Zhou, Jing   II-482
Zhou, Junwen   I-464
Zhou, Libei   I-312
Zhou, Mingnan   I-592
Zhou, Peng   II-343
Zhou, Rui   I-134
Zhou, Wei   II-524
Zhou, Wendy   I-495
Zhou, Xiaoguang   II-524
Zhou, XiaoHu   I-48
Zhou, Xiaomin   II-383
Zhou, Yinghua   II-322

Zhu, Chongchong   II-21
Zhu, Li   II-429
Zhu, Nan   I-569
Zhu, Pufan   I-660

Zhu, Yan   I-13
Zou, Chang   I-318, I-327
Zu, Lijun   I-238
Zuo, Yan   II-284

Printed in the United States
By Bookmasters